MSU-WEST PLAINS
GARNETT LIBRARY

DATE DUE

			PRINTED IN U.S.A.

Why We Fight

Why We Fight

CONGRESS AND THE POLITICS OF WORLD WAR II

Nancy Beck Young

 University Press of Kansas

© 2013 by the University Press of Kansas

Published by the University Press of Kansas (Lawrence, Kansas 66045), which
was organized by the Kansas Board of Regents and is operated and funded by
Emporia State University, Fort Hays State University, Kansas State University,
Pittsburg State University, the University of Kansas, and Wichita State
University

Library of Congress Cataloging-in-Publication Data

Young, Nancy Beck.
Why we fight : Congress and the politics of World War II / Nancy Beck Young.
pages cm
Includes bibliographical references and index.
ISBN 978-0-7006-1917-7 (cloth : alk. paper)
1. World War, 1939–1945—United States. 2. United States—Politics and
government—1933–1945. 3. World War, 1939–1945—Causes. 4. United States.
Congress—History—20th century. I. Title.
D742.U5Y68 2013
940.53'1—DC23
2012044371

British Library Cataloguing-in-Publication Data is available.

Printed in the United States of America

10 9 8 7 6 5 4 3 2 1

The paper used in this publication is acid-free and contains 30 percent
postconsumer waste. It meets the minimum requirements of the American
National Standard for Permanence of Paper for Printed Library Materials
z39.48-1992.

For Thomas

Contents

Preface

Some of my earliest memories are of the give-and-take that exists at the core of American democracy, the electoral process. Being the oldest child of older parents who were very active in politics at the grassroots level meant that I had heard many a campaign speech, attended innumerable election night watch events (complete with a big black chalkboard where votes were tallied), sat quietly at precinct and county conventions, and been kissed by politicians—all before I entered public school, let alone registered to vote. Former senator Ralph Yarborough (D-TX) was a guest in our home, and we visited with Lyndon B. Johnson at his ranch once while he was president and over a dozen times after he retired. After I could vote I became an election precinct worker and relished sitting in the back room to count the ballots (old paper ballots with the names of detested candidates often scratched out with a pen or pencil).

I came of age at the moment of transition from New Deal and Great Society liberalism to Reagan-era conservatism. Growing up I asked lots of questions, especially about what politicians did after they went to Washington, D.C., and my parents took me seriously, providing the answers as best they understood them. Many people who knew me at a young age assumed a political career was in my future. I participated in state and national campaigns, once even writing a letter to the editor of the *Corsicana Daily Sun*. In that 1983 special election for the old Sixth Congressional District in Texas, Phil Gramm had resigned the seat as a Democrat and announced he would run for election again but as a Republican. There were countless candidates, mostly liberal and moderate Democrats hoping to prevent the district from going Republican. A man who saw my letter wrote me with a check to give to the candidate I had endorsed. He noted he was moved to do so because of my youthful enthusiasm for the liberal reformer. Gramm won that election, a signal of the shift away from the solid Democratic South to the GOP, a cause and a consequence of the demise of the moderate political order whose formation I explore here.

Two factors dissuaded me from pursuing politics as a career. First, I knew that I was too liberal to be successful in the place Texas was becoming in the 1980s. My parents' generation of "yellow dog" Democrats—as in "I would sooner vote for a cur yellow dog than a Republican"—was giving way first to "boll weevils" and "blue dogs" and later to Republicans who cared little for sustaining the economic order of the New Deal or expanding the social justice liberalism of the Great Society. More important, I had grown fascinated with the politicians who governed the United States in the middle of the twentieth century.

I became determined to explain the pragmatic liberalism of midcentury that evolved from the 1930s through the mid-1970s, when it faded in proportion with the rising antistatism of American voters. In an earlier book I chronicled the career of one key member of Congress, Wright Patman, who embodied the economic liberalism of his generation. He entered Congress as more a demagogue than a pragmatist, but I detected a significant shift in his political style during World War II. As such, I searched for literature that would explain the larger dynamics of the institution at this critical juncture in American political development. I found nothing that was satisfactory, so the seed was planted for this book. Initially, my questions were rather broad: what accounts for legislative effectiveness, what is the proper role for congressional deliberation during wartime, and what role does ideology play in the process. As I did more research and started writing, the project gained focus and took its current form: an explication of the New Deal's fate during the war and the role of moderates in creating a liberalism in praxis that privileged economic policy over social justice policy.

In the process of gathering materials for *Why We Fight,* I have accumulated numerous debts, and it is my pleasure to acknowledge the many people and institutions who have made this book possible. Though I first conceptualized this book when working on my dissertation, I did not begin work in earnest until 2003. During the 2003–2004 academic year I was fortunate enough to be a fellow at the Woodrow Wilson International Center for Scholars in Washington, D.C. This center is an ideal location for academics interested in the history of politics and public policy, and while there I received much encouragement and support from several individuals: Lawrence C. Dodd, Kent Hughes, Anne Pitcher, Philippa Strum, and Donald Wolfensberger. In the years since I was a Wilson Fellow, Flip Strum has become a valued mentor, and I am forever grateful for her warm friendship and encouragement. I also benefitted from the work of a wonderful research assistant, Erin K. Fitzpatrick. A special word of thanks goes to the Honorable Lee Hamilton for his work in fostering an intellectual community where conversations flowed freely and all views were welcome. Being at the Wilson Center enabled me to conduct research at the Center for Legislative Archives, National Archives, where I was able to examine the records of all the congressional committees active during the war years. Richard Hunt, the director of the center, William Davis, Rodney Ross, and Ed Schamel all provided immeasurable assistance. I also did a significant amount of work in the Manuscripts Division at the Library of Congress, and I am grateful to the archivists there who filled many a request for boxes with good cheer.

Archivists across the country at numerous university archives made my visits productive and enjoyable. I want to thank the professionals at the Alderman Library, University of Virginia; American Heritage Center, University of Wyoming; the Bentley Historical Library, University of Michigan; Carl Albert Congressional Research and Studies Center Congressional Archives, University of Oklahoma; Chester Fritz Library, University of North Dakota; the Department of Archives and History, Arizona State University; the Dolph Briscoe Center for American History, University of Texas at Austin; K. Ross Toole Archives and Special Collections, University of Montana; the Kansas State Historical Society; the Lilly Library, Indiana University; the Richard B. Russell Library for Political Research, University of Georgia; the Southern Historical Collection, University of North Carolina; Special Collections, Brigham Young University; Special Collections, Georgetown University; Special Collections and Archives, University of Kentucky; University Archives Political Collections, University of Colorado; the Utah State Historical Society; and the W. S. Hoole Special Collections, University of Alabama. I have also spent extensive time in several presidential libraries while researching this book, specifically the Abraham Lincoln Presidential Library, the Herbert Hoover Presidential Library, the Franklin D. Roosevelt Presidential Library, the Harry S Truman Presidential Library, the Dwight D. Eisenhower Presidential Library, and the Lyndon B. Johnson Presidential Library. I am grateful to everyone at each of these institutions who kindly shared their wisdom with an often harried researcher trying to make time to look at just one more box, and I would like to say a special word of thanks to Dennis Bilger, Rick Ewig, Carolyn Hanneman, Matthew C. Hanson, David M. Hays, Evan Hocker, Karen Jania, Virginia H. Lewick, Elizabeth Safly, Matt Schaefer, Lynn Smith, Randy Sowell, Sheryl B. Vogt, William K. Wallach, Pat Wildenberg, and Cindy Worrell. Librarians at McKendree College and at the University of Houston have been generous with their time, and my appreciation goes to Becky Bostian, Bill Harroff, Debbie Houk, Alex Simons, and Liz Vogt.

In addition to the very generous support from the Woodrow Wilson Center, I have benefitted from financial support from a host of different institutions. David Brailow, Jim Dennis, Gerald Duff, and Dennis Ryan of McKendree College always made sure I had the money I needed for research travel and the time I needed to write. I am appreciative for the following research grants: the Harry S Truman Research Grant; the Mark C. Stevens Fellowship from the Bentley Historical Library, University of Michigan; and the University of Wyoming American Heritage Center Travel Grant. I also want to thank the University Press of Florida for permission to reprint portions of a chapter I contributed to the volume Stephen R. Ortiz edited, *Veterans' Policy, Veterans' Politics: New Perspectives on Veterans in the Modern United States.* A small section of my chapter from that book, "'Do Something for the Soldier Boys': Congress, the G.I. Bill of Rights, and the Contours of Liberalism," appears in the epilogue here.

Many individuals have read portions of this book, talked with me about my ideas, commented on conference papers that grew into chapter drafts, and provided crucial advice throughout the research and writing process. I would like to acknowledge the help I received from Don E. Carleton, Patrick Cox, Jewell Fenzi, Lewis L. Gould, Waldo Heinrichs, Richard Lowitt, Kristie Miller, Iwan Morgan, Stephen R. Ortiz, Martha Patterson, Bruce Schulman, R. Hal Williams, Randall Woods, and Julian Zelizer. Richard McCulley deserves especial recognition for the countless conversations we have had about this book and the innumerable drafts he has read. Several colleagues at the University of Houston have been very supportive of my work, and I would like to express my gratitude to Kathleen Brosnan, Hannah Decker, Steven Deyle, Sarah Fishman, Mark Goldberg, John Mason Hart, Philip Howard, Susan Kellogg, Kairn Klieman, James Kirby Martin, Martin Melosi, Natalia Milanesio, Thomas O'Brien, Catherine Patterson, Monica Perales, Joseph Pratt, Raul Ramos, Linda Reed, and Eric Walther. James Schafer, Landon Storrs, and Todd Romero went above and beyond the call of duty, especially in the last few months of revision. The department's staff and the staff at McKendree College have helped in large and small ways. I offer many thanks to Donna Butler, Kristin Deville, Richard Frazier, Linda Gordon, Lorena Lopez, Gloria Turner, and Daphyne Pitre.

Students at McKendree College and the University of Houston have listened with much charity and good will as I have tried out my ideas on the many classes I have taught over the years. At McKendree I benefitted from a number of talented research assistants: Rachel Brandmeyer, Carl Florczyk, Josh Hollingsworth, John Jurgensmeyer, Erin McKenna, Dawn Pedersen, Matt Sherman, and Dana Vetterhoffer. I tested ideas on students in several UH undergraduate courses, U.S. History since 1977, the Age of Roosevelt, Liberals versus Conservatives: American Politics from FDR to the Present, and Texans in Washington. In each case the students helped me deepen my thinking about the themes of my book. Students in several graduate seminars have asked probing questions and challenged my conclusions in ways that caused me to tighten my arguments. I am especially appreciative of the efforts of Jordan Bauer, Brenda Broussard, Tracy Butler, Matt Campbell, Sandra Davidson, John Goins, Kyle Goyette, Devethia Guillory, Chris Haight, Brittany Hancock, Debbie Harwell, Bernice Heilbrunn, Ashley Jordan, Kristen Contos Krueger, Guillermo Nakhle, Andrew Pegoda, Natalie Schuster, Becky Smith, Kristi Stephens, Joe Thompson, Stephanie Weiss, Kristen Williams, and Tim Wyatt.

I have many debts that I owe to the University Press of Kansas. Fred Woodward is a scholar and a gentleman. He is the ideal editor, and his knowledge and skills have made this a better book. I am grateful to the two anonymous readers who have given generously of their time to read and evaluate my work. Their comments and questions pushed me to think more deeply about my arguments and make significant improvements in the final stages of work on this book. I am also appreciative of Larisa Martin's work in overseeing the production process, Susan Schott's efforts to market the book, Martha Whitt's skillful copyediting, and Mary Brooks's hard work preparing an index.

Family and friends have provided much encouragement over the years of working on this book. I would like to thank John K. Beck Jr., Shari Beck, John K. Beck III, Rudy Beck, Sarah Beck, Thomas Clarkin, Josiah Daniel III, Susan Daniel, Margie Foster, Tom Foster, Debbie Ham, Jon Lee, Susan Peterson, Michele Reilly, Cheryl Robinson, Clark Robinson, Mary Standifer, Bob Young, and Sherry Young. My parents have nurtured and supported my academic pursuits throughout my life. Words cannot express what they mean to me. My mother, Kenna Beck, and my father, John K. Beck Sr., have been my biggest supporters. Unfortunately, my father did not live to see the publication of this book, but had he done so he would have placed it prominently on his coffee table for all to see and told everyone he knew about it, perhaps more than once. My husband, Mark E. Young, a talented historian in his own right, has helped in countless ways from tending to household chores and making sure dinner was on the table to assisting with research and reading many, many drafts of the manuscript. My son, Thomas E. Young, was born in the middle of my work on this book, and is already showing an interest in political history and geography. He puts things in perspective with his joyous smiles and never-ending questions, one of which has been when will I finish with my papers—the many drafts of this book—so that I can play with Legos. I could never have finished this book without the love, friendship, support, and criticism of my friends, family, and colleagues. This book is better for their many contributions; any flaws that remain are mine alone.

Why We Fight

Introduction

Do moderates matter? Why and how did moderates and conservatives use World War II to revise the New Deal? Conversely, why and how did moderates join with liberals to preserve the New Deal? Congress became the nexus of this conflict between liberals and conservatives about the nature of the state, making the World War II years crucial for understanding postwar politics. Moderate lawmakers in ways not possible a decade earlier limned and constrained but also preserved the New Deal. I contend the New Deal was a revolution with moderate and radical phases, and that its aftermath, in other words the period of retrenchment and reaction, occurred during World War II. Here I am borrowing from Crane Brinton's *The Anatomy of Revolution*, but the analogy carries nicely to this period of American political history.[1] I assert that we cannot fully appreciate the nuances of American politics in the sixty years from World War II through the end of the twentieth century without careful explication of how the legislative branch redefined the New Deal in the decade following its creation. The early 1940s was a critical moment of transformation from the hopeful, experimental welfare state liberalism of the 1930s to the vital center warfare state liberalism of the 1950s.

My title, which refers to the famous war-era propaganda films directed by Frank Capra, references the myriad ideological, partisan, regional, and institutional conflicts not only among lawmakers but also between the legislative branch and the White House. The numerous honest congressional differences with the executive branch have been airbrushed out of the story in deference to the presidency-centered literature that too often dominates the study of modern American politics, especially by historians on the left who have written on Franklin D. Roosevelt. By revisiting the Roosevelt era from the fresh perspective of Congress, the war-era legislative battles appear in a new light. Long-serving members knew FDR too well by the 1940s, and most had grown to hate him as he they. Even though lawmakers resented Roosevelt for his arrogance toward them, there were no "good guys" and no "bad guys," only principled politicians doing what they believed to be best for the country. Congress fought because the members believed in the democratic freedom to debate, disagree, and decide. They discounted the Roman statesman Cicero's observation, "In time of war, law is silent," instead debating and legislating about the problems of the day. This messiness and the corresponding mistakes in American democracy, especially concerning issues relating to social justice where congressional policy was out of sync with American war aims, mirrored what the war was about. The dean of the Capitol press galleries during the war years maintained, "This is a Congress of fighting men, women . . . fighters for American democracy. . . . The Congress of the United States is not—and never has been—a 'rubber stamp' Congress. It has been a Congress of men of steel and explosiveness, many chosen because of their military records."[2]

During the war years, Roosevelt and Harry S Truman faced a fractious Congress riven by hardcore conservatives and liberals (New Dealers), a state of affairs that empowered moderates—mostly Democrats but Republicans also—to cut deals on war-related economic policies but not on issues of pluralism and social justice. This wartime political dynamic established the dominant patterns for postwar politics: the solidification but never complete acceptance of New Deal statism. The contentious legislative-executive contest for power shaped national politics for the remainder of the twentieth century. At its core the partisan debate between liberals and conservatives has been about the scale, scope, and purpose of the federal government, an old conflict rooted in the founding of the government but with new import in the aftermath of the New Deal revolution.[3]

Postwar bickering over the purpose of government intensified during the Truman, John F. Kennedy, Lyndon B. Johnson, and Richard M. Nixon administrations when reformers pushed to expand the concept of New Deal liberalism to include issues like health care, civil rights, environmental protections, and welfare reform, mirroring the 1940s with heightened peevishness on Capitol Hill and with moderate lawmakers often becoming the kingmakers. At moments where fewer changes to the role of the state were discussed, most notably during the 1950s when Dwight D. Eisenhower was president, the tensions in Congress and between the legislative and executive branches ebbed somewhat. Though ideological debates about what the state should and should not do spiraled in the post-Watergate era of conservative ascendancy, the legislative role changed dramatically because of the demise of the seniority system in Congress and the movement of conservative southern Democrats into the Republican Party. Therefore, I assert that the patterns lawmakers established in the 1940s continued unabated through the mid-1970s whereby moderates determined the direction of national politics and the nature of reform. A new institutional dynamic emerged in Congress after the 1970s whereby the left and the right polarized and consolidated, leaving far fewer moderates to find the compromise necessary to enact successful reform initiatives.

Partisanship dominated wartime politics, as did strains between the branches of government. While a conservative coalition of some Republicans and some Democrats undid parts of the New Deal, particularly those agencies designed to put people back to work, a liberal-moderate coalition consolidated much of the New Deal according to a center left construct. Members of Congress in the majority party fought and won a dual war in the 1940s: preserving but not expanding the New Deal and providing for a military victory. In the process, lawmakers contested presidential power mongering because some conservatives believed an expanded presidency to be as dangerous as the New Deal. Roosevelt had merged the twentieth-century trend toward strong presidents and a weakened Congress. This development chafed moderates and conservatives in Congress, but Rep. Robert L. "Muley" Doughton (D-NC) claimed, "I am not defending the President who may be exercising too much war power, but the situation, bad as it is, is not as bad as it would be if we were ruled by Hitler."[4]

My work clarifies what the New Deal really meant for those lawmakers who constructed it and then revised it. The second half of this equation is as important as the first. Many of the same lawmakers who implemented the New Deal in the 1930s believed by the 1940s it should be narrowed. Junior lawmakers elected in or after 1938 typically agreed, and their votes were key to the transformations described in this book. Of the 819 members of Congress who served between 1941 and 1945, 368 lawmakers had held office during the New Deal years and just 295 had been in Congress in the heady 1933–1935 period. Of those, only 55 consistently voted with the liberals in the 1940s. The war-era Congress was a very different institution than the Depression-era one it replaced, deserving study in its own right for its contributions to the evolution of the New Deal, itself a nebulous construct that shifted in meaning multiple times in the 1930s. Conservatives in Congress wanted to rid the body politic of dangerous New Deal experimentalism by the 1940s, or as Rep. H. Carl Andersen (R-MN) put it, "now is the time to lop off a dead branch of the New Deal tree," but moderates and liberals disagreed.[5]

In all the twentieth century wars, ritualistic invocations of nonpartisanship occur just after the onset of hostilities, and then politics as usual recurs immediately. Because World War II is understood as "the Good War" fought by the "Greatest Generation," too much focus has been placed on sentiments such as those recorded in the *New York Times* on December 8, 1941: "Gone is every sign of partisanship in the Capitol of the United States. Gone is every trace of hesitancy and indecision. There are no party lines today in Congress." The illusion of cooperative congressional behavior masked the internecine party warfare over issues ranging from strikes, economic regulation, and anti-Communist red-hunting to race, gender, and refugee policies. Senate Minority Leader Charles McNary (R-OR) reflected, "Yes, it is true that when we get a Democratic administration we get into a world war. Maybe it is to cover up their domestic sins."[6] A close look at Congress during the most consensual war in American history will reveal that politics thrived in World War II because members of Congress fought two wars, the well-known war against the Axis powers and the less well-known war about the New Deal. Lawmakers quarreled not primarily to impede progress but to find compromise, behavior in sync with a society and government based on free speech.

I demonstrate how scaling back on certain domestic reforms was an essential compromise liberals and moderates made in order to institutionalize the New Deal economic order. Congress, not executive branch officials, controlled this process, and they did not fully depress the lever for change until the war years, a development that I argue was inevitable. Indeed, examination of the period reveals a bifurcated record of accomplishment and failure. In certain policy domains (taxation, rationing, military oversight, labor management policy, and postwar economic conversion) Democrats held together their coalition and preserved the New Deal economic order. Doing so was no small feat. The result: some policies and programs were rejected—including the Civilian Conservation Corps, the National Youth Administration, and the Works Progress Administration—but others—like the Wagner Act, Keynesianism, and economic regulation—were institutionalized (at least until the 1970s and 1980s with the rise of modern conservatism). Policymaking remained productive despite, and sometimes because of, the vituperative partisanship. These quarrels resulted from the freedom to debate; the participants understood the end game was legislation, not simply ideological vindication.

On other issues (refugee policy, the persistence of racial discrimination, and hunting Communist spies) the discord proved insurmountable. A minority of congressional conservatives used legislative procedures to stifle liberal domestic policy. Indeed, conflicts concerning such social matters never dominated the New Deal order within Congress and were not important enough for moderates in that body to waste their political capital on, especially when struggles about the economy were intense and, from their perspective, more relevant to the war effort. While these political developments might seem unremarkable at first glance, in actuality they prefigure postwar attitudes toward liberalism. Departure from the economic radicalism of the 1930s made the New Deal economy more sympathetic to capitalism and also facilitated postwar rights-based liberalism benefitting groups previously marginalized in the American state: people of color, women, and gays and lesbians. This development generated even more passionate outbursts from conservatives, who drew from the modern rhetoric of anti-statist opposition refined in the 1940s. For example, Rep. Karl Mundt (R-SD) insisted, "The New Deal Santa Claus has an unpleasant but inevitable habit of calling back with due bills for the gilded presents which he leaves on the doorsteps of the people."[7]

Congress reflected the divisions within the country over the various war programs and over the ever more powerful presidency. Congress, more than the president, encapsulated the national political and social consciousness, for good and for ill, meaning that lawmakers collectively held the same range of values and prejudices as did average Americans. So explained Sen. Carl Hayden (D-AZ), "The Representatives and Senators in Washington are simply a good cross section of the general public. If the purpose to be served by our system of government is to assure the election of only intellectual giants to the Congress, then I am afraid that in our democracy as we know it that purpose will never be achieved."[8]

Lawmakers acted on constituent priorities. Members of Congress remain in office by keeping aware of what voters in their districts are thinking, and while presidents often see legislators as parochial, they provide a good reflection of shifting public opinion on the local level. Congress also takes direct pressure from lobbyists and citizen protests. One caveat worth making is that Congress in the 1940s was not truly representative of the national population. Congressional districts were stacked in favor of rural areas over cities since the Supreme Court did not mandate "one person, one vote" until twenty years later. In the South, African Americans and many poor whites were disenfranchised. Few women served in Congress, and those who won election often found themselves on the margins of an "old-boy" institution governed by the seniority system.

This imperfect Congress with its imperfect representation of the nation nonetheless legislated the important shifts that had occurred in national politics in the 1930s and 1940s. Members of Congress learned an overriding lesson from the New Deal: productive policy could be crafted when the White House and Congress worked in tandem as was the case in the so-called first 100 days of the Roosevelt presidency and again in the so-called second New Deal of 1935. Congressional authors of the New Deal included a sometimes bizarre combination of liberal Democrats and southern segregationists, with both groups advocating economic liberalism in the early and mid-1930s. Such a fragile coalition based more on self-interest than on principle could easily break, and break it did in the 1940s. These fissures first appeared early in Roosevelt's second term when he asked for legislation to reform the Supreme Court by expanding its membership. He fell flat because there was scant cooperation with Congress. The record of legislative and executive cooperation in the 1940s is mixed: the two branches were most often in pursuit of common purpose over economic mobilization matters while there was almost no attempt at compromise on social justice legislation. These results were no accident. Scholars have long acknowledged that Roosevelt abandoned support for New Deal reforms midway through the war. What is less well known is the process by which liberal and moderate lawmakers made a similar shift.[9]

Though grammatically Congress is a singular noun, functionally it is not. Congress is composed of two separate, often contentious institutions, the House and the Senate, the former with 435 members and the latter with ninety-six during the war years. In addition to the two dominant political parties, Democrats and Republicans, a scattering of third-party members played a not insignificant role in legislative debates. Just as important, members divided according to ideology, schisms that crossed party lines. Moreover, region functioned as a secondary factor, shading the ideological divisions.

Wartime partisanship, another determinative factor, was not a simple clash between Democrats and Republicans but was as much about cross-party factionalism, ideological differences, and intra-party conflicts. Congressional Democrats never cohered into a homogeneous party in the 1930s, a problem that intensified in the 1940s. These internal divisions resulted from size, geography, and ideology. Two contradictory trends emerged. The Democratic Party both nationalized its influence and regionalized its leadership in the 1930s and 1940s with liberal, moderate, and conservative southerners exercising power. Democratic priorities differed from region to region and fractious domestic politics resulted.[10]

Congressional liberals during the war years believed in the New Deal, the importance of an activist federal government, and the centrality of economic reform and regulation to prevent a capitalist oligarchy from taking over the United States. War-era congressional liberals were less unified on questions of individual rights and social justice. Nor were liberals of one mind regarding capitalism, with some retaining the anticapitalist animus of the early 1930s and some accepting the inevitability of capitalism in the United States. Liberal leaders included Sens. Robert Wagner (D-NY), George W. Norris (I-NE), Robert M. La Follette Jr. (P-WI), Hiram Johnson (R-CA), and James E. Murray (D-MT). La Follette, a Progressive Republican, was acknowledged among administration Democrats and Senate leaders as "one of the best we've got."[11] Liberals hailed from across the country. Northeastern liberals tended to be urban and have immigrant, working-class districts and constituents who identified as consumers. Southern and western liberals shared a concern about their regions as colonial economies for the northeast. As such, they wanted a strong state to encourage industrial growth in their regions, but they also sympathized with rural producers, sometimes putting them at odds with northeastern liberals. Midwestern liberals evolved from the progressive, insurgent political leaders of the early twentieth century. They fluctuated between northeastern liberals and southern and western liberals depending on the issue.

This complicated range of views makes it difficult to talk about liberals as a coherent group. I have used roll call voting data to more precisely understand liberal behavior by looking at the difference between economic and social justice liberals. Economic liberals endorsed the statist solutions embodied in the New Deal and wanted the federal government to continue to exert a strong regulatory role in the nation's economy. Social justice liberals avowed the need for federal policies, again statist in orientation, that equalized rights and opportunities in a pluralist nation. There were fewer of the former than the latter, but the majority of the latter served in the House, not the Senate, thus diluting their power to effect civil rights reform. In the absence of presidential leadership, the Senate through the filibuster had near veto power over social justice legislation. The economic issues that Congress addressed were all directly related to the war and often also reinforced the New Deal ethos. Of the economic liberals 216 were Democrats and 34 were Republicans while 63 were southerners, 89 were northeasterners, 72 were midwesterners, and 31 were westerners. Wartime efforts at social justice reform proved even more divisive in part because no one of notable stature pushed this agenda for greater individual rights or fought against the wartime red-baiters. There was divergence among members who were liberal on economic issues and members who were liberal on social justice issues. Of the social justice liberals, 189 were Democrats and 158 were Republicans while 34 were southerners, 130 were northeasterners, 134 were midwesterners, and 54 were westerners. Only 32 senators and 142 House members fell in both categories.[12]

Overcoming isolationism, a key component of conservatism since the end of World War I, proved to be the biggest obstacle for conservatives. Republican leaders—Sens. Gerald P. Nye (ND), Robert A. Taft (OH), and Arthur Vandenberg (MI)—had been important isolationist critics of the drift toward war in the late 1930s. As with liberals, conservatives were not limited to one political party or to one region of the country. Northeastern conservatives represented the concerns of the privileged industrialists and the financial elite and they advocated for smaller government, lower taxes, and fewer benefits for labor unions. Southern conservatives were more motivated by race than by economics though they did endorse statist solutions for agriculture and regional industrialization.

The war legitimated a newer mode of conservatism that built on the low-tax, antiregulatory GOP agenda from the 1920s. What emerged in the 1940s appeared primarily antistatist, and it functioned in opposition to the New Deal, abandoning all appeals to isolationism by the time of the Pearl Harbor attack. As it evolved during World War II, the new conservatism constituted a bridge to the modern conservatism of the late twentieth century by arguing against social justice reform in ways that were reminiscent of progressive-era ethnocultural politics. During the early 1940s, conservatives achieved their greatest successes in thwarting social justice reform, and these triumphs resulted because few non-southerners, regardless of region or identity, were willing to defend a civil rights agenda.

This Pyrrhic victory must be juxtaposed against the twin conservative goals where they met with defeat: deconstructing the New Deal and reducing the power of the presidency. As such, wartime conservatives opposed existing New Deal policy and did not propose new policy. Among Republicans, Sen. Eugene Millikin (R-CO) expressed the views of many in his party, blaming the New Deal for "attacks on the Congress designed to bring it into disrepute as an institution of our Government." Wartime conservatives most wanted to stop the federal government leviathan from becoming permanent and eliminating individual economic liberty. They were unhappy with both the bureaucratization of government and increasing authority for the White House. Presidential usurpations of the legislative process, specifically the increased reliance on executive orders, political initiatives not vetted by the legislative branch, intensified this complaint. During his presidency, Roosevelt not only signed 3,728 executive orders, he also turned them into a device for unilateral policymaking initiatives. In 1945, the Senate Judiciary Committee passed a resolution condemning the president for his "grabs of power." Sen. Taft lamented the need for a strong Congress to legislate domestic policy and not become "the mere shell of a legislative body."[13]

Partisan discord functioned as an opening wedge for conservatives to challenge the New Deal liberal order, work that required moderate compliance. In the 1940s, though, moderates were not stooges of the conservatives. By their very nature, moderates are not ideologues but are often the antithesis of such. The war enabled pragmatic moderates to dominate the political process, and these center-left politicians forged a liberalism in praxis that shifted the country away from welfare state liberalism and toward warfare state liberalism. Indeed, the 1940s were different from the 1930s in important ways: whereas public support for liberal reform waned during the war, a decade earlier conservatives had been in retreat. Instead, the exigencies of wartime governance created conditions where moderates were empowered. In the middle of the vehement statist versus anti-statist debates, the war necessitated a third way of nonideological compromise. When something had to be done, when doing nothing was not an option, the limited statist approaches that moderates advocated proved the least unappealing. Indeed, moderates privileged governing over endless quarrelling. Studying how wartime moderates broke this inertia clarifies the importance of the 1940s to understanding American political development. While ideologues shaped the contours of debate, moderates determined the results and enabled legislation to be passed.

Moderates proved key to sustaining a revised but still liberal economic order; on social justice questions moderates were less reliable, typically aligning with conservatives, especially in the Senate. Conservatives win when politicians from the center abandon liberal views, and the unspoken conservative agenda in the 1940s and since has been to move the center to the right. With liberal and moderate victories on the economic front but conservative and moderate triumphs on the social justice front, a calculus emerged that presaged the political battles for the remainder of the century, and the political center began shifting rightward, assuming a center-left position that was muted in comparison with the New Deal era.

The fluidity of moderates—who they were and why they shifted from left to center and sometimes to right on the various economic issues before Congress—explains the extraordinarily dynamic and contentious environment within national politics. Because this was a battle decided by the center, such omissions elide understanding of midcentury politics. Moderates, often decried for occupying the inchoate middle, held the balance of power in the 1940s and often determined what policy areas prevailed and what did not. Indeed, moderates succeeded in preserving the core of the New Deal economic reforms but never sufficiently coalesced to influence the social justice reform initiatives. Discerning a pure set of moderate principles is impossible because pragmatic compromise governed moderate political mores. There were about twice as many House Democrats as Republicans in this category, 115 and 53 respectively, but in the Senate Democrats far outnumbered Republican moderates, 30 and 9. Moreover, moderates were geographically dispersed in both chambers. Their collective longevity in Congress was comparable with other ideological factions. However, they were more willing than liberals to view New Deal programs as temporary experiments and they were more willing to trim or eliminate in deference to the war effort. The result was an incomplete victory for both conservatives and liberals, one that exaggerated the ideological contests between the two for the remainder of the century. Indeed, the transformation to modern conservatism was rooted in the ideologically neutral behavior of moderates and was evolutionary, dating back decades earlier to the World War II era.[14] Put simply the ideological wars that came to dominate the American political landscape in the last four decades of the twentieth century germinated in the 1940s.

The chapters that follow look at congressional politics, governance, and the policy formation process in what was the defining decade of the twentieth century. This method reveals the nuances of partisanship and the reasons for a bifurcated record on economic and social justice policy. Policy success and policy failure stand in bold relief against each other. Part 1 of *Why We Fight* sheds new light on economic policies with clear ties to the war effort. Chapter 1 defines the complicated institutional and historical context by exploring congressional procedure at midcentury and the parameters of congressional behavior from World War I through the New Deal, in other words the key antecedents for what happened between 1941 and 1945. Three chapters on taxation, rationing, and labor laws reveal just how difficult passage of these necessary wartime measures was. Lawmakers were never able to isolate the debate to the questions at hand but instead used the need for additional taxation, the construction of a command economy, and the challenges of manpower mobilization as proxy issues to fight what was for them a war about the New Deal and the role of the federal government in American life. These chapters precede the second part of *Why We Fight*, and they show the fragility of wartime liberalism, clarifying why, when, and how reform ended. Only from this context can the failures to enact wartime social justice reform be understood.

In Part 2 three chapters explore refugee policy, civil rights, and anti-Communist red-baiting, revealing a potent racial conservatism too powerful for the moderates and liberals to overcome. Not only did these issues have less direct impact on the outcome of the war, but, more important, they seemed disconnected from the core of the New Deal, making them expendable to moderates in Congress. The congressional contribution to these policy struggles was significant, yet little is known of these events because one of the conventional arguments about American politics is that Congress lost power to the executive branch in war making. Through my new look at World War II we see this is not quite the case. Finally, an epilogue explores how the partisan dynamics established in the 1940s shaped national politics through the 1970s when the seniority system was eliminated, conservative southern Democrats began their migration to the GOP, and the ongoing Cold War intervention in Vietnam ended. World War II then becomes the template for understanding the history of the twentieth century, one where politics and war merged and warfare state liberalism replaced the welfare state.

World War II catapulted the United States from a third-rate military power to one of two leading superpowers. An equally important conversion occurred at home in the realm of national governance. Nevertheless, the role of Congress in this transformation has yet to be examined. The World War II congressional generation saw everything—depression, war, and then Cold War. These incredibly varied experiences changed the members of Congress and the institution in which they served. Informal and cordial part-time lawmakers sharing quarters in the capital city's many hotels disappeared, and, because of the partisan politics of moderation, a professional, modern, even imperial Congress of full-time lawmakers unwilling to cede an ounce of control to the newly powerful imperial presidency emerged. These alterations to New Deal liberalism, especially a revitalization of congressional moderates, illustrate how America's national lawmakers responded to and were transformed by the last great worldwide military conflagration.

1. The World before the War

In small and large ways World War II changed life in Washington, D.C., the center of national politics. The U.S. Capitol was not exempt from war, and indeed the scene mirrored the realities of congressional warfare about the New Deal. Soon after Pearl Harbor heavy machine guns were installed on roofs of the government office buildings, an unhidden military secret. Within the Capitol, signs reading "Reserved—for Military Use" blocked stairways and corridors normally open for passage. Before visitors could access the galleries they had to be inspected by the Capitol police, as did all packages brought into the building. Agnes V. O'Mahoney, the wife of one senator, wrote in a newspaper column about the soldiers "with metal helmets and fixed bayonets" guarding the capitol and other key sites in the city, including bridges on the Potomac, the city waterworks, and the apartments and hotels where some members of Congress lived. Such military realities sharpened the legislative disputes, but understanding them requires an overview of what Washington, D.C., had been like before the war.[1]

Journalist Frank McNaughton's unpublished memoranda for *Time* magazine speak volumes about the changes in Congress. Although he worked in the Washington bureau for *Time,* an opinionated news magazine that criticized the Roosevelt administration, McNaughton had close connections with midwestern liberals and he sympathized with Franklin D. Roosevelt and Harry S Truman. McNaughton nonetheless had earned the respect of the Republican publisher of the magazine, Henry Luce, because he nurtured a network of Capitol Hill and executive branch sources. He sometimes was an invited guest to Speaker Sam Rayburn's (D-TX) hideaway office, the Board of Education, where many important war-era political bargains were struck. McNaughton defined Pearl Harbor as a distinctive moment dividing two periods in U.S. history, concluding "an era of moral bankruptcy, utter confusion, spineless mediocrity. Anything would do in that era. Boondoggling, shade-tree censuses, WPA diaper-pinning projects, 'the only thing we have to fear is fear itself.' It was a rude awakening. There is a hell of a lot more to fear than fear." McNaughton's critique of social democracy paralleled the views of the moderate and conservative lawmakers who trusted him with information about the internal workings of Congress, for by the 1940s many of those members had rejected part or all of the New Deal welfare state and worked to remake their Frankenstein's monster of the 1930s into a more palatable warfare state.[2]

Because McNaughton viewed the challenges of the 1940s as serious, he was not sanguine in the weeks after Pearl Harbor, quipping, "Did you ever see a whorehouse when the madam was away and the girls were trying to run the business? This is it!" McNaughton was not suggesting that the "madam" or the "girls" reflected particular branches of the government. Instead, the metaphor of wartime Washington, D.C., as an unsupervised whorehouse described the extensive congressional fighting with the president, between the House and the Senate, and among the various ideological factions of lawmakers, but it does not convey why those fights mattered. Agnes O'Mahoney explained, "Debate and controversy is the day by day work of Congress."[3]

What follows is a dual examination of the congressional world before the war, focusing first on the institutional context and second on the historical context. Understanding something about the interior workings of Congress as it evolved in the mid-twentieth century is central to appreciating the political nuances of the 1940s. The complexity of Congress makes studying the institution difficult. It involves multiple players without a clear center of power and, to the uninitiated, arcane rules and technical procedures that matter very much to how political battles are conducted. Without knowledge of the role of committees, the discharge petition, filibusters, or cloture rules, it is impossible to grasp the ins and outs of partisan battles.

Members of Congress in the 1940s lived and worked according to the seniority system in which committee chairs and the leadership in the two chambers earned their positions by length of service, not by a majority vote. Argued Sen. Bennett Champ Clark (D-MO): "A man has to learn to be a Congressman just as he has to learn to be a blacksmith, a carpenter, a farmer, an engineer, a lawyer, or a doctor. A new Congressman must begin at the foot of the class and spell up." As such, southerners held a disproportionate number of committee chairs, a fact that remained true in the war years. Of the 819 lawmakers who served during World War II, 237 were midwesterners, 245 were northeasterners, 228 were southerners, and 109 were westerners. In the 1920s, Dixie politicians had been more likely to retain congressional seats than their northern, western, and midwestern counterparts, so in any given Congress the ratio of non-southerners to southerners is higher. For example, of the 562 members who sat in the 77th Congress (the number is greater than 531 because of replacements resulting from death and resignation) just 167 were southern, or 29 percent of the membership. Between 1941 and 1945, southerners chaired about half of the forty-seven standing committees in the House, and a comparable percentage of the thirty-three standing Senate committees. During these years, southerners held an overwhelming percentage of major committee chairs in both chambers. Additionally, southerners assumed key leadership positions in both chambers, meaning that the seniority system, which functioned as the Democratic Party's ruling order in the House, was intrinsically

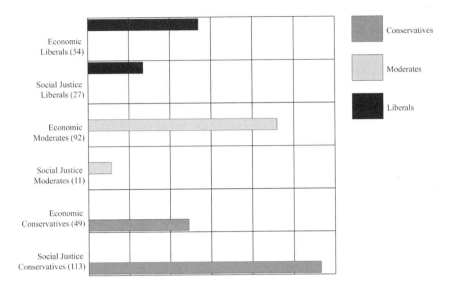

Chart 1.1: Southern Ideological Diversity, U.S. House of Representatives. Data for this chart are derived from analysis of key economic policy roll call votes from the war era.

linked to southern political mores. The one-party South was not ideologically uniform but was factionalized, as Charts 1.1 and 1.2 show. A majority of politicians from this region held moderate to liberal views on the economy and conservative views on social justice issues. Since southerners dominated congressional politics this dichotomy shaped the war-era debates about the New Deal.[4]

An informal coalition between conservative southern Democrats and conservative Republicans evolved in this era. Some liberal lawmakers even attributed Roosevelt's first vice president, John Nance Garner of Texas, with partial authorship of the coalition. Such accusations played into stereotypes, though, because the partisan and geographic identity of lawmakers was much more complex than suggested by this calculus of a conservative coalition, and in fact its reputation surpasses its importance for war-era politics. A careful exploration of roll call voting from the war years suggests a more complicated story regarding the identity of conservatives than the standard assumptions that Republicans and southern Democrats dominated the right wing of the political spectrum. As Charts 1.3 and 1.4 show, economic conservatives in the House included more northeasterners than southerners, 71 and 49, respectively, and in the Senate there were slightly more southerners than northeasterners, 19 and 15. Social justice conservatives more obviously hailed from the South, especially in the House. While there were more Republican social justice conservatives in the House than Democratic ones,

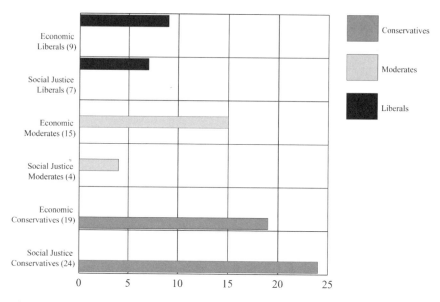

Chart 1.2: Southern Ideological Diversity, U.S. Senate. Data for this chart are derived from analysis of key economic policy roll call votes from the war era.

174 and 115, in the Senate, Democrats outstripped Republicans, 38 to 25, again calling into question whether the conservative coalition continued into the 1940s in the same form in which it emerged in the late 1930s.[5]

Critics then and since have denigrated this legislative structure for being undemocratic, but such criticisms are facile. The House both set and revised its rules by a simple majority vote every two years, but it preserved seniority as a reasonable way of determining committee chairmanships. It is true that seniority benefitted southerners because they so often were reelected, but it also allowed long-serving liberals, progressives, and mavericks to rise who might never have prevailed in a vote within their caucus. Since the southerners constituted the largest voting bloc in the Democratic caucus, they likely would have won votes to chair the committees (especially since moderate and liberal Republicans would have voted in their own caucus). Liberals might have blocked a particularly reactionary chairman but could then have suffered the same consequences. And is "merit" the likely alternative to seniority? The history of Congress since the 1970s suggests party loyalty trumped merit in many leadership contests.

In addition to the seniority system, other characteristics of the midcentury Congress played a key role in shaping wartime politics, notably the important differences between the two chambers. The rules of the Senate permitted unlimited debate, but those of the House did not. This made the filibuster

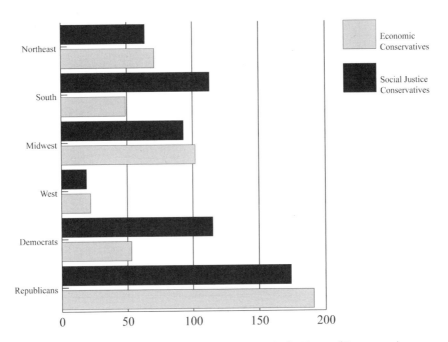

Chart 1.3: The Geography of Congressional Conservatism in the House of Representatives. Data for this chart are derived from analysis of key social justice policy roll call votes from the war era.

possible in the upper chamber. Antidemocratic, the filibuster enabled a minority in the Senate to block votes on legislation deemed unacceptable to them but otherwise likely to win passage on a simple majority vote, the then normal operating procedure in the upper chamber. During the 1940s, the filibuster was the tool southern segregationists used to block civil rights measures. Breaking a filibuster, a procedural vote called cloture, required an affirmative vote of two-thirds of the Senate—sixty-four members—in the 1940s. The filibuster functioned then as a support system maintaining the power of the institution's oligarchs not unlike the "emergency superstructure of frank ungainly steel" that kept the Senate chamber from falling in on itself.[6]

The House, lacking the filibuster, was less likely to allow southern segregationists to dominate procedure and policy. As a result, the chamber often took more moderate positions on legislation than did the Senate, and it seemed more responsive to the public than did the Senate. Still, the House was no bastion of perfect democracy. The Rules Committee determined how and under what conditions legislation would be debated on the floor. It could subvert the majority will by limiting time for debate or the number and type of amendments

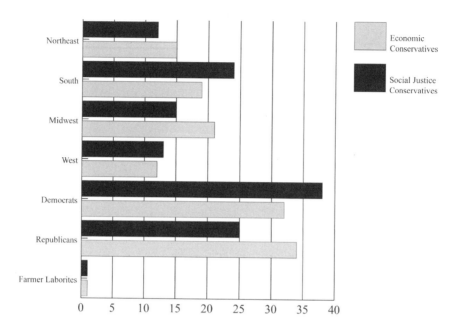

Chart 1.4: The Geography of Congressional Conservatism in the Senate. Data for this chart are derived from analysis of key social justice policy roll call votes from the war era.

permitted from the floor. Moreover, it, along with jurisdictional committees, could block legislation from being moved to the floor, leaving proponents only one remedy: the discharge petition, which required the signatures of 218 members to force a floor debate.[7]

The leadership in the House during the war era appeared more substantive and serious than in the Senate. Both institutional structure and personality explain this result. The House has always been more hierarchic than the collegial Senate, and the Senate has been less tolerant of a top-down leadership. One journalist acknowledged, "In the House the facts of life are considerably closer to the surface. If Joe Doakes thinks Bill Blow is a son of a gun he gets up and says so, and none of your 'distinguished Senator from so-and-so' stuff. Members tell one another off in a roughhouse atmosphere." The rules of the House give great power to the Speaker, in contrast to the limited authority that Senate rules give the majority leader. Sam Rayburn, the no-nonsense Speaker of the House, oversaw his chamber not so much as a dictator but through personal respect and loyalty from the members. Alben Barkley (D-KY), the Senate majority leader, was the antithesis of Rayburn in that he did not command respect from senators. Said one observer, the Kentuckian "acts like a man who is working awfully hard and awfully earnestly at a job he doesn't particularly like."[8]

Other important lawmakers included Joseph W. Martin, Jr. (R-MA) and Charles McNary (R-OR), the minority leaders in the House and the Senate. Martin was a conservative Republican interested in reforming House procedure to increase the power of the minority, while McNary was popular, bipartisan, and effective. The White House worked with him, telling McNary its legislative strategy. House majority leader John W. McCormack (D-MA), an Irish Catholic, hailed from Boston, and he worked closely with Rayburn. Beyond the formal leadership structure in the two chambers, individual lawmakers asserted themselves as leaders because of their policy prowess. For example, Robert L. Doughton (D-NC) and Walter George (D-GA), the chairs of the House Ways and Means Committee and the Senate Finance Committee, dominated much of the debate about wartime tax and fiscal policy. The war made other members of Congress into national heroes. Most significantly, Harry S Truman (D-MO), who chaired an important Senate oversight committee to monitor the defense industries, gained the credibility through his war work to become vice president and later president.

To study Congress is to study the myriad individuals who practiced democracy on a daily basis. Their work involved the formal and the informal, with the latter being as important as the former to achieving policy success. Papers of war-era lawmakers are full of cross-party Christmas cards and other similar statements of the comity that was a necessary prerequisite for moderates to dominate the liberalism in praxis that remade the New Deal. For example, Elbert D. Thomas (D-UT) opined: "If the people in our country realized that men in the Senate learn to appreciate one another . . . they would have greater faith in our Senate. . . . Men who reach the Senate love their country more than anything else." The politicians who populated Capitol Hill at midcentury were among the most colorful and substantive ever to serve in Washington, D.C. Analysis of the congressional gadflies—Sen. Theodore Bilbo (D-MS), Rep. Vito Marcantonio (AL-NY), and Sen. William Langer (R-ND), as examples—cannot be divorced from consideration of the congressional workhorses like Rayburn, Sen. Robert A. Taft (R-OH), and Sen. Robert M. La Follette Jr. (P-WI). A diverse cast of astute politicians with complicated motivations dominated Congress. They perfected the politics of partisanship and compromise. Rayburn declared: "We call this a people's war, and it is well to remember that the Congress is the people's Congress. It is in the Congress that out of the clash of contending opinions is forged the democratic unity of a democratic people."[9]

The informal aspects of congressional life—the clubbiness, the fraternities, and the socializing—played a significant, if often hidden, role in policy outcomes. These factors, as much as committee assignments and floor debates, determined the kind of institution Congress was at midcentury. Lawmakers divided themselves into a number of categories or blocs that sometimes had no obvious relationship to partisan politics, among which were included membership in fraternal organizations like the Masons and the Rotary Club and invitations to drink in Rayburn's hideaway office, the Board of Education. For some, place of residence in the district mattered. For example, the Mayflower Hotel provided quarters to a number of important economic moderates, most notably Walter George, while the Shoreham Hotel and the Wardman Park Hotel housed several leading liberal senators. Given the reality of the war with which they dealt on an almost daily basis, past military service mattered; approximately one-third of the members of Congress had served in the military, 197 out of 531 members. A comparable percentage of lawmakers had relatives serving in World War II, giving rise to the War Parents Association, a group of members with children in military service.[10]

Buffoonery and bellicose behavior caused the institution's image to suffer vis-à-vis the president, though. Character-driven behavior and idiosyncrasy were still welcome; the Congress had not yet evolved into a collection of junior executives in Brooks Brothers suits. For example, "Cousin" Nat Patton (D-TX), a backbench congressman who called everyone "Cousin," had been drinking beer in the kitchen of the House dining room one day. Patton pulled a pocket knife on columnist Drew Pearson, who had belittled Patton, "You beat me, you beat me. You God damned sonofabitch." Similarly unpleasant anecdotes reveal gender discrimination in Congress. Rep. Clare Hoffman (R-MI) became angry that the table reserved for him in the House restaurant was not to his liking, so he told the woman on duty, "If you were a man I'd slap you." She responded, "Go right ahead. Don't let my dress interfere with you. And I guarantee you if you do, the flag will fly at half mast until they can get you back to Michigan!" When lawmakers from Michigan heard of the incident, they refused to eat with Hoffman.[11]

Members of Congress were not without the capacity for reflection upon problems within the institution. Sen. Joseph C. O'Mahoney (D-WY) made a national radio address on June 17, 1942, in which he discussed the subject of what was wrong with Congress. He attacked the centralized power given to the White House, arguing instead "the legislative power, rather than the executive or judicial, has always been recognized as the basis of democracy." He refuted charges that Congress had "impeded the war effort." O'Mahoney believed "exactly the reverse." He cited congressional warnings about pending shortages of critical materials in the 1930s, proposed legislative remedies, and presidential rebuttals. "The record is clear," reasoned O'Mahoney. "The nation would have plenty of rubber and there would be no prospect of nation-wide gasoline rationing . . . if the authority which the Congress gave years ago had been used." Whereas O'Mahoney used temperate, thoughtful speech to criticize the administration, when Rep. William Lemke (R-ND) demagogued the issue, he furthered the caricature of Congress as unequal to the challenges before it. "I shall call a spade a spade," professed Lemke regarding the executive branch bureaucracy. "There are too many book educated specialists from Harvard and Columbia Universities. These are more foreign minded than American minded. They would substitute the Hitler form of government for the American. They believe in regimentation, in bluff, and in bluster."[12]

Examination of wartime congressional staffing, albeit not necessarily the most glamorous subject, reveals the difficulty lawmakers had with the bureaucracies and why the administration viewed Congress as a "rubber stamp." The small size of their staffs was not sufficient for the sort of work required in the 1940s. The president even suggested to no avail that funds be appropriated for the Speaker and the vice president to hire one additional secretary each. At the end of the war, a total of 356 clerks worked for all the House and Senate committees, with a payroll under a million dollars. Most of the congressional aides were not professionally trained but were patronage appointments, sometimes relatives, spouses, and even mistresses. Lawmakers grew dependent on the professionally trained, borrowed staff from the agencies that they criticized to do the wartime work required of Congress. For example, at the outset of the war, in fiscal year 1941, 211 officials from federal agencies were detailed to work for committees of Congress. One other small note exemplifies the antiquated procedures of the wartime Congress. In 1943, the Senate Appropriations Committee studied whether or not senators should be authorized to make long-distance telephone calls at government expense. Likewise, as noted in Charts 1.5 and 1.6, the professional preparation of the members themselves varied widely. Just over half the members of Congress had legal training, but from institutions ranging from Ivy League universities to Y.M.C.A. night schools, a fact that often left lawmakers stymied when facing down the experts from the executive agencies in committee hearings. Indeed, sometimes lawmakers behaved badly toward the executive branch staff that intimidated them. For example, Harvard Law School graduate, David Ginsburg, the general counsel for the Office of Price Administration, recalled years later how members of Congress attacked him for being Jewish.[13]

These realities shaped the way members of Congress interacted with the White House and, more importantly, the strategies FDR's lobbyists used in their work on Capitol Hill. Rarely were Roosevelt's liaisons with Capitol Hill not in need of hazardous duty pay, so intense could the feuding between the legislative and executive branches be during the war years. Henry Morgenthau once explained to his wife: "somebody would have to be the ham in the sandwich as between the President and Congress, and I was expecting to be it."[14]

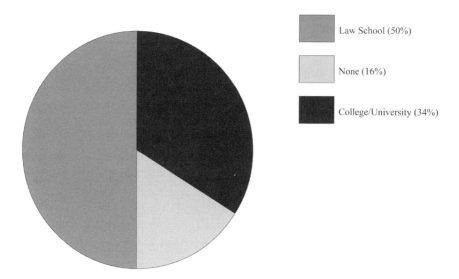

Chart 1.5: College Education. Data for this chart are drawn from the Congressional Directory, *77th Congress–79th Congress.*

Over the course of the war years, Roosevelt deployed four different categories of lobbyists to sway Congress, with varying degrees of success. First, there were the agency officials, individuals like Leon Henderson, a longtime New Dealer who was the first director of the Office of Price Administration, and John Kenneth Galbraith, who began his career in the 1930s and went on to advise Democratic presidents for much of the rest of the century. These men, often liberal purists in their commitment to the New Deal and often trained at elite colleges and universities, did not appreciate the pragmatic, messy underside to democracy as practiced in the halls of Congress. Henderson especially rankled lawmakers, so different was his mien than that of congressional power brokers.[15]

Second, some members of the administration, for example Jesse Jones, the director of the Reconstruction Finance Corporation and later secretary of commerce, had close ties to the moderate and conservative Democratic leaders in Congress. One journalist called him the "transmission belt of the Administration. . . . This is because Jesse knows which side his bread is buttered on; Jesse knows the advantages of getting along with the boys." Third, there were the administration's political gurus, men like Thomas "Tommy the Cork" Corcoran and James Rowe. Both Corcoran and Rowe maintained close friendships with lawmakers while also being committed New Dealers. Their fingerprints on legislative lobbying for the White House are much less visible, Corcoran especially, because they did so much of their work for the president over the telephone.[16]

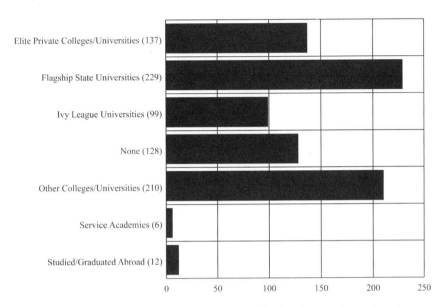

Chart 1.6: College Education by Institution Type. Data for this chart are drawn from the Congressional Directory, *77th Congress–79th Congress.*

Finally, as the war wore on, Roosevelt turned to former members of Congress to fill posts in his mushrooming administration, most notably the "assistant president" James F. Byrnes, Prentiss Brown, and Fred Vinson. Byrnes and Vinson proved more than able in their executive branch work, having spent time in the federal judiciary after leaving Congress and before going to the White House. Brown was another story; he gained a presidential appointment after suffering a bitter defeat for reelection in 1942 and was never able to speak forcefully for the White House, so much did lawmakers expect him to be a ninety-seventh senator representing the views of Capitol Hill within the administration.[17]

The congressional immaturity compared with the executive branch stands in stark relief when examined alongside changing patterns in federal expenditures and the vast proliferation of executive agencies. As such, Roosevelt viewed Congress as provincial and unimaginative, not alert to the emerging role of U.S. leadership in the world. According to one estimate coming out of Sen. Gerald P. Nye's (R-ND) office, the U.S. government had spent $71,303,000,000 between 1789 and March 4, 1933. During Roosevelt's first eight years in office the U.S. government spent another $63,774,000,000. Between June 1, 1940, and April 1, 1941, the U.S. government spent $39,177,000,000 on national defense according to the National Defense Advisory Commission.[18]

Such spending matters were constantly in the minds of lawmakers. Rep. Clinton Anderson (D-NM) observed, "I could begin to see, when I came to Washington, that money as I had known it was likely to change in its character. I had not been here very long until we voted seven billion dollars, then five billion dollars, then ten billion dollars. No Congress ever voted money in such amounts." By looking at the average annual expenditures for the ten years preceding and the ten years following each major war since the American Revolution, Anderson criticized war-induced spending sprees. The War of 1812 and the Mexican War both saw a rough doubling of expenditures, in the first case from $9 million and in the second case from $26.2 million. For the Civil War spending increased over five-fold, from $60.1 million to $332.5 million. The Spanish American War, though, was the most frugal period. During World War I, spending increased almost six-fold, from $696.9 million to $3.9 billion. As such, Anderson predicted an annual budget of $12 billion in the immediate postwar years. He used these figures to call for wise fiscal management by Congress to avoid unnecessary ballooning of the budget. Even so, Congress paid scant attention to the annual need to raise the debt ceiling, complying each year after Pearl Harbor with little debate.[19]

Other lawmakers had a different view of war funding. Sam Rayburn lectured that military de-escalation in the 1920s played an important role in the needed expenditures in 1940s. "There was not a ship laid down during the Hoover Administration. We are becoming prepared just as fast as it is humanly possible to do. No republic is ever prepared for war when there is no trouble in the world, but we know there is trouble now and we are preparing," Rayburn avowed. "Naturally, it takes a lot of money to do this, and I do not see how the public debt can be reduced and carry out this preparedness program at the same time."[20]

Looking at data on the size and scope of the national security system, and the place of Congress within it, reveals the magnitude of the challenges before the legislative branch and why wartime policy was so contentious. For example, the proposed total federal expenditures for fiscal year 1941 paint a stark picture of how unready for war the country was and how important New Deal spending remained in the national economy. Out of Roosevelt's total proposed budget of just over $8.4 billion, which included spending cuts of approximately $500 million, only $1.8 billion was allocated for national defense while $6.3 billion went to various New Deal spending programs. The federal deficit was just under $2.2 billion. By war's end the deficit was nearly $270 billion. For fiscal year 1945, the federal government spent over $100 billion, 90 percent of which went to the war effort.[21]

Following the story of the war and the federal budget forward to the end of the 1940s shows just how successful conservatives in Congress were at redirecting federal spending away from the New Deal into national defense. President Harry Truman's proposed budget expenditures for fiscal year 1950 totaled $41.9 billion, with $21 billion allocated for national security and just $2.4 billion for social welfare, $1.7 billion for agriculture, and $2.3 billion for housing, education, labor, finance, commerce, and industry. While defense spending went from 21 percent of the budget in fiscal year 1941 to 50 percent in fiscal year 1950, spending on New Deal–style initiatives remained flat in total dollars appropriated, but shrunk significantly as a percentage of government outlays: down from 75 percent to just 15 percent of the budget.[22] Certainly international conditions explain the continued spending on national defense, but the reduced prioritization of New Deal social welfare programs cannot be attributed solely to postwar prosperity. Some conservatives and moderates in Congress, as I argue in this book, worked hard in the 1940s to delegitimize the welfare state liberalism of the 1930s and replace it with a less expansive warfare state liberalism disassociated from social welfare problems.

A survey of military manpower combined with a count of the number of congressional committees engaged in military oversight reinforce this point. In 1940, the U.S. Army ranked eighteenth in the world, larger than Bulgaria, but nothing to suggest the role it would play in World War II or the half century that followed.[23] Just as the military and the federal budget were unready for war so was Congress. Its committee structure provided little opportunity for streamlined military and national security oversight. In the House there existed the Committees on Foreign Affairs, Merchant Marine and Fisheries, Military Affairs, and Naval Affairs with direct oversight responsibilities. Additionally, the Committees on Ways and Means and Appropriations were critical because of their role in raising and appropriating the funds needed to fight the war. The five special and select committees created in the House for oversight purposes typically functioned more to obstruct than to facilitate U.S. military success, with the most important being the Select Committee to Investigate Acts of Executive Agencies beyond the Scope of Their Authority and the Select Committee on Un-American Activities. The former existed solely to attack the New Deal and expenditures for it, and the latter searched for Communists in the federal government with tactics intended to discredit the New Deal. A similarly diffuse system of committee jurisdiction existed in the Senate with the Committees on Foreign Relations, Military Affairs, and Naval Affairs all overseeing aspects of the defense program. Additionally, the Senate created three special committees—Special Committee to Investigate the National Defense Program, Special Committee to Investigate Gasoline and Fuel-Oil Shortages, and Special Committee Investigating Petroleum Resources—with the most important being the first, which Truman chaired.

An example showing the peculiarities of the seniority system further illustrates congressional unreadiness for military oversight. In September 1941, the House leadership faced a crisis that had the potential to harm the military appropriations process. Edward T. Taylor (D-CO), the eighty-year-old chair of the Appropriations Committee, passed away. Most House members expected that the mantle would pass to Clifton Alexander Woodrum (D-VA), Taylor's unofficial stand-in as chair for the last four years. Clarence Cannon (D-MO) also wanted the post. Both Cannon and Woodrum had entered Congress the same year and had gone on the Appropriations Committee the same year, but according to the alphabet, Cannon's name was listed first. Despite his conservative leanings on domestic questions, Woodrum enjoyed presidential backing. He worked equally well with Republicans and he avoided partisan excesses, but Cannon, "a psychopathic case" primarily concerned with agricultural funding and parity pricing schemes according to Woodrum, "sees everything, virtually, from a partisan angle."[24]

Said Woodrum privately, "He puts in a perfunctory appearance at national defense hearings, no more; asks a couple of questions to get his name in the record, then hides out." Other committee members concurred with this assessment. Journalists covering Congress worried that Cannon was ill equipped to manage national defense appropriations through the lower chamber. Nonetheless, the House leadership, Rayburn and McCormack, bent to the will of lawmakers and the rule of seniority, not the president, and supported Cannon over Woodrum. When Cannon gained the post, he also claimed the chairship of the deficiency appropriations subcommittee, key to war funding, despite the fact that Woodrum had been doing all the work for years. The disappointed Woodrum complained in an off-the-record interview, "For years I've been doing the work here, while others get the credit. If he wants to be chairman of deficiencies, carry the flag, let him do the work. I didn't mind doing it for Taylor. He was in poor health, aged. Let Cannon do the work." Woodrum expected that Rayburn would eventually ask him to take over the defense spending bills, and according to *Time* magazine journalist Frank McNaughton, he planned "to tell Rayburn that he thinks he's a hell of a heel."[25]

The institutional portrait of Congress, then, on the eve of the war suggests that the legislative branch still had one foot in the older verities of the late nineteenth- and early twentieth-century procedures and another in mid-twentieth-century modernization. As such, lawmakers were less certain of the wisdom of making the New Deal permanent. This reality helps explain and contextualize the two major arguments of this book regarding the primacy of congressional partisanship and its impact on economic and social justice policy, specifically the role of moderates in preserving a New Deal orientation regarding the former and blocking passage of the latter. Lawmakers were a product of place: the states and districts they represented but also the Capitol building where they worked. Here Pennsylvania Avenue proved itself as a definitive piece of real estate, a concrete ribbon more often separating than connecting Capitol Hill with the White House.

The historical context, though, matters as much as the institutional context. The political legacy of World War I, the 1920s, and the New Deal shaped the policy deliberations between 1941 and 1945 because many of the congressional workhorses of the war years had cut their legislative teeth, so to speak, in the three preceding political periods. As Charts 1.7 and 1.8 show, of the forty-five leading committee chairs and leadership officials just seven came to Congress when Franklin D. Roosevelt was president and only another eight in the Herbert Hoover administration. The remaining thirty entered Congress during or before Calvin Coolidge was in the White House with a few gaining election when Theodore Roosevelt was president. When the totality of congressional membership is examined a different picture emerges, one where the majority of the membership was elected in 1938 or later. The context for congressional war policy is multifaceted. Because World War I marked the emergence, albeit hesitantly, of the United States as a world power, some appreciation of the congressional role in that conflict is in order. The story for the 1920s is different: Democratic leaders elected in that decade learned the politics of opposition and partisanship because Republicans controlled both the legislative and executive branches from 1921 through 1931. Equally important, the domestic political realignment of the 1930s instituted not only an era of Democratic hegemony but also a more activist federal government. These developments require explication, as does the process by which 1930s' politicians first legislated neutrality and then repealed it. Indeed, the Great War caused many Americans, in and out of Congress, to rethink the virtues of world involvement. Finally, the impact of Pearl Harbor on domestic politics merits consideration. National politics, like all other aspects of American life, changed on December 7, 1941.

A generation before Pearl Harbor, President Woodrow Wilson led a divided country into the Great War. In 1917, many Americans still held a nineteenth-century view of the world, one in which a young and vigorous United States remained free from corruption by the old and lethargic Europe. This vision had deep roots, reaching back into the earliest days of the Republic. In 1797, George Washington had cautioned Americans against the dangers of entangling alliances abroad. Such ideological currency combined with the state of near constant warfare in Europe led President James Monroe to institute the Monroe Doctrine, which declared Europe should remain out of American affairs and cease colonization efforts in the Western Hemisphere. These two grand declarations combined with internal conflicts over slavery and expansion westward helped Americans construct the myth of isolation from world politics.[26]

The Great War debunked this myth. At first, the war seemed far removed

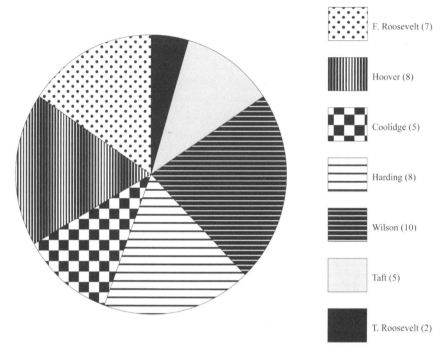

F. Roosevelt (7)

Hoover (8)

Coolidge (5)

Harding (8)

Wilson (10)

Taft (5)

T. Roosevelt (2)

Chart 1.7: Administration When Committee Chairs and the Leadership Entered Congress. Data for this chart are drawn from the Congressional Directory, *77th Congress–79th Congress.*

from the United States. The fighting began in August 1914 after a Serbian nationalist assassinated the Austrian Archduke Francis Ferdinand. The local, political murder triggered a series of convoluted secret treaties of mutual defense into operation so that Serbia's struggle for freedom from the Austro-Hungarian Empire became a world war with the domination of Europe as the ultimate prize. The European powers divided into two warring alliance systems: the Central Powers, which included Germany, Austria-Hungary, the Ottoman Empire, and Bulgaria, and the Allied Powers, which included Great Britain, France, Russia, Serbia, Italy, Greece, Montenegro, Portugal, and Romania. President Wilson instructed the American people to remain impartial in their thoughts and their actions. Prior to U.S. entry into the war in 1917, members of Congress blamed Wilson's policies for Germany's submarine warfare, and they pursued isolationist legislation such as banning American travel on belligerent ships and implementing a "water's edge" defense policy. Wilson called his congressional critics "willful men."[27]

On April 2, 1917, in an address to a joint session of Congress asking for a war

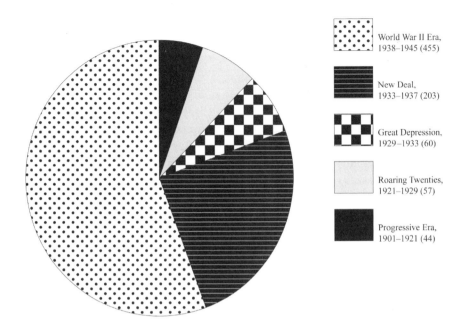

Chart 1.8: Political Era When All Members of the 77th through 79th Congresses Gained Election. Data for this chart are drawn from the Congressional Directory, *77th Congress–79th Congress.*

declaration, Wilson told lawmakers "civilization itself" was "in the balance." He attested, "The right is more precious than the peace, and we shall fight for the things which we have always carried nearest in our hearts,—for democracy, for the right of those who submit to authority to have a voice in their own governments, for the rights and liberties of small nations." Insurgents and progressives in Congress doubted Wilson's call to turn war into an international progressive movement. They could not reconcile military action abroad with the traditional republican values upon which American democracy was based. Days after Wilson addressed Congress, Sen. Robert M. La Follette Sr., a progressive Republican from Wisconsin, affirmed a responsibility "to vote and act" his "convictions on questions" regarding war. "Quite another doctrine has been proposed by the newspapers of the country," he warned. "It is the doctrine of standing behind the president, without inquiry as to whether he is right or wrong. I have never subscribed to that doctrine and I never shall." Likewise, Sen. George W. Norris (R-NE) avowed, "I feel that we are about to put the dollar sign on the American flag." His critics rejoined with cries of "treason." The final vote on the war declaration encapsulated the divided public opinion, as the measure carried by a margin of 373–50 in the House and 82–6 in the Senate.[28]

During the war, a sectionally divided Congress, especially Democrats, focused energy on both social and economic policy questions while also critiquing the military effort. It placed harsh restrictions on the rights of both citizens and immigrants. Convinced by wartime propaganda that recent immigrants from southern and eastern Europe posed a danger to civilization, Congress implemented a literacy test for new arrivals. The Trading-with-the-Enemy Act, the Espionage Act, and the Sedition Act severely limited citizenship rights for all Americans. In response, isolationist insurgents questioned the administration's war policy, lambasted congressional deference to Wilson, and advocated progressive reforms such as a war profits tax. Regarding military matters, Congress reduced its credibility because too many members flatly opposed massive troop movements to Europe. Said one leading senator about White House and War Department plans for the American Expeditionary Force in April 1917, "Congress will not permit American soldiers to be sent to Europe."[29]

American soldiers went, fought, and, along with the Allies, reached an armistice-inducing stalemate by November 1918, a result that did little to assuage congressional concern. Animosity regarding the Treaty of Versailles and presidential power left a potent legacy for shaping legislative behavior on the eve of World War II. President Wilson made errors in the negotiation of that treaty: he took no important Republicans or Senators to Paris, and he failed to consult with the Senate about the progress of the secretive treaty negotiations. Some lawmakers charged he had exceeded his constitutional duties.[30] Once the treaty had been hammered out at Versailles, the Senate was in no mood to approve it. The usage of obstructionist tactics to defeat the treaty influenced congressional-executive relations in constructive and destructive ways.

What legacy did this episode leave for Congress in future wars? First, even though Wilson lost the battle, the president gained preeminence over Congress in the realm of foreign affairs. He advocated reform while his critics espoused a negative and reactive creed. Sen. Henry Cabot Lodge (R-MA), the most important opponent of the League of Nations, concluded: "'Very great men' are extremely rare. Mr. Wilson was not one of them."[31] Second, the irreconcilables learned the limits of their power to influence foreign and domestic policy in World War I. Their story remains important for the World War II era because several of these lawmakers were again significant critics of wartime policy, but the tactics that worked in 1918–1919 did not meet with success in the late 1930s for conditions, internally and externally, were very different.

The aftermath of the Great War shaped partisan allegiances in the 1920s and 1930s. Politicians in the 1920s had retreated from the domestic and international progressive movement of the early twentieth century, especially Woodrow Wilson's struggle for the League of Nations.[32] Those progressive politicians who remained in Washington found themselves outnumbered by lawmakers who touted business efficiency, rationalization, and cooperation—not regulation. The stock market crash and the Great Depression, however, created conditions when political experimentation regarding the economy was again welcome, and New Deal reforms forever remade the relationship between state and society.

Just as danger lurks when Congress is used as a singular noun so also should the same caution apply to the New Deal, which was an evolutionary, not singular, political development forged in a Congress with partisan, ideological, and regional differences not unlike those found a decade later during the war years. Because there were many different New Dealers in and out of Congress, lawmakers in the 1940s were again able to remake this political culture. On the surface, the New Deal seemed the product of crisis and of FDR's advisors, but in reality, Congress discussed many of its intellectual antecedents during the 1890s and the Progressive Era: agricultural relief, labor protections, and business regulation. Histories of the New Deal have ignored or downplayed the congressional contributions to the activism of the 1930s. In fact, members of the legislative branch midwifed most of the New Deal into existence, and when the nation found itself in another crisis the following decade—World War II—liberal and moderate members of Congress saved what they could of that New Deal from extinction.

So what was the New Deal and why was it important to Congress? This amorphous, pragmatic, often Keynesian economic program resulted from Democratic Party concerns about inequities among various organized interests within society, especially with regard to how the economic privations of the Great Depression worsened class stratification. Two concentrated bursts of legislative activism—one in 1933 that was moderate in approach and a second in 1935 that encompassed a comparatively more radical phase of reform—produced most of the New Deal. Initially many of the programs sought relief and recovery from the Depression, while more of the later initiatives offered long-term systemic reforms.

The congresses of the New Deal period, with the exception of the first few weeks of the FDR administration, were divided over policy issues. And New Deal programs lacked ideological coherence, instead reflecting the urgency of the moment and the experimental approach to reform. If there was a unifying principle among the laws of the New Deal, the focus on state action and statist solutions to the Great Depression was it. While it is true that the electoral process had brought in more ideological conservatives after 1938, earlier in the New Deal conservative Democrats, some from the South and some not, joined with Republicans to circumscribe the liberals' plans for social welfare legislation and creative, reformist approaches to relief (Social Security and the WPA, as examples). Other southerners with a progressive bent, Sam Rayburn is a good example, worked hard to ensure strict legislation retarding corrupt practices in the financial sector of the economy (the Securities Act, the Federal Communications Act, the Securities and Exchange Act, the Public Utilities Holding Company Act, and the Rural Electrification Act). Regarding the economic issues, progressive Republicans, populist southern Democrats, and labor-oriented northern Democrats crafted statist solutions that were usually compromised and sometimes at odds with one another. The incongruities between partisan and ideological identities, then, were extant in the 1930s—and the New Deal (if there is such a thing) reflected that miasma of opinion.

To understand the New Deal's fate during World War II, though, a new way of thinking about it is needed. Grouping its various agencies according to whether or not a specific program made direct payments to individuals is the first step. Such a categorization explains why some programs remained controversial and others did not. Programs primarily designed to make direct payments to Americans included the Agricultural Adjustment Administration, the Federal Emergency Relief Administration, the Civilian Conservation Corps, the Public Works Administration, the Works Progress Administration, and Social Security, to name a few. Equally important, New Deal programs that addressed structural economic problems and thus made no direct income transfers to the people included the Federal Deposit Insurance Corporation, the Securities and Exchange Commission, the Tennessee Valley Authority, the National Labor Relations Board, and the Rural Electrification Administration. Overall, programs in the first category encountered greater citizen and political criticism than those in the second group. Even when the public and lawmakers attacked the latter, efforts to scale back or eliminate these programs proved less successful than campaigns against the agencies that made direct payments to needy Americans, with the AAA, Social Security, and the NLRB being noteworthy outliers.[33]

The New Deal established the federal government as a broker among various organized interests within society, specifically big business, the labor movement, and large farmers. When Congress enjoyed excessively heavy Democratic majorities early in the decade, the loudest critics attacked the New Deal for its moderation not its liberalism. Left-leaning lawmakers outside the two mainstream parties were the most flamboyant in the 1930s. Several liberal blocs, regional in scope and rooted in a radical past, rejected the modern, corporate order. The Progressive Republicans and the Progressive Insurgents, Senate factions that Midwestern and Western politicians dominated, found an ally in Franklin D. Roosevelt. For a brief historical moment, the various liberal blocs helped move the administration leftward. Even Republicans acceded to the new Democratic schema, especially the president's Depression-fighting initiatives, but they disparaged it at the same time. By 1936, congressional Republicans, who had grown restive under the new Democratic order, used the solidarity between the White House and the Democratic leadership to attack the "supine surrender of Congressional prerogatives to Executive dictation."[34] In the election of 1938, a conservative revival, many progressives and liberals met with defeat. While over eighty liberal congressmen lost their seats, the most well-entrenched and powerful bloc members remained in Congress. As conservatives became emboldened late in the decade, the New Deal received heightened attacks from the right as well. The fights over these policies helped shape the ideological, factional, and partisan cleavages within Congress during the 1930s and 1940s.

Two important congressional trends connected New Deal with World War II politics: increased tensions between the executive and legislative branches and the ideological warfare in Congress. As a result, power dynamics in Congress underwent change. When he became Speaker in 1940, Rayburn sought acknowledgments from the White House of legislative equality, indicating Democratic congressional support for the president never meant acceptance of a supplicant's role toward his patron. Presidential requests of Rayburn and Majority Leader McCormack for more cooperation struck a sour note for the Texan found little to criticize in his chamber's efforts at collaboration. Moreover, the infamous conservative coalition of Republicans and Southern Democrats proved its influence in 1937 when three Republicans and five Democrats on the Rules Committee delayed consideration of a labor reform measure. The Rules Committee thus abandoned its responsibility of moving bills to the floor and instead became an agent of minority obstruction, according to one student of Congress. Success propelled the coalition to expand its reach. Labor protections, social security and healthcare matters, and civil rights initiatives incited the conservative coalition to action. Although this negative approach to lawmaking attracted few adherents, cantankerous representatives embraced such practices during and after the 1940s.[35]

The legislative-executive schism and the conservative coalition both were born of frustrations regarding the perceived excesses of FDR's liberalism. As the New Deal unfolded, tensions between the legislative branch and the executive branch intensified. That divide positioned the president to characterize himself as "hero of the masses" striving against "sectionally controlled" parties and "congressmen harnessed to their localities."[36] Roosevelt's favorable public image heightened the inter-institutional difficulties. The resultant exasperations occurred against the backdrop of America's changing relationship with the world and continued into the 1940s in ways that often proved counterproductive.

Depression-era foreign policy constituted perhaps the most important factor determining the parameters of the ideological war in Congress in the 1940s. Prior to Pearl Harbor, unilateralism and neutrality dominated congressional foreign policy. The United States never enjoyed perfect isolation; by the Roosevelt era, revolutions in trade, immigration, transportation, exportation of democratic ideals, communication, and territorial expansion rendered any such introduction of total isolationism impossible. Indeed, isolationists never attacked American cultural ties to Europe, diplomacy per se, or foreign trade. Still, supportive politicians used the word "isolationism" without qualification in the 1930s to codify neutrality. Their modest goals reflected a progressive bent, not an obstructionist mentality. The League of Nations and Wilson's advocacy of collective security still irked these lawmakers, who endorsed a foreign policy guided by national self-interest, much as had been sought by the founders and embodied in the Constitution. Isolationists in the 1930s married unilateralism with avoidance of war. The seemingly incompatible juxtaposition succeeded because faith in the two concepts—combined with fear of permanent international commitments—transcended geographical, political, class, and ethnic divides.[37]

By 1935, a war about war began within the federal government. Deteriorating international relations convinced President Roosevelt that a more vigorous American foreign policy was necessary. Congress, though, authored neutrality legislation replete with isolationist values. The 1934 Nye Committee investigations into war profiteering in the 1910s provided important context. Members of Congress, still overwhelmed with the domestic economic problems, were less sanguine about the future of international relations than FDR. Both congressional moderates and bomb-throwers alike advocated isolationism. In the fall of 1938, Georgia Democratic senator Richard Russell told his mother, "We have no business in other peoples [sic] quarrels, most of which had been the subject of many wars and hundreds of years of controversy long before Columbus ever sailed." So as tensions rose in Europe, Congress implemented strict neutrality as a safeguard against war. Ironically, given the trouble neutrality legislation ultimately created for the administration, credit for first suggesting that approach goes to FDR, who asked the Nye Committee to draft a bill. Between 1935 and 1939, Congress enacted five different neutrality laws to prevent the conditions that had caused American entry into World War I: a mandatory embargo on arms shipments to all belligerent nations, a declaration that Americans traveling abroad on ships registered to belligerent powers did so at their own risk, a ban on loans to warring nations, an extension of the embargo provisions to the Spanish Civil War, and finally a law that made neutrality permanent and instituted a two-year "cash and carry" proviso for nonmilitary trade with belligerent nations. Even though impetus for the laws came from the White House, Roosevelt opposed strict neutrality, favoring instead a flexible approach.[38]

In the midst of the neutrality debate, Congress considered other more radical antiwar measures. Rep. Louis Ludlow (D-IN) advocated a constitutional amendment to require a national referendum for declarations of war. Ludlow's proposal contained but one exception: it permitted congressional war declarations after attacks on American soil. He explained to one constituent, "If we cannot trust the people themselves, who must fight and die and pay the bills, whom can we trust?" Ludlow's amendment, which was stalled in committee, almost made it to the House floor for a vote in the winter of 1937 when tensions with Japan escalated following the bombing of the *Panay*, an American gunboat escorting three Standard Oil Company ships up the Yangtze River. Proponents of the measure gained signatures for a discharge petition, but White House intervention ultimately blocked the measure. Roosevelt condemned the Ludlow Amendment, telling then House Speaker William B. Bankhead (D-AL), the "impracticable" proposal "would cripple any President in his conduct of our foreign relations." Bankhead read the letter to his House colleagues and advocated the wisdom of trusting Congress to declare war as required in the Constitution. On the strength of these arguments, House members rejected the discharge petition by a vote of 209 to 188.[39] Some commentators read the vote as a victory for presidential hegemony over foreign policy, but a different interpretation is needed. In reality, members of Congress defeated the Ludlow Amendment because they wanted to retain their prerogatives within the foreign and domestic policy process.

On September 1, 1939, Germany invaded Poland and the war was on. At that time Walter George, the number two man on the Senate Foreign Relations Committee, was in New York City recuperating from cataract surgery. Temporarily blind and bedridden, he received two visitors, Bernard Baruch and Jesse Jones, who had come to gain his assessment of what the United States should do and report to the president. Once their mission was clarified, George stressed they should "go back and tell the President to call a special session of Congress, ask for repeal of all the embarrassing and restrictive provisions of the Neutrality law. I will be out of the hospital in a few weeks, and I shall support with all of my strength the administration's request."[40]

Congress passed the last Neutrality Act in early November 1939, lifting the embargo on military trade and permitting cash and carry. Members of Congress avoided explaining the real reason for neutrality reform—salvation for Britain and France—and preferred to couch their votes in terms of protecting America from war participation. As the isolationists lost favor in Washington, they took the fight to the American people. Created in 1940, the America First Committee advocated an American defense policy that left Europe to solve European conflicts. Several members of Congress, such as Sens. Burton K. Wheeler (D-MT), Robert Rice Reynolds (D-NC), Nye, Clark, David I. Walsh (D-MA), and Rep. Hamilton Fish (R-NY), worked closely with the committee. A leading journalist with *Time* magazine branded these lawmakers as anti-Semitic or worse in his pri-

Sam Rayburn and Alben Barkley talk with reporters after leaving the White House where they had discussed revisions to the neutrality legislation, July 5, 1939. Courtesy Library of Congress, Prints & Photographs Division, photograph by Harris & Ewing [reproduction number, LC-DIG-hec-26963].

vate notes. Wheeler was nothing more than a political opportunist with presidential ambitions. Reynolds, who associated with Nazi sympathizers, "has no more patriotism than a hog." Furthermore, isolationism proved a financial and public relations boon for Nye. Clark suffered "an extreme case of psychological bile." "A great soldier in his day," Fish had transformed into an "unprincipled, self-seeking devious demagogue." The isolationist lawmakers lacked any real allegiance to America First; instead "they are using it, just as it uses them."[41] Congress as an institution suffered.

By the summer of 1940, the war in Europe had become so desperate that FDR sought all available methods for helping the British except a congressional declaration of war. He acted without congressional authorization when he negotiated the destroyer-bases deal whereby the United States provided Great Britain with fifty World War I–vintage destroyers in exchange for military bases in Newfoundland, Bermuda, and the British West Indies. This policy heightened tensions about American foreign policy. Isolationists from both parties expressed outrage even as the congressional leadership applauded the president. Sen. D. Worth Clark (D-ID) called the deal "an act of war" while Rep. Harold Knutson (D-MN) complained, "The whole world's gone crazy." Still the isolationists faced increased public criticism. In response, Wheeler blamed the administration for manipulating public opinion toward the eastern, intellectual, aristocratic, interventionist perspective, terming the president's team "a little handful of men so out of touch with public opinion that they couldn't be elected to the office of dog-catcher."[42]

Raising an army in 1940 proved even more controversial. Isolationists fought bitterly with congressional interventionists. Simplistic assessments of Congress as isolationist and the president as interventionist constitute a faulty explanation of the legislation's passage. Initial discussion of the measure came from interested citizens outside the government. Lawmakers endorsed the plan before FDR. Collaboration, then, not capitulation is the better way to understand passage of the draft. The Burke-Wadsworth selective service legislation enjoyed bipartisan sponsorship by Sen. Edwin R. Burke (D-NE) and Rep. James W. Wadsworth (R-NY), both known for their criticisms of FDR and the New Deal. Another proponent, Senate insider James F. Byrnes (D-SC), remarked the bill had but a "Chinaman's chance" in an election year. It provided for a one-year term of service and prohibited the use of troops outside the Western Hemisphere.[43]

Burke-Wadsworth passed the Senate on a bipartisan vote of 58 to 31 with strong southern, border, New England, and mid-Atlantic state support. On the House side, Sam Rayburn, Wadsworth, and Andrew Jackson May (D-KY) retained the bill in committee until Senate passage. Rayburn explained to one constituent, "If it were possible to raise a sufficient number of men by voluntary enlistment and they would come from all sections in equal percentages the selective service might not be necessary. In our section of the country, men are volunteering but this is not so in many other sections. Therefore, the bill to carry out compulsory military service will have my support." The House debate occurred after the announcement of the destroyer-bases deal, giving opponents additional fodder. Frances P. Bolton (R-OH) declared, "If Mr. Roosevelt can do what he wants with our destroyers without consulting Congress, and we give him our boys, God alone knows what he will do with them." Despite numerous peace marchers and the fulminations of the isolationists, Rayburn and his forces secured House passage by a vote of 263 to 149. The House vote followed the same bipartisan and geographic divides as found in the Senate.[44]

Enactment of Burke-Wadsworth proved congressional foresight regarding questions of national security, and Congress prepared for war in other ways. It increased appropriations for the army and the navy, removed limits on profits within war contracts, authorized construction of new munitions plants, and facilitated government supervision of plants that would not participate in rearmament.[45] These trends toward military preparedness became issues in the fall elections because the war had worsened.

The Nazi control of Western Europe and the Battle of Britain generated a new, cynical political calculus in the United States. Politicians framed their campaigns with war rhetoric and, at the behest of Republicans, lawmakers adopted a "war schedule" with few recesses but little substantive work, or as one key Democrat said, "'They're just . . . jackassing around.'" Walking to the chamber for quorum calls annoyed "old men members and the fat ones." One such Republican bellowed: "'By God, boys, we've oversold the country on this staying in session.'" Electoral realities caused some members to ignore these inflated demands. An unidentified Republican told his party's minority leader: "'Sorry, I'm tied up here [back home]. If there's a roll call on recess, pair me against it.'" Others benefitted politically from the extended session. Playing up the demands of national defense caused one member to "arrange to cut his finger and have to go to the hospital here if Congress adjourned." Rather than emphasize New Deal successes, the Democrats, reacting to their losses in the 1938 midterm election, ran a pro-business campaign. In 1940, FDR defeated internationalist Republican Wendell Willkie because the European war worsened throughout the year and because voters preferred a seasoned president at the helm, especially one who that year promised not to send American boys to fight a foreign war. Congress remained strongly Democratic, and the election results did little to alter the prospects of war.[46]

More than any other foreign policy decision before December 7, 1941, the Lend-Lease bill ensured that the United States would eventually go to war. It provided a mechanism to aid the near-broke allied nations, specifically England, with munitions and reflected Roosevelt's insistence that American security hinged on British survival. Emblematic of the shifting power base within the government, this bill originated with Roosevelt, who included the measure as part of his annual message to Congress. Lawmakers ultimately enacted it in such a way as to preserve the constitutional prerogatives of the legislative branch. While cruising in the Caribbean in December 1940, the president received a letter from Winston Churchill explaining England's budget crisis. After several days of thought, Roosevelt outlined what became Lend-Lease. Secretary of the Treasury Henry Morgenthau termed it one of the president's "brilliant flashes," and his treasury department plotted how to implement the idea. The measure was numbered H.R. 1776 because John McCormack, the House author, feared reprisals from his Irish Catholic constituents if it bore his name. The symbolic bill number may have saved McCormack grief in Massachusetts, but it did nothing to stint the isolationist-internationalist divide in Congress even though its sage critics privately acknowledged the need for the program. For example, House Minority Leader Martin, known for his isolationist leanings, contended at a White House leaders conference, "'Mr. President, I don't care what you do. Just don't let England fall.'" His public actions did not correspond with this sentiment, for he approved GOP opposition to the measure and he voted against it.[47]

Mainline or moderate Democrats behaved in an equally predictable fashion. In a nationwide radio address Alben Barkley defended the Lend-Lease bill. "Upon what other shoulders can Congress place the responsibility of acting in this emergency?" he asked. "We cannot hold a town meeting every time England or Greece or China may need an airplane or a tank." Privately, some pro-administration Democrats were less certain. In early February 1941, Richard Russell told his mother: "I am scared to death of this bill and have worried over it more than I ever have any piece of legislation."[48]

Isolationists regarded the vote on this measure as the last chance to avoid war. But with amendments in place preserving congressional foreign policy prerogatives, the House passed the measure easily. Before the bill went to committee in the Senate, Wheeler called it "the New Deal's triple A foreign policy—plow under every fourth American boy." In response, interventionists dubbed Wheeler as a "Twentieth Century Benedict Arnold." Senatorial isolationists termed the bill congressional abdication when they waged war in the Senate Foreign Relations Committee hearings. Most of the committee members favored the bill, but they had to maneuver it around the committee's filibustering isolationist minority. Walter George, the chair of the committee, refused to let the debate "take all session." Despite the isolationists' best efforts, the measure passed the committee by a vote of 15 to 8, and the full Senate, 60 to 31.[49]

That Roosevelt prevailed in this fight was no surprise. He only sent legislation to Congress when confident of a victory. Matters about which Congress seemed likely to rebel received an executive branch solution. Moderate members of Congress worried about this monumental shift. "Well the old lease-lend is out of the way insofar as legislation is concerned and I am so happy about it. I never got as tired of a debate in my life. It was a contest between the two sides trying to see which could scare the American people worse," explained Russell. "I sometimes wonder what is to become of our country if our people have become so soft that public opinion is to be formed and directed through fright." Doughton of North Carolina noted superior administration information about the foreign policy problem, but he still cautioned: "I fear that the course being pursued by our Government tends to get us into war rather than keep us out." Rep. John Dingell (D-MI), though, had a bold suggestion: "why not ship [the isolationist senators] prepaid to Hitler? If the authority does not go that far I will gladly pay the freight."[50]

Perhaps even more contentious than Lend-Lease was the fight over draft extension in the summer of 1941. Given that conditions in Europe and Asia had worsened in the year since the Selective Service was created, the administration, the Democratic leadership, and Republican internationalists agreed Congress must retain in service the 900,000 men who had been drafted in the fall of 1940 and who would otherwise be released in a month. Sen. Lister Hill (D-AL), the majority whip and the administration's "strong man Friday back in the cloakrooms," believed, wrongly as it turned out, the measure would pass easily because "'men who voted for the draft act can't afford not to vote for it. It would be suicide.'" The upper chamber approved the bill by a vote of 45 to 30 on August 7. It added a $10 pay raise, bringing soldier pay to $40 a month, despite administration objections. House critics later castigated the pay hike as "a glorified W.P.A."[51]

Decided momentum for the Axis powers—the Vichy government in France declared its allegiance to Hitler, the Russians struggled in the East, and U.S.-Japanese relations deteriorated—became the context for the House debate. "'The Germans ought to begin mopping up about the time the bill gets well into the House,'" said Hill. "'That will change a lot of minds.'" Indeed, on the day after House consideration of the bill began, the *New York Times* ran the following front page headline: "25 Soviet Divisions Lost in Ukraine Trap, Soviets Say; Russians Raid Berlin Twice." As a result, May, the House sponsor of the bill, insisted on an unlimited extension of service even though Rayburn told him, "By God, you can't pass this bill. Go out and draft an amendment extending the service for 18 months." Even so, Rayburn knew that he needed the votes of twenty Republicans to balance projected Democratic defections. The GOP divided as to whether emergency conditions existed and thus whether it should fight or accede to the president's wishes. Martin understood the importance of the legislation, but because he also shared isolationist fears he did nothing to help Rayburn find GOP votes. Isolationists within the party were much less placid. They sought to defeat the bill by defeating all amendments.[52]

Rayburn proved his parliamentary and political brilliance on August 12, 1941, when the lower chamber voted whether or not to retain the draftees. Rep. Dewey Short (R-MO), a former preacher who led the floor fight against draft extension, later explained, "'Rayburn moved fast and used every parliamentary device possible on that vote.'" At the time of the vote, however, Short was much harsher: "'Congress just doesn't trust this bastard Roosevelt.'" After the roll had been called, vote counters on both sides of the aisle sensed the tension that crackled throughout the chamber. One member clamored to change his vote from aye to nay while another sought to record a late aye vote. Short requested a recapitulation of the vote, ostensibly to check for errors. Rayburn, though, refused to entertain the motion until after the vote had been announced, freezing the results at 203–202. The isolationists questioned Rayburn's integrity after the Speaker declared: "There is no correction in the vote. The vote stands, and the bill is passed. Without objection, a motion to reconsider is laid on the table." An irate Short "demand[ed] recognition" so that he could move for a reconsideration of the vote. When Rayburn refused him, Earl Michener (R-MI) made a parliamentary inquiry and told Rayburn "there is no use getting excited about this." The Speaker rejoined, "The Chair trusts the gentleman from Michigan does not think the Chair is excited." Several Republicans then denied that Rayburn had laid the motion to reconsider on the table, which prompted the Speaker to end the matter: "The Chair does not intend to have his word questioned."[53]

Geographic division explains the Republican vote. Of the 21 Republicans voting in favor of the bill all but one, a Minnesotan, came from the Northeast or California. Of the 133 Republicans voting against the bill, 85 were not from either coast. Additionally, many Republicans (and Democrats) doubted the severity of the war. Equally significant, the party leadership did not take a strong stand in this debate. Explained Joe Martin, "I regarded it as one of those fights in which one comes out stronger if one loses than if one wins." Other Republicans disagreed. "'The Republican party has got its ass in a sling,'" said New Deal critic Leland F. Ford (R-CA) privately. "'I think the party is killing itself. Here we have plenty of issues. This administration is developing a bastard brand of state socialism. There's a damned good issue in upholding the right of a man to work without paying tribute (union dues) to anyone. Suppose Japan touches off a war—it may come tomorrow. Well, we haven't got an excuse.'" Democratic breakdowns were more complex. Regarding the majority party cleavages, Rayburn and McCormack privately gave a range of reasons for the 65 Democratic nay votes, including local politics, promises to men of service age that the draft was for but one year, concerns about reelection, and "'God damned dirty politics.'"[54]

While Congress needed a recess after this fight, lawmakers refused to adjourn for more than three days at a time because "exhausted as it is, bedeviled and rudderless, Congress—the majority of it—doesn't trust Franklin D. Roosevelt, wants to get back quick if it thinks necessary," explained McNaughton. In order to facilitate a month-long break for the majority of the members, a "watchdog squad" remained in town and held brief sessions every three days in which nothing more was accomplished than a reading of the minutes "by a droning clerk." The time off gave members a chance to reconnect with voters, who tended to be supportive of the war regardless of party. Said Sam Rayburn in an off-the-record interview: "I talked to a hell of a lot of people, all kinds of people, people I know. And I'm telling you they are not isolationists. They want to know what in the hell's the matter up here. They are criticizing those who voted against lend-lease, against extension of the military service. They don't see how in hell anybody can vote against an army at a time like this."[55]

In addition to the passage of draft extension, Congress dismantled other isolationist policies that fall, and they passed a measure providing for the arming of merchant ships. In late September 1941, Roosevelt and the congressional leaders debated whether to repeal all neutrality legislation or whether to strip it of substance. Rayburn privately advised, "You know how it is, there's a lot of sentimental appeal in the word neutrality. The isolationists would get up and holler like hell about neutrality, and the public would get wrought up about it. If we go at it the other way, just leave the act on the books and cut the guts out of it with amendments, at least they can't holler" about the demise of neutrality. Meanwhile, Sen. Kenneth McKellar, a "demagogic, patronage-grabbing" Tennessee Democrat, introduced legislation repealing all the neutrality laws. The move angered Senate Foreign Relations Committee chair Tom Connally. "God damn old Kenneth. He oughtn't have done that. He ought to have waited and let me introduce the administration bill after we know what the President wants. I don't see why he had to rush in this way and muddy things all up," fumed the Texan. In the fall, country and Congress divided down the middle on the question of intervention. Unity of purpose came only after an attack on American soil, and even then it proved to be a chimera.[56]

Realizing the inevitability of war, congressional and administration leaders moved ahead with contingency plans. By December 4, Rayburn spoke with the press about congressional strategy "when the war starts" without hedging his statements. Forging workable coalitions would prove his biggest challenge as a wartime Speaker. Despite the popular mythology of the war, Congress never spoke with one voice. Even in the outraged days immediately after December 7, competing strategies emanated from Capitol Hill. Dewey Short clamored, "Hell, it's the only thing to do. Shoot the God damned living Hell out of [the Japanese]." Other congressional leaders blamed Germany for the war. For example, in the December 8, 1941, issue of the *New York Times*, the organization Fight for Freedom ran a full-page advertisement headlined, "It's America First, *Now!*" Sen. Carter Glass (D-VA) was listed as honorary chairman of the organization, the first time he had lent his name to an advocacy group. The advertisement depicted the Japanese attack as nothing more than "a last desperate effort of Hitler to turn American attention from the center of war against our world. That center is Berlin." It continued: "War has chosen us. It is our duty to understand the full and terrible scope of that war. While fighting Japan to the death, we must remember that Berlin prompted this attack, that Berlin is the meaning of this attack, that Berlin is the world enemy and the world danger."[57]

Roosevelt signing the declaration of war against Japan, December 8, 1941. Standing left to right: Rep. Sol Bloom (D-NY), Rep. Luther Johnson (D-TX), Rep. Charles A. Eaton (R-NJ), Rep. Joseph W. Martin Jr. (R-MA), Vice President Henry Wallace, Speaker Sam Rayburn (D-TX), Rep. John W. McCormack (D-MA), Sen. Charles McNary (D-OR), Sen. Alben Barkley (D-KY), Sen. Carter Glass (D-VA), Sen. Tom Connally (D-TX). Courtesy the Associated Press.

When Roosevelt delivered his historic "Day of Infamy" speech to a joint session of Congress, he received Republican and Democratic applause. Noted one observer, "Only a few sat on their hands—Hiram Johnson of California, William Lambertson of Kansas, Ulysses S. Guyer of Kansas." In making his ten-minute speech Roosevelt appeared "firm" and "grim" with "no show of weakness, no lack of confidence." McCormack offered this post-mortem: "The President at his best; the House at its best." Once the resolution calling for a declaration of war had been introduced and referred to committee, McCormack moved to suspend the rules so immediate passage could be won. Rayburn asked if a second was needed, and Martin said yes. Jeanette Rankin (R-MT), a pacifist who served in Congress in 1917 and voted against U.S. entry into World War I, tried to object. After Rayburn refused to entertain her motion, McCormack took twenty seconds to condemn the "dastardly attack" and conclude, "This is the time for action." Next, Martin read a speech he had written at three in the morning calling for unity, an end to strikes, and a vigorous war effort. After the cheering for Martin's oration ceased, Democrats called for a vote, and Rayburn respectfully promised "It won't be long. Let us maintain order at this time particularly." Fish gained the floor next, spoke in favor of the war, and indicated he would join the services and fight with a "colored" unit as he had done in World War I. When Rankin again tried to speak, Rep. Dingell yelled out, "Sit down, sister."[58]

Later, after the House began voting on the resolution, a smiling Rankin responded "no" when her name was called. Hisses resonated throughout the chamber. Other members of Congress who had earlier shared her isolationist sentiments tried to change her mind, but she insisted there was no proof an attack had occurred. Instead, she suggested the reports might be nothing more than Roosevelt-inspired propaganda. Said George H. Bender (R-OH) in an off-the-record comment, "The woman is crazy. I never heard such talk. She doesn't believe we have been attacked. She's nutty." It took less than an hour for the war resolution to pass both houses of Congress. Observed one journalist, "There were no tears. The tension was not as dramatic as when the House passed the amendments to the Neutrality Act. Why? Because this time, America had been attacked, and Congress' will was not to be doubted. Its will was to declare war, fight like Hell."[59]

The grandeur of the war declaration and the use of inclusive, sweeping language suggests a reality that never existed on Capitol Hill. Instead the four years that followed revealed a sometimes strident, often partisan Congress that used the war for its own political ends—preserving the New Deal, destroying the New Deal, ensuring congressional independence vis-à-vis the presidency, finding common ground with the White House, and waging war on the other chamber. Treatments of the war era Congress have either celebrated the mythical unity or attacked the supposedly destructive partisanship when they should commemorate the wonders of democracy functioning at its best against the backdrop of total war. When thorough study is given to congressional economic, social justice, and reconversion policy in the era of World War II, an imperfect picture results, as is to be expected. Indeed, contemporary imperfection against the promise of future perfection was and remains the thesis of American political history.

Part One

Bringing Home the Bacon: Congress and the Economics of War

2. "We'll Get Down and Fight" over Resource Management

"God damn it! Where is the fleet? In hiding? What is it doing? Why doesn't Frank Knox tell the whole truth? The President seems to think that all problems can be solved in terms of a dollar. God damn it, that isn't the answer," fumed Sen. Tom Connally (D-TX) a month after the attack on Pearl Harbor. "We won't buy this victory. We'll get down and fight and bleed and scratch and claw for it." A Washington fixture since 1917, Connally had garnered a reputation as something of a gadfly, appearing on the Senate floor for debate in his trademark black frock coat, black string tie, and thick long white hair with a flip at the end. While pompous, he disdained mediocrity. Often serious, his overall persona caused many to underestimate him. He preferred work on economic and diplomatic policy but was an important behind-the-scenes leader of southern senatorial opposition to civil rights.[1]

Connally was correct about the fighting and bleeding necessary for victory, but incorrect about the importance of money and thus the role of Congress as the keeper of the purse strings in the United States. Resource management, especially taxation and price control, bedeviled lawmakers throughout the 1940s. For moderate and liberal Democrats these most important domestic political concerns embodied the reformist political economy constructed in the New Deal years, making the decisions about the wartime economy into matters larger than funding and feeding the troops but also retaining what had been won in the 1930s. Conversely, for conservative Democrats and Republicans, taxation and rationing became a mechanism to attack the New Deal. In these struggles, the moderates prevailed and a liberalism in praxis emerged that was center left in orientation and that privileged statism over antistatism. Conservative congressmen learned, much to their chagrin, that the New Deal was too powerful to be erased, while liberal congressmen lamented it was not powerful enough to be expanded. Moderate lawmakers who brokered the compromises over taxation and rationing made the New Deal ethos—meaning reliance on an activist regulatory government—a permanent part of the American polity, but in an altered form skewed away from welfare and toward warfare.[2]

The war in Congress was about money: how much and through what methods should war costs be charged to taxpayers; how will prices be determined and goods rationed; and finally how shall the military be held accountable in a democracy? Overshadowing all of these specific questions about the work of Congress were larger, more important debates about the fate of the New Deal and the nature of the state. How powerful should the state be? The manner in which Congress asked and answered this question merged the congressional wartime battles over ideology—liberals versus conservatives—and institutional structure—Congress versus the president and House versus Senate—in a contest over the meaning of the Constitution in the twentieth century. While liberals in Congress embraced statism as a solution to the problems that bedeviled the United States, conservatives were much more suspect. Was not statism the common denominator among the Axis powers? This left moderates in Congress—a shifting group often difficult to define—to forge the compromises necessary for passing wartime tax and price control legislation. In much of the literature on state development in the twentieth century Congress has been assigned a negative role, but such characterizations are not entirely accurate. Indeed, lawmakers compelled President Franklin D. Roosevelt and the mushrooming federal bureaucracy to scale back some of the more grandiose plans for empowering nonelected experts. More important, Congress constructed a resource management policy regarding taxation and price control that made permanent a circumscribed but still activist state.[3] This process cannot be understood apart from the war, which provided the contextual backdrop and the reasons for the congressional arguments about resource management. Indeed, debates about these questions all predated Pearl Harbor, but that tragedy gave each a new frame of righteous anger.

Outrage in Congress was near universal. Rumors of utter destruction, the loss of eight battleships at Pearl Harbor, the ruination of the navy, and the inability to regroup and win the war in the Pacific swarmed the halls of Congress. Some searched the executive branch bureaus for information, and others besieged the White House with demands for an investigation of Pearl Harbor. Nothing assuaged the congressional concerns in the first months of the war. Members of Congress looked to the administration and found nothing but chaos, or as one reporter termed it, "a political Punch-and-Judy show."[4]

Sen. Walter George (D-GA) had been in Washington since 1922, long enough to learn the importance of restraint. Nonetheless, he adopted a defeatist pose. "The whole thing is confusion. We face a fearful struggle." Sometimes referred to as "Mr. Coca-Cola," George was one of the leaders of the Southern bloc in the Senate. No friend of the president, George survived FDR's efforts in 1938 to purge conservative Democrats from power when he easily gained reelection. George was crucial to the success of resource management legislation in Congress. Smart and deliberative, George was a master of tax policy, his domain as chair of the Senate Finance Committee. "The most powerful man in the senate," was how Sen. Lister Hill (D-AL), an economic liberal as long as regional issues did not skew the debate, described George. "When he gets up to speak, he is one man who always changes votes." He had a reputation for being gentle and kind, rarely losing his temper. He disliked the Washington social life. He did not even own the silk hat common in midcentury Washington. He shared an apartment in the Mayflower Hotel with his wife, "Miss Lucy." For entertainment, they saw a movie every month or so and a play a few times a year at the National Theater. He was a social drinker, but never a drunk. His secretary of ten years, Christie Bell Kennedy, willingly argued with him on all subjects of congressional importance. She was "his master and confessor, a veritable priest for a Baptist Senator." One pundit said she "manages the office much as Joe Stalin runs Russia."[5]

Congressional anger and mistrust of the executive branch played a hugely important role in the politics of resource management in wartime Washington, D.C. The turmoil of the 1930s and the momentous shifts in approach to governance had not been lost on Congress. Indeed, Roosevelt's efforts to dominate national politics—sometimes successfully as with key New Deal reforms like banking and Social Security and sometimes unsuccessfully as with failed policy initiatives like court packing in 1937—had left many in Congress weary of the president. The coming of the war, though, meant Congress did not have the luxury of divorcing itself from the White House. Quite the contrary, the ability of the two branches to cooperate and develop effective tax and rationing policies might more than anything else determine the fate of the United States in the war especially since the country was the arsenal of democracy for the free world. To understand how this process unfolded requires careful explication of Congress's understanding of itself and its role in the federal government on the eve of the war.

Days after the attack on Pearl Harbor, Hatton Sumners (D-TX), chair of the House Judiciary Committee and a vociferous critic of what he had termed FDR's dictatorial ambitions during the Supreme Court packing fight of 1937, worked with Attorney General Francis Biddle on legislation expanding Roosevelt's wartime powers: the bill revived the Great War–era Overman Act, which granted Woodrow Wilson substantial authority to rearrange federal government offices and agencies; it provided unchecked presidential authority over war contracts; and it reinstituted the 1917 Trading with the Enemy Act.[6] These legislative decisions made early in the war resulted from lessons learned during World War I about the perils of obstructing the White House. Seasoned members of Congress understood that a neutered president would mean a neutered nation. The country survived a generation earlier because the obstruction against President Wilson happened at the end of the war over the nature of the postwar peace. Should the pre–Pearl Harbor obstruction continue into the war itself, interventionists in Congress understood that the results could be dire. Compromise on resource management policy was vital even if it meant sustaining the New Deal. The alternative of an Axis victory was not tenable. This knowledge learned from the Great War as much as any other factor explains why the vituperative partisanship of the war years sometimes resulted in policy compromises beneficial both to the war effort and to the sustenance of the New Deal. In other battles, typically dealing with social justice policy where the outcome was much less directly related to the war effort, conservative and moderate lawmakers were much less likely to compromise.

Lawmakers provided Roosevelt with what some termed "dictatorial powers" because he asked for a "bill to cover everything from hell to breakfast" and because the country and the world needed it. Still the thought of giving the architect of the New Deal this power terrified conservatives in Congress. Deliberation of the law provided an important juxtaposition between what Congress believed to be true about the balance of power in the federal government and what it knew was necessary to win the war. Most lawmakers spoke critically off the record about the administration, but on the record had nothing but praise for the president. The First War Powers Act was approved on December 18, 1941, and another omnibus war powers bill passed the following year. Later Sam Rayburn (D-TX) explained this situation to a constituent: "This talk of the abdication of Congress, of its rights and authority, I assure you is much more paper and radio talk than any thing else. . . . Congress cannot administer the laws it passes nor fight the wars it declares."[7]

By implicitly acknowledging Roosevelt's preeminent role in the federal government, Congress unintentionally established the presidency as hierarchically superior to the legislative branch. As a result lawmakers become the "whipping boy" for political problems with resource management.[8] This image was unfair. Congress was not abdicating but was revealing itself to be a mature deliberative body when it added to Roosevelt's power. The war necessitated the political deference to the White House, but this short-term solution constituted an institutional mistake from a long-range perspective. It further entrenched a presidency-centered orientation to the federal government, which created as many problems as it solved in the second half of the twentieth century and which contributed to the unhelpful dichotomy between the proponents of big and small government.

In the first half of March 1942 the volume of critical mail to Congress tripled, and by May 1942, only 33 percent of Americans, according to the Gallup Poll, believed Congress was doing a good job. Another 40 percent rated congressional performance as fair. No doubt progress, or lack thereof, in the war shaded this public dyspepsia, for the Philippines fell to Japan in May 1942 and the Bataan Death March had begun a month earlier in April. Victory later that May in the Battle of the Coral Sea proved insufficient to rally American confidence. Voters had a long list of grievances related to wartime resource management. The public did not like "useless expenditures" by lawmakers unwilling to "'quit playing politics'" with price control and wartime strikes. For some letter writers Congress was at fault, for others the executive, and still others blamed "the government" more generally. Letter writers did not understand the functioning of Congress within the federal government. For example, Rep. Hale Boggs (D-LA) spoke off the record, "They write as if they thought I am telling General Marshall how to run this war, as if I see the President every day." Still this anger about the warfare state in the supposed "good war" provided Congress with opportunities and challenges.[9]

Conservatives tried to use public discontent to blast the administration for its assertion of unprecedented powers and for the proliferation of executive agencies. Here FDR was cagey, creating the new agencies without much authority but with overlapping jurisdictions. The situation made for an ineffective flow chart but also a difficult target for critics, leaving Congress and not the popular president the most likely foil for public protests. A concerned Rep. Jesse P. Wolcott (R-MI) articulated the challenges before Congress. "This is serious. Congress undoubtedly is due for some blame. It hasn't done its full duty, and at times it has failed to assert its independence when it should have done so," Wolcott expounded. "But Congress is one branch of democratic government. Let it be ridiculed into impotence and you have the Reichstag exactly as it was when Hitler came in power."[10]

Speaker Rayburn was perhaps the most important lawmaker in the politics of resource management. He told journalists: "Congress is being criticized, but Congress has given the President every law he has asked for defense purposes." Rayburn defied easy political categorization. He described himself as a "progressive conservative or a conservative progressive." During the war, he worked hard to maintain the New Deal redistributive economy as a fundamental component of the American state, but to do so he often brokered compromises between the most extreme factions within the House. More than that, he believed in constructive legislation, recounting on numerous occasions that "any jackass can kick a barn down, but it takes a good carpenter to build one." In a speech to a group of Detroit businessmen, Rayburn contended: "I believe in free enterprise. I do not believe that the government of the United States ought to do anything that individuals or groups can do. . . . I believe in just as little interference by government in people's business as is possible. Mark my words, I said 'as is possible.' . . . Sometimes we have to pass statutes that look rather cruel in order to make the pistol-toting minority behave."[11]

Conversely, the Senate majority leader, Alben Barkley (D-KY), a moderate liberal who had been in Congress since 1913, enjoyed a reputation for oratory, dating back to his school years when supposedly "his teachers discovered he had a speaking voice that could awaken sleeping hogs in the next county." Indeed,

Barkley was more known for talking than leading. His ascension to the leadership post in 1937 resulted not because of his popularity and respect in the Senate but because FDR had written his "Dear Alben" letter, implicitly telling the Senate to elect Barkley instead of Pat Harrison (D-MS), the lawmakers' choice for majority leader. One journalist reasoned: "The President should never have been mixed up with that. The Senate is entitled to elect its own leader. That was when the southerners started getting angry." In his years as leader, according to another political journalist, "Barkley has run up an imposing record as a lumbering oaf."[12]

Rayburn exerted his leadership not via brute force but through the respect of his colleagues in the House. By reputation, he was "painfully honest" and humble. A story about his baldness illustrates this point. Once a newsboy tried to sell Rayburn a magazine that he did not want. The boy told him, "You'd better buy one, Mister. There's a good article there about Speaker Rayburn." Rayburn replied, "Well, I don't think so much of that bald-headed fellow." The boy countered, "Lissen, if you had used your head as much as he's used his, you wouldn't have any hair either!" Rayburn bought two magazines. Such behavior in Washington made it difficult for House members to turn him down when he sought their help with a crucial bill. Members of Congress knew that Rayburn viewed the institution with religious reverence. Though he did not enjoy the Washington, D.C., social circuit, Rayburn relaxed with his close Texas cronies, all House Democrats, at his modest apartment: Wright Patman, Fritz Lanham, Luther Johnson, and Lyndon Johnson. Rayburn preferred to eat and serve to guests canned chili made by Gebhardt's, a San Antonio company. His favorite topics for conversation included Texas history and politics. He enjoyed reading Confederate history and dime western novels. A confirmed bachelor save for a failed almost three-month-long marriage in 1927, Rayburn treated his employees as his surrogate children.[13]

In Rayburn's famous Capitol hideaway office, the Board of Education, the Speaker drank, but lightly. He added a splash of Scotch to a glass of water and sipped it throughout the evening. His second-in-command in the House, John W. McCormack (D-MA), avoided alcohol. McCormack was first elected to Congress in 1928, serving a South Boston district with a heavy Irish working-class population. He quickly developed a close relationship with John Nance Garner of Texas, then the Democratic leader of the House. The two men were fierce partisans and also devoted poker players. His relationship with Rayburn was equally close, and McCormack's support had been crucial to Rayburn's election as majority leader in 1937.[14]

On Rayburn's counsel, Roosevelt instituted weekly meetings with the congressional leadership. Once the war came, Rayburn insisted to Roosevelt that further New Deal activism must be abandoned, and all energy must be devoted to winning the war, meaning that no new social programs like national health care should be introduced, *not* that existing New Deal programs should be eliminated. On that point, Rayburn told former congressman John McDuffie, "Everybody here, there and everywhere seem to want to stop spending money on non-essentials and I believe the folks here are sincere about it, . . . but you know from your experience here how very hard it is to stop a Government agency when once started. I do think for the fiscal year 1943 we will save or refuse to spend somewhere from three quarters of a billion to one billion dollars." He was a consistent and steadfast defender of the president. Rayburn was often the first to speak in White House conferences. Nor was he shy to disagree with the president or his colleagues. However, when a decision had been made about strategy, Rayburn supported the majority consensus whether he had convinced the others to support his position or not. Roosevelt ceased holding the meetings in January 1943, and presidential-legislative relations suffered.[15]

Rayburn's GOP counterpart in the House, Rep. Joseph W. Martin Jr. (R-MA), was first elected to the U.S. House of Representatives in 1924. Martin advocated the economic conservatism of small-town business interests. He became minority leader in 1939, and he implemented a variety of procedural reforms that made for a more effective opposition party including the use of the whip system to enforce party discipline, an activist steering committee to craft a centralized party message, liaison work with the Republican National Committee, and research committees to bring a partisan interpretation to the issues that were before the Congress. Though he was a strong partisan, Martin was also unassuming. When vacationing on Cape Cod during a spring 1945 recess of the House, he arrived at his hotel before his room was ready for check-in. The manager directed him to wait in his private office so he could read the newspapers. A few minutes later a woman rushed into the room and said to Martin, "Oh, there you are! How did you happen to come in here?" Martin replied, "The manager told me to wait here." The woman said next, "Well, I like your looks and I think you will do. I can give you $80 a month and your living," to which Martin answered, "I consider that very liberal." The woman concluded, "You may wait and see my husband." She returned mortified a few minutes later and asked, "Why did you not tell me who you were?" "You never asked me," replied Martin. He did not get the job of gardener after all.[16]

Prior to Pearl Harbor, Congress approached resource management from a parochial perspective. For some lawmakers, that meant pork for developing businesses in their districts and states. In the run-up to the war, lawmakers spent much time strategizing how to get the most federal dollars for defense projects in their districts. Attesting that a centralized defense industry was dangerous for the country, Sen. Arthur Capper (R-KS) made a subtle, region-wide appeal: "Unless

Rep. Joseph W. Martin Jr. leaving the White House in 1945. National Park Service, Abbie Rowe, Courtesy of Harry S Truman Library.

the Middle West is developed to some considerable extent industrially . . . , the Nation faces the danger of having a vast interior of backward . . . [and] impoverished peoples." Sen. Prentiss Brown (D-MI) argued for federally funded shipping facilities in the northeast. Sen. Harry S Truman (D-MO) was more blunt. He told a Kansas City businessman, "I believe that with proper organization Missouri can get its proper piece in the set-up." Sen. Arthur Vandenberg (R-MI), though, complained about pork projects, "The American people are entitled to some protection from such political exploitation."[17]

Other lawmakers used the war as a device to realign home-front politics and priorities. What emerged was a war between liberal and conservative lawmakers and with Congress against the administration over the fate of the New Deal economy. "There is another principle I believe all should agree on," stressed Sen. Robert A. Taft (R-OH). "There should be a truce on the controversies regarding social legislation. No additional public expenditures and no additional government regulations should be authorized unless absolutely essential for the war." Rep. Robert L. "Muley" Doughton (D-NC) told a supporter of the National Youth Administration that it and other New Deal agencies "were only created as temporary emergency agencies and never intended to be permanent. Now when employment is as great as it has been almost in our history and when the states are amply able to educate and care for the young people, it seems to me that these emergency expenses should at least be temporarily suspended." Others struggled to protect the New Deal in wartime. For example, Sen. Joseph C. O'Mahoney (D-WY) promised that he would do everything in his power to protect the Farm Security Administration from Sen. Harry Byrd (D-VA), who wanted it abolished.[18] These contradictory views toward resource management made it easier for liberals and moderates to retain statist solutions but without the ideological underpinnings of the 1930s. A liberalism in praxis governed congressional decisions about the war economy, one that was pragmatic, not ideological, a distinction that made possible cooperation with moderates.

As the opposition party, the GOP advocated clearer, more consistent objectives than the ideologically diverse Democrats regarding resource management. Even while GOP lawmakers saw a domestic policy advantage in the war—it could be a tool to destroy the New Deal—that advantage could not be sustained if the party hindered the war effort. Taft avowed: "We must contribute everything— every effort, every thought, and every constructive force—to the winning of the war. That comes first." He did not want Republicans trying to micromanage war strategy. For Taft and the GOP, though, there were other resource management concerns, namely, "that in handing over to the Chief Executive necessary emergency powers for use during the war provision is made to reclaim those powers for Congress and the people once the conflict is won."[19]

The battles over resource management were the most intractable of the war years and they began well before the attack on Pearl Harbor with Roosevelt working on fiscal mobilization as early as 1939. Ideological and legislative-executive tensions dominated these quarrels. Conservatives looked to eliminate the New Deal political economy and moderates wanted to curtail the most experimental aspects of it. Similarly lawmakers were collectively aggrieved over constriction of congressional power and authority in the Roosevelt era. The fighting about resource management thus reflected legitimate ideological differences as well as constitutional conflicts about how power was shared between the executive and the legislative branches. Though the outcome of these conflicts was crucial for the future of politics in the United States, for average citizens the subject of the arguments—higher taxes and rationing—were what mattered. Careful consideration of wartime politics reveals there was far less sacrifice in the United States than in any of the other principal belligerents. Indeed, the partisan battles over resource management in Congress and between the legislative and executive branches mirrored the more miserly attitudes found in the population. As Fred M. Vinson, a former member of Congress and a wartime administrator with the Office of Economic Stabilization, put it, "Each of us is likely to be slightly more eager to hold down the other fellow's prices, wages or profits, and to raise the other fellow's taxes."[20]

This war about the New Deal involved significant skirmishing over what one scholar has termed the "rickety" prewar tax structure. In 1939 only 4 million income tax returns were filed, leaving most Americans out of the tax system. The fiscal demands of the war became unavoidable by the spring of 1941, but the policy answers were less certain. The rate of tax collections perhaps more than anything else would determine the sustainability of the New Deal, increasingly a luxury for conservatives with new wartime fiscal demands on the federal government. Democrats wanted to collect the bulk of wartime taxes from higher wartime profits as well as from corporations and the wealthy while conservatives advocated an equitable or shared sacrifice to pay new taxes. Patriotism, then, becomes a key motivating factor for conservative politicians who otherwise would not have supported higher taxes, and did not in the 1930s. Moreover most members of Congress joined with individual and corporate taxpayers in protesting higher rates for pragmatic reasons of electoral survival, for concerns about creating a too powerful state, and for fear funding would go to social reform. At issue was whether to implement an Excess Profits Tax as proposed by the Treasury Department or an increase in the normal tax rates or a special defense tax as the business community desired. The president, though, worried that the tax bill under consideration would permit too many corporations to escape taxation. FDR subtly shifted the focus, arguing that "the overwhelming majority of our citizens want to contribute something directly to our defense and that most of them would rather do it with their eyes open than do it through a general sales tax." Earlier in the year, though, a slight majority, 54 to 46 percent, favored a federal sales tax, and that percentage hovered around 50 percent as the war wore on. By the spring of 1944, though, majorities in both parties favored a federal sales tax over even higher income taxes.[21]

Even while lawmakers grappled with tax policy, other resource management issues demanded the attention of Congress. Never did the legislative branch have the luxury of dealing with wartime policy one issue at a time. Instead the layering of problems made the pursuit of solutions all the more difficult. Within the realm of resource management, lawmakers embraced a range of duties beyond taxation and rationing, including congressional oversight of how taxpayer dollars were spent, especially by defense contractors. "Fox-faced" Harry S Truman of Missouri, described as the "bogeyman to all national defense chiselers," personified wartime oversight. After hearing stories about waste in the defense industry, Truman took it upon himself to tour the country. He learned that defense contractors were paid fixed rates whether or not they delivered their products efficiently. He also discovered that the majority of war contracts were going to large eastern firms. Arguing that this waste and corruption was detrimental to national security, Truman convinced his colleagues to create an investigatory committee. The Special Senate Committee to Investigate the National Defense Program was formed in March 1941 and was responsible for investigating waste in the defense industry. It was a bipartisan operation that did not discriminate, but its budget paled in comparison with what the government had issued in war contracts in 1940, $15,000 compared with $10 billion. Because there was no integrative war cabinet such as the one that failed miserably during the Civil War, the Truman Committee remained the best oversight tool of the Congress. It became a cover to avoid any additional oversight reform, leaving Congress to use ad hoc methods that pitted committees and the two chambers in competition for publicity and furthering the power disparity between Congress and the president.[22]

While the investigative function of the Truman Committee proved glamorous for Congress and helped create a favorable impression of at least this feature of its work, the other resource management issues generated less positive reviews from voters. Indeed, citizen discontent about taxation and rationing policy encouraged the legislative, ideological war. The very complexity of constructing policy as opposed to investigating waste meant that debate about the issues of taxation and rationing was often heated and vitriolic even as all in Congress agreed to the general principles of increased taxes and some form of price control. In 1941, the outlines of both fights were established. More conservative lawmakers wanted business-friendly tax policies, concerned that too-high tax rates would be destructive of American capitalism and perhaps the ability of the United States to prevail in the war. Liberals in Congress, and the administration for that matter, wanted wartime fiscal policies to be an extension of the New Deal, specifically confiscatory of excess profits. Similarly, those who opposed the shifting of additional power to the executive branch tended to oppose the application of New Deal economics to the war era. This complex calculus recurred in the various arguments over taxation and rationing policy.

The federal government employed an evolutionary approach to taxation and rationing policy development but consumers not producers were the targeted beneficiaries. As such, the congressional war about resource management was fought on the terrain of the New Deal. Historians of the consumer culture have shown how the emergence of this economic world order portended a significant political realignment that was more fully realized in the postwar era, one reflected in the New Deal order and one that privileged consumers not only in fiscal policy but also in social programs. The shift was not without controversy as southern Democrats and others who represented the older producing order chafed at new policies disadvantaging their constituents in favor of urban workers and consumers. Still, the politics of the consumer culture allowed these otherwise disenfranchised or under-enfranchised, African Americans and women, to assert themselves as citizen consumers. Tax and rationing policy tightened and formalized this connection, which played an integral role in making the New Deal order a permanent, if constrained, feature in the national political economy. Citizen consumers stood with the moderates and liberals defending the New Deal and against the southern conservatives who fought a rearguard action to thwart the reforms of the 1930s and protect rural Americans.[23]

The first phase of rationing policy was implemented in February 1941, when Roosevelt created the powerless Office of Price Administration and Civilian Supply to control inflation even though it lacked statutory authority, a move that met with public approval. Leon Henderson was at the helm. A bombastic, combative man weighing in at 200 pounds, Henderson was known for sitting behind his desk during the sultry summer months wearing nothing but his boxer shorts. He was also a New Dealer to the core interested in making the federal government more the product of bureaucracy and less of Congress. Before the attack on Pearl Harbor lawmakers began debating the anti-inflationary Emergency Price Control Act, but they did not enact the measure until January 1942. This debate about rationing and price control cannot be understood outside the context of southern concern for agricultural price structures. In February 1941, Sen. John H. Bankhead (D-AL) wrote his Senate colleague Ellison D. "Cotton Ed" Smith (D-SC) and argued for "a new cotton program" to compensate for "the loss of practically our entire foreign market for cotton." Southern lawmakers introduced other components of what would later generate so much criticism of the Office of Price

Administration (OPA), namely demands for parity.[24] In Congress too often the fighting about price control was really a series of questions about whether to accept or reject a modern economy, whether producers or consumers should be privileged, and whether the New Deal regulatory state would be cast aside as a temporary experiment in a moment of domestic crisis or made the center of the nation's political economy.

The tax wars in 1941 gained more attention and were first to receive some resolution. Citizen disagreement over appropriate tax policy further riled congressional tempers, for in January 1941 only 51 percent of the American people believed all households not on relief should pay income taxes for the war effort; 41 percent opposed such a tax policy. According to a Gallup Poll in August, a majority of Americans believed that lower income earners, defined at $3,000 a year, should pay $140 in income taxes while proposed legislation set the rate at only $11. Currently such individuals paid no taxes. The polls revealed similar answers for middle-income earners, with respondents indicating $1,123 instead of $998 should be the rate for those making $10,000 per year, but when asked about upper-income earners the respondents advocated lower tax rates than currently proposed: $24,000 instead of $52,738 for those making $100,000 per year. This trend of public support for higher taxes than recommended by the government for low-income workers and lower taxes than recommended by the government for high-income workers continued, but polling also showed Americans wanted to pay for defense expenditures with additional taxation.[25]

Doughton told a constituent, "What is a heavy peacetime tax is not necessarily a heavy wartime tax or an emergency tax." Faced with the challenge of finding additional revenue sources to fund heightened demands for national defense in 1941, members of the House Ways and Means Committee, the legislative body in which all tax legislation originates, crafted a complex bill to meet these needs, but the committee never transposed administration wishes into legislation. Instead it fought the Treasury Department proposals as did the Senate Finance Committee. One clause in the bill called for married people with two incomes, regardless the source, to file joint income tax returns. Doughton reportedly told the press that the joint returns provision was "the easiest way to get money without the committee 'loosing sleep.'"[26] Such returns threatened to increase significantly the tax rates for middle-class and wealthy Americans. As a result loud cries of protest emanated from diverse constituencies—male economic elites and feminists. The proposed solution in part pitted the economic liberalism of the New Deal era, the foundation upon which the modernization of American governance rested, against feminist demands for preserving women's economic independence, a significant component of what would become the rights revolution of the 1960s.

From a legislative perspective, the most notable and important foe was

Speaker Rayburn. He used the prerogative of his office to protect the interests of Texas, one of the eight community property states (the others were Arizona, California, Idaho, Louisiana, New Mexico, Nevada, and Washington). He had conversed with Sen. Connally about how to defeat the provision. Although Connally was on the Senate Finance Committee and would have an opportunity to fight against it there, he was the only community property state senator on the panel and he believed the best chance for eliminating joint returns lay with the House. As such, Rayburn worked closely with the administration to encourage President Roosevelt's opposition to the measure.[27]

The fight in the House Ways and Means Committee and the full House ultimately became a contest about the continuation of the economic liberalism of the New Deal. The characteristics linking these seemingly dissimilar perspectives were belief in individual autonomy and responsibility. After the Ways and Means Committee voted out the tax bill—including the provision for joint returns—by a 15–10 tally, the measure went to the full House. Republicans in the House chafed under the mechanism the House Rules Committee established for debating the tax bill, which required authorization by the tax committee for all floor amendments. Joe Martin called it a "'gag rule'" but assured reporters that the GOP would oppose the procedure not the policy: "'We can't afford to vote against this bill.'" At the same time, the minority members of the Ways and Means Committee issued their report on the tax bill to the public, which read like a legal brief against the New Deal's "extravagant spending and reckless borrowing." At stake, the Republicans insisted, was "the credit of the nation." The Minority Report included substantive statistics about the increased and often "hidden" taxes implemented during the 1930s, when tax receipts more than doubled from $3.1 billion in fiscal year 1934 to $7.6 billion in fiscal year 1941. For that same period, expenditures rose accordingly—from $6 billion to $12.7 billion—as did the deficit and the debt—from $2.8 billion to $5.1 billion and from $27 billion to $48.9 billion, but the administration had not asked the Appropriations Committee for ways to trim expenditures. This data convinced the GOP that "the finances of the nation—which are its first line of defense—were in a critical condition before the present emergency began."[28]

Because there was so much pushback against the tax bill, especially from powerful community property state lawmakers, Rules Committee chair Rep. Adolph Sabath (D-IL) indicated he would call another meeting of his committee but stated that was "'all I promised.'" The next day, Doughton and his forces sought a semi-closed rule for debating the tax bill, which in effect would permit separate consideration of the joint returns clause but would still prevent other amendments not sanctioned by the committee. The full House approved the rule by a 204–167 vote, with a majority of Democrats voting yea and a majority of Republicans voting nay. Two Ways and Means Committee Republicans spoke in favor of the measure, reminding their colleagues that when the GOP had held the majority they had used closed rules for such debates and as a result Democrats should enjoy the same privilege. Speaking for "'the new generation of Republicans,'" Jesse Wolcott disagreed with the "'reprehensible'" tactic. Daniel Reed (R-NY) attacked the "boondoggle tax" bill by lambasting the New Deal. Were it not for the $25 billion squandered on public works in the 1930s, he charged, there would be ample revenue for national defense. Reed quoted an unnamed Cabinet member who had "stated publicly that the American people were 'too damn dumb' to understand Roosevelt's financial policies."[29]

During the House floor debate, though, the fate of the joint returns provision became tenuous. Lawmakers made speeches about how the joint returns clause would hamper the advance of women's rights. Republicans and conservative Democrats also used the debate to question the merits of New Deal fiscal policy. Said Rep. Fred L. Crawford (R-MI), "[they] have presented to the American public an allegedly painless national defense program" devoid of sacrifice. President Roosevelt made matters difficult for Doughton when he released a letter opposing the joint returns provision, the method for calculating the excess profits tax, and reducing the income tax exemption rates. According to one source, Doughton viewed the letter as a "near betrayal" for he had assured Republicans on the Ways and Means Committee that the president would not be "'sticking his fingers into this tax bill.'" Done reading the letter, Doughton prepared for a "showdown" with Roosevelt and the House Democratic Leadership—Speaker Rayburn and Majority Leader McCormack—who had "openly lobbied against the committee's joint returns proposal."[30]

A "red-faced and mad" Doughton greeted his committee. He was "an old-style, old-school politician, [who] believed in House leaders supporting their committee" as was the norm under the seniority system. He told his colleagues the letter from Roosevelt and another from Treasury Secretary Henry Morgenthau "'is a terrible hurt. . . . Why didn't they bring this up before we got the bill on the floor?'" Doughton's bilious response was typical of the relationship between lawmakers and the administration when its lobbyists, the president included, sought policy that was indigestible to a majority in Congress. He blamed Rayburn for convincing FDR to write the letter, which the president then used to "belt the committee on its refusal to accept the Treasury excess profits, its failure to lower income tax exemptions." Said Doughton, "I understand [Rayburn] was down to the White House" about taxes a few days before the letter arrived. Doughton asserted he would not "stand for this." A ninety-minute debate ensued before the committee rejected each proposal within the Roosevelt letter. The committee asked Doughton to retort "'nothing doing'" to the president, and the chair gladly accorded to their wishes. The "crusty" North Carolinian made 100 copies of his

Rep. Robert L. Doughton. Courtesy Library of Congress, Prints & Photographs Division, photograph by Harris & Ewing [reproduction number, LC-USZ62-136521].

reply along with the White House correspondence and disseminated it among the press corps, telling them, "'You think it's a pretty good letter, hey boys? Well, you can have all the copies you want. Take some to your friends.'"[31]

When the August 4 floor debate occurred, the bulk of the fighting was over an amendment to remove the joint returns clause from the tax bill. That measure passed by a roll call vote of 242–160, a setback for House economic liberals who contributed 100 of the nay votes and 71 of the yea votes but a victory for feminist critics of the bill. The tax bill itself then passed easily by a roll call vote of 370–29. As a result, the Senate never gave serious consideration to joint returns. The most significant feature of Senate action on the tax bill was the inclusion of a mechanism to control government spending. Careful examination of this amendment reveals crucial differences among moderately conservative House members from the South like Doughton and conservative southern Democrats in the Senate like Byrd. Doughton blamed "the people back home" for many of the "needless expenditures," not Congress, because constituents "constantly clamor for and demand larger and larger appropriations." Because "our Government has undertaken financial obligations of the most colossal magnitude," Byrd used the global realities of war to demand fiscal restraint at home. Byrd secured an amendment to the Revenue Act of 1941, creating a Joint Committee for the Reduction of Non-Essential Federal Expenditures. The Senate passed the tax bill 67–5 on September 5.[32] The Byrd Committee, as it became known, typified the congressional conservatives' war on FDR and the New Deal during the 1940s while it also identified wasteful tendencies in federal spending, blaming congressional liberals and the White House. Its mere existence retarded not only liberal economic policy but also liberal social policy, indirectly at least, during the war years by providing conservatives with a legitimate justification—wartime fiscal discipline—for their ideological crusades.

The Revenue Act of 1941 lowered the exemption rate and increased taxes on upper-income earners, in keeping with the wishes of Congress. The president had wanted to eliminate even more deductions and to tax gross income. These positions were something of a role reversal because typically during the war years Roosevelt wanted to tax the wealthy, and the conservatives in Congress, in keeping with public opinion, wanted shared sacrifice across the board. The House approved the conference committee report without a roll call vote on September 16, 1941, and the Senate followed suit the next day.[33] No key player controlled the outcome, but the result was statist, pragmatic, and center left.

At the same time lawmakers were using taxes to fight a proxy war against the New Deal, a similar battle was brewing about price control. Prior to the introduction of what became the Emergency Price Control Act on August 1, 1941, executive branch officials met extensively with congressional leaders, rewriting the bill six times. Because most Americans believed their country to be "a land of chronic surplus" prior to the attack on Pearl Harbor, there was little if any public support for the controls. Once created, though, the OPA became the most important example of the wartime extension of New Deal regulations, and the agency's work was well funded with a budget on par with the Social Security Board and the Department of Labor. The New Deal liberals who held key positions within the OPA viewed the agency as a tool to extend the federal government into areas of the political economy that had proven difficult before. As such, a substantial minority of conservatives in Congress used the wartime battles over price control to dispute one of the three tenets of modern liberalism, that consumption was a prerequisite for economic vitality, not production.[34]

The House leadership disapproved the price control bill the administration wanted even as they supported the concept of price control. Henry B. Steagall (D-AL), in the words of one reporter, "practically disowned the bill" that he was sponsoring for the administration. While Steagall told the press it was important to control prices, he also agreed that farm income as well as crop prices must be protected. Rayburn and McCormack were unsure that the House would pass the bill, and told Henderson so. Meanwhile, moderate Democrats Wilbur Mills (AR), Mike Monroney (OK), Albert Gore (TN), and Paul Brown (GA) wanted to add wage controls to the legislation even though this was in keeping with the GOP strategy. Though pragmatically a fair position, this strategy diverged from the consumer-oriented liberalism of the New Deal because it threatened workers and because it negated the redistributive economics of Roosevelt's closest supporters. Gore, a disciple of Bernard Baruch and a leader of the group, believed in an across-the-board freeze of wages, prices, rents, and commissions. According to Mills, Rayburn did not really care if the measure made it to the House floor. The speaker sent the bill to the Banking and Currency Committee knowing it would encounter problems there.[35]

As committee chair, Steagall vacillated, running "one of the most leisurely outfits in Congress, if not the most leisurely." Meetings scheduled for 10:00 a.m. typically did not begin until 11:30 a.m. Members wrangled "interminably over minor points of language." The committee had "to hear every fact and every theory." Steagall, though, was not a student of the legislation debated in his committee or of economics generally, preferring instead to spend as much time as possible near his Ozark, Alabama, home with his foxhounds. The administration's problems with Steagall were compounded because the ranking Republican, Jesse Wolcott, a liberal in his party who acknowledged that some price control was necessary, was among the best economic minds in Congress.[36]

Late September 1941 found Congress in a contemptuous and disaffected state with regard to the politics of price control. Members of the House Banking and Currency Committee showed their disregard for the administration bill with lax attendance and "desultory" questioning of witnesses at the committee hearings. Farm state lawmakers hoped to either remove agriculture from controls altogether or to increase the percentage of parity permitted as the ceiling for farm income. Those lawmakers who paid attention learned as much as they could about price control, and they used that background to good effect in the many wartime struggles over price control. Sam Rayburn worried, "I don't know what we can do, but I do know it is going to be tough. But we are going to try to pass something, and I think we will."[37]

In early October, Congress watchers doubted that effective price control legislation could pass the House, but rising prices that fall convinced the Banking and Currency committee chair that action was needed. Serious impediments remained: lobbying from special interests representing industry and commodity producers and an inept administrative strategy to combat inflation. These conditions did not inspire House Banking and Currency Committee leaders to write a strong bill representing a consensus position, so they began with the bill that Henderson wrote. This decision displeased Roosevelt and the administration, but a month later, Rayburn told Steagall to report the price control bill and be ready for a floor debate. Furthermore, Rayburn indicated Steagall should get an open rule, meaning all amendments would be welcomed. This approach differed significantly from the closed rule floor management plan for tax legislation. Rayburn had no choice because the House leadership did not know the administration preferences beyond the Henderson bill, it lacked regional consensus within the Democratic Party, and it faced a GOP more ready to politick the debate than with taxes. Of these problems, the lack of knowledge regarding White House strategy suggests two things: that FDR's lobbying efforts on Capitol Hill were insufficient and that a Democratic government was in disharmony. In an off-the-record interview, Rayburn declared, "Henry Steagall didn't do such a bad job getting that bill out as he did. He's got a hell of a hard committee to work with there." Rayburn acknowledged the lack of wage controls in the bill, explaining that "the God damned Republicans, they'd all vote against it, try to pin it on the Democrats that they were anti-labor." The Speaker promised "to get some kind of a bill through the house, but God knows what it will be." Though he did not know what Roosevelt wanted in the bill, he knew Morgenthau had threatened a second major tax bill if price control was not accomplished. This "shotgun in the closet," Rayburn contended, was no way to legislate.[38]

Leon Henderson complained that the price control bill reported out of the House Banking and Currency Committee was "entirely unsatisfactory." The House panel had weakened enforcement authority. It also added an amendment by Paul Brown that instituted a price floor for agricultural produce, a measure which would almost surely push prices higher and harm consumers. John McCormack had told Henderson "there would be a hell of a fight on the bill on the floor, that he was lucky to get any kind of a bill." McCormack realized that the GOP would control the outcome because Democrats were divided. Though McCormack would not admit it, his remarks indicated he had discussed the matter with Roosevelt and the president had promised to veto any measure akin to the House Banking and Currency Committee bill.[39]

Off the record, McCormack hinted, "There may be some things that we may let the Senate do." Much of the difficulty in the House resulted because of Republican strategy to use the issue for political purposes. McCormack explained, "You tell me what the Republicans will do; I'll tell you what we can pass. My guess is that they'll vote for every amendment to hamstring the bill." Nonetheless, McCormack hoped that key provisions regarding the buying and selling of commodities and the licensing of dealers could be restored. Rayburn was less sure: "Hell's fire, I'm not going to ask these farm boys to cut their throats. . . . If these farm boys were to exempt wages in the bill, and then vote against the Brown amendment, there'd be a lot of them that wouldn't come back."[40]

So bad was the floor debate in the House that Democratic leaders meeting in the Speaker's lobby had adopted the refrain, "a number and a title to send to the Senate," just enough to let Carter Glass (D-VA), the acting chair of the Senate Banking and Currency Committee, revive a workable bill. "Walrus-mustached" Sen. Cotton Ed Smith, an opponent of price control, sat in the back of the House chamber for the debate. Steagall could do very little to blunt the attack on his committee's bill. Gore introduced his bipartisan bill with the GOP-favored comprehensive controls including wages. The House voted to kill the Gore substitute with just 63 in favor and 218 opposed, but the GOP held the upper hand. Rayburn and McCormack asserted just how dire the situation was. They encouraged speedy passage of any bill with the long-term plan of fixing matters in the conference committee. A bill no one liked full of problematic amendments with Republican sponsorship passed 224–161. As Chart 2.1 shows, Southern Democrats split fairly evenly with only a slight majority voting for the bill; more important those southern Democrats who voted against the bill constituted the majority of the Democratic opposition to the bill. Republicans, though, provided two-thirds of the opposition and the majority were midwesterners. The politics of agriculture more than the conservative coalition dictated this outcome given the significant southern divisions over the bill. Sam Rayburn admonished, "Hell, with the House in this frame of mind, we've got to take what we can get, then hope that the Senate will do better. This thing is horribly messed up."[41]

Political conditions were only marginally better in the Senate, though. Glass had no intention of reporting out the House bill. As a long-time admirer of Baruch, he wanted something much more akin to the Gore bill, which never gained traction in the House. The main goal of the Senate Banking Committee, though, was to restore Henderson's powers, which the House had eliminated. Sen. Prentiss M. Brown (D-MI) led the fight for the administration against an array of forces: the cotton senators, Southern Democrats led by Connally, Richard B. Russell (GA), and George, generally all sane conservatives but for the issues of cotton prices and race; the GOP for partisan reasons; lobbyists for the dairy, livestock, and cotton interests; and farm bloc senators who believed this the one chance to help farmers make money. As Sen. O'Mahoney explained at the end of the war agrarian grievances were not without merit. While 23 percent of the U.S. labor force worked in agriculture, this sector received but 7 percent of the national income. O'Mahoney compared these statistics with those for manufacturing, which employed 22 percent of the U.S. labor force while earning 26 percent of the national income. Inflationary amendments were proposed, including Bankhead's to require the price administrator to gain prior approval from the secretary of agriculture for controls affecting agricultural commodities and another linking parity to an index of urban wages. When polled in September 1941,

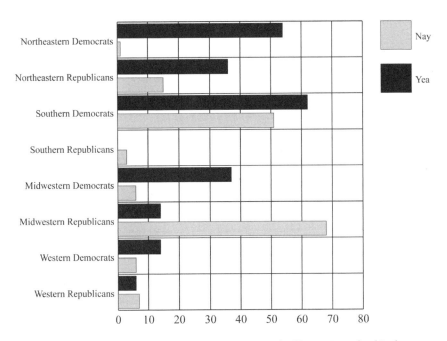

Chart 2.1: Regional and Party Identification—Price Control Bill, 1941. Data for this chart come from analysis of the November 28, 1941 record vote in the House of Representatives. See Congressional Record, 77th Congress, 1st session, 9247.

52 percent of American farmers answered that they were earning enough for the production of their chief crop, suggesting that politicians more than farmers advocated for the legislation favorable to farm prices. During the Senate vote, Edward A. O'Neal of the American Farm Bureau Federation lobbied members outside the chamber, and took a position in the gallery. He told a senator, "You had better get busy. There's God in the Gallery!"[42]

Passage of the bill followed the entry of the United States into the war, revealing just how important an attack on American soil was for the way Congress conceptualized resource management policy. As one government official later noted, "Pearl Harbor found the United States with no rationing plans, no rationing organization, and no real appreciation of the indispensability of rationing in a genuine all-out war effort." In the end, the Senate approved the inflationary Bankhead amendment, 48–37, and the bill, 84–1, making a conference committee necessary. Northeasterners and westerners almost universally opposed the Bankhead amendment, but southerners and midwesterners split their votes as Chart 2.2 reveals. The *New York Times* editorialized, "After the attack on Pearl Harbor the Senate passed a price-control bill that was in most respects a great

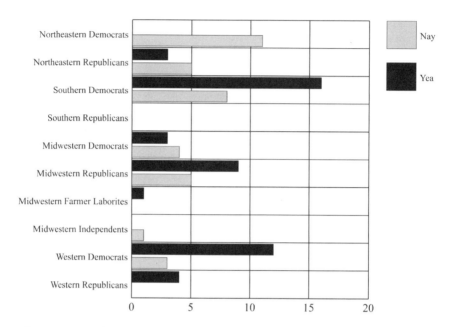

Chart 2.2: Regional and Party Identification—The Bankhead Amendment. Data for this chart come from analysis of the January 9, 1942, record vote in the Senate. See Congressional Record, *77th Congress, 2nd session, 189.*

deal worse," than the House bill. Senate changes included support for a single price administrator whereby the House vested such authority with a five-person board; manipulation of commodity prices through a program of buying and selling; and a requirement that commodity sellers be licensed. The matter of whether price control politics should be vested with one person or a board was really a debate about the unpopular Henderson. During the conference committee deliberations Roosevelt pressured House conferees to moderate the most extreme Senate provisions. He did so with effective and creative use of executive branch staff, measures that angered opponents of the bill, both conservative Republicans and New Deal Democrats who wanted more for farmers. During the conference committee meetings on the price control bill, Prentiss Brown and Alben Barkley drew advice from David Ginsburg, known in Washington as "Leon Henderson's ace legalist." Ginsburg then discussed with Henderson the ongoing deliberations, who used the information to plot strategy with Rayburn and McCormack so they could lobby the conferees from the lower chamber. They achieved only modest success. The House voted its approval of the conference committee report—which followed the Senate version of the bill—289–114. The Senate concurred, 65-14. Roosevelt later castigated Bankhead for authoring the amendment that gave the secretary of agriculture a veto over the decisions of the OPA administrator, inquiring of him, "Did you ever read the *Merchant of Venice?* I remember something about a fellow who wanted his pound of flesh."[43]

The Emergency Price Control Act became law on January 31, 1942. It created the OPA, authorized the agency to control prices and rents, and prevented any agricultural price control below 110 percent parity. The law was not sufficient to contain the wartime problems within the American economy, even though it was born of statist, pragmatic thinking about resource management. Within three months, the OPA announced General Maximum Price Regulation, or General Max as it was commonly known, on April 29, 1942. Some scholars have even suggested that the real congressional purpose for the Emergency Price Control Act was an across-the-board increase in agricultural prices, not the implementation of price controls, and the House bill evidenced that point. Here the conflict between the older producer economy and the newer consumer economy could not have been more apparent. Conservative lawmakers, though, saw the administration's motives as a quest for too much power. Taft complained Roosevelt and the executive branch were "still busy asking for every power they can think of, whether they need it or not."[44]

General Max proved insufficient to manage the wartime economy, leaving Roosevelt and Congress in agreement that wage controls were needed. In the middle of July 1942, Rayburn described a private conversation with Roosevelt in which the president said that the price situation was out of hand. Rayburn said, "He's pretty worked up over it, and he ought to be. I told him that if he sent anything up here, it would have to be forceful. I told him it would have to be something more than a letter to a committee chairman or a message to the speaker. He'd have to send a message to the Congress, and make it a hard, ringing one." Rayburn hoped the problem, or at least the strategy for solving it, would be decided at the next meeting with the president. He hinted, "The President very definitely has in mind legislation to freeze wages. Of course there's got to be legislation. We've got to do something or we're going to have the God damnedest blowup this country ever saw, and it'll cost us billions of dollars."[45]

For Southern Democrats like Rep. John E. Rankin (D-MS), the politics of price control were directly related to preservation of the New Deal order, or at least those parts linked to the agrarian economy, which were at odds with other parts of the New Deal order, the consumer economy. Southern Democrats had a very different understanding of how the New Deal should be revised than did party members from other regions. Moreover southern Democrats failed to grasp the contradictions between preserving farm income, largely determined by the price of foodstuffs, and protecting purchasing power for industrial workers who needed cheap food to make ends meet. Rankin told his constituents during the

1942 congressional elections: "I am opposed to giving any man, or set of men, the right or the power to fix the price of cotton below the cost of production." He compared farm income with industrial wages. "A farmer gets on an average of 1¢ an hour," Rankin averred, for work that required "toiling in the hot sun." He concluded, "I am not trying to take anything away from the man who works for a daily wage. I am simply trying to raise the farmers' income up . . . and to give the farmer his share of the nation's prosperity."[46]

On September 6, Roosevelt sent Rayburn a "confidential" telegram urging his speedy return to Washington to attend to wage and price control legislation. After a White House meeting with Barkley, McCormack, and Rayburn to discuss strategy for the legislation, Roosevelt asked Congress to come back to town earlier than scheduled to enact an "over-all stabilization" program of prices, salaries, wages, and profits to replace General Max. Food prices alone were increasing over 1 percent each month. He argued: "It not only would be unfair to labor to stabilize wages and do nothing about the cost of food; it would be equally unfair to the farmer" whose "wife buys many articles of food at the store for the use of her own family, and high prices hurt her pocketbook as much as that of the city housewife." He gave Congress an ultimatum, demanding they act by October 1, or he would. Rayburn and other leading lawmakers had previously told the president he could and should tackle the problem with an executive order, such was his power as commander in chief. They feared the congressional war would escalate. Roosevelt, though, wanted a legislative solution or at least legislative cover. He knew if he acted independently he would suffer the blame should the measure fail, but if deliberated by Congress, lawmakers would share the criticism. Ultimately, the congressional debate was over the meaning of parity, policies dating back to 1933, and Roosevelt told Senate liberals the standard was "good . . . for war. To recalculate parity now, and to offer the public 100 percent of a new and higher parity, would be to offer stabilization, yet destroy the possibility of achieving it."[47]

Members of Congress chafed at Roosevelt's ultimatum. Sen. Robert M. La Follette Jr. (P-WI) complained FDR had "placed a pistol at the head of Congress." Taft was even more contemptuous of the president: "I regret that the president has yielded to advisors who have so little respect for the Constitution. The doctrine that is asserted leaves Congress as a mere shell of a legislative body." They believed he had acted because of negative public opinion regarding lawmakers, and that he had devised the October deadline as a mechanism to make Congress look bad even though the administration had done nothing to solve the problem. Lawmakers trusted neither the president nor his proclivity for changing positions. Initially, he had opposed wage controls, but now he wanted them. Others noted that he had not rejected union demands for wage increases while also

Rep. John Rankin and Rep. Edith Nourse Rogers. Courtesy Library of Congress, Prints & Photographs Division, photograph by Harris & Ewing [reproduction number, LC-DIG-hec-25936].

opposing pending legislation to control wartime strikes. Said Gore, who had wanted a comprehensive bill the first time out, "I just don't trust him. He had a chance to get wage controls in the first bill. . . . The farm bloc would not have been able to write in these parity formulae if it had not become evident that the administration intended to do nothing about advancing wages." Prentiss Brown spoke critically of Rayburn's proposal to give Roosevelt blanket authority for price control: "We could never take that. The Senate wouldn't pass it. That just won't do."[48]

Legislative leaders, including Barkley, Rayburn, Brown, Robert Wagner (D-NY), Steagall, Wright Patman, and Brent Spence (D-KY), met with FDR about price stabilization. They told the president it would be difficult to pass a bill, and several of the senators—Wagner, Barkley, and Brown—controverted the Rayburn approach, which was also what Roosevelt wanted. Still when Rayburn left the meeting he had hope the president would follow his strategy recommendations.

He told one of his legislative lieutenants: "We tried to convince [Roosevelt] before we left Washington that he could do whatever he wanted about stabilization without asking for legislation. He finally agreed and said when he did he would send the report to Congress on what he had done, which I think is the wise thing." Ultimately, Henry Steagall introduced the House bill for inflation controls, and it was a sop to the farm bloc, providing that the parity floor be based on all production costs, including labor. It would raise the parity calculation 110 percent above the current level and would eliminate the existing parity provisions. Brown introduced the Senate bill, and it contained a minimum of the president's demands: stabilization of agricultural prices and industrial wages at current levels. Brown defended the White House stipulations for a "time limit on a rather slow-moving Congress" and asserted "action is vital and vital now."[49]

When there was no new price control bill ready for his signature on October 1, FDR was angry. He longed for 1933 when he had been able to get important bills in a matter of days; the results then were the product of symbiotic legislative-executive relations characterized by a shared ideology and willingness to experiment. Such sentiments were gone by the war years. At one point during the war, Franklin D. Roosevelt observed to Eleanor Roosevelt, "I think the country has forgotten we ever lived through the 1930s." He was not at all cooperative with the leadership team on Capitol Hill. He told the press of his tour around the country, its defense plants and military installations. He spent time recounting his visit with "my old friend" John Nance Garner, who had been vice president from 1933 until 1941, and before that a long-serving, widely respected member of Congress. FDR insisted that Garner, long allied with the farm bloc in Congress, agreed the cost of living needed to be contained. Rayburn, a protégé of Garner and a political ally of the former vice president, was furious with FDR's October 1 press conference, calling it "a hell of a thing to do, and it has got to stop. We have a hard enough time up here carrying the load for him without any blasts like that, that are totally undeserved and uncalled for. Hell, we put this bill through for him, and he's getting just about what he wants. And then he kicks us this way." Rayburn claimed that he could have killed the bill in the Banking and Currency Committee if he had wanted to but that he had done everything to get the legislation through for the president. Connally said that if he were a Republican he would "make a two hour speech directed right at the White House this afternoon and I'd say plenty." Wolcott, who had worked very hard for the bill, declared, FDR "can go to hell. That's what we ought to tell him, and believe me, if this weren't war he'd be told plenty quick."[50]

Brown said of the passage of the price control bill, which addressed both prices and wages, "I have never known of a measure in which the voice of the people was such a potent factor in final passage of the bill." Contemporary scholars and practitioners had a different explanation, though, one that blamed farmers and work-ers for unwillingness to take a cut. The Economic Stabilization Act, passed just one day after the administration deadline, provided the White House additional au-thority over prices and wages, but agriculture was still privileged even though the 110 percent parity formula was rescinded. The politics of price control grew in dif-ficulty throughout the war years because the OPA functioned as the proxy for the New Deal. Through its work stabilizing prices, the OPA helped to strengthen the nonagrarian components of the New Deal. This caused congressional critics of the New Deal to heap invective on the agency, which had not only fought to limit farm income but also was committed to expanding the power of the federal gov-ernment, institutionalizing redistributive politics.[51]

At the same time FDR pushed Congress to perfect price control, he also chal-lenged lawmakers to adopt a much more progressive income tax. As with price control, lawmakers moved too slowly for the White House. Despite the administra-tion's preference that Congress follow the 1941 Revenue Act with more tax leg-islation before the March 1942 filing deadline, there was no early completion of the 1942 Revenue Act. Blame lay with both the executive and legislative branches. Secretary Morgenthau waited until March to send to Congress the administration bill, which provided for increased taxes on individuals and corporations, payroll deductions, higher social security taxes, elimination of the oil depletion allow-ance, and an end to exemptions for interest earned on municipal bonds. Law-makers ultimately delayed action for seven months on the unpopular bill. Meanwhile, in a message to Congress, Roosevelt called for a $25,000 limit on after-tax individual incomes. He told Congress on April 27, 1942, "Discrepancies be-tween low personal incomes and very high personal incomes should be lessened," arguing that "in time of this grave national danger, when all excess income should go to win the war, no American citizen ought to have a net income, after he has paid his taxes, of more than $25,000 a year." Sober thinking about war mobiliza-tion limited the congressional will to pursue the administration's radical tax ini-tiatives, which targeted corporate wealth. Because Congress refused to enact the salary limitation, Roosevelt issued an executive order, citing the authority granted him under the price stabilization legislation.[52]

Lawmakers in the two chambers wanted to pass the tax bill in 1942 before the midterm elections to prove their courage to take controversial action, and to de-flect growing GOP criticisms of Democratic tax policy. When Congress returned to town in early September, Walter George introduced a plan for what he called the victory tax. It was a 5 percent withholding tax, and it included provisions for postwar rebates. It did not differentiate among taxpayers according to family sta-tus, number of dependants, or medical expenses so critics lambasted its regressive inclusion of working-class families. The Senate Finance Committee revised the

George proposal regarding the surtax, making it more favorable to low-income surtax payers. To compensate, the committee also increased rates for high-income surtax payers. In all the Senate layered the tax bill with approximately 500 amendments while generating less revenue than the administration had requested, $7 instead of $8 billion. Gaping loopholes remained in the tax code, but the 1942 Revenue Act was inclusive and progressive, satisfying demands of both conservatives and New Deal liberals. It became the foundation of wartime tax policy. Most Americans became taxpayers as a result of it. Furthermore, corporate and excess profits taxes were increased, the latter from 60 to 90 percent.[53]

One unintended result of the tax and price control wars was the increasing congressional hostility to the administration, which by the end of 1942 extended beyond specific policy quarrels to include a general disapproval of presidential policies and presidential discourse with Capitol Hill. For example, Rayburn and Mills expressed serious discontent with the administration's management of the war, which in the fall of 1942 saw Japan launch a major offensive against the U.S. position at Guadalcanal that did not turn in the favor of the Americans until after the midterm congressional elections. Rayburn predicted that after the midterms lawmakers would attack the president on military decisions just as he had attacked them on issues like taxes and inflation. At the same time Roosevelt praised Rayburn, "the speakership has assumed a special importance because of the gravity of the issues with which you have continually had to deal. Keep up the good work. The country has need of you." More ominously, Mills argued: "They have blamed every failure on Congress, and the administration has made it harder, not easier, for the Democrats to retain their control. . . . These bureaucrats seem to think now that our only job is to appropriate the money they ask, that we haven't a right to question anything they do. That is a hell of a notion. Congress criticized during the last war and with some pretty damned good results."[54] These views belie the ability of Congress and the executive branch to work together on questions of resource management. The complex Democratic coalition proved durable even when key members in it distrusted other key members, including the president, and it confirmed the ability to operate over the separation of powers and coalition-rending fights about the meaning of the New Deal. Congressional Democratic success on resource management early in the war defined what was and was not possible in the highly charged partisan war over New Deal liberalism.

3. "Congress DOES Have Power" over the President

"Of course, we'll try to run the rascals out. There will be plenty of domestic issues for the 1942 campaign. The woods are full of weeds. There will be plenty of issues, non-defense spending, waste, and such things as that," declared Senate Minority Leader Charles McNary (R-OR) at a Republican conference four days after Pearl Harbor. "I have no doubt that we will find something to campaign on. There's the matter of efficiency in the government."[1] As few as five days earlier, foreign policy and isolation were the standard GOP issues deployed against Franklin D. Roosevelt and the Democrats. War changed all that, making possible a partisan attack on the New Deal and statism, one that exacerbated tensions among liberal, moderate, and conservative Democrats and encouraged the development of a liberalism in praxis that was not driven by ideology but by the need to govern. Though in the ten months following Pearl Harbor, moderate and liberal Democrats had sustained the New Deal political economy, they did so by making war issues primary. Republicans, though, never hesitated to blame Democrats for failures in the war, arguments that ran parallel to presidential criticism of the legislative branch.

Speaker of the House Sam Rayburn (D-TX) contended Congress should not be blamed for Axis ascendancy in the war for it had provided all legislation the White House requested. "Congress cannot run the war and knows it," Rayburn asserted. "The war must be run by experienced people who have made a life study of it." Still, Rayburn understood the crucial role of Congress in the nation's military efforts, and he believed maintenance of strong Democratic majorities was vital. He was optimistic about Democratic chances in 1942, too much so. He played a leading role in fundraising for Democratic congressional candidates, bringing in more money than ever before. Of the $100,000 raised, $75,000 came from Texas. He told his brother-in-law, "They can all thank me and the people of Texas." Rayburn's attitude toward the White House was much stingier, complaining "the President has not been helpful to us" by "indict[ing] the whole Congress."[2]

Rayburn's optimism about the elections emanated from his center left pragmatism, but he underestimated the difficulties he had faced in the last two years. Welding the peacetime government into a fist of steel proved most difficult for congressional moderates, the faction in Congress who would determine the fate of New Deal statism in this process of mobilizing Capitol Hill for its wartime duties. As Rayburn argued before the elections, Congress, meaning moderates, had cooperated with the White House. Administration insiders saw matters differently. Said Interior Secretary Harold Ickes, "Congress is a menace and it looks as if the president would have to sustain heavy losses on the political front."[3] The challenges intensified after the 1942 midterm elections, and it became much more difficult for the center to hold. The result: further constriction of New Deal liberalism away from its social welfare roots and toward the new warfare state. The process by which this happened involved more wartime fights over resource management policy, but with fewer Democrats for the congressional leadership to deploy.

The post-election landscape made wartime congressional moderates all the more important. Definition of this category relies as much on disposition of the lawmakers as on ideology, meaning who were the compromisers and who were the purists. Center left moderates possessed the political pragmatism necessary for compromise. They cared more for results than being right all the time, perfecting a pragmatic liberalism during the war that consolidated but narrowed the New Deal. Moreover, these individuals appreciated the importance of the New Deal order as a permanent change in the national political economy but were not wedded to its particulars as crafted in the 1930s. Instead, moderates believed that the same political creativity that gave birth to the New Deal should be employed to revise it in the war and postwar eras. Experimentation became increasingly contentious in 1943 and 1944, though, as the demands of the war intensified. Moderates more than liberals believed new rules were necessary for the political economy, making them more likely to cooperate with conservatives.

The story of this transformation begins with the midterm elections. Voters were restless. Battlefield progress seemed elusive at the time even though the results of military action in 1942 paved the way for an Allied victory in 1945. More important, the public hated living in a command economy with rationing, price control, new government regulations limiting commerce and trade in the private sector, and rising prices. Government agencies to manage the war economy seemed impotent, and the Republican Party ran against the domestic war effort, attacking specifically New Deal rhetoric by liberals in Congress. Changed economic circumstances since 1932 abetted Republican strategy; the primary issues that drew voters to Roosevelt and the Democrats, depression and unemployment, had disappeared because of war-induced prosperity. Voters who needed federal government relief programs in the early 1930s blamed themselves for their economic failures, not larger systemic forces, and they credited themselves when they found good jobs in war plants in the early 1940s, not the warfare state that replaced the New Deal welfare state. Moreover, wage and price controls angered both workers and farmers, two key constituencies for the Democrats. Republican mastery of the issues was only one reason for the Democratic debacle in 1942, though. Turnout was low that year; just 28 million people voted, down from 50 million in 1940. Relocation for military service and for work more than any other factor explained this disparity, which disproportionately affected Democrats.[4]

The resource management problems before Congress intensified as the war progressed, causing lawmakers to command more forcefully their constitutional role and intensify the ideological warfare in Washington, D.C. The 1942 midterm congressional elections were an important turning point if for no other reason than the number of conservatives in Congress swelled. Thus, the congressional warfare over resource management in the years after 1942 was not fought exclusively between conservatives and the moderate-liberal coalition, but instead also included increased discord between moderates and liberals. As a result, during the remaining years of the war it became more difficult for moderates to defend the New Deal–oriented fiscal policies in wartime taxation and price control. At the same time lawmakers were bolder in their challenges to Roosevelt's expansion of new presidential powers. Moderates in Congress redefined the New Deal as a warfare state that was, to be sure, dependent on a strong federal government to invest in the economy, but more for the purpose of national defense and less for social welfare.

Democratic National Committee Chair Edward J. Flynn did his party no favors when on the eve of the 1942 midterm elections he sermonized that only the Axis powers would benefit from a GOP Congress. Remembering what happened to Woodrow Wilson in 1918 and his own ill-fated effort to purge conservative Democrats in 1938, President Franklin D. Roosevelt simply said voters should choose representatives who would support the government's war effort. It fell to Sam Rayburn to make a more positive argument for retaining congressional incumbents. He told Americans in a national radio address, "Your Congress has provided the legislative strength necessary to wage this total war. The Congress has given the President, the War Department, the Navy Department, War Production Board, and every other war agency every law and every dollar necessary for the prosecution of the war."[5]

The election of 1942 might well be considered the first postwar election even though the United States had been at war for less than a year and would fight for almost three more years before it ended. In 1942 moderates and conservatives forced a redefinition and constriction of liberalism away from the experimental approaches of the 1930s, previewing what would dominate domestic politics in the postwar years. The policy decisions in the newly elected 78th Congress reflect this development. But in other very real ways the 1942 contest was decided because voters feared the war was being lost, not won. The wisdom of the island-hopping strategy in the Pacific Theater was not yet apparent. The Battle of Guadalcanal, then a stalemate, was not decided in favor of the United States until early 1943. Moreover U.S. troops had yet to land in North Africa and begin Operation Torch. Had either of these military developments been timed with the political clock the 1942 elections might well have been a victory for the Democrats.[6]

Conservatives and Republicans benefitted from voter frustrations with an executive that overreached on issues regarding the domestic economy, labor relations, and wartime social policies. Voters rewarded those politicians they believed most likely to abet the congressional pushback against executive interference. The GOP encouraged such behavior, running against the conduct of the war. One big-city daily, the *Los Angeles Times*, editorialized that the changes in Congress and the national government would be significant. Paraphrasing from the work of other political pundits, the *Times* alleged that if the "prophecies of all the optimists" were correct, "it ought to provide us with just about everything from unlimited butter to a Republican president in 1944." Among the more specific and occasionally humorous predictions were wiser spending policies, greater congressional involvement in national policy, a curtailment of benefits for organized labor, pay-as-you-go tax reform for tax filers, no further social security programs, reduced power for the president, elimination of New Deal programs, and finally "less Eleanor."[7]

After the 1942 midterm elections a more conservative Congress arrived in Washington, D.C. Democrats maintained a 222–209 House majority, with four independents. The Democratic majority in the Senate was 57–38 also with four independents. The GOP upsurge, though, obscures heightened difficulties for moderate Democrats frustrated with heavy-handed administration tactics. On the eve of the midterms key Democratic leaders were irate with FDR regarding his tax and price control policies. Diminished Democratic numbers, especially administration-friendly Democrats, weakened the party in Congress and limited the negotiating strength of Capitol Hill Democrats vis-à-vis the White House. Even when FDR lost he won, or at least it was a draw, with the tie going to the White House.[8]

One issue that captured voter attention, and anger, was the president's $25,000 salary limitation executive order, which the new Congress killed in March 1943. Both the president and Congress understood that the proposal applied to just one in 50,000 Americans, but both branches of government viewed the measure as symbolic. FDR wanted to win the support of organized labor, while conservatives in Congress clamored for approval from business interests. Here was a safe fight Congress could have with the president without jeopardizing the war effort, but still trimming his presidential powers and helping shift the direction of the nation's political economy away from Washington and toward the private marketplace. Moderates were caught in the middle.[9]

A related message of the 1942 election involved anger with the mushrooming federal bureaucracy for interfering in people's private lives. New wartime bureaucracies gained a degree of exemption from criticism because of their centrality to the war, but New Deal bureaucrats enjoyed no such luxury. Nor did wartime agencies like the Office of Price Administration (OPA), for it restricted liberty of contract in the domestic economy. The election did not mean the death of the New Deal, but of its most experimental aspects. Most observers recognized that components of the reforms from the 1930s were popular and needed, including the Securities and Exchange Commission, the Agricultural Adjustment Administration farm programs, the Reconstruction Finance Corporation, public power, reciprocal trade, the Federal Deposit Insurance Corporation, the good neighbor policy with Latin America, wage and hour legislation, Social Security, the Wagner Act, and the Public Utilities Holding Company Act, all measures that in varying degrees attempted systemic reform. Those parts most in jeopardy were the Work Projects Administration, the Farm Security Administration, the Civilian Conservation Corps, and the National Youth Administration, all entities that paid direct benefits to needy recipients. Indeed, Americans were split on whether various New Deal programs should be eliminated because of the war: 54 percent favored discontinuing the Civilian Conservation Corps, 38 percent favored discontinuing the National Youth Administration, and 43 percent favored eliminating farm benefits. *Time* magazine journalist Frank McNaughton reasoned: "The New Deal has reached a point where it must be digested. The public and Congress has been fed for ten years on this butterscotch rich diet of reform, and the fare is getting nauseating, particularly with the more rugged meat of a global war to chow upon."[10]

Moreover, wartime agencies charged with emulating statist New Deal values—among which were the OPA, the Office of War Information (OWI), and the Office of Civil Defense (OCD)—earned the enmity of conservative lawmakers. The OPA's supposed sins involved economic regulations that continued the New Deal ethos while the OWI and the OCD came in for attacks because of a focus on moral, ideological, and political issues. Conservatives in Congress held nothing back. They despised the director of the OCD, James Landis, in part because he cooperated with Eleanor Roosevelt to host a White House party for African American employees of the agency when the segregated Wardman Park Hotel refused to accept his guest list. Rep. Joe Starnes (D-AL) called the OWI's domestic work "a stench to the nostrils of a democratic people." Sen. Robert A. Taft (R-OH) had in his files a list of OWI staff who had worked for the leftist publication *PM*. Attached to the list was a dossier on each named employee. These documents noted the liberal and supposedly Communist affiliations of each individual. The congressional assault on the OWI was then in part a calculated effort to thwart liberals from writing the national narrative and controlling public policy during the

"The Roll Back Season." Berryman cartoon depicting congressional eagerness to eliminate executive branch agencies with a New Deal orientation, June 20, 1943. Courtesy Library of Congress, Prints & Photographs Division, Clifford Berryman Collection [reproduction number, LC-DIG-ds-02874].

war years.[11] Lawmakers were never able to eliminate the OPA, so central was its work to the war, but the OWI and the OCD were disbanded in 1945 during the waning months of the war.

The midterm elections had a significant impact on the identity of Congress. The new GOP lawmakers, many from the educated middle-class business community, shared a hatred of New Deal statism and liberalism, be it ideological or pragmatic. This economic perspective proved to be equally important in the debates that followed regarding resource management as was the defeat of key Democratic leaders. In the Senate, three committee chairs were beaten: William J. Bulow (D-SD), the chair of the Civil Service Committee; Prentiss M. Brown (D-

MI), the chair of the Claims Committee; and H. H. Schwartz (D-WY), the chair of the Pensions Committee. Moreover Brown was considered a "star member" of the Banking and Currency Committee. Other notable defeats in the Senate included Clyde Herring (D-IA), who was on the Banking and the Finance panels, but was not quite the workhorse; James H. Hughes (D-DE), who was on Banking and Judiciary; Josh Lee (D-OK), who was on Foreign Relations and Military Affairs; George Norris (I-NE), who was a hard worker on Agriculture and on Judiciary; and William H. Smathers (D-NJ), who was a "mediocrity" on Banking, Finance, and Judiciary.[12]

Seven House committee chairs were defeated: Guy L. Moser (D-PA), chair of the Census Committee; William H. Larrabee (D-IN), chair of the Education Committee; Leo Kocialkowski (D-IL), chair of the Insular Affairs Committee; Charles Kramer (D-CA), chair of the Patents Committee; Martin F. Smith (D-WA), chair of the Pensions Committee; Milton A. Romjue (D-MO), chair of the Post Office and Post Roads Committee; and Wilburn Cartwright (D-OK), chair of the Roads Committee. Furthermore, seven of fourteen Democrats on the House Ways and Means Committee were beaten, most of whom were administration Democrats. Ways and Means Committee chair Robert L. "Muley" Doughton (D-NC) told a former member of the committee that his contribution to the committee was missed. Of the new members only Wilbur Mills (D-AR) and Albert S. Camp (D-GA) were making a mark. Doughton bemoaned, "Confidentially, our Committee on the Democratic side is the weakest it has been in years." The committee chair defeats reflected a national retreat from liberalism and the New Deal. Only nine Southern Democrats were defeated, and all but one were replaced with other Democrats. This meant that few if any powerful committee chairs presiding over panels vital to the war effort were rejected by the voters because 64 percent of the leading House and 66 percent of the leading Senate committees were in the hands of Southern Democrats. It also meant there were fewer left-of-center Democrats with seniority to sway the moderates and deflect the conservatives. After the midterm elections, Minority Leader Joseph W. Martin, Jr. (R-MA) promised extensive use of conferences and conversation to keep members in line. He affirmed to a journalist, "Don't mistake it, we are going to run the House. They can't ever hold the Democrats together, and we will always have the balance of power on controversial issues."[13]

Rayburn disagreed: He told a Texas political friend, "You and I had fathers that taught us how to be a Democrat and how to stay in there and pitch when the going was hard. In times like these people are depressed and unhappy. The party in power must take it." The ramifications of increased GOP strength appeared first with regard to the organization of the House, and they showed mathematically just how much potential power the conservatives had and exactly why pragmatic moderates might search for compromise with Republicans more frequently than with liberal Democrats. Martin wanted Democrats to have only a margin of one on House committees, but Rayburn refused. He insisted that both the fifteen to ten majority for the Ways and Means Committee and the ten to five majority on the Rules Committee remain in place. On the remaining committees the Democrats would have a two- or three-seat majority. Martin demanded that there would be no more New Deal measures. Rayburn was adamantly opposed to Martin's request for a committee to look into the war effort. The Texan argued: "I'll be god damned if we are going to have any joint committee, and let them put on a lot of flannel mouths that will be blabbing everything they know. The military affairs committee has a right to information, but you start loading up a general committee, and the reporters that you can't trust . . . will begin running around digging up stuff."[14]

Given the Republican strength in the new Congress, and the absence of five Democrats when the vote was taken, some worried Rayburn might not be reelected as Speaker of the House. The Republicans nominated Martin. There were a few interesting moments in the voting. House Majority Leader John W. McCormack (D-MA) was so involved in a conversation that initially he forgot to vote for Rayburn, saying "present" but correcting himself with a "Rayburn" vote. Rayburn said nothing when it was his turn to vote, and Martin only voted "present." After forty-five minutes of voting, Rayburn prevailed by a margin of eleven votes, 217–206. Martin gave a unity speech and led Republicans in singing happy birthday to Rayburn, who blushed even as he smiled. Rayburn put the executive branch on notice, arguing that "we must have teamwork between the executive departments and the legislative branch of government," demanding "the hill must be consulted."[15]

At the Senate Democratic Conference, the official party caucus, on January 7, Kenneth McKellar (D-TN) took revenge on Alben Barkley for an incident in late 1942 when Barkley had had McKellar arrested and brought back to the Senate chamber as part of a quorum call. That action severed their friendship for as one journalist said of McKellar, "[he] nurses a heart as unforgiving and in some respects as bitter as any Tennessee mountain feudist that ever leveled a squirrel rifle on the neighbor down the trail." Another observer described McKellar as "sour-tempered, narrow-minded, and irrevocably tied to the antidemocratic machine of Boss Ed Crump." McKellar challenged Barkley over the nomination for permanent secretary of the Democratic Conference, and his candidate, hard-nosed Francis T. Maloney (D-CT), was elected. This test was just a warm-up for McKellar's real purpose, a resolution requiring that the Democratic Steering Committee membership no longer be appointed by the majority leader but by the conference.[16]

McKellar also wanted the Steering Committee to meet more frequently and to be more representative of all Senate Democrats. Barkley responded to the resolution with a thirty-minute speech. His eyes were damp with tears, his voice quivered, and his rage was apparent to all. Barkley asserted, "If this resolution is approved, it will constitute a repudiation of my leadership in the Senate. It would be a repudiation of me. In such circumstances, I could not do anything but resign as majority leader, and I would resign." Barkley prevailed by a vote of 33–20. Next Walter George (D-GA) introduced a resolution, which could best be understood as a Democratic declaration of independence against the bureaucracy. It called for all legislation to be vetted through the Steering Committee before going before the full Senate. George maintained that such a process would prevent intraparty ideological splits and more important prevent the Republicans from controlling the Senate. Barkley immediately agreed, and the resolution passed unanimously. The consequence was less liberal legislation because all positions along the ideological continuum were present in the Democratic Party. Said Sen. Ernest W. McFarland (D-AZ): "I think that it is the sentiment of a majority of the Democrats that the bureaucratic reign is over. . . . Those days are over. The Democrats have decided that they'll not let a bill that will split the party and cause a lot of bad feeling come up on the floor. We'll just kill it quietly."[17]

The Republican success in 1942 put the Capitol Hill leadership team into a defensive posture so as to protect the president's program. "I doubt that there will be much domestic legislation put before Congress," admitted Rayburn. "We'll probably have only the war program, with the regular appropriations. There will be a tax bill, but outside of that, I doubt that the domestic program will amount to much." No objections would be raised over military appropriations, but Rayburn expected "on the domestic appropriations for the regular agencies, there will be a lot of fighting, and we'll probably be beaten a number of times, maybe pretty often." He expected New Deal programs like the NYA and the WPA to "be knocked higher than a kite." Such assessments did not reflect his views of the merits of these New Deal agencies but the politics of what was possible in wartime, for the Speaker was on record as a strong supporter of such programs. Other members of Congress had professed for at least two years that national defense spending made New Deal relief programs unnecessary. He explained, "We will have a technical majority, but for all practical purposes, we haven't even a working majority." McCormack was just about as bleak in his assessment, though he did not think the Wagner Act and the wage and hour legislation were in jeopardy because he believed the Republicans coveted the labor vote.[18]

Rayburn blamed Leon Henderson and other bureaucrats for the loss of about fifteen to twenty-five seats in the House. His criticism reflected the congressional animosity toward the expert advisors Roosevelt employed in the executive branch, sentiments that resulted from the failure of such individuals to appreciate the challenges of electoral democracy and from the dismissive manner some employed when lobbying Congress. Rayburn feared that Roosevelt would not cease advocating for domestic programs, and Prentiss Brown agreed, suggesting the president had learned nothing from the election. Continuing his theme of blaming the administration, and specifically the bureaucracy, Rayburn proclaimed a new congressional independence for the 78th Congress, saying that lawmakers would begin writing legislation again and would not pass bills as sent from the executive branch.[19]

The meaning of the Republican victory for legislative-executive relations remained unclear. Would Roosevelt appreciate the new partisan calculus in Congress or would he insist on operating as he had prior to the election? Presidential strategy would determine the intensity of constitutional conflict between the executive and legislative branches. Frustrated Democratic leaders used the occasion to push their agenda with the White House, and they achieved some success. On December 6, 1942, five House Democrats—Clarence Cannon (MO), Clifton A. Woodrum (VA), Robert Ramspeck (GA), James M. Barnes (IL), and Wright Patman (TX)—and five Senate Democrats—Scott Lucas (IL), Joseph Guffey (PA), Lister Hill (AL), Theodore Francis Green (RI), and Abe Murdock (UT)—met with President Roosevelt at the White House. One Senate moderate complained that the House delegation contained too many southerners thus not representing the myriad Democratic views in the lower chamber. Despite the question over composition of the delegation, these lawmakers intended to have their say. They did not want Roosevelt to dominate the conversation, as he typically did. They discussed the problems with Henderson's leadership of the OPA. Because Henderson was an avowed New Dealer and because he wanted to use the New Deal–inspired OPA to extend the New Deal philosophy of government into the war years, Henderson never was popular with conservatives in Congress. Furthermore, his arrogance and disrespect for elected officials hurt his reputation with moderates and even some liberals. Finally, after the congressional delegation "went down and read the riot act to him," the president fired Henderson, causing at least one other wartime bureaucrat to insist Henderson had been "cruelly treated."[20]

FDR had originally planned for his 1943 State of the Union address to be a forceful brief for postwar domestic reform. Rayburn and McCormack argued with him and with James F. Byrnes, a former U.S. senator from South Carolina and Supreme Court justice, the new director of Economic Stabilization, stressing that such a speech would be read as a declaration of war on Congress and would poison the 78th Congress for the duration of its tenure. They also requested that the president should not come to Capitol Hill to deliver the speech, that it was too dangerous to have the entire government gathered under one roof. Roosevelt heeded the advice on the first point, but not the second. Republicans and Democrats clapped throughout the speech, especially when Roosevelt spoke of progress in the war and plans for permanently disarming the Axis powers. In the last two months the Allies had defeated the Germans in North Africa, and the Soviets were winning the Battle of Stalingrad. While he acknowledged government responsibility for "cradle to the grave" social security, he did not endorse a specific plan.[21]

Rep. Howard Worth Smith (D-VA) made his own contribution to the congressional war on the administration in January 1943, when he introduced a resolution to investigate all the executive branch agencies. His extremist approach to warring with the administration actually revealed the limits of how much the Democratic leadership wanted to challenge FDR, and a rare occasion after 1942 when moderates rebuked conservatives. Rayburn said of it, "Why look at the damned thing. It allows an investigation of anything. I told Howard Smith I knew damned well I couldn't find five men with the wisdom and intelligence to make an investigation of this kind." Smith wanted to investigate whether government regulations had exceeded the intent of Congress. Rayburn complained, "This committee would be higher than the Supreme Court. . . . I don't know what he is after, but I know this would tie the government agencies in a knot." Smith made his antistatist resolution sound necessary, but he explained there were no particular targets he had in mind. He suggested there would be public support for such a policing of the administration. Smith moderated plans for his investigatory resolution, recalibrating it to eliminate any idea that Roosevelt was his target. The revised resolution passed, and Smith used his committee to investigate and harass the OPA, long a target of Congress regardless of ideology. Privately Rayburn indicated that the new draft was "not bad."[22]

While conservative Democrats were scheming about how best to defeat the New Deal, Roosevelt was out of the United States attending a conference with Winston Churchill at Casablanca. At this meeting, Roosevelt had less power than Churchill, and he attempted to remedy that situation by announcing to the press at the end of the negotiations an unconditional surrender would be required to end the war. This declaration surprised Churchill for they had not discussed the decision. Back in Congress, though, lawmakers found other reasons to criticize the conference. Wrote Sen. Richard B. Russell (D-GA) to his mother, "I believed that Stalin and Chang Chai Shek [*sic*] were there also. I hope much good will come of the conference but before long one must be had with S. and C.K.S. in attendance. From all I can hear the Chinese feel that they have been neglected and we must remember they were attacked years before we were."[23]

A couple of months after his return from Casablanca Roosevelt hosted a reception for the new members of Congress. Rayburn and Lyndon Johnson (D-TX) had advised him to do so. These moderate Texans emphasized the importance of the president making an individual, human connection with members of Congress, especially those who had been elected for the first time in 1942. They reasoned the contact with the president would make it much more difficult for new, conservative members to lambast the administration. One of the new Republicans overestimated the importance of her views to the White House. Rep. Clare Boothe Luce (R-CT) went through at least three drafts of her screed accepting Roosevelt's invitation while other guests replied with one or two sentences. Luce told the president that the new Congress was "utterly patriotic. In our love of our country, no aisle divides us." Because she worried that her fellow freshmen lawmakers would not feel comfortable telling the president what they thought about public policy matters, Luce equated her views with the GOP agenda. She asserted herself in part because her husband was publishing magnate Henry Luce. The White House wrote Luce in advance of the reception informing her the affair was a social not a political event. At the March 1943 reception, Roosevelt's greeting of Luce was "frosty." A Republican congressman who witnessed the exchange said, "I'll swear to Christ I could almost see his thumb giving her the old 'move along' signal!" Once Luce had been dispatched, Roosevelt regaled new members in groups of a dozen or so with talk of his attendance at the Casablanca Conference. So eager was the president to court the new members that he nearly disclosed national defense information, declaring once, "We've got to open Burma up. We've got to do it." Rayburn and McCormack judged the evening a success, but they were not willing to predict what impact it would have on congressional-executive relations or on partisan bickering.[24]

The first substantive issue with which the new Congress dealt was tax relief, and the legislative approach to it was not in sync with White House wishes, suggesting that goodwill measures like the White House social had minimal impact. Demands for relief from the high wartime taxes had increased sufficiently that by 1943 Congress gave serious consideration to a federal income tax withholding procedure. Congressional work on this issue, though, was in sync with the views of Americans whereby 50 percent supported an income tax withholding system as early as the summer of 1942, and that figure increased significantly with Democrats and Republicans each giving over 80 percent support to such a plan as the calendar moved closer to the income tax filing deadline in 1943. Of the 12.5 million new taxpayers that year few knew how to file or even that they owed the federal government money. Henry Morgenthau and his Treasury Department employees ruminated on the impact of prosecuting 5 million Americans for nonpayment of taxes. In and out of Congress solutions were sought to ease the burden on new taxpayers. The Ruml plan, named for its author Beardsley Ruml, the chair of the New York Federal Reserve Bank, provided for forgiveness of a year's worth of taxes and implementation of a payroll tax withholding system to make the income tax payment easier. He said tax forgiveness would not matter until Judgment Day, at which point "no one will give a damn." Roosevelt and New Deal liberals in Congress cared very much. Tax forgiveness curtailed the progressivity of wartime tax policy and made social spending for New Deal programs more difficult to sustain. The statist Ruml Plan was decidedly not ideologically liberal, but the process by which it became law reflects the liberalism in praxis of congressional moderates. Its enactment was not without controversy. Indeed, there was little agreement about how best to proceed. The first twenty-five witnesses before the House Ways and Means Committee all had different plans. Moreover the chairs of the two tax committees, George and Doughton, both economic moderates, were nonetheless divided. George wanted withholding but Doughton was more negative. Criticizing editorial writers for ginning up public opinion, he groused: "I do not feel that it is equitable to skip taxes that people are able to pay and which the Government desperately needs."[25]

The House Ways and Means Committee drew opprobrium when it reported a tax bill that provided a 20 percent withholding tax and had no tax forgiveness provision. Republicans offered a floor amendment providing for the Ruml plan. Doughton described the Ruml plan as a GOP effort to earn "capital" with voters. He viewed the Treasury plan with comparable enmity. Excluding tax forgiveness, it allowed taxpayers three years to pay their 1942 taxes and it implemented pay-as-you-go for 1943 tax collections. He told one supporter, "I fought it to the limit of my ability. We have never had as much trouble with any tax bill, and the trouble resulted from so much rotten poison propaganda." Democrats believed that GOP support for the Ruml plan was payback for the financial interests that had funded their races in the 1942 midterm elections. Still the majority party did not have the political capital to prevail. After a lengthy debate on March 30, 1943, the House on a party line vote rejected the Ruml amendment, which required the collection of two years' taxes in one year, with 198 yeas and 215 nays, and then it sent the bill back to committee for further study.[26]

Doughton named a bipartisan subcommittee to forge a compromise, which met daily, including Sundays. One of the subcommittee members, Harold Knutson (R-MN), said, "The rest of the committee attends church and prays for us." Doughton told Rep. John H. Folger (D-NC), "Our Committee has brought out the best bill we could evolve with respect to a pay-as-you-go, collection-at-the-source tax plan. In a way it involves some forgiveness, and in a way it does not." The committee bill resulted from bipartisan compromise, and it reflected what Rayburn had earlier argued about the changed ideological makeup of Congress: "I have been telling our folks that things had to get just so bad before they could get better. Some of our Republican brethren are beginning to realize that sense-less criticism and sniping with no constructive suggestions are getting them in a hole it will take them a good while to dig out of."[27]

Once Ways and Means reported out its new bill, House lawmakers faced a choice between the committee's bill, which reflected the administration's wishes that there be no tax forgiveness, and a measure introduced by Rep. Frank Carlson (R-KS), which embodied the Ruml plan. Southern Democrats, typically administration supporters of a liberal tax policy, were unable to deflect the conservative initiative. The debate was heated and demagogic. On May 4, the House defeated the Carlson bill, 206 against 202 in favor on a party line vote. Next, the House defeated the Ways and Means bill, 230–180, by voting to send it back to committee. Instead, the House passed a "dark horse" bill that implemented withholding and eliminated 75 percent of the tax assessments from 1942, affecting 90 percent of taxpayers. The House passed this bill, 313–95, but the Senate was nonplussed with the partial abatement. Sen. George indicated his committee would not use the murky compromise measure the House passed but would start fresh with a bill that included the conservative but statist Ruml plan.[28]

When the Senate Finance Committee reported its bill, the measure replicated the failed Carlson bill from the House. The full Senate agreed, passing the Ruml-inspired legislation by a vote of 49–30 on May 14. All but three of the nay votes came from a center left coalition dominated by southern Democrats, but another eighteen Democrats, mostly non-southern, joined with the Republicans to pass the more conservative approach. Roosevelt criticized the Senate bill harshly, noting working-class Americans would bear the burden of tax forgiveness much more acutely by paying higher future tax bills, and he threatened a veto. Roosevelt's words were just enough to convince Democratic House members to defeat the Senate bill, 194 in favor and 202 against, making a conference committee necessary to solve the tax standoff. The conference committee remained deadlocked for days. Roosevelt had Byrnes, a former senator with many friends on Capitol Hill, speak with House conferees and let them know he would accept 75 percent forgiveness if that was the best that could be done. Byrnes reported, "Doughton was so anxious to get a bill that if I made this statement to him, he would be encouraged to compromise at a higher percentage." This duplicitous tactic worked. Finally on May 25, conferees reached an agreement for partial abatement only, a muted victory for the administration and the moderate Democrats who held out against the Ruml plan. The conference committee merged parts of the Senate bill with a 75 percent abatement of the 1942 tax bill, and an elimination of the tax liability for those owing under $50. The latter provision was a recommendation from Sen. Harry Byrd (D-VA), no liberal, but it also deflected Roosevelt's harsh criticism of the Ruml plan for burdening lower-income tax filers. The House ap-

"The Forgotten Man." Cartoon by Berryman showing House support for the Ruml Plan and administration opposition. Joining the administration is Rep. Robert L. Doughton. The public is shown without defenders, April 1, 1943. Courtesy Library of Congress, Prints & Photographs Division, Clifford Berryman Collection [reproduction number, LC-DIG-ds-02875].

proved the conference committee report 257–114 on June 1. The Senate followed suit the next day, 62–19.[29]

Though statist, the Current Tax Payment Act of 1943 was a win for congressional conservatives, specifically House Republicans from the Northeast and Midwest who played a key role in first demanding tax abatement and who opposed forcing payment of two years of taxes in one year. As Chart 3.1 shows, a clear party divide shaped the outcome of the bill, but the chart also reveals that the majority of tax liberals were southern Democrats. Had Democrats from other regions supported their party and president, Roosevelt might have gotten all that he wanted from this bill. The administration almost immediately began working on a new tax bill to further increase government revenue.

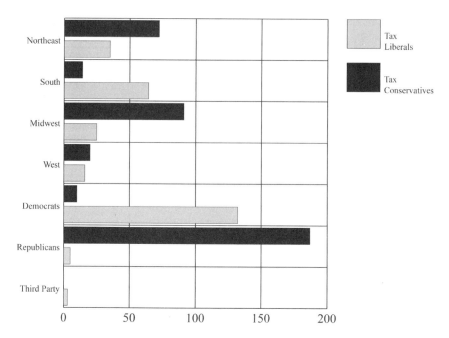

Chart 3.1: Ideology and Tax Policy in the House of Representatives, 1943–1944. Data in this chart are drawn from analysis of roll call votes regarding tax policy in the 78th Congress.

In Congress, the stress of the war took its toll on lawmakers. Sen. Russell wrote his mother of the difficulties in Washington, D.C. He attested that he had spent an hour searching for a new suit and new clothes. Stores were completely sold out. He had equal difficulty getting clean clothes back from the laundry in less than two weeks. He complained of the "unusually hot and sweaty weather we have been having" and the need for "a larger stock of shirts and underwear than is usually necessary." Russell solved his problem by "putting in for a new ration card here so you need not worry about it." Russell also noted severe shortages of meat and gasoline. "The other day I stood in line for 40 minutes and when I was only about 3 cars from the tank the gas gave out," Russell grumbled. "There were cars for several blocks behind me and 3 policemen to maintain order and see street crossings were clear. We couldn't have imagined that 3 years ago, could we."[30]

Russell's difficulties exemplified the problems with price control, a necessary wartime program that was not working. In the spring of 1943, President Roosevelt issued an order to "hold the line" against inflation, calling for a 6 percent rollback to September 1942 levels and blocking further wage increases. Both a military and a political necessity, the continuation of price control linked the New Deal economic order with Democratic visions for postwar liberalism through its consumer protections. If inflation went unchecked, Roosevelt worried, unions would push for higher wages. Here the president faced off against a Congress where the majority of lawmakers sympathized with farmers as producers but not workers, or farmers for that matter, as consumers. Conservative Democrats and Republicans worried about producers, an economic class increasingly being devalued in the modern American state. They shifted their attacks in 1943 to a federal government program created in 1942 to make subsidy payments to agrarian producers and to prevent inflation for consumers. This short-term solution involved substantial government intervention in the working of the economy, statist policies that conservatives disapproved. Throughout the war years farm groups and farm bloc lawmakers bitterly opposed the program for artificially lowering prices. The Reconstruction Finance Corporation and the Commodity Credit Corporation purchased commodities and sold them below market value. Because the Commodity Credit Corporation would soon require congressional reauthorization, it became the target for conservative congressional invective.[31]

Some lawmakers, specifically Sen. George and Rep. Hampton P. Fulmer (D-SC), demanded that the president move authority for food to Chester C. Davis, the War Food Administrator. Here, George and Fulmer were trying to trade for an executive branch official with whom they believed they could work. Just as FDR used executive branch staff to manipulate Congress, so also did lawmakers try to manipulate the administration. They made the request through James Byrnes, knowing that Davis did not want responsibility for food prices and rationing. Byrnes rejected the proposal on Roosevelt's behalf. Roosevelt heightened tensions when he declared subsidies were the best method to hold prices in check. Lawmakers neither agreed with the president nor ceased their own strategies. Former senator and OPA chief Prentiss Brown, though, was confident that the subsidy program would remain intact. "The battle will be won in the Senate. I think the House is lost, but I'm going to do some talking with Bob Taft and John Bankhead [D-AL], and I am pretty sure that they will not repeal the rollback that has been started," explained Brown. "They can't very well do that, and they realize it. . . . The blame would be right on Congress."[32]

Meanwhile, Republicans successfully pushed through the House funding cuts for the OPA. Like much of the congressional warfare over price control this too was a fight between urban and rural, consumers and producers. GOP economic philosophy merged with the policy priorities of Southern Democrats and other farm bloc lawmakers who wanted farmer producers to earn higher prices. The cut in OPA funding "was just the chickens coming home to roost." Lower chamber lawmakers were angry, according to Robert Ramspeck, that Prentiss Brown had not "start[ed] a real housecleaning in OPA" to "root out the old Leon Henderson gang."[33]

Conservative House critics of the OPA disliked numerous aspects of the agency, not the least of which was the manner in which its staff treated lawmakers when they lobbied Congress. The congressional war on the OPA was as much about the New Deal as it was dislike of the president and his administrative style. Ramspeck contended, "He [Brown] got rid of (J. Kenneth) Galbraith and one or two others like Dave Ginsburg and John Hamm, but OPA is still lousy with the fellows who thought and still act like Leon Henderson is running the show." To force the issue conservatives amended the legislation to prevent the payment of salaries to "anyone who has not had practical business experience of five years in the field in which he is working for OPA. That amendment would compel OPA practically to disband and start all over again, and it would raise hell, but that is how the House is thinking." Ramspeck justified the strategy "because there is a tremendous amount of public dissatisfaction with the way OPA has been administered by young, impractical lawyers, professors and economists who know business theory but don't know a damned thing about business' practical problems."[34]

As a result, the House passed amendments to the OPA, which "would wreck the price control program." One critic of the OPA, Rep. A. L. Miller (R-NE) complained that of the 61,000 employees in the OPA, 2,700 were lawyers. In comparison, he noted Herbert Hoover ran the Food Administration during World War I with 3,000 employees, while England used only a dozen lawyers during World War II. Ramspeck divulged, "The revolt was a lot worse than we expected; we knew we were up against a hell of a fight, but we didn't expect anything like this." The farm bloc was adamant that the agricultural sector deserved higher prices. They were unwilling to accomplish that result with subsidies or rollbacks; instead, they wanted the market to determine price structures—an antistatist view. When the House vote occurred, there were 99 members absent from urban areas where the natural inclination was to maintain the OPA. The absent lawmakers made it impossible for Democrats to beat back the Republican challenge.[35]

In early July 1943, Roosevelt sent a stinging veto message to Congress, castigating the bill for encouraging inflation and food shortages even though it extended the Commodity Credit Corporation and eliminated the subsidy program. Per the request of the House leadership, Roosevelt gave advanced warning of his veto. Rayburn, McCormack, and Ramspeck put the Whip Office to work. McCormack said of Ramspeck, a southerner: "He has a national mind, he is a hard worker, he is able in debate." McCormack viewed him as a loyal New Dealer who would not try to block the legislative machinery. The House leadership had a two-fold purpose in supporting the president: doing no harm to the war effort but just as important securing a political advantage in the ongoing constitutional conflict between the legislative and executive branches. They believed, "We can't let Congress take a chance on this; the veto has got to be sustained. Then if there is inflation, the blood will not be on Congress." The leadership, working out of Ramspeck's office, wired absent, urban lawmakers, ordering them back to the city. The House Republicans voted almost unanimously to override the president. McCormack was angry. He expounded, "By God, it was sickening to see Republicans vote this as a political issue." The veto was sustained in the House, 228–154, short of the two-thirds required to override. Though all but a handful of Republicans supported the override effort, a majority of southern and midwestern Democrats voted not the party line but the occupational line of their agrarian constituents. It became incumbent upon Congress to find a temporary solution. Pragmatic moderates and liberals opted for an emergency extension of the Commodity Credit Corporation for six months and enough conservatives agreed after which Congress left Washington, D.C., for a summer recess.[36]

This episode showed the flaws in FDR's strategy of appointing Brown, a former senator, to run the OPA. Conservative and moderate lawmakers were as hard on him as they had been on Henderson, so key was neutering the OPA to this cross-party ideological faction. While lawmakers succeeded in ruining Brown's tenure as OPA chief, they did not win their assault against the agency. FDR tapped former advertising executive and state director of the OPA in Connecticut, Chester Bowles, to replace Brown, who resigned in October 1943. Bowles assumed the post in November.[37]

Washington and the world changed while Congress was on its summer recess in 1943. Mussolini fell from power and the Japanese lost Kiska. The long summer vacation had been Sam Rayburn's idea. He wanted lawmakers to get some rest and hear from their constituents. He believed that the fall of 1943 and the spring of 1944 would be a crucial test for lawmakers, and he wanted them ready. The 1,281 days since September 21, 1939, when Germany invaded Poland, Congress had met and worked 1,261 days, excluding Sundays.[38]

When lawmakers returned, the interrelated issues of subsidies, inflation, and rationing remained problematic. Government expenditures on subsidies spiraled; by December 1943, such spending surpassed $1 billion. Patman attributed opposition to subsidies as the result of "a lot of the people [who] want to get rich out of this war and get rich right quick." Meanwhile, William Lemke (R-ND) merged his attack on federal spending for Lend-Lease and on home-front rationing when he complained of the shipment of 600,000 diapers to the Middle East. "While American mothers were denied, the Arab mothers did not know what to do with the diapers. Arab babies are not quite as modest as ours. They don't use them. So the Arab ladies thought they were American headgear. They used them for bonnets."[39]

By the end of 1943, Rayburn had grown concerned that the steady worsening of the congressional war with the president would harm the country. Though his relationship with the president was close and productive—Rayburn even sent the president a mess of small-mouth bass during the summer recess—he acknowledged that the 78th Congress had become an anti-administration Congress. "No. I can't see very much hope of improving the situation between Congress and the White House. I can't see it at all," intoned Rayburn. "But I'm trying to think about it in terms of the welfare of the country, not so much in political terms." He blamed the Republicans for "handling every goddam proposal and issue from the standpoint of politics." Discontent with the OPA made it difficult to keep Democrats in line. Rayburn sighed,

> I've been able to go among them and get a vote on almost anything, but I can't even touch them on these farm issues. I've gone downtown and talked to Byrnes and Vinson and Bowles and pleaded with them to remove whatever irritants they can. I've told Bowles for God's sake not to ration anything that doesn't absolutely have to be rationed, to get rid of the kind of people that cause all these little complaints, and then for God's sake to get on the radio and tell everybody what he's done.

Ironically, given that he had pushed for the congressional recess, Rayburn argued lawmakers were "paying too much attention to all the little bellyaching that goes on back home."[40]

In one small way Roosevelt eased these tensions when in December 1943 he announced that "Dr. Win the War" would replace "Dr. New Deal." The declaration pleased conservative, antistatist critics of the administration in Congress. Kenneth McKellar wrote Roosevelt: "I have just read in the morning paper that you had stated that our slogan for the next campaign must be 'Win the War' and that the 'New Deal' had performed its functions and would not be the slogan in the next campaign." Concluding "I think this is excellent," McKellar advised that "we should conciliate in every way all Democrats," meaning abandonment of the liberal social agenda. The president indicated there were limits to his compromise with conservatives. "I am sure that when victory has been accomplished," FDR countered, "All of us can unite in . . . end[ing] the economic as well as political isolation."[41]

The fight over subsidies for agriculture became a metaphor for expanded state power, with proponents of subsidies generally favoring statist solutions. Even so, most Americans, including farmers, did not understand the federal wartime program for farm subsidies. So divided was the Congress over CCC legislation that they avoided debate on the issue for over a day to instead give eulogies for two deceased members. When they did have them the debates were acrimonious and unproductive. Because there had been no permanent solution to the subsidy problem in 1943, lawmakers plotted what should be done in 1944. Moderates and conservatives sympathetic to agriculture complained of intense administration "pressure" and propaganda. The CCC had been set to expire at the end of December, and all Congress managed was an extension of the agency until mid-February 1944. A lack of consensus remained a key challenge. Too often partisan politics guided the process, especially with a presidential election looming. Even some otherwise conservative Democrats defended subsidies, here putting country ahead of ideology. Southern economic moderate Sen. Allen Ellender (D-LA) pronounced the total cost of living during the first four years of World War II was 25.4 percent less than in World War I. He contended subsidies were "an essential tool to do the stabilization job which must be done if we are to win the war and win the peace." Republicans had to make no such choices between partisanship and policy. For example, Rep. Louis E. Miller (R-MO) blamed the inflation problem on both New Deal and World War II spending decisions. "The purchase of next year's election is under way. That is what the subsidy program is intended to do. So let's call things by their right names," Miller avowed. Indeed, the subsidy issue became a major complication for presidential-legislative relations in early 1944. Much like in the summer of 1943 legislation was introduced and passed to eliminate subsidies; again Roosevelt vetoed the bill, and again his veto was sustained. The impasse was handled with another temporary fix: extension of the CCC through June 1945.[42]

Washington insiders believed that the "real fight" would be over extension of the Price Stabilization Act, which was due to expire on June 30, 1944, and which codified the OPA's authority to pay subsidies. Farm bloc lawmakers opposed the use of subsidies for foodstuffs to contain the cost of living, believing that prices could go higher were it not for the artificial control. They planned to use this legislation to trim the subsidy program. Jesse Wolcott (R-MI), known as a friend of the farm lobby who also appreciated the need to stabilize prices, was readying for battle. He wanted hearings. Wolcott did not want the controversial matter left until the last minute when the administration could force its way with Congress. He said, "We are not going to defeat price control. Hell, nobody wants that. But we want time to write a real bill. Look how they have been doing on the CCC, waiting until the last minute."[43]

Before the OPA issue could be solved—that problem drug into the summer so Wolcott did not get his way—the war in Washington degenerated early in 1944 over the meaning of FDR's words in a veto of the Revenue Act of 1943. The bill raised new revenue, readjusted social security taxation, and provided for defense contract renegotiation. It only raised an additional $2.3 billion in taxes whereas

"That Mouse is enough to Scare any Elephant." Berryman cartoon depicting Minority Leader Joseph W. Martin Jr. trying to contain the Republicans in Congress, who are shown running in fear from an administration request for new taxes drawn in the form of a mouse, October 21, 1943. Courtesy Library of Congress, Prints & Photographs Division, Clifford Berryman Collection [reproduction number, LC-DIG-ds-02876].

the administration had wanted $10.5 billion in new taxes, no doubt hoping to make up for the revenue lost to the Current Tax Payment Act of 1943, which forgave the bulk of taxes from 1942. Speaking of the Revenue Act of 1943 liberal senator Robert M. La Follette Jr. (P-WI) protested Congress had "labor[ed] for months to bring forth a mouse." Partial context for the tax veto fight was Roosevelt's veto of the anti-subsidy bill, which he had criticized as the "high cost of living measure."[44] Congressional conservatives were willing to let FDR win only so many quarrels in their constitutional conflict about the political balance of power in Washington, D.C.

The tax bill veto was the first ever of a president against a general revenue bill, suggesting just how divided the Democratic president was from his Democratic Congress on wartime resource management. Democrats debated whether the nation's fiscal policies should be redistributive and whether and to what degree the New Deal ethos should be continued. On February 21, Rayburn, McCormack, Wallace, and Barkley met with FDR in his White House bedroom about the legislation. At such meetings Roosevelt was in bed wearing his old gray bathrobe. Barkley, who loved to give speeches, typically talked more than Rayburn or Mc-Cormack, but Roosevelt trusted the taciturn Rayburn. The president indicated he would veto the legislation, and he read portions of his message. Barkley, Rayburn, and McCormack argued with the president not to veto the bill; Wallace said nothing. Roosevelt seemed unmovable, and a dismayed Barkley, unable to sway the president, told him: "It's perfectly obvious that you are going to veto this bill and there's no use for me to argue with you any longer about it." The next day, February 22, a stinging, intemperate veto message, harsher than the one legislative leaders heard the previous day, arrived at the Capitol, suggesting that the president had become tone deaf in his congressional dealings on tax policy. Barkley read the message three times, growing madder with each reading. He conferred with George and Doughton, neither of whom had been advised of the president's plan. Every Democrat he consulted was irate, suggesting just how unified moderates and conservatives were in Congress at that moment. The rage was not about statism or even the liberalism in praxis that often guided congressional action but was more about a decade of simmering animosity toward the president, not his policies but his personality.[45]

Earlier lawmakers had rejected the administration tax bill because a majority of Congress agreed with Walter George's warnings about confiscatory taxation, a reflection of congressional pragmatism: "You can tax forever if the taxes are properly adjusted, but you can confiscate only once. When taxes become confiscatory, they are destroying all sources of revenue for the government, unless it is assumed that the government is going over into the realm of business itself, that the whole system of economics is going to change from one of free enterprise to state Socialism or something approaching it."[46]

In his February 22, 1944, veto message, Roosevelt disputed legislative claims that the tax bill provided $2,100,000,000 in new revenues because it also eliminated automatic increases in the Social Security tax, yielding $1,100,000,000. He complained other tax relief measures in the bill would cost the Treasury at least $150,000,000. "In this respect it is not a tax bill but a tax relief bill," contended FDR, "providing relief not for the needy but for the greedy." He termed the numerous "indefensible special privileges to favored groups"—mining, logging, natural gas, steel, and commercial aviation—as "dangerous precedents for the future." Roosevelt also used the veto message to hit hard at Congress for its insis-

tence on the Ruml plan in the previous year and for not providing tax code simplification in the pending bill. "The Nation will readily understand that it is not
the fault of the Treasury Department that the income taxpayers are flooded with
forms to fill out which are so complex that even Certified Public Accountants
cannot interpret them," carped Roosevelt, who revealed his contempt for Congress. "No, it is squarely the fault of the Congress of the United States in using
language in drafting the law which not even a dictionary or a thesaurus can make
clear." The journalist Allen Drury compared the veto message to a "mad dog
snarling at the postman."[47]

Doughton and Harold Knutson, the ranking Republican on the Ways and
Means Committee, issued a joint press release after the president's veto was announced. In it, the two argued that the president had posed for Congress "the
question whether the taxing power shall continue to be exercised by the duly
elected Representatives of the American people, or whether such power is to be
surrendered and turned over to, or be dictated by, a small group of irresponsible
theorists in the Treasury Department." For lawmakers, the veto presented a fight
against "government by Executive decree." Whereas the president wanted a tax
increase on all corporate profits, Congress only wanted to tax the war profits of
corporations. "The President's proposal . . . would threaten the solvency of all
business and undermine its ability to provide jobs when the war ends," criticized
Doughton and Knutson. Regarding the president's comments about the tax
forms, the two lawmakers noted, the Treasury Department prepared the forms.
"We trust he will direct the Treasury to adopt a more cooperative attitude," said
Doughton and Knutson, "and cease trying to obstruct when it cannot dictate."[48]

The more newsworthy and important protest came from the Senate. Barkley
took especial umbrage at the president's remarks, making the war between Congress and the executive personal. In an off-the-record interview, Barkley reasoned,
"The more I thought about it, the more convinced I became that the point had
been reached where something had to be done. It seemed that things had reached a
point where the President was taking every opportunity and going out of his way
to belittle and slap Congress around. . . . How could I face the Senate thereafter,
having failed to protest against such an assault?" After eating a light supper,
Barkley began typing his reply, using the "hunt-peck-and-cuss" method. He
drafted four pages that evening, and dictated eleven more the next morning. No
one but Barkley's wife and his stenographers knew of the message before its delivery.[49]

Only seven pages of his speech had been typed when it was time to speak before the Senate. He told his typist to work "like the devil is after you!" Secretaries
typed frantically and pages were delivered to Barkley on the Senate floor when
they were completed. On three occasions Barkley neared the end of his last typed

page, waiting on a new delivery. According to one reporter, "It made him nervous, heightened his emotion. When he had finished, he was nearly exhausted. He had no idea he would get such an ovation; it nearly broke him down."[50]

In his forty-five-minute speech rebutting Roosevelt's veto message, Barkley declared that the president's arithmetic regarding the revenue bill came from "a mind more clever than honest." At issue was the freeze on social security taxes. Roosevelt opposed the freeze and suggested the additional revenues would accrue to the treasury, but Barkley believed otherwise: "I had never regarded the moneys procured by this tax as anything but a sacred fund" for the stated purpose of the legislation. Regarding fault for the complex tax forms, Barkley avowed Congress had legislated according to "the language of the Treasury Department, through its so-called experts." Because the president dismissed the revenue from the tax bill as nothing more than a "small piece of inedible crust," Barkley countered the $2.25 billion exceeded the entire U.S. debt prior to World War I and more than doubled the annual expenditures of the federal government prior to World War I. He fumed at Roosevelt's statement about relief for the greedy. "This statement, Mr. President, is a calculated and deliberate assault upon the legislative integrity of every Member of Congress." He stressed his record of support for the administration. "I have carried that flag . . . with little help here on the Senate floor," noted Barkley, "and more frequently with little help from the other end of Pennsylvania Avenue." He then announced his intent to resign as Senate majority leader at a conference of the Democratic majority the next day. Senators cheered wildly for Barkley. Only a handful of loyal administration Democrats sat mute.[51]

His actions earned him the accolades of conservative Democrats, one of whom sponsored the resolution declaring Democratic fealty for Barkley. Indeed, the episode rehabilitated Barkley with the Senate and Congress with the public. "It occurred to me that the pleasure of the smiling Senators was not so much the result of any statesmanship on the part of Senator Barkley, as it was from the fact that what he had done could not help but be embarrassing to the President of the United States," Murdock described the scene in the Senate chamber. "The cherubic face of Senator Byrd was glistening. His smile was uncontrolled. . . . Senator Smith could not have been more pleased with a doubling in the price of cotton. Senator McKellar had a complacent grin on his face, and even on the face of Senator George dignity had been replaced by an enthusiastic smile. The Republican Senators could hardly contain themselves." Scott Lucas said of the veto: "The message was too rough on the fellows. You can't be calling them crooks." He indicated he would vote to override the veto even though he had intended to support FDR. "I have to live with Barkley and these fellows and I just can't butt my head against a stone wall," explained Lucas. "I wish the President would look over the messages which are written for him, but he is too busy with world affairs."[52]

Roosevelt was shocked with the ferocity of Barkley's speech, but he presumed the matter would blow over quickly until Eleanor Roosevelt and James Byrnes convinced him otherwise. When Roosevelt gave White House secretary Stephen T. Early a letter to be delivered to Barkley, he told his secretary to "ask him if he would mind if I gave it [the letter] out at the White House through you, or if he prefers, that he give it out himself." In the letter Roosevelt told Barkley of his hope that Senate Democrats would not accept Barkley's resignation, or if they did, "I sincerely hope that they will immediately and unanimously reelect you." Additionally, Roosevelt told Barkley, "I regret to learn from your speech in the Senate on the tax veto that you thought I had in my message attacked the integrity of yourself and other members of the Congress. Such you must know was not my intention." Roosevelt intimated that a difference of opinion "does not mean we question one another's good faith." Though he acknowledged no person could ignore his or her core principles, Roosevelt suggested that Barkley had agreed to disagree at the private White House meeting but had later decided to launch a public protest in the Senate.[53]

When Barkley received the short missive from the president asking him not to resign, the Kentuckian responded with a two-page letter. Barkley termed the letter "gracious" and he thanked Roosevelt for his "prompt disavowal of any intention to reflect upon my own or the integrity of other members of the Congress." Barkley explained that since the Democrats had unanimously reelected him, he would be returning to his post. He concluded, "I fervently trust that this incident may be instrumental in bringing the Executive and Legislative Departments closer together in fullest cooperation to the end that we may win this terrible war at the earliest possible moment."[54] When Barkley spoke of "this terrible war" he meant the conflict in Europe and Asia, but just as important was the war in Washington. How would it end and what impact would it have on democracy?

Announcing "make way for liberty," Connally led a committee of senators—Millard Tydings (D-MD), David I. Walsh (D-MA), and himself—to tell Barkley he had been reelected majority leader. Liberty meant voting against the president, and on February 25 the Senate easily overrode the veto of the tax bill 72 to 14, with an increased cushion of 26 additional votes for the bill than had been cast when the Senate originally passed the measure. The House had already voted to override the veto 299–95 on February 24. The fourteen senators—Democrats Homer T. Bone (WA), Theodore F. Green (RI), Joseph T. Guffey (PA), Lister Hill (AL), Harley M. Kilgore (WV), James Mead (NY), Robert Wagner (NY), Abe Murdock (UT), James Murray (MT), Claude Pepper (FL), Elbert Thomas (UT), Jim Tunnell (DE), and Mon Wallgren (WA), and Republican William Langer (ND)—who voted to sustain the veto were not viewed as powers in the Senate by Washington journalists, but they were moderates and liberals. "The Senate is being maneuvered and run by men who do not like the President," expounded one journalist. George provided further analysis of the revolt in 1945, saying Roosevelt and Treasury Secretary Morgenthau "insisted on combining taxes with New Dealism, even in wartime," a policy unacceptable to conservatives in any case and one that moderates could not support after Roosevelt's veto message. Here Roosevelt more than any conservative lawmaker thwarted his New Deal ambitions by overreaching his executive authority.[55]

Sam Rayburn said in a not-for-attribution interview that the president paid too much attention to "bad advice from some smart alecks he has around him," meaning his well-educated, liberal-minded advisors with no appreciation for how Congress functioned. Such individuals had convinced Roosevelt, Rayburn believed, that based on his bipartisan record of cooperation with a GOP legislature during his days as New York's governor that he could achieve success with a GOP Congress during World War II. Rayburn elucidated: "Well, when Roosevelt gets a Republican Senate and House, he'll find out that Albany was the bush league and this is the major league. They'll start right in to gut him. If he takes this lesson to heart, it may have a very salutary effect. But if he persists in sending such messages to Congress, there will just be a hell of a fight."[56]

By mid-March, Congress had perfected the salient points made during the Barkley rebellion. An episode of the *American Forum of the Air* provides a good example. Rep. Carlson argued: "I think we must keep in mind that Congress has passed seventeen tax bills in eleven years. We have just passed tax bill on tax bill, without any regard as to their effect on individuals, and their complexity. . . . We must remember that, as Mr. [Wilbur] Mills suggested, there were 4 million taxpayers in 1939, and 52 million this year." Mills explained, "Perhaps the Congress in the past has been too willing at times to let policy matters be determined outside of the Congress. Most of the policy that is involved in the tax law, at least since I have been in Congress, has been determined more or less by some expert who has been employed by the Treasury."[57]

Indeed the congressional war with the administration continued in the summer of 1944 when lawmakers debated a bill to extend the Price Stabilization Act and the OPA for eighteen months. The situation in the House Banking and Currency Committee had not improved since Henry B. Steagall's (D-AL) death the previous November. Brent Spence (D-KY), the new committee chair, was "a rather sad figure," who was in the pocket of the administration and "depend[ent] on the younger and more nimble-witted members of his committee. . . . The ranking Republican, Jesse P. Wolcott of Michigan, thinks ten times before Spence can start scratching his own head." In the House, Wolcott said that the hearings on the extension of the Price Stabilization Act were meaningless where the committee was stacked in favor of the administration, and he claimed conservatives should rewrite the bill from the House floor. A further worry for the administration was Howard Worth Smith, whose committee examining executive department expenditures was "cooking up a fistful of gimmicks as yet undisclosed to throw into the price bill when it reaches the floor." A rabid anti–New Dealer, Smith had long hated the OPA in part because it interfered with the rents he collected on his investment properties in Virginia but more so because he distrusted this level of federal intervention in the economy. Just as problematic in the Senate, Bankhead, described as "fact and statistics-stuffed," led the fight for the cotton bloc on the price stabilization legislation. They were, according to Frank McNaughton, "working on the price control lid with every crowbar, pry, gimcrack and gadget at their command to lift it up and let the steam start blowing high, wide and handsome."[58]

The House Banking and Currency Committee rejected all of Smith's proposed amendments to the price stabilization legislation. Because the conservative coalition controlled the Rules Committee, though, there was still a chance for Smith to kill the bill. His allies on the Rules Committee, described by McNaughton as "the most unblushing bunch of legislative pirates in Congress," reported the price stabilization legislation with a rule permitting the Smith bill as a substitute. This made Sam Rayburn and the rest of the House leadership angry. John J. Cochran (D-MO), confined to a wheelchair the previous year because of a double amputation of his legs, yelled that the Rules Committee "has set itself up as a super-duper committee assuming control over the various legislative committees of the House" in its quest to "embarrass the administration." Rayburn disliked having to discipline the committee but he abhorred its actions, stating, "I do not want to take away any of the rights of the Committee on Rules, and I do not want the Committee on Rules to take away the rights, prerogatives, and privileges of other standing committees of the House." Because of his firm leadership the House voted against the rule permitting consideration of the Smith legislation even though it permitted unlimited amendments to the OPA bill. This forced a bipartisan quartet of Banking and Currency Committee members working for the committee bill to keep their supporters on the floor and to be knowledgeable about all possible attack amendments. These lawmakers—Spence, A. S. Mike Monroney (D-OK), Patman, and Wolcott—defended the OPA, the administration, continuation of a New Deal regulatory economy, and consumers over producers, but they were not among the most liberal members of the House, revealing the importance of center left moderates in holding the balance of power and redefining the political economy of the nation. The moderates won an important victory: the OPA was extended through June 30, 1945. Said McNaughton, "Sam Rayburn, almost single-handed, had saved the price stabilization bill from one of the most unblushing guerilla raids ever planned against it."[59]

The OPA extension legislation produced quite a row in Congress during the summer of 1945. Moderate Democrats maintained: "It would be a cruel mockery to keep it this far and then abandon the nation to inflation with the end of the war very near," but Republicans countered, "It should be completely revamped. It is an un-American, illegitimate child. It was promulgated by a clique here in Washington that think more of foreign institutions than of their own." Wolcott tried but failed to get the legislation amended so that the OPA would expire after six not twelve months. Rayburn went to the floor of the House to speak on behalf of the bill. Rayburn's remarks were sufficient to fend off the Wolcott attack. Another amendment moved food pricing authority from the OPA to the Agriculture Department. Clinton Anderson (D-NM), already confirmed as the new secretary of agriculture but still serving in the House, declared, "I will not run from any responsibility, but I don't want to be a policeman." In the end, Congress easily reauthorized the OPA subsidy program in part because most farm organizations had changed their views and endorsed government regulation as healthy for the economy.[60]

The two struggles over extending the OPA in the summer of 1944 and the summer of 1945, though not without their vitriolic moments, reflected just how much and how little the 1944 tax rebellion changed Congress. During that episode moderate and conservative lawmakers fought a jurisdictional battle with the administration. By 1944 an informal coalition of center left moderates and conservatives that made pragmatic choices about liberalism and about state power reclaimed control of American politics to a degree unseen since William Howard Taft was president. During the Woodrow Wilson years progressives dominated the ideological wars in Congress while for the better part of the 1920s conservatives triumphed. With the Great Depression and the election of Franklin D. Roosevelt, though, came a bold reaffirmation of liberalism as the predominant governing ideology. A three-way struggle among liberals, moderates, and conservatives began in the late 1930s and continued into the war years. The moderate alliance with conservatives ultimately played a more important role in defining U.S. politics into the postwar years according to a liberalism in praxis than the often-maligned conservative coalition, but victory regarding ideology did not bring a jurisdictional triumph. Instead for all of Congress's efforts to assert its coequal role with the president the burgeoning imperial presidency presented a major, ongoing challenge to lawmakers interested in following the edicts of the Constitution regarding governance.

4. "A Lesson to the President": Labor Legislation

Labor politics proved the most contentious of the wartime resource management issues before Congress, but lawmakers ultimately crafted moderate policies unwelcome both to the liberal unions and to the conservative business community. Partisanship and pragmatism dictated this result. The legislative process functioned here not despite but because of partisanship, which forced compromise and a moderate solution. With the United States provisioning the Allied military effort gridlock was not an option. Both sides realized in this dispute that the war was a political opportunity to refashion labor policy. Studying the tenacity of the conservative war on labor, which began in the late 1930s and continued into the postwar years, reveals much about the wartime liberalism in praxis and the conversion of the New Deal welfare state into a warfare state. Wartime labor politics helped pivot the national political culture in ways that prevented a return to a pre–New Deal ethos and secured retention of the reforms won in the 1930s. In this crucial policy domain then, moderates and liberals consolidated the victories from the 1930s.

During World War II Congress revised extant policy and did not capitulate to the administration. Unlike taxation and price control where the administration had clear goals, Franklin D. Roosevelt and his advisors proved reticent regarding most of the major wartime labor debates, with the Fair Employment Practices Committee (FEPC) being the exception. This lack of substantive administration input encouraged the devolution of ideological warfare on Capitol Hill, and it suggests how labor politics functions as a bridge to the study of social justice politics. Ideological debates about labor involved more than just battles over union rights but also included racial and gender questions about manpower mobilization. Here the key question was whether the state could compel work in a total war, and, if so, who could and should be compelled. Just as important was the question of whether the state could and should coerce employers to disregard gender and race. No clear answers emerged, but the questions added new tensions to the already fraught ideological warfare in Congress.[1]

In June 1941, the liberal-leaning Senate Committee on Education and Labor concluded that sufficient workers "will not be available without training a vast number of new men or diverting labor from nonessential civilian uses." The simple need for maximized production became complicated by longstanding prejudices regarding race and gender, making worker mobilization for victory over fascism all the more difficult. Because the White House preferred to forge a wartime labor policy without much congressional input, discord between the two branches escalated. Conservatives used the war to attack labor rights won in the 1930s. To understand and evaluate the complex policies Congress crafted requires careful evaluation of seemingly disparate topics: the creation of the FEPC, arguments about manpower mobilization, the use of Japanese-American internees as forced laborers, the importation of Mexican workers through the bracero program, and the passage of antistrike legislation over a presidential veto. Only through viewing these issues collectively can an accurate picture of wartime labor policies be drawn. The resulting image reveals not only the powerful racial, gendered, and class considerations given to wartime labor policies but also the importance of these debates to the reconfiguration of ideology away from the reformist, liberal New Deal ethos and toward a moderated version of those concepts.[2]

The difficulty of overcoming labor quarrels was reflected in a brawl between two members of Congress. On February 22, 1945, John E. Rankin and Frank E. Hook, Democratic congressmen from Mississippi and Michigan, respectively, who represented the two extremes of their party, became involved in a vicious shouting match on the House floor over the merits of the Congress of Industrial Organizations (CIO) and its political action committee. Hook, a friend and beneficiary of organized labor, called Rankin a "God damned liar" on the House floor, which propelled Rankin to punch Hook. The fight was one-sided. It took three members to separate the two men. The fight symbolized the ideological conflict between liberals and conservatives. Democratic Whip Robert Ramspeck's (GA) motion to adjourn probably prevented further fisticuffs. Majority Leader John W. McCormack (D-MA) and Eugene E. Cox (D-GA) tried to calm Hook and Rankin down, but Cox also spoke out against Hook in public, suggesting he should be removed from Congress. Adam Clayton Powell (D-NY) made a similar public attack against Rankin, arguing he was a fascist. McCormack convinced Hook to apologize and Cox extracted a similar promise from Rankin. Hook's words of contrition seemed genuine, according to observers. Rankin, though, spoke briefly, without feeling. He even challenged his colleagues by arguing, "If I had violated the rules of the House there was a way to call me to the bar of the House and discipline me. . . . I was not responsible for what occurred yesterday and I make this statement to let you know how I feel." Rankin did not earn points with his colleagues for his "sour, emetic" words, but Hook received hearty applause when he completed his statement.[3]

The congressional war on labor began in the late 1930s when southern Democrats ceased supporting the administration and the Democratic Party on labor questions. Debate about and passage of the Fair Labor Standards Act in 1938 proved the last straw for southern lawmakers. In 1939, Howard Worth Smith (D-VA), who was described as being "wily as a coyote," became the chair of the committee to investigate the National Labor Relations Board (NLRB). Said one supporter: "Unionization through compulsion is a terroristic doctrine that smacks of the rankest Stalinism." The committee existed only to attack the New Deal and the labor reforms associated with the Wagner Act. Smith's criticism of the NLRB for its presumed political activities previewed a strategy that conservative Democrats and Republicans would follow during the war years: charging political irregularity to discredit New Deal programs. Mary T. Norton (D-NJ), chair of the liberal-leaning House Committee on Labor, challenged the work of the Smith Committee, arguing it duplicated the work of the labor committees in Congress, that it wasted taxpayer money, and that it had uncovered "little [information] of fundamental importance." She criticized the Smith Committee's strategy for proposing amendments that would in effect repeal the Wagner Act. "It would seem much more honest to bring in a bill to repeal the law in its entirety," Norton asserted. "The issue would then be clear-cut." But conservatives did not use that strategy in part because they would not win and in part because the ideological warfare was more important than repeal. Wrangling about the issue continued for much of the remainder of 1940 with no resolution in sight. Even the committee's final report proved divisive. The liberal minority complained that the investigation had not been "an impartial fact-finding investigation" but had intensified the internecine congressional warfare, harming national security.[4]

Perhaps the most significant tension running through Congress during the 1940s, at least regarding labor politics, involved not the issue of strikes but the conflict about who should and should not be working. In the total war of World War II lawmakers never agreed to mobilize all adults capable of working even while they voted to retard the right to strike for those who did. Congressional reticence to enact manpower mobilization legislation was out of sync with public opinion, with 61 percent of the population supporting total war mobilization in a March 1942 Gallup Poll. In subsequent polls the figure fluctuated but never fell under 50 percent.[5] These contradictory policies resulted from the ideological politics of Congress, but such debates need also to be framed by military mobilization policies because the production of war material was the leading U.S. contribution to the Allied war effort.

In 1941 military planners had sought 215 divisions, but as the war progressed this figure was scaled back to just 90 divisions with the argument being that the U.S. contribution to an Allied victory would be in munitions production more than military personnel. Even though 43 million men between the ages of eighteen and sixty-five had registered for the draft, the military only wanted those under twenty-six, and with some in this category exempt for reasons of physical limitations, family circumstance, and responsibilities in the civilian workforce, the number of men likely to see military service was under 30 million. Because of congressional action, agricultural not factory workers received more generous deferment options, totaling 2 million compared with approximately a third that number for factory workers (ironic given the ongoing congressional spleen over the shortage of agrarian workers). Young volunteers often served in the cadet training programs the military brass had created in case they faced a future manpower shortage, but this practice proved harmful to efforts to mobilize the civilian workforce. To solve the problem in December 1942 Roosevelt charged the War Manpower Commission (WMC), directed by Paul McNutt, with overseeing both the selective service system and the civilian mobilization efforts. Under these policies, 16 million Americans served in the military by war's end.[6]

Mobilizing domestic workers was never easy or smooth. Unemployed and underemployed Americans took advantage of the heightened demand for war workers, migrating freely to places like Henry Ford's Willow Run outside of Detroit, Michigan, and to Henry Kaiser's shipyards in California where defense jobs were plentiful and financially rewarding. These habits hindered production, because there was little stability in the workforce, causing some in Congress to advocate manpower mobilization akin to the drafts of labor common elsewhere in the world. Approximately 10.5 million new workers took jobs during the war. These men and women far outstripped civilian workers among the other Allied and Axis nations, building 299,293 aircraft, 40 billion bullets, 634,569 jeeps, 6.5 million rifles, 7,333 seagoing vessels, and 88,410 tanks. Comparing just aircraft production explains the important American role in the Allied victory in this air war: Germany built 111,767 aircraft, Japan 69,910, and Great Britain 123,819.[7]

The success of American industry is a postwar not a wartime story, though, making it all the more puzzling that the FEPC and other measures intended to increase worker mobilization were controversial. The FEPC troubled members of Congress on several levels. For the conservative coalition, it was an attack on the system of Jim Crow and therefore unacceptable. For lawmakers generally, it was another example of the executive branch preempting congressional prerogatives. Finally, it revealed significant congressional hypocrisy. Richard B. Russell (D-GA), himself a conservative Democrat and a segregationist, had among the many notes and partial drafts of speeches within his papers a particularly telling attempt to play on the racism of the elite regardless of political ideology. Russell suggested the near universal absence of African American employees in Congress would put "Congress out of commission." Russell contended the problem was equally bad for white-collar workers in the White House. He argued, "The Senate and the President also would be subject to fine and arrest by the FEPC because of their obvious refusal to nominate and confirm negroes to be ambassadors from the United States to foreign countries. How many Members of the Senate would vote to confirm the nomination of Negroes to be United States ambassadors to Great Britain, France, Russia, China, Denmark, Sweden, or . . . other foreign countries?"[8]

The issue was much less humorous for African American activists in the NAACP, who lobbied Congress throughout the war years, first for an investigation of the systemic discrimination against minorities in the defense industry, and then for increased funding and permanent status for the FEPC. In late December 1940, Walter White, the NAACP secretary, and William Hastie, a government official and the dean of the Howard University School of Law, discussed which senators were most likely to sponsor a resolution calling for an investigation into war plant discrimination. In addition to wanting regional and partisan balance, they also sought lawmakers who were in good standing with organized labor. One key challenge would be getting segregationist southern senators to authorize funding for the investigation.[9] Such deliberations continued for the ensuing months to no avail. When FDR signed the executive order creating the FEPC, the matter became moot.

Roosevelt finally demanded the drafting of the executive order when it became obvious no other strategy would prevent a march on Washington that A. Phillip Randolph and the Brotherhood of Train Car Porters had threatened. White House aide Joseph L. Rauh Jr. was given the assignment. His boss, Wayne Coy of the Office of Emergency Management, told him, "Get your ass over here, we got a problem." When Coy asked Rauh to draft the order, Rauh replied, "Any idiot can write an executive order, but what do you want me to say?" The draft was based less on efficacious policy choices and more on the political need to stop Randolph's march. Executive Order 8802, signed on June 25, 1941, required components of the federal government with vocational and defense production training programs to eliminate all discriminatory employment practices. It also banned employers with federal government contracts from discriminating. The last provision of the order created the FEPC, placing it under control of the Office of Production Management. Its staff totaled eleven part-time workers, and its annual budget was $80,000. Moreover, it lacked punitive power. Rep. Norton, one of the staunch proponents of a permanent FEPC, held: "In my country, no man should be denied the right to find a job, support his family, and get ahead economically as far as his capabilities will carry him."[10]

For different reasons Congress was just as unwilling to mobilize women as workers even though economic necessity drove women into the workforce at high rates. Because women's organizations did not necessarily view workplace access as a civil right worthy of a major congressional lobbying effort, there was much less pressure externally on Congress for liberalizing work opportunities for women. Furthermore, the workplace discriminations against women were much more subtle than those African Americans faced, leaving this issue as one of tertiary importance for lawmakers. Entrenched social mores and biases about how children should be reared made difficult the shift toward federally funded daycare centers, the policy that Congress could most effect to encourage more working women. The Lanham Act, a broad-based wartime federal public works program that included appropriations for daycare, never proved popular with working women because of the location of the facilities and the cost of the care. Nor was there the congressional will to fix these problems. Indeed, Congress spent more time considering women's work not from the perspective of industrial mobilization but in military service. The attack on Pearl Harbor pushed lawmakers and War Department officials to take seriously Edith Nourse Rogers's (R-MA) bill for the creation of the Women's Army Auxiliary Corps. The range of congressional criticism reflected ingrained social biases about women. Complaints included female enlistees who married while in service, the failure to provide a mechanism for court martial, the entry of women with children, and women who wanted the uniform for reasons of social status.[11]

The racial and gender prejudices that shaped congressional labor policies were more complicated than the black, white, female dichotomies most often discussed. The presence of a small concentrated Japanese American population on the West Coast and the almost complete lack of a congressional criticism of the decision to intern this demographic segment of American society led western lawmakers to view Japanese Americans as a ready labor source. For members of Congress, at least those representing districts with shortages of agricultural workers, internment was less a civil rights issue and more a labor issue, and, ironically, one made possible by the state structure formed during the New Deal, because it was the Works Progress Administration that constructed most of the camps. Western lawmakers, especially those from the regions where most of the camps were placed, viewed the internees as a cheap source of labor, albeit coerced, to replace the men who either left the region for better paying defense jobs elsewhere in the country or for military service. Unless the Japanese American internees could be used to solve the labor problems, westerners were not interested in hosting the camps. For example, James E. Murray (D-MT) heard numerous protests from Montanans about proposals to move Japanese Americans to the mountain west. Murray told a journalist with the *Miles City Star* that recruiting Japanese American workers had been made difficult by "the statement . . . that Japanese evacuees would be met with firing squads if they came into Montana." He argued for the "immediate, full employment of this labor on war work" and against the "wholesale evacuation on racial or national lines," claiming that was "Hitler gospel."[12]

For conservatives in Congress, racial distinctions in labor policy involved the relative exploitability of each ethnicity. Because African Americans sought the right to work in settings white conservatives disapproved such lawmakers fought the FEPC, but the circumstances of Japanese Americans were very different. Congressional policy toward Mexican workers followed the pattern of Japanese Americans, not African Americans. The Japanese American population was not sufficient to sate the western demand for agricultural workers. As such western landowners clamored for relief programs. They desired the right to employ Mexican immigrant labor, but whereas the federal government preferred the bureaucratically and administratively layered bracero program whereby immigrant agricultural workers had to be processed through Mexico City, landowners and farm managers preferred the simple migration of Mexicans across the border with limited state intervention.

Labor shortages were such that a congressional committee investigated the problem and its impact on national defense. The Tolan Committee announced in late May of 1942 that there was a surplus of migrant agricultural workers unable to get to new work sites because of rationing-related transportation problems. John Tolan (D-CA) endorsed national planning regarding agricultural labor, but this recommendation never gained congressional popularity in large part because landowners preferred a racially exploitative system of labor. Indeed, American authorities negotiated with the Mexican government for the temporary migration of Mexicans under the bracero program. According to the agreement signed on August 4, 1942, protections for Mexican workers—including prohibitions against military service and discrimination and guarantees for housing, transportation, and wages that would be consistent with the prevailing rates—were "suggested," not required. The agreement listed the Farm Security Administration within the Department of Agriculture as the primary employer and individual farm owners as sub-employers. Employment contracts for work were to be rendered in Spanish.[13]

The process did not work smoothly. Sen. Carl Hayden (D-AZ) was infuriated: "I will be frank to say that I have never seen an example of so much buck-passing, red tape, delay, shifting of responsibility, and of plain failure to get anything done." Hayden complained: "Thus far the farmers . . . have received nothing except an explanation of what cannot be done." Similar criticisms emanated from the mountain west and the Rio Grande Valley of Texas. After Tom Connally (D-TX) lobbied for relief for agrarian growers, the Mexican–United States Agricultural Commission was established, which had as its purpose cooperation between the two nations on agricultural policy.[14] Ultimately Congress devoted less attention to the bracero program than to other labor questions. Recruiting foreign workers seemed less important to conservative lawmakers than waging an ideological war about domestic workers.

As the world war worsened early in 1941 so did the legislative war on labor, which challenged the labor reforms of the 1930s. Even pragmatic liberals like Speaker Sam Rayburn (D-TX) believed "the National Labor Relations Act has been badly administered. . . . Instead of moving up on the thing gradually as they should have, they plunged forward and disrupted things and disgusted people." Electing not to challenge the Wagner Act, conservatives pushed for wartime anti-strike legislation, a compromise position that was more obtainable but also reflective of the fact that the labor revolutions of the New Deal could not be obliterated. The two labor committees, both dominated by moderates and liberals sympathetic to labor, assumed a mediation role. Countless letter writers besieged the committees and Congress appealing for and against additional controls on union activity. Labor activists launched an important first strike when Philip Murray, the president of the CIO, presented Elbert D. Thomas (D-UT), who chaired the Senate Committee on Education and Labor and possessed the disposition of a "professor and a missionary," with a detailed plan for steel production. Murray promised that "total steel output in the interests of National Defense" would result from his plan. Thomas, though, responded with nothing more than a polite acknowledgment. Meanwhile, Smith lobbied Norton to discharge his bill to amend the Wagner Act, arguing that there had been sufficient hearings the previous year. He implied that dilatory tactics would force him to seek a discharge petition. Norton answered, "I would advise you that we have not had an opportunity to discuss this bill in the Committee as yet but I shall be glad to do so at the very first opportunity." Hatton Sumners (D-TX) revealed the new congressional priorities at the April 3, 1941, meeting of the House Judiciary Committee when he told the members of his changed attitude regarding antistrike legislation. Whereas Sumners had earlier asked lawmakers "to refrain from introducing antistrike legislation," he then announced "members should introduce whatever bills they desire."[15]

Such bills put moderate lawmakers on the defensive. The president of the American Federation of Labor threatened Robert L. Doughton (D-NC) that these measures would breed "hatred and enmity in the minds and hearts of labor toward Congress and the government." Doughton replied, "I do not see how" pending antistrike legislation, "which applies only to Defense Industries, could in any way abridge the rights of labor—a thing I would by no means be willing to do." Furthermore, Harry S Truman (D-MO) told one labor union official antistrike measures have "been brought about by Labor itself." To a constituent, Truman wrote, "There are some people who are so violently opposed to fair labor standards that they cannot discuss the thing from an unbiased standpoint, and there are Communists and radicals in the labor set-up who cannot see anything good in a man who saves his money and makes a profit." He wondered "whether either one of them are worth saving" because the "logical conclusion" was fascism or communism "and there is not any difference in them. It is simply government by thuggery."[16]

Years later Connally delineated how he became involved in antistrike legislation. He recounted that both Undersecretary of the Navy James V. Forrestal and President Roosevelt came to him, begging him to introduce antistrike legislation. The law permitted the president to seize control of factories whereof the ownership was unwilling to undertake wartime production. There was, though, no corresponding law providing for drafting of striking workers. Whether or not Connally's claims were true, substantial evidence proves the enmity between John L. Lewis, who had already led wartime strikes while threatening more, and the White House. Lewis, the leader of the United Mine Workers (UMW) and former president of the CIO, had by the start of World War II broken with FDR. After ensuring Roosevelt's reelection victory with union votes in 1936, Lewis grew increasingly skeptical, even campaigning against Roosevelt in 1940. He realized the potential of the war to retard labor's victories under the New Deal. He led a successful month-long strike in the spring of 1941 that ended the regional wage differential in the Appalachian coalfields. Connally recalled Roosevelt telling him, "The Senate Labor Committee is under the complete domination of labor unions. They'll never let a strike control bill out. That's why I'm asking you to do it through the Judiciary Committee."[17]

Smith and Connally had little tolerance for their critics, but theirs was not an easy alliance. The Senate as a whole tended to take a more moderate position on strike control legislation. Smith told a supporter how the labor bills he had authored had been "promptly chloroformed in the Senate." He expressed his inability to get approval for further investigations into the NLRB. "I am afraid that, until the Administration is willing to do something about the outrages being perpetrated upon the American people by organized labor, it will be impossible to get anything through Congress." Even though his legislative proposal was less extreme, Connally criticized labor's excesses, insisting "the great mass of American labor has no sympathy with certain labor leaders who seek to seize the Nation's extremity to improve their own selfish ends. . . . John L. Lewis breathes defiance to the government. He rudely and arrogantly demands that his will alone shall control. The government cannot tolerate such an attitude." Indeed, Congress never had much respect for Lewis. Sam Rayburn believed for years that the president should "destroy" the recalcitrant labor leader.[18]

Because "presidents leave much unsaid," the journalist Westbrook Pegler published an open message to Congress, declaring the institution "a sorry counterfeit of a legislative body in a republic. You are an enemy to the very body which you constitute." He lambasted Congress for ceding its independent legislative authority to the will of the president. "You have been saying yourselves that it is impossible to pass any laws to put down the brazen rascalities and plots of the crooked unioneers because the President won't let you. Isn't that a fine confession from men who are supposed to represent the civic honor and courage of the people of a great republic?" asked Pegler. On the same day that Pegler's column appeared in the local papers, the conservative Judiciary Committee agreed that "no action would be taken" on pending labor legislation. Proponents of the measure had other ideas, and the House passed the Smith bill on December 3 by a vote of 252–136. Here the conservative coalition deserves credit for the result: the majority of southern Democrats supported the bill as did the majority of Republicans. The lawmakers in the upper chamber did not share the zeal of the House for labor restrictions. The Smith bill languished in the Senate even though 73 percent of the American people supported a government prohibition against strikes in the defense industry, blaming foreigners for the nation's labor problems.[19]

Knowing that the chair of the Senate Labor Committee disapproved of the Smith bill, Harry F. Byrd (D-VA) wrote Elbert Thomas and issued that letter as a press release. This strategy relied on public opinion to help move the bill through. Byrd urged immediate hearings for the Smith bill. He asserted the large majority the bill gained in the House signified "an overwhelming demand on the part of the people of America that the Congress of the United States take immediate, effective, and constructive action to curb strikes in defense industries, which have done so much to sabotage the defense program of our country." If there was any hope of achieving a legislative solution before Christmas, he explained, the Senate must act on the bill and not another Senate measure. Passage of a separate Senate bill would require action again in the House. He averred that "the emergency now confronting us" necessitated Senate action on this "vital legislation . . . [for] our program of national defense."[20]

Smith took to the airwaves to explain the legislation. He had been scheduled in advance to appear on the *American Forum of the Air* for the evening of December 7, 1941. The program continued as arranged, but the shadow of Pearl Harbor hung over the broadcast. Smith used the emergency to add gravitas to his demands for antistrike legislation. He said he "welcome[d] cool, calm, honest, constructive criticism" but had only received "infuriated blasts and bombastic threats." He contended that his bill would require a thirty-day intent to strike or lockout notice; authorize a secret ballot on any strike vote with results publicized; reiterate the illegality of using intimidation and violence to prevent someone from working; outlaw pickets at workers' homes; prohibit picketing by third parties, ban strikebreaker interference with peaceful pickets; cease jurisdictional strikes, sympathy strikes, and boycotts; compel union registration of certain information, including all fees and dues charged of workers, data on elections, census of membership, open bookkeeping, and proof that there were no felons, Communists, or subversives in leadership positions; and halt all further efforts to impose closed shops on industry. Unions that violated these provisions would lose their rights under the National Labor Relations Act and would be subject to an injunction. Smith cautioned that the closed shop was the most dangerous threat to the freedom of American workers. He stressed that at the war's conclusion, were current trends not checked, veterans could return and be jobless, but these arguments were not sufficient to move lawmakers to action. The year ended with no further action on the antistrike bill.[21]

In early January 1942, Connally came back to Washington, D.C. He passed out 25 cent El Producto cigars to reporters, made wisecracks, but was "hot as a firecracker underneath" about congressional inaction on antistrike legislation. He promised he would call up his plant seizure bill even though "certain quarters" opposed it. Walter George (D-GA) agreed antistrike legislation "must be" enacted. Both Connally and George noted their contempt off the record for the industry-labor agreement not to strike. Smith condemned the agreement openly, saying it did not "amount to a damn." In an article for the *American Bar Association Journal,* Smith reasoned, "No private organization within our midst, which has such a potential power for the destruction of this nation, should be tolerated or permitted to exist either in peace or in war."[22]

Liberal lawmakers responded to the conservative assault on labor. In a debate about the forty-hour workweek, James E. Murray blamed propaganda, "editorial half-truths and deliberate untruths," and the corporate profit motive for the effort to roll back protections for labor. He opined that strikes had nothing to do with work slowdowns, but instead the problem lay with inadequate supplies. Of 8 million defense workers, Murray argued, less than 100 were on strike at that moment. He disputed the point that soldiers at Bataan, who were subjected to the infamous death march following the fall of the Philippines and who received no more than $21 a month, were proof that domestic workers needed no wage and hour protections. "The American soldier will not be overjoyed to learn now that his family's income is proposed to be still further cut and his service to your country used as the flimsy excuse," Murray avowed. "And all this in the face of the fact that industry is making scandalous profits."[23]

By the spring of 1942, the Washington correspondent for the *St. Louis Post-Dispatch* termed the "barometer reading" of constituent mail to members of Congress to be "stormy with probable squalls." Legislation limiting workers' right to strike prompted much of this letter writing, and one Missouri congressman, John J. Cochran (D-MO), received from 5,000 to 6,000 letters a month. He told the press that he discounted "inspired" communications from members of organizations in favor of "those in the words of a writer who is known to the Congressman either personally or by reputation." Other members of Congress had complaints about the volume and content of mail, if for no other reason than the angry tone. An irate South Dakota voter queried Elbert Thomas, "By what right do you suppress legislation passed by 65 percent majority in the House? By what right do you submit to dictation from the executive branch of government? . . . Is it possible that through these actions elections are being bought with tax money? YOU KNOW THE ANSWER."[24]

Once the United States entered the war, the predominant labor policy debates shifted from the antistrike bill to the more draconian manpower mobilization proposal for legislation authorizing the state to compel citizens to work. This statist concept received much attention and little satisfactory resolution in Washington, D.C. Unlike the more typically liberal statist solutions from the 1930s, the manpower issue crosscut the ideological spectrum. It functioned as a stalking horse for the antistrike legislation, because manpower mobilization was even more controversial than the antistrike bills. A debate on the *American Forum of the Air* typified the difficulties of compelling defense work in a democracy. Ideological debates about the nature of the state, specifically how much power should be granted to the federal government and how much should remain with the states, shaped the problem of maximizing worker output. The struggle for manpower mobilization, though, did not neatly conform with traditional liberal or conservative schisms. Rep. Wesley E. Disney (D-OK) described the problem as a debate about the meaning of and access to democracy: "I think the States and the legislatures and the courthouses are where democracy is. This thing up here is the superstructure of democracy. Down there is where democracy is, where you and I, the humblest citizen, has a right to assert himself. This system, federalized, turns the individual over to an administrative system where he has no legal right to assert himself and no recourse to the ballot."[25]

While neither liberals nor conservatives liked the "compulsory regimentation of our people" under manpower legislation, lawmakers who favored such proposals spoke to the necessity of meeting the problem before it intensified. Supporters believed the "peacetime free competition in the labor market" would not prove sufficient during the world war. The biggest challenge to passing manpower mobilization, though, was the Management-Labor Policy Committee of the WMC. Rep. James Wadsworth (R-NY), who had helped push through the selective service legislation in 1940, was a strong proponent of manpower mobilization. He insisted that suspension of the labor laws was as necessary in wartime as were wage controls. Wadsworth affirmed, "When, under a man power law, the President orders a machinist to leave his present occupation and report to another factory, he must not, upon arrival, be told that he must join a union before he can go to work." He doubted any legislation could be passed without strong presidential support. He concluded, "We must wait until the President and his advisors come out openly for such a program. They may do it after [the 1942] election. I dunno."[26]

Robert A. Taft (R-OH) spoke to the National Republican Club about wartime labor issues. His remarks show how the manpower bill could be divorced from ideology. Taft, a conservative, fulminated against a statist bill that compelled work not because he sympathized with unions but because he loathed the power the legislation would give to the executive branch. Taft described the calls for manpower mobilization as typical of the "unjust criticism of labor" heard frequently in wartime Washington. He explained, "The typical argument is that labor ought to be conscripted; that if boys are drafted at $21.00 a month, labor ought to be made to work for $21.00 a month. Of course if that argument applied to labor, it can be applied just as well to everybody in this room. We can conscript the entire population, which is just what Mr. Hitler has done in Germany." Taft argued such drastic measures were unnecessary. Because "we are fighting for a democratic system of government," Taft stressed, "unless it is absolutely essential to our existence, we don't want to suspend any more of our own freedom than necessary."[27]

In February and March of 1942, Grenville Clark, a wealthy New York attorney who advocated for intervention in World War II, conscription legislation in 1940, and then full manpower mobilization after Pearl Harbor, first began working on a legislative solution to the manpower crisis. By the end of the spring, he had sent a draft of proposed legislation to the president. Roosevelt replied favorably to Clark on June 13, 1942, and indicated he would have the WMC study the proposal. After several months the commission issued a negative report. As a result, Clark worked with Republicans Wadsworth and Warren Austin (R-VT) to draft a manpower mobilization bill for congressional consideration. Clark noted, "It wasn't feasible to get leading Democrats to sponsor the Bill in the absence of word from you."[28]

Indeed, Harley Kilgore's (D-WV) views proved Clark's point when he recommended against manpower mobilization legislation, but not for reasons of antistatism. Because he chaired a subcommittee of the Truman Committee, and because he was a moderately liberal senator, his position carried weight and revealed the complex intersection of ideology and labor policy. Kilgore's subcommittee claimed, "Compulsion in this field should be the very last resort in a democracy such as ours, and then should be used only in very specific and well-defined areas." Instead of passing manpower legislation, Kilgore and other moderate and liberal Democrats—Claude Pepper (D-FL), Truman, Tolan, and Murray—promoted placing all aspects of the U.S. economy not directly related to the military "under one civilian roof," a statist proposal. They called for the creation of an Office of War Mobilization, which would be authorized to assume the functions of the War Production Board, the Selective Service System, the Office of Economic Stabilization, and procurement for all branches of the military. Pepper promised to push forward with this legislative fight despite presidential opposition because of the conservative turn the voters took in the 1942 midterm elections. He asserted: "The people have expressed dissatisfaction with loose organization." When FDR did create the Office of War Mobilization (OWM) later in 1943, the new executive agency had far less authority than the lawmakers had hoped; instead of replacing the extant agencies Kilgore and his colleagues alluded to, the OWM only coordinated policy across agency lines. It did little to change the wartime economic balance of power, which benefitted industry and the military.[29]

Advocates of manpower legislation did not view this administrative reorganization as a useful substitute, and they pushed forward with their bill. The Austin-Wadsworth bill had numerous opponents from the time it was introduced in 1943. WMC chair Paul McNutt did not like it, even though he had endorsed national service legislation in 1942. Nor did the legislative committees with jurisdiction over the military or the Truman Committee. In an interview, Truman praised the mobilization effort on the home front. He noted, though, that waste and inefficiency were inevitable and necessary by-products of the rapid mobilization: "War is waste—waste of manpower and material." There were less thoughtful criticisms of Austin-Wadsworth. For example, conservative Republican Clare Hoffman of Michigan pronounced, "I certainly have no intention of voting for the Austin-Wadsworth bill. We have altogether too much regimentation."[30]

Wadsworth worried that planning for the domestic labor market did not compare with planning for battle. He recognized that while the Congress could not determine the size of the army or navy, for example, "it should lay down the principles" for requiring service "behind the lines" as well as in the military. That Congress had not yet passed a manpower mobilization bill, Wadsworth alleged, was the fault of the White House, which had "discouraged" such initiatives. Moreover, Wadsworth bragged the bill would ensure "there can be no such thing as a closed shop or union dues applicable to men who take orders and go where they are sent." This argument further linked the manpower mobilization crusade with the antistrike crusade. To critics who suggested his manpower mobilization bill was a draft of labor only, Wadsworth replied that the government had already "assumed full control over private industry engaged in producing munitions of war" through taxation, rationing, and the letting of defense contracts, making a draft of capital and production unnecessary.[31]

Congress was paralyzed when it came to solving the ideologically divisive manpower problem in 1943. Too few members had the political courage to tackle the problem. Furthermore, the administration showed little interest in the controversial issue. After lengthy hearings, Congress tabled the Austin-Wadsworth bills. There was no interest in calling them up to the floor in either chamber, but technically the bills remained pending. Still, Wadsworth was hopeful. He observed that "scarcely any of the members or senators replied with a flat negative" when polled about the legislation. Wadsworth apprised a supporter that the president's failure to ask Congress for manpower mobilization legislation was an example of "mal-administration of some of the powers conferred upon the Executive Branch of the Government by acts of Congress." As such, he held Congress should "go ahead and enact laws which in its judgment are vitally important in this great crisis. In other words, the Congress should do its duty." Clark cautioned Wadsworth that he doubted the manpower bill could be passed as long as it included language that retained McNutt in power, a position that would be "repugnant" to many newspaper editors and to the labor movement.[32]

Wadsworth later noted that even though FDR had privately given his personal support for manpower mobilization, "we can't get him to speak out loud about it and apparently some of his intimate advisors are urging caution." Both the United States Chamber of Commerce and the National Association of Manufacturers pushed for a volunteer system, which McNutt supported, slowing momentum for the Wadsworth legislation. "The truth is there is a streak of timidity running through this whole crowd," Wadsworth contended. "How long they will continue to suffer from this state of mind I do not know. In the meantime, the war effort suffers and more men will die."[33]

The better part of 1943 was devoted to manpower hearings in the House and Senate Military Committees. Despite support from the War Department and the Maritime Commission, the bill was not reported to the floor of either chamber. Indeed, the U.S. government did not follow the example of its allies and its foes in the war and require national service. Early in 1944, Austin and Wadsworth put together a detailed list of what their revised national war service legislation, written with an expiration date of May 1, 1945, would and would not do. One journalist described the measure as "a package of potentially totalitarian dynamite," but Austin and Wadsworth countered, "It would provide for . . . total mobilization of all our skills, and of our man and woman power." They believed such legislation would show Americans "the equal liability of all in the war effort." Included in the measure were safeguards against "the evils of unbalance, hoarding, piracy, absenteeism, inadequate training for management and supervision, . . . and such shortages as those in agriculture." Other benefits included an end to confusion regarding government production orders, the introduction of "due process of law" in place of "executive acts" ensuring that "if any 'mobile' person" refused "to perform his assigned duty, punishment could be applied only after conviction

. . . in our courts of justice." Men between the ages of eighteen and sixty-five and women between eighteen and fifty would be required to register. The lawmakers professed it would "preserve the right to join or not to join any union," but they did not win enough converts to pass the bill into law.[34]

When the manpower bill is contrasted with legislative policy toward the FEPC, much irony is revealed about the congressional war over labor politics. Neither were members of Congress willing to mobilize all able workers nor did they want to ban workplace discrimination against African Americans. The creation of the FEPC and plans for its expansion in 1942 drew intense and harsh criticism from most southern congressmen, but this phase of the debate did not spill over into the whole of Congress. These lawmakers enjoyed such power in Congress and with the administration that they forced Roosevelt to maim the FEPC within a year of its creation by folding it into the WMC and giving WMC officials operational authority over the FEPC, but they were never able to obliterate the agency. Abetting the southern Democrats was Paul McNutt, the director of the WMC and, though a liberal New Dealer, no friend of African American civil rights, though he did support using blacks as war workers. Within Congress, the existence of the FEPC caused some lawmakers not normally given over to such behavior to engage in race baiting. Wright Patman (D-TX) reported on a meeting he and Ramspeck had had with McNutt about the manpower shortage. McNutt had argued that African American employment must be maximized, but Patman countered that if the administration did not "cease giving" African Americans and Jews "an advantage over the other people, that they would soon find themselves carrying the banner for these two minority groups alone." Patman stressed, "We, as Democrats, should have the support of all minority groups that we can get, but we cannot afford to sacrifice . . . in order to keep them." Patman was not alone in his views. Richard Russell attested: "The FEPC is the most sickening manifestation of the trend that is now in effect to force social equality and miscegenation of the white and black races on the South. I have fought this organization for all I am worth, but I am afraid that we are going to be licked." Moreover, the opponents of the FEPC enjoyed organizational and motivational advantages because northern and border state lawmakers, regardless of party, often refused to be publicly associated with the NAACP, a major defender of the FEPC.[35]

While such concerns typified the thinking of southern Democrats, there was little public controversy in Congress about African Americans and the FEPC until an appropriation for that agency became necessary in the summer of 1943. The FEPC became an issue because Roosevelt yielded to pressure from the NAACP and other civil rights agencies to recast the FEPC again. In May 1943 the president used an executive order to reform the committee, making it more powerful in the process. The new FEPC was made a part of the Office of Emergency Management, and it received a budget of $500,000. By that point, Congress generally was restive and angry about what it termed administrative excess. The increased number of Republicans in Congress further intensified the backlash against the administration. Funding for the FEPC, then, became an ideal target for conservatives. Instead of trying to kill the FEPC outright, a battle they knew they would lose, conservative lawmakers in 1943 and 1944 attacked its appropriations.[36]

Many of the same conservatives who fought the FEPC lobbied for antistrike legislation. Animosity toward strikes was pervasive in the 78th Congress following the 1942 midterm elections. According to a confidential draft for the Truman Committee, "our government has the right and duty to tell, not ask, labor . . . that there shall be no stoppage of work in essential industry." But because this committee was more balanced in its outlook, the report also acknowledged "government must recognize that when it tells labor not to exercise during wartime its right to strike, it is depriving labor of its chief weapon with which to force management to be fair to labor. Government must, therefore, assume a duty to labor to see that it gets fair and square treatment."[37]

In 1943, John L. Lewis led the UMW in a series of strikes—in May, June, and October—demanding a $2 a day wage increase, which gave Connally the cover to push for antistrike legislation. Roosevelt ordered the strikers back to work after the first stoppage and in a May radio address affirmed striking workers were abetting the Axis powers. Lewis hoped to break the previous bargains reached between the government and the unions over wartime wages and prove the efficacy of wartime strikes, commenting at one juncture, "we want stabilization of the mine workers' stomachs." Others in the country saw it differently, with *Stars and Stripes* announcing, "John L. Lewis, damn your coal-black soul" and members of Congress demanding he be tried for treason. Connally's bill drew on the conservative belief that supposedly unscrupulous labor leaders like Lewis were responsible for strikes and needed to be checked. Roosevelt's private views of Lewis were not much different from those of Congress. The president even remarked once that he "would be glad to resign as President if Lewis committed suicide," but in public he conceded Lewis was a rightfully elected union leader. Because it was driven by congressional anger and not thoughtful policy remedies and because there was no negotiation with the White House to craft an effective measure, what became the War Labor Disputes Act, better known as the Smith-Connally Act, actually encouraged more workers to bring grievances against employers.[38]

Connally's "toothless" bill, which did nothing more than authorize decisions FDR had already made, had been languishing in the Senate Judiciary Committee. Angry about Lewis, senators amended and passed a much stronger version of the Connally bill, knowing that even a 64 percent majority of labor union members favored a policy forbidding strikes in war plants. The "fat, bumbling" majority leader, Alben Barkley (D-KY), could do nothing because he faced a tough reelection bid in 1944, and an effort to recommit the bill back to committee for further study, equivalent to killing it, failed, 27 in favor and 52 against. Southern Democrats and Republicans accounted for most of the nay votes. Next Republican senators Taft and John A. Danaher (CT) successfully introduced a forceful amendment authorizing prison time for persons who incited strikes, giving statutory imprimatur to the War Labor Board (WLB), granting it subpoena power, and providing judicial enforcement for WLB rulings. The tougher bill troubled both the White House and the labor movement when it passed the Senate by a vote of 63 to 16 on May 5, 1943. Next, Connally pressed the House to act quickly so the new law could be used against Lewis's coal strike. He insisted, "It announces a clear-cut policy of the Congress."[39]

When it was sent to the House for action, "ample 'Aunt'" Mary T. Norton, a friend to the labor movement and the chair of the House Committee on Labor, asked that the bill be referred to her committee. Rayburn refused. He sent it to the House Military Affairs Committee instead where the chair, "bald, eagle-beaked," and conservative Andrew Jackson May (D-KY), was sure to support and strengthen the Connally bill. May's committee was known as "one of the most obstreperous, hell-raising committees in the House." As the House Military Affairs Committee deliberated the Connally bill, it amended it with every provision possible from the old Smith bill that the House had passed in December 1941. May's committee argued the "urgen[cy]" of addressing the problem especially since there was but a fragile truce in the coal workers' strike. Speaker Rayburn even told a leading Texas newspaper publisher:

> Next week, the House will be given an opportunity to vote on a measure to curb strikes. I am waiting to see how some people are going to vote who have been howling the loudest and criticizing the Administration for not stopping strikes. I am of the clear opinion that our Republican brethren, or at least a majority of them, will not even vote to adopt a rule for consideration of the bill. Watch and see. I really want something done myself.[40]

Smith promised he would be "battling for the Lord" to pass the amended Connally bill when it went to the House floor. Meanwhile the labor unions were fighting for its defeat, and they convinced some members to oppose the bill who had earlier supported it. The floor manager was May, who faced constant political challenges from Lewis and the UMW. He told the press he wanted to "take" John L. Lewis "and stop those strikes against National Defense." Assisting him were Smith, William M. Colmer (D-MS), Carl Vinson (D-GA), and dozens of others. Smith, May, and the others were unsure of whether they would prevail because the Republicans were interested in the labor vote in 1944. Equally problematic was the vocal administration opposition to the bill. In an off-the-record interview, Sam Rayburn suggested the bill might be sent back to committee on the strength of GOP votes. His prediction proved erroneous. The House passed a bill even stronger than the Senate bill on June 4 by a 233–141 vote with the votes of southern Democrats and about 80 percent of the Republicans.[41]

Connally stressed that there was no chance of the Senate accepting such a strong bill. The only hope for legislation, he explained, was for the bill to go to a conference committee. Connally did so to prevent Elbert Thomas from taking the two bills—Smith's strong House bill and the more moderate Connally Senate bill—to his committee for revisions. Connally told Thomas a story about when Uncle Remus went fishing to explain why a conference committee was the only option: "He caught a little perch about two inches long. . . . It was slimy and still alive and it began to flirt and flip and jerk around. Uncle Remus exclaimed, 'Little fish, what in the world is the matter with you? Why are you cutting up so much? I ain't going to do nuthin' to you but gut you.' And that's what the Labor Committee wants to do to the anti-strike bills."[42]

Both chambers approved the conference committee report on Smith-Connally, which was stronger than the weak Connally bill but not as harsh as the House revisions. Journalist Frank McNaughton concluded, "The ironic aspect of this whole fight is: John L. Lewis fattened on Roosevelt labor policies, and Roosevelt fattened on John L. Lewis' early political assistance; Roosevelt's opposition kept Congress for three years from taking a sock at Labor; John L. Lewis' coal strike goaded Congress into such a rage that something had to be passed; all union labor gets socked in the process." But the irony went further than that. Labor unions were so eager to defeat Smith-Connally, a measure they termed fascistic, that they never realized it was a weak bill.[43]

Sam Rayburn spoke with Postmaster General Frank Walker on the telephone and "told him for Christ's sake to get somebody to see the president and tell him not to veto the [Smith-Connally] bill, that it would set Congress afire, cost the Democrats votes in the next election, play hell with the fast fading cooperation between Congress and the executive, cost the administration votes on other issues that might come up later." Ramspeck wrangled with Byrnes about the same point. Connally lobbied the White House via telegram even though he chaired one of the most important wartime committees, the Senate Foreign Relations Committee, and had ready access to the president via telephone or Oval Office visits. He realized the president would not change his mind, so preparations began for the override vote. Indeed, Roosevelt issued his veto on June 25, 1943, despite his approval of the goals of the bill. He quarreled with the provisions that required workers to file an intent to strike and that imposed a thirty-day cooling-off period before strikes could begin, arguing such policies would encourage strikes, not minimize them.[44]

The context for the override of the Smith-Connally bill was a Congress in need of a vacation and time to think about the large issues before the country. Congressional pique over the apparent slights from the administration, especially the executive's tendency to intrude into congressional prerogatives, left lawmakers feeling they had no role to play in governance. Furthermore, partisan division between Republicans and Democrats and factional division between the farm bloc and the consumer-labor bloc hindered legislative effectiveness. More important, the congressional leadership lacked an independent voice, too long had it spoken almost exclusively for the president. Rayburn privately suggested that the veto would be overturned in the House. He was unhappy that labor was not being treated in the same fashion as farmers, business people, and others in the economy.[45]

During House debate on another bill, Clifton Woodrum (D-VA) announced that the veto had been overridden in the Senate, 56 to 25, with the votes of the conservative coalition carrying the day: "Our armies in the field are winning glorious victories. Today, in the minds of many American citizens, we are about to lose an important battle on the home front. . . . It is time for action in this body, not tomorrow, not Monday, but today." In this struggle lawmakers declared independence from what they viewed as a dictatorial White House. Past history suggested how difficult it was for Congress to exert independent leadership during wartime. During the Civil War Congress suffered when it created a committee on the conduct of the war. It looked just as bad during World War I when it investigated Woodrow Wilson's fitness for duty. The House override vote was overwhelming, 244–108, and again drew on the conservative coalition. Congressional decisions regarding this issue resulted from a hyper-attenuated memory of the last decade, and also from keen awareness of public opinion. Indeed, 67 percent of Americans surveyed supported the Smith-Connally Act a month after it was passed.[46]

Perhaps the biggest problem was the lack of liaison between the White House and Capitol Hill. While Roosevelt had spoken out for labor legislation in the past, he had never addressed the movement critically, and he did not do so during the war years. His only legislative suggestion was a draft of all men under sixty-five to work in the coal mines. The purpose there was not so much to enact a bill but to embarrass Congress; lawmakers could not refuse such a bill when it had voted to draft men for military service. Rayburn bemoaned, "My God! What would old Andy Jackson have done to John L. Lewis? And wouldn't he have signed this bill in 20 minutes?" Similarly, Doughton explained, "I hope the action of Congress will have a salutary effect upon the entire labor situation and also be a lesson to

This July 13, 1943, Ding Darling cartoon, "Dear, dear, we do hope we haven't forgotten anybody," suggests that labor leaders, politicians, and government officials have all worked against the war effort. Courtesy of the Jay N. "Ding" Darling Wildlife Society.

the President, who, I think, has been entirely too lenient with some of the arrogant labor leaders, especially John L. Lewis."[47]

Some Congress watchers deemed the passage of the antistrike bill as counterproductive for the war effort while others termed it a constructive victory for lawmakers. Connally recounted that Roosevelt was not bothered by the override vote. He hinted that the president had one set of views publicly and another privately with the latter being more conservative. Rayburn was pleased with the vote to override the veto of the Smith-Connally Act. In fact, he was prepared to cast a tie-breaking vote, if necessary, to overturn the president. His views were not anti-administration but reflected his opinion that the labor movement was not sufficiently sacrificing for the war effort, showing a congressional preference for warfare state liberalism over welfare state liberalism. He had warned the president months before that the House would not long tolerate strikes and threats of strikes.[48] The impact of the Smith-Connally Act was more symbolic than real. Conservatives won passage of a law curtailing strikes, but the act's details were imprecise. Still, liberals incorrectly viewed Smith-Connally as a defeat, shaping attitudes toward the remaining labor policy issues: the FEPC and manpower mobilization.

The FEPC funding issue returned in 1944. Richard Russell introduced an amendment to the Independent Offices Appropriations Bill, saying of his measure, "I hope it wipes out the Fair Employment Practice Committee." The Russell amendment eliminated funding for agencies more than a year old that existed without congressional authorization. While the ploy threatened approximately thirty executive agencies created by presidential decree, the FEPC received most of the notice, but lawmakers also complained about the OPA, the WLB, the Office of War Information, and the War Food Administration. Russell made his attack on the FEPC into a debate about the proper functioning of the federal government—statism versus antistatism—and not into a racial diatribe, helping gain non-southern supporters for his cause. Moreover, by offering the amendment to a funding bill that had to be passed, Russell increased the likelihood his crusade against the FEPC would meet with success. This strategy merged well with the constitutional struggle members of Congress waged with the administration. The Georgia senator said his objective was to "stop the executive department from legislating."[49]

The NAACP worked hard for the FEPC. Roy Wilkins, an NAACP official, sent a carefully worded letter to Carter Glass (D-VA). Wilkins told a colleague: "I have no illusions about what effect the letter will have upon Glass and others like him on the Committee." In his letter to Glass, Wilkins stated African Americans did not oppose "the sound theory" requiring annual evaluations of executive agencies by Congress. The issue was instead the use of such a process to abolish the FEPC.

Tom Connally, Walter George, Richard B. Russell, and Claude Pepper. Courtesy Library of Congress, Prints & Photographs Division, photograph by Harris & Ewing [reproduction number, LC-DIG-hec-23959].

"We believe that this announcement, this singling out of the FEPC from among some thirty-odd agencies," avowed Wilkins, "will tend to prejudice a fair hearing of the claims of the Agency when it does appear before the Senate Appropriations Committee." The NAACP told the members of the Senate Subcommittee that approved the Russell amendment: "It was a shock to read that you voted to abolish the Fair Employment Practice Committee. We are, therefore, asking you to give us your comment on the action taken by the sub-committee. We would appreciate also if you would indicate your position on the work of the FEPC and more specifically whether you favor an adequate appropriation to continue this vital work."[50]

While race certainly played a role in the debate over the Russell amendment, tensions between the executive and legislative branches were just as important. Indeed, the range of lawmaker opinion reflected the difficulty of solving the problem. Said Chapman Revercomb (R-WV), "My consideration of the proposal will be with respect to all of the numerous agencies created by executive edict. It is definitely my view that agencies of government should be created by act of Congress and not by executive direction."[51]

Sen. Harold Burton (R-OH) clarified he had helped postpone the effective date of the Russell Amendment until July 1, 1944, a maneuver that gave Congress more time to approve the work of the FEPC. Burton explained to Wilkins, "The survival of the FEPC therefore now depends upon action to be taken on a budget estimate submitted by the President for an appropriation to be included in the War Agencies Appropriation Bill. This is pending in the House of Representatives and has not yet been before the Senate." Meanwhile the House approved the $500,000 appropriation for the FEPC. The debate was not without rancor. Sam Hobbs (D-AL) insisted the "Fair Employment Practices Committee [is] prevent[ing] white people from obtaining jobs." The amount requested for the FEPC was but a "pittance" in the words of Walter White, compared with the $98 billion budget for the war effort in 1945.[52]

When the Senate Appropriations Subcommittee met, it voted 3–2 to eliminate the FEPC funding from the War Agencies Appropriation Bill. Of the ten absent subcommittee members, eight had been on record favoring the FEPC appropriation. White called the vote a "travesty on democratic process. Substantial majority of full appropriation committee have indicated approval of FEPC item. Advised full committee vote Monday. Imperative majority favoring appropriation attend meeting and vote for restoration of this item." Indeed, the full committee voted in favor of funding the FEPC, sending the matter to the Senate floor.[53]

According to notes taken by NAACP officials who observed the Senate floor debate, the Southern demagogues behaved badly, revealing that race politics more than labor politics animated their opposition to funding the FEPC. James Eastland (D-MS) complained that during the many hearings on funding the FEPC, white stenographers had been forced to take dictation from "burr headed niggers." (The quote was changed to read "Negroes" in the *Congressional Record*.) Theodore "The Man" Bilbo (D-MS) gave an incoherent speech that attacked a host of people, religions, ethnicities, and institutions, including African Americans, Jews, the NAACP, Howard University, A. Phillip Randolph, Walter White, Treasury Secretary Henry Morgenthau, Eleanor Roosevelt, and New York Mayor Fiorello LaGuardia, among others. After suggesting that 2.5 million African Americans should be deported to Liberia, Bilbo advocated making Eleanor Roosevelt queen of that nation. Finally, he called on whites to undertake mob violence in Washington, D.C., to preserve residential segregation. During John McClellan's (D-AR) speech the word "nigger" recurred numerous times. McClel-

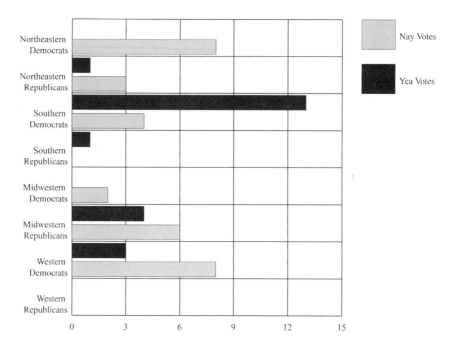

Chart 4.1: Region and Party Identification—The Russell Amendment. Data for this chart come from analysis of the June 20, 1944, record vote in the House of Representatives. See Congressional Record, *78th Congress, 2nd session, 6271.*

lan called the FEPC a "public nuisance" and a "public liability to race relation-ships and unity here at home" because "every complaint that comes from the Ne-gro is also a complaint against a white man." Guy Gillette (D-IA) walked over to McClellan, shook his hand, and congratulated him on his talk. This behavior notwithstanding the Senate passed the $500,000 appropriation bill without Rus-sell's amendment having rejected that initiative 22 to 31. Scant Republican coop-eration with southern Democrats, as depicted in Chart 4.1, suggests that the conservative coalition did not play a role in this vote. The wartime FEPC survived another assault from southern conservatives. Lawmakers did nothing, though, about making the agency permanent.[54]

By the new year, the manpower issue was again on the congressional radar. Said Sen. James M. Mead (D-NY), the guest host of the *American Forum of the Air* and the chair of the Senate Committee Investigating National Defense (following Truman's election as vice president), "Manpower is an eight-letter word that car-ries tremendous meaning for America today." While Mead assured the audience that manpower issues had not adversely affected the troops as yet, he also noted 40 percent of war production was behind schedule. He argued, "The war must not last even an hour longer because we did not supply enough. Our production goals must be met." An official with the WMC instructed that the production problems resulted because "you cannot stockpile workers," meaning that changed production needs occurred faster than shifts in the workforce.[55]

After much discussion of the numbers of workers and soldiers needed for the war effort, the debate became partisan. Sen. Owen Brewster (R-ME) recommended that Democrats push as Roosevelt suggested for the mandatory registration of all 4-Fs into the civilian workforce. Rep. Hook countered, "We don't agree that there is a shortage because of the fact that if the Government agencies, labor and management, would cooperate together for the utilization of labor there would be no shortage and no need for any draft." Brewster then tried to turn the remark into a criticism of FDR, suggesting the country had made a mistake when it reelected him in 1944. "Now we have got to do the best we can with him," concluded Brewster. Hook asserted that simply requiring the 4-Fs to work in defense industries was unrealistic propaganda because many would not pass the health requirements for employment there, either. Mead suggested the problem was a disagreement between those who wanted mandatory national service legislation and those who believed that the more effective use of existing workers would ameliorate the shortages.[56]

Events in the European theater affected debate about national service legislation. The Battle of the Bulge, which began in December 1944 when Germany penetrated the Allied position in the Ardennes and temporarily regained parts of Belgium and Luxembourg, ultimately ended in victory for the Allies. Nonetheless, when Germany first launched its attack, the Battle of the Bulge frightened American policymakers. After the Battle of the Bulge started, the military brass began making the erroneous argument that production bottlenecks in the United States jeopardized the war effort. May, R. Ewing Thomason (D-TX), Elbert Thomas, Walter G. Andrews (R-NY), and Austin stressed that Congress simply would not consider a national service bill. One senator, Edwin C. Johnson (D-CO), contended, "The key to this manpower situation is Elbert Thomas. You watch the way Elbert jumps and you'll know whether the president really wants national service or not." In early January Thomas did nothing to suggest Roosevelt favored passage of the bill even though he had spoken positively about it in December. Debates on the subject would only bring "a hell of a fight," according to one inside observer. Too many important constituencies were dead-set against the legislation, including organized labor and the farm lobby. Furthermore, optimism that the war in Europe would soon end meant that there would be less need for additional manpower, so reasoned the lawmakers.[57]

They did not prevail. Rayburn was ready to take the manpower legislation to the House floor in late January 1945. He was not willing to have the bill referred back to committee, a sure death sentence. In an off-the-record interview, Rayburn averred, "I'll be God damned if I know how the bill will come out." Of especial difficulty were amendments to ban the closed shop and to make the FEPC permanent. As such, Rayburn concluded, "Those amendments may play hell. But we are going to pass some kind of a bill and check it up to the Senate. General [George C.] Marshall and Admiral [Ernest J.] King, when they talked to us Wednesday at the Library of Congress, said enough for me, and for anybody with any brains. We're up against God damned hard fighting and Congress knows it. Now it's up to Congress to do its part." Without mentioning specific legislation, General Marshall had called for 900,000 new troops in the next six months. Rayburn concluded, "There's no other way to get them than to take some out of factories, and to replace them with men who are not now willing to take defense jobs. By God, I don't know what it will be, but we're going to pass something. We've got to. Maybe we can work it out in conference." When Rayburn spoke on the floor on January 31, he stressed, "Any amendment placed on this bill that is going to lose it a large block of votes, is a dangerous amendment." Thanks to Rayburn's cloakroom lobbying and a strong floor argument against amending the bill the manpower legislation survived the House chamber, passing on February 1 by a vote of 246–167.[58] With the exception of southern Democrats who overwhelmingly supported the bill all other regions divided their votes on manpower.

The bill faced challenges in the Senate. Joseph C. O'Mahoney (D-WY) assumed the vagaries in the bill should bring its defeat. The authorization of an "unknown agency to carry out this work" most troubled O'Mahoney. He maintained: "I think that any legislation which is based upon so important a subject as the conscription of manpower should be absolutely definite and clear, and I don't believe that Congress should give to any central agency in Washington authority to deal." Others hit even harder against the bill. William Lemke (R-ND) insisted: "Last week the lower House passed the May Bill—should be called the Slave Bill. The passage of this bill was made possible only because of false propaganda. There is no shortage of manpower, but there is a shortage of bureaucratic intelligence."[59]

The Senate version of the manpower bill, passed on March 8 by a 63–16 vote, proved unsatisfactory to the House and to the president because it was ineffective. Despite his yea vote Richard Russell concluded, "It is as inadequate for dealing with this problem as would be a resolution adopted by a ladies sewing circle." In an off-the-record interview, Sam Rayburn presumed the House would fight against the Senate bill until "hell freezes over thick." There was no chance, he predicted, of the House approving "that c—p that they passed. We'll get a bill that is a bill or the Senate will take the blame for it." Likewise, Wadsworth complained to General George E. Patton that the Senate replaced the House national service bill with a weak substitute that "isn't worth the paper it is written on. It misses the whole point" that "every competent adult civilian" should work in industry or agriculture and thus support the military. "They tell me that I am urging slave labor. If this is slave labor then you are in command of an army of slaves and we would better quit the whole show."[60]

The House manpower bill treated compulsion as the solution whereas the Senate bill demanded efficient bureaucratic planning. A Senate conferee said the compromise was "a holy terror. . . . It has more teeth than a shark. It's worse than anything either the Senate or the House ever dreamed up," but Ewing Thomason, a House conferee, disagreed, calling it "a pretty good omelette, especially since it includes many features of the House bill." The conference committee report drew more from the House bill than the Senate bill. Leading senators advocated that their colleagues reject the conference committee report and insist on the Senate bill. Majority Whip Ramspeck asked Democratic members to be present on Tuesday, March 27, 1945, for consideration of the conference report for the manpower bill, requiring Americans to work or fight, but no action was taken. Roosevelt lobbied Congress to pass the manpower legislation even though it was not the same as what had been initially introduced. Nonetheless, the Senate rejected the conference committee report on the manpower legislation, and while it appointed a new conference committee delegation, the certainty of victory in Europe signaled the demise of the legislation. FDR's death on April 12, 1945, further stymied the manpower mobilization bill. After Truman's ascension to the presidency there were no further demands for the bill.[61]

At the same time Congress deliberated the manpower bill, the NAACP renewed its lobbying campaign for the FEPC. In 1945, civil rights activists called for protecting the wartime agency and creating a permanent FEPC. Part of the strategy involved hitting hard those lawmakers who had promised support in the campaign but had reneged after securing reelection. One civil rights advocate charged, "Senator Robert A. Taft today stands self condemned as a political chameleon,—a pre-election friend and a post-election foe." Taft objected to the NAACP criticism of him, declaring, "There is no plan of collaborating with the Southern Senators on any issue, and certainly you can count on the unanimous support of the Republicans in the Senate for any reasonable bill to create a Fair Employment Practices Commission." Roy Wilkins of the NAACP told Herbert Brownell, the chairman of the Republican National Committee, "Today Senator Taft says it was never intended that this bill should have any 'teeth' in it and that he will not support a bill with any compulsory features. You can understand that this looks to Negro voters throughout the nation like the well-known double-cross."[62]

Rep. Norton moved the legislation through her committee but had difficulty getting it on the floor. When she tried to force the FEPC bill out of the Rules

Committee, she tussled with the reactionary Cox. After Norton pointed to discrimination against "certain groups," Cox asked "Who?" She retorted, "You can't be serious! The Negro, of course." They wound up in a shouting match so loud that the committee stenographer could not record the proceedings. Later during her testimony, Norton argued, "I have been chairman of the Labor Committee for a long time, and I think the Rules Committee has been most unfair to the Labor Committee. Why are you gentlemen so determined to be so unfair?" Her arguments were not sufficient to gain a rule for the bill; Norton had to gain signatures on a discharge petition to secure a floor debate and vote.[63]

At the behest of the NAACP, President Truman wrote to Adolph Sabath (D-IL), the chair of the House Rules Committee, on June 5, and declared his support for the Norton bill, which provided for a permanent FEPC. Doing so was rare for a president, and Truman escaped criticism only because he had been a member of Congress. He castigated the House Appropriations Committee for failing to fund the FEPC because it had not been created by Congress: "The principle and policy of fair employment should be established permanently as a part of our national law. . . . I therefore urge the Rules Committee to adopt a rule permitting the legislation to be voted upon by the members of the House as quickly as possible."[64]

Among the many challenges to the permanent FEPC legislation was the failure to have a quorum in the House Rules Committee. NAACP officials lobbied Joseph W. Martin Jr., the House Minority Leader, to ensure that GOP lawmakers on the committee were present at the next meeting. Three Republicans had been absent when the quorum was not achieved, leaving Sabath, the committee chair, to tell the press, "I just haven't got the members here to do anything about it." The House Rules Committee blocked the permanent FEPC legislation from moving to the House floor, despite President Truman's lobbying. Civil rights activists then shifted their efforts to the Senate where they hoped that reviving the funding for the FEPC in the National War Agencies Appropriations Bill would at least sustain the temporary FEPC. After Clarence Cannon (D-MO) affirmed that the Rules Committee had blocked inclusion of the wartime FEPC in such legislation, Norton professed, "It took a lot of courage to come before this House and tell us that the Rules Committee, or a few members of the Rules Committee, were running the entire House!"[65]

Proponents of the program continued fighting for its life. During a late June 1945 Senate filibuster against the FEPC, Theodore Bilbo promised that he would talk "until the FEPC is dead." He had help. Eastland's June 29 race baiting stirred up tremendous resentment among African American soldiers fighting abroad for he erroneously charged that African American soldiers had raped as many as 5,000 German women. The NAACP publicized many of the letters of protest. One soldier argued, "Your system for scuttling democracy at home by smearing a minority on the nation's Senate floor and talking the FEPC 'to death' truly must arouse misgivings in the small countries who must look to the United States for leadership." Sgt. Duwayne Corzine was equally blunt: "This is a hard pill to take after seeing what happened to our American troops. . . . The Germans weren't shooting just white troops; they were killing American soldiers. . . . I believe if a few bombs had fallen in the Mississippi area it probably would have changed the Senator and his followers on the type of politics they are offering the American Government."[66]

The NAACP fought the Senate filibuster over the FEPC legislation, sending a telegram to the nation's leading newspapers that concluded the move was akin to "treason." During the debate Sen. Dennis Chavez (D-NM) insisted, "Death on the battlefield does not differentiate between the Jew, the Negro, the Mexican, and the so-called Anglo-Saxon." Later he referred to his own ethnicity, refuting the not-so-subtle contention of white southerners that only white people could be Americans. The filibuster failed after Barkley negotiated a compromise: Bilbo and the reactionaries agreed to forego the filibuster if the bill was amended to lower the FEPC's funding to $250,000. This measure passed on a sectional vote, 42–26, with southerners shouting their displeasure. The FEPC's strongest supporters still viewed this move as a "mortal blow" because the appropriation was not sufficient to sustain the agency. Bilbo retorted that "one cent" was too much to give the FEPC.[67]

House conservatives had other plans, though, and they amended the War Agencies Appropriation Bill so that funding for the FEPC would be restricted to dismantling the agency. In response supporters of the FEPC stripped the funding for ten other agencies. The appropriation for the FEPC passed both houses of Congress on July 12 without a record vote. The legislation was ambiguous as to what the fate of the FEPC would be once the war ended. Lawmakers failed to act on legislation creating a permanent FEPC.[68]

Looking at the congressional wars over the FEPC, manpower mobilization, and antistrike legislation as part of a larger story as opposed to separate legislative struggles reveals just how conflicted lawmakers were about wartime labor policy. The U.S. victory in the war became an excuse for some lawmakers to justify the decisions they did and did not make. For example, in the last year of the war O'Mahoney avowed: "The people of America, without compulsion, without forced labor, have outproduced all of the totalitarian countries. We have built more ships, more airplanes, more guns, we have produced more ammunition and more food than all of our enemies, Germany, Japan and Italy. We . . . have been able to supply huge quantities of war material to Russia too. We . . . have made a record of output that has been beyond all imagination."[69]

Indeed, this heroic story has minimized memory of the contentious wartime

debates about antistrike legislation generally and manpower mobilization legislation specifically, shading appreciation for how lawmakers forged a liberalism in
praxis when addressing the complicated questions about labor politics. Manpower
mobilization failed because laborers and managers agreed they did not want a statist program whereby the government assigned workers to particular duties and because, by 1944, the Allied war effort was prevailing over the Axis.[70] Instead, the
congressional wars about labor politics were a cautionary tale encapsulating several major themes of wartime politics: the ideological conflict between liberals and
conservatives over the power of the federal state, the debate about the New Deal's
future, and the institutional, constitutional struggle between Congress and the
president over determination of the domestic political agenda. That there was no
clear decision on either matter suggests just how divided Congress and the nation,
by proxy, were over what should be the outcome of a domestic, congressional war
devoid of slogans comparable to those used in the international war against fascism. Pragmatic not ideologic solutions were all that could be had.

The results of congressional combat on the labor battlefield appeared unclear
at the time. The intersection of race and conservatism dictated congressional
debate about the forced labor of Japanese American internment camp residents,
the reliance on Mexican American immigrant workers for the bracero program,
and the fate of the FEPC, but conservatives did not always get their way, prevailing
regarding Japanese Americans and Mexican Americans but less so regarding the
FEPC. That Congress funded the FEPC, albeit at meager rates, proved an
important victory for preserving and even expanding the New Deal ethos in
halting fashion to include some provisions for individual rights. The manpower
and antistrike debates also left a complicated legacy for the New Deal. Liberals
decried the former as antiwar but also some conservatives opposed it because the
bill vastly increased the power of the federal government. Moreover, while FDR
had initially been cool to manpower mobilization, by 1945 he supported it. His
advocacy did not convince all congressional liberals, and the failure of the bill
should be judged as a victory for the New Deal ethos. Finally the Smith-Connally
Act presents further challenges for assessing the impact of World War II for the
New Deal. Liberals fought hard against the bill but could not prevent its passage.
Still, Smith-Connally was more a propaganda victory for conservatives than a
policy loss for liberals. In sum, the conflicted and contradictory legacy of war-era
labor policy must be judged a narrow victory for moderates and liberals in the
retention of the New Deal. The question remained whether these arguments
would be compelling when Congress debated social politics.

Part Two

Human Rights or Human Wrongs? Congress, Pluralism, and Social Justice

5. "The Dregs of Europe": A Conflicted Refugee Policy

On June 4, 1941, Rep. M. Michael Edelstein (D-NY), a fifty-three-year-old, two-term House member, died of a heart attack outside the House chamber. Five minutes earlier he had delivered a speech refuting charges from Rep. John E. Rankin (D-MS) that "Wall Street and a little group of our international Jewish brethren" were pushing the United States into World War II. Edelstein countered, "Hitler started out by speaking about 'Jewish brethren.' It is becoming the play and the work of those people who want to demagogue to speak about 'Jewish brethren' and 'international bankers.'. . . The fact of the matter is that the number of Jewish bankers in the United States is infinitesimal." He criticized his colleagues for making Jews into a "scapegoat" for the world's problems. "I say it is unfair and I say it is un-American," asserted Edelstein. "As a member of this House I deplore such allegations, because we are living in a democracy. All men are created equal regardless of race, creed or color; and whether a man be a Jew or Gentile he may think what he deems fit." Edelstein revealed the varieties of racial and ethnic prejudice in Congress that girded the ideological war about the nature of the state. Conditions got so bad that Speaker Sam Rayburn (D-TX) had to call for order several times.[1]

Edelstein was both a controversial and a "gentle" figure in the House, and the circumstances of his death highlight the problem of an insular anti-Semitism predicated on anti-immigration, anti-refugee views. The Jewish refugee problem, a humanitarian concern that brought tremendous challenges to the United States, threatened the nation's racial order as the political ruling class in Congress saw it and caused the congressional wars to look very different than when the debates addressed economic politics. Even though lawmakers disagreed about refugee policy, an inchoate majority opposed statist solutions that would have ameliorated the crisis for European Jews but advocated statist measures to limit immigrant rights. Race and racial prejudice not governmental theory dominated. Moreover, because Franklin D. Roosevelt was unwilling to do much to alleviate the problem, this issue produced little warfare between Congress and the administration. Indeed, the liberal defenders of Jewish refugees were a leaderless group lacking sufficient voice and heft to challenge administration inaction and congressional indifference. As such, the battles about refugees were fought to a stalemate on Capitol Hill even as Jewish Zionists in the United States incorrectly believed that New Deal rhetoric about protecting society's weakest members would extend to Hitler's Jewish victims.[2]

Two important factions in Congress dominated the immigration and refugee policy debates the anti-restrictionists, who supported a liberal refugee policy, and restrictionist anti-Semites, who did not. There were more of the latter than the former. While none of the proponents of immigration reform for refugees linked the cause with the New Deal, most had been moderate and liberal New Dealers and they advocated similar expansions of state power to address this problem. Likewise, the restrictionists never used anti–New Deal rhetoric to defend restrictive immigration policies, even though most had opposed the Roosevelt reforms in the 1930s. The parallel positions on the New Deal and on refugee policy, then, suggests that the penumbra of the New Deal shaded refugee policy in subtle but important ways. Certainly the inability of the Congress to develop an effective refugee policy typifies the failure of New Deal liberals to transform that ideology toward a rights-based liberalism.[3]

Political Zionists—typically Protestants, not Catholics—some Jewish politicians, and some liberal lawmakers with urban, immigrant districts composed the anti-restrictionists. Self-promotion more than commitment to mitigating the refugee crisis motivated political Zionists, a polyglot group, representing the full ideological spectrum: rural and urban districts, districts with a fairly homogenous population of white and Protestant voters, and districts with multiple ethnicities and multiple religious traditions. That said, some characteristics dominated this bloc. With the exceptions of Claude Pepper (D-FL) and Alben Barkley (D-KY), none of the leading anti-restrictionists were from the South, and with the exception of Hamilton Fish (R-NY) and Edith Nourse Rogers (R-MA), all were liberal Democrats. Furthermore, all the House members except Rogers were from New York. Only Rogers and Fish had districts that were not entirely urban. The remaining New Yorkers represented immigrant neighborhoods in New York City. The Senate anti-restrictionists—Barkley, James E. Murray (D-MT), Harry S Truman (D-MO), Carl Hayden (D-AZ), Pepper, Edwin C. Johnson (D-CO), and Robert Wagner (D-NY)—were motivated more by political ideology than state voter demographics. Political Zionism then was a very fractious issue in Congress, one that proved more contentious than the struggle over the New Deal and the liberal political order.[4]

One key difficulty in using New Deal liberalism to abet a refugee policy resulted from the hesitancy of Jewish lawmakers, otherwise New Dealers, to lead the fight. Rep. Emanuel Celler (D-NY) and Rep. Samuel Dickstein (D-NY), as examples, realized that the efforts of Jews and liberals in the years before 1941 to challenge the anti-Semitic faction would fail and would bring more restrictionist legislation, so popular were the views of the latter. Indeed, Jewish lawmakers were

Rep. John Kerr and Rep. Samuel Dickstein with an opera singer. Courtesy Library of Congress, Prints & Photographs Division, photograph by Harris & Ewing [reproduction number, LC-DIG-hec-22296].

not always the most vocal anti-restrictionists. For example, Rep. Sol Bloom (D-NY) was a moderate. He did not like it when other Jewish members of the House "made God Damned fools of themselves" by calling for a more aggressive foreign policy against Adolf Hitler. In mid-September 1941, Bloom contended, "You never catch me doing that. I know that I've got to be on guard every minute. . . . Some Jews don't watch their step enough."[5]

Political Zionists responded to and relied on activists outside Congress who supported Zionist calls to make Palestine into a Jewish homeland, but according to leading anti-restrictionist lawmakers, there was scant difference in the views of Zionists and Jews regarding the designation of Palestine as a Jewish homeland. American Zionists who were Jews educated both Jews and Christians in the United States about the movement's Palestinian mission, with Rabbi Stephen Wise being an important leader. Abba Hillel Silver, another leading American Zionist and a frequent congressional lobbyist, reasoned, "We cannot truly rescue the Jews of Europe unless we have free immigration to Palestine." Silver's advocacy of free immigration, then, better than anything else encapsulated the congressional debate: would Jews from Europe before Pearl Harbor have access to the United States and after Pearl Harbor would they have access to Palestine?[6]

Vocal congressional restrictionists, often bold to the point of arrogance, were much more homogenous than the anti-restrictionists, all coming from the South and all conservative Democrats who rarely supported the administration, except on wartime economic questions. Their public anti-Semitism proved possible because of the much larger silent majority of moderates who did not object. Most of the congressional anti-Semites attained their goals without broadcasting their beliefs. Indeed, silent supporters of conservative views proved the difference in each of the social policy conflicts in the 1940s, but unlike economic policy where the moderates could broker compromise, there was not an identifiable contingent of social policy moderates, so polarizing were these issues. When discussing with Roosevelt and the cabinet what could be done to ameliorate conditions for Jewish refugees in March 1938, then vice president John Nance Garner noted that if Congress could vote by secret ballot it would outlaw all immigration. As another example, Rankin learned nothing from his role in Edelstein's death. Later in the war, he blocked passage of a private bill that would have permitted the entrance of one Jewish refugee family, whose sons were already in America, in the army, and scheduled to be deployed overseas. Moreover, restrictionist lawmakers peppered Congress with bills between 1939 and 1943 designed to thwart the efforts of the Zionists and convince Roosevelt he should not advocate a refugee policy.[7]

The divisions in Congress reflected the contradictory strengths and weaknesses of democracy. While democratic governance requires the freedom to debate, unthinking, vituperative arguments divorced from efforts to compromise are not beneficial to democracy. In *The Federalist* number ten, James Madison had pronounced the safeguarding of competing interests as essential. Madison and the other architects of the Constitution did not intend Congress to speed through the passage of legislation but to deliberate carefully. By the 1940s, too many members of Congress had forgotten the adverb in the previous sentence, opting instead for hot-headed, passionate outbursts or secretive attempts at subterfuge, both designed to deflect democratic outcomes, especially when there was a leadership void as was true with social policy.[8]

These problems aside for a moment, Congress still passed one crucial test in the war era—reflection of what the American people believed. The failure to develop a refugee policy was the result of democracy, albeit misguided, in action. As Dickstein explained, had Roosevelt pushed in the late 1930s for open borders then Congress most likely would have enacted even more restrictive immigration legislation. He understood that lawmakers were responding to the will of the American people not the realities of Hitler's menace. Congressional anti-Semitism was a function of democracy. Rudimentary as they were, polls taken in 1938 and again in 1943 reflect an overwhelming opposition, approximately 75 percent, to immigration or refugee admittance into the United States.[9]

In other ways, the American public appeared anti-Semitic. Polls in 1937 and 1939 indicated that a significant minority, 38 and 45 percent, respectively, believed anti-Jewish attitudes were increasing in the United States. More troubling, in April 1938, 48 percent of Americans answered that European Jews were partially responsible for the actions Hitler had taken against them. The following year, over half of Americans surveyed indicated support for segregating Jewish people in the United States with 10 percent advocating the humane deportation of all Jews in the country. By the mid-1940s, after news of the Holocaust was publicized, the percentage indicating Jewish Americans had too much influence in the country rose to over 50 percent. Public anti-Semitism appeared higher in urban areas and in the Northeast.[10]

This complex context made it all but impossible for Congress to act on the most significant wartime humanitarian challenge before it: construction of a meaningful rescue policy for Jewish refugees in the years before 1942. Historians deduce that it would have been easier logistically to rescue the Jews before 1941, during the refugee phase of the Holocaust, than in the extermination phase that followed, but explication of the congressional discord shows why this was impossible. In either period, though, the challenges were immense, especially when viewed from the perspective of Congress. Prior to American entry into the war and the late 1942 reports of the wholesale murder of millions of Jews, imagining what Hitler was doing was all but impossible for Gentiles unaffected by his murderous rampage. Nor was it likely that the anti-Semitic faction of Congress could be dissuaded by the Zionist faction.[11]

The war-era refugee debates, then, reflected the center right social justice conservatism of many lawmakers, a development that only aggravated partisan discord. This conservatism, which derived in part from racial prejudice, was not unique to debates about Jewish refugees, but also permeated efforts to implement civil rights reform in the 1940s. Congressional conservatives who opposed statist solutions for the Jewish refugee crisis then practiced what modern historians might call the politics of whiteness, privileging white Americans over Americans of Southern and Eastern European origin as well as Mexican Americans, African Americans, and Asian Americans, even though such a term would be foreign to an audience from the 1940s.[12] Here, unlike in economic policy debates, no immediate military imperative and no leader enough above the stature of any member of Congress highlighted the need for action. The one exception was the brief debate and easy passage in 1943 of legislation repealing the Chinese Exclusion Act. This exception both proves the rule and also reinforces racial readings of debates about refugees and immigration. Moreover, analysis of these debates shows that Congress as much or more than the State Department thwarted policies to protect Jewish refugees even when there was strong evidence of horrific actions taking place. Racial conservatism joined with partisanship and the constitutional conflict with the executive to produce stasis. Inaction in this policy bailiwick enabled Congress to determine the policy trajectory regarding refugees especially because FDR did not actively seek remedies for European Jews.

To understand these points requires knowledge that the Edelstein tragedy was not an isolated episode. Congress watchers had detected an upsurge in anti-Semitism, hearing more often references to "the Jew bastard" and other racial epithets in the years before the war. Bloom cried when he discussed the problem. Indeed, congressional bias rendered him legislatively impotent. Bloom could not even move legislation from the committee he chaired—House Foreign Affairs— to the floor for fear that members would use ethnic prejudice to derail his initiatives. Dickstein, the chair of the House Immigration Committee, had the same problem, and was dubbed "Dickswine" by conservatives for his attacks on fascism. He blamed the "professional restrictionists" for perennially blocking all reform initiatives. In 1939, it took intervention from Rayburn, then the majority leader, and Speaker of the House William B. Bankhead (D-AL) to ensure that Rep. Adolph L. Sabath's (D-IL) appointment as chair of the House Rules Committee survived blocking efforts.[13]

Anti-Semitism was most potent among southern Democrats, which meant that much of the congressional leadership shared this prejudice. Bloom described most of the southern Democrats as anti-Semitic, but also noted that they did not advertise their prejudices. Even Rayburn did not have a perfect record on this subject. He expressed his private hatred for two Jewish members of the House: Celler and Dickstein. Close associates of Rayburn insisted he was not anti-Semitic, but Frank McNaughton, a journalist for *Time* magazine, noted that Ted Wright, Rayburn's clerk, was "the bitterest anti-Semite I have seen in years. . . . He hates them all."[14]

According to journalists who covered Capitol Hill, congressional anti-Semitism flowed from multiple sources: FDR's reliance on Jewish advisors, including Secretary of the Treasury Henry Morgenthau; Morgenthau's employment of Jewish people, "giving this race the control of money"; Jewish predominance throughout the executive branch agencies; southern and western congressional frustration at not being able to place Gentile job seekers in federal employment; a perception that Jews were radicals and Communists (typically New Deal advocacy was sufficient for some congressional conservatives to brand Jewish policy advisors in this manner); and fear of "giving these brilliant, young and liberal fellows too much power, too much prestige" especially after they had made ill-prepared members of Congress look bad in committee hearings. McNaughton concluded, "I think probably the main source of anti-Semitism in Congress is not hate per se, but primarily a feeling of inferiority—mentally and financially—to many of the Jews, and this translates itself by a process of rationalization into undercover attacks on the Jews."[15]

During the 1930s and 1940s, a minority of Congress fought an ideological war against the anti-Semitic restrictionists and their silent, moderate supporters with the goal being refugee assistance for European Jews. As early as 1933, congressional anti-restrictionists began a public dialogue condemning Hitler's persecution of the Jews. Eleven months before Pearl Harbor, Barkley told a Cleveland, Ohio, audience on January 18, 1941, the war was not about "adjust[ing] a boundary in Europe, or elsewhere" but was "a war against racial and national integrity. . . . It is a war to control the world, politically, economically, territorially and intellectually." In November 1941, he made another speech where he asserted, "We cannot escape the result of this *holocaust.*"[16]

Barkley's words, specifically the use of the term "holocaust," introduce anew the question of what did officials in the U.S. government know and when did they know it regarding Hitler's war crimes against the Jews. The Barkley speech combined with countless other bits of evidence suggests a generalized knowledge of Hitler's murderous intent well before the United States became a combatant. For example, Sen. Joseph C. O'Mahoney (D-WY) fumed to a constituent about the "unmitigated outrages" of the recent "German pogrom" against Jews in Europe. The Senate Immigration Committee, a conservative, restrictionist panel, maintained a clipping file that augments the evidence of just how much key members of Congress knew about the atrocities in Europe. Examples of articles in the file include "4,500,000 Anxious to Flee Austria, Conference Told," *Washington Evening Star,* July 7, 1938; "Refugee Director Leaves for London," *Washington Herald,* August 11, 1938; "Law to Aid Persecuted of Germany May Be Put Up to Georgia's Russell," *Atlanta Constitution,* November 30, 1938; and "Roosevelt Finds Quotas Limit Aid," *New York Times,* November 18, 1938. Despite this evidence, the anti-immigration mood in Congress remained strong.[17]

Indeed, conservatives in Congress advocated new immigration restriction legislation, arguing the American state did not have a role to play in this international dilemma. Ironically, though, these conservatives crafted statist solutions to deny political rights to immigrants as part of a much broader campaign to retard the civil liberties of citizens. Between January 1939 and January 1941 there had been seventy restriction bills introduced in Congress with nine enacted into law. Rep. Martin Dies (D-TX), a reactionary anti-Communist, told the president, "Aliens are entering this country illegally without any great difficulty. Under the loose methods by which refugees are admitted, agents of foreign powers are coming in under the guise of refugees." The Smith Act, named for Rep. Howard Worth Smith (D-VA) and also known as the Alien Registration Act, was the most important of the restriction initiatives. Smith intended much more than simply registering immigrants who had not yet become citizens. He wanted to displace so-called immigrant radicals from politics and labor unions, which conservatives associated with the New Deal. Smith avowed the law was needed to protect the military from Communists. When critics charged that his measure was "red-baiting," he retorted that he was "fighting the devil with fire." Tom Connally (D-TX) managed the Alien Registration Act in the upper chamber. The Senate bill shifted the locus for registration to the post offices from federal courts to allow citizen vigilantes to force registration. Said Connally, "I can imagine such a man calling up the postmaster and saying, 'Has Old Man Bohunk over here ever registered as an alien? If not, we want to know, and we will see that he comes in.'" Connally's reasoning bore an eerie likeness to the actions that facilitated many a lynching in the South. When Roosevelt signed the bill, he tried to soften its anti-democratic implications with the argument that it was "for the protection of the loyal aliens who are . . . guests" of the United States. Passage of the Smith Act cannot be understood apart from the larger context of prewar isolationism and citizenship restriction measures, nor should it be separated from the conservative war about ideology. Indeed its passage shows that conservatives were not always opposed to increasing the power of the state, especially if such actions resulted in delegitimizing liberalism and emboldening a conservative vision of the state.[18]

The political dynamics of the interwar years, including depression, isolationism, nativism, racial prejudice, and anti-Semitism, made difficult any thoughtful attempt at rescue of the European Jews in the late 1930s. The Jewish community was divided on *what* should be done, and Congress was divided over *whether* anything should be done. Of those lawmakers sympathetic to the plight of the Jews, some members of Congress championed a Zionist solution while others concentrated on securing permanent residency for Jewish visitors already in the United States or on related immigration status concerns. Still others espoused creation of a Jewish army to fight in Europe. Finally, once the United States entered the war, and especially after the more generalized "discovery" of the Holocaust, lawmakers deliberated the fate of Jewish refugees from Nazism, keying their efforts on opening Palestine to homeless and stateless Jews. Inertia governed most of these debates. The cross purposes at which lawmakers worked suggests much about why Congress rendered itself impotent on this most important issue. Sol Bloom said it best when he reasoned that there was not a Jewish problem but instead a "non-Jewish problem," meaning that the difficulties Jews faced were the making of non-Jews and could only be solved with the policy leadership of non-Jews.[19] Policy debates in the war years proved Bloom's thesis; the U.S. Congress failed to

Rep. Howard Worth Smith and William M. Leiserson, the chair of the National Labor Relations Board. Courtesy Library of Congress, Prints & Photographs Division, photograph by Harris & Ewing [reproduction number, LC-DIG-hec-27799].

ameliorate Bloom's "non-Jewish problem" for many of the same reasons of prejudice and center right social justice conservatism that had gone into making it in the first place.

In 1938, the U.S. government acknowledged there was a refugee problem for European Jews. That March, the State Department, which was widely believed to harbor anti-Semitic views, issued a statement indicating a willingness to work with other governments to facilitate "emigration from Austria and presumably from Germany of political refugees." Additionally, the government allowed for unlimited extensions for visas of persons already in the United States. Sen. Wagner sought an audience with Roosevelt, stating "I didn't know what the President can do but, politically, it is pretty important to me. . . . I know he won't like this but we all have to do things to help ourselves and I really am concerned about the terrible time they are having over there."[20]

Later that year in November, Roosevelt expressed his hopes that the number of refugees permitted into Palestine would be increased. This very small step accomplished nothing for Jews seeking to leave Europe. Before German Jews faced the discriminatory non-policies of the United States, they had to find a solution to the discriminatory policies of Germany, namely that Jews could take no more than RM 200 in foreign currency out of the country, an amount insufficient to gain admission to the United States. In 1937, the figure was reduced to RM 10. Between 1933 and 1939, approximately 370,000 Jews emigrated from the greater German Reich. Only 60,000 obtained visas to go to the United States from either Germany or Austria, but likely more Jews made it to America after seeking transit through an intermediary country. Furthermore, between 1933 and 1943, a total of 168,128 Jews came to the United States on permanent visas. The total number of immigrants for the same period was 499,998. Another 43,944 Jews entered the United States on temporary visas. The immigration numbers for Jews in the ten years after Hitler came to power were reduced by half from the 1920s and were just an eighth of the total for the pre–World War I era. Some scholars have argued that even Jews were unaware of what awaited them after *Kristallnacht*, a coordinated destruction of Jewish neighborhoods in Germany that occurred November 9–10, 1938. Synagogues and homes were burned and windows were broken. The German Sturmabteilung, commonly known as the SA Storm Troopers, in and out of uniform led the rampage, which resulted in ninety-one Jewish deaths. A quarter of the Jewish men still in Germany were arrested and sent to concentration camps.[21]

Kristallnacht and Hitler's actions eight months earlier when Germany annexed Austria convinced some of the Jewish lawmakers who had previously not taken a role in the struggle between the restrictionists and the anti-restrictionists to call for reforms to the U.S. immigration laws. In 1938, Celler shocked the Zionist leadership in the United States when he introduced legislation that would eliminate quotas for refugees, the ban on persons likely to become public charges, minors traveling without their parents, and persons for whom passage was paid by an organized group. Congressional Zionists feared that negative reaction to this bill would make it impossible for the administration to pursue efforts on the margins to assist Austrian Jews. The bill was not given a hearing even though Dickstein chaired the House immigration panel, an otherwise conservative committee. Of additional concern was the spate of bills from restrictionists calling for severe cuts in the quota system. In 1939, restrictionist senator Robert Rice Reynolds (D-NC) read two and a half pages of advertisements from immigrants seeking work in the United States. As such he declared all immigration should be blocked because the country was still recovering from the ravages of the depression. Others called for the deportation of all aliens in the United States. Congress even defeated legislation to simplify naturalization for aliens already living in the United States who had children serving in the U.S. military.[22]

Political Zionism in Congress was not wholly a positive thing, stemming as much from prejudicial as from equalitarian thinking. Indeed, the restrictive U.S. immigration policy led to the realization that Jews needed somewhere to go. Jews and non-Jews rarely discussed the United States as a potential destination. Instead the failure of Great Britain, which held the mandate over Palestine, to liberalize Jewish immigration there became the target. Emanuel Celler complained to a journalist with the *Jewish Chronicle of London,* "It would truly be a cruel hoax on Jewry were Palestine to be divided" since it offered "the only refuge for us Jews." Sen. James E. Murray (D-MT) agreed repudiation of the mandate would "constitute a real catastrophe for these unfortunate refugees who are being despoiled of their property and ruthlessly forced from their homes."[23]

Congressional Zionists from Protestant, Catholic, and Jewish backgrounds reflected at best a myopic understanding of the challenges Jews faced. While this Zionism pushed some lawmakers further in support of Palestine as a Jewish homeland, it also contributed to the emergence of a U.S. Middle East policy that ignored Arab concerns. In February 1941, Wagner told Sen. Carter Glass (D-VA) of his efforts to revive the Zionist, Christian-dominated American Palestine Committee (APC). Ultimately 68 members of the U.S. Senate had signed on, including the leadership. Soon 200 members of Congress championed its mission as did various members of the Cabinet, several former presidential candidates, 15 governors, and key labor leaders. Wagner solicited Roosevelt's endorsement for the APC, asking the president's secretary to have FDR prepare a public statement. By the end of 1942, support for the American Palestine Committee had swelled in Congress, with lawmakers pushing the president to no avail to promote Palestine as a Jewish homeland.[24]

Leaders from the Arab National League, an organization founded in 1936 by Arab Americans to protect Arabs in Palestine, lobbied against the APC. They noted the importance of Middle Eastern oil to the Allied war effort and stressed that the Zionist goal in Palestine was "the most important cause for Arab resentment." Officials with the Arab National League maintained that there were serious concerns about Palestine as a Jewish refuge: "There are many other larger tracts of land throughout the globe that may be opened to Jewish Refugees without stirring trouble. Will you not help us in promoting Anglo-Arab good will by refraining from supporting political Zionism?" When Sen. Murray received this letter, he detailed his commitment to humanitarianism. Vocal support for Zionism was easier for American politicians than opening U.S. borders to Jewish refugees, especially in the late 1930s.[25]

"Do you think they are going to liquidate the Jews?" Rep. Cliff Clevenger (R-OH) posed this question to a witness before the House Immigration and Naturalization Committee. That the witness answered yes is significant. That Dickstein, the committee chair, concluded, "At the rate Hitler is going he can liquidate anything" is more significant. That this exchange took place in July 1939 is still more significant, suggesting a new and earlier timeline for what the government should have known and when it should have known it and also suggesting the importance of seniority as a tool in Congress to thwart consideration of policy reform when inaction and antistatism were preferred by conservatives and some moderates. Indeed, Noah M. Mason (R-IL), no liberal, said of the committee, "The whole damned committee is stacked with conservatives on both the Democratic and Republican sides."[26]

In the late 1930s, the House Committee on Immigration and Naturalization heard countless private bills for legalizing the U.S. residency of Eastern European Jews and German refugees already in the United States on temporary visas. Private bills differed from legislation designed for the general public in that the provisions only applied to the individuals named in the bills. Careful examination of these previously untapped hearings tells an important story about the congressional war between the powerful immigration restrictionists and the weaker anti-restrictionists, namely congressional indifference to human suffering in the abstract. Those with leverage in Congress cared far more about economic than social policy, making it difficult for lawmakers to see evidence of the Holocaust when action by the United States could have saved millions. For example, when the House Immigration and Naturalization Committee debated the status of individual Jews residing in the United States, members typically paid more attention to the legality of their entry than to the political realities facing Jews in Europe.[27]

Those seeking aid and those with political connections knew whom in Congress to approach for help and whom not to approach. The papers of sympathetic lawmakers are replete with countless tales of woe. Conversely, few such missives were sent to lawmakers oblivious to the problem or actively opposed to aiding Jewish refugees. For example, over 150 German and East European Jews wrote to Sen. Truman, sometimes directly and sometimes through an intermediary, for assistance leaving Europe or remaining in the United States. The correspondence was clinical and bureaucratic in nature. There was very little follow-up to determine the fate of the plaintiffs, suggesting the limits of compassion even among the anti-restrictionists.[28]

Sen. Lister Hill (D-AL) proved an exception when he had connections with the refugees seeking assistance. He worked extensively on one such case for a number of years. In the summer of 1940, he explained the transportation problems involved, namely that Jewish refugees had to travel by commercial steamer out of the port at Lisbon, Portugal. Moreover, Americans leaving the European war zone had priority for securing passage to the United States. The Montgomery, Alabama, cotton merchant who was lobbying Hill regarding this particular case opined, "This is a groundhog case. It is urgent, and if I ever wanted your assistance, I want it in this case." Hill replied: "I certainly am distressed to learn that your nieces have been removed to a concentration camp and again assure you if there is any possible way in which I can help you procure immigration visas for them, I will be glad to do so." The necessary visa was obtained for one of the women in April 1941, but the other died in a concentration camp before her rescue could be organized. The case of David Maisel reveals the haphazard appeals process for families without direct connections to Washington politicians. Maisel's two brothers already lived in the United States, in Mobile, Alabama, to be exact, and they used their friendship with the local sheriff and a local banker to deliver pleas to Hill. The senator said he would do what he could, but promised little given the "strict" immigration laws.[29]

Landmark immigration legislation passed in the 1920s, the Immigration Act of 1924, had established a restrictive quota system based on nationality and implicitly race, making this laborious process necessary. Then proponents of restriction propounded that immigrants who could not be assimilated, read to mean those from southern and eastern Europe, would reduce the American standard of living and harm the "basic strain" of the nation's population. The new law required usage of the 1890 census to calculate the quotas. Because 1890 was the last census prior to the massive southern and eastern European immigration to the United States, quotas for entry from that region of Europe were incredibly small, approximately 15 percent of the total number of immigrants permitted in any given year. This new policy codified a hierarchical construct of whiteness that left Jews out of the category of preferred immigrants. A decade or so later, Jews in Germany and Eastern Europe found it nearly impossible to escape to the United States given these racial policies. Proponents of the 1924 reform were partially guided by eugenics, but they also hierarchized Europeans by nationality to create white as a race separate from nonwhite. Ultimately, heredity trumped scientific racism, and this thinking still dominated social justice conservatism in Congress in the late 1930s and the 1940s. This mindset made any legislative fix nearly impossible. For example, Dickstein proposed the creation of a "pool quota," which would have combined the unused quota allocations and distributed them to migrants from countries with minuscule quotas. He only wanted to help "the better class of immigrants from countries which are discriminated against and let them come in and join their dear ones." Family reunification, not a blanket refugee policy, guided Dickstein, whose idea drew "strong opposition" from southern Democrats, center right social justice conservatives who "were always against immigrants on the general grounds that they did not like them."[30]

Meanwhile, Rep. Hamilton Fish (R-NY), an economic conservative with strong humanitarian views, waged war against Roosevelt's "complete refusal to make Hitler's genocidal racial policies an issue, his absolute silence while millions died." Fish recounted his unsuccessful efforts in 1933 to pass a resolution condemning German "economic persecution and repression of Jews." Later Fish took bolder steps to ease the problem. In 1939 while traveling in Europe on congressional business he received a request from an attorney, Fanny Holtzman, seeking visas for German Jews wishing to enter the United States. Fish explained that a legislative solution was not possible. When they spoke on the phone the next day Holtzman told Fish the refugees seeking visas were dismissed as "hysterical Jews." Fish replied angrily, "What are they supposed to do, stand by calmly and wait for Hitler to kill them?" Fish then took the next plane from London to Berlin. Holtzman had already told the American Embassy a powerful congressman was on his way. The two happened upon the following solution: Fish sponsored countless temporary tourist visa applications so that the Jewish refugees could come to the New York City World's Fair. At the same time he was procuring tourist visas for German Jewish refugees, Fish was also undertaking secret, unauthorized diplomatic relations with the British and the French to try to have space opened for 2 million refugees in Africa. Fish believed that Palestine was not a viable solution because of Arab opposition. His efforts drew the ire of the White House. Roosevelt wrote to Bernard Baruch, "I wish this great Pooh-Bah would go back to Harvard and play tackle on the football team. He is qualified for that job."[31]

Such problems resulted from the government's failure to recognize refugees as a distinct category. The weakened U.S. economy, State Department anti-Semitism, and immigration law led American consuls to be stringent with the granting of visas to Jews from Germany and Eastern Europe. In the mid-1930s, Labor Department officials, who were charged with oversight of the Immigration and Naturalization Service, accused the State Department of encouraging American consuls to compete to see who could admit the fewest immigrants. On average, national quotas went 90 percent unfilled. Dickstein blamed the American consuls abroad for making immigration to the United States difficult. After traveling throughout Europe, he advocated a simplified application process. He was especially angry about the use of "improper questions" to block potential immigrants "on the mental examination." Instead, the policies tightened further in the summer of 1940 when Immigration and Naturalization Services was moved to the Justice Department for national security reasons. All U.S. consular offices in Germany were closed in 1941.[32]

One newspaper editorialized in 1939 about the refugee crisis in the United States, complaining that in the previous year more refugees had come to America than anywhere else in the world. At issue was the use of temporary visas, which could be renewed an unlimited number of times, for entry. With immigration counted this way, the paper concluded there had been a 300 percent increase in immigration since 1933. The editor estimated 8 million people needed to leave Europe for political or racial reasons, an eerily close prediction of the number of people who would be killed in the camps.[33]

An aide to Rep. Robert Ramspeck (D-GA) disagreed. He contended the commitment to immigration restriction had not "been changed one iota since the first outburst in Germany." He continued, "The laws are enforced just as fairly and just as vigorously as ever. I emphasize this to set at rest rumors of wholesale evasions." Noting the many requests for help, the aide affirmed lawmakers could do nothing "except to provide information." He overlooked the obvious legislative solution. Acknowledging the need for immigration reform, Sen. Carl Hayden (D-AZ) averred, "Discussion of this question has been dominated by two classes of extremists, those who would exclude all immigrants . . . and those who would exclude none." A solution could only be found through compromise, impossible when the ideological war raged, when no effective leaders emerged, and when no one demanded a solution for reasons of military necessity.[34]

The lack of a centrist position on immigration made for strong opposition to the one legislative proposal designed for more than just one person. In early 1939, Sen. Wagner and Rep. Rogers introduced unpopular legislation authorizing the immigration of 20,000 German refugee children, aged fourteen and under. The nonquota entries would occur over a two-year period. *Kristallnacht* was the inspiration for Wagner-Rogers. The legislation provided that none of the children would become public charges. Wagner asserted, "This resolution would be the most immediate and practical contribution by the American people to the cause of human freedom." While lawmakers were still deliberating the measure, private organizations engaged in relief work among children began developing a strategy to implement the legislation should it pass, including the selection process in Germany and placement in the United States. Meanwhile, Roosevelt's response to the Wagner-Rogers bill was to write on the pertinent memorandum, "File No Action."[35]

Still, a joint House-Senate immigration subcommittee studied the legislation and heard from lawmakers and some celebrities, most notably the actress Helen Hayes. Organized labor and "patriotic organizations" charged that the measure should be rejected because of continued economic problems in the United States. While the United States was unwilling to act Great Britain adopted 5,000, and the Netherlands took an additional 1,700. Private polling of Senate opinion suggested there was little chance for passage. Initially only twenty-one senators favored the bill. Another twenty-four expressed opposition, while the remaining fifty-one would not answer. Many of the senators who would not give their opinion of Wagner-Rogers had stated their opposition to any kind of immigration reform

Sen. Robert Wagner, Helen Hayes, and Rep. Edith Nourse Rogers. Courtesy Library of Congress, Prints & Photographs Division, photograph by Harris & Ewing [reproduction number, LC-DIG-hec-26517].

that would admit more people to the United States. The bill died in committee, so well organized were the social justice conservatives fighting the measure. Not even the State Department dared to endorse Wagner-Rogers. It failed because the legislative restrictionists prevailed. None had qualms, though, about absorbing British children in 1940 who were victims of the blitz.[36]

Some of the anti-restrictionists were not willing to give up after the defeat of Wagner-Rogers. They proposed legislation that would open Alaska to settlement by refugees. Many of the same arguments were used here, but there were new criticisms as well. Alaska politicians were upset with the measure even though it promised substantial funding for developing the territory. They did not approve of the forced placement of refugees, who would not be eligible to move throughout the United States. Nor were the organizations and publications that had espoused Wagner-Rogers enthusiastic about this measure. Indeed, once the Wagner bill and the Alaska bill were defeated, the only remaining method with any hope of success was the use of private bills, a tepid at best solution because the only beneficiaries were those already in the United States who had political connections. Of the just under 400 private bill cases heard by the House Immigration and Naturalization Committee between 1937 and 1941, almost 30 percent were considered in 1937–1938, 50 percent in 1939–1940, and just over 19 percent in 1940–1941. Few if any were enacted into law.[37] These hearings reveal not only the extent of the congressional quagmire, but more important the outlines of Hitler's final solution.

At a 1939 hearing about permanent residency for two Germans, Dickstein asked if they could return to Germany, and Charles Jasper Bell (D-MO) replied, "It would mean the concentration camp." Another man hoping for refuge in the United States told the House Immigration and Naturalization Committee, "I am a Jew. I cannot go back to Germany." Such statements require a clear explication of how the concept of the concentration camp was understood in the United States in 1939, not late 1942 after publication of the final solution, or 1945 after liberation of the camps. During debate on an alien detention and deportation bill in 1939, Rep. Vito Marcantonio (AL-NY) maintained: "What makes a concentration camp? Is it the barbed-wire fence that makes a concentration camp? That does not make a concentration camp. . . . Imprisonment without due process of law is concentration camp imprisonment."[38]

The politics of immigration resulted in some most strange positions. Dickstein, the chair of the committee and a defender of Jewish refugees, argued, "I do not want it to appear . . . that we would be establishing a precedent because as you know we could have thousands and thousands of similar cases." During one debate, Albert E. Austin (R-CT) questioned why the committee was spending time on this problem. "What is the use, Mr. Chairman, of taking up the time of the Committee when we know positively there is nothing to be done with them," Austin observed. "Now here is a case in point. We can be Hitlerized if we want to and send this man back to Germany where he will be sent to a concentration camp and probably be shot with his wife and children. Why not leave them here?" Edward J. Shaughnessy, an official with the Labor Department, told the committee there were few good options. None could be deported to Germany because it was at war; or to Poland because the United States had not recognized the Russian-German division of Poland following the Hitler Stalin pact; or to the eastern European countries Hitler had conquered because they no longer existed as nation-states. Shaughnessy explained that the problem could only accumulate as long as the world was at war. Once hostilities concluded, he noted, the options would include a recalculation of the quotas or blanket immunity for all. He continued that the total number of cases could increase during the war, but he also noted that only "one-half of one per cent [were] criminals." The lawmakers voted to approve the bill, and residency for the family.[39]

Much speculation ensued about the timing of and reasons for the arrivals, especially by center right social justice conservatives. Debate about relief for Morris Schwartz proved most interesting. Rep. Charles Kramer (D-CA) elucidated, "He cannot go back to Austria, because he is a Jew. . . . He is another one of those cases of a man without a country." Schwartz had been in the United States when Austria fell to Germany, but Robert Poage (D-TX) was not satisfied with the explanation, noting he had come after Austria fell to Germany, "with the intention of staying to defraud the United States." In the case of a Romanian man who worked as a grain importer and exporter, Rep. A. Leonard Allen (D-LA) opined about impoverished Americans in the same field. "I think we should take care of our own people in the grain business first. I may be selfish, but it is an American selfishness." He ignored the earlier testimony that established the family's wealth, approximately $250,000. No action on the case would require the family to report monthly to the State Department, but Allen countered, "That won't hurt them." At a July 1941 hearing, Dickstein criticized the government's immigration rules: "They have got 4,000 questions and forms, and it would take eight lawyers, two from Philadelphia and two from New York and three from California" to have hope of admission.[40] The debate reflected the bankruptcy of Congress, especially in a committee that was unwilling or unable to admit and act on what it knew about Hitler's murderous intentions toward the Jews.

Once the war began the debates about immigration subsided. After Pearl Harbor, the number of private bill hearings regarding Jewish refugees plummeted to zero, but concern for Jews worldwide remained. Zionist lawmakers next fought to form a Jewish army, a more popular endeavor than any of the private bills. Advocates shared few common ideological views and were not always even on the same side of the question about immigration and citizenship. Raising a Jewish army did not threaten the racial status quo in the United States, the ideological balance of power, or the debates about the New Deal. Additionally Zionist lawmakers intensified the efforts to have Palestine opened to Jewish immigration from war-ravaged Europe. Writing for the American Palestine Committee, the liberal Wagner asked lawmakers to "support repeated request [that] Palestine Jewry . . . be organized in fighting force under their own flag." Sen. Theodore G. Bilbo (D-MS), a social justice conservative, told Wagner: "I endorse the proposition one hundred percent and I trust the British Government will authorize immediate enlistment, equipment and training of Jews and let them get on the firing line at once because of all the races on earth they have been sinned against the most." Legislative Zionists lobbied in private and public for a Jewish army. Truman, a moderate, ignored the full ramifications of the proposal, and alleged "American citizens ought to serve in the American Army." Meanwhile the liberal Pepper gave a major speech at Carnegie Hall in New York City where he asked, "Who, more than the Jews, deserve the honor of the battle's scars?"[41]

A majority of lawmakers never answered in the affirmative, though. On November 24, 1942, Gabriel A. Wechsler of the Committee for a Jewish Army wrote to Sol Bloom about the deterioration of conditions in Europe. According to an Associated Press report of that date, Heinrich Himmler, Nazi Gestapo chief, had called for the murder of half the Jewish population of Poland by December 1942. Wechsler noted a subsequent Associated Press report from the next day that 2 million of the 4 million Jews in the German-controlled areas of Europe had been exterminated. He questioned Bloom: "CAN ANYONE NOW DENY THE STATELESS AND PALESTINIAN JEWS THE RIGHT TO FIGHT BACK AS JEWS?" The answer, at least from an American perspective, was yes. Part of the reason for the failure of this crusade was the opposition of other leading American Jews, who professed the movement for a Jewish army was Zionist in inspiration, revealing Zionism as a more contentious philosophy than liberalism.[42]

Confirmation of the Holocaust only created further divisions about how best to rescue the Jews. Earlier Truman affirmed in April 1942: "The main effort is now for the United States to win the war as quickly as possible." The next year, after knowledge of the camps and their purpose was widespread, Truman noted the difficulty of even finding safe haven for refugees with the wartime dislocations. Other lawmakers appeared prostrate to do anything significant about the problem even as they bragged of their hard work on the issue. Sol Bloom bemoaned, "Permit me to advise you that if everyone, Jew or non-Jew, was doing as much as I am doing to relieve the terrible situation throughout the world today, the situation would be relieved immediately." To another constituent, Bloom declared that even the $50 million appropriation in the 77th Congress to assist "the distressed peoples of the Axis occupied countries" had been nothing more than a gesture since "it has proved impossible to obtain any assurance that any supplies sent to these unfortunate people would be permitted to be used by them."[43]

Still, the dawning realization of Hitler's schemes for exterminating Europe's Jews caused heightened debate about what must be done during and after the war. In November 1942, Elbert Thomas (D-UT) argued, "The problem of the Jewish homeland is thus a world problem. It is not just a Jewish problem. Freedom for the Jews should not be considered separate from freedom for other people." In early March 1943, the Senate passed a resolution similar to one that the British Parliament had passed stating its fury over Germany's slaughter of 2 million Jews, all empty words given the prewar decision.[44]

For the most vehement Zionist lawmakers more was necessary, but hopes that international diplomacy would provide a solution were dashed. When Roosevelt made plans to attend the Bermuda conference on International Refugees, he took no press and only two members of Congress, Sen. Scott W. Lucas (D-IL) and Rep. Bloom. The third delegate was the president of Princeton University, Dr.

Harold Dodds. Breckinridge Long encouraged the nominations of Bloom and Lucas to the U.S. delegation to the Bermuda conference. He chose them because he understood they would not push for a refugee policy but would support the State Department. Similarly, Roosevelt refused to invite Dickstein to serve on or accompany the delegation. Bloom took much criticism from the Yiddish press for his collaboration with the State Department. It called him "a shabbas goy," an insulting term reserved for non-Jews who performed work forbidden to orthodox Jews loyal to their faith.[45]

Because the Bermuda conference failed to satisfy Zionists, the Committee for a Jewish Army of Stateless and Palestinian Jews, which was created by Peter Bergson, a Zionist activist, and chaired by Sen. Edwin C. Johnson (D-CO), took out a full-page advertisement in the *New York Times* arguing "democracy cannot connive with the slaughter of millions of innocent civilian people—the Jews in Europe." The advertisement called for the United Nations to "now <u>do</u> something if these words of pity are to be more than empty lies." Specifically, the advertisement called for creation of a UN agency to "<u>deal, not with refugees outside Hitler's reach, but with the Jewish people under his yoke today.</u>" The Committee recommended the immediate movement of Jews from the region under German control to Palestine or some "temporary refuge." It also renewed the campaign for a Jewish army of stateless and Palestinian Jews. Truman complained that the advertisement "can be used to stir up trouble where our troops are fighting," especially among Arabs in North Africa. "We want to help the Jews," Truman asserted, "and we are going to help them but we cannot do it at the expense of our military maneuvers."[46]

Even though much of the work of the conference was subject to military censorship, Lucas addressed his colleagues on May 6, 1943, two days after the advertisement ran in the *New York Times*. With sarcasm and irritation, he noted "what is made clear by the advertisement is the fact that the persons who wrote it profess to know more about the report than does the committee which sat in Bermuda for some 11 or 12 days." Lucas contended, "This kind of advertisement plays into the hands of Adolf Hitler." In the discussion that followed, several of the senators listed in the advertisement purported their ignorance of it prior to publication and their disagreement with it after publication. James J. Davis (R-PA) termed the advertisement "untimely, unnecessary, and unhelpful." In a letter that he sent to his Senate colleagues, Johnson also condemned the advertisement. Later Truman told Stephen Wise, "It is fellows like Mr. Bergson who go off half cocked in matters that affect strategy of the whole world that cause all the trouble." The *New York Times* advertisement troubled Truman, who worried it would "be used to stir up trouble where our troops are fighting. . . . That ad was used by all the Arabs in North Africa in an endeavor to create dissension among them and caused them to stab our fellows in the back." A few intrepid Zionists in Congress did not back down when Lucas took umbrage at the *New York Times* advertisement. Sen. William Langer (R-ND) charged on the floor, "2,000,000 Jews in Europe have been killed off already and another 5,000,000 Jews are awaiting the same fate unless they are saved immediately."[47] Outrage about anti-Semitism produced few tangible results while exacerbating partisan congressional animus.

Still, the problem of Jewish refugees proved intractable. By summer 1943, Zionist lawmakers began calling for a plan to rescue the Jews in Europe still under Hitler's control. These efforts were bipartisan and defied categorization according to any of the cleavages within the war-era Congress. Zionist leaders lobbied Congress along a partisan divide, encouraging a bipartisan solution. Abba Hillel Silver aligned with the GOP while Stephen Wise, a partisan Democrat, lobbied the other side of the aisle. Rep. Will Rogers Jr. (D-CA) said the Jewish problem needed to be debated as an issue for humanity and not simply another item on "the dossiers of the diplomats." Rogers called for the creation of a rescue organization under the auspices of the United Nations. He argued, "There are enough open spaces and unpopulated areas to accommodate 4,000,000 tortured human beings." Palestine provided the best option, he suggested.[48]

This last phase in the congressional debate over Jewish refugee policy was the most important for charting the political course from war to postwar. Late in the war, Zionist lawmakers, a more encompassing but less well defined group than the liberal anti-restrictionists, fought hard for resolutions advocating the rescue of Jews in Europe and declaring U.S. support for Palestine as a Jewish state. The arguments were heated, and they previewed postwar debates about the same issue, which ultimately led to U.S. support for the creation of Israel in 1948. More important, when Congress inserted itself in the contentious politics of the Middle East it did so in large part because of interest group lobbyists representing foreign entities, making this policy domain unique for the era. The results further destabilized partisan cleavages in Congress and contributed to political discord in Washington, D.C. Because there was no dominant voice in the war era about this matter, the restrictionists carried the day, at least until the war ended. The discovery of the death camps proved that the brutal facts about man's inhumanity could function as a better leader than any president or member of Congress.

In late 1943, a bipartisan group of House lawmakers introduced the Baldwin-Rogers resolution, named for Reps. Rogers and Joseph Clark Baldwin (R-NY), requiring the president to name a commission with diplomatic, economic, and military experts to develop plans to save the remaining European Jews from destruction. The resolution made no mention of Palestine as a destination for refugees. Sen. Guy Gillette (D-IA) authored an identical resolution in the Senate. Despite the fact that he was at loggerheads with Gillette over an unrelated civil rights issue, Sen. Robert A. Taft (R-OH) cooperated with the Iowan on the resolution in the Senate. The two were a study in opposites with Gillette vociferous and Taft taciturn. The three lawmakers drew their inspiration from Peter Bergson, leader of a fringe, right-wing Zionist group, revealing the importance of interest group lobbying to the congressional policymaking process. Their effort attracted significant media attention but did not enjoy the unified support of all Jewish organizations in the United States. Wise lobbied hard against the resolution, leading Rogers to reply that his approach prevented politicizing the humanitarian rescue mission with political controversy over Palestine. One conservative Republican insisted that passage of the resolution would only bring further harm to the Jews, an opinion widely held in the government and the military. Critics of the resolution swore that if FDR and Secretary of State Cordell Hull were in fact doing all that was possible then a new agency was unwarranted. This resolution was controversial in the main because of the regressive views a vocal majority of Congress held on questions of immigration. *The New Republic* reasoned that if conservatives in Congress went unchecked, "we may come to regard the alien and sedition laws as the keystone of our civil liberties."[49]

Hearings on Baldwin-Rogers began in the House, and Bloom was not an ally. He used the hearings in his committee to attack the Emergency Committee to Save the Jewish People of Europe, the fringe group that had encouraged lawmakers to introduce the measure. Zionists disliked the resolution because it did not call for Palestine to be the Jewish homeland. The first battles were in the House where Bloom held a grudge for attacks against the Bermuda Conference. He stressed that the cost of rescue, approximately $2,000 per person, made it prohibitive. One Yiddish-language newspaper averred, "It is truly difficult to understand why it is such a life and death matter for Congressman Bloom to dig up arguments against the resolution." Pressure mounted, and Bloom later came out in favor of Baldwin-Rogers. This was not sufficient. Too many House lawmakers believed untrue claims from Long that the State Department's Intergovernmental Committee had been working in secret and achieving great results. They thus looked for ways to shelve the resolution without losing Jewish support, specifically publicizing the Long testimony. The strategy backfired when Long came in for tremendous criticism over his mendacious statements. Celler carped that Long "drips with sympathy for persecuted Jews, but the tears he sheds are crocodile." Nonetheless, Bloom's House Foreign Affairs Committee stalled in its consideration after Long suggested the measure was unnecessary, showing the pivotal role of seniority and committees to congressional outcomes.[50]

Division within the Jewish community was also a factor in Senate deliberations. Gillette complained, "I wish these damned Jews would make up their minds what they want. I could not get inside the committee room without being buttonholed out here in the corridor by representatives who said that the Jewish people of America did not want passage of this resolution." Connally affirmed hearings were unnecessary, but he tried to delay a vote until right before Christmas. Supporters of the measure—Gillette and Thomas—took advantage of his absence, called up the measure, and obtained a unanimous vote in favor. The committee report claimed the matter was not a "Jewish problem" but was a "Christian problem" demanding the immediate efforts of "enlightened civilization." Two days before the full Senate was to consider the resolution, Roosevelt signed an executive order creating the War Refugee Board, which was a victory for proponents of Rogers-Baldwin.[51]

Jewish constituents next lobbied Congress on behalf of a Senate resolution offered by Wagner and Taft providing for unlimited Jewish immigration into Palestine leading to the creation of a Jewish state there. Wagner acknowledged the need "to right the tragic plight of the Jews of the Old World and help them rebuild their ancestral homeland." The measure proved as much or more controversial than Baldwin-Rogers. Connally wrote Stimson and Hull for their opinions. Hull wanted to avoid a commitment one way or the other because there was no definitive Palestine policy. He asked Stimson to tell Connally that the resolution threatened military success. Stimson hinted that even public hearings posed a danger. In case Congress passed the resolution anyway, the State Department let Arab diplomats know the president would not view it as binding. Testimony from General George C. Marshall cinched the fate of Wagner-Taft. Marshall told the Senate Foreign Relations Committee that such a resolution would create great difficulty in the Muslim world. Marshall agreed to testify because of the military gravity of the situation and because no other witness would have the same credibility. After Marshall made his appearance the senators who heard the remarks voted unanimously to table Wagner-Taft. Sen. Arthur Vandenberg (R-MI) asserted: "He may be wrong: but he <u>might</u> be right—and the chance is <u>not</u> worth taking when the lives of tens of thousands of our American soldier sons are at stake." Later, Taft suggested the role oil played in the administration's thinking. "If the desire for oil is to prevail over the interests of the Jewish people in Palestine, I see no reason why it should not prevail indefinitely, for oil will become a more and more scarce commodity and the importance of the oil fields in Arabia will apparently increase," Taft naively avowed. "If the Palestine problem is settled right, why can't we hope for as much oil from Arabia as if it is settled wrong?"[52]

Additional drama came when Roosevelt questioned Marshall's testimony and hinted his support for Palestine as a homeland for Jewish refugees. Vandenberg argued, "I think our <u>civilian</u> 'Commander-in-Chief' had <u>better</u> 'give credence' to our real <u>military</u> Commander-in-Chief if we are to win this war with maximum speed and minimum casualties." The president's behavior on this question was a classic

FDR political ploy whereby he tried to retain a public image of supporting an intractable political position while using General Marshall to ensure defeat of the resolution because of military necessity.[53] It also revealed why so many in Congress—Democrats and Republicans—fought a war with the administration during the 1940s. Not only did lawmakers resent presidential intrusion in the legislative domain, but also they chafed against FDR's duplicitous leadership strategies.

Domestic and foreign protests continued. The U.S. government received complaints about the pending resolution from the Iraqi government. In response, Speaker Rayburn even wrote the president, warning of the "danger" of Iraqi politicking but assuring the president he had the situation "in hand." Such efforts did not dissuade Wagner, who emphasized: "Congress for over a century has decided questions on its own without interference from foreign countries." His indignant reaction measured congressional discomfort with interest group lobbying, especially when the source was foreign, nonwestern, and nonwhite. Stressing the resolution was "prejudicial to the successful prosecution of the war," Stimson asked Bloom to block the measure. Lawmakers tabled the resolution in an executive session.[54]

That September, Taft wrote to Stimson to inquire whether or not the War Department would maintain its objections to a resolution calling for "the free entry of Jews into" Palestine. While action was not forthcoming in the Senate, the House Committee on Foreign Affairs reported the resolution providing for a Jewish homeland in Palestine on November 30, 1944, but it stripped the all-important modifier "Jewish" before the noun "commonwealth." Wagner complained to Roosevelt that the Palestinian Resolution was being delayed in the Senate Foreign Relations Committee: "In view of the fact also that nearly four hundred Senators and Representatives are directly quoted in a House Document as favoring this Resolution it will be most unfortunate in my opinion, if this legislation is defeated in the Senate on the basis of the alleged opposition by you." Roosevelt told Wagner and Connally why it would be unwise to enact the resolution. The already large population of 500,000 Jews in Palestine combined with the additional million who hoped to immigrate there were "of all shades—good, bad and indifferent." Believing legislative action would exacerbate the situation, Roosevelt cautioned Jewish migrants to Palestine would be met by "approximately seventy million Mohammadans who want to cut their throats the day they land."[55]

A majority of the Senate Foreign Relations Committee wanted to vote in favor of the resolution, but Connally delayed until Secretary of State Edward Stettinius could explain his opposition to the measure. On December 8, 1944, Connally told his committee that while the State Department had been helping European Jews by assisting the War Refugee Board, it remained opposed to the Palestine resolution. The mixed messages from the administration were unacceptable to Zionist members of the committee. Vandenberg told a constituent the situation was "ex-actly the same" as in the spring when Secretary of War Stimson "partially with-drew his previous military objections (in a very equivocal letter)" only to have Roosevelt and the State Department "emphatically insist[ing] (behind the scenes and confidentially) that there ought to be no Congressional action on a contro-versial international issue of this nature at the present time." Vandenberg told of the demands that the administration make a public statement against the resolu-tion as the price of a committee vote against it. To solve the problem, Vanden-berg wrote a substitute resolution without the strong language of the original measure. Vandenberg's replacement gained passage, but by a narrow vote and over the harsh protests of the backers of the original resolution, who termed the Vandenberg offering as "'worse than no action at all.'"[56]

In late December 1944, the Iraqi government sent a message to the Senate For-eign Relations Committee and the House Foreign Affairs Committee, arguing: "Iraq and the other Arab countries consider Palestine to be an Arab country. . . . The Iraqi Government cannot remain as a spectator of the tragedy which the Zionists wish to enact on the stage of the world." The Iraqis objected that the pending Palestinian Resolution ran counter to the "principles of the Atlantic Charter and violates all the lofty principles of humanity." They blamed "Zionist propaganda" for overwhelming American lawmakers and blinding them to the Arab perspective. The Iraqis intimated: "The principle of interference in the des-tiny of the countries of others is an extremely dangerous one. This war is raging to exterminate that principle and to bring about justice among the peace-loving nations."[57]

The Palestine resolution stalled in Congress in the early months of 1945, and events in Europe following V-E Day were not unlike an earthquake in reconfigur-ing the topography of this debate. When Allied soldiers liberated the many Ger-man concentration camps a new and more terrifying level of knowledge about the Holocaust seeped out to the West. Hitler's systematic program to eliminate every Jew in Europe began in June 1941 immediately after Germany invaded the Soviet Union. Thousands and thousands of Jews were killed every day, and by war's end 6 of the 8 million European Jews had been murdered, victims of Hitler's maniacal fantasies of a master race and his insatiable quest for political power. Though Germans responsible for this machinery of death left meticulous records, the best accounts of what the Holocaust meant come from those people who sur-vived, the witnesses.[58]

On April 30 and May 1, 1945, members of Congress and their staffs screened a short film recounting Nazi atrocities. This formal introduction to the realities of the Holocaust provided stark, visual evidence to the remaining members who were not included on the congressional inspection tour, which had visited several

of the camps a few days earlier. Sens. Barkley, Walter F. George (D-GA), Elbert
Thomas, C. Wayland Brooks (R-IL), Kenneth S. Wherry (R-NE), and Leverett
Saltonstall (R-MA) along with Reps. R. Ewing Thomason (D-TX), James P.
Richards (D-SC), Edouard V. Izac (D-CA), James W. Mott (R-OR), Dewey Short
(R-MO), and John M. Vorys (R-OH) comprised the Joint Congressional Committee that made the inspection trip. General George C. Marshall and General
Dwight D. Eisenhower had requested the visit. Eisenhower told Marshall: "We
are constantly finding German camps in which they have placed political prisoners where unspeakable conditions exist. From my own personal observation I can
state unequivocally that all written statements up to now do not paint the full
horrors." The military leadership wanted a delegation of lawmakers and journalists to see the atrocities *before* they were cleansed from the record.[59]

Out of the 100 or more camps located in Germany and German-controlled
territory, the members of Congress visited only three of the major camps—
Buchenwald, Dora, and Dachau. Located slightly north of Weimar, Germany,
Buchenwald opened in 1937. Approximately a quarter of a million people from all
over Europe were imprisoned there. The overwhelming majority of Jewish prisoners there had been marched out in early April 1945 prior to the arrival of American troops. Originally a subcamp of Buchenwald, Dora was located in central
Germany and functioned as a forced labor camp. Its prisoners were removed
prior to the arrival of the Americans. Dachau was the oldest of the concentration
camps, established in 1933 to house political prisoners and located about ten miles
northwest of Munich. SS concentration camp guards were trained there. Like the
other two camps visited by the congressional delegation, the Germans had tried
to move prisoners out of the camp prior to the arrival of American troops, and
7,000 of the 67,665 prisoners there were sent on a death march.[60]

In a clinical statement for the press that described the horrors of the camps,
the committee noted the four classifications of prisoners: political prisoners, ha-
bitual criminals, conscientious and religious objectors, and persons in prison for
failure to work. "Although differing in size they all carried into effect the same
pattern of death by hard labor, starvation, disease, brutality, gas chambers, and
filthy and unsanitary conditions which meant inevitable death eventually to every
imprisoned person," noted the committee.

> We found hundreds of dead bodies piled around and scattered
> promiscuously and thousands still alive who will either die or would have
> died except for their liberation by the American armies. We found in each
> case that the supervision of the camp was carried out by the criminal tactics
> of the SS troops who, in addition to their own brutality, assigned some of the
> punitive duties to the prisoners, especially the habitual criminals who had

charge of barracks in which all types of prisoners were subject to their vicious and inhuman methods.[61]

The language in the committee report prepared the world for the war crimes trials that would later be held at Nuremberg. "We found this entire program constituted a systematic form of torture and death, administered to intellectual political leaders and all others, including the Jews who would not embrace and support the Nazi philosophy and program. We found the extent, devices, methods and conditions of torture almost beyond the power of words to describe." The committee concluded: "They reached depths of human degradation beyond belief, and constituted no less than organized crime against civilization and humanity for which swift certain and adequate punishment should be meted out to all those who were responsible."[62]

In his spiritual autobiography, Elbert Thomas revealed how the horrors of what he witnessed affected him. "My Americanism and my Mormonism were the most shocked. Here was a man representing a religion and a nation whose fundamental principles are based upon the concept of the worth of the individual. I was invited to observe situations where individual rights, personal dignity, and governmental protection of the individual were shattered. . . . Those experiences hurt me spiritually." Other members of the inspection tour were less philosophical and more visceral in their reactions. Vorys noted that not only was he an "eyewitness" but also an "ear and nose witness" to "the nauseating revulsion" of the camps.[63]

On Wednesday, May 9, 1945, the Jewish members of Congress (excepting Sabath who was ill and Bloom who was in San Francisco deliberating the United Nations Charter) met in Celler's office with various government officials about the plight of the Jews recently liberated from concentration camps in Germany and Eastern Europe. They agreed that Eisenhower should be asked to designate Jewish liaison officers to help handle the various refugee issues resulting from life in the concentration camps.[64]

The members of Congress who visited the liberated concentration camps spoke before their respective chambers in mid-May 1945. Barkley read the committee's report to the Senate as did Thomason in the House. Barkley lamented, "We saw the victims, both dead and alive, of the atrocities practiced at these camps. We saw the process of liquidation by starvation while it was still going on. We saw the indescribable filth and smelled the nauseating stench before it was cleaned up, and we saw a number of victims of this liquidation process actually die." Short was so repulsed with what he saw that he talked for over half an hour without notes of any kind. The "spellbound and horrified" listeners in the galleries applauded as did the lawmakers when he finished talking. Said one ob-

Sen. Alben Barkley touring Buchenwald concentration camp, April 25, 1945. Courtesy National Archives, photograph by Department of the Army.

server: "It took Short to tell it in the most brutal, most violent, most dramatic way." Short spoke of "the unutterable stench of rotting human flesh piled in mountainous windrows, the sight of human eyes glazed with the insensibility of a dying dog, of human whimpers at some little touch of kindness, of souls in which the lights had gone out and only the cinders remained." Short concluded that he would "never forget the bestiality that he found in Germany."[65]

Lawmakers who had been committed to opening Palestine to Jewish settlement redoubled their efforts after hearing the joint congressional committee's report about its visit to the concentration camps. "For as the Resolution points out, the use of anti-Semitism as an instrument in the lust for power has enabled Fascist forces to destroy democratic governments and institutions and to menace the peace of the world," Rep. Andrew L. Somers (D-NY) told his colleagues. "You will recognize that this Resolution is an expression of traditional American sentiments based on justice and righteousness." The key components of the resolution included recognition of a Jewish state in Palestine, granting international legal rights to the new state, repatriation of Jewish people to Palestine, and political independence for the new country. Not until December 1945 did Congress approve the Palestine resolution.[66]

With the war in Europe over, Wagner and Taft urged that Jews not "be made a football of power politics" but instead be granted easy access to Palestine. Uncritical reading of the arguments on behalf of Jewish settlement in Palestine make the lawmakers in question seem more enlightened than their reputations merit. Sen. Thomas C. Hart (R-CT) explained that the majority of Senate support for the Palestine resolution was not about the fate of "a chunk of desert" but the votes of Jewish Americans. Hart was one of a very few lawmakers who feared support for the resolution would "bring us the hatred of 200 million Muslims." Careful examination of the hearings into the few Jewish refugee camps established in the United States suggests the role racism and prejudice played in the struggle to open Palestine to the Jews.[67]

Beginning in the summer of 1944, the military had brought some refugees to the United States in order to relieve pressure in Italy and make the escape of other refugees from Germany and Eastern Europe possible. In the summer of 1945, the House Immigration and Naturalization Committee held a series of hearings at the various camp locations in the United States, and determined the "prisoners" to be "pure, good souled, loving, Christian people—some of Jewish faith and some of Catholic faith who just ran away from their homes and abandoned their property for the purpose of self-preservation." The War Relocation Authority, the same agency that administered the Japanese internment camps, oversaw this process. One such camp was located at Fort Ontario near Oswego, New York. Members of the committee expressed concern that the camp residents might still hold allegiances to Nazism or fascism, but the camp official who testified disagreed. The majority of refugees were in fact stateless Jews. The citizenship rights granted to babies born in American camps concerned members of Congress. Dickstein ultimately provided enough pressure that the camp residents were permitted permanent residency in the United States.[68] The unfolding of this small drama paralleled all the previous immigration and refugee debates of the war years in that it was solved on an ad hoc basis.

Members of Congress struggled with questions about refugees and immigration because all too often they considered such issues according to a racial hierarchy. Unlike policymakers earlier in the century who created the restrictive quota system, though, World War II–era officials were willing to amend the racial constructs of immigration and citizenship policy for reasons of military necessity, as in the case of repeal of the Chinese Exclusion Act, but not for reasons of humanitarian rescue, as in the case of prewar Jewish refugees. For example, one member of Congress complained about policies that would result in the admission of "the 'dregs' of Europe" to the United States.[69] The prevalence of such characterizations of Jewish refugees in Congress ensured that the restrictionist, anti-Semitic faction would always trump the Zionist, anti-restrictionist politicians, at least when there was any chance for rescue. This realization is all the more tragic because the hearings before Dickstein's committee in the late 1930s prove beyond a doubt that Congress had definitive evidence of Hitler's murderous intent when there was still a possibility for rescue. Complex reasons intimately related to an often perverse institutional culture meant there was no will to act on in the horrific knowledge of the Holocaust.

6. A "Virtual Black-Out of Civil Liberties" and the Politics of Prejudice

"We will not be misled by the vicious propaganda of the enemy nor deviated by ancient or superficial disagreements either geographical, racial or religious," so said Senate Majority Leader Alben Barkley (D-KY) in a 1942 speech honoring the national service of African Americans. Barkley was correct to note the patriotism of people of color during World War II, but neither did Americans generally nor a majority of Congress admit this conspicuous fact. The fulminations of racist southern demagogues dominated the political discourse and prevented an expansion of New Deal economic liberalism to include civil rights liberalism.[1]

Racist rhetoric masked another more potent gambit less focused on oratory and more on tactical maneuvers. In the late 1930s, realizing the inevitability of civil rights reform, southern senators developed a strategy of delay that they buttressed with frequent references to constitutional principles and an antistatist governing philosophy. Disproportionate power in Congress through the seniority system allowed southern lawmakers to hijack the committee structure and prevent legislative action. Their efforts were crucial to the fate of New Deal liberalism in the war years. For example, Rep. John E. Rankin (D-MS), "a little man with bush hair and a hallelujah voice," declared in a reelection speech, "We are now in the midst of the greatest war of all time." Though he meant the military battles of World War II, the rest of his remarks suggest a dual meaning: the antidemocratic efforts to maintain the Jim Crow South. Then he segued into a vile attack on African Americans. He wanted the Red Cross to retain racial labels on blood, blaming "these radical parlor pinks" for not respecting white southern prejudices. Rankin asserted, "The Red Cross is standing firm. . . . We are not going to have the blood of other races injected into the veins of our white boys."[2]

Lawmakers refused to enact new laws protecting the civil rights of African Americans, and the White House, which viewed civil rights claims as an impediment to the war effort, never pushed for reforms. FDR's inaction endeared him to hardly any in Congress, especially liberals who resented his lack of leadership. This dangerous calculus exacerbated partisanship and proved an incubator for social justice conservatism, leaving the southern Democrats in Congress behind the attitudinal shifts in the region. By the 1930s, fewer not more local white southern leaders openly defended practices like lynching. Moreover, U.S. foreign policymakers worried about the negative impact of racism at home on war aims abroad. How could the country pronounce itself to be the bastion of democracy while apartheid-like conditions permeated the South? The answer: it could not. U.S. war aims abroad to advance democracy globally were incongruous with domestic policy, which furthered discrimination and prejudice. While making this argument, the NAACP deployed its strategy of effecting change through congressional lobbying and court challenges, not mass action. Thus, interest group lobbying proved even less effective than in the Jewish refugee and immigration debates. The lack of tangible results did not dissuade additional lobbying, but this new style of advocacy politics further destabilized the political system, aggravating the partisanship and enraging conservative critics of the New Deal. The predominant southern device within Congress for preserving the racial status quo was the filibuster. This "instrument of minority rule," as one observer phrased it in the 1940s, constituted an effective tool for ensuring the poll tax remained inviolate and that there be no federal legislation outlawing lynching, the terroristic practice of the white South toward interracial challenges to the racial status quo.[3]

Indeed, southerners controlled much of the debate about civil rights questions even if they did not represent the majority of Congress or the country. Strategies ranged from the behind-the-scenes leadership of senators such as Richard B. Russell (D-GA) and Tom Connally (D-TX) to the public demagoguery of Rankin and others not embarrassed by social justice conservatism. At the end of the 1940s, one Washington columnist explained the southern congressional strategy as implemented by Russell: "Leads the best disciplined bloc in the Senate. Keeps a Southern Senator on the floor on sentry duty every minute the Senate is in session to make sure nothing is put over on the South."[4]

Individuals and organizations reflecting a diverse range of the political spectrum had been working against the barbarous practice of lynching for decades. As W. E. B. DuBois noted, there had been approximately 3,000 lynchings between 1900 and 1946, but only 135 persons were convicted for these crimes. Initially, the struggles had been focused on the court of public opinion and included the work of black and white southern women, namely Ida B. Wells and Jessie Daniel Ames. By the 1930s, the anti-lynching issue, which had first been introduced in Congress in 1918, had attracted increased congressional attention, but Franklin D. Roosevelt had never exerted the political capital necessary to bring the question to a vote. Given the power of the seniority system and the southern control of key committees, he knew that he needed white southern Democratic support for the New Deal, so he compromised, overlooking southern hypocrisy on the issue. In 1934, Sen. Tom Connally (D-TX) criticized pending anti-lynching legislation for authorizing federal punishment of lynchers, and when he attacked the 1940 version of the bill for failing to include such provisions, NAACP leaders characterized his response as "thoroughly dishonest." Fifty-five percent of the public with an opinion favored the proposed federal lynching law in February 1940.[5]

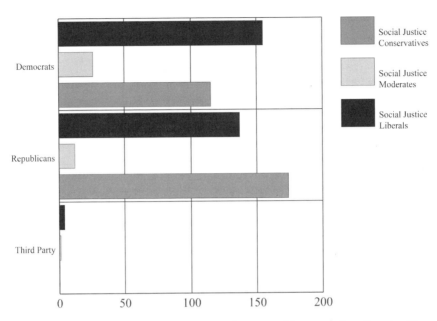

Chart 6.1: The Southern Strategy in Congress—The House of Representatives. Data for this chart are derived from analysis of key social justice policy roll call votes from the war era.

As the world crisis worsened, the southern congressional defensiveness about lynching intensified. In January 1938, Russell told John Boykin, the Georgia Solicitor General, "Have concrete evidence so called antilynch bill first step in legislative program aimed at South supported by Communist Party." By December 1938, Connally emerged as one of the southern leaders in the fight against antilynching legislation. While Connally functioned as the "brains" of the southern opposition to the anti-lynching legislation and the anti–poll tax legislation, individuals like Rankin and Sen. Theodore "The Man" Bilbo (D-MS) were "the chief gunmen for the poll-tax system in Washington." The southern strategy relied on an informal alliance with Republicans, who used the relationship to hurt the Democratic Party, but on roll call votes the alliance was more fictive than real, as Charts 6.1 and 6.2 show. The Republicans who voted to obstruct social justice measures counted for approximately half of the party's strength in the two chambers, but when particular roll calls are examined, the bulk of the Republican social justice conservatives earned that designation for their support of the Dies Committee's anti-Communist agenda not their opposition to civil rights legislation. The number of social justice liberals who were also Republican cannot be overstressed; the GOP was as divided on civil rights and pluralism as was the Democratic Party. Social justice moderates were inconsequential. Charts 6.3 and

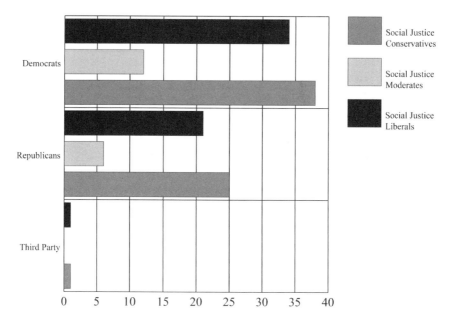

Chart 6.2: The Southern Strategy in Congress—The Senate. Data for this chart are derived from analysis of key social justice policy roll call votes from the war era.

6.4, though, evaluate the problem regionally. The non-southern votes against civil rights came from the Northeast and the Midwest, not the West, in the House, but in the Senate a comparable number of westerners, northeasterners, and midwesterners opposed civil rights. Nevertheless Sen. Joseph F. Guffey (D-PA) described the combination of southern Democrats and northern Republicans as an "unholy alliance" and he charged the southern Democrats with being a "Fifth Column" movement within their party.[6]

Connally glossed over the cooperative relationship with Republicans and instead reckoned, "Some anti-Southern Democrats always thought they could pick up more home votes by attacking us southerners rather than by attacking Republicans." He earned a reputation for his gruff manner regarding the subject. Walter White, secretary of the NAACP, complained that Connally "badger[ed] the witnesses" testifying in committee "pretty much as a small town attorney would treat a penniless and friendless Negro." Connally kept a list recording senatorial votes on cloture on the anti-lynching bill that, ironically, had been prepared by the NAACP. In January 1939, Connally asked the Tuskegee Institute to send him a detailed report on all lynching cases for 1939 along with a "statement of number of cases in which officers prevented lynching and statement as to whether socalled lynchings showed any cases in which victim was taken from officers." Connally

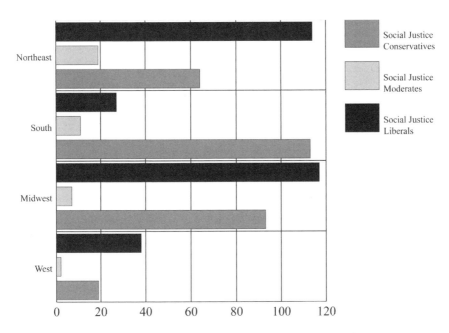

Chart 6.3: Regional Cooperation and the Southern Strategy—The House of Representatives. Data for this chart are derived from analysis of key social justice policy roll call votes from the war era.

also encouraged his southern senatorial colleagues to provide him with information about lynchings in their states.[7]

The Texan wrote to the editor of the *Sheriff's Magazine of Texas:* "I wish you would advise the sheriffs and peace officers through your columns of the implications and effects of the pending Anti-Lynching Bill. I am sending you a copy of this bill and I hope you will peruse it. It is leveled not against those who take part in mob action but against sheriffs and peace officers and the tax-payers of a county." Connally acknowledged his role as "spokesman in resisting and fighting its passage." He requested that Texas sheriffs who had prevented mob actions against prisoners in 1939 write him the facts of the cases so that it could be used to "combat the bill." Connally suggested that the magazine note only two lynchings happened in 1939, but "on the other hand, there were numerous cases in which peace officers prevented lynchings and thereby showed that more could be effected through the responsibility and vigilance of these local peace officers than from any Federal legislation. Won't the sheriffs of Texas communicate with Senator Connally and advise him respecting this matter." Connally's statement in the Texas sheriff's magazine was published.[8]

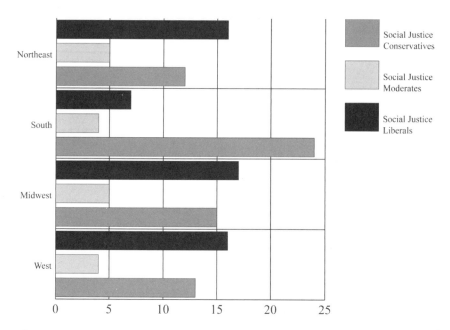

Chart 6.4: Regional Cooperation and the Southern Strategy—The Senate. Data for this chart are derived from analysis of key social justice policy roll call votes from the war era.

Southern Democrats disguised their race-driven opposition to anti-lynching legislation with arguments that the problem was insignificant in statistical terms. Said Connally to Ames, with whom he was friendly, "Thank you for sending me the clippings respecting the alleged lynching in Georgia, which was later proved a myth." To another reformer, Connally avowed, "The House of Representatives voted down an amendment to have the law also cover gangster murders and killings, which constitute mob action just as much as the so-called lynchings. This reveals its political and partisan aspect." On another occasion, Connally discredited the reform proposal as "legislation based on race purely for political effect." Yet, in the same sentence he stressed, "I have no prejudices whatever against the colored race."[9]

Whereas Connally tried to show lynching was no longer an issue, Sens. Robert F. Wagner (D-NY) and Arthur Capper (R-KS) and Reps. Joseph A. Gavagan (D-NY) and Hamilton Fish (R-NY), all proponents of anti-lynching legislation, sponsored a report about the new characteristics of lynching, noting white southerners had gone "underground" with the ugly practice because "Public opinion is beginning to turn against this sort of mob activity." Earlier in the century, hundreds and sometimes thousands of people treated such events as a public spectacle. Midcentury lynchings deviated from turn-of-the-century practices in that they often were "done quietly so as not to attract attention, draw publicity. Thus those who must rule by terror and intimidation turn to new methods." This shift in practice was the consequence of an effective campaign by the NAACP and other groups to demonize lynching as the most brutal of acts. After a real or fictitious crime had been charged, "A few white men gather, formulate their plans, seize their victim. In some lonely swamp a small body of men do the job formerly done by a vast, howling, bloodthirsty mob composed of men, women and children. The word is then passed that the matter has been handled." The report concluded, "Countless Negroes are lynched yearly, but their disappearance is shrouded in mystery, for they are dispatched quietly and without general knowledge."[10]

Debates about the lynching bill became partisan when Rep. Arthur Mitchell (D-IL), the only African American in Congress, carped that Republican support for the bill was not genuine but was an attempt to "buy back" the black vote for the GOP. His remarks angered GOP lawmakers. Hamilton Fish inquired whether Mitchell's charge meant black votes could be bought. Mitchell expressed outrage at the idea. He attacked the Republican Party for its history of false promises to help blacks advance. His arguments reflected a larger political realignment occurring within the African American electorate away from the GOP and to the Democrats, despite the racial conservatism of southern Democrats. The party of Roosevelt became attractive to African Americans because the New Deal order had had a more positive impact on blacks than decades of Republican policies. Both within the early New Deal's anticapitalist phase and its later articulation of individual rights were liberal ideals offering a promise of improvement for African Americans. "The day has come when you cannot fool the Negro like you used to," Mitchell asserted. "There are some of us who have the courage to tell the truth. We know who our friends are and we are going to stand by them."[11]

The partisan warfare was not contained within Congress but also included moderate lawmakers squabbling with the NAACP. By late April 1940, White and Barkley were at war with one another, making it difficult to obtain results in the Senate, even for a weak bill. The federal anti-lynching legislation that Congress debated but never approved during the war years authorized federalizing the crime when state authorities failed to act, a statist solution discomfiting to states' rights lawmakers, who favored local authority over federal authority. Nonetheless, Barkley fumed over White's "inexcusable misstatements" and lack of respect for the "utmost courtesy" he had shown the NAACP, revealing an expectation of deference from White not uncommon in southern white men with regard to African Americans. This mattered politically as well because Barkley, while not among the more powerful majority leaders in Senate history, influenced the Senate agenda. Moreover, he possessed a unique position in that he was southern, moderately liberal in his political orientation, and willing to support anti-lynching legislation. Because the bill could not survive a filibuster and because important war measures were pending, Barkley saw no reason for a floor debate. He complained of White's pressure tactics: "you caused to be published in the 'Louisville Defender', a colored newspaper, . . . the statement that I was holding up a vote on this bill, that I was opposed to it, that ever since last November I had refused to confer with you or Senator Wagner about it." Barkley accused White of planting the erroneous story "for the purpose of attempting to build a fire under me by sort of local intimidation."[12]

White retorted that "a great many people throughout the country" resented "the manner in which this legislation for years has been kicked about in the Senate." Furthermore, he fumed that the obstructionist tactics in the Senate had cost taxpayers $460,000 in 1938 when a seven-week filibuster prevented consideration of any legislation. White also gave Barkley substantial evidence of his unsuccessful efforts to schedule a meeting with the Senate supporters of anti-lynching legislation, ironic since all parties proclaimed the same goal. The NAACP wanted the anti-lynching bill to be made a top priority. He suggested Barkley and the Senate leadership lacked the "moral courage to oppose the brazen tactics of the minority."[13]

Regarding the feud, White told a supporter the Democratic leadership did not want to debate the anti-lynching bill during an election year. He asserted that Barkley's attitude was typical of "most southern white men, and even a great many northern white men" for he "believed that Negroes could be soft-soaped." White and the NAACP saw through Barkley's strategy and maintained pressure for legislative action, which caused Barkley to "los[e] his temper . . . [and] wr[i]te that intemperate and wholly unfounded letter and, either consciously or subconsciously, believed as most southern white men do that when a white man speaks to a Negro the latter is going to accept the white man's statement." In September 1940 the controversy between Barkley and the NAACP worsened when some African American newspapers reported that the Kentucky senator had said the anti-lynching bill was a "dead horse." Barkley denied the comment, but the result was the same.[14]

After the war began, proponents of the anti-lynching legislation tried but failed to use the international situation as justification for reform. In a radio speech, Sen. Wagner condemned the "virtual black-out of civil liberties" around the globe. He stressed that the United States must synchronize its global propaganda with its internal policies. "If we are to vindicate our proud position as the foremost example of a functioning democracy, if in the eyes of the world we are to practice what we preach," Wagner avowed, "we must put an end to the barbarous practice of lynching. . . . To ignore the menace of the lynching mob is to acquiesce in the tactics by which dictators rode to power." The NAACP was more bold in its pronouncements. One NAACP official telegrammed Roosevelt: "Three lynchings within five days in Mississippi are as much sabotage of our nation's war effort as a bomb in an airplane factory or a shipyard. Nothing angers and embitters thirteen million American Negroes like lynching. Nothing delights the Axis powers more."[15]

Much more congressional attention was given to the anti–poll tax bill than the anti-lynching bill. Repeal of the poll tax threatened to upend the political structure in the South by enfranchising African Americans as full citizens and voters whereas the anti-lynching bill only struck at the use of violence to maintain white hegemony in the region. Black voting rights, conservative southern white politicians feared, would not only upend the power dynamics in their states but also the moderate political order in Washington, D.C., that gave them so much power through the seniority system. During the war years, eight southern states used the poll tax as a prerequisite for voting: Alabama, Arkansas, Georgia, Mississippi, South Carolina, Tennessee, Texas, and Virginia. The taxes seemed low, between one and two dollars, but they were cumulative and subject to penalties for periods of nonpayment. Officials with the NAACP estimated as many as 10 million Americans were disenfranchised as a result. Even the small sums charged were beyond the means of sharecroppers and the worst-paid urban workers. Among African Americans, the former earned as little as ten to fifteen cents a day while the latter only commanded ten to fifteen cents an hour. In Mississippi only 2,000 African Americans out of a population of 1.8 million voted.[16]

Rep. Lee E. Geyer (D-CA) was the first member of Congress to introduce an anti–poll tax bill. He did so in August 1939 at the behest of the Southern Conference for Human Welfare, a Birmingham, Alabama–based organization that attempted to implement New Deal–style reforms in the South. Geyer sponsored the bill only after no liberal southern Democrat would. Introduced as an amendment to the Hatch Act of 1939, a measure that checked political corruption, the Geyer bill only applied to the general election for federal races, a limited but statist measure. Liberal senator Claude Pepper (D-FL) introduced a wholly different anti–poll tax bill that year. The Pepper bill was much more direct. It posited the unconstitutionality of the poll tax. As such, the Pepper bill would have eliminated the poll tax in primary and general elections whether they be federal or state contests, also statist but much more aggressive. Subsequent anti–poll tax bills were based on the Pepper model. Sen. Harold Burton (R-OH) discounted the use of the poll tax as a factor to determine voting qualifications. He postulated, "I believe that a person is equally qualified to vote whether or not at the moment he has a few dollars in his pocket." A Michigan congressman complained that the poll tax provided disproportionate power to southern lawmakers, and certainly the elimination of people of color from southern voter rolls along with the region's one-party politics abetted the lengthy congressional service of many southerners in Washington, magnifying the ideological strains of the war years even though there was no clear non-southern liberal versus conservative dichotomy on this aspect of racial politics. Just under 40 percent of the longest-serving lawmakers, twenty or more years, were southerners from poll tax states. One-third of the committee chairs in the Senate and just over that percentage in the House were from poll tax states. Furthermore, poll tax state lawmakers held the gavel for four of the ten most significant House committees.[17]

In the spring of 1941 a Gallup Poll captured national and regional perspectives about the poll tax. Sixty-three percent of Americans regardless of region advocated abolition of the poll tax, but the results were different in the South. A bare majority, just 51 percent, of southerners in the five states without the poll tax (Florida, Kentucky, Louisiana, North Carolina, and Oklahoma) supported its repeal while 59 percent of those southerners in the eight states with the poll tax opposed repeal. Ironically, 53 percent of southerners in states with the poll tax who had not paid it endorsed its retention.[18]

One key strategy for preserving the status quo came from the specious argument that the poll tax was not a disincentive to voting in general elections. The truth of the statement masked the one-party reality of midcentury southern politics whereby elections were decided in the Democratic Party because there was no viable GOP in the region. For example, Sen. Carter Glass (D-VA) told a journalist of the tens of thousands of Virginians who did not vote even though they paid the tax. "I have been thoroughly convinced that it is not the poll tax which prevents people from voting in Virginia," Glass averred, "but indifference to the right of suffrage." The following year conservative senator Burnet R. Maybank (D-SC) made the same point about poll tax payment rates and voter turnout. He alleged the poll tax was actually a "Revenue Measure" to fund public education. He concluded, "In my opinion it is unfortunate that the Federal Government is again interfering in the financial business of the Sovereign States."[19]

Lawmakers advocating poll tax repeal began working in earnest on the issue after Pearl Harbor. Pepper lobbied hard with his colleagues most likely to support the anti–poll tax bill. Southern opponents of reform believed otherwise. For example, Bilbo called the anti–poll tax bill a "rape" of the "constitution." His vituperative, hate-filled racist rhetoric against civil rights was a sharp departure from the economic liberalism that dominated his political career in the 1930s as a southern New Dealer, revealing exactly how easily social justice conservatism could trump economic liberalism and enable the constriction of the New Deal. Sober southerners like Harry F. Byrd (D-VA) and Kenneth McKellar (D-TN) op-

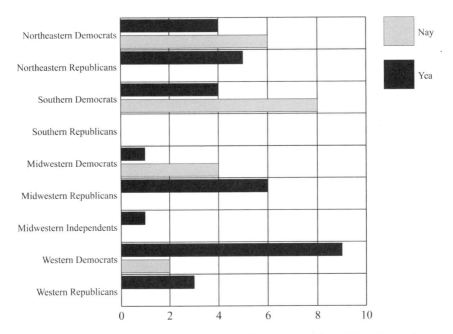

Chart 6.5: Region and Party Identification—The Soldier Vote and the Poll Tax, Senate. Data for this chart come from analysis of the August 25, 1942, record vote in the Senate. See Congressional Record, *77th Congress, 2nd session, 6971.*

posed the filibuster as one more thing that would make the Congress look bad. They also feared that it would be a tool the Axis could exploit. Similarly, Rep. John Sparkman (D-AL), otherwise a moderate, called the anti–poll tax bill a "lynching of constitutional law" that must be stopped in the Senate.[20]

Any consideration of the anti–poll tax initiative during the war years needs also to include the soldiers' vote controversy for efforts to ease access to the ballot, for the military refracted disagreements about the poll tax. A 1942 bill to make possible the right to vote for members of the service included a provision to suspend poll tax collections for those individuals. Sen. Charles W. Brooks (R-IL), who offered the amendment in the Senate, contended, "We have drafted these men. We have reached into the states to put them into the service and to tell them where they must go to serve. We have an equal responsibility now to preserve their rights for them. 'Political restrictions as usual' are over." The measure passed the Senate 47–5 on August 25, but the vote on the amendment to remove poll tax collections earlier that day was much closer, 33–20, with almost as many northeastern as southern Democrats opposing the amendment as Chart 6.5 shows. No Republicans voted nay and few voted at all, revealing that the conservative coalition was not operative in this debate. Southern votes for passage of the bill resulted because of two reasons: fear that opposing it would be depicted as antipatriotic and knowledge that the law would have no impact on the 1942 elections in the region for it would not go into effect until after the Democratic primaries, the only meaningful election in the one-party South.[21]

Several themes emerged, all showing the complexity of a global war for domestic politics, especially partisan divisions over ideology. Rep. John F. Hunter (D-OH), a backer of the soldiers' vote legislation, complained that southern Democrats worried such measures would be a wedge for gaining consideration of the anti–poll tax legislation. Hunter noted that Roosevelt privately supported the soldiers' vote legislation even though he had not done so publicly. Regarding the controversy over legislation to exempt soldiers from payment of any required poll taxes, Pepper argued, "This has not yet become an idealistic or an ideological war on the part of the United Nations, because we are finding ourselves hamstrung almost every time we turn with some kind of restraint, or discrimination, or inconsistency, or paradox which pollutes the purity of any idealism which we might profess." Rep. Robert Ramsay (D-WV) insisted that the remaining isolationist bloc in Congress was "secretly but bitterly" opposed to the soldiers' vote bill out of fear that such votes would lead to their collective defeat. "All the isolationists are bushwhacking the bill. They don't dare oppose it openly, so they object to it on constitutional grounds. And after the Senate stuck in the poll tax amendment, they wanted to bet me that the bill would never become law. I don't know that it will become a law, but we are going to make a real fight for it."[22]

In late August, the House had passed a soldiers' vote bill without provision for repealing the poll tax. An aid to Speaker Sam Rayburn (D-TX) explained to the speaker: "After a great deal of skullduggery on the part of Major [Alfred] Bulwinkle [D-NC] and Otis Bland [D-VA], we got the Soldier's Vote Bill to conference today." There House conferees agreed to endorse the Senate bill. Rankin was the sole holdout. He bellowed, "This measure is a monstrosity, shoved through in the name of the American soldier, who did not ask for it. It is an attempt to wipe out the election laws as well as the registration laws of the various states." Center right social justice conservatives used the states' rights defense to mitigate their otherwise noxious, anti-democratic arguments to maintain the electoral status quo in the South. Rankin concluded electoral reforms such as soldiers' vote legislation and anti–poll tax legislation were "part of a long-range communistic program to change our form of government . . . and to take the control of our elections out of the hands of white Americans in the various states and turn them over to certain irresponsible elements." The House passed the conference committee report 248–53 on September 9, not so much for reasons of civil rights but as a war measure, suggesting just how little support existed in Congress for social and humanitarian reform in wartime and just how important the argument of military necessity was for overcoming the partisan gridlock that otherwise stagnated the national government in the 1940s. The New Deal welfare state was no more; a warfare state emerged in its place and policy decisions flowed from evaluations about military impact.[23]

Navy Secretary Frank Knox opposed overseas balloting for soldiers for fear that the practice might reveal secrets to the enemy. In response, Sen. Clyde Herring (D-IA) reasoned: "The ballots could go along with letters from the mothers of the boys. Mail from home doesn't reveal any information to the enemy and neither would the ballots. . . . Of course it will require a little more work for some of the people in the War and Navy departments to handle the war ballots." Herring stressed, "These cocktail party soldiers and sailors here in Washington" needed "to do some work for the boys who are doing the fighting." He wanted to make sure the war and navy departments adhered to new statutes regarding suffrage, arguing "they'd damned sure better not violate an act of Congress." Still, the mechanism for soldier voting was weak and it was enacted so late that only 28,000 soldiers used it to vote.[24]

Even as Congress managed to pass a weak soldiers' vote bill in 1942, it was much less successful with the anti–poll tax legislation. Getting the anti–poll tax bill to the House floor proved more difficult because the Judiciary Committee refused to discharge the bill. Work on a discharge petition had begun in the summer, but proponents were well short of the required 218 signatures, a simple majority of the House membership. According to an NAACP poll of friendly House members released in July 1942, thirty-eight signed a discharge petition for the Geyer poll tax bill, another four said they would sign, two expected to sign, four were giving consideration, and nine indicated they could not sign. Other members gave an array of responses from "pledges [of] support" to promises to "keep views in mind" and "will give consideration when before [the] House." Joseph W. Martin Jr. (R-MA), the Minority Leader, said he "does not sign petitions unless approved by Rep. Conf." The statement lacked political courage because as minority leader he had no small influence within the Republican conference, but it also reflected a degree of legislative independence from interest group lobbying, which functioned through tactics of group coercion. According to a September 1942 report by Walter White, thirty additional signatures were needed to force a floor debate regarding the Geyer anti–poll tax bill. Rep. Gavagan worried that Geyer's death on October 11, 1941, meant the bill would have to be abandoned. Interested lawmakers met in conference to devise a compromise whereby Congress continued to consider the measure through the remainder of that session.[25]

Cliff Clevenger (R-OH) was the 218th member of the House to sign a discharge petition freeing the anti–poll tax amendment from the House Judiciary Committee. He had been opposed to the discharge petition as an agent of disunity in wartime, but the partisan arguments caused him to rethink his position. He intimated, "There was a lot of demagoging going on regarding this issue. There was a lot of political heat on it, and it was being used against some of the boys, Republicans, in their districts. I decided we had just as well drag it out on the floor and vote on it. You can't quote me on this, but in any number of districts the poll tax was a political issue." He indicted northern Democrats, saying they pushed the bill for partisan and racial reasons to court African American voters. "Republicans in the north who hadn't signed the petition were having that used against them," Clevenger affirmed. "I decided to stop it." Democratic leaders were afraid to discuss the issue. Majority Leader John W. McCormack (D-MA) attested that northerners had no complaint with using the poll tax for a revenue measure but were troubled with its use to restrict African American voting. Even Rep. Robert C. Ramspeck (D-GA) said off the record that the South would be better off without the poll tax, but he exhorted an antistatist solution whereby the tax should be eliminated at the state level not by the federal government. Other southerners were more typically outspoken against the bill. Sam Hobbs (D-AL) implored: "I tell you that the day this is passed, property values in many Southern states will be depressed 50 percent. You will have negro Senators and Representatives, or the negro will dominate the elections. The purchase of votes will flourish, and elections will be more corrupt."[26]

A range of organizations lobbied for the anti–poll tax bill beyond the NAACP. An official with the National Federation for Constitutional Liberties told Rep. Sol Bloom (D-NY), "We join the great majority of the American people in commending you for signing Discharge Petition #1, assuring democratic consideration of the Geyer anti-poll tax bill." Said the legislative chair of the New York League of Women Shoppers, a consumer and labor advocacy organization, "Beating the poll tax is an integral part of beating Hitler and the Axis." Virginia Foster Durr, the executive vice chairman of the grassroots National Committee to Abolish the Poll Tax, told Bloom, "Abolition of the undemocratic poll tax system is a magnificent chance to tell the people of the whole world that the United States is indeed the hope of all freedom-loving people." Bloom promised Durr, "I shall be on the floor of the House of Representatives on October 12th, and shall support the Geyer Anti-Poll Tax Bill to its fullest extent." When asked to attend a local candidates' forum scheduled for October 13, Bloom replied, "Which is more important, the anti-poll tax bill or the member-candidates night dinner of the Grand Street Boys'? I am betting on the anti-poll tax bill, so I don't think I will be back in time to be with you tonight." The full House approved the measure, 254–84. The fight was much more heated than the vote totals suggest. "I think we are

Democracy's Turnstile

Dr. Seuss drew this anti–poll tax cartoon for PM *where it appeared on October 12, 1942. Courtesy Dr. Seuss Collection, MSS 230, Mandeville Special Collections Library, UC San Diego.*

coming to a showdown in America as to whether we are going to preserve democracy or not," Hatton Sumners (D-TX), the chief House strategist against the re form, importuned.[27] Indeed, making the argument that poll tax retention was democratic took moxie and exemplified the boldness of racial conservatives.

Passage of the anti–poll tax bill faced another challenge in 1942 from an otherwise erstwhile supporter of civil rights. Sen. Joseph C. O'Mahoney (D-WY) disagreed with the legislative strategy for eliminating the poll tax, preferring instead a constitutional amendment as the only legal way to accomplish that goal. He said of his opposition to the anti–poll tax bill, "Many supporters of the poll tax system would rather have the bill than the amendment because they know that the amendment would put an end once and for all to the poll tax system." Later, O'Mahoney denied that Congress had any authority "to fix the qualifications of electors even for federal office." Moreover, O'Mahoney noted the historic usage of the poll tax, citing the property requirements in the early days of the American republic. O'Mahoney argued, "Of all organizations the American Civil Liberties Union should support the Constitutional amendment approach [to repeal the poll tax]. It is the Constitution which protects civil liberties against waves of passion."[28]

Regarding the Pepper anti–poll tax bill, seventeen senators polled by the NAACP said they would support the measure, none indicated opposition, four said they would give it careful consideration, but only two said they would vote for cloture. Pro–poll tax senators used a variety of methods to prevent a cloture vote, especially absenting themselves from the chamber to prevent a quorum. For example, on November 14, when the Senate could not achieve a quorum, Barkley asserted, "There seems to have taken place an exodus from the Senate equal to the exodus of the Children of Israel from Egypt." After noting there were sufficient senators in town to make a quorum, Barkley instructed the vice president to issue arrest warrants to be executed by the sergeant at arms. Kenneth McKellar, an old friend of Barkley, was one of the senators arrested. The Tennessean was irate at being dragged out of his Mayflower Hotel apartment.[29]

Interference with the cloture vote also resulted in drama for the GOP. Walter White lambasted Minority Leader Charles McNary (R-OR) for not voting cloture to end the filibuster, maintaining it "means death to the bill." McNary fumed to a delegation of NAACP activists: "A man by the name of White sent me the most insulting letter I have ever received containing the words 'conspiracy,' etc; this man White is doing more harm to Negro rights than any other single person in the country." His disagreement with White resulted because he was playing politics with the anti–poll tax bill. He believed it made no sense to help non-southern Democrats pass the bill because there would be no political credit for the Republicans. Instead, he was willing to help kill the bill in 1942 and then pass it later when the Republican Party could earn the credit. George W. Norris (I-NE) dismissed McNary's strategy as dishonorable. The NAACP responded with a telegram to Minority Leader Martin, claiming that opposition to cloture and a decision to abandon the anti–poll tax bill would "have enormous repercussions for years to come. Newspapers charge coalition between Senate Republicans and filibusterers. We ask you as chairman Republican National Committee to take appropriate action." Not voting cloture, the NAACP stressed, was equivalent to "denial of right to participate in government to those who are being asked to fight and die to preserve that government. Republican party will be held responsible if it is a party to scuttling of bill."[30]

Because of the seniority system the defenders of the poll tax controlled the Senate. While the Senate Judiciary Committee had voted the bill out, it had done so with proxy votes. Only nine of the eighteen members had been present for the vote. When supporters of the anti–poll tax legislation tried to bring the bill to the floor, Sen. Wall Doxey (D-MS) made a point of order, challenging that it had not been properly reported out of committee. During debate on the point of order, Connally and others who supported the poll tax turned the discussion into the merits of the bill. They were prepared to debate the point of order until the adjournment of the second session of the 77th Congress. Connally, though, never spoke with the loudest anti–poll tax voice in the Senate. He did not wish to "stand behind a desk and make of fool of himself like Bilbo" but instead operated with the cover of secrecy in the Senate cloak room. He negotiated with Republicans, who favored anti–poll tax legislation but who also wanted southern Democratic help voting against New Deal agencies. Proponents could do nothing to stop the southerners because a cloture vote could not be taken on a point of order debate. Instead, cloture was only an option when the filibuster was being used to halt a vote on legislation. Ultimately an agreement was struck to drop the point of order, bring up the bill, and allow a cloture vote, but not with enough time to allow absent lawmakers to return to Washington.[31]

As this strategy was being deployed, Connally and others spared no victims. Connally was at his worst when he called Norris a "lame duck" because Norris had recently been defeated in his reelection bid. Norris's eyes filled with tears and he protested Connally's words, to no avail. McNaughton proclaimed: "To Tom Connally, Theodore Bilbo, Kenneth F. McKellar, Richard B. Russell, belong the dubious honors of tying the Senate into a knot, bringing it into disgrace in the eyes of the nation, rendering it impotent in wartime, and thus defeating legislation intended to strike off the feudalistic political shackles that load down thousands and millions of persons in the poll tax states. The Senate yesterday reached government by minority obstruction." The fight also frayed the nerves of senators and further harmed comity among lawmakers.[32]

On November 23, the cloture vote failed in the Senate, 37 in favor and 41 opposed, far short of the two-thirds necessary to stop the filibuster. As depicted in Chart 6.6, southern Democrats relied not just on Republicans but also on Democrats from other regions to prevent cloture as only 9 voted nay and 15 yea. After the cloture vote failed, Capper told White: "This is about the toughest proposition that has come before the Congress for several years so far as the interests of your people are concerned. I am glad you are planning to have the bill reintroduced. I believe there will be a better chance for favorable action in the next Congress." Stressing that he "did not kill the Anti-Poll Tax Bill," McNary explained, "the bill came up at the wrong time, at the end of the session, which really invited a filibuster." The success of a filibuster had much to do with timing, making it easier to talk legislation to death at the end of a session with the clock about to expire anyway. McNary revealed his supple and malleable views, attempts to curry favor across the ideological spectrum, when he defended the filibuster as a crucial mechanism for the support of minority rights.[33]

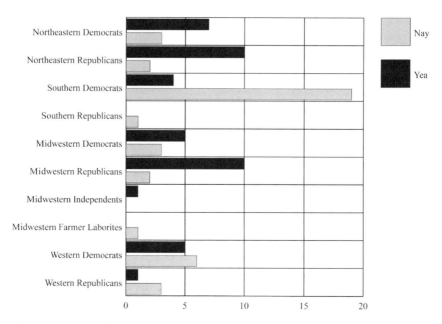

Chart 6.6: Region and Party Identification—Senate Cloture Vote on the Anti–Poll Tax Bill. Data for this chart come from analysis of the November 23, 1942, record vote in the Senate. See Congressional Record, 77th Congress, 2nd session, 9065.

This racial conflict between liberals and conservatives carried forward into 1943. When the 78th Congress first worked to organize its committees in January 1943, the Democrats on the House Ways and Means Committee, which functioned as a committee on committees and made appointments to all the other committees, recommended Vito Marcantonio (AL-NY) by a 9–6 vote for the House Judiciary Committee, one of the more conservative and more important House committees especially for consideration of wartime civil rights measures. Marcantonio wanted on the committee because he planned to introduce anti–poll tax legislation and force a vote early in the session, thus making a Senate filibuster much more difficult. When the matter went before the Democratic Caucus, the southerners were prepared. Even though the seniority system offered some protection against advancing liberal legislation, southerners did not want another proponent of the anti–poll tax bill and the anti-lynching bill on the all-important Judiciary Committee, especially Marcantonio. One observer said Robert L. "Muley" Doughton (D-NC), the Ways and Means chair, looked like he had "swallowed a fly" when he spoke for Marcantonio. Rep. Lyle Boren (D-OK) termed it a "corrupt bargain" made in exchange for American Labor Party support of Democrats in New York, and he cited numerous examples from Marcantonio's speeches that proved, at least in his mind, that Marcantonio was at least "pink" if not a Communist. The caucus refused to go along with the recommendation from the Ways and Means Committee, and Doughton was even angrier than Marcantonio. Doughton felt like the House leadership, which had initially pushed for Marcantonio, had betrayed him when they did not fight for him in the caucus. Marcantonio's assessment of the situation was not mild: he swore his defeat was the result of "domestic fascists," meaning southern Democrats, who held their offices because of the poll tax.[34]

Despite this setback, Marcantonio sponsored the anti–poll tax bill in the House. White worried that Marcantonio's sponsorship would cause some members of Congress to forego signing a discharge petition or voting on the floor. Virginia Foster Durr divulged to White, "The Congressmen agreed among themselves on this particular Bill. I understand the reason being chiefly that the Republicans did not want to support a Democratic Bill and the Democrats did not want to support a Republican Bill, and they all felt this was the best solution." She understood that Rep. George H. Bender (R-OH), leader of the informal group pushing the reform, would take care of lobbying Republicans about the Marcantonio bill, that seventy-five people had already signed the discharge petition, and that the labor unions would give the measure "one hundred percent" support. In addition to Bender, the congressional coalition backing the Marcantonio bill included Warren Magnuson (D-WA), Joseph C. Baldwin (R-NY), Gavagan, William L. Dawson (D-IL), Marcantonio, Charles La Follette (R-IN), Walter Ploesser (R-MO), Karl Stefan (R-NE), and Thomas E. Scanlon (D-PA). Still, there was much difficulty getting an anti–poll tax bill introduced in the Senate in 1943. Neither Sens. Harley M. Kilgore (D-WV) nor John A. Danaher (R-CT) were willing, and Burton, no longer a Judiciary Committee member, was not viable given the importance of that committee to the outcome. Homer Ferguson (R-MI) was considered as a likely sponsor, even though he was a rabid anti–New Dealer, revealing the vicissitudes of ideology from economic issues to social issues and providing further evidence why social issues were more difficult to pass in the 1940s.[35]

Typical of the lawmaker response to NAACP pleas for signatures on the discharge petitions for the anti-lynching and anti–poll tax bills was what John J. Cochran (D-MO) said, "I am not in favor of legislating by petition." Others like J. Percy Priest (D-TN) elaborated the point: "I feel there has been in many respects a tendency in the last few years to destroy legislative machinery of the Congress. Judiciary and legislative committees in many instances have been circumvented by special committees of one kind or another, and more and more there is a growing tendency to bring legislation to the floor through the discharge petition route." Priest reasoned that during war when unity was required it made no sense to push for divisive legislation that "would no doubt result in a bitter filibuster" in the Senate. Such arguments were situational. No opponent of tax or rationing legislation used such rhetoric.[36]

Bender lobbied Walter White to redouble his efforts on behalf of the anti–poll tax bill. He told the NAACP secretary that with 180 signatures on a discharge petition only thirty-eight more lawmakers needed to sign in order to force a floor vote. He advocated the continued lobbying by interested national organizations as the only viable strategy. Someone in White's office penned on the letter, "If you can give us names of those who haven't signed who come from northern and border states where N vote, we can concentrate on them."[37]

The NAACP had difficulties keeping its congressional coalition together. Rep. James V. Heidinger (R-IL), who had worked hard during the last session of Congress for anti–poll tax legislation, was unwilling to sign the discharge petitions for the new anti–poll tax bill and the anti-lynching bill in 1943. He insinuated, "The Administration wants to say that it passed an anti-poll-tax bill in the House but, acting in bad faith, will order it killed in the Senate." Heidinger also complained that southern blacks continued to support the white Democrats who held power in the region, a conclusion that begs credulity since most southern blacks could not vote. Furthermore, he noted the only organizations supporting anti–poll tax legislation were the CIO and the Railroad Brotherhoods, labor unions that had opposed his reelection bid. The NAACP representative who spoke with Heidinger concluded, "My impression of Heidinger is that, for one thing, he appears to have been left out of the picture. . . . It is entirely possible that if he can be made to feel important . . . he might come through." Heidinger was not the only representative to complain of labor support for anti–poll tax legislation. Jamie Whitten (D-MS) avowed that such interference "make[s] it much more difficult for us who consider ourselves liberal in the South as we struggle to free the poor people in the South and admit them to the economic life of the region and to participation in its political process."[38]

By May 5, 1943, 208 House members had signed a discharge petition for the anti–poll tax bill, leaving just ten signatures to be gained to force a floor debate. But matters were more complicated than this calculus suggested because southern Democrats were lobbying those who had already signed the discharge petition to rescind their support. As such, Rep. Bender asked the NAACP to sound the "fire alarm" and help move the bill to the floor. Bender prevailed. On May 6, sufficient signatures were collected and the bill was scheduled for floor debate on May 24. Bender credited the "remarkable" effort of the NAACP and other supportive national organizations for the success of the discharge petition, but he also cautioned that the battle was not over. The dangers that remained included crippling amendments and large absentee rates on May 24, preventing a vote. Bender told White the best method for foiling this strategy was constituent mail. He also stressed the importance of the NAACP and asked White to keep working.[39]

All "hell broke loose" in the House gallery on May 25, 1943, during the anti–poll tax bill debate. Before lawmakers voted 265–110 to pass the anti–poll tax bill over the negative votes of almost exclusively the southern Democrats, Evan Owen Jones, a white sailor on forty-eight hours' shore leave, had been sitting silently and angrily watching the proceedings for over an hour. He leapt to the railing in the gallery and yelled out to the lawmakers below: "Mr. Speaker, I demand the right to be heard." Lawmakers scurried about on the floor unsure how to respond, but Jones continued, "I'm a man from the service. Do I have the floor?" Rep. Bulwinkle, who had been in the chair, replied "No," but Jones did not relent: "Why should a man be taxed to vote? Why should a man be taxed to vote when he can fight without paying? I speak for the thousands who can not be here. I would like to ask you, why does a man have to pay tribute for the right to vote?" Two doormen for the House tried to get Jones off the railing. Ultimately, he was taken to the capitol police guardroom where he was lectured for his intemperate behavior. Jones remained unapologetic. "These people are fighting the Civil War all over again," Jones contended. "They should be spending their time fighting this war. California wants one thing, Pennsylvania wants something else, and Alabama wants something else. We've got to work together more to help this country." He stressed his patriotism but concluded, "We are fighting to keep it the best government and Congress ought to do its part." One journalist argued, "It was the best speech of the whole debate." In a few minutes Jones lay bare the hypocrisy that typified much of the war being fought in Congress.[40]

There were a number of strategies developed to pass the anti–poll tax bill in the Senate. Because the House bill passed in May 1943 was identical to the bill the Senate Judiciary Committee reported favorably in 1942, Marcantonio urged, "Those who want poll tax repeal should press for the Senate Judiciary Committee to report my bill out with all possible speed. We need no hearings on the bill." Bender told White how to pass the anti–poll tax bill in the Senate. "I am convinced that to beat the filibuster, which Senator Bilbo has promised us in the Senate, it will be necessary to pledge every Senator to vote for cloture," Bender professed. "I urge you to do everything humanly possible because I am convinced that this measure can be passed at this session, but it will only be done if every Senator realizes that the entire Negro vote will be cast on this issue in 1944." Rep. Baldwin, the floor leader for the anti–poll tax bill in the House, advised White that he would "do what I can personally with Senator McNary" in order to move the bill to the Senate floor on a cloture vote. McNary was on record opposing cloture votes but supporting the legislation. Thurgood Marshall researched the various occasions in the late 1910s and the 1920s when McNary either signed petitions for or voted for cloture.[41]

Even though the anti-lynching bill had proven more intractable than anti–poll tax legislation, liberal lawmakers still sought to outlaw the barbaric process. Increased episodes of white on black violence in the spring and summer of 1943 did little to convince lawmakers of the need for the new law. The Addsco shipyards in Mobile were the scene of a brutal white on black riot in late May 1943. The city's population had increased by 60 percent because of wartime employment. The shipyards had notoriously discriminated against black workers, but when a small number of African American employees had been promoted to welders, a large mob of angry whites attacked them. Quickly the violence spread throughout the city, leaving eleven blacks hospitalized. The rebellion was quelled only after Addsco management moved its African American workforce to separate facilities. In Los Angeles, when a gang of white sailors attacked some Mexican American youths wearing zoot suits with whom they were in competition for the same girls, a riot lasting almost a week ensued in early June. Over sixty Mexican Americans were arrested, but no whites were detained. The city council responded by making the wearing of the zoot suit illegal. Similar white on black episodes of violence erupted in Beaumont, Texas, a few weeks later on June 15. False rumors of rape and violence spurred a white mob of 2,000 workers from the Penn Shipyards and Consolidated Steel Shipyards to render untold violence in the African American section of the city. The governor of Texas declared martial law before the violence ended. Three people were killed, several dozen wounded, and approximately twenty homes and businesses owned by blacks were burned down.[42]

In June 1943, White told friendly members of Congress why the discharge petition for the anti-lynching bill was crucial: "It has been the hope of opponents of lynching that this loathsome practice would be eliminated, particularly during the time when the nation is engaged in fighting the lynching psychology and practices of Nazi Germany and Japan." He then disclosed that the "tragic growth of mob violence within recent weeks . . . threaten[ed] to become a nation-wide crisis." Arguing that state and local solutions to racial violence were impractical and unlikely to work, White concluded, "The record demonstrates that these promises have not been kept."[43] Still, Congress lacked the courage to outlaw the poll tax or the practice of lynching, statist measures that moderates were unwilling to link to the burgeoning warfare state.

These examples were repeated elsewhere throughout the United States, with the most famous conflict occurring in Detroit, then the fourth-largest city in the nation and the place where 35 percent of the nation's ordnance was manufactured. A year earlier *Life* magazine had proclaimed: "Detroit is Dynamite. It can either blow up Hitler or blow up the U.S." Thousands and thousands of poor blacks and whites from the Midwest and the South poured into Detroit for better-paying defense jobs, and they were greeted with inadequate housing and deteriorating living conditions. On June 20, a bloody three-day riot began when black and white Detroiters gathered and scuffled in the Belle Isle park on a Sunday afternoon. Later that evening a riot began on the Belle Isle bridge connecting the park with southeast Detroit. Rumors of race war spread in both the black and white communities with the opposite race being blamed for the violence. Siding with whites, law enforcement officials murdered 17 African Americans and no whites. A total of 34 people were killed, 25 of whom were black. Over 600 were injured, and thousands were jailed. Federal troops were required to quell the riot. In the period from spring 1943 through early summer 1943 over 1,100,000 days of work were lost to racial bigotry, prompting CBS News to devote an hour-long program to the problem of racial hatred and its impact on the war effort.[44]

In the fall of 1943 consideration of a soldiers' vote bill distracted Congress from anti-lynching and anti–poll tax measures. Earlier that year, Majority Leader McCormack argued to Rayburn, "One of the most important duties confronting us . . . is the duty and responsibility of allowing the boys in the service to exercise their suffrage. While we passed a bill last year designed to accomplish that it was ineffective. Another election will come up in 1944 and certainly everything should be done to enable those who want to exercise their suffrage to do so with as little inconvenience as possible."[45]

Roosevelt supported the Green-Lucas soldiers' vote bill, which was first introduced in June in the House of Representatives. While it did not promise an immediate solution to racial disfranchisement, the fact that lawmakers considered a measure to expand federal control of the electoral process nonetheless threatened the racial status quo in the South. Instead of creating a powerful federal mechanism for soldier voting, lawmakers added a "milk-and-water" antistatist amendment sponsored by Sens. James Eastland (D-MS), John McClellan (D-AR), and McKellar, which left states in control of the elections machinery. As such the negative votes came from liberals not conservatives. It passed the Senate 42–37 in December, and, with this change, the bill was sent to the House. This Senate bill was, according to one journalist, "a mockery" because roughly half the state legislatures were not willing to meet until after the 1944 election. Rayburn told a journalist: "Now, we've got a chance to fight on the soldier vote issue too." Tension between the House and the Senate was almost as strong as wartime partisan rancor. "It's just ridiculous, what they did in the Senate. Everybody knows the States can't handle that or if they try to the soldiers just won't get the chance to vote," Rayburn affirmed. "I think the House will be able to set up some kind of Federal system, and I think . . . it will be done by someone attacking John Rankin as being against the Negro vote. He'll be charged with barring the votes of the entire armed forces on account of that prejudice. And I think that with such tactics we can carry a compromise that will give us a fairly decent bill."[46]

Congress was in a stalemate regarding anti–poll tax and soldiers' vote legislation when it adjourned at the end of 1943. Discord, fighting within the Democratic Party in Congress and between congressional Democrats and the Democratic president, had grown so severe one careful observer cautioned, "Out of the complex personalities of 96 men are rising prejudices and dislikes which could, under some circumstances, seriously handicap the country. . . . It was apparent this afternoon that mere dislike is turning, in some cases, into active hatred as the soldier-vote issue becomes embroiled in the growing, general bitterness between the White House and the Hill."[47] The same divisions regarding increased federal power versus states' rights and social justice liberalism versus social justice conservatism characterized the debates in 1944. The reformers who wanted the two policy changes faced opposition from the constitutionalists and the states' righters. The former pretended support for soldiers' vote and anti–poll tax legislation but maintained the reforms must be initiated through amendment to the Constitution. The latter were even less sincere, arguing their goal was preservation of minority rights, but they meant the minority rights of white southerners, not the minority rights of African Americans.

The anti–poll tax bill, O'Mahoney said, had "nothing to do with the war," and the soldiers' vote bill, he held, was "wholly an emergency bill and applies only during the war. I believe that when the federal government . . . takes young men out of their states, puts a gun in their hands and sends them off to war, it has a right at the same time to protect them from the loss of their vote, just as it has attempted to protect them against the loss of their jobs." Other lawmakers viewed the soldiers' vote bill differently. When Edward H. Moore (R-OK) hinted that the soldiers' vote bill was nothing but a plot to gain a fourth term for FDR, Scott Lucas (D-IL) took to the floor and challenged Moore's motives and character, in clear violation of Senate rules. He was reprimanded, accepted it, and continued, stating Moore "has not had a single constructive thought since he has been in the Senate."[48]

O'Mahoney concluded that a constitutional amendment was the best solution to the problem of granting the vote to soldiers. Moreover, he derided the states' rights bill that had passed the Senate in December. O'Mahoney indicated a willingness to work with Lucas and Sen. Theodore Francis Green (D-RI), the authors of the original soldiers' vote legislation, "because I think they have done an excellent job." He queried every governor in the country asking whether they supported his proposed constitutional amendment regarding the soldiers' vote issue. The reaction to O'Mahoney's plan was mixed. "I do not believe it is advisable to introduce a constitutional amendment at this time. I think it would only have a tendency to further cloud the importance of passing the Lucas-Green bill at the earliest possible moment," Lucas argued, noting the need for a new law within thirty days. O'Mahoney discounted the arguments that there was not time for implementing a constitutional amendment, noting that since prohibition repeal had been accomplished in 368 days "a soldier vote amendment could now be ratified in at least one-fourth of the time." Barkley advocated mixing the two strategies, but John McCormack told O'Mahoney, "Congress would be derelict in its duty if it failed to meet the situation and to pass a real, effective bill" for soldier voting. Sam Rayburn acknowledged O'Mahoney's plan without comment on its merits.[49]

Meanwhile, Green and Lucas introduced a new soldiers' vote bill on January 11, 1944, which provided federal oversight for continued state-level voting procedures for soldiers. The measure was a substitute for the states' rights soldiers' vote bill, which received Senate approval in December. The new Green-Lucas bill called for cancellation of the poll tax for soldiers voting on federal races: president, Senate, and Congress. This new attempt at compromise retained the foundations of the 1942 soldiers' vote law, which waived state voting requirements, but it also provided no penalties for states that violated the proposed new law. Because the states' rights bill had already passed the Senate, though, Majority Leader McCormack reasoned it would take a "political miracle" to gain the ballot for soldiers. He believed there was no chance the House could undo the "meaningless and ineffective" Senate bill. Indeed, when this new measure went to the Senate floor, it faced harsh attacks from states' rights senators.[50]

Given the confusions surrounding the soldiers' vote legislation, Roosevelt decided to issue a statement. He eviscerated the states' rights bill before the House and endorsed the revised Green-Lucas bill in the Senate. He wrote that the states' rights bill was a "fraud" perpetrated on the soldiers even as he conceded "this is solely a legislative matter." The message drew boos from Republicans when the clerk read it to the House, and in this instance the legislature's institutional war on the administration became personal. The statement angered lawmakers who looked at the military ranks of their children, often serving as privates, compared with the president's children, all officers. One senator opined, "Roosevelt says we're letting the soldiers down. Why God damn him. The rest of us have boys who go into the Army and Navy as privates and ordinary seamen and dig latrines and swab decks and his scamps go in as lieutenant colonels and majors and lieutenants and spend their time getting medals in Hollywood. Letting the soldiers down! Why that son of a bitch."[51]

Roosevelt delivered the statement because the House was on the verge of passing the states' rights bill that had cleared the Senate in December but that the Senate had informally rejected in the new year when it deliberated the revised

Green-Lucas offering. Most political observers agreed that the outcome could turn the results of the 1944 presidential and congressional elections, for the soldiers were believed to lean heavily to the Democratic Party. Even Republicans admitted that if Roosevelt were not running then the bill would pass easily.[52]

In early February, the House refused to rewrite the states' rights bill even though over 100 members of the House signed a petition stating their support for Rep. Eugene Worley's (D-TX) soldiers' vote bill, a statist, federal ballot measure like the various Green-Lucas bills. Clinton Anderson (D-NM) circulated the petition among House Democrats. He condemned the partisan bickering about this legislation, which pitted moderates and liberals against conservative Democrats, many of whom shared similar concerns as the GOP. Doughton worried about the soldiers' vote bills, which gave the federal government authority for the election machinery, because "people are frequently more interested in state and local elections than in national elections, and to turn over our entire voting machinery to national authorities, the state abdicating, I am not certain would be a sound policy." On February 3, after rejecting the Worley measure primarily with Republican votes, 168–224, the House passed the states' rights bill by a vote of 328–69 in a session that lasted until 10:58 p.m. Going against the conservatism of his region, Clifton Woodrum (D-VA) declared, "The spectacle you are making here tonight is not adding to the prestige of the House of Representatives."[53]

Five days later, the Senate passed the revised Green-Lucas measure, 47–38, and included a hybrid federal-state mechanism. As Chart 6.7 shows almost as many southern Democrats voted for it as against it, making the Republicans the primary source of negative votes and revealing that the conservative coalition played but a scant role in this outcome. When the various soldiers' vote bills went to conference committee, the negotiators for the two chambers were deadlocked. Worley, the leader of the House conferees, proposed first that the portions of the 1942 soldiers' vote legislation suspending the poll tax be repealed, second that only the federal ballot be sent to soldiers whether they requested it or not, third that states would be authorized to determine the validity of such ballots, and fourth that every effort would be made to make state ballots available to those who requested them. The next day Rankin balked, but Worley told the press, "Somebody has changed his mind; we're right back where we started." Said one journalist of the deliberations, "just a little handful of familiar, thoroughly human men, sitting down around a table and slugging it out for what they believe in. This democracy, as commonplace and well-worn as an old shoe, is sometimes more moving than it knows."[54]

On the last day of February the conferees reached near-unanimous agreement with Rankin, the only remaining holdout. According to the conference report, governors in states without absentee ballot laws had until October 1 to authorize

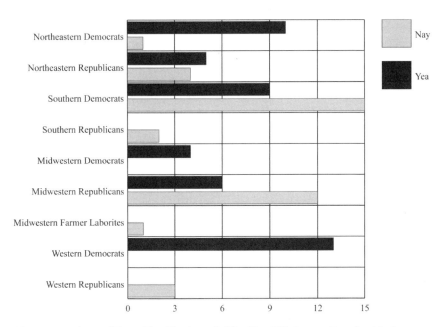

Chart 6.7: Region and Party Identification—Soldier Vote Bill, Senate. Data for this chart come from analysis of the February 8, 1944, record vote in the Senate. See Congressional Record, 78th Congress, 2nd session, 1406.

the federal ballot for their states. Governors of states with absentee ballot laws had the same deadline to authorize the federal ballot. Soldiers from such states wishing to use the federal ballot had to certify that they had applied for but had not received a state ballot as of October 1. Worley argued there was no valid constitutional argument to be made: "Under this plan, the federal ballot is made merely supplemental to the state ballot." Advisors to the president recommended he veto the bill. Before deciding whether to sign the soldiers' vote bill, termed by critics a states' rights measure, Roosevelt polled the nation's governors about what steps were being taken to make federal ballots available to the soldiers. Of the forty-two governors who responded to the president, six—those from California, Maryland, North Carolina, Florida, Alabama, and Kansas—indicated state laws already permitted the federal ballot, in one case, Alabama, with substantial restrictions. Thirteen said no action would be taken toward usage of the federal ballots. Twelve—from Vermont, Utah, Massachusetts, New Mexico, Indiana, New Hampshire, Rhode Island, New Jersey, Nebraska, Maine, Oklahoma, and Connecticut—suggested that likely measures would be taken to permit federal ballots. Six state governors did not reply: South Carolina, Tennessee, Michigan, Texas, Wyoming, and Oregon.[55]

Almost no one liked the conference committee report. An unnamed states' rights Democrat told journalist Allen Drury that Roosevelt had maneuvered the legislation to prevent another Democrat from challenging for the presidency. "He uses you and then he throws you away. Why, hell, I could no more be one of these ass-kissing New Dealers! He'll be your friend as long as he can get what he wants out of you, and then it's good-by. That's not for me," said the Senate Democrat who articulated views that explain why and how the New Deal order was revised and narrowed in the 1940s when it took a more permanent, moderate form. "I'm a Democrat, and I'll always remain a Democrat, but I'm not a New Dealer. And I think that's true for the majority of the Democratic Party."[56]

Philip Murray, president of the CIO, told members of Congress that the conference committee report on the soldiers' vote bill was "a technical absurdity which will actually disfranchise the few servicemen who were enfranchised by the 1942 act.... As Senator Green has said: 'It is better to have no bill at all than one which decreases the number of those who vote and makes it harder rather than easier.'" Congress and the White House, though, never came to terms regarding the legislation. Roosevelt never relented from his demand for a federal voting mechanism while lawmakers were equally adamant it should remain under state jurisdiction. After Congress approved the conference committee report, it became law without Roosevelt's signature. While he did not want to veto "that fool bill" neither did he want to put his name on it. In the election about half of the 11 million Americans in uniform submitted their state ballots, while far fewer soldiers voted the federal ballot, just under 112,000 soldiers.[57]

The states' rights law did not eliminate the larger anti–poll tax debate even though most senators hoped that the poll tax battle could be avoided, so tired were they of this ideological and increasingly unproductive war. They realized a filibuster against legislation to extend the vote at home would be problematic in the middle of a war being fought for the expansion of democracy. The white supremacist senators were not in a mood to yield, though, causing one journalist sympathetic to the anti–poll tax argument to ruminate at the end of April:

All the groups who want to force the Senate into a filibuster are gradually achieving success.... The strange, the peculiar, the tragic thing about it is that all this they demand in the name of democracy, and indeed and admittedly in the name of democracy it should be done. If they were at all interested in the practical mechanics of the thing, however, if they had taken the time in all this shouting about democracy to study the Senate and find out how democracy actually operates in the hard, practical business of corralling votes, they would know that it cannot be done now.... They just haven't got the votes.[58]

Social justice conservatives were winning this debate, and a Supreme Court decision in 1944, *Smith v. Allright,* further emboldened them. In this case the justices ruled the white primary, a mechanism created in Texas at the turn of the century, and its underlying premise that primary elections were private and not state affairs where black voting could be denied, unconstitutional. Connally characterized the *Smith v. Allright* decision as "outrageous. It overruled a unanimous opinion of the Court rendered in 1935. Joining in the former opinion were such Judges as Holmes, Brandeis, Hughes, Vandeventer, McReynolds, Stone, Butler, etc. Stone, in the recent decision reversed himself. Recently I had a long talk with Justice Roberts about the matter. He feel[s] outraged." Burnet Maybank gave a speech on April 13, where he used blunt language. "The White people of the South will not accept these interferences. We are proud of our section. We know what is best for the white people and the colored people. We are going to treat the Negro fairly, but in so doing we do not intend for him to take over our election system or attend our white schools," Maybank underscored. "Regardless of any Supreme Court decisions and any laws that may be passed by Congress, we of the South will maintain our political and social institutions as we believe to be in the best interest of our people."[59]

In May 1944 Russell told his mother of his concerns about the voting rights debate. "The old poll tax is going to be pushed on us again next week. I certainly dread to go through with this fight again, but we have no alternative," Russell concluded. "These professional reformers from the outside are determined to run the Southern States as they think they should be operated, and a surprising number of our own people seem to be willing to turn it over to them. I am afraid that these agitators, both within our State and without, will eventually cause us serious difficulties that are altogether unnecessary." Southern senators blamed the CIO and Communists for the pressure to enact the anti–poll tax bill, but proponents of the reform were just as concerned about what they termed nefarious tactics. For example, Wagner complained of "disquieting rumors of deals and of bargains and of clandestine agreements" to withdraw the bill should the cloture vote fail. He contended, "I cannot believe that any members of this Senate would attempt an agreement which would prevent the orderly operation of democracy." White southerners took a different view. Sen. Ellison D. "Cotton Ed" Smith (D-SC) ranted, "I'm still for white supremacy and those who don't like it can lump it. Those who vote for me I'll be much obliged. Those who don't can go to hell."[60]

When Pat McCarran (D-NV) first called the anti–poll tax bill to the floor of the Senate for debate, an agreement had already been reached about a filibuster, the cloture vote, and the abandonment of the legislation. Because congressional proponents of the poll tax bragged of having thousands of amendments, each requiring debate, a prearranged strategy for the floor was necessary to prevent social justice conservatives from halting all Senate business. Years later Connally recalled of the many filibusters and the failure of the supposed Senate majority to break them, "if the advocates of the anti-lynching and anti-poll tax bills had been serious, they could have defeated us. All they had to do was call continuous sessions around the clock. . . . Their purpose was served not by getting the bills passed, but by creating a fuss in which they could pose as heroes." After its initial introduction there was a week of casual filibustering, enough for the social justice conservatives to make a point with their white southern constituents. Likewise, the cloture vote allowed Senate liberals to make their case with labor and African American voters. The southerners were prepared to filibuster until "hell froze over" were it not for the deal. Journalists covering Congress determined, "It's a deal all the way through, and the most sensible one under an impossible set of circumstances" with demagoguery on both sides. Bill Langer (ND), the lone Republican proponent for the bill declared, "everybody's sick of this. Let's get rid of it."[61]

At the end of the cloture debate Claude Pepper shouted that the majority must rule. Connally made a forceful, predictable argument against the motion to vote cloture, which would require the Senate to "put its hand and heads in the stocks": "I don't want to see this Senate commit suicide. This is a motion for the Senate to strip itself of one of its greatest prerogatives in government. If you want to tie the hands of the Senate, vote for this motion. I hope the Senate will not vote thus to strike the strength from its arms, the impulses of its brain from the repository (tapping his forehead) of its intelligence!" According to one journalist, "A generous scattering of negroes" attended the debate. Not a sound was heard in the chamber during the roll call. The southerners prevailed, 36–44, rebuking the moderates and liberals who failed to achieve even a bare majority let alone a two-thirds majority to force an end to the filibuster. Though proponents of anti–poll tax legislation tried again in 1945, their efforts were for naught. This war for expanding democracy at home was lost. Center right social justice conservatives in Congress triumphed over congressional liberals and an executive that did not wish to fight. Moderates became the fulcrum. For example, Sam Rayburn, the speaker and a moderate, told conservative Georgia Democratic representative Eugene E. Cox, "I think my [reelection] race is going all right although they are hollering negro, negro, FEPC and etc."[62] This exchange and the fate of the anti–poll tax legislation exemplifies why Congress was never able to compromise and enact functional legislation addressing social policy problems. Put simply, no one cared enough to make it happen.

Still, the NAACP, the most vocal organization working for civil rights in the 1940s, used this congressional intransigence to try to bring more liberals into Congress, but this strategy drew ire from conservatives. In the late summer of 1944, Sen. Robert A. Taft (R-OH) expressed anger over NAACP literature scoring the voting records of members of Congress regarding support for African American issues. "This exact technique is taken directly from that of the Communists and the New Republic. It assumes without any justification that a vote on certain legislation is against the negro because it happened to be at variance with the position of the NAACP," Taft averred. "It is perfectly clear to me that Walter White is cooperating 100% with the left wing organizations in and has fortified his right to speak for the negro in America in any question in which the New Deal is involved." Moreover, Taft complained that such assessments were being used for political purposes for the presidential election that fall.[63]

Americans generally were displeased with the outcome of this domestic congressional war. A Brooklyn woman, Josephine Piccolo, wrote to Bilbo, "I find it very hard to believe that you are an American citizen and much, much harder to believe that you are allowed to enter the doors of the U.S. Senate." Bilbo replied, calling the woman, "My Dear Dago." He queried what she was "griping about" since she lived in New York City, and concluded she should "keep [her] dirty proboscis out of the other 47 states." When Rep. Marcantonio insisted that Bilbo apologize for addressing Piccolo as "My Dear Dago," the Mississippi senator retorted, "Hell, no." Instead he attacked Marcantonio as an "ex-Communist and political mongrel"; Marcantonio countered that Bilbo was a "domestic Fascist." The next day Bilbo pronounced that instead of apologizing to Piccolo, she should seek forgiveness from him for what he described as her intemperate words. Moreover, he concluded that the use of the term "dago" was not considered insulting in the South. "It is generally used without any suggestion of contempt."[64]

Bilbo wrote to his Senate colleagues and denied that he had ever denigrated "Jews, Italians, Poles, Catholics and others as a class, as a nationality or as a denomination." He did admit to making scathing comments about specific people "because of their advocacy of what, in my opinion, are the most vicious and un-American Legislative concepts." Bilbo admitted his use of harsh words against white people who endorsed social integration, "thereby leading to miscegenation, intermarriage and mongrelization of both the white and black races. With the respect and love that I have for the Caucasian blood that flows not only in my veins but in the veins of Jews, Italians, Poles, and other nationalities of the White race, I would not want to see it contaminated with Negro blood." He trumpeted "any decent, self-respecting Negro resents the contamination of his blood with the white man's blood. My whole effort is a fight against the mongrelization of the two races in America and the social intermingling of the two races can lead only to that."[65]

The inability of Americans in or out of Congress to stifle such rhetoric became obvious. The president of the NAACP, Fred H. M. Turner, told Russell, "A simple recital of the truth will no longer stop the lies of Senators Bilbo and Eastland.

And, since they hide behind the shield of Congressional immunity, there is no legal redress for the people they have slandered. Yet, if the honor and dignity of the United States Senate is to be maintained, something must be done." Turner advocated "open censure" by other members of the Senate, which "will show them the contempt in which every decent American holds them. We ask you to have nothing to do with them. Do not even offer them the courtesy of 'Good morning'. Ignore them as completely as they have ignored the sensitivities of the people they have slandered. Have all the other senators join with you in this silent treatment, so that the effect will be even greater." Bilbo's use of his Senate letterhead to spread his intemperate and vile rhetoric caused some Americans to write to other senators to enlist their aid in a campaign of censure and impeachment against the Mississippi firebrand. Said Arthur Capper (R-KS) in response to one such missive: "I do not approve his sentiments for one moment. I regret to say, however, there is nothing that I can do about it. . . . I have been here 26 years, and in that time I have never heard of any effort being made to stop a United States Senator from making such use of Senate stationery as he might see fit."[66]

This tragic story highlights the considerable shifts in American politics, which resulted from the ineffectiveness of the liberal and moderate majority in thwarting the hate rhetoric of a minority of the conservative minority. The consequence was an intensification of the congressional war on all other social and economic fronts. Dissonance between the nation's war aims and its social justice policies regarding race and civil rights at home grew louder, making the ideological extremists within Congress less likely to compromise and more likely to fight. This warfare over issues of civil rights weakened democracy as a whole in the United States. Speaker Rayburn, no integrationist, despised the demagoguery of John Rankin. He viewed his behavior as "counterfeit." He doubted that the demagogues even believed their own rhetoric.[67] Thus, the dichotomy between liberals and conservatives was more a symptom and less a cause of the politics of prejudice. The core issue was about power and who held it within the Congress and the country. This power struggle fed the ideological wars and the institutional wars between the White House and Congress, and it made a major contribution to the war era constriction of liberalism while also teaching conservatives that the merger of social and economic opposition to New Deal reform initiatives held much potential for the postwar era.

7. "Saving America for Americans": The Fascistic Origins of the Second Red Scare

Historians have argued for decades about the origins and architects of McCarthyism. In the many efforts to implode the notion that Sen. Joseph McCarthy (R-WI) sired the second Red Scare, though, scholars have given too little attention to the role of Congress during World War II. A major theater in the congressional war about ideology, though, involved fighting against communism. In this, the earliest iteration of the postwar Red Scare, anti-Communist rhetoric was little more than a convenient, if somewhat ironic, bludgeon given that the Soviet Union was a U.S. ally. The earliest anti-Communist activists targeted the New Deal in the continuing congressional assault on liberalism and the statist policies developed in the 1930s.

The leading wartime anti-Communist, blond and tall Martin Dies (D-TX) or "der Fuehrer" as close allies called him, gained a reputation as a buffoon for his leadership of the House Un-American Activities Committee. For decades historians have dismissed his findings because his methods were without merit. More recent interpretations suggest Dies had discerned the broad outlines of Communist activity in the United States even if his particular conclusions were wrong. These debates have overlooked the more important matter of Dies's intent—to halt the New Deal, not to root out communism—and his impact on wartime and postwar politics—merging the ideological and institutional war Congress fought in the 1940s in one assault against the New Deal.[1]

Dies's activities are another example of congressional policies responsible for the shift away from experimental New Deal economic liberalism and to the much more circumspect vital center, warfare state liberalism of the postwar years. More than any other congressional conflict explicated in this book, the demagoguery of the Dies Committee sealed the fate of the New Deal in the 1940s and beyond. Though in chronologic time most of the events described in this chapter occurred before Pearl Harbor, in political time Dies's activities connect the late 1930s much more directly than previously understood with the 1950s, making it necessary to examine this component of the congressional world war at the end of the story. Indeed, the significance of Dies's work only emerges after a full consideration of congressional bushwhacking about the economy and about other social justice struggles. The House Appropriations Committee reified Dies and his analysis of

Witness before the Dies Committee giving Rep. Martin Dies the "Heil Hitler" salute, August 12, 1938. Courtesy Library of Congress, Prints & Photographs Division, photograph by Harris & Ewing [reproduction number, LC-DIG-hec-24930].

New Deal liberalism in 1943 to prove overall congressional acceptance of the committee's work, which lawmakers affirmed again in 1945 with an overwhelming vote to make the committee permanent.

Years later McCarthy said Dies was "a heroic voice crying in the wilderness" who had been "damned and humiliated and driven from public life." Dies's nickname, der Fuehrer, was not the only tantalizing but inconclusive evidence of his political loyalties. According to one scholar who published a biography of Dies in 1944, there was "little evidence" the Texan "understands or believes in American democracy." Moreover, Felix Frankfurter informed the White House of a $20,000 payment to Martin Dies's campaign manager from a German national advocating increased trade between Hitler's government and the United States. In response, President Franklin D. Roosevelt ordered an FBI investigation of Dies, revealing White House defensiveness vis-à-vis Dies's charges. Attorney General Francis Biddle, however, was unable to prove the link, but patterns of liberal weakness in the face of often specious conservative charges emerged, suggesting Dies not only helped sire McCarthyism but also the political modus operandi of modern conservatives whereby liberalism itself became the sin. Only Roosevelt had the power to "spike Dies" as Biddle put it, and Roosevelt never accomplished that feat. Instead, by acting as if Dies was powerful, the administration empowered him, and a conservative methodology for discrediting liberals that remained potent into the early twenty-first century.[2]

Dies and his allies hated Roosevelt and the statist roles the federal government assumed in the 1930s. Moreover, he disapproved the manner in which the nation's political economy, its domestic priorities, and its foreign policy changed as a result of the New Deal and the war. In 1963, Dies wrote, "We lost World War II." By that he meant "we didn't destroy the idea of a powerful central government, controlling and dominating our lives, our business, and our political thought." During the early years of the New Deal, Dies had supported Roosevelt, but he broke with the administration over Roosevelt's plan in 1937 to enlarge the Supreme Court and the sit-down strikes in Michigan that year, which had been made possible by New Deal labor legislation passed two years earlier. Even when he was a New Dealer, though, Dies was also a nativist, arguing for the deportation of radical aliens. Key targets of the Dies Committee were high-, mid-, and low-level New Dealers within the executive branch and in the wider world, those who seemed most vulnerable to the charge of communism. He hit hardest against the National Labor Relations Board, Leon Henderson, the Federal Communications Commission, and labor unions, specifically the CIO.[3]

Obviously unpopular with liberals, Dies's behavior sometimes discomfited conservative southern Democrats, too. Three of the best attorney legislators in the House, all conservative Democrats—Eugene E. Cox (D-GA), Hatton W. Sumners (D-TX), and Howard Worth Smith (D-VA)—had acknowledged "privately" according to one journalist "that Dies and his committee have trampled civil rights heavily. They admit that, but in the same breath they bring up the stock argument that after all the committee has done good." That Cox, Sumners, and Smith all disliked the New Deal and the president gives the assertion that the committee "has done good" an important and layered meaning.[4] These conservative Democrats, then, disliked Dies's methods, but they approved his results.

Not only did the committee foment anti–New Deal tendencies, it was also culturally conservative, predicting another postwar political development. For the Dies Committee, cultural issues about race and gender were framed with an anti-Communist rhetoric. A report from Robert Stripling, a committee investigator, revealed the intersections of racism, sexism, and anti-communism in the Un-American Activities panel. He contended that the Washington Branch of the American Peace Mobilization was filled with government employees who were closet Communists. While many Communists did join the organization, so did workers, students, and others committed to the cause of peace. It folded soon after Hitler invaded the Soviet Union. "Young white girls in the American Peace Mobilization are instructed to play up to Negroes, by sleeping with them if necessary, in order to bring them into the movement. They are told their reward will come in five years when the Communist Party rules America," Stripling expounded. "At social parties which followed the meetings, white girls sat kissing Negro men, and were observed making a point of dancing affectionately with all Negroes who attended." After spinning a tale that the APM was pushing African Americans into the defense industry so they could file charges of discrimination, Stripling concluded, "It appears that the Communist Party is using the APM as a spearhead in its attack on the U.S. Defense Program."[5]

Dies tested the rhetoric and the methodology that McCarthy and others perfected in the postwar era. For example, the language of "coddling" Communists, being "soft" on the threat of the Soviet Union, and noting "reliable evidence" that could not be "disclose[d] at the present time" all emerged during Dies's tenure as chair of the committee. Moreover, the phrase, "I have here in my hand" for which McCarthy became famous, was also a Dies Committee device. Dies once remarked, "the most effective weapon" against subversion was exposure because "we can trust public sentiment to do the rest." Careful analysis of the Dies record suggests the formula could be rewritten: circulation of rumors conflating a legitimate political ideology—liberalism—within the mainstream of the American political tradition with communism—a political ideology that for better or for worse terrified many Americans—damaged the New Deal coalition and narrowed the options for reformers in the postwar era. Even while the House leadership disdained Dies, it legitimized his charges when naming the Kerr Committee, a subcommittee of the House Appropriations Committee, to investigate Dies's findings regarding the supposed employment of Communists within the federal government. Conservative members of Congress agreed that the war should be about preserving American institutions and values, and they implied New Deal liberalism was actually foreign and antithetical to the nation's political tradition. For example, John E. Rankin (D-MS) argued, "We want neither Fascism, Nazism, nor Communism in this country. They are all symptoms of the same disease. They are a kind of international malaria; one of them is the chill and the other is the fever of the dying liberties of mankind."[6]

The Kerr Committee findings attracted little attention outside Congress, but its existence and its conclusions, both far less demagogic than the Dies Committee, made mainstream the anti-Communist rhetoric within the institution of Congress. For this reason, Harold Ickes, secretary of the interior and presidential confidante, characterized the Kerr Committee as "'a vicious political campaign'" in which members of Congress hoped "'to smear and to discredit the Administration, irrespective of the cost to the war.'" Ickes had no warm feelings for Dies or his committee, either. In his diary, he had called the Texan "an ass." Wartime political anti-communism garnered scant public attention in large part because the military alliance with the Soviet Union made such rhetoric dangerous to the war effort and because political antifascism seemed more in keeping with the nation's war aims.[7]

The Dies Committee became the progenitor of all things anti-Communist and anti–New Deal even though it was created to fight fascism following a German spy trial and violent outbreak at a Madison Square Garden rally of the German American Bund, an organization of right-wing American fascists in sympathy with Hitler's Germany. In 1938, the FBI had discovered a ring of New York City–based Nazi spies, some of whom had infiltrated the U.S. military and defense plants. Eighteen of the spies were indicted and tried for their crimes. Years later Dies recalled that the House leadership and the administration selected him to introduce the resolution creating the committee because of his reputation as a Roosevelt supporter. According to the Texan, Speaker William B. Bankhead (D-AL) told Dies he had Roosevelt's private support. To the leadership in the House, men who were creatures of the seniority system, the committee seemed a safe place to put Dies, already known for his demagoguery. There he could be controlled and his ability to harm the war effort limited. When the House authorized the Dies Committee by a vote of 191–41 on May 26, 1938, most did not foresee the partisan ends to which Dies would guide the panel, but this was false complacency. Rep. John W. McCormack (D-MA) warned Dies away from demagogic behavior, and the Texan promised that he would not oversee "a three-ring circus." Some House members noted privately that Dies worked "with a bazooka in one hand" and "a fireball in the other." Indeed, Dies described himself as the "'President of the House Demagogues' Club.'" A newspaper columnist for the *Washington Star* dismissed Dies's early efforts as ludicrous: "For any congressional body to hang its investigation of 'un-American activities' on an attempt to demonstrate that radical sentiments are widespread and growing comes close to basic un-Americanism. 'Who shall guard our guardians themselves?'" When he made known his intent to search for Communists as well as fascists, the funding for the new special committee was reduced from a proposed $100,000 to just $25,000, a sum Dies regarded as "paltry" and insufficient. Dies blamed then Majority Leader Sam Rayburn (D-TX), whom he described as partisan and "one of the most ambitious" politicians in the House. After Dies made a national radio address the original $100,000 was restored. Congress appropriated almost $500,000 between 1938 and 1943 for the various Dies Committee investigations and another $300,000 for similar inquiries by the Justice Department.[8]

"Country Boy Makes Good!" Berryman cartoon critical of the Dies Committee, February 1, 1939. Courtesy Library of Congress, Prints & Photographs Division, Clifford Berryman Collection [reproduction number, LC-DIG-ds-02877].

The Dies Committee lost no time in asserting its authority. Dies's first major hearing was into the German-American Bund. He soon turned his attention to organized labor, and at one point even called for the impeachment of labor secretary Frances Perkins, a New Deal loyalist, who had helped draft social security legislation and minimum wage laws. Its hearings were never balanced; instead, the only witnesses called to testify were those supportive of the Dies agenda. Liberal committee member Jerry Voorhis (D-CA) concluded, "The Dies Committee, in my opinion, got off to a bad start" because it took testimony, much of it partisan, from witnesses that were not "competent," and never assessed objectively the "validity" of the charges.[9]

Beginning in June 1940, Dies pushed hard for the administration to endorse legislation retarding the action of "fifth column" organizations in the United States. Dies wanted Roosevelt to create a Home Defense Council with representatives of the Dies Committee working in tandem with the FBI, the Army's Military Intelligence Division, and the Office of Naval Intelligence. J. Edgar Hoover disdained Dies's meddling in what he believed was his turf. He warned that Dies's demagoguery would "give momentum to the so-called Fifth Column hysteria." The FBI monitored the various requests from the committee for information. In response Dies told the White House: "I do not believe adequate steps are now being taken or that government agencies understand the technique and strategy being employed by agents of Stalin, Hitler, Mussolini, and Japan in the United States." Hoover tried but failed to get the attorney general to convene a grand jury to investigate Dies. Neither did Dies have all the backing of all his committee members; Rep. John Dempsey (D-NM) even called Hoover to say "he was not in sympathy with the procedure Dies has taken nor with the remarks that Dies has made about the Bureau." A public jousting match ensued, and Dies parlayed the feud into a private White House meeting with Roosevelt, despite warnings from the president's advisors not to see the Texan.[10]

At their late November 1940 meeting, the president endorsed the work of the Dies Committee, but he quashed the Texan's call for a comprehensive federal employee loyalty program. Roosevelt had a stenographer record a transcript of the meeting. The president began the meeting by insisting on "some kind of demarcation between administration work and investigatory." He disputed the wisdom of charging congressional committees with investigating subversion. At the conclusion of their meeting Dies stressed his willingness to cooperate with the executive, but he also complained he had "been denounced" and "have had to pay a pretty high price for what I have done." He told reporters when he left the White House he was satisfied with the meeting and he would be making no changes to committee procedures. Several days after the meeting Dies arranged for Voorhis to function as liaison between the committee and the White House "in order to avoid any possible friction or misunderstanding." Even though the transcript proves otherwise, Dies later quoted Roosevelt as saying at their meeting, "I look upon Russia as our strongest ally in the years to come." Dies used this supposed statement from the president along with another quote he attributed to Roosevelt—"several of the best friends I have are communists"—to argue "the views he expressed that day . . . shed much light on subsequent events. They . . . explain the concessions to Stalin and post-war policies with regard to Soviet Russia."[11] This event proved administration critics could make a false characterization of the president seem true by repeating it often enough.

The Dies Committee contained two liberal Democrats, two conservative Democrats, and two conservative Republicans. J. Parnell Thomas (R-NJ) was one of the

Republicans and he, Dies, and Joe Starnes (D-AL) were the most important members. Starnes, a schoolteacher turned congressman, was of limited intellect. On one occasion he compared the American Revolution favorably with the Russian Revolution, arguing that no one had been killed in the former. Equally stunning, when a witness before the Dies Committee made reference to Christopher Marlowe, Starnes queried, "You're quoting from this Marlowe. Is he a communist?"[12]

Procedural practices within the Dies Committee were loose and without regularity. As a result, the staffing of the committee deserves some mention. Dies's first hire was a young Texan, Robert E. Stripling, who had known the congressman before he moved to Washington, D.C., and who volunteered to work for free when committee funding was in doubt. Committee research director J. B. Matthews had had a storied career before signing up with Dies. A former Methodist missionary and a teacher, Matthews had earlier identified with socialism and Marxism. He got his job with Dies after giving ten hours of testimony before the committee in executive session. He taught Dies the importance of building a massive filing system with names of suspected Communists. Among the individuals he charged was child actress Shirley Temple. He once noted, "To me a letterhead of a Communist front is a nugget." Dies and his committee had other sources for their information, namely the FBI. As early as 1938, the FBI began feeding evidence to at least Rep. Thomas so that charges could be publicized, showing that even though Hoover disdained aspects of Dies's methodology he recognized the usefulness of Dies as a demagogue. Subcommittees of one or two, with investigatory power, were common. Such flux gave Dies inordinate power.[13]

The most important evidence of all in disproving recent arguments that the Dies Committee should be viewed as a legitimate hunter of communists comes from observing the lack of meaningful change in his strategy after the signing of the Nazi-Soviet Pact, a 1939 agreement between Germany and the Soviet Union whereby the two nations agreed not to take up arms against each other, or after the attack on Pearl Harbor. Because Dies's anti-communism was about domestic politics, he sounded in 1941, 1942, and 1943 much as he had in 1938 and 1939. Indeed, he began making charges of long lists of Communists working in the government. In January 1940, Rep. Dempsey reported to presidential advisor James Rowe there was no list of Communists working in the federal government despite Dies's numerous claims to the contrary. Even with evidence from Dempsey that Dies had no list of Communists in the government, the press continued to publish his salacious charges. Dies told the press that some of the people held jobs with significant authority. He also broke down the number of alleged Communists in each government department. On June 28, 1941, Congress passed the appropriation bill for the Justice Department. Contained within it was $100,000 for investigating subversive tendencies among federal government employees. In October 1941, Dies sent a list of 1,124 names to Attorney General Biddle of the people who he believed were Communists or fellow travelers, more in one year than McCarthy ever "identified." An even more significant fact about the list were the names on it—Alger Hiss and Harry Dexter White—who became infamous in the postwar years when charges they were Communists dominated headlines. That Dies did not make a case against either Hiss or White further suggests the weakness of his committee's actual investigative efforts and even abilities. The Texan nonetheless expounded: "Our government, by its aid to Russia on the eastern front, has opened up for Stalin a new western front right here in the capital of America."[14]

The administration began its own loyalty investigation within the federal government to stymie Dies. Only two persons from Dies's list were terminated from their government jobs for subversive behavior. Dies rejected the FBI findings by arguing the agency had not administered a proper investigation. Voorhis had a very different understanding of the situation. He insisted, first, that the FBI was the only entity qualified to investigate subversion, and, second, that "whoever the real Nazi, Japanese, fascist, or communist agents were, they would not be people whose names were publicly listed as members of controversial organizations." Nevertheless, Dies claimed the administration was harboring subversives on the federal payroll.[15]

Dies had done his most effective work in 1939 two years before the United States entered World War II. Even when he did correctly identify the existence of Communists within the country, among a minority of the CIO union, in the Federal Theater Project, and in a host of front groups, his methodology was as un-American as were the supposed actions of his targets. Dies's biggest accomplishment was the September 1939 hearing that resulted in U.S. Communist Party leader Earl Browder's conviction for traveling to the Soviet Union on a forged passport. Moreover, Dies identified the anti-Semitic activities of the German-American Bund, even if he did not spend concomitant time on ferreting out fascists as he did Communists. He also identified some of the individuals who worked in Communist espionage networks throughout the New Deal. By 1940, Dies had reverted to politically inspired attacks on New Dealers, especially the CIO. More important, he ceased holding hearings, instead functioning as a subcommittee of one. Where there had been fifty-three hearings in 1938 and sixty-one in 1939, the number fell to twenty-three in 1940, and by 1942 there were none. Those hearings held in 1943 did not include Dies. Dies's health problems—he had had a nervous breakdown in 1941—played a role in the pattern of hearings.[16]

Key members of Congress found Dies's charges without merit. Rep. Adolph Sabath (D-IL) told FDR that additional congressional funds for the Dies Committee was wasted money. He also tried to convince the press that the president shared those views, a strategy that worried the White House because "a good many people in this country are for the Committee and there wouldn't be 20 votes against it in the House." Still, in January 1940 Sabath planned to delay hearings on a resolution to extend the Dies Committee for an additional year. His justification was Dies's absence from Washington, D.C. "I think that the Country will be safe if we wait until Dies returns before considering this Resolution," Sabath avowed. "I feel that the Department of Justice has a better organization than Dies ever can expect to have and I don't believe in unnecessary duplication. . . . After all, Dies has had enough publicity for any and all purposes and perhaps he will be still in demand for public speeches and writing magazine articles." The Speaker intervened and forced Sabath to call a meeting. Roosevelt agreed there was no option but to "let the resolution go through."[17]

Rayburn and McCormack explained that Dies's methods harmed the reputation of the federal government and had hampered consideration of the price control legislation, one of the most important issues before the wartime Congress. Even FDR had publicly attacked Dies for his "sordid" ways, but the president had his limits. He wished not to be the reason for Dies's defeat. Dies's antipathy toward the Democratic Party troubled McCormack, who had chaired an investigation into subversion in the early 1930s. For all the demagoguery Dies exhibited in his committee, he had not introduced a single piece of remedial legislation. Said McCormack off the record, "Why, damn it, when I conducted an investigation of subversive activities, it was an investigation. It resulted in legislation. And we didn't make victims of innocent people."[18]

William Dudley Pelley was one of the few fascists the committee investigated. He formed the Silver Legion, a "patriotic fraternity," in 1933 "to propagandize exactly the same principles that Mr. Dies and this committee are engaged in prosecuting right now." Pelley admitted that he believed "Mr. Hitler had done an excellent job in Germany for the Germans." He agreed that relocation of all American Jews into one city in each state was a good method for addressing "the Jewish question," but he drew the line at sterilization. At the conclusion of the Pelley testimony Starnes protested just enough to separate the Dies Committee from Pelley but never did the Dies Committee push for remedial action against Pelley or his ilk.[19]

Discussion between a committee member and a committee staffer about a report on fascist threats to the United States reveals how domestic political bias regarding the New Deal and not anti-subversion guided the work of the committee. Rep. Thomas told Stripling: "Read both the report on the Axis Front movement in the United States and the supplemental inserts in detail, and my conclusion is that the main body of the report is excellent, but that both the introduction and Inserts 1 and 4 read like either a New Dealer's pipe dream or the minutes taken down at one of Washington's nudist meetings." Thomas complained that Eleanor

Roosevelt, Henry Wallace, and Jerry Voorhis might have written it, and that he would withhold his support until revisions were made. "You and Doc Matthews better get together and write the introduction all over again," Thomas advised. "The less Jerry Voorhis has to do with it, the better I'll like it. By all means show him this." Upon reflection, Thomas concluded he had been too critical of Voorhis, but he nonetheless declared: "Jerry could render a much greater service to our committee if he would just get wise to the fact that this nation's greatness is the result of individual sweat and toil and thrift, and not the result of uneconomic, sociological, crackpot ideologies." After the revisions were complete, Thomas approved the report.[20]

Contemporary public opinion polls suggest that Americans held a nuanced view of the Dies Committee. In a March 1939 poll of those aware of the Dies Committee only 26 percent considered Communist activities important enough to merit investigation. Respondents viewed Nazi activities, at 32 percent, and war propaganda, at 42 percent, as more significant. The following year, public opinion shifted with 70 percent of Americans surveyed with an opinion endorsing inquiries into Communist activities but only 30 percent suggesting Nazi activities should be studied. If nothing else the Dies Committee attracted significant media attention from its inception, claiming over 500 column inches of space in the *New York Times* over a two-month period in late summer, early fall 1938. Dies both helped manufacture that shift and used it to foster his publicity-seeking investigations. He reported at the end of 1939 that he received thousands of letters a day from supporters. Dies understood the importance of positive public relations if he was to prevail in his anti-Communist crusade. One of his favorite contacts was right-wing anti–New Deal newspaper columnist Westbrook Pegler, an ally in the wartime crusade against liberal statism.[21]

Opposition to the Dies Committee became politically untenable for members of Congress from all but the safest of districts, revealing that Dies functioned outside the boundaries of the seniority system, celebrated for its hierarchical control of congressional behavior. By early 1941, Rep. John Coffee (D-WA) told an ACLU colleague, "'those of us liberals who have fought the Dies Committee from its inception have stuck our necks out just about as long as we felt it is justified. The main issue raised against me in my campaign was my opposition to the Dies Committee.'" Moreover, those who did challenge the committee did so less for ideological reasons but because of geopolitical concerns. Even Roosevelt appreciated the difficulties of challenging Dies. His words about the Texas demagogue suggest an entirely different approach to congressional relations than was normally true for FDR, who often tried to mold Congress in his image. He told Vito Marcantonio (AL-NY), "I want to be absolutely correct in not interfering in any way with purely congressional business that I am not able to say anything."[22]

Enough lawmakers endorsed the Dies Committee to preserve its place on Capitol Hill. Liberals either overlooked the civil liberties abuses or viewed them as inconsequential in comparison with other war-related issues. The press of more important war measures on the congressional docket meant liberal and moderate Democrats never disbanded the Dies Committee. For example, New York Democrat Sol Bloom, a civil rights advocate and the chair of the House Foreign Affairs Committee, could not attend a Rules Committee hearing on the future of the Dies Committee because of simultaneously scheduled Lend-Lease revision hearings. Inaction combined with moderate and conservative acquiescence entrenched the Dies Committee in American politics. Rep. Robert L. Doughton (D-NC) told Rep. Clarence Cannon (D-MO), the chair of the Appropriations Committee: "I have not always agreed with everything that Mr. Dies has done and said, [but] I do believe that his Committee has rendered a nation-wide service and shall gladly vote to increase the [Committee's] appropriation."[23]

Dies's incessant search for publicity led to the creation of the Kerr Committee. On February 1, 1943, Dies indicted the government for its failure to purge Communists from the executive agencies. The Texas demagogue defended himself against charges that his committee work aided and abetted the Axis powers. He named thirty-nine executive branch employees as dangerous subversives unworthy of federal jobs. He threatened that the Appropriations Committee could deny funding for salaries if the individuals were not removed by other means. Dies lumped "bureaucrats" together with "crackpots" and "Communists" as defenders of "totalitarianism." Dies's speech forced the media and the House to examine his charges, but not all of his colleagues concurred. Kentucky Democrat Brent Spence told a steel worker and union official that the Dies Committee no longer "perform[ed] any functions for which it was created, but has gone on snooping investigations beyond the powers granted it." He decried the failure to hold "speedy and public trial[s]" and the abandonment of the presumption of innocence. Others like newly elected Fred Busbey (R-IL) agreed with the Texan. Busbey told Dies, "I personally believe the work you and the committee" have undertaken to be "the most important of our whole program, and it should not only be continued but expanded."[24]

This controversy caused some in the House to push for the elimination of compensation for the thirty-nine individuals Dies had named. On February 5, the House rejected such an amendment to the Treasury and Post Office Departments appropriation bill (the first appropriations bill before the new Congress) by a vote of 146–153. Another amendment, banning payment of salary to William Pickens of the Treasury Department, passed easily. Controversy erupted when lawmakers learned that Pickens was African American. Even though Dies and Cannon read off the twenty-one supposed Communist-front organizations with which Pickens had allegedly worked, northern and Republican lawmakers would not cooperate with what one congressman compared to a lynching. Cannon brokered a compromise. He named a five-person subcommittee of the Appropriations Committee to study the charges and to give each of the thirty-nine individuals a chance to testify. The majority and minority leaders endorsed the solution, and House members agreed. Concurrently, the House extended the Dies Committee for an additional year by a 302–94 vote.[25]

Days later Dies spoke on the radio to a national audience. His rhetoric reflected an appreciation of the totalitarian forces that had brought on the world war and a simplistic attempt to argue similar trends were extant in the United States. After criticizing the "revival of the pagan and materialistic conception of the nature of the state," Dies asserted, "federal bureaucrats have been gradually taking over the functions of state and local governments." Though he acknowledged the need for an expanded federal government to fight the war, he believed this new power should be temporary and should not bear on domestic programs. Just as he disliked the New Deal welfare state so also did he oppose a permanent warfare state. Dies intimated his committee should play a central role in preventing Communists from "infiltrat[ing]" these new agencies. Dies asked his audience to write and tell him whether they agreed with his contentions: "the fight that I have made during the past four and a half years is more than a fight against subversive groups and organizations. In the larger and more important sense it is a fight for survival of constitutional government and the preservation of your God-given rights as American citizens."[26]

What Dies and other conservatives saw as defense of American liberties, liberal activists characterized very differently. The president of the NAACP, at the behest of his board of directors, telegrammed John McCormack and Joseph W. Martin Jr.: "character assassination, professional lynching, and intimidation of public officials by the Dies clique must be stopped. . . . The conduct of the men responsible for this attack would be more becoming to agents of the Gestapo than it is to those acting in the name of the American Congress. Let there be no mistake. This outrageous action is but an opening gun in a direct assault against American liberalism."[27]

The House resolution that created the Kerr Committee in February asserted "present association or membership" as well as "past association or membership" in subversive organizations would be sufficient for dismissal. Conservative Democrat John H. Kerr of North Carolina chaired the panel. Clinton Anderson (NM) and Albert Gore (TN) were the other two Democratic members. Frank B. Keefe (WI) and David Lane Powers (NJ) assumed the two minority seats. Anderson explained the Kerr Committee's mission to one witness: "this is not an examination to determine whether you have done your work well or have not done your work well. The only question involved, if the Chairman will permit me to say this, is whether or not you have belonged to associations of a subversive character. It is not a question of whether your own activities have been subversive." The Kerr Committee relied on materials from the FBI and the Dies Committee to conduct its inquiry.[28]

Each of the Kerr Committee hearings was dubbed executive and confidential with witnesses appearing via invitation not subpoena. Witnesses were not allowed to bring counsel nor were colleagues from their employing agencies permitted to attend. Initially, the Kerr Committee passed along the charges to its witnesses before their appearance, but halted that practice after the first two witnesses. Kerr claimed on the House floor that witnesses already knew the charges because they came from Dies's speech to Congress in February, but actually the charges that Kerr and his colleagues used came from a confidential document different from what Dies had used for his February 1 speech. Kerr granted witnesses the right to introduce supporting documents with their statements, but witnesses could not question the motives of the Dies Committee.[29]

The Kerr Committee defined subversive activity, something that Congress, the attorney general, and the courts had not done: "'Subversive activity in this country derives from conduct intentionally destructive of or inimical to the Government of the United States—that which seeks to undermine its institutions, or to distort its functions, or to impede its projects, or to lessen its efforts, the ultimate end being to overturn it all. Such activity may be open and direct, as by effort to overthrow, or subtle and indirect, as by sabotage.'" One contemporary critic blasted the definition for its imprecision, suggesting that Republican Party diatribes against Democrats might be found treasonous under this wording. A decade after the fact, former attorney general Francis Biddle attacked the thoughtless pursuit of subversives in government, especially the definition that the Kerr Committee drafted. "Ambiguous words, these. They might well be construed to include reciprocal trade agreements, federal health programs, or even criticism of the recent increase in salaries of government officials."[30]

Even though Cannon promised that the Kerr Committee would not be a "'star chamber,'" none of the thirty-nine individuals called to testify had ever been accused of Communist Party membership. Instead, their "crimes" involved affiliation with Communist-front organizations, as defined by the Dies Committee and/or the FBI; public utterances disparaging laissez-faire capitalism; and praise of either the Soviet Union or the Spanish Loyalists who fought and lost a civil war against the fascist government of Francisco Franco in 1939. Most troubling, the committee never clarified the standards it used to determine guilt or innocence. Comparisons of the thirty-six who were cleared against the three who were found guilty of subversive behavior revealed little difference in patterns of membership and political activity.[31]

Once the Kerr hearings were announced, many asked for an opportunity to testify and for a fair investigation. Joseph A. Facci, an employee of the Foreign Language Division of the Office of War Information, who was among those to be investigated by the Kerr Committee, demanded of Cannon, "not to be condemned without an opportunity to defend myself. I stand ready and eager to undergo any investigation, but I ask for a fair democratic investigation with an opportunity to present evidence in my defense."[32]

Because Dies and his cronies had overreached, colleagues and friends of the targets responded. Both institutions and individuals loyal to the accused asked Kerr and Dies for a fair hearing and for acknowledgments of innocence. For example, when the Dies Committee charged Columbia University professor Goodwin B. Watson with Communist leanings, Watson's academic colleagues rallied to his defense. Said Irving E. Bender, a Dartmouth College psychologist, "The attack is completely unjustified and does much discredit to a committee which we have assumed was safeguarding American interests and American citizens." Watson even took his case to the court of public opinion in a letter to the *New York Times* after the Kerr Committee branded him as subversive. Rep. Francis D. Culkin (R-NY) came to civil rights activist Mary McLeod Bethune's defense when she ran afoul of the Dies Committee for supposed association with Communists. Culkin told Kerr of her school for African American girls, Bethune-Cookman College: "I am informed that religion and church services play a daily part in the work of this institution. May I say in conclusion that I have been a supporter of the Dies Committee from the beginning and voted to continue it yesterday." African American labor leader A. Philip Randolph, the president of the Brotherhood of Sleeping Car Porters, reached a less charitable conclusion. He affirmed that Dies, a Texan, made the accusations because of his racism and because he, in his "traditional belief that a Negro should be docile about the wrongs that are heaped upon him, cannot understand her militant spirit. He therefore considers Mrs. Bethune . . . as a part of a subversive movement." Randolph concluded that such charges would not "caus[e] Negroes to become less militant in their fight for their rights and for the status of first-class citizenship in America."[33]

The Kerr Committee addressed a variety of supposedly subversive topics in its hearings—academic study of the Soviet Union, religious beliefs, defense of the Loyalists in the Spanish Civil War, civil rights advocacy, and gender relations to name a few. The Kerr Committee encouraged the naming of names of others with supposed subversive tendencies. It did not ask its witnesses to assuage their guilt by widening the circle of suspects, but it relied on the testimony of other future professional witnesses who made a career out of naming names in the postwar Red Scare. For example, Dr. Frederick L. Schuman, a German political analyst with the Federal Communications Commission, faced suspicion because noted anti-Communist and anti-Semite Elizabeth Dilling had listed him as a Communist supporter in the pamphlet, "Culture and the Crisis," but he denied authorizing any such use of his name. Schuman's offense involved writing a doctoral dissertation at the University of Chicago. His subject was American policy toward Russia since 1917, and since he published it with International Publishers, a press with a substantial Russian studies list, his loyalties were questionable to conservatives in American politics.[34]

Because the Kerr Committee had not yet begun its hearings, on April 7, Rep. Everett McKinley Dirksen (R-IL) complained about the subcommittee's apparent inaction. He used the State, Justice, and Commerce Appropriation bill to frame his remarks, importuning that Kerr's delay hindered congressional deliberations. "The House has shown admirable restraint and patience in letting this matter reside in that committee for a determination. But 60 days have elapsed," Dirksen stressed. "Other appropriation bills will be submitted and they will include the names of some people on whom there has been a report by investigators of our own committee and whose names I propose to bring into this well unless some action is taken reasonably soon." At that point, Rep. Hamilton Fish (R-NY) asserted that "we were led astray" by Cannon and the Appropriations Committee, who had promised that the subcommittee would act expeditiously. Since the Kerr Committee was holding morning and afternoon hearings, Anderson implored "What more would the gentleman require of us?" Dirksen remained adamant that a preliminary report was necessary, but Anderson countered, "you cannot give a preliminary report as to whether a man is a fit or unfit person to stay on the pay roll."[35]

Keefe, a member of the subcommittee, articulated some additional challenges, "We have had a great deal of difficulty getting the charges presented to the committee. All of the charges against all of these people are not before the committee yet. It has taken the Dies committee a tremendous amount of work in order to assemble this information and submit it in proper form to our committee." After more quibbling from his colleagues, Keefe retorted, "If you think it is any little peanut job you have another guess coming. . . . This committee is trying to be fair." Kerr supported Keefe's analysis. "On April 1 we had only one case from the Dies committee which was full and complete and included recent testimony before the Dies committee. The accused in this one was heard before us the next day." After more bickering, the House debated and passed the appropriations bill.[36]

This fight only escalated congressional passions regarding subversion, and Ickes increased his pressure on Kerr to dismiss the charges as unfounded. He averred, "Congressman Dies sees membership in certain organizations as positive proof that the employee is a member of the Communist Party or plans to subvert the Government of the United States. This I think is unwarranted." Ickes held that the supposed Communist-front organizations had among their members "American citizens who are of unimpeachable loyalty and integrity." Ickes declared that even "the churches and the country clubs" had Communist members. No one person, Ickes stressed, could replicate the FBI's investigatory resources before determining whether to join an organization. He then cited several examples of members of Congress who had either been members of or had worked with the organizations that Dies singled out as subversive.[37]

The stigma of congressional accusation influenced personnel decisions that should have been beyond the purview of the legislative branch. To avoid the Kerr Committee imbroglio, some executive branch officials terminated the accused employees working under their authority. For example, Leo T. Crowley, an administration official with the FDIC and various wartime agencies, dismissed an employee whom Dies had accused of being a rhythmic dancer sympathetic to the Soviet Union. Another individual on the Dies Committee list of thirty-nine asked to be excused from his appearance before the Kerr Committee, explaining that while he was not and had never been a Communist he no longer worked for the federal government.[38]

The Kerr Committee conducted hearings in this fraught environment, and it added to the tension. Some of the testimony revealed the ridiculous nature of equating liberalism with communism. Texan Arthur E. Goldschmidt, an official with the Interior Department's Division of Power, testified about his donations to the Washington Friends of Spanish Democracy. When he had his dog bred, explained Goldschmidt, many of his friends wanted to buy a puppy. "I did not want to make any money out of my dog's puppies, or out of my friends. At the same time there were more people who wanted puppies than there were puppies. So I sold the puppies to those people," and donated the money to "the war-stricken people of Spain."[39]

The Great Depression and the New Deal had caused many policy activists to reexamine fundamental questions about American democracy. Flirtations with socialism and communism along with criticisms of the political status quo were common in the 1930s. For example, Kerr grew angry when Marcus I. Goldman of the U.S. Geological Survey decried the lack of opportunity for the one-third of Americans ill housed, ill clad, and ill nourished, phrasing Roosevelt himself had used in his second inaugural address in 1937 to argue for even more New Deal reforms. "I am asking you for your personal opinion," Kerr intoned, "if in this great country of ours, which has one-half of the wealth of the world, does half of the business of the world, contributes more to education and uplift of the people of this country than all the balance of the world—now can you conceive under circumstances of that kind that one-third of the people of this country haven't had a fair chance?" Goldman did not waver: "Well, they haven't."[40]

Still other Kerr Committee hearings reveal the undercurrent of gender bias within the politics of anti-communism. Dr. Maurice Parmelee, an economist with the Board of Economic Warfare, affirmed that Dies had misconstrued his writings. Dies had targeted Parmelee because he viewed him as a "crackpot." When the Dies Committee had examined Parmelee's writings about gender relations, especially his book *Nudism in Modern Life,* the House members had behaved as if they were twelve-year-old boys. Parmelee intimated that the charges of subversion against him were based on the books and articles that he had written over a period of thirty-five years, including *Bolshevism, Fascism and the Liberal-Democratic State,* and *Farewell to Poverty.* When questioned as to whether he advocated nudism, Parmelee replied, "in some respects I was favorably disposed to nudism. It was my view that nudism is valuable for health, . . . but I am certainly not an advocate of nudism in the sense that on the street it should be widespread or universal." He acknowledged to the committee that the church was "an impediment to the development of nudism," as he had written in the book. This argument was not persuasive. Nor was his assertion that women exchanged virginity at marriage for a life of economic security. Parmelee challenged the worldview of the subcommittee members. Anderson reasoned, "the habit of Dr. Parmelee of going to apartments where there are men and women who remove their clothing and sit around in the nude is not subversive. . . . It sickens me with him as a man, but it did not persuade the Kerr Committee to vote against him on the charge of being subversive."[41]

By the middle of May, the Kerr Committee had finished deliberating some of its cases and had concurred with the Dies Committee findings regarding Goodwin B. Watson, Robert Morss Lovett, and William E. Dodd Jr. As a result, on May 17, 1943, Kerr offered a rider to the urgent deficiency appropriations legislation, barring the payment of salaries to Dodd, Watson, and Lovett. Emanuel Celler (D-NY) attacked the measure as "rather dangerous. We should think very deeply before we vote approval of the so-called ouster of liberals from various executive departments of the Government." Celler described legislative anti-communism as "hysteria" and "witch burning." While no one disputed general congressional spending authority, legitimate questions ensued as to the constitutionality of this unprecedented action. Certainly, Congress could not withhold the salary of a president or a member of the Supreme Court if it disagreed with that individual's policies. When first debating whether or not Congress had the power to deny salary payments to individuals it labeled as subversive, one member declared, "'If a man is an employee of this Government and if some people have seen fit to question his loyalty, and knowing, as I do, that he has no property right in the job which he holds, why can I not, as a Member of this House, vote to have him taken from the payroll?'"[42]

Next, Keefe began a spirited defense of the Kerr Committee and an equally vigorous attack on Dodd, Watson, and Lovett. The legality of the Kerr Committee deliberations hinged on whether or not the judgments had been judicial in character. Keefe attested that its entire function had been judicial. The committee, though, never applied the methods of American jurisprudence to its procedures. Furthermore, even if it had, the Constitution bans Congress from acting in a judicial fashion. Argued one observer: "Few principles of American public law are better established . . . than the principle that a legislature may not exercise powers of trying and punishing individuals. When, as in the present instance, the individuals in question are charged with no violation of law, and are therefore not subject to trial even by the courts, the definitive character of this prohibition can scarcely be open to debate."[43]

The following day, the House returned to the urgent deficiency appropriations bill. Kerr pronounced: "I think the committee fully understands the implications involved in one branch of the Government attempting to remove an employee of another branch." He attested that his subcommittee had not been created to fire people. "The House Committee on Appropriations is simply bringing here to this Congress and giving you the facts as it has found them, saying to you, 'Gentlemen, these are the facts. The duty devolves upon you now to say whether or not these men named in the amendment are fitted to be employees of the United States Government,'" avowed Kerr. "I contend that the proposition before the House is an elementary one. It does not involve the question of impeaching anybody." Kerr denied that the "employees under investigation" had "property rights in their offices." Said Kerr, "One Congress can take away their rights given them by another." The House approved the rider 318–62.[44]

Journalists criticized the rider as a bill of attainder (legislative imposition of punishment without a judicial trial), and House moderates and liberals went on the attack. The *New York Times* ridiculed the House for its acceptance of the Kerr Committee recommendations. In an editorial, the paper berated the Kerr Committee because "the 'evidence' in question was not made available to the House. Yet that august body voted to deprive Dr. Lovett and his colleagues of their rights. One wonders what country this is in which such things can take place. . . . Perhaps the Senate, which has still to act in this matter, will reassert the ancient rights and decencies of which we have been so proud." Ickes used another line of reasoning to attack the Kerr Committee. He told the press about Lovett's patriotism: "'He is a genuinely good man. His only son was killed in action at Belleau Wood in the last war. He was born an American, has lived as an American for seventy-three years, and today deserves American treatment from his government and not the type of liquidation that is enforced in conquered European countries.'"[45]

A dispute erupted between the two chambers of Congress, showing the boundless congressional warfare involved jealousy between the House and the Senate mixed with ideology. No liberal, Kenneth McKellar (D-TN) noted that the Senate refused to adhere to the House provisions because it had not been privy to the evidence that the Kerr Committee studied. McKellar wrote Kerr that no one testified to the Senate Appropriations Committee in favor of the rider, so the committee "simply struck it out so that the matter might go to Conference." McKellar complained, "We were told that you had taken evidence but that it had never been printed and had been kept confidential by your Committee. I should think this evidence should be furnished the Conferees." After the Senate unanimously rejected the rider, on June 8 Cannon pushed for its inclusion. Equally adamant, the Senate insisted on its deletion two days later.[46]

The Kerr Committee responded to its critics in the Senate and in the public with a unanimous statement. The committee delineated its righteousness vis-à-vis the Dies Committee: "Up to this point the Committee on Un-American Activities had not given the persons charged any hearing," whereas the Kerr Committee ensured "each accused person an opportunity to appear and be heard." The committee offered "no apologies for writing a definition of subversive activity," reminding the public that neither the Attorney General nor the Congress nor the courts had defined the term. The committee refuted all charges that it had prevented witnesses from having an attorney even though the executive session testimony revealed otherwise. The Kerr Committee characterized its actions as "wise and fair and expedient."[47]

On June 15, Kerr told his House colleagues that the Senate was wrong to state that the subcommittee's evidence and transcripts had been held in secret. "The transcripts have been available at all times to any and all of the Members of the Congress," professed Kerr. "The exhibits in these cases are voluminous and are and have been available to all Members of Congress, but to deliver them from one office to another would require trucks or wheelbarrows to transport them."[48]

The disagreement went to a conference committee with the upper chamber claiming on June 24 that the House position was unconstitutional and un-American. When the lower chamber prevailed, the measure went back to the two houses for what should have been final approval but stubborn lawmakers reenacted the earlier scenario, leading to a second conference committee on June 28. By that point, most were willing to compromise because the deficiency appropriation bill required immediate attention. Unfortunately, the two chambers could not agree on how to draft that compromise, and the measure went through three more conference committees before a solution could be found. Publication of the Kerr Committee transcripts encouraged a sufficient number of Senators to accept the re-vised rider, which eliminated the three salaries unless Roosevelt sent nominations for the three individuals to the Senate by November 15. The upper chamber voted 48–32 to approve the report and the House concurred on July 3.[49]

The Kerr Committee episode, while forgotten by most students of the second Red Scare, nonetheless gave credibility to the wartime anti-Communist dema-goguery of the Dies Committee. It also showed a certain lack of responsibility by lawmakers who were willing to sacrifice the legitimate fiscal needs of the war-fare state by postponing passage of appropriations legislation to indulge anti-Communist hysteria. Ostensibly created to calm the passions that the Texan had inflamed, the Kerr Committee instead gave the issue substance, revealing that the ideology of conservative anti-communism had secured a place in the antistatist tool kit and that the moderate reconceptualization of the New Deal order em-braced ideological politics when the arguments were conservative in bent. Put differently, whereas the moderate coalition took center left positions on the econ-omy typically it skewed toward center right on social justice issues.

Throughout the war years, a majority of the House had been willing to leave the Dies Committee in place, neither taking it too seriously nor worrying about its abuses. When Dies named thirty-nine individuals on the federal payroll as subversive risks, he crossed a line. Some in Congress and the public enjoined that he be stopped and others exhorted that the subversives be stopped. Because enough lawmakers wanted to curtail funding for the salaries of all the individuals Dies named, the House Appropriations Committee launched its investigation. The Kerr Committee, though, never quite balanced between the two radically op-posed constituencies. It favored the anti-Communist politics that Dies had per-fected. Furthermore, it shared Dies's tendency to combine a host of liberal positions under the umbrella of subversive activity. Thus, even though the Kerr Committee dismissed the majority of the charges Dies had brought to the House floor, the fact that it took seriously what was nothing more than ideological dem-agoguery made that political style attractive and profitable, intensifying the ideo-logical war in Congress while doing nothing to settle the institutional war with the executive branch.

After the Kerr Committee investigation subsided, the Dies Committee had less influence on Capitol Hill. It attempted but a few investigations in 1944 of the Civil Service Commission, the CIO PAC, and the National Citizens' PAC. In January 1944, Dies tried to mount an investigation of the CIO's political activity. "The CIO fought Dies from hell to breakfast when he ran for Senator in Texas" earlier in the 1941 special senatorial election to replace the deceased Morris Sheppard, noted one journalist, "and undoubtedly did him some considerable harm. Between the labor organization and the Texas demagogue there is a deep bond of mutual hate, disrespect, and disgust." Later in life Dies even insisted that the wartime defense industries located in his district had been placed there to increase the union vote against him. Moreover, Dies charged, the administration began a politically motivated investigation of his Internal Revenue Service filings to try to force him from office.[50] But Dies's deteriorating health and the unwillingness of Congress to begin another specious witch hunt blocked this latest attempt at war against the New Deal.

When Dies announced he would not run for reelection in 1944, his aides told journalists off the record that he had a tumor on his larynx, a diagnosis that turned out to be false. Later Dies said of his retirement, "I felt that the country had been given all the funds it needed to defeat Communism, and I asked myself 'what more can I accomplish under a hostile Administration?'" Frank McNaughton wrote of Martin Dies, "Dies' larynx is his life; he has a good set of brains, he's wily, but he has always preferred to rely, instead, upon his voice box and now that it has developed an ailment, a new, less-raucous, more thoughtful and less garrulous Dies must emerge." Prior to his illness, Dies commanded hefty fees on the lecture circuit, earning over $50,000. "This money he said he was going to use to establish a Dies Foundation for Americanism," McNaughton noted. "If the Foundation is functioning it is Martin Dies' quietest activity." Dies's book, *The Trojan Horse in America*, was published in 1940 and earned between $3,000 and $5,000. Committee staffer Matthews was the actual author of the book. Moreover, circumstantial evidence suggests Dies profited in other ways from his chairmanship, namely by accepting bribes not to hold hearings or otherwise charge individuals with Communist activity. Similarly, his biographer suggests he took bribes to charge individuals he otherwise would have ignored. This funding came through honoraria for his public speeches for higher than normal amounts.[51]

Dies's departure from Congress did not harm his brand of conservatism, suggesting that anti-communism as a weapon against New Deal liberalism knew no bounds. Thomas contended, "The withdrawal of Martin Dies is both unexpected and regrettable. He will be missed by a large majority of the House Members." He advised that the committee would continue to work for the remainder of the 78th Congress but that the new 79th Congress seated in 1945 would have to decide the fate of the committee beyond that date. "As the ranking Republican Member of the Committee, I personally believe that the House of Representatives will find it necessary to have such a Committee," Thomas asserted, "and I further believe that the House should give serious consideration to the advisability of establishing a permanent standing Committee on un-American Activities with a highly trained and permanent staff. My convictions on this matter are based upon the present underground strategy now in operation by certain of the subversive and un-American groups within our midst."[52]

Upon his retirement, Dies exhorted: "We cannot repeat too often or emphasize too strongly the grave danger our country faces from the enemies within our gates. If we are destroyed as a free country I am confident it will come from within." He named "a powerful coalition of New Dealers, communists, socialists and racketeers" as culprits, noting their dominance of the government, organized labor, and industry. "They are united in a common aim to destroy our constitutional Republic and substitute some form of dictatorship. They are succeeding to an extent which few citizens realize," Dies argued. "Indeed our Government has already been changed by intrigue and subterfuge. We are rapidly becoming an inefficient expensive and meddling bureaucracy, which is the beginning of dictatorship. If this trend is to be reversed the people must shake off their indifference and complacency."[53]

Though the Kerr Committee investigation and Dies's retirement from Congress were the most significant reasons for the decline of the committee in the latter half of the war, Allied military victories also muted briefly the passions that encouraged criticism of the administration. The successful D-Day landings on June 6, 1944, the beginning of the final Allied assault against Germany, brought a new, optimistic attitude to Congress about the war and its impact on national politics. Journalists with newspapers and the radios began calling members of Congress as early as 4 a.m. on June 6, 1944, for comments about D-Day. Lawmakers wanted the best source possible, so some asked to meet with Roosevelt. Speaker Rayburn made such a call at 8:45, and he was the only member of Congress asked to the White House that day. The Texan met with Roosevelt an hour later in the president's bedroom. The two conferred for thirty-five minutes, with Roosevelt relating the demise of the first line of German coastal defenses and a lower than expected Allied casualty count.[54] These temporal developments had little long-term impact on the ideological wars in Washington, D.C., though.

In 1945 moderate and liberal Democrats were intent on ending the Dies Committee. Cochran complained that the Dies Committee had spent $667,500, and should be reconsidered with the new session of Congress in 1945. He acknowledged that "this expensive agent of Congress" had "done some good," though, especially in permitting military intelligence officials access to its files. "Frawsy headed" Rep. John Rankin had other ideas. Known as a skillful parliamentarian he moved that the Dies Committee be made a permanent committee on the first day of the new Congress. His motion was offered as an amendment to the rules of the House. Normal procedure for changing the status of a committee required consideration in the Rules Committee, but Rankin took advantage of the fact that the Rules Committee had not yet been formed to demand that his amendment be debated by the full House. Moreover lawmakers could not vote against the amendment without also voting against all the House rules, an impossible dilemma. Few in the House expected such a maneuver from Rankin regarding a committee all believed would be eliminated. Making HUAC a permanent investigatory committee broke precedent. Never before had Congress made an investigative committee into a standing committee.[55]

Majority Leader McCormack cautioned, "Mark what we are doing. This is not a question of establishing an investigating committee to investigate conditions that arise from time to time; it is a question of amending the rules of the House to provide for a permanent standing committee that does not consider legislation, but has one subject, one field, the field of investigating and making a report." Rankin countered that the new committee would have legislative and investigative functions, but he did not specify what. Moreover giving HUAC a legislative function would not be easy for matters like sedition, espionage, and sabotage were within the purview of the Judiciary Committee. Instead Rankin relied on fear to win his argument. He admonished that opponents of the committee wanted to have its political dossiers destroyed, harming the nation's security in the process. Dies had even done his part regarding this argument. After announcing his retirement, he reminded his colleagues of the massive files his committee had collected. By a vote of 208–186 the House reconstituted the Dies Committee as a standing committee. As Chart 7.1 shows an overwhelming majority of the nay votes came from Democrats, but because southern Democrats joined with Republicans on this issue the conservative coalition prevailed in Rankin's bid to entrench the Dies Committee in the machinery of Congress.[56]

In a "NOT FOR ATTRIBUTION" interview, Speaker Sam Rayburn maintained that approximately thirty or forty Democrats groused after the vote that they opposed the Rankin maneuver but could not afford to vote no on a roll call against the Dies Committee. Because of the strength of the conservative coalition of southern Democrats and Republicans Rankin did not have to lobby for his position. He knew the measure would pass given what one journalist termed the "bigotry" of lawmakers. McCormack privately reasoned that Dies's activities benefitted the Republicans. "He was responsible for the defeat of Democrats by the dozen. This committee, under the guise of protecting liberties, can and will be a constant threat to individual liberties," said McCormack. "Suppose in a year or two from now, the chairman and committee—and nobody knows who it might be—decide that the Negro is un-American? Or the Catholics? Or the Jews? Or Protestants or Irish?" McCormack worried that the desire "to make a record" caused investigative committee chairs to make reckless choices. "I think this is a dangerous threat to democracy, for it may clothe some clever, unscrupulous man

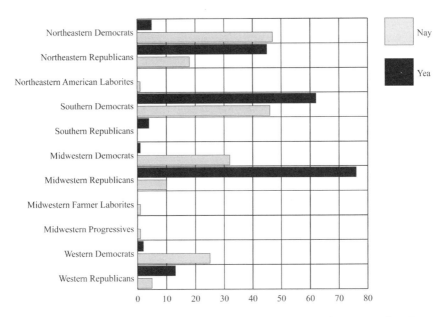

Chart 7.1: Region and Party Identification—Dies Committee, House of Representatives. Data for this chart come from analysis of the January 3, 1945, record vote in the House. See Congressional Record, 79th Congress, 1st session, 15.

with the authority, the power and prestige of Congress, in reaching his own ends. . . . Furthermore, this committee gives an opportunity for the development of dangerous public opinion. The Dies Committee proved that many times." The House leadership took steps to minimize the impact of the conservative coalition over the permanent HUAC, by establishing the ratio of Democrats to Republicans as six to three not five to four. Furthermore, Rayburn plotted to keep Rankin off the committee. He tried but failed to get John McCormack to serve as chair of the committee and Joe Martin as ranking minority member. Instead the chairship went to Edward J. Hart (D-NJ), a New Dealer.[57]

The first seven years of HUAC, when Dies was its chair, proved terribly important toward establishing the direction of postwar politics. Though disliked by the House leadership, including fellow Texan Rayburn who had an abiding and bitter hatred for Martin Dies, Dies nonetheless wove his committee into the institutional fabric of the U.S. Congress and national politics, leaving a valuable inheritance for the next conservative politician interested in manipulating the Communist issue to constrict the political opportunities for liberals. Instead of being controlled by the seniority system, Dies manipulated it to his own ends by exploiting the ideological debates about the New Deal order. Less than a year after he left Congress Dies told his good friend, right-wing journalist Westbrook Pegler, "The pendulum always swings. I know that our findings were right and fully supported by the evidence. I have always felt confident . . . we would be fully vindicated." Starting in 1950 Sen. Joseph McCarthy exploited and exaggerated Dies's legacy for four tumultuous years, but after he overreached HUAC continued to crusade against Communists as "the good gray dean of exposure" as one contemporary observer phrased it until its demise in 1975.[58]

Dies's contributions to the ideological war within Congress and the legislative war on the administration were immense. More than any other conservative tactic used in the 1940s to discredit liberalism and the Roosevelt administration, implications that the statist political reforms of the 1930s drew in part at least from Communist inspiration proved decisive. Liberals in Congress and the administration had no effective response for Dies and his committee, proving the power of anti-Communist demagoguery in American politics. The lessons for conservatives in the postwar era were obvious and apparent: if Dies could gain that much traction during a period when the United States and the Soviet Union were allies, what limits were there to Dies's tactics after that alliance crumbled? Dies willed to the postwar anti-Communists a method and a language through which liberalism could be discredited. His work to that end far surpassed any of the economic conservatives during the 1940s or the social conservatives who fought against refugee and civil rights reforms. Through wartime anti-communism center right and conservative politicians in Congress gained a foothold in their crusade against statist political solutions, one that slowly expanded and threatened the center left warfare state iteration of the New Deal order made permanent in the 1940s.

Epilogue:
The World the War Made

What did Congress learn about the balance of power among liberals, moderates, and conservatives? How did these wartime discoveries shape the New Deal order and the institutional, constitutional struggle between Congress and the White House for the immediate and the long term? The answers to these questions and the results of the two-front congressional war in the 1940s vary according to which model of executive-legislative relations from the 1930s is applied. In the economic policy wars including resource management issues like taxation, price control, and labor policy, Franklin D. Roosevelt and moderate and liberal lawmakers followed the New Deal model of 1933 and 1935, whereby cooperation engendered center left results. To be sure, forging compromise was never easy and all but impossible on questions of labor policy, but in contrast with wartime social justice debates, the results were palpable and they sustained the core of the New Deal economic order.

Social justice issues—immigration and refugee policy, civil rights, and civil liberties—proved impossible to solve, solidifying a center right model and suggesting why the moderate New Deal order formed in the 1940s could not prevail indefinitely. The moderates who controlled national politics in the U.S. Congress through the mid-1970s never were able or even willing to fuse economic liberalism with social justice liberalism. Complicated reasons rooted in the war explain this result. First, the White House devoted the majority of its attention to grand strategy, and in any case understood no liberal result was possible given the racial conservatism of the southern Democrats, who held a disproportionate number of leadership positions. Second, moderates and even some liberals who advocated such reforms deemed them of secondary or tertiary importance compared with wartime resource management issues vital to an Allied victory. Liberals acceded to this pragmatic compromise only because they believed social justice reforms to be possible at war's end. While perhaps necessary to victory over the Axis powers, the decision meant little ammunition remained to fight for social justice reform in a weary nation and a weary government. Third, the two-front congressional war intensified, making consensus impossible. Finally, while there were advocates for a host of social justice reforms, no national leader emerged, leaving these struggles to follow in reverse the pattern first established in 1937. Then Roosevelt found himself without congressional allies or followers for additional New Deal reforms, specifically judicial reform, because he did not seek accommodation with lawmakers. During the war liberal advocates of social justice reforms functioned as a leaderless army with no general and more importantly no commander in chief: Roosevelt had abandoned these proposals because they had scant chance of success.

Liberal and moderate lawmakers used the war to prevent a complete dismantling of the New Deal, preserving its core reforms, while moderate and conservative lawmakers did the same to cast aside some of its most experimental, relief-oriented programs. This result institutionalized an emboldened government bureaucracy, a development that by no means satisfied conservative and some moderate members of Congress, who believed that swollen powers for the executive branch impinged on the constitutional authority of Congress and the freedoms of average Americans. Liberal and some moderate lawmakers typically approved the programmatic results of a stronger executive branch, making their war with the White House very different from the one conservative lawmakers fought. Put simply, when moderates and liberals chafed under Roosevelt's perceived excesses, they viewed such scenarios in situational terms, not necessarily as a systemic crisis, whereas conservatives saw the president's behavior longitudinally as a problem unyielding in its declension. Euphoria over an Allied victory had little impact on the war between Congress and the White House, and hostility about the proper scale, scope, and function of the federal government became a defining characteristic of postwar politics.

During the war years, conservatives in Congress developed a language of opposition that put liberals on the defensive and empowered politicians in the center and on the right. This trend was most obvious in the political confrontations over wartime civil rights initiatives and in the quarrels about the Dies Committee. Conservatives used both social issues to question the totality of liberalism, especially its emerging focus on individual rights. Challenging the federal leviathan proved easier when politicizing social issues rather than quarrelling about economic policy. The former often remained a question of absolutes while the latter involved gradations of statism. Even so, conservatives did not waste their rhetorical thrusts during the struggles about economic policy. The liberal and moderate defense of wartime regulations narrowed the boundaries and possibilities of liberalism for the postwar era, though, converting the welfare state of the 1930s into the warfare state of the 1940s and beyond. By redefining the interventionist state of the 1930s away from its experimentally liberal and redistributionist focus and toward a more neutral emphasis on national security, moderates made a powerful federal government less threatening to the capitalist order and rendered the conservative economic aims more difficult to achieve.

World War II for Congress then was about whether the primary locus of power in the United States should be with the states or the federal government and whether the federal government should engage in liberal, redistributive economic policy. Those that took a statist view were also the defenders of the New Deal and of social justice. Said one Washington observer of the "deep and fundamental conflict" over states' rights, "This argument will never be settled by Congress so long as there are diehard Southerners, Northern liberals, and Republicans hepped up on the chance to play politics in an election year." These conditions encouraged the conservative coalition, which bedeviled moderate and liberal Democrats. Speaker Sam Rayburn (D-TX) remarked, "I really think some of them [conservative Democrats] are going to get ashamed of themselves being advertised weekly about joining in with the Republicans." Such views overlook another important truism, that is the essential conservatism of the American people as reflected in congressional politics. Indeed, 65 percent of Americans surveyed in May 1945 agreed with the statement that more power for Congress would be positive for the country. States' rights had as much to do with race as with antistatist economics and with hostility toward the administration. In a letter from the last years of the war, Rayburn explained the hierarchical governing ethos of congressional moderates that privileged seniority and congressional expertise vis-à-vis the executive branch: "We have many of our laws administered by people who are sometimes incapable and others who are 'too big for their britches.' I spend a great deal of time trying to straighten out mistakes that have been made. Sometimes I am successful, sometimes I am not."[1]

So how did the war change American politics?[2] Yes, the New Deal coalition remained intact and yes, the federal government grew more omnipotent, but beyond this surface level examination, the core of American politics also seemed very different in 1945 than before the war came to the United States. While Roosevelt remained personally popular in the 1930s, the conservative coalition was ascendant and the New Deal was in retreat. The war made possible preservation of the New Deal *and* the emerging moderate political order that dominated postwar politics. Study of wartime congressional politics nonetheless suggests there were battles afoot in the first half of the 1940s for the future of national politics as important as those being fought in North Africa, the South Pacific, and ultimately on the beaches of Normandy through to Berlin.

The assessment of victory in the congressional battles requires a nuanced interpretation unlike similar evaluations of the actual World War II battlefields where the difference between victory and defeat was more obvious, suggesting why exactly it is crucial to answer the question that frames this book—why do moderates matter—for neither conservatives nor liberals were in control of war-era politics. Moderates were ascendant, and this often unheralded political middle more than anything else determined the fate of both economic and social justice policy during and after World War II. The dominant role of moderates also explains why partisanship thrived in the early 1940s. The vitriol from the left and the right had a target audience, moderates who proved themselves open to persuasion. Moderates shaped the story both of a war's end—over the fate of the New Deal as it was constructed in the 1930s—but also of another's beginning—protracted warfare over the nature of the federal government in the modern era. Here liberals and conservatives adopted a siege strategy, which produced no clear winners. Put simply, congressional moderates ended one war in the 1940s while congressional liberals and conservatives began another. Nothing short of the future of American politics was at stake.

What follows is an explication of how the political order forged in the early 1940s governed national politics for the next thirty years. The moderate-dominated system, based on statist solutions and a liberalism in praxis, shaped the reconversion process, most notably passage of the GI Bill for war veterans instead of an extended cradle-to-grave system of social security for all Americans. The emergence of the United States as a superpower remade domestic politics according to the warfare state model, preventing a return to the liberalism of the 1930s. World War II redefined the New Deal political system that lasted for the next three decades. To solidify its role in this political universe, Congress implemented internal institutional reforms with the Legislative Reorganization Act of 1946. The ensuing political battles of the Harry S Truman, Dwight D. Eisenhower, John F. Kennedy, Lyndon B. Johnson, and Richard M. Nixon years reveal the undulations and ultimate demise of the moderate order. Its death had multiple causes: the end of the seniority system in 1975 and the passing of the generation that perfected it, the steady but more gradual realignment of the South from one-party Democratic politics to one-party Republican politics, and exasperation with the successful liberal civil rights and Great Society reforms emanating from the moderate order. More effective governance did not result; instead polarization and a reduced willingness to compromise characterized national politics by the century's end.

Studying postwar economic reconversion reifies the arguments about the war's impact on the New Deal. Public debates about veterans' policy, and secretive efforts to fund the Manhattan Project, two of the most significant issues before Congress, merged the otherwise separate strands of economic and social policy into warfare state liberalism. The result: a mediated New Deal ethos unfolded that was less liberal and less experimental but still attuned to the need of providing for the general welfare. Lawmakers privileged veterans. "We are going to have to do something for these soldier boys when they come back," declared Speaker

Rayburn. "They're fighting this war for us, and we're not going to put them on the street corners selling apples when they get back here." His plan for veterans' benefits both projected the outline of what would become the GI Bill but also revealed a preference for rural social values, including a nation dominated by small yeoman farmers. Rayburn revealed eclectic ideological beliefs, first in a powerful federal state funding social largesse, and second a preference for a Jeffersonian democracy, suggesting that the wartime ideological battles settled none of the disagreements in Congress but only reformulated them for adjudication in the postwar era. "We've got to buy them farms," Rayburn proclaimed. "The government will have to finance this program" through loans at cost. "I'll tell you that will build up the backbone in this country and solve a lot of economic problems."[3]

Because the GI Bill enjoyed support from veterans' organizations and passed Congress with relative ease, too many have assumed that it was not controversial. The debate was not about whether or not to have a GI Bill but whether it should be a template for a more generalized social welfare system. Even though the GI Bill assumed a foundational role in the moderated warfare state of postwar America, its conservative congressional supporters in no way viewed it as a tool to advance the New Deal liberalism or the welfare state that they so despised from the 1930s and that they had retarded during the war years. As Senate Minority Whip Kenneth S. Wherry (R-NE) put it, "The New Deal and this Administration is having its wings clipped and from now on you can expect Congress to continue the clipping."[4]

Presidential overreach became a synonym for New Deal excess in the minds of conservative and many moderate lawmakers. As such, postwar policy choices reflected lessons Congress learned in its earlier struggles with the executive branch. Congressional moderates had long since deemed New Deal experimental liberalism dangerous and had balanced national politics between 1930s liberalism and a variegated conservatism that merged antistatist economic arguments with racial prejudice. Here the vital role of moderates in the nation's political economy becomes clear. By taking a middle path between destroying the New Deal and expanding the New Deal, lawmakers solidified a centrist reform tradition, one that veered left on economic policy but toward the right on social justice questions. This shift in Congress proved most controversial, and programs like the GI Bill emerged because of what conservatives were willing to do, not because of what liberals wanted to do. Sen. Robert A. Taft (R-OH) laid out a conservative philosophy for addressing postwar domestic issues that explains why a majority of lawmakers drew a sharp line between enactment of the GI Bill and rejection of health care: the former was limited and federalized and the latter—conservatives and many moderates feared—would be nationalized. Weakening the role of state and local government in public life, as Taft argued the New Deal had done, threatened the sustainability of democracy. The result, he avowed, was a dangerous separation of the federal government from "the folks at home."[5]

The demise of social security expansion legislation tells a larger, more important story about liberalism during the war years. Participation in the war did nothing to encourage additional legislative support for an expansive social security program but did cause some in Congress to begin debating reconversion and its meanings for the state. Less than two weeks after the attack on Pearl Harbor, Congress turned its attention to reconversion—specifically programs to protect soldiers and veterans: relief from mortgage and debt foreclosure, hospitalization and rehabilitation, national service life insurance, and increased pensions for veterans. These measures did not challenge capitalism in the same way that an expanded social security program did.[6] Regardless of ideology, veterans' politics had benefits for lawmakers. Moderates and conservatives used the issue to constrict the New Deal welfare state while liberals relied on veterans' politics to expand the welfare state. In this ideological struggle, the moderates and conservatives prevailed.

After passage of the GI Bill Sen. Ernest McFarland (D-AZ) told an audience listening to the *American Forum of the Air,* "We worked with the idea of giving the veteran the opportunity to help himself. It was the determination of all that the veterans of World War II should not be the recipients of the neglect and indifference suffered by the veterans of World War I upon their discharge." The GI Bill included provisions for low-interest home loans, funding for education, and loans to purchase a business. Liberal journalists acknowledged its limited statism, with the *New Republic* writing, "The bill does not contemplate making the veteran a permanent ward of the government; it seeks to speed his rapid reintegration into civilian life." Evaluation of the GI Bill in context with the larger program for economic reconversion reveals that liberals did not want veterans' programs when liberalism was ascendant; only when conservatives dominated did liberals use veterans' policy as a Trojan horse to get state expansion back on track as was the case in 1944. Here liberals succeeded with their immediate but not their larger goals.[7]

The GI Bill embodied the new warfare state liberalism, not the defunct welfare state liberalism of the 1930s. It was the most important wartime economic and social reconversion policy with which Congress was publicly involved, but privately a select group of legislators worked on an entirely different matter that was more vital for determining how the war ended—funding for the development of the atomic bomb. Congressional sustenance of the Manhattan Project served as a metaphor for the redefinition of a 1930s welfare state into a warfare state. The seniority system permitted moderate congressional leaders to shroud their actions not only from the general public but also the full membership of Congress. Moreover, this episode shows just how easily congressional leaders abandoned partisanship when patriotism demanded it. The selective rejection of partisanship for the sake of national defense became a component of the postwar moderate system forged in the early 1940s because war, in the form of the Cold War, along with Korea and Vietnam, remained a constant through 1975 when the seniority system, the Vietnam War, and the moderate congressional order all ended. It was no irony, then, that the permanent New Deal order was born in war and that it fell apart when significant changes in the tenor of the Cold War brought an end to U.S. military engagement abroad.

Before the attack on Pearl Harbor, Secretary of War Henry L. Stimson communicated with Congress about weapons developments. The most important such conference during World War II took place in Speaker Rayburn's office, with just a handful of attendees: Rayburn, Majority Leader John W. McCormack (D-MA), and Minority Leader Joseph W. Martin Jr. (R-MA). Briefing them were Secretary Stimson, Army Chief of Staff George C. Marshall, and Vannevar Bush, the director of U.S. scientific research and development. Efforts to build the atomic bomb were revealed. While the Manhattan Project had been extant since 1941, by the date of the meeting some lawmakers on the House Appropriations Committee had discerned the War Department's subterfuge of taking project funding from other appropriations. The purpose of the meeting was to get cooperation from the leadership to maintain the secret. Rayburn recalled, "They said if we could get the thing, we won't have to invade Japan, we could save the lives of 500,000 Americans, lives and limbs." Marshall and Stimson painted a grim picture of a German victory should the Third Reich develop the weapon first. They asked for $1.6 billion, requesting that the purpose of the funding never be revealed. Rayburn and McCormack worked on Appropriations Committee Chairman Clarence Cannon (D-MO) and Martin gained the silence of the ranking Republican member John Taber (NY). Martin described the effort as "the greatest gamble of the war." While he put country ahead of party other Republicans did not. Rep. Albert Engel (R-MI) politicized the most sensitive issue of the war, a classified, controversial weapons program that was viewed by its advocates as the salvation of American democracy. He functioned as a one-man watchdog, critiquing what he saw as excessive spending and excessive stealth.[8] Engel failed in his immediate quest to gain access to the Manhattan Project, but, whether he was trying or not, he won an important victory for the GOP when he crafted a rhetoric of opposition for debates about national security, not just domestic politics. Questioning the loyalty of the opposition became a feature of the postwar moderate order, one that stifled liberal reforms that could be equated with the new enemy, communism.

When Harry Truman inherited the presidency upon Roosevelt's death, he also inherited a Congress that was at sea. The legislative branch had had enough of presidential dictation; they wanted input into the crucial postwar transitions. Lawmakers believed legislative reorganization constituted a prerequisite for all other policy matters. There was no interest on the part of the moderate power structure, though, to change in any meaningful way the seniority system. In 1945 and 1946 only congressional outsiders viewed the seniority system as a problem; the leadership believed it and the committee structure that girded it needed expansion. Indeed, the emphasis was less on reform of procedure so as to benefit an ideologically pure agenda and more on modernizing Congress and equalizing its status with the presidency.[9]

Wartime observers of congressional procedure complained of a "planless" institution struggling "to meet the needs of a complex swift-moving world; but its organization is cumbersome and slow-moving, and there is much overlapping and duplication of work. It is a body without a responsible head. . . . One group points out that if Congress does not change it will lose more of its leadership to the Executive and lose more of the public's esteem." Limited congressional staffs during the war forced lawmakers to borrow personnel from executive agencies and depend on measures that had been drafted in the White House. To address the power disparity between Capitol Hill and the White House, Congress created the Joint Committee on the Organization of Congress in 1944 and tasked it with writing legislation that would reclaim congressional preeminence in the national government.[10]

Lawmakers were not of one mind about how legislative reorganization should proceed. Two key members who assumed responsibility for the reform process, Sen. Robert M. La Follette Jr. (P-WI) and Rep. Mike Monroney (D-OK), solicited input from Congress. Four years earlier, Sen. Taft summed up the problems Congress faced. "To a certain extent the attack on Congress seems to be inspired by the administration," Taft explained. "People don't seem to realize that Congress is the administration, that the Democratic Party has a two-thirds majority in both Houses, and that the President is the leader of the Democratic Party." Administration Democrats saw matters differently. "I disagree with those critics who believe that Congress is lacking in intelligence or patriotism," said James F. Byrnes, who advocated larger, more professional congressional staffs and better congressional pay to reflect the demands of "modern" times. He promoted having fewer congressional committees with all members doing important work and the creation of a congressional cabinet whereby committee chairs met with the president. He suggested that members of the president's cabinet appear before Congress to answer questions about legislation. Finally, "this reduction of committees would concentrate responsibility," said Byrnes. The budgetary demands on Congress during the war propelled many of the demands for reform. Sen. Alexander Wiley (R-WI) wrote to Sen. Harry F. Byrd (D-VA) about the proposed budget of $109 billion as his evidence, noting that the amount was half of all the nation's expenditures between 1789 and the start of the war: "Senator, our machinery for considering such a tremendous budget is obviously inadequate." He called for the creation of a joint House and Senate Budget Committee, which would propel "modernization of Congressional machinery, not a jerry-built modernization, but an intelligent program."[11]

The Legislative Reorganization Act of 1946 proved thinner than what reformers wanted. It worked to the benefit of the leadership and as such aided the moderate political order. Extensive hearings in the Joint Committee on the Organization of Congress in 1945 focused on strategies for increasing efficiency and public support for the institution. Excluded from consideration were any efforts to attack seniority, the filibuster, or the balance of power within Congress. Such omissions made sense. Moderates did not see a significant problem with these key characteristics of midcentury lawmaking but instead endorsed professionalizing the legislative branch. Said Rayburn, "A great national legislature cannot safely rely on the technical assistance and advice which private interests are willing to provide." Still, committee functionality was made more efficient, the number of committees was reduced, and the size of congressional and committee staffs was increased. Lawmakers gained greater oversight through the reformed committee structure, and the law provided for two new joint committees on economic policy and budgetary matters. Reformers were unable to do more than these patchwork repairs to speed procedures; only a minority wished to examine "the whole problem of its [congressional] relationships with the Executive and the public, and try to see its task in a day when Federal power is still growing" largely because there was such a stark schism within Congress over *whether* that growth of power was desirable. The statist versus antistatist conflict hampered efforts to achieve substantive procedural reforms.[12]

Simultaneously with legislative reorganization the government debated other reforms that had been postponed during the war—full employment, labor policy, civil rights, and universal health care. These negotiations tested the moderates because the proposed measures were predicated on a continuation of the New Deal order as formulated in the 1940s. The moderates again functioned as kingmakers even though Republicans regained control of both chambers of Congress after the 1946 midterm election. This conservative victory meant centrist politicians had fewer options than at the start of the decade. Was the country center left in orientation as the moderates behaved or had it shifted farther right because of wartime quarrels about social justice policy?

The disagreement about full employment helps answer this question. Advocates of this legislation came from the liberal, New Deal wing of the Democratic Party, and they viewed planning as a key federal responsibility to prevent future economic downturns. Conservatives dismissed the arguments as smacking of socialism and any potential policies for implementing full employment as a hindrance to free enterprise. The Employment Act of 1946 that Congress passed proved weak in comparison with what liberal administration officials like Leon Keyserling had first suggested. One journalist contended, "The Senate gave [Truman] a crust, the House gave him a crumb, and the conferees gave him two crumbs," or as Alben Barkley put it, lawmakers had gone on record saying a man had "the right to get a job if he can find one."[13]

The midterm congressional elections in 1946 changed the partisan landscape in Washington, D.C., lessening moderate cooperation with liberals and increasing moderate cooperation with conservatives. The Republicans took a 51–45 advantage in the Senate and a 246–188 advantage in the House, leaving Truman without an opportunity to forge a collaborative relationship with the congressional majority. Moderates held less power. Even Rayburn, the embodiment of the moderate political order, considered leaving the leadership because he feared an intensification of partisanship beyond what had characterized the war years. He told President Truman, "I will be freer to take the floor when your program really needs me than to be in the position of yapping with every little fellow who jumps up on the republican side."[14]

Much of that "yapping" involved labor legislation. More moderate convergence with conservatives happened in 1947 when lawmakers debated and passed the Taft-Hartley Act, a measure that retarded the rights of workers as authorized in the Wagner Act of 1935, a keystone New Deal measure. The hundreds of committee hearings and publications about communism and strikes in industrial plants provided context for enactment of Taft-Hartley. Not only was the problematic House Committee on Un-American Activities sounding the tocsin, but also the previously liberal-minded House Committee on Education and Labor gave comfort to conservatives and moderates worried about labor having too much power. Additionally, other House and Senate committees held hearings on related subjects.

The hue and cry from industry groups and trade associations against the Wagner Act intensified with the war's end. Even most liberals appreciated that legislation would be passed to curb the power of labor, but they denied the necessity for such changes. Truman had few choices; fearing any bill limiting the prerogatives of labor, he did nothing as the Republicans put together a bill. His self-imposed exile from the debate meant that the only liberal and moderate voices to be heard came from the Democratic minority in Congress, which further empowered the conservatives. When the bill reached the White House, Truman vetoed it and a successful override by Congress solidified the president's support with liberals and labor while also further dividing the political poles in Congress.[15]

The conservative assault on labor shaped the context for the 1948 presidential election, a key contest in determining the ideological balance in Congress. Truman made policy choices that defined the Republicans as the voice for the special interests and the Democratic Party as the guardian for the common man. This strategy crystallized when Truman called the 80th Congress into a special session during the summer of 1948. He realized that Taft, a conservative and the titular head of the GOP in Congress, had views far to the right of Thomas Dewey, the former governor of New York and the Republican nominee for president. Truman asked the Congress to go ahead and enact the major provisions within the Republican Party's statist platform—federal education funding, inflation controls, public housing, social security expansion, and urban renewal—noting that if the country needed these reforms there was no reason for the Republican Congress to wait until a Republican president could be elected and inaugurated. For Taft and the other conservative Republicans who held sway in Congress, these liberal and moderate measures were anathema. No legislation was enacted that summer, and Truman won the presidency in 1948 campaigning as much against the so-called "do nothing Congress" as against Dewey.[16] Moderate Democrats who governed Congress in the first half of the decade and who remained leaders in their party did not tolerate "do nothing" Republicanism even if through their liberalism in praxis they had often sought the least powerful statist solution.

When Truman prevailed in the 1948 presidential election he not only defeated Dewey the Republican but also Progressive Party candidate Henry A. Wallace, who siphoned off some liberals from the Democratic Party, and Dixiecrat candidate Strom Thurmond, who gathered in votes from some southern Democrats. Moreover his ballot strength proved sufficient to help his party reclaim both houses of Congress. Rumblings in Washington, D.C., suggested that there might be a purge of the Dixiecrats, a rumor that Rayburn denied. Instead, the two extremes of the party, southerners and liberals from the North and the West, needed each other for legitimacy. Southern Democrats knew they would never have power should they merge with the Republicans. Likewise, the liberals in 1949 understood that any efforts to create a labor party would be for naught.[17] Thus in a somewhat strange manner the 1948 elections further entrenched the mediated, pragmatic style of liberalism developed in the war years, but there was never a satisfactory relationship between the president and his party on the Hill sufficient to enact a more ambitious liberal agenda beyond the extant New Deal.

Two issues more than anything else from Truman's Fair Deal threatened controversy and the delicate partisan divide in Congress: civil rights and national health care. Truman knew there was no chance for social justice legislation so he acted with executive power: issuing orders to create a commission on civil rights, to desegregate the military, and to desegregate the federal bureaucracy and introducing amicus curiae briefs before the Supreme Court in the *Shelley v. Kramer* case and the *Brown v. Board of Education* case. His instincts were proven correct when the Senate refused to amend its cloture rules, making it harder to block the obstructionist filibuster and signaling there would be no merger of economic liberalism with social justice liberalism. The impact of this defeat reached beyond the president's civil rights program to include most of the social welfare issues included in the Fair Deal, especially health care.[18]

Truman first mentioned health-care reform in 1945. He returned to the issue in 1949, but his results were dismal. Arguments about cradle-to-grave social welfare, which would include a national system of health care, cemented the conservative and moderate alliance at the expense of liberals. Because medical care was not costly in the middle of the twentieth century, there was no significant economic argument to be made for the reform, the one policy area where moderates had been willing to cooperate with liberals. Instead, national health care too closely resembled the social reform programs of the New Deal that conservatives, especially those on the Dies Committee, had branded as socialist. Indeed, the American Medical Association insisted federal provision for health care would destroy individual incentive. Said one observer of the debate: "The majority of Congress, and especially its leaders or key men, abhor 'free' benefits, but HAVE been sold on and accept the social insurance approach restricting benefits by formula to those paying."[19]

Truman's efforts to expand New Deal liberalism in the postwar era met with no success, but neither did conservative efforts to roll it back. Even the much-lamented Taft-Hartley Act had very little impact on labor politics. Tensions crackled in Congress, between the two chambers, between the two parties, and among the various factions. Heightened charges of socialism were hurled against the Democrats generally and Truman's Fair Deal proposals specifically. Said Rep. Daniel A. Reed (R-NY), "I believe that the Congress and the American people have had enough of this . . . back-door approach to State Socialism." Sen. Taft agreed, contending the 81st Congress was more "radical" than the previous one controlled by Republicans. He based his argument on the declining numbers of conservative Democrats and the rising numbers of liberals in the party, specifically three freshmen senators: Paul Douglas (IL), Hubert Humphrey (MN), and Lyndon B. Johnson (TX). Of the three Johnson was the only one with wartime congressional service, and only Johnson fully appreciated the liberalism in praxis forged in the war years, ultimately implementing it in grand fashion when he reached the presidency in the 1960s. Journalists who covered Capitol Hill, though, argued the 81st Congress "was one of moderation. At times, it seemed hopelessly moderate to the point of incapacity to act." There were real accomplishments, though—constructing the policy infrastructure of the Cold War, public housing legislation, an increase in the minimum wage, agricultural reform, and expansion of social security—and they were born of moderate cooperation.[20]

The election of Dwight Eisenhower and a Republican Congress in 1952 portended significant shifts in Capitol Hill partisan politics. Conservatives, especially those who ran party affairs in Congress, viewed the election as an opportunity to roll back or eliminate the New Deal. Because Eisenhower was not a doctrinaire Republican, he did not always find ready accord with the more conservative GOP leadership in Congress. The impact of this divide between president and party on political moderation and the New Deal order became apparent after the 1954 midterm congressional elections when Democrats regained control of the House and the Senate. Eisenhower enjoyed a much more productive relationship with the Democratic leaders of the House and the Senate, Speaker Rayburn and Majority Leader Lyndon B. Johnson, than he did with any of the Republican leaders, Martin, Charles Halleck (IN), Taft, William Knowland (CA), and Everett McKinley Dirksen (IL). Of Knowland Eisenhower once wrote in his diary, "In his case there seems to be no final answer to the question, 'How stupid can you get?'"[21] Eisenhower's bipartisan cooperation with Rayburn and Johnson epitomized the political style that moderates forged during the war years; the Democratic leaders did so because they had observed the differences in the 1930s and 1940s from when FDR worked with Congress and when he did not, and they knew mutuality between the two branches constituted a key component of the moderate New Deal order they inhabited. Eisenhower most needed Democrats to hold off those Republicans who threatened the tenuous Cold War consensus, and Rayburn and Johnson needed the president to protect as much of the New Deal as possible. In these efforts their bipartisanship was subject to suspension, especially on the part of Rayburn and Johnson if they found an opportunity to secure an advantage for more liberal policies.

Both Rayburn and Johnson maintained their Democratic independence, criticizing Eisenhower's administration when it suited their purposes. For example, Rayburn gave a radio and television address in September 1954 where he charged, "If there is one word in the English language that would properly describe this Republican Administration, it is the word, 'Inept.'" The following month, though, the two Texans protested when Eisenhower spoke critically about congressional Democrats, alleging, "Your statement of last night is an unwarranted and unjust attack on the many Democrats who have done so much to . . . defend your program from attacks by members and leaders of your own party." They hypothesized that Eisenhower's "new position of rigid, unswerving partisanship" resulted from "the frantic pleas of your political advisors to come to the rescue of a party fearful of repudiation by the voters." Rayburn and Johnson concluded, "We assure you, as the leaders of the Democratic party in Congress, that as far as we are concerned there will be no Cold War conducted against you."[22]

The Democrats did take control of Congress in 1954, and they did not wage a cold war against the president. To do so would have been foolish partisan excess when Democratic objectives could be obtained through softer methods, or as Johnson liked to quote from the book of Isaiah in the Bible, "Come now, let us reason together." Indeed, he proved his mastery of bipartisan political compromise with tactics that often also relied on skillful manipulation of Senate rules and personalities. The odds were against him; he was a novice majority leader in 1955 and with a presidential election the following year neither party was interested in legislating very much for fear of handing the opposition a victory or a campaign issue. Johnson was interested in legislating, though. Moderation did not mean stagnation to Johnson. Among the 1,300 bills he shepherded through the upper chamber were measures dealing with trade, wages, and public housing. Passage of the housing bill illustrates how Johnson perfected the politics of moderation. He prevented a coalition of southern Democrats and Republicans from passing the weak administration bill in favor of a stronger measure that authorized construction of almost double the number of housing units, 135,000 in three years as opposed to 70,000 in two years. Johnson kept his strategy hidden as was normative under the seniority system, and liberal organizations, including the Americans for Democratic Action, wrongly criticized him for capitulating to the Republican assault on liberalism. Johnson won, playing "the Senate like a well trained violin virtuoso" according to journalist John Steele.[23]

Johnson took bolder steps in 1956 and 1957. At this juncture, he knew his political career depended on passage of liberal legislation. By creating a façade of bipartisanship—Senate Democrats were instructed to amend Republican, administration bills to make them more liberal, not to introduce their own measures—Johnson orchestrated victories in Social Security legislation, funding for medical research and school construction, water conservation, and road construction. The Democrats lost on other matters, including agriculture, taxation, and immigration. The 1957 Civil Rights Act exemplifies the challenges before Johnson. The Texan realized that a perfect bill, what the liberals wanted, could not be had, but that a weak bill, one with no tangible benefits for African Americans, might survive a Senate filibuster making it easier to secure meaningful reform in a future Congress. The result was just that, and Sen. Douglas complained that it "was like soup made from the shadow of a crow which had starved to death." These results won Johnson few friends among Senate liberals, who rejected his bipartisanship as harmful to the party's chances in 1958 and 1960. An advisor to Johnson recommended, "Some serious thought has to be given on how to deal with the 'liberals.' They do not have the capacity to present a serious challenge to the present Democratic leadership. But they do have the capacity—by constant hammering—to portray the present leadership as 'parochial' and 'sectional' in the eyes of the country unless something is done."[24]

The 1958 congressional election brought a cohort of liberal purists to Washington, D.C.—primarily from the Northeast and the West and including Sens. Philip Hart (D-MI), Thomas Dodd (D-CT), Ernest Gruening (D-AK), Ralph Yarborough (D-TX), Edmund Muskie (D-ME), and Reps. Julia Butler Hansen (D-WA), Ken Hechler (D-WV), and John Brademas (D-IN)—men and women who had little tolerance for the war-era liberalism in praxis. The younger generation of congressional liberals disdained Rayburn and Johnson for cooperating with Eisenhower. Two decades later they played a key role in the death and burial of the New Deal political order. They allied with other liberals elected since the end of the war and with liberal advocacy groups, and they argued that procedural reform was as important as attention to specific liberal issues like civil rights. This split in the Democratic Party threatened the continued effectiveness of moderate, left of center bipartisanship, but Republicans were equally suspicious of the Democratic leadership. At a White House meeting of Republican legislative leaders, Minority Leader Martin spoke critically about Rayburn. "But I wouldn't be lulled to sleep by anything Mr. Rayburn says, because he's playing politics this year. That may be an understatement!"[25]

Postwar liberals who lacked the experience of legislating in the 1930s and 1940s suffered from myopia regarding the necessity of compromise for enacting liberal reform. This problem suggested that the World War II system, which had worked so well by institutionalizing the New Deal, was fated to fade away in the decades that followed. Liberal calls for purity contained the seeds of destruction for the Democratic Party; there were not enough Democrats in Congress or the country to rule without the conservative southern bloc and without the seniority system, both sometimes problematic stumbling blocks to liberal reform but also both necessary to that same outcome. Rayburn and Johnson teamed together to forestall the demise of the moderate order for another decade and a half. Success for Rayburn and Johnson hinged on thwarting conservative Democrats, the other major target that younger liberals in the party attacked in the 1950s. In the House, these liberals were most angry about the Rules Committee and in the Senate the filibuster.

By 1961, Rayburn wanted a larger Rules Committee so that the conservative Democrats under the leadership of Chairman Howard Worth Smith (D-VA) could no longer block party legislation. The fight was especially significant to Rayburn because many Washington observers criticized his moderate record during the late 1950s, with the *New Republic* avowing "seventy-eight-year-old Speaker Rayburn is no longer the master in his house." Rayburn failed to control the conservative and liberal wings of his party, making him appear less like a leader and more like a relic from the past. He needed the win to prove his mettle to the newly elected Democratic president, John F. Kennedy, and he savored the notion of defeating Smith, long a thorn in his side.[26]

On the eve of the new Congress no one knew what Rayburn would do or what strategy would best resolve the Rules Committee dilemma, especially since Democrats had lost twenty-one seats in Congress even though they won the presidency. Control of the Rules Committee would determine the fate of the Kennedy legislative program for housing, education, civil rights, minimum wage, and health care. Whereas the moderate political order that Rayburn had overseen for two decades was forged to protect New Deal economic reforms, increasingly liberals yearned for social justice and civil rights reforms. The fight about the Rules Committee in 1961 better than anything else reflected this pivot. Smith not only had opposed retention of the New Deal political economy in the 1940s but also he was a virulent foe of racial equality. Privately Rayburn understood that meaningful civil rights legislation was imminent and necessary, but his main objective was control of his chamber. The eight-to-four split between Democrats and Republicans on the committee was not sufficient to guarantee Democratic outcomes because the nebulous conservative coalition of some Republicans and some southern Democrats usually controlled the committee.[27]

Before the inauguration Rayburn advised that the Democratic Caucus not appoint any committees other than Ways and Means, he cautioned the incoming Kennedy administration to stay out of this internal House matter, and he ignored suggestions that the most conservative Democrats be removed from the committee, opting instead to push for the enlargement of the Rules panel. This strategy was in keeping with Rayburn's preference to find the center in political disagreements. Rayburn believed this alternative was "the way to embarrass nobody if they didn't want to be embarrassed." Rayburn asserted, "The issue is very simple. Shall the elected leadership of the House run its affairs, or shall the chairman of one committee run them?" After monitoring Democratic views Rayburn explained: "Hell no. We're going to vote. . . . The only way to avoid a vote is for me to abdicate and I won't do it. If they lick me, that's that. For the next three months, I'll have those who vote against me come to my office, and there'll be more ass-kicking than they ever dreamed possible." Rayburn prevailed on January 31 when the House voted 217–212 to expand the Rules Committee.[28]

The vote constituted a personal victory for Rayburn and approval of a strong speakership. Rayburn noted, "When the House revolted against Speaker Cannon in 1910, they cut the Speaker's powers too much. Ever since I have been Speaker, I have been trying to get some of that power back for the office." For Bolling, though, it "was . . . 'the end of the beginning'—a step toward making the Rules Committee an instrument of the majority party in the House." It was also the beginning of the end to the moderate New Deal political order forged during World War II. During his brief term Kennedy struggled with a recalcitrant Congress that remained under the sway of conservatives. That he lost control of Congress even after Rayburn's dramatic victory in the Rules battle resulted for a variety of complex reasons: Rayburn's death in November 1961, a power vacuum in Congress that conservatives filled, and Kennedy's lack of prowess over legislative matters. As such, his domestic reform agenda was stalled at the time of his assassination on November 22, 1963.[29]

"Let us continue." Lyndon B. Johnson spoke those words in his first major presidential address, a speech to a joint session of Congress on November 27, 1963. He did not mean Congress should continue its lack of action on domestic issues. Instead, he wanted lawmakers to get busy and enact a cornucopia of legislation, all inspired by the liberal reform initiatives that had been discussed for at least the last twenty years: civil rights; health care; federal funding for education; space exploration; environmental protections; consumer protections; funding for the arts, humanities, and sciences; poverty prevention programs; urban renewal; mass transit; and public broadcasting.[30] As arguably the best legislative president in U.S. history Johnson personified the delicate compromises, the arm-twisting, and the timing that would be necessary to achieve results, besting FDR's results in 1933, 1935, and even on wartime economic policy by working collaboratively with Congress. Moreover, because of his tenure in the U.S. Senate as majority leader Johnson appreciated the vast, quantifiable differences between flowery ideological rhetoric and the pragmatic deal making that girded significant legislative victories.

First elected to Congress in 1937, he had absorbed the political milieu of the war years whereby moderates compromised with liberals to sustain the New Deal. In his own administration, Johnson orchestrated reforms greater than those of the New Deal era, and he knew he would need cooperation from liberals and moderates in both parties. Moreover, Johnson's civil rights agenda required lawmakers to break one key precedent established in the war years—willingness to act on economic but not social justice issues—raising the question of how his Great Society agenda would affect the tenuous New Deal political order.

Johnson himself blew wide open the spirit of moderation when determining the strategy for passing civil rights legislation in 1964. Instead of encouraging compromise with the southern congressional Democrats who would have preferred to water the bill down to nothingness, akin to the Civil Rights Act of 1957, Johnson endorsed a bold measure: "I made my position unmistakably clear: We were not prepared to compromise in any way. . . . I knew that the slightest wavering on my part would give hope to the opposition's strategy of amending the bill to death." The president met with the key lobbyists for all the civil rights organizations to make sure they knew he would never surrender, that the bill must stay on the floor until it passed, and that the Senate would undertake no other business until the measure was signed into law.[31]

Majority Leader Mike Mansfield (D-MT), a western liberal but not an outspoken proponent of civil rights, oversaw the Senate debate. When the Senate doorkeeper announced the arrival of the bill from the House where it had passed days earlier, Mansfield told his colleagues: "I should have preferred it had the civil rights been resolved before my time as a senator or had it not come to the floor until afterward. . . . Great public issues are not subject to our personal timetables; they do not accommodate themselves to our individual preference or convenience. They emerge in their own way and in their own time. . . . The time is now." Mansfield proved cagey but never duplicitous in his management of the bill. He did not send it to the Judiciary Committee where the chair, James O. Eastland (D-MS), was a rabid racist, but instead Mansfield used an arcane rule to force the bill's immediate consideration by the whole Senate. He cautioned Richard Russell (D-GA), a leading segregationist, of his strategy well in advance. The debate, which lasted eighty-three consecutive working days, was the longest in Senate history. Johnson worked closely with his allies on the Hill. He understood that he had to place himself and the prestige of the presidency on the frontlines of this battle for the soul of the nation, but also that he had to let "my colleagues," meaning the members of Congress, take the glory for victory. Moreover, he counseled Sen. Humphrey to maintain a "dignified" debate that was respectful toward both the "heritage of Lincoln's party" and "the integrity of the Senate as an institution." Johnson did not want liberal senators to challenge the "motives of Republicans or Southern Democrats."[32]

When Humphrey, already widely discussed as a likely vice presidential nominee in 1964, suggested Johnson would be willing to see the House bill weakened, the president corrected him, and newspaper stories sensationalized the exchange. Later Johnson told Humphrey, "I wasn't giving any unshirted hell anyway. I was just clarifying that I want to be awful careful. . . . I think you could get by with repealing the goddamn bill." Here the president made an oblique reference to the benefit of the doubt given to northern liberals like Humphrey and the assumption of racial guilt given to southerners regardless of ideology.[33]

Cloture, the vote to stop the filibuster, would determine success or failure for the liberals, and Johnson knew Dirksen and the southern Democrats would be the key players. His respect for Dirksen was mixed with disdain, especially when the Illinois senator made critical remarks in the press about Johnson and his lifting of his pet beagles by their ears. Johnson fumed to Mansfield, "It's none of his damn business how I treat my dog and I'm a hell of a lot better to dogs and people than he is." Johnson's firmness had a political purpose; he communicated to Dirksen there would be no compromise and that it would be the Republican minority leader's responsibility to secure the needed GOP votes. He also flattered Dirksen, "You're worthy of the land of Lincoln and a man from Illinois is going to pass the bill and I'll see that you get the proper attention and credit." With Dirksen on board, the only remaining challenge came from the southern Democrats. Russell attested the legislation would cause the federal government to grow even larger and assume qualities of socialism. "Every Negro citizen possesses every legal right that is possessed by any white citizen," Russell avowed, "but there is nothing in either the Constitution or Judaeo-Christian principles or common sense which would compel one citizen to share his rights with one of another race at the same place and at the same time."[34]

More than two-thirds of the senators disagreed, voting for cloture, and assuring that a strong civil rights bill would pass. Later, after Lyndon Johnson signed the bill into law on July 2, 1964, he made a point of calling and thanking those members of Congress who voted for the historic measure. One of those calls was to Rep. Jake Pickle (D-TX), who held Johnson's old congressional seat. Pickle feared his courageous vote would end his political career (it did not), so he went out and got very drunk. As such it took many hours for Johnson to track him down. When the two crusty Texans finally conversed they agreed that the passage of civil rights would send reverberations throughout the South, causing the region to switch its political allegiances to the Republican Party for a generation.[35]

Their only error was the timetable; Republican dominance of the South post-

1964 lasted for several generations, and the Civil Rights Act of 1964 as well as its companion piece, the Voting Rights Act of 1965, hold a unique legacy in modern American political history. Johnson hoped that enforcement of civil rights would not be vindictive, and he also exhorted that voting rights receive the bulk of the attention. He believed suffrage was crucial to black advancement, so he quietly sent a voting rights bill to Congress in 1965 even though he doubted its prospects in Congress, especially because of the voting rights protests in Selma, Alabama. In March 1965 when Johnson addressed lawmakers in what his biographer called his greatest speech he declared, "We shall overcome," causing almost all the members to give him a standing ovation. The Voting Rights Act became law later that summer in the strong form Johnson had originally proposed.[36]

Passage of both could not have happened outside the political system lawmakers forged in the 1940s, but ironically this success ensured the demise of the politics of moderation. An electoral backlash against the merger of New Deal economic liberalism with Great Society social justice liberalism meant the congressional midterm elections in 1966 were a disaster for Democrats across the ideological spectrum. The GOP elected forty-seven new House members and three new senators, two of the latter in the South. Not only was liberalism in retreat but also southern Democrats. These results were a harbinger of what the next decades would bring, but they did not cause an immediate end to the Great Society. Johnson continued to work his magic with the legislative branch in 1967 and 1968, winning more important liberal reform laws including air pollution, public broadcasting, truth-in-lending, and fair housing, and proving the tenacity of the war-era liberalism in praxis, especially when liberal pragmatists were at the helm. So by the end of the 1960s the moderate order was and was not durable.[37] The ultimate victory that merged New Deal economic liberalism with Great Society social justice liberalism, then, spelled defeat for the political order that made it all possible, but only if Johnson or someone like him was no longer in the White House.

Nixon's presidency added further strain to the domestic political mores forged in the 1940s and solidified in the succeeding decades, with the politics of moderation imploding one year after Nixon left the White House. Nixon had become the liberal bête noir for the way in which he entered the House of Representatives in 1947. His upset victory against liberal hero Rep. Jerry Voorhis (CA) in 1946 and his defeat of Rep. Helen Gahagan Douglas (CA) in a red-baiting campaign four years later in a U.S. Senate race earned him the enmity of liberal Democrats as did his relentless pursuit of Alger Hiss, whom he charged with being a Communist. As such liberal Democrats mistrusted President Nixon even when his administration sponsored reforms that otherwise might have been popular with the left. The Family Assistance Plan, a failed attempt to reform welfare by providing a minimum family income for those under the poverty level and by not punishing two-parent families is perhaps the best example. By the early 1970s the combination of liberal anger with the Richard Nixon administration, pushback against Great Society reforms by the so-called "silent majority," and a belief by liberal reformers that conservatives in Congress were using systemic means, namely the seniority system and the conservative coalition, to thwart passage of the progressive legislation resulted in heightened agitation for institutional reform as a first step toward additional policy reform.[38]

Moderates usually determined the outcomes of the partisan disagreements that had dominated American politics from the late 1940s through the mid-1970s. Even though this system worked, and worked quite well, few were happy with it by the early 1970s. The civil rights revolution and the widening of the social welfare state in the 1960s stand out as stark exceptions to the longer-term trends of postwar politics. Liberals believed that they had made too little progress addressing social and economic inequities while conservatives fulminated over liberal excess. The combination of Johnson's expansive reform ambitions with liberal hostility toward Nixon especially after revelations of the Watergate scandal proved too much for the system to sustain itself. Both poles of the political spectrum demanded more ideological limpidness in politics. The messy middle had resulted in decades of opacity, a condition purists no longer tolerated. Liberals increasingly believed were it not for the moderate-dominated seniority system better, more all-encompassing reforms could be won whereas conservatives, who had disdained the modern welfare state from its birth, took the emergence of the silent majority—middle-class Americans who criticized Vietnam and civil rights protesters along with federal government social welfare programs—in the late 1960s as proof that the public wanted no more liberal experimentation and social engineering.[39]

So how and why did the era of moderate equilibrium dissipate? The election of 1974 and its aftermath, meaning the arrival of the "Watergate babies" in Washington, D.C., remade the internal workings of congressional politics and seems a logical end point for considering the impact of World War II on postwar politics. The seventy-five new Democratic House members and the five new Democratic Senate members had all run against corruption in Washington. Of course Nixon and Watergate were the primary targets, but the seniority system also generated substantial invective. Indeed, Democrats wrongly believed Nixon's crimes in the Watergate imbroglio would open the door for another wave of liberal reform. After taking office, liberal Democrats avowed that institutional reform must precede policy reform so they set out to clean house, literally, by deposing several longstanding committee chairs in the lower chamber, but reforms were less drastic in the Senate where some liberalization had already happened. There younger and more liberal members gained greater access to important committees, hearings were opened to the public, and the requirement for cloture was reduced from two-thirds to three-fifths. The freshman lawmakers teamed with more senior liberals, some of whom had been in Congress since the late 1940s, and these results indicated that the postwar liberals had done a better job of mentoring junior members than had the moderates and conservatives who embraced the seniority system, an ironic development since the seniority system had long relied on committee chairs and the leadership hierarchy giving tutelage to promising freshmen.[40]

The hyper-partisan political milieu of the federal government in the decades after 1975 can best be understood as the unintended consequences of otherwise well-intended reformers. There were flaws with the seniority system to be sure—abuse of power by committee chairs, silencing of more liberal voices on committees run by conservatives, and control of Congress by moderates and conservatives even as the chambers as a whole skewed center left in ideological orientation—and its demise in the 1970s was but one part of larger efforts to make the federal government more democratic. Other major reforms to the governing structure in the 1970s included shifts in the presidential nominating process that took power away from party elites and tried to move it to the grass roots, systematized investigations of political corruption, greater access to governmental information, and a wider role for public interest groups in the policy process.[41] All born of liberal efforts to root out corrupt practices and to cast sunshine on the process of governance, the procedural reforms of the 1970s meant that moderates and the concept of moderation in national politics became less and less important.

Moreover, the decline of the moderate helped encourage the entire political spectrum to polarize and to move rightward by century's end. Without the seniority system and without a more conservative wing of the Democratic Party, which was mostly southern (though not all southerners were conservative and not all conservatives were southern), the moderate order was crippled. Another consequence of the civil rights victories in the 1960s was the slow but steady southern realignment into a one-party Republican region, another crucial factor in the demise of moderation as the Democratic Party without its southern flank and without its seniority system became more uniformly liberal. Finally, since moderates had become the hallmark of the Democratic Party the question remained whether Republicans would also employ this governing style. By the 1970s the GOP was restive from four decades of Democratic dominance of national politics, so opposition not cooperation appeared more popular to younger Republicans entering the federal government in the 1970s and later.

Nor can the end of war be overlooked in appreciating the downfall of the moderate order. The year 1975 was an important turning point in the Cold War. On April 30, 1975, the last American left Saigon and the Vietnam War ended. War had midwifed the moderated iteration of the New Deal order into existence in the early 1940s, and the combination of the Cold War, the Korean War, and the Vietnam War nurtured it in the three decades that followed. While the Cold War continued for another fourteen years its tenor shifted, becoming more of an extreme fluctuation between arms buildup and efforts at arms control not unlike the increasingly nuclear style of late twentieth and early twenty-first century American politics. Instead the "shadow of war" as one historian phrased it effectively framed national politics from the late 1930s and early 1940s onward, encouraging partisan conflict balanced with moderate-driven compromise. Warfare state liberalism replaced welfare state liberalism, typically minimizing the reform impulse, especially in the 1940s and 1950s, but also making possible for one brief moment an unprecedented burst of liberal reform in the 1960s.[42]

Most important and often forgotten, the liberalism in praxis of the moderates worked. Both the New Deal and the Great Society were products of the seniority system and pragmatic compromise, and no comparable period of liberal or conservative reform for that matter has resulted since the dismantling of it in 1975. This matters. World War II partisanship and the constricted liberalism that resulted from action on the economy and intransigency on social questions reflected the contesting views of both the American people and the Congress. This is why midcentury lawmakers fought. They did not agree about a statist economic order or a statist system of social justice and civil rights. By fighting and respecting both the freedom to debate and the results of the fights, though, they found consensus. That it was manufactured and artificial matters less than its discovery and its application to policy: an increased statist economy in the war years; tepid efforts at social welfare, civil rights, and social justice in the postwar presidential administrations of Truman and Eisenhower; and a profusion of genuinely liberal social welfare and civil rights reform in Johnson's Great Society, the product of presidential cooperation with Congress.

The moderate order dictated messy, but result-oriented debates. Congress fought because debating oiled the machinery of democracy, and the moderate-dominated liberalism in praxis of midcentury worked for over thirty years, not because it was perfect but because of its flaws: the moderate order was never able to make permanent the merger of economic liberalism with social justice liberalism. When the two were joined, temporarily, in the Johnson era, two decidedly contradictory forces clashed. The triumph of statist-oriented liberalism encouraged its own death and its coroners were not only antistatist conservatives but also process-oriented liberals uncomfortable with the New Deal order. The last decade of the New Deal order proved two things. First, moderates matter to political outcomes. Second, success begat failure.

Notes

ABBREVIATIONS USED IN THE NOTES

AHC	American Heritage Center, University of Wyoming, Laramie, Wyoming
ASU	Department of Archives and Manuscripts, Arizona State University, Tempe, Arizona
BHL	Bentley Historical Library, University of Michigan, Ann Arbor, Michigan
BCAH	Dolph Briscoe Center for American History, University of Texas at Austin, Austin, Texas
BYU	Special Collections, Brigham Young University, Provo, Utah
FDRL	Franklin D. Roosevelt Library, Hyde Park, New York
GU	Special Collections, Georgetown University, Washington, D.C.
HHPL	Herbert Hoover Presidential Library, West Branch, Iowa
HSTL	Harry S Truman Library, Independence, Missouri
KRTA	K. Ross Toole Archives and Special Collections, University of Montana, Missoula, Montana
KSHS	Kansas State Historical Society, Topeka, Kansas
LBJL	Lyndon B. Johnson Library, Austin, Texas
MD, LC	Manuscript Division, Library of Congress, Washington, D.C.
NAACP Papers	National Association for the Advancement of Colored People Papers on Microfilm
NYT	*New York Times*
OF	Official File
PPF	President's Personal File
PPI	Post-Presidential Individuals File Series
RBRL	Richard B. Russell Library for Political Research and Studies, University of Georgia, Athens, Georgia
RUSHR, NA	Records of the United States House of Representatives, National Archives, Washington, D.C.
RUSS, NA	Records of the United States Senate, National Archives, Washington, D.C.
SHC	Southern Historical Collection, University of North Carolina, Chapel Hill, North Carolina
S/VP Papers	Harry S Truman Papers, Papers as Senator and Vice President
UKL	Special Collections and Archives, University of Kentucky Libraries, Lexington, Kentucky
UND	Chester Fritz Library, University of North Dakota, Grand Forks, North Dakota
USHS	Utah State Historical Society, Salt Lake City, Utah

UVA   Alderman Library, University of Virginia, Charlottesville, Virginia
WSHSC   W. S. Hoole Special Collections, University of Alabama at Tuscaloosa,
             Tuscaloosa, Alabama

INTRODUCTION

1. Crane Brinton, *The Anatomy of Revolution* (New York: W. W. Norton, 1938). See also
Neil A. Wynn, "The 'Good War': The Second World War and Postwar American Society,"
Journal of Contemporary History 31 (July 1996): 463–482.

2. Allen Drury, *A Senate Journal, 1943–1945* (New York: McGraw-Hill, 1963), 4–5; Mary
L. Dudziak, *War-Time: An Idea, Its History, Its Consequences* (New York: Oxford
University Press, 2012), 3 (first quote); William P. Kennedy, *America's Fighting Congress,* S.
Doc. no. 78-94 at 3 (Washington, D.C.: Government Printing Office, 1943) (second quote).

3. See David Plotke, *Building a Democratic Political Order: Reshaping American
Liberalism in the 1930s and 1940s* (New York: Cambridge University Press, 1996) for a
political scientist's treatment of the politics of ideology during this period. He finds the
1930s, not the 1940s, to be the defining decade for midcentury politics and "progressive
liberalism" to be the driving force behind this political development.

4. Robert L. Doughton to W. S. Graybeal, July 7, 1943, in Robert L. Doughton Papers,
SHC.

5. *Congressional Record,* 78th Congress, 1st session, 6967.

6. "United We Stand," *NYT*, December 9, 1941; Charles McNary to Roy Gill, December
24, 1941, in "December 1941," Box 19, Charles McNary Papers, MD, LC.

7. *Congressional Record,* 78th Congress, 1st session, 6966, 7063.

8. Carl T. Hayden to J. F. Yandell, April 8, 1942, in Folder 40, Box 248, Carl T. Hayden
Papers, ASU. See also *Building America,* vol. 10, no. 2, in "Congress—Maloney Committee,
1942–1945," Box 515, Robert A. Taft Papers, MD, LC.

9. Ronald C. Moe and Steven C. Teel, "Congress as Policy-Maker: A Necessary
Reappraisal," *Political Science Quarterly* 85 (September 1970): 443–470; Abe Murdock,
notes on meeting [c. December 6, 1942], in Folder 35, Box 16, Abe Murdock Papers, BYU.

10. Richard W. Waterman, "Institutional Realignment: The Composition of the U.S.
Congress," *Western Political Quarterly* 43 (March 1990): 81–92.

11. Alan Brinkley, *Age of Reform: New Deal Liberalism in Recession and War* (New York:
Alfred A. Knopf, 1995), provides the best assessment of liberalism in the 1930s and 1940s.
Telephone conversation between Thomas Corcoran and Lister Hill, June 9, 1945, in "1945
June 1–15," Box 335, President's Secretary's Files Summaries of Conversations (Thomas
Corcoran), Harry S Truman Papers, HSTL.

12. These statistics are derived from a careful evaluation of key roll call votes from the
war years. For details on my methodology, see the Essay on Sources.

13. Remarks for Republican campaign caravan: Westminster, Colorado July 8, 1944,
Greeley, Colorado, July 8, 1944, Longmont, Colorado, July 13, 1944, Littleton, Colorado,
July 15, 1944, in Folder 6, Box 4, Eugene Donald Millikin Papers, University Archives
Political Collections, University of Colorado, Boulder, Colorado (first quote); Scott C.

James, "The Evolution of the Presidency: Between the Promise and the Fear," in *The Executive Branch,* Joel D. Aberbach and Mark A. Peterson, eds. (New York: Oxford University Press, 2005), 30; Frank McNaughton to Bill Johnson, March 25, 1944, in "January–March, 1944," and McNaughton to Johnson, April 21, 1944, in "April 16–30, 1944," both in Box 6, and McNaughton to Johnson, July 6, 1943, in "July 1943," Box 5, all in Frank McNaughton Papers, HSTL; Lister Hill to Franklin D. Roosevelt, March 14, 1942, and Roosevelt to Hill, March 17, 1942, both in PPF 3927, FDRL; McNaughton to Johnson, May 29, 1944, in "May 16–31, 1944," Box 6, McNaughton to Don Bermingham, January 19, 1945, in "January 16–31, 1945," Box 8 (second quote), both in McNaughton Papers, HSTL; National Archives, "Federal Register, Administration of Franklin D. Roosevelt (1933–1945)," http://www.archives.gov/federal-register/executive-orders/roosevelt.html; Robert A. Taft to Herbert Hoover, January 12, 1943, in "Taft, Robert A., Correspondence—1943–1944," Box 233, PPI, Herbert Hoover Papers, HHPL; "The War Powers of the President," in "Presidential Powers and Usurpation, 1942," Box 754, Taft Papers, MD, LC (last quote).

14. These statistics are derived from a careful evaluation of key roll call votes from the war years. For details on my methodology, see the Essay on Sources.

1. THE WORLD BEFORE THE WAR

1. Frank McNaughton to David Hulburd, Wartime Washington, December 26, 1941, in "December 16–31, 1941," Box 2, Frank McNaughton Papers, HSTL; "A Wyoming Woman in Washington," Agnes V. O'Mahoney, December 19, 1941, in "O'Mahoney, Agnes V., 'A Wyoming Woman in Washington,'" Box 14, Joseph C. O'Mahoney Papers, AHC.

2. Robert Herzstein, *Henry R. Luce: A Political Portrait of the Man Who Created the American Century* (New York: Scribner's, 1994), 250, 254, 304; McNaughton to Hulburd, January 2, 1942, in "January 1–15, 1942," Box 2 (quote), and McNaughton to Bob Elson, January 6, 1949, in "January 1–15, 1949," Box 17, both in McNaughton Papers, HSTL. For further evidence of his relationship with congressional leaders see McNaughton to Lou Rayburn, July 4, 1946, in "Rayburn: Personal," Box 3R325, Sam Rayburn Papers, BCAH.

3. McNaughton to Hulburd, January 2, 1942, in "January 1–15, 1942," Box 2, McNaughton Papers, HSTL; O'Mahoney, "A Wyoming Woman in Washington," July 9, 1943, in "O'Mahoney, Agnes V., 'A Wyoming Woman in Washington,'" Box 14, O'Mahoney Papers, AHC.

4. *Building America,* vol. 10, no. 2, in "Congress—Maloney Committee, 1942–1945," Box 515, Robert A. Taft Papers, MD, LC, Washington, D.C. (quote); E. Pendleton Herring, "First Session of the Seventy-Fourth Congress, January 3, 1935, to August 26, 1935," *American Political Science Review* 29 (December 1935): 985–986; O. R. Altman, "Second Session of the Seventy-Fourth Congress, January 3, 1936, to June 20, 1936," *American Political Science Review* 30 (December 1936): 1086–1088; Floyd M. Riddick, "American Government and Politics: Third Session of the Seventy-Sixth Congress, January 3, 1940, to January 3, 1941," *American Political Science Review* 35 (April 1941): 285. For more details on war-era members of Congress, see the *Congressional Directory,* 77th–79th Congresses. I

define the South as the eleven former Confederate states plus Kentucky, Oklahoma, and West Virginia. Additionally, I define the Northeast as Connecticut, Delaware, Maine, Maryland, Massachusetts, New Hampshire, New Jersey, New York, Pennsylvania, Rhode Island, and Vermont; the Midwest as Illinois, Indiana, Iowa, Kansas, Michigan, Minnesota, Missouri, Nebraska, North Dakota, Ohio, South Dakota, and Wisconsin; and the West as Arizona, California, Colorado, Idaho, Montana, Nevada, New Mexico, Oregon, Utah, Washington, and Wyoming. I define the major Senate committees as Agriculture and Forestry, Appropriations, Banking and Currency, Education and Labor, Finance, Foreign Relations, Judiciary, Military Affairs, and Naval Affairs. I define the major House committees as Agriculture, Appropriations, Banking and Currency, Education, Foreign Affairs, Judiciary, Labor, Military Affairs, Naval Affairs, Rules, and Ways and Means.

5. Barbara Hinckley, *The Seniority System in Congress* (Bloomington: Indiana University Press, 1972); Nelson W. Polsby, *How Congress Evolves: Social Bases of Institutional Change* (New York: Oxford University Press, 2005); Maurice B. Tobin and Joan Shaffer, *Hidden Power: The Seniority System and Other Customs of Congress* (New York: Greenwood Press, 1986); James T. Patterson, *Congressional Conservatism and the New Deal: The Growth of the Conservative Coalition in Congress, 1933–1939* (Lexington: For the Organization of American Historians by the University of Kentucky Press, 1967); Joseph Guffey to Franklin D. Roosevelt, July 29, 1939, in Joseph Guffey Papers, Washington and Jefferson College, Washington, Pennsylvania.

6. Sarah A. Binder and Steven S. Smith, *Politics or Principle? Filibustering in the United States Senate* (Washington, D.C.: Brookings Institution, 1997); W. Lee Rawls, *In Praise of Deadlock: How Partisan Struggle Makes Better Laws* (Washington, D.C.: Woodrow Wilson Center Press, 2009); Gregory J. Wawro and Eric Schickler, *Filibuster: Obstruction and Lawmaking in the U.S. Senate* (Princeton, N.J.: Princeton University Press, 2006); Allen Drury, *A Senate Journal, 1943–1945* (New York: McGraw-Hill, 1963), 22 (quote).

7. For more on the functioning of the Rules Committee in this era, see Bruce J. Dierenfield, *Keeper of the Rules: Congressman Howard W. Smith of Virginia* (Charlottesville: University Press of Virginia, 1987).

8. Drury, *A Senate Journal*, 11, 161.

9. Elbert D. Thomas to Arthur Capper, July 31, 1944, in "T," Box 31, Arthur Capper Papers, KSHS (first quote); McNaughton to Bill Johnson, September 2, 1943, in "September 1943," Box 5, McNaughton Papers, HSTL (second quote).

10. "Love thy Neighbor as Thyself," Folder 31, Box 8, and List of Rotarians, Folder 23, Box 9, both in J. Edgar Chenoweth Papers, Special Collections, University of Colorado, Boulder, Colorado; Styles Bridges to Members of the Senate, March 25, 1944, in "Bridges, Styles," Box 28, Harold Burton Papers, MD, LC; William P. Kennedy, *America's Fighting Congress*, S. Doc. 78–94 (1943).

11. Drury, *A Senate Journal*, 2; McNaughton to Eleanor Welch, September 15, 1944, in "September 1–21, 1944" (first quote) [Report by Frank McNaughton], September 1944, in "September 22–30, 1944," both in Box 7, McNaughton Papers, HSTL (remaining quotes).

12. Joseph C. O'Mahoney Speech, "What's the Matter with Congress," June 17, 1942, in

"Speeches, June 17, 1942" (first five quotes), and Congress and the Bureaucracy, December 8, 1942, in "Speeches, December 8, 1942," both in Box 267, O'Mahoney Papers, AHC; William Lemke, Doings in Congress, February 3, 1943, in File 1, Box 28, William Lemke Papers, UND (remaining quotes).

13. David Brinkley, *Washington Goes to War* (New York: Alfred A. Knopf, 1988), 196–197 (quote), 206; Herring, "First Session of the Seventy-Fourth Congress," 996; Roosevelt to Sam Rayburn and Alben Barkley, December 3, 1940, in PPF 474, FDRL; Roger H. Davidson, "The Advent of the Modern Congress: The Legislative Reorganization Act of 1946," *Legislative Studies Quarterly* 15 (August 1990): 368; Report of Departments and Independent Establishments Regarding Detail of Personnel to Congressional Committees, n.d., in "Detail of Department Clerks," 77th Congress, Senate 77A-F2, Box 42, and Clerk to Theodore Francis Green, May 15, 1943, in "Correspondence C," 78th Congress, Senate 78A-F2, Box 70, both in Senate Committee on Appropriations, RG 46, RUSS, NA; author's notes from Seminar—New Work on the New Deal, April 15, 2004, Woodrow Wilson International Center for Scholars, Washington, D.C.

14. Allan M. Winkler, *The Politics of Propaganda: The Office of War Information, 1942–1945* (New Haven, Conn.: Yale University Press, 1978), 70.

15. John Kenneth Galbraith, *A Life in Our Times: Memoirs* (Boston: Houghton Mifflin, 1981); Richard Parker, *John Kenneth Galbraith: His Life, His Politics, His Economics* (Chicago: University of Chicago Press, 2007); Joseph P. Lash, *Dealers and Dreamers: A New Look at the New Deal* (New York: Doubleday, 1988).

16. Jesse H. Jones and Carl H. Pforzheimer, *Fifty Billion Dollars: My Thirteen Years with the RFC, 1932–1945* (New York: Macmillan, 1951); Drury, *A Senate Journal*, 176 (quote); David McKean, *Tommy the Cork: Washington's Ultimate Insider from Roosevelt to Reagan* (Hanover, N.H.: Steerforth Press, 2004), 131–189; Michael Janeway, *Fall of the House of Roosevelt: Brokers of Ideas and Power from FDR to LBJ* (New York: Columbia University Press, 2004); Jordan A. Schwarz, *The New Dealers: Power Politics in the Age of Roosevelt* (New York: Alfred A. Knopf, 1993).

17. David Robertson, *Sly and Able: A Political Biography of James F. Byrnes* (New York: W. W. Norton, 1994); James E. St. Clair and Linda C. Gugin, *Chief Justice Fred M. Vinson of Kentucky: A Political Biography* (Lexington: University Press of Kentucky, 2002), 123–155.

18. Memorandum, in "Defense Program, 1936–1944 and Undated," Box 11, Gerald P. Nye Papers, HHPL; Robert Higgs, *Crisis and Leviathan: Critical Episodes in the Growth of American Government* (New York: Oxford University Press, 1987), 272–274; Rexford G. Tugwell, *The Democratic Roosevelt: A Biography of Franklin D. Roosevelt* (Garden City, N.Y.: Doubleday, 1957), 645. For more on World War II spending and the growth of government, see James T. Sparrow, *Warfare State: World War II Americans and the Age of Big Government* (New York: Oxford University Press, 2011), 119–159, 261–264. For data on the rise of government revenues as a percent of the gross national product, see John Wallis, "American Government Finance in the Long Run, 1790–1990," *Journal of Economic Perspectives* 14 (Winter 2000): 61–82. For more on the proliferation of the executive branch during the war, see Matthew J. Dickinson, *Bitter Harvest: FDR, Presidential Power, and the Growth of the Presidential Branch* (New York: Cambridge University Press, 1996), 117–203.

19. Clinton Anderson to Louis C. Ilfeld, November 17, 1941, in "Inflation," Box 459, Clinton Anderson Papers, MD, LC; Sparrow, *Warfare State*, 127.

20. Rayburn to O. J. Colwick, July 26, 1940, in "1940 General—Miscellaneous Correspondence," Box 3R281, Rayburn Papers, BCAH.

21. C. E. Noyes, "Spending vs. Economy: A Ten-Year Record," *Editorial Research Reports 1940*, vol. 1 (Washington, D.C.: CQ Press, 1940), Retrieved from http://library .cqpress.com.ezproxy.lib.uh.edu/cqresearcher/cqresrre1940030100; Sparrow, *Warfare State*, 127; Michael French, *U.S. Economic History since 1945* (Manchester, England: Manchester University Press, 1997), 50, gives a different, much lower figure of $47.6 billion; "Record of the 79th Congress (first session), 1945," *Editorial Research Reports 1945*, vol. 2 (Washington, D.C.: CQ Press, 1945), retrieved from http://library.cqpress.com .ezproxy.lib.uh.edu/ cqresearcher/cqresrre1945122100.

22. Harry S Truman, Annual Budget Message to the Congress: Fiscal Year 1950, January 10, 1949, in John T. Woolley and Gerhard Peters, *The American Presidency Project* [online], Santa Barbara, Calif.: University of California (hosted), Gerhard Peters (database), http://www.presidency.ucsb.edu/ws/?pid=13434 .

23. J. Garry Clifford and Samuel R. Spencer Jr., *The First Peacetime Draft* (Lawrence: University Press of Kansas, 1986), 11.

24. McNaughton to David Hulburd, September 19, 1941, in "September 16–30, 1941," Box 1, McNaughton Papers, HSTL.

25. Ibid.

26. Naturally, diplomatic historians have presented a much more complex picture of American foreign affairs, but scholarly interpretations matter little when considering the belief systems of average Americans and their elected representatives in Congress. For some of the most significant writing about nineteenth-century diplomatic history, see Wai-chee Dimock, *Empire for Liberty: Melville and the Poetics of Individualism* (Princeton, N.J.: Princeton University Press, 1989); Thomas Hietala, *Manifest Design: American Exceptionalism and Empire*, rev. ed. (Ithaca, N.Y.: Cornell University Press, 2003); Kristen Hogansen, *Fighting for American Manhood: How Gender Politics Provoked the Spanish-American and Philippine-American Wars* (New Haven, Conn.: Yale University Press, 1998); Reginald Horsman, *Race and Manifest Destiny: The Origins of American Racial Anglo-Saxonism* (Cambridge, Mass.: Harvard University Press, 1981); Michael Hunt, *Ideology and U.S. Foreign Policy* (New Haven, Conn.: Yale University Press, 1987); Walter LeFeber, *The New Empire: An Interpretation of American Expansion, 1860–1898* (Ithaca, N.Y.: Cornell University Press, 1963); Anders Stephanson, *Manifest Destiny: American Expansion and the Empire of Right* (New York: Hill and Wang, 1995); Robert W. Tucker and David Hendrickson, *Empire of Liberty: The Statecraft of Thomas Jefferson* (New York: Oxford University Press, 1990).

27. For background on the war and its origins, see David Fromkin, *Europe's Last Summer: Who Started the Great War in 1914?* (New York: Alfred A. Knopf, 2004). For America and the war, see Lloyd E. Ambrosius, *Wilsonian Statecraft: Theory and Practice of Liberal Internationalism during World War I* (Wilmington, Del.: SR Books, 1991); Robert B. Bruce, *A Fraternity of Arms: America and France in the Great War* (Lawrence: University

Press of Kansas, 2003); Edward M. Coffman, *The War to End All Wars: The American Military Experience in World War I* (New York: Oxford University Press, 1968); Robert H. Ferrell, *Woodrow Wilson and World War I, 1917–1921* (New York: Harper & Row, 1985); Ellis W. Hawley, *The Great War and the Search for a Modern Order: A History of the American People and Their Institutions, 1917–1933,* 2nd ed. (New York: St. Martin's Press, 1992); Jennifer D. Keene, *Doughboys, the Great War, and the Remaking of America* (Baltimore, Md.: Johns Hopkins University Press, 2001); David M. Kennedy, *Over Here: The First World War and American Society* (New York: Oxford University Press, 1982); Stephen Vaughn, *Holding Fast the Inner Lines: Democracy, Nationalism, and the Committee on Public Information* (Chapel Hill: University of North Carolina Press, 1980); David R. Woodward, *Trial by Friendship: Anglo-American Relations, 1917–1918* (Lexington: University Press of Kentucky, 1993); Robert H. Zieger, *America's Great War: World War I and the American Experience* (Lanham, Md.: Rowman & Littlefield, 2000). Harry Carr, "Export of Munitions Condemned, Defended," *Los Angeles Times,* January 6, 1916; Lewis L. Gould, *Progressives and Prohibitionists: Texas Democrats in the Wilson Era* (Austin and London: University of Texas Press, 1973), 161–165; Wilson quoted in David A. Horowitz, *Beyond Left and Right: Insurgency and the Establishment* (Urbana: University of Illinois Press, 1997), 22–24.

28. Wilson quoted in Thomas J. Knock, *To End All Wars: Woodrow Wilson and the Quest for a New World Order* (New York: Oxford University Press, 1992), 121–122, 131. See also Alan Dawley, *Changing the World: American Progressives in War and Revolution* (Princeton, N.J.: Princeton University Press, 2003), and James T. Kloppenberg, *Uncertain Victory: Social Democracy and Progressivism in European and American Thought, 1870–1920* (New York: Oxford University Press, 1986). "Keen Debate for 13 Hours," *NYT,* April 5, 1917 (remaining quotes); "Text of War Resolution Adopted by Senate and the Detailed Vote upon Its Passage," *NYT,* April 5, 1917; "Seek to Explain Miss Rankin's 'No,'" *NYT,* April 17, 1917.

29. Kennedy, *Over Here,* 69, 76–80, 93 (quote), 96–97, 103, 144–190; Horowitz, *Beyond Left and Right,* 25–27.

30. Knock, *To End All Wars,* 189–190; Herbert F. Margulies, *The Mild Reservationists and the League of Nations Controversy in the Senate* (Columbia: University of Missouri Press, 1989), x–xiii, 8; John Milton Cooper Jr., *Breaking the Heart of the World: Woodrow Wilson and the Fight for the League of Nations* (New York: Cambridge University Press, 2001); Ralph Stone, *The Irreconcilables: The Fight against the League of Nations* (Lexington: University Press of Kentucky, 1970), 1–3, 13, 23, 24, 29, 31, 41–43, 49, 70–76, 95, 99, 100, 115–127, 178–182.

31. Henry Cabot Lodge, *The Senate and the League of Nations* (New York: C. Scribner's Sons, 1925), 226.

32. See for example, Ferrell, *Woodrow Wilson;* Hawley, *The Great War.*

33. Theodore J. Lowi, *The End of Liberalism: The Second Republic of the United States,* 2nd ed. (New York: W. W. Norton, 1979). The TVA's political difficulties did not appear until the 1950s.

34. Altman, "Second Session of the Seventy-Fourth Congress," 1086 (quote); Karl

Mundt, "A Strong Opposition Is Needed," *Vital Speeches of the Day* 7 (September 1, 1941): 696–698; Richard E. Darilek, *A Loyal Opposition in Time of War: The Republican Party and the Politics of Foreign Policy from Pearl Harbor to Yalta* (Westport, Conn.: Greenwood Press, 1976).

35. C. Dwight Dorough, *Mr. Sam* (New York: Random House, 1962); Booth Mooney, *Roosevelt and Rayburn: A Political Partnership* (Philadelphia: Lippincott, 1971); Alfred Steinberg, *Sam Rayburn: A Biography* (New York: Hawthorn Books, 1975); Anthony Champagne, *Congressman Sam Rayburn* (New Brunswick, N.J.: Rutgers University Press, 1984); D. B. Hardeman and Donald C. Bacon, *Rayburn: A Biography* (Austin: Texas Monthly Press, 1987); Lewis L. Gould and Nancy Beck Young, "The Speaker and the Presidents: Sam Rayburn, the White House, and the Legislative Process, 1941–1961," in Roger H. Davidson, Susan Webb Hammond, and Raymond W. Smock, eds., *Masters of the House: Congressional Leadership over Two Centuries* (Boulder, Colo.: Westview Press, 1998), 181–221; O. R. Altman, "Second and Third Sessions of the Seventy-Fifth Congress, 1937–38," *American Political Science Review* 32 (December 1938): 1103–1104; Alan Brinkley, *The End of Reform: New Deal Liberalism in Recession and War* (New York: Alfred A. Knopf, 1995); Ira Katznelson, Kim Geiger, and Daniel Kryder, "Limiting Liberalism: The Southern Veto in Congress, 1933–1950," *Political Science Quarterly* 108 (Summer 1993): 283–306; Patterson, *Congressional Conservatism and the New Deal*; David L. Porter, *Congress and the Waning of the New Deal* (Port Washington, N.Y.: Kennikat Press, 1980).

36. O. R. Altman, "First Session of the Seventy-Fifth Congress, January 5, 1937, to August 21, 1937," *American Political Science Review* 31 (December 1937): 1082 (quotes); Susan Dunn, *Roosevelt's Purge: How FDR Fought to Change the Democratic Party* (Cambridge, Mass.: Belknap Press of Harvard University Press, 2010).

37. Manfred Jonas, *Isolationism in America, 1935–1941* (Ithaca, N.Y.: Cornell University Press, 1966), 1–31; Robert A. Divine, *The Illusion of Neutrality* (Chicago: University of Chicago Press, 1962), 1–56; William Appleman Williams, "The Legend of Isolationism in the 1920s," *Science and Society* 18 (Winter 1954): 1–20; Thomas N. Guinsburg, *The Pursuit of Isolationism in the United States Senate from Versailles to Pearl Harbor* (New York: Garland Publishing, 1982), 51–109.

38. Richard B. Russell to Mother, October 2, 1938, in "Personal Family Papers 1938," Box 41, Winder Series, Richard B. Russell Papers, RBRL; Divine, *Illusion of Neutrality*, 57–122, 185–186; for background on isolationist thought in the seven years preceding Pearl Harbor, see Jonas, *Isolationism in America*; See for example David M. Kennedy, *Freedom from Fear: The American People in Depression and War, 1929–1945* (New York: Oxford University Press, 1999), 381–425; U.S. Congress, House of Representatives, Committee on Foreign Affairs, *American Neutrality Policy*, 74th Congress, 2nd session, 1936.

39. Louis Ludlow to James A. Crain, January 21, 1935, in Box 1, Louis Ludlow Papers, Lilly Library, Indiana University, Bloomington, Indiana (first quote); Donald Francis Drummond, *The Passing of American Neutrality, 1937–1941* (Ann Arbor: University of Michigan Press, 1955), 57–59; Cordell Hull to Sam D. McReynolds, January 8, 1938, in United States, Department of State, Press Releases, Microfilm Edition; Roosevelt to

William B. Bankhead, January 6, 1938, in "House Blocks Vote of People on U.S. War," *Christian Science Monitor*, January 10, 1938 (remaining quotes).

40. McNaughton to Johnson, July 6, 1943, in "July 1943," Box 5, HSTL.

41. Wayne S. Cole, *America First: The Battle against Intervention, 1940–1941* (Madison: University of Wisconsin Press, 1953), 23; McNaughton to Hulburd, September 26, 1941, in "September 16–30, 1941," Box 1, McNaughton Papers, HSTL (quotes); "War and Peace: Follow What Leader?" *Time* (October 6, 1941): 18–20; U.S. Congress, House of Representatives, Committee on Foreign Affairs, *American Neutrality Policy*, 76th Congress, 1st session, 1939, 14–15; Divine, *Illusion of Neutrality*, 286–335; Drummond, *The Passing of American Neutrality*, 106–111. For background on these lawmakers see, Donald John Cameron, "Burton K. Wheeler as Public Campaigner, 1922–1942" (Ph.D. dissertation, Northwestern University, 1960); Richard T. Ruetten, "Burton K. Wheeler of Montana: A Progressive between the Wars" (Ph.D. dissertation, University of Oregon, 1961); Julian M. Pleasants, *Buncombe Bob: The Life and Times of Robert Rice Reynolds* (Chapel Hill: University of North Carolina Press, 2000); Cole, *Senator Gerald P. Nye*; Dorothy G. Wayman, *David I. Walsh: Citizen Patriot* (Milwaukee, Wisc.: Bruce Publishing, 1952); Hamilton Fish, *Memoir of an American Patriot* (Washington, D.C.: Regnery Gateway, 1991).

42. Hedley Donovan, "Isolationists Call Destroyer Swap 'Act of War,' None Hopes to Halt It," *Washington Post*, September 4, 1940 (first two quotes); Guinsburg, *The Pursuit of Isolationism in the United States Senate*, 243–245 (third quote).

43. Clifford and Spencer, *The First Peacetime Draft*, 1–7, 83–101 (quote is on p. 84); David L. Porter, *The Seventy-Sixth Congress and World War II, 1939–1940* (Columbia: University of Missouri Press, 1979), 127–171.

44. Rayburn to Topsy Russell, August 22, 1940, in "1940 Bills Selective Service," Box 3R279, Rayburn Papers, BCAH (first quote); Clifford and Spencer, *The First Peacetime Draft*, 200–225 (second quote).

45. Felix Belair Jr. to Hulburd, September 25, 1940, in "Belair, Felix, Jr., 1940–1943," Box 20, McNaughton Papers, HSTL; Porter, *The Seventy-Sixth Congress and World War II*; Flanagan to Hulburd, May 4, 1940, in "Flanagan, [no first name], 1940," Box 21, McNaughton Papers, HSTL.

46. John W. Jeffries, *Wartime America: The World War II Homefront* (Chicago: Ivan R. Dee, 1996), 147, 150; Ernest Havemann to Hulburd, October 11, 1940, in "Havemann, Ernest, 1940," Box 22 (quotes), and Belair to Hulburd, September 25, 1940, in "Belair, Felix, Jr., 1940–1943," Box 20, both in McNaughton Papers, HSTL; John Morton Blum, *V Was for Victory: Politics and American Culture during World War II* (New York: Harcourt Brace Jovanovich, 1976), 262–265; Kennedy, *Freedom from Fear*, 454–464.

47. Drummond, *The Passing of American Neutrality*, 208–212 (first quote); Warren F. Kimball, *The Most Unsordid Act: Lend-Lease, 1939–1941* (Baltimore, Md.: Johns Hopkins University Press, 1969), 151–152; Doyle W. Buckwalter, "The Congressional Concurrent Resolution: A Search for Foreign Policy Influence," *Midwest Journal of Political Science* 14 (August 1970): 434–458; McNaughton to Hulburd, August 15, 1941, in "August 1–15, 1941," Box 1, McNaughton Papers, HSTL (second quote).

48. "The Real Meaning of the Lend-Lease Bill," Speech of Alben W. Barkley, February 10, 1941, in "'The Real Meaning of the Lend-Lease Bill' Senator Alben Barkley, February 10, 1941," Alben Barkley Papers, UKL; Russell to Mother, February 5, 1941, in "Family (IDR) 1941," Box 42, Winder Series, Russell Papers, RBRL.

49. Kimball, *The Most Unsordid Act,* 195–229; Guinsburg, *The Pursuit of Isolationism in the United States Senate,* 247–274; "Wheeler Sees War in Bill," *Los Angeles Times,* January 13, 1941; Mark Lincoln Chadwin, *The Hawks of World War II* (Chapel Hill: University of North Carolina Press, 1968), 212–215; Cole, *America First,* 47; Gerald P. Nye to Robert E. Wood, January 16, 1941, in "America First Committee: Correspondence 1941, January–April," Nye Papers, HHPL (quotes); Guinsburg, *The Pursuit of Isolationism in the United States Senate,* 247–274; "Wheeler Sees War in Bill," *Los Angeles Times,* January 13, 1941.

50. Cole, *America First,* 65–66; Russell to Mother, March 11, 1941, in "Family (IDR) 1941," Box 42, Winder Series, Russell Papers, RBRL; Robert L. Doughton to Robert W. Winston, May 23, 1941, in File 893, Box 25, Robert L. Doughton Papers, SHC; John Dingell to Roosevelt, March 11, 1941, PPF 7449, FDRL.

51. "1940 Proviso Cited," *NYT,* July 16, 1941; "Senate Defeats Taft Draft Plan, Faces New Curb," *NYT,* August 6, 1941; Jerry Greene to Hulburd, July 18, 1941, in "Greene, Jerry, 1941–1942," Box 21, McNaughton Papers, HSTL (quotes); "Senate Votes to Extend Draft Term to 2 Years," *Los Angeles Times,* August 8, 1941; Frederick R. Barkley, "Vote Is 203 to 202," *NYT,* August 13, 1941.

52. Greene to Hulburd, July 18, 1941, in "Greene, Jerry, 1941–1942," Box 21, McNaughton Papers, HSTL (first two quotes); "25 Soviet Divisions Lost in Ukraine Trap, Soviets Say; Russians Raid Berlin Twice," *NYT,* August 9, 1941; McNaughton to Hulburd, August 15, 1941, in "August 1–15, 1941," Box 1, McNaughton Papers, HSTL (last quote); "Draft Extension Bill Wins Republican Support in House," *Christian Science Monitor,* August 12, 1941; *Congressional Record,* 77th Congress, 1st session, 6995–7077; Hardeman and Bacon, *Rayburn,* 261–270; George Stockton Wills, "Mr. Speaker and the Call to Arms: The Role of Sam Rayburn in the 1941 Extension of the Selective Service Act" (M.A. thesis, University of Virginia, 1962); McNaughton to Hulburd, August 15, 1941, in "August 1–15, 1941," Box 1, McNaughton Papers, HSTL.

53. Wills, "Mr. Speaker and the Call to Arms," 76 (first quote); McNaughton to Hulburd, August 15, 1941, in "August 1–15, 1941," Box 1, McNaughton Papers, HSTL (second quote); *Congressional Record,* 77th Congress, 1st session, 6995–7077 (remaining quotes). Two points of clarification should be remembered regarding Short and the Republicans: first, one voting with the losing side may not make a motion to reconsider, and second, since Rayburn had already dispatched such a motion, another could not be entertained for that particular measure. See Asher C. Hinds, *Hinds' Precedents of the House of Representatives of the United States, Including References to Provisions of the Constitution, the Laws, and Decisions of the United States Senate* (Washington, D.C.: Government Printing Office, 1907–1908).

54. Joe Martin, as told to Robert J. Donovan, *My First Fifty Years in Politics* (Westport, Conn.: Greenwood Press, 1975), 97 (first quote); "House Vote on Draft Bill," *NYT,* August 13, 1941; McNaughton to Hulburd, August 15, 1941, in "August 1–15, 1941," Box 1,

McNaughton Papers (remaining quotes). See also, "The Congress: State of Mind," *Time* (August 25, 1941): 15–17; Arthur H. Vandenberg Jr., ed., *The Private Papers of Senator Vandenberg* (Boston: Houghton Mifflin, 1952), 15; "House Vote on Draft Bill," *NYT*, August 13, 1941.

55. "Congress Hopes for 2-Week Rest," *NYT*, August 18, 1941; McNaughton to Hulburd, August 15, 1941, in "August 1–15, 1941" (first three quotes), and McNaughton to Hulburd, September 18, 1941, in "September 16–30, 1941" (last quote), both in Box 1, McNaughton Papers.

56. McNaughton to Hulburd, September 27, 1941, in "September 16–30, 1941," Box 1, McNaughton Papers, HSTL (quotes). See also Robert Dean Pope, "Senatorial Baron: The Long Political Career of Kenneth C. McKellar" (Ph.D. dissertation, Yale University, 1975); Thomas T. Connally, as told to Alfred Steinberg, *My Name Is Tom Connally* (New York: Thomas T. Crowell Company, 1954), 246; "Ballot Is 50–37," *NYT*, November 8, 1941; Robert C. Albright, "Freedom of Seas Is Restored to Shipping after President Appeals to House and Promises Sterner Attitude on Strikes," *Washington Post*, November 14, 1941; Cole, *America First*, 162–166, 198–199; Wayne S. Cole, *Charles A. Lindbergh and the Battle against American Intervention in World War II* (New York: Harcourt, Brace, Jovanovich, 1974), 229.

57. McNaughton to Hulburd, December 4, 1941 (first quote), and McNaughton to Hulburd, December 8, 1941 (second quote), both in "December 1–15, 1941," Box 1, McNaughton Papers, HSTL; "It's America First, *Now!*," *NYT*, December 8, 1941 (remaining quotes); Chadwin, *The Hawks of World War II*, 164–165.

58. McNaughton to Hulburd, December 8, 1941 (multiple letters), in "December 1–15, 1941," Box 1, McNaughton Papers, HSTL (first through fifth quotes and remaining quotes); *Congressional Record*, 77th Congress, 1st session, 9519–9537 (sixth and seventh quotes); Fish, *Memoir of an American Patriot*, 93–94. For background on the United States and the start of the war, see David Reynolds, *From Munich to Pearl Harbor: Roosevelt's America and the Origins of the Second World War* (Chicago: Ivan R. Dee, 2001); Robert A. Divine, *Roosevelt and World War II* (New York: Penguin Books, 1970); James McGregor Burns, *Roosevelt: The Soldier of Freedom* (New York: Harcourt Brace Jovanovich, 1970); Waldo Heinrichs, *Threshold of War: Franklin D. Roosevelt and American Entry into World War II* (New York: Oxford University Press, 1988); Warren F. Kimball, *The Juggler: Franklin Roosevelt as Wartime Statesman* (Princeton, N.J.: Princeton University Press, 1991).

59. McNaughton to Hulburd, December 8, 1941 (multiple letters), in "December 1–15, 1941," Box 1, McNaughton Papers.

2. "WE'LL GET DOWN AND FIGHT" OVER RESOURCE MANAGEMENT

1. Frank McNaughton to David Hulburd, January 1, 1942, in "January 1–15, 1942," Box 2, Frank McNaughton Papers, HSTL (quotes); Thomas T. Connally, as told to Alfred Steinberg, *My Name Is Tom Connally* (New York: Crowell, 1954); Merle L. Gulick, "Tom Connally as a Founder of the United Nations" (Ph.D. dissertation, Georgetown University, 1955); David Leon Matheny, "A Comparison of Selected Foreign Policy Speeches of

Senator Tom Connally" (Ph.D. dissertation, University of Oklahoma, 1965); Lionel V. Patenaude, "Garner, Sumners, and Connally: The Defeat of the Roosevelt Court Bill in 1937," *Southwestern Historical Quarterly* 74 (July 1970): 36–51; Janet Schmelzer, "Tom Connally," in *Profiles in Power: Twentieth-Century Texans in Washington,* Kenneth E. Hendrickson Jr. and Michael L. Collins, eds. (Arlington Heights, Ill.: Harlan Davidson, 1993); Frank Herbert Smyrl, "Tom Connally and the New Deal" (Ph.D. dissertation, University of Oklahoma, 1968).

2. The role of Congress in this process has only been partially recognized. See George B. Galloway, "Leadership in the House of Representatives," *Western Political Quarterly* 12 (June 1959): 437; Andrew H. Bartels, "The Office of Price Administration and the Legacy of the New Deal, 1939–1946," *Public Historian* 5 (Summer 1983): 5–6; Robert Higgs, *Crisis and Leviathan: Critical Episodes in the Growth of American Government* (New York: Oxford University Press, 1987), 196–236. For more on the rise of the warfare state, see Michael S. Sherry, *In the Shadow of War: The United States since the 1930's* (New Haven, Conn.: Yale University Press, 1995); Bartholomew H. Sparrow, *From the Outside In: World War II and the American State* (Princeton, N.J.: Princeton University Press, 1996); Brian Waddell, *The War against the New Deal: World War II and American Democracy* (DeKalb: Northern Illinois University Press, 2001).

3. Higgs, *Crisis and Leviathan,* 211; Amy Bentley, *Eating for Victory: Food Rationing and the Politics of Domesticity* (Urbana: University of Illinois Press, 1998), 14; Meg Jacobs, *Pocketbook Politics: Economic Citizenship in Twentieth-Century America* (Princeton, N.J.: Princeton University Press, 2005), 190; James T. Sparrow, *Warfare State: World War II Americans and the Age of Big Government* (New York: Oxford University Press, 2011). For representative accounts that malign the role of Congress in the development of the liberal state, see James T. Patterson, *Congressional Conservatism and the New Deal: The Growth of the Conservative Coalition in Congress, 1933–1939* (Lexington: For the Organization of American Historians by the University of Kentucky Press, 1967); Alan Brinkley, *The End of Reform: New Deal Liberalism in Recession and War* (New York: Alfred A. Knopf, 1995); John Morton Blum, *V Was for Victory: Politics and American Culture during World War II* (New York: Harcourt Brace Jovanovich, 1976), 221–254. Students of the postwar era have found a much more engaged Congress but this study locates the engagement earlier than these works. See for example David M. Barrett, *The CIA and Congress: The Untold Story from Truman to Kennedy* (Lawrence: University Press of Kansas, 2005); Robert David Johnson, *Congress and the Cold War* (New York: Cambridge University Press, 2006); Julian E. Zelizer, *On Capitol Hill: The Struggle to Reform Congress and Its Consequences, 1948–2000* (New York: Cambridge University Press, 2004); Julian E. Zelizer, *Taxing America: Wilbur D. Mills, Congress, and the State, 1945–1975* (New York: Cambridge University Press, 1998).

4. McNaughton to Hulburd, December 26, 1941, in "December 16–31, 1941," and McNaughton to Hulburd, January 23, 1942, in "January 16–31, 1942," (quote), both in Box 2, McNaughton Papers, HSTL.

5. McNaughton to Hulburd, January 1, 1942, in "January 1–15, 1942," Box 2 (first quote); McNaughton to Bill Johnson, July 6, 1943, in "July 1943," Box 5 (remaining quotes), both in McNaughton Papers, HSTL; James P. Fleissner, "August 11, 1938: A Day in the Life of

Senator Walter F. George," *Journal of Southern Legal History* 9 (2001): 55–101; Josephine Mellichamp, *Senators from Georgia* (Huntsville, Ala.: Strode Publishers, 1976), 230–239; Luther Harmon Zeigler Jr., "Senator Walter George's 1938 Campaign," *Georgia Historical Quarterly* 43 (December 1959): 333–352; Susan Dunn, *Roosevelt's Purge: How FDR Fought to Change the Democratic Party* (Cambridge, Mass.: Belknap Press of Harvard University Press, 2010), 152–178.

6. McNaughton to Hulburd, December 17, 1941, in "December 16–31, 1941," Box 2, McNaughton Papers, HSTL.

7. McNaughton to Hulburd, December 12, 1941, in "December 1–15, 1941" (first two quotes); McNaughton to Hulburd, December 17, 1941, in "December 16–31, 1941"; McNaughton to James McConaughy for Havemann, February 14, 1942, in "February 1942," all in Box 2, McNaughton Papers, HSTL; Hal H. Smith, "Summary of the Legislation Enacted in the First Session of the 77th Congress," *NYT*, January 2, 1942; "Wider War Powers Win Vote of House," *NYT*, February 28, 1942; Higgs, *Crisis and Leviathan*, 205–207; Sam Rayburn to R. T. Wilkinson, January 19, 1943, in "Political, National," Box 3U45, Sam Rayburn Papers, BCAH (last quote). Congress refused to pass a third war powers bill in 1942.

8. Franklin D. Roosevelt had talked during the war about his desire to have a few handy "whipping boys," and though he did not name Congress as one of his targets, the record indicates that lawmakers often filled that unwelcome void. See Kenneth S. Davis, *FDR, the War President, 1940–1943: A History* (New York: Random House, 2000), 630.

9. "Gallup and Fortune Polls," *Public Opinion Quarterly* 6 (Autumn 1942): 475; McNaughton to Hulburd, March 13, 1942, in "March 1942," Box 2, McNaughton Papers, HSTL (quotes); David M. Kennedy, *Freedom from Fear: The American People in Depression and War, 1929–1945* (New York: Oxford University Press, 1999), 526–532. Contemporary literature on Congress suggests that the more Americans know about the institution, the more they disapprove of it because Americans do not like to see the messiness of democracy at work. See John R. Hibbing and Elizabeth Theiss-Morse, *Congress as Public Enemy: Public Attitudes toward American Political Institutions* (New York: Cambridge University Press, 1995). Polls from the war era are somewhat more nuanced, ranging from favorable, to mixed, and to negative views of congressional job performance. Consistently high in war-era polls was a measure of public unawareness of who their congressman was, what positions s/he took on the issues, and whether s/he was doing a good job, with the percent of respondents in these categories ranging from 30 to 40 percent. This range of responses suggests a greater reliability should be attributed to the responses than perhaps Hibbing and Theiss-Morse accept despite the statistics demonstrating a significant minority was disengaged from the legislative process. See Hadley Cantril, ed., *Public Opinion, 1935–1946* (Princeton, N.J.: Princeton University Press, 1951), 133–135, 790, 929–939.

10. McNaughton to Hulburd, March 13, 1942, in "March 1942," Box 2, McNaughton Papers, HSTL (quotes); Higgs, *Crisis and Leviathan*, 203. For more on executive branch organization, see Matthew J. Dickinson, *Bitter Harvest: FDR, Presidential Power, and the Growth of the Presidential Branch* (New York: Cambridge University Press, 1996), 117–203.

11. McNaughton to Hulburd, March 20, 1942, in "March 1942," Box 2 (first quote), and

McNaughton to Johnson, September 2, 1943, in "September 1943," Box 5 (second quote), both in McNaughton Papers, HSTL; D. B. Hardeman and Donald C. Bacon, *Rayburn: A Biography* (Austin: Texas Monthly Press, 1987), 376 (third quote). See also Anthony Champagne, *Congressman Sam Rayburn* (New Brunswick, N.J.: Rutgers University Press, 1984); Edward Oda Daniel, "Sam Rayburn: Trials of a Party Man" (Ph.D. dissertation, North Texas State University, 1979); C. Dwight Dorough, *Mr. Sam* (New York: Random House, 1962); Lewis L. Gould and Nancy Beck Young, "The Speaker and the Presidents: Sam Rayburn, the White House, and the Legislative Process, 1941–1961," in Roger H. Davidson, Susan Webb Hammond, and Raymond W. Smock, eds., *Masters of the House: Congressional Leadership over Two Centuries* (Boulder, Colo.: Westview Press, 1998), 181–221; Kenneth D. Hairgrove, "Sam Rayburn: Congressional Leader, 1940–1952" (Ph.D. dissertation, Texas Tech University, 1974); Dwayne Lee Little, "The Political Leadership of Speaker Sam Rayburn, 1940–1961" (Ph.D. dissertation, University of Cincinnati, 1970); Booth Mooney, *Roosevelt and Rayburn: A Political Partnership* (Philadelphia: Lippincott, 1971); "The Battle on the Home Front during the War and After," Sam Rayburn speech, January 31, 1944, in "Rayburn, Sam 4 of 4," Box 52, LBJA, Lyndon B. Johnson Papers, LBJL (last quote).

12. David Brinkley, *Washington Goes to War* (New York: Alfred A. Knopf, 1988), 209 (first quote); Robert E. Kennedy to Mr. Finnegan, February 24, 1944, in "Off Record Letters, 1944," Box 2, Robert E. Kennedy Papers, AHC (second quote). See also Alben W. Barkley, *That Reminds Me* (Garden City, N.Y.: Doubleday, 1954); Jane R. Barkley, *I Married the Veep* (New York: Vanguard Press, 1958); Polly Ann Davis, *Alben W. Barkley, Senate Majority Leader and Vice President* (New York: Garland Publishing, 1979); James K. Libbey, *Dear Alben: Mr. Barkley of Kentucky* (Lexington: University Press of Kentucky, 1979); Donald A. Ritchie, "Alben W. Barkley: The President's Man," in *First among Equals: Outstanding Senate Leaders of the Twentieth Century*, Richard A. Baker and Roger H. Davidson, eds. (Washington, D.C.: Congressional Quarterly, 1991), 127–162; McNaughton to Johnson, September 2, 1943, in "September 1943," Box 5, McNaughton Papers, HSTL (last quote).

13. McNaughton to Johnson, September 2, 1943, in "September 1943," Box 5, McNaughton Papers, HSTL (quotes); Hardeman and Bacon, *Rayburn,* 121–131; Secretary to Speaker Rayburn, June 26, 1945, in "Chili," Box 3R318, Rayburn Papers, BCAH.

14. Ibid. See also Lester I. Gordon, "John McCormack and the Roosevelt Era" (Ph.D. dissertation, Boston University, 1976); Garrison Nelson, "Irish Identity Politics: The Reinvention of Speaker John W. McCormack of Boston," *New England Journal of Public Policy* 15 (Fall/Winter 1999/2000): 7–34. For more on the import of the relationship between Rayburn and McCormack, see Anthony Champagne, *The Austin-Boston Connection: Five Decades of House Democratic Leadership, 1937–1989* (College Station: Texas A & M University Press, 2009), 102–124.

15. Rayburn to John McDuffie, February 24, 1942, in "1942 General 'M,'" Box 3R292, Rayburn Papers, BCAH; McNaughton to Johnson, September 2, 1943, in "September 1943," Box 5, McNaughton Papers, HSTL.

16. Agnes V. O'Mahoney, "A Wyoming Woman in Washington," April 27, 1945, in

"O'Mahoney, Agnes V., 'A Wyoming Woman in Washington,'" Box 14, Joseph C. O'Mahoney Papers, AHC (quotes). See also William A. Hasenfus, "Managing Partner: Joseph W. Martin, Jr., Republican Leader of the United States House of Representatives, 1939–1959" (Ph.D. dissertation, Boston College, 1986); James J. Kenneally, *A Compassionate Conservative: A Political Biography of Joseph W. Martin, Jr., Speaker of the U.S. House of Representatives* (Lanham, Md.: Lexington Books, 2003); Joe Martin, as told to Robert J. Donovon, *My First Fifty Years in Politics* (New York: McGraw-Hill, 1960).

17. Arthur Capper to J. D. Turner, March 29, 1941, in "National Defense Plants," Capper to Edward Stettinius, July 6, 1940, in "National Defense Advisory Council," both in Box 15, Arthur Capper Papers, KSHS; Prentiss Brown to Josiah W. Bailey, March 25, 1941, in "Miscellaneous," 77th Congress, Senate 77A-F7, Box 144, Senate Committee on Commerce, RG 46, RUSS, NA; Harry S Truman to Lou Holland, August 15, 1940, in "National Defense—Lou E. Holland (President of Mid Central War Resources Board)," Box 116, S/VP Papers, HSTL; Arthur Vandenberg to Charles C. Johnson, March 7, 1942, in Reel 3, Arthur Vandenberg Papers on Microfilm, BHL. An additional measure of how the war became a vehicle for regional transformation is in Gerald D. Nash, *World War II and the West: Reshaping the Economy* (Lincoln: University of Nebraska Press, 1990), and Neil R. McMillen, *Remaking Dixie: The Impact of World War II on the American South* (Jackson: University Press of Mississippi, 1997).

18. Miscellaneous notes, in "New Dealism and Truce, 1941–1943," Box 728, Robert A. Taft Papers, MD, LC; Robert L. Doughton to Mollie Roberts Jones, November 28, 1941, in File 941, Box 26, Robert L. Doughton Papers, SHC; O'Mahoney to Dear Friend, January 17, 1942, in "Speech, January 20, 1942," Box 267, O'Mahoney Papers, AHC; John Morton Blum, *Roosevelt and Morgenthau* (Boston, Mass.: Houghton Mifflin, 1972), 430.

19. Untitled manuscript, n.d., in "New Dealism and Truce, 1941–1943," Box 728, Taft Papers, MD, LC.

20. W. Elliot Brownlee, *Federal Taxation in America: A Short History*, 2nd ed. (New York and Washington, D.C.: Cambridge University Press and Woodrow Wilson Center Press, 2004), 108–109; Mark H. Leff, "The Politics of Sacrifice on the American Home Front in World War II," *Journal of American History* 77 (March 1991): 1297 (quote).

21. Richard Polenberg, *War and Society: The United States, 1941–1945* (Philadelphia: Lippincott, 1972), 27 (first quote); Steven R. Weisman, *The Great Tax Wars: Lincoln to Wilson: The Fierce Battles over Money and Power That Transformed the Nation* (New York: Simon and Schuster, 2002), 353–354; Mark H. Leff, "Taxing the 'Forgotten Man': The Politics of Social Security Finance in the New Deal," *Journal of American History* 70 (September 1983): 359–381; Blum, *V Was for Victory*, 228–229; see for example, William C. Wardlaw Jr. to Richard B. Russell, February 26, 1941, in "Members of Congress, 3," 77th Congress, Senate 77A-F10, Box 167, Senate Committee on Finance, RG 46, RUSS, NA; Franklin D. Roosevelt to Doughton, July 31, 1941, in Doughton Papers, SHC (last quote); George H. Gallup, *The Gallup Poll, Public Opinion, 1935–1971*, vol. 1, *1935–1948* (New York: Random House, 1972), 272, 333, 345–346, 418, 436–437.

22. McNaughton to Hulburd, December 18, 1941, in "December 16–31, 1941," Box 2, McNaughton Papers, HSTL (quotes); Donald H. Riddle, *The Truman Committee: A Study*

in Congressional Responsibility (New Brunswick, N.J.: Rutgers University Press, 1964), 12–31; Arthur M. Schlesinger Jr. and Roger Bruns, eds., *Congress Investigates: A Documented History, 1792–1974,* vol. 4 (New York: Chelsea House Publishers, 1975), 3115–3136; Truman to Lou Holland, April 24, 1941, in "National Defense—Lou E. Holland (President of Mid Central War Resources Board)," Box 116, S/VP Papers, HSTL; Bruce Tap, *Over Lincoln's Shoulder: The Committee on the Conduct of the War* (Lawrence: University Press of Kansas, 1998).

23. Brinkley, *The End of Reform,* 137–271; Lizabeth Cohen, *A Consumers' Republic: The Politics of Mass Consumption in Postwar America* (New York: Alfred A. Knopf, 2003), 5–15, 62–109; Jacobs, *Pocketbook Politics,* 1–11, 179–220.

24. Higgs, *Crisis and Leviathan,* 203; Brinkley, *Washington Goes to War,* 52–53; Jacobs, *Pocketbook Politics,* 182–184; Gallup, *The Gallup Poll,* 273; Caroline F. Ware, *The Consumer Goes to War: A Guide to Victory on the Home Front* (New York and London: Funk and Wagnalls, 1942); Julius Hirsch, "Evaluation of Our Wartime Price Control," *Journal of Marketing* 8 (January 1944): 281; John H. Bankhead to Ellison D. Smith, February 13, 1941, in "Farm Legislation, 1941," 77th Congress, Senate 77A-F1, Box 33, Senate Committee on Agriculture and Forestry Papers, RG 46, RUSS, NA (quotes); H.R. 4694, Commodity Credit Corporation, House of Representatives, Committee on Banking and Currency, Tuesday, May 13, 1941, in Minute Book, 77th Congress, House Committee on Banking and Currency Papers, RG 233, RUSHR, NA.

25. Gallup, *The Gallup Poll, Public Opinion,* 258, 269, 281, 331–332.

26. Doughton to E. L. Sandefur, May 17, 1941, Doughton to Josephus Daniels, February 26, 1942, and Doughton to W. D. Kizziah, June 6, 1941 (first quote), all in Doughton Papers, SHC; Frank J. Dawson to Doughton, June 15, 1941, in "[Joint Income Tax Return]," 77th Congress, House of Representatives 77A-F37.1, Box 323, House Committee on Ways and Means, RG 233, RUSHR, NA (last quote); Blum, *Roosevelt and Morgenthau,* 434.

27. "Tax Ruling on Couples," *NYT,* January 31, 1941; "Joint Return Plan Studied for Revenue," *Washington Post,* June 12, 1941; "Joint Returns Favored," *Wall Street Journal,* June 13, 1941; "Joint Return May Be Abandoned," *NYT,* July 8, 1941; "Penalizing Marriage," *NYT,* July 19, 1941; "Mandatory Joint Returns," *Wall Street Journal,* July 10, 1941; "Boston C. of C. against Joint Returns for Taxes," *Christian Science Monitor,* July 21, 1941; "Pound Scores Tax Plan," *NYT,* July 21, 1941; "Tax Plan Viewed as Immoral," *NYT,* July 15, 1941; Mary Hornaday, "Intimate Message: Washington," *Christian Science Monitor,* July 16, 1941; "Joint Income Tax Attacked by Merchants," *Christian Science Monitor,* July 16, 1941; "Roosevelt Favors Treasury's Program on Excess Profits Levy," *Wall Street Journal,* July 16, 1941. For the committee hearings, see U.S. Congress, House of Representatives, Committee on Ways and Means, *Revenue Revision of 1941,* vol. 1, 77th Congress, 1st session; U.S. Congress, House of Representatives, Committee on Ways and Means, *Revenue Revision of 1941,* vol. 2, 77th Congress, 1st session.

28. Henry N. Dorris, "Joint Return Kept in Defense Tax Bill," *NYT,* July 21, 1941; "House Group to Oppose Tax Bill 'Gag Rule,'" *Christian Science Monitor,* July 25, 1941 (first two quotes); "Text of Minority Report on Tax Bill," *NYT,* July 26, 1941 (remaining quotes).

29. "Way Is Opened to Fight Joint Income Return," *Christian Science Monitor,* July 30,

1941; Henry N. Dorris, "Tax Bill Delayed by Revolt over Joint Returns for Married," *NYT,* July 30, 1941 (first quote); Henry N. Dorris, "House Adopts 'Semi-Closed' Rule Providing Vote on Joint Tax Return," *NYT,* July 31, 1941 (remaining quotes); *Congressional Record,* 77th Congress, 1st session, 6459–6466.

30. *Congressional Record,* 77th Congress, 1st session, 6466–6487 (first quote), 6523–6561, 6598–6652; "Joint Tax Filing Fought in House," *NYT,* August 1, 1941; Roosevelt to Doughton, July 31, 1941, OF 962, Government Revenue Bills, 1941, Box 2, FDRL; McNaughton to Hulburd, August 2, 1941, in "August 1–15, 1941," Box 1, McNaughton Papers, HSTL (remaining quotes).

31. McNaughton to Hulburd, August 2, 1941, in "August 1–15, 1941," Box 1, McNaughton Papers, HSTL (quotes); Doughton to Roosevelt, August 2, 1941, OF 962, Government Revenue Bills, 1941, Box 2, FDRL.

32. *Congressional Record,* 77th Congress, 1st session, 6731–6733; Alice Kessler-Harris, *In Pursuit of Equity: Women, Men, and the Quest for Economic Citizenship in 20th-Century America* (New York: Oxford University Press, 2001), 340 n. 38; Doughton to Ralph P. Hanes, October 6, 1941, in File 926, Box 26, Doughton Papers, SHC (first three quotes); Reduce Non-Essential Federal Expenditures, Address by Hon. Harry F. Byrd, November 7, 1941, in "Speech by Phone, November 7, 1941," Box 363, Harry F. Byrd Papers (last quote), and Harry F. Byrd to Carter Glass, September 18, 1941, in Box 246, Carter Glass Papers, both in UVA; *Congressional Record,* 77th Congress, 1st session, 7377.

33. Doughton to Jere Cooper, August 29, 1941, in Doughton Papers, SHC; Brownlee, *Federal Taxation in America,* 109; Sparrow, *From the Outside In,* 103–104; Harold G. Vatter, *The U.S. Economy in World War II* (New York: Columbia University Press, 1985), 102–112; *Congressional Record,* 77th Congress, 1st session, 7432; *Congressional Record,* 77th Congress, 1st session, 7442.

34. Paul M. O'Leary, "Wartime Rationing and Governmental Organization," *American Political Science Review* 39 (December 1945): 1089 (quote); Meg Jacobs, "'How About Some Meat?': The Office of Price Administration, Consumption Politics, State Building from the Bottom Up, 1941–1946," *Journal of American History* 84 (December 1997): 911; Michael W. Flamm, "The National Farmers Union and the Evolution of Agrarian Liberalism, 1937–1946," *Agricultural History* 68 (Summer 1994): 55; Cohen, *A Consumers' Republic,* 62–85; Jacobs, *Pocketbook Politics,* 86, 175, 179–220.

35. McNaughton to Hulburd, August 1, 1941, in "August 1–15, 1941," Box 1, McNaughton Papers, HSTL (quotes); W. H. Lawrence, "Price Curb Bill Sent to Congress Sets July 29 Base," *NYT,* August 24, 1941; Ellison D. Smith to J. Roy Jones, August 1, 1941, in "Price Fixing, 1 of 2," 77th Congress, Senate 77A-F1, Box 34, Senate Committee on Agriculture and Forestry Papers, RG 46, RUSS, NA.

36. McNaughton to Hulburd, August 1, 1941, in "August 1–15, 1941," Box 1, McNaughton Papers, HSTL.

37. McNaughton to Hulburd, September 26, 1941, in "September 16–30, 1941," Box 1, McNaughton Papers, HSTL (quotes); U.S. Congress, House of Representatives, Committee on Banking and Currency, *Price Control Bill,* pt. 1, 77th Congress, 1st session; U.S. Congress, House of Representatives, Committee on Banking and Currency, *Price Control*

Bill, pt. 2, 77th Congress, 1st session; Roland A. Young, *Congressional Politics in the Second World War* (New York: Columbia University Press, 1956), 91.

38. McNaughton to Hulburd, October 3, 1941, in "October 1–15, 1941," Box 1, McNaughton Papers, HSTL; Henry B. Steagall to Roosevelt, November 7, 1941, in OF 327, Price Fixing, 1941, Box 2, and Roosevelt to Steagall, November 8, 1941, in PPF 474, both in FDRL; McNaughton to Hulburd, November 6, 1941, in "November 1941," Box 1, McNaughton Papers, HSTL (quotes); Lawrence, "Congress to Debate Price Control," *NYT*, November 9, 1941.

39. McNaughton to Hulburd, November 7, 1941, in "November 1941," Box 1, McNaughton Papers, HSTL.

40. Jerry Greene to Hulburd, November 14, 1941, in "Greene, Jerry—1941–1942," Box 21 (first quote), McNaughton to Hulburd, November 21, 1941, in "November 1941," Box 1 (remaining quotes), both in McNaughton Papers, HSTL.

41. McNaughton to Hulburd, November 28, 1941, in "November 1941," Box 1, McNaughton Papers, HSTL (quotes); Henry N. Dorris, "Over-all Control of Prices Beaten in House, 218–63," *NYT,* November 26, 1941; *Congressional Record,* 77th Congress, 1st session, 9060–9089, 9095–9141, 9145–9182, 9198–9247.

42. O'Mahoney to H. P. Beirne, January 17, 1945, in "Farm Credit Administration," Box 54, O'Mahoney Papers, AHC; Gallup, *The Gallup Poll,* 297; McNaughton to Hulburd, December 13, 1941, in "December 1–15, 1941," Box 2, McNaughton Papers, HSTL (quote); U.S. Congress, Senate, Committee on Banking and Currency, *Emergency Price Control Act,* 77th Congress, 1st session.

43. O'Leary, "Wartime Rationing and Governmental Organization," 1089 (first quote); "Travesty of Price Control," *NYT*, January 24, 1942 (second quote); Leon Henderson to Roosevelt, January 12, 1942, in OF 327, Price Fixing, January–May, 1942, Box 2, FDRL; "Conferees Debate on Two Major Bills," *NYT*, January 12, 1942; Robert A. Taft to Herbert Hoover, January 3, 1942, in "Taft, Robert A., Correspondence and printed material, July, 1941–1942," Box 232, PPI, Herbert Hoover Papers, HHPL; Frederick R. Barkley, "Price Bill Change Upheld by House," *NYT*, January 27, 1942; Henry N. Dorris, "Senate Approves Price Control Bill," *NYT*, January 28, 1942; McNaughton to Hulburd, January 23, 1942, in "January 16–31, 1942," Box 2, McNaughton Papers, HSTL (third quote); Edward L. Schapsmeier and Frederick H. Schapsmeier, "Farm Policy from FDR to Eisenhower: Southern Democrats and the Politics of Agriculture," *Agricultural History* 53 (January 1979): 362 (last quote); James MacGregor Burns, *Roosevelt: The Soldier of Freedom* (New York: Harcourt Brace Jovanovich, 1970); *Congressional Record,* 77th Congress, 2nd session, 189, 242, 688–689, 693–725.

44. Hirsch, "Evaluation of our Wartime Price Control," 281; John D. Black and Charles A. Gibbons, "The War and American Agriculture," *Review of Economics and Statistics* 26 (February 1944): 41; Vatter, *The U.S. Economy in World War II,* 89–101; Higgs, *Crisis and Leviathan,* 208; Taft to Hoover, January 24, 1942, in "Taft, Robert A., correspondence and printed material, July 1941–1942," Box 232, PPI, Hoover Papers, HHPL.

45. Hirsch, "Evaluation of our Wartime Price Control," 281; McNaughton to McConaughy, July 16, 1942, in "July–August 1942," Box 3, McNaughton Papers, HSTL (quotes).

46. John E. Rankin Speech, August 24, 1942, in 77th Congress, House of Representatives 77A-F39.1, Box 335, House Committee on World War Veterans Legislation, RG 233, RUSHR, NA; Cohen, *A Consumers' Republic,* 62–109; Jacobs, *Pocketbook Politics,* 179–220.

47. Roosevelt to Rayburn, September 6, 1942, in PPF 474, FDRL (first quote); Roosevelt to the Congress of the United States, September 7, 1942, in U.S. Congress, Senate, Committee on Banking and Currency, *Stabilizing the Cost of Living,* 77th Congress, 2nd session, 1942, 1–6 (second through fourth quotes); Higgs, *Crisis and Leviathan,* 209; McNaughton to McConaughy, September 9, 1942, in "September 1942," Box 3, McNaughton Papers, HSTL (fourth quote); Roosevelt to Robert F. Wagner, September 16, 1942, in "1942 Roosevelt, Franklin D. Correspondence," Alben Barkley Papers, UKL (remaining quote).

48. Frederick R. Barkley, "Roosevelt Stirs Congress by Threat to Act on Prices," *NYT,* September 8, 1942 (first two quotes); McNaughton to McConaughy, September 11, 1942, in "September 1942," Box 3, McNaughton Papers, HSTL (remaining quotes).

49. Rayburn to A. L. Bulwinkle, August 31, 1942, in "1942 Congressman Correspondence To and From," Box 3R290, Rayburn Papers, BCAH (first quote); McNaughton to McConaughy, September 12, 1942, and September 16, 1942, both in "September 1942," Box 3, McNaughton Papers, HSTL; C. P. Trussell, "Rival Measures," *NYT,* September 15, 1942; Roosevelt to Steagall, September 16, 1942, in PPF 474, FDRL; "Wage Limits Seen," *NYT,* September 9, 1942 (remaining quotes).

50. Kennedy, *Freedom from Fear,* 644 (first quote); Burns, *Roosevelt: The Soldier of Freedom,* 260; Roosevelt, Excerpts from the Press Conference, October 1, 1942, in John T. Woolley and Gerhard Peters, *The American Presidency Project* [online], Santa Barbara, Calif.: University of California (hosted), Gerhard Peters (database), http://www.presidency .ucsb.edu/ws/?pid=16307 (second quote); McNaughton to McConaughy, October 1, 1942, in "October 1–15, 1942," Box 3, McNaughton Papers, HSTL (remaining quotes).

51. Statement by Senator Brown as he appears on Universal News, in "Universal Newsreel Statement, October 6, 1942," Box 11, Prentiss Brown Papers, BHL; Black and Gibbons, "The War and American Agriculture," 19–20; Higgs, *Crisis and Leviathan,* 210; Cohen, *A Consumers' Republic,* 62–109; Jacobs, *Pocketbook Politics,* 179–220.

52. Roosevelt to Doughton, November 1, 1941, OF 962, Government Revenue Bills, 1941, Box 2, FDRL; Polenberg, *War and Society,* 27; Brownlee, *Federal Taxation,* 109–111; Blum, *V Was for Victory,* 229; Roosevelt, Message to Congress on an Economic Stabilization Program, April 27, 1942, in Woolley and Peters, *The American Presidency Project* [online], (quotes); Leff, "Politics of Sacrifice in World War II," 1299.

53. McNaughton to McConaughy, August 28, 1942, in "July–August 1942," McNaughton to McConaughy, September 9, 1942, McNaughton to McConaughy, September 10, 1942, both in "September 1942," all in Box 3, McNaughton Papers, HSTL; Polenberg, *War and Society,* 28; Brownlee, *Federal Taxation in America,* 112; Blum, *V Was for Victory,* 230; Sparrow, *From the Outside In,* 104; Young, *Congressional Politics,* 128–130.

54. Roosevelt to Rayburn, September 16, 1952, PPF 474, FDRL (first quote); McNaughton to McConaughy, October 20, 1942, in "October 16–31, 1942," Box 3, McNaughton Papers, HSTL (second quote); Kennedy, *Freedom from Fear,* 548–561.

3. "CONGRESS DOES HAVE POWER" OVER THE PRESIDENT

1. Frank McNaughton to David Hulburd, December 12, 1941, in "December 1–15, 1941," Box 2, Frank McNaughton Papers, HSTL.

2. Sam Rayburn to C. R. Starnes, November 12, 1942, in "1942 Statements and Views," Box 3R296 (first two quotes), and Rayburn to W. A. Thomas, October 19, 1942, in "1942 Political Texas," Box 3R296 (remaining quotes), both in Sam Rayburn Papers, BCAH.

3. Harold Ickes to Lady Bird Johnson, August 13, 1942, "LBJ 1943–1944," Box 161, Harold Ickes Papers, MD, LC.

4. John Morton Blum, *V Was for Victory: Politics and American Culture during World War II* (New York: Harcourt Brace Jovanovich, 1976), 229–234; John W. Jeffries, *Wartime America: The World War II Home Front* (Chicago: Ivan R. Dee, 1996); Richard Polenberg, *War and American Society: The United States, 1941–1945* (Philadelphia: Lippincott, 1972), 187–192.

5. Blum, *V Was for Victory,* 225, 231–232; Richard E. Darilek, *A Loyal Opposition in Time of War: The Republican Party and the Politics of Foreign Policy from Pearl Harbor to Yalta* (Westport, Conn.: Greenwood Press, 1976), 53; Clipping, "Rayburn Asks Fair Hearing for Congress," in PPF 474, FDRL (quote); Susan Dunn, *Roosevelt's Purge: How FDR Fought to Change the Democratic Party* (Cambridge, Mass.: Belknap Press of Harvard University Press, 2010).

6. David M. Kennedy, *Freedom from Fear: The American People in Depression and War, 1929–1945* (New York: Oxford University Press, 1999), 782. For a contrary view suggesting liberal potential for electoral success in the immediate postwar years, see Jonathan Bell, *The Liberal State on Trial: The Cold War and American Politics in the Truman Years* (New York: Columbia University Press, 2004), 1–45. Bell ultimately acknowledges that the Cold War eliminated this political path.

7. "Our New Cornucopia Congress," *Los Angeles Times,* January 6, 1943.

8. Donald A. Ritchie, ed., *Minutes of the U.S. Senate Democratic Conference, 1903–1964, Fifty-Eighth Congress through Eighty-Eighth Congress* (Washington, D.C.: U.S. Government Printing Office, 1998), 363. Some scholars wrongly claim that nothing of significance changed with the 1942 elections because voting patterns, policy debates, and party platforms remained relatively constant. See for example Jeffries, *Wartime America,* 145–169. For more on the soldier vote issue, see Chapter 5, which examines the issue within the context of racial prejudice, a key determinant for the outcome.

9. Mark H. Leff, "The Politics of Sacrifice on the American Home Front in World War II," *Journal of American History* 77 (March 1991): 1299–1306.

10. George H. Gallup, *The Gallup Poll, Public Opinion, 1935–1971,* vol. 1, *1935–1948* (New York: Random House, 1972), 331; McNaughton to James McConaughy, November 21, 1942, in "November 20–30, 1942," Box 4, McNaughton Papers, HSTL; Blum, *V Was for Victory,* 234–240; George McJimsey, *The Presidency of Franklin Delano Roosevelt* (Lawrence: University Press of Kansas, 2000), 249; Lizabeth Cohen, *A Consumers' Republic: The Politics of Mass Consumption in Postwar America* (New York: Alfred A. Knopf, 2003),

62–109; Meg Jacobs, *Pocketbook Politics: Economic Citizenship in Twentieth-Century America* (Princeton, N.J.: Princeton University Press, 2005), 179–220.

11. Donald A. Ritchie, *James M. Landis: Dean of the Regulators* (Cambridge, Mass.: Harvard University Press, 1980), 112; Allan M. Winkler, *The Politics of Propaganda: The Office of War Information, 1942–1945* (New Haven, Conn.: Yale University Press, 1978), 70; Kerry B. Fosher, *Under Construction: Making Homeland Security at the Local Level* (Chicago: University of Chicago Press, 2009), 25; Employees of the Office of War Information Who Were Formerly on the Staff of *PM*, n.d., in "Office of War Information, 1943," Box 732, Robert A. Taft Papers, MD, LC; Wendy L. Wall, *Inventing the "American Way": The Politics of Consensus from the New Deal to the Civil Rights Movement* (New York: Oxford University Press, 2008), 115–118.

12. McNaughton to McConaughy, November 6, 1942, in "November 1–6, 1942," Box 3, McNaughton Papers, HSTL; Blum, *V Was for Victory*, 234.

13. Robert L. Doughton to R. M. Duncan, October 16, 1943, in Robert L. Doughton Papers, SHC; McNaughton to McConaughy, November 6, 1942, in "November 1–6, 1942," Box 3, McNaughton Papers, HSTL.

14. Rayburn to Robert Lee Bobbitt, February 26, 1943, in "1943 Political National," Box 3R300, Rayburn Papers, BCAH (first quote); McNaughton to McConaughy, November 20, 1942, in "November 20–30, 1942," Box 4, McNaughton Papers, HSTL (last quote).

15. McNaughton to McConaughy, January 7, 1943, in "January 1–15, 1943," Box 4, McNaughton Papers, HSTL. The party division in Congress during the 78th Congress was 222–209 with two Progressives, one American-Laborite, and one Farmer-Laborer.

16. McNaughton to McConaughy, January 8, 1943, in "January 1–15, 1943," Box 4, and McNaughton to Bill Johnson, March 25, 1944, in "January–March, 1944," Box 6 (first quote), both in McNaughton Papers, HSTL; Jennings Perry, *Democracy Begins at Home: The Tennessee Fight on the Poll Tax* (Philadelphia: Lippincott, 1944), 273 (second quote). The details of McKellar's arrest are discussed in Chapter 5 because the issue being debated was the anti-poll tax legislation.

17. Ritchie, ed., *Minutes of the U.S. Senate Democratic Conference*, 365; McNaughton to McConaughy, January 8, 1943, in "January 1–15, 1943," Box 4, McNaughton Papers, HSTL (quotes).

18. McNaughton to McConaughy, November 21, 1942, in "November 20–30, 1942," Box 4, McNaughton Papers, HSTL (quotes); McNaughton to McConaughy, December 17, 1942, in "December 1942," Box 4, McNaughton Papers, HSTL; Rayburn to Malcolm Hatfield, March 19, 1940, in "General Correspondence," Box 3R281, Rayburn Papers, BCAH; Doughton to Charles A. Taylor, January 3, 1941, Doughton Papers, SHC.

19. McNaughton to McConaughy, November 21, 1942, in "November 20–30, 1942," McNaughton to McConaughy, December 17, 1942, in "December 1942," and McNaughton to McConaughy, January 7, 1943, in "January 1–15, 1943," all in Box 4, McNaughton Papers, HSTL.

20. Abe Murdock, notes on meeting, December 6 [c. 1942], in Folder 35, Box 16, Abe Murdock Papers, BYU; Wright Patman to Sam Rayburn, December 17, 1942, in "Mr. Patman's Personal File, 1942," Box 129A, Wright Patman Papers, LBJL; Harry S Truman to

Bill, December 20, 1942, in "National Defense Committee, December 1942," Box 120, S/VP Papers, HSTL (first quote); Donald M. Nelson, *Arsenal of Democracy: The Story of American War Production* (New York: Harcourt, Brace, 1946), 124 (last quote); Cohen, *A Consumers' Republic*, 62–109; Jacobs, *Pocketbook Politics*, 179–220.

21. McNaughton to McConaughy, January 7, 1943, in "January 1–15, 1943," Box 4, McNaughton Papers, HSTL.

22. McNaughton to McConaughy, January 29, 1943, in "January 16–31, 1943" (first two quotes), and McNaughton to Johnson, February 5, 1943, in "February 1–19, 1943," both in Box 4, McNaughton Papers, HSTL (last quote); Roland A. Young, *Congressional Politics in the Second World War* (New York: Columbia University Press, 1956), 107–108.

23. Richard B. Russell to Mother, January 29, 1945, in "Family (RBR to IDR) 1943," Box 42, Winder Series, Richard B. Russell Papers, RBRL.

24. Clare Boothe Luce to Franklin D. Roosevelt, March 2, 1943, in File 9, Box 389, Clare Boothe Luce Papers, MD, LC (first quote); Stephen Early to Luce, March 8, 1943, in OF 419, Congress of the United States, January–March 1942, Box 4, FDRL; McNaughton to McConaughy, March 12, 1943, in "March 1–15, 1943," Box 5, McNaughton Papers, HSTL (remaining quotes).

25. Gallup, *The Gallup Poll*, 338, 359, 366, 371, 376–377, 381; Jeffries, *Wartime America*, 33 (first quote); W. H. Lawrence, "President Favors Pay-as-You-Go Tax, But Not Ruml Plan," *NYT*, January 9, 1943; "Ruml Tax Plan Bill Ready for New Congress," *Chicago Tribune*, January 5, 1943; Doughton to W. D. Kizziah, February 9, 1943, in Doughton Papers, SHC; Walter George to Florence M. Weinstein, January 23, 1943, in "Tax Letters (January 22–23, 1943)," 78th Congress, Senate 78A-F10, Box 115, Senate Committee on Finance, RG 46, RUSS, NA; Doughton to George W. Coan, January 28, 1943 (last quote) and Doughton to R. A. Doughton, February 10, 1943, both in Doughton Papers, SHC; U.S. Congress, House of Representatives, Committee on Ways and Means, *Individual Income Tax*, 78th Congress, 1st session; James T. Sparrow, *Warfare State: World War II Americans and the Age of Big Government* (New York: Oxford University Press, 2011), 126. Assessments of George's and Doughton's political ideology regarding economic issues comes from a thorough evaluation of the key roll call votes for the war years.

26. McNaughton to McConaughy, March 13, 1943, in "March 1–15, 1943," Box 5, McNaughton Papers, HSTL; Doughton to Josephus Daniels, March 15, 1943 (first quote), Doughton to John Hanes, March 17, 1943 (second quote), both in Doughton Papers, SHC; McNaughton to McConaughy, March 27, 1943, in "March 16–31, 1943," Box 5, McNaughton Papers, HSTL; William R. Thom to Doughton, April 15, 1943, in Doughton Papers, SHC; *Congressional Record*, 78th Congress, 1st session, 2742–2772.

27. McNaughton to McConaughy, April 17, 1943, in "April 1–22, 1943," Box 5, McNaughton Papers, HSTL (first quote); Doughton to John H. Folger, May 1, 1943, in Doughton Papers, SHC (second quote); Rayburn to John J. Cochran, March 5, 1943, in "1943 Congressmen Letter to and from, A–D," Box 3R298, Rayburn Papers, BCAH (last quote).

28. Gilbert Stewart Jr., "Carlson of Kansas," *Wall Street Journal*, May 3, 1943; McNaughton to Hulburd, May 6, 1943, in "May 1943," Box 5, McNaughton Papers, HSTL; "House Abates 75% of '42 Income Tax; Ruml Plan Beaten," *NYT*, May 5, 1943 (quote); U.S.

Congress, Senate, Committee on Finance, *Current Tax Payment Act of 1943,* 78th Congress, 1st session; *Congressional Record,* 78th Congress, 1st session, 3915–3958.

29. "Fight to Head Off Ruml Plan Mapped by Administration," *NYT,* January 11, 1943; John Fisher, "Ruml Tax Wins Senate O.K.," *Chicago Tribune,* May 15, 1943; White House Press Release, May 17, 1943, PPF 1484, FDRL; "FDR Attacks Ruml Plan and Indicates Veto," *Chicago Tribune,* May 18, 1943; John H. Crider, "Senate's Tax Bill Defeated in House on Threat of Veto," *NYT,* May 19, 1943; James F. Byrnes to Roosevelt, May 26, 1943, PSF: Subject File, Byrnes, James F., Box 97, FDRL; John H. Crider, "Sure of Adoption," *NYT,* May 26, 1943; W. Elliot Brownlee, *Federal Taxation in America: A Short History,* 2nd ed. (New York and Washington, D.C.: Cambridge University Press and Woodrow Wilson Center Press, 2004), 114; Bartholomew H. Sparrow, *From the Outside In: World War II and the American State* (Princeton, N.J.: Princeton University Press, 1996), 104–105; Young, *Congressional Politics,* 130–136; *Congressional Record,* 78th Congress, 1st session, 4395–4448, 4566–4580, 5128–5167, 5203–5211; Fred Vinson to Roosevelt, July 10, 1943, OF 137a, Taxes— Income Taxes, 1943–1944, Box 9, FDRL.

30. Russell to Dear Mother, June 6, 1943, "Family (RBR to IDR), 1943," Box 42, Winder Series, Russell Papers, RBRL.

31. Julius Hirsch, "Evaluation of Our Wartime Price Control," *Journal of Marketing* 8 (January 1944): 282; John D. Black and Charles A. Gibbons, "The War and American Agriculture," *Review of Economics and Statistics* 26 (February 1944): 44; Barton J. Bernstein, "Clash of Interests: The Postwar Battle between the Office of Price Administration and the Department of Agriculture," *Agriculture History* 41 (January 1967): 46; Meg Jacobs, "'How About Some Meat?': The Office of Price Administration, Consumption Politics, State Building from the Bottom Up, 1941–1946," *Journal of American History* 84 (December 1997): 918 (quote); Herbert Hoover to Joe Martin, January 18, 1943, in "Martin, Hon. Joseph W., Correspondence, 1935–1950," Box 143, PPI, Herbert Hoover Papers, HHPL; James MacGregor Burns, *Roosevelt: The Soldier of Freedom* (New York: Harcourt Brace Jovanovich, 1970), 340–341; Jacobs, *Pocketbook Politics,* 197–200; Young, *Congressional Politics,* 110; Cohen, *A Consumers' Republic,* 62–109; Alan Brinkley, *The End of Reform: New Deal Liberalism in Recession and War* (New York: Alfred A. Knopf, 1995), 137–271.

32. McNaughton to Johnson, June 18, 1943, in "June 1943," Box 5, McNaughton Papers, HSTL.

33. "The OPA Crisis," *The American Forum of the Air,* July 4, 1943, in "1943, June– September," Box 315, Theodore Granik Papers, MD, LC; McNaughton to Johnson, June 19, 1943, in "June 1943," Box 5, McNaughton Papers, HSTL (quotes). While scholars including Alan Brinkley have argued such actions reveal a Congress out of touch with the economic reality of the war, the point is an unfair criticism playing to the trope of the conservative coalition and avoiding substantive analysis of complex and complicated congressional politics. Brinkley himself later celebrates the success of the wartime economy, in which the OPA played a central role. See Brinkley, *The End of Reform,* 140–148, 176.

34. Ibid.

35. Ibid.

36. McNaughton to McConaughy, June 10, 1942, in "June 1942," Box 3 (first quote) and

McNaughton to Johnson, July 2, 1943, in "July 1943," Box 5 (remaining quotes), both in McNaughton Papers, HSTL; *Congressional Record*, 78th Congress, 1st session, 7051–7055.

37. Howard B. Schaffer, *Chester Bowles: New Dealer in the Cold War* (Cambridge, Mass.: Harvard University Press, 1993), 7–24.

38. McNaughton to Johnson, September 2, 1943, in "September 1943," Box 5, McNaughton Papers, HSTL.

39. Michael W. Flamm, "The National Farmers Union and the Evolution of Agrarian Liberalism, 1937–1946," *Agricultural History* 68 (Summer 1994): 68; Patman to Judson Pryor, November 19, 1943, in "Office of Price Administration," Box 1337A, Patman Papers, LBJL; William Lemke, Doings in Congress, December 1, 1943, in File 1, Box 28, William Lemke Papers, UND.

40. Rayburn to Roosevelt, July 16, 1943, PPF 474, FDRL; Ray Brecht to Johnson, December 10, 1943, in "December 1943," Box 6, McNaughton Papers, HSTL (quotes).

41. Kenneth McKellar to Roosevelt, December 24, 1943, and Roosevelt to McKellar, December 29, 1943, both in PPF 2910, FDRL.

42. Gallup, *The Gallup Poll*, 420; Allen Drury, *A Senate Journal, 1943–1945* (New York: McGraw-Hill, 1963), 7; Harlan J. Bushfield to Charles L. McNary, January 8, 1944, in "January 1944," Box 21, Charles McNary Papers, MD, LC (first quote); Young, *Congressional Politics*, 113–114; "Subsidies and the Cost of Living," *The American Forum of the Air*, December 14, 1943, in "1943, October–December," Box 315, Granik Papers, MD, LC (second and third quotes); Brecht to Johnson, January 15, 1944, in "Brecht, Ray—1944–1947, [1 of 2]," Box 20, and McNaughton to Johnson, February 18, 1944, in "January–March, 1944," Box 6, both in McNaughton Papers, HSTL; *Congressional Record*, 78th Congress, 2nd session, 1873–1874.

43. McNaughton to Johnson, February 18, 1944, in "January–March, 1944," Box 6, McNaughton Papers, HSTL (quotes); Brent Spence to Agnes K. Moriarty, March 11, 1944, in "OPA, Rent Control, 1944," Box 12, Brent Spence Papers, UKL.

44. Drury, *A Senate Journal*, 56 (first quote); McNaughton to Johnson, February 25, 1944, in "January–March, 1944," Box 6, McNaughton Papers, HSTL (second quote).

45. Ibid.; Sparrow, *From the Outside In*, 106; Brownlee, *Federal Taxation in America*, 114; Burns, *Roosevelt: The Soldier of Freedom*, 433–434; Alben W. Barkley, *That Reminds Me* (Garden City, N.Y.: Doubleday, 1954), 169, 172 (quote).

46. McNaughton to Johnson, July 6, 1943, in "July 1943," Box 5, McNaughton Papers, HSTL.

47. Roosevelt to the House of Representatives, February 22, 1944, in Doughton Papers, SHC; Drury, *A Senate Journal*, 85; Brownlee, *Federal Taxation in America*, 114. Congress passed tax simplification legislation in April 1944.

48. Press Release, February 23, 1944, in "Legislation—Tax Bill Veto, 1944," Box 15, Spence Papers, UKL.

49. McNaughton to Johnson, February 25, 1944, in "January–March, 1944," Box 6, McNaughton Papers, HSTL (first quote); Barkley to Charles B. Rutan, March 18, 1944, in "Politics—Resignation as Majority Leader of the U.S. Senate, 1944, Mc, Favorable," Barkley Papers, UKL; Barkley, *That Reminds Me*, 173 (last quote).

50. Barkley, *That Reminds Me,* 174 (first quote); McNaughton to Johnson, February 25, 1944, in "January–March, 1944," Box 6, McNaughton Papers, HSTL (second quote).

51. "The War Revenue Bill," Speech of Hon. Alben W. Barkley of Kentucky in the Senate of the United States, February 23, 1944, in "Barkley Speeches, 'The War Revenue Bill,' by Senator Barkley, February 23, 1944," Barkley Papers, UKL (quotes); C. P. Trussell, "Congress Rebels," *NYT,* February 24, 1944; *Congressional Record,* 78th Congress, 2nd session, 1964–1966.

52. McNaughton to Johnson, February 25, 1944, in "January–March, 1944," Box 6, McNaughton Papers, HSTL; Murdock, notes on meeting, February 24, 1944, in Folder 35, Box 16, Murdock Papers, BYU (first two quotes); Kennedy to Mr. Finnegan, February 24, 1944, in "Off Record Letters, 1944," Box 2, Robert E. Kennedy Papers, AHC (remaining quotes).

53. George W. Robinson, "Alben Barkley and the 1944 Tax Veto," *Register of the Kentucky Historical Society* 67 (July 1969): 198; Doris Kearns Goodwin, *No Ordinary Time: Franklin and Eleanor Roosevelt, The Home Front in World War II* (New York: Simon and Schuster, 1994), 487; Roosevelt to Steven Early, February 23, 1944, in "Politics—Roosevelt, Franklin D., February 23, 1944," (first quote), John Cutter to Barkley, and attached, in "Barkley Speeches, 'The War Revenue Bill,' by Senator Barkley, February 23, 1944" (remaining quotes), all in Barkley Papers, UKL.

54. Barkley to Roosevelt, February 24, 1944, in PPF 3160, FDRL.

55. McNaughton to Johnson, February 25, 1944, in "January–March, 1944," Box 6, McNaughton Papers, HSTL (first two quotes); C. P. Trussell, "Taxes Voted Law 72–14 in the Senate," *NYT,* February 26, 1944; "Senate Reelects Barkley Majority Leader," *NYT,* February 25, 1944; Young, *Congressional Politics,* 136–143; *Congressional Record,* 78th Congress, 2nd session, 2013–2021, 2048–2051; McNaughton to McConaughy, in "January 16–31, 1945," Box 8, McNaughton Papers, HSTL (last quote).

56. McNaughton to Johnson, February 24, 1944, in "January–March, 1944," Box 6, McNaughton Papers, HSTL.

57. "How Can We Simplify Taxes?" *The American Forum of the Air,* March 14, 1944, in "How Can We Simplify Taxes," Box 253, Granik Papers, MD, LC.

58. McNaughton to Eleanor Welch, November 6, 1944, in "November 1944," Box 7 (first two quotes), and McNaughton to Johnson, April 14, 1944, in "April 1–15, 1944" (third quote), and McNaughton to Johnson, June 2, 1944, in "June 1–8, 1944" (remaining quotes), both in Box 6, all in McNaughton Papers, HSTL; Jacobs, *Pocketbook Politics,* 213.

59. McNaughton to Johnson, June 9, 1944, in "June 9–30, 1944," Box 6, McNaughton Papers, HSTL (first and last quote); *Congressional Record,* 78th Congress, 2nd session, 5465–5473 (second, third, and fourth quotes); Young, *Congressional Politics,* 114–120; McNaughton to Welch, June 16, 1944, in "June 9–30, 1944," Box 6, McNaughton Papers, HSTL; "The New Price-Control Bill," *NYT,* June 23, 1944; Jacobs, *Pocketbook Politics,* 212.

60. "Should OPA Be Remodeled?" *The American Forum of the Air,* June 19, 1945, in "1945, June–December," Box 316, Granik Papers, MD, LC (first two quotes); McNaughton to Don Bermingham, June 22, 1945, in "June 1–27, 1945," Box 9, McNaughton Papers, HSTL (last quote); Young, *Congressional Politics,* 120–122.

4. "A LESSON TO THE PRESIDENT":
LABOR LEGISLATION

1. Other scholars have considered this problem. See for example James T. Sparrow, *Warfare State: World War II Americans and the Age of Big Government* (New York: Oxford University Press, 2011), 162–166. Sparrow contends the federal government never fully ameliorated race and gender discrimination because of limited state capacity and insufficient political will. This chapter provides a nuanced reassessment, suggesting the problem was less about limited intestinal fortitude and more about deeply held partisan differences over whether such power should be exercised in the first place.

2. Paul A. C. Koistinen, "Mobilizing the World War II Economy: Labor and the Industrial-Military Alliance," *Pacific Historical Review* 42 (November 1973): 443–478; Domestic Economic Developments, June 19, 1941, in "Miscellaneous and Correspondence L," 77th Congress, Senate 77A-F9, Box 157, Senate Committee on Education and Labor, RG 46, RUSS, NA; Alan Brinkley, *The End of Reform: New Deal Liberalism in Recession and War* (New York: Alfred A. Knopf, 1995), 201–226; Justin Hart, "Making Democracy Safe for the World: Race, Propaganda, and the Transformation of U.S. Foreign Policy during World War II," *Pacific Historical Review* 73 (February 2004): 49–84; Thomas A. Guglielmo, "Fighting for Caucasian Rights: Mexicans, Mexican Americans, and the Transnational Struggle for Civil Rights in World War II Texas," *Journal of American History* (March 2006): 1212–1237. Political arguments about the FEPC are included in this chapter, not Chapter 5 on the Politics of Prejudice, because there is an important difference between the FEPC, certainly a civil rights initiative as much as a labor reform, and the other civil rights bills proposed during the war. The FEPC was the only such measure to receive an affirmative vote from Congress when funding bills were introduced. To be sure, southerners demagogued their unique brand of racial conservatism, but they were unable to stop the continuation of the agency whereas they did block anti–poll tax and anti–lynching legislation. The soldiers' vote laws considered in Chapter 5 were not primarily about race and civil rights, but those debates nonetheless bring the anti–poll tax legislation into sharper focus. Other scholars of race and the war have likewise assessed the FEPC as a labor question. See Daniel Kryder, *Divided Arsenal: Race and the American State in World War II* (New York: Cambridge University Press, 2000).

3. Frank McNaughton to Don Bermingham, February 23, 1945, in "February 1945," Box 8, Frank McNaughton Papers, HSTL (quotes); *Congressional Record,* 79th Congress, 1st session, 1368–1373; Merl E. Reed, *Seedtime for the Modern Civil Rights Movement: The President's Committee on Fair Employment Practice, 1941–1946* (Baton Rouge: Louisiana State University Press, 1991), 166; Ira Katznelson, Kim Geiger, and Daniel Kryder, "Limiting Liberalism: The Southern Veto in Congress, 1933–1950," *Political Science Quarterly* 108 (Summer 1993): 283–306.

4. McNaughton to Bill Johnson, January 27, 1944, in "January–March 1944," Box 6, McNaughton Papers, HSTL (first quote); Walter A. Bruce to Howard Worth Smith, September 1, 1939 (second quote), and Harold W. Metz to Charles A. Halleck, September 15, 1939, both in Charles A. Halleck Papers, Manuscripts Department, Lilly Library,

Indiana University, Bloomington, Indiana; see for example, "For Release 12:00 Noon, Thursday, March 7," March 6, 1940, and "For Release March 9, 1940," Statement of Honorable Mary T. Norton, Chairman of the House Committee on Labor, on the Smith Amendments to the National Labor Relations Law, (third through fifth quotes), both in "Committee Reports, Statements, etc.," Box 220, Howard W. Smith Papers, UVA; Landon R. Y. Storrs, *Civilizing Capitalism: The National Consumers' League, Women's Activism, and Labor Standards in the New Deal Era* (Chapel Hill: University of North Carolina Press, 2000), 177–205; Statement of Minority, January 3, 1941, in "Correspondence with Minority Members," Box 220, Smith Papers, UVA (last quote).

5. George H. Gallup, *The Gallup Poll, Public Opinion, 1935–1971*, vol. 1, *1935–1948* (New York: Random House, 1972), 324–325, 329, 343, 353, 403–404, 431, 448.

6. David Kennedy, *Freedom from Fear: The American People in Depression and War, 1929–1945* (New York: Oxford University Press, 1999), 631–637.

7. Ibid., 637–655; Sparrow, *Warfare State*, 163.

8. Untitled typed notes, n.d., in "File #1, FEPC Speech File, 1944–1946," Box 31, Subseries A, Series III, Richard B. Russell Papers, RBRL.

9. Walter White to William H. Hastie, December 31, 1940, in Reel 24, Part 13, The NAACP and Labor, 1940–1955, Series B, NAACP Papers, MC, LC. For more details on the impetus for the FEPC, see Herbert Garfinkel, *When Negroes March: The March on Washington Movement in the Organizational Politics for FEPC* (Glencoe, Ill.: Free Press, 1959); Lucy G. Barber, *Marching on Washington: The Forging of an American Political Tradition* (Berkeley: University of California Press, 2002), 108–140; White to Warren Barbour, January 30, 1941, in Reel 24, Part 13, Series B, NAACP Papers, MD, LC.

10. Andrew Edmund Kersten, *Race, Jobs, and the War: The FEPC in the Midwest, 1941–46* (Urbana: University of Illinois Press, 2000), 17–20 (first two quotes); p. 212, in "Norton, Mary T.: manuscript, Madam Congresswoman the Memoirs of Mary T. Norton of New Jersey," Box 17, Lorena Hickock Papers, FDRL (last quote).

11. William M. Tuttle, *Daddy's Gone to War: The Second World War in the Lives of America's Children* (New York: Oxford University Press, 1993), 70, 75–76; D'Ann Campbell, *Women at War with America* (Cambridge, Mass.: Harvard University Press, 1984), 72–84, 224; Virginia Office of Civil Defense Committee on Child Care, *The War and Virginia's Children* (Richmond, Va.: Virginia Committee on Child Care, Office of Civilian Defense, 1944), 1; Susan E. Riley, "Caring for Rosie's Children: Federal Child Care Policies in the World War II Era," *Polity* 4 (Summer 1994): 655–675; Pat McCarran to Mrs. Robert E. Dutton, May 15, 1944, in "Labor and Federal Security I," 78th Congress, Senate 78A-F2, Box 72, Senate Committee on Appropriations, RG 46, RUSS, NA; Sonya Michel, *Children's Interests/Mothers' Rights: The Shaping of America's Child Care Policy* (New Haven, Conn.: Yale University Press, 1999), 118, 134–135, 143–144, 175, 180, 193–194; Elizabeth Rose, *A Mother's Job: The History of Day Care, 1890–1960* (New York: Oxford University Press, 1999), 166–170; Emilie Stoltzfus, *Citizen, Mother, Worker: Debating Public Responsibility for Child Care after the Second World War* (Chapel Hill: University of North Carolina Press, 2003), 46; Emily Yellin, *Our Mothers' War: American Women at Home and at the Front during World War II* (New York: Free Press, 2004), 109–198; U.S. Congress, House of

Representatives, Committee on Military Affairs, *Women's Army Auxiliary Corps,* 77th Congress, 2nd session, 1942, 5, 7.

12. James E. Murray to C. E. Lanstrum, March 20, 1942, in File 20, Box 301, Murray to W. F. Flinn, June 29, 1942, in File 10, Box 651 (first quote), and Murray to Louis Bromfield, May 8, 1942, in File 17, Box 41 (remaining quotes), all in Series 1, James E. Murray Papers, KRTA. The historiography of Japanese American internment does not address western congressional eagerness to exploit further the internees as forced laborers in western agriculture, though one recent account—Brian Masaru Hayashi, *Democratizing the Enemy: The Japanese American Internment* (Princeton, N.J.: Princeton University Press, 2004), 16–19, 88–90, 207–208—does address federal government interest in employing internees on projects facilitating land and water development in the West. Another important, recent account is Greg Robinson, *By Order of the President: FDR and the Internment of Japanese Americans* (Cambridge, Mass.: Harvard University Press, 2001). Robinson spends more time with the role of Congress than does Hayashi, but he focuses on the evidence regarding pressure for evacuation, support for internment, and hostility to internees. See Robinson, *By Order of the President,* 92, 97, 100, 103, 106, 109–110, 116–117, 133–134, 140–141, 159, 164, 179, 192, 194–195, 203–204. Other recent and classic treatments of internment include Roger Daniels, *Concentration Camps U.S.A.: Japanese Americans in World War II* (New York: Holt, Rinehart, and Winston, 1971); Richard Drinnon, *Keeper of Concentration Camps: Dillon S. Myer and American Racism* (Berkeley: University of California Press, 1987); John Howard, *Concentration Camps on the Home Front: Japanese Americans in the House of Jim Crow* (Chicago: University of Chicago Press, 2008); Peter H. Irons, *Justice at War* (New York: Oxford University Press, 1983); Eric L. Muller, *American Inquisition: The Hunt for Japanese American Disloyalty in World War II* (Chapel Hill: University of North Carolina Press, 2007). Jason Scott Smith notes the role of the WPA in the internment of the Japanese Americans. See Smith, *Building New Deal Liberalism: The Political Economy of Public Works, 1933–1956* (New York: Cambridge University Press, 2006), 222–231. Smith contends that this development disproves earlier arguments that the war had the potential to revitalize the New Deal's "social democratic potential" (p. 231).

13. John H. Tolan to the Speaker and Members of the House, May 22, 1942, in "Investigations, 1937–1940," Box 388, George W. Norris Papers, MD, LC; Arrangement for the Temporary Migration of Mexican Agricultural Workers to the United States, August 4, 1942, in Carl Hayden Papers, ASU (quote). Significant scholarship exists on Mexican American labor history more generally in this period and on the bracero program specifically. From this literature evolves a compelling picture of the degradations Mexican and Mexican American workers faced in the United States during these years. Among the best works are Deborah Cohen, *Braceros: Migrant Citizens and Transnational Subjects in the Postwar United States and Mexico* (Chapel Hill: University of North Carolina Press, 2011); Ronald L. Mize and Alicia C. S. Swords, *Consuming Mexican Labor: From the Bracero Program to NAFTA* (Toronto: University of Toronto Press, 2011); Zaragosa Vargas, *Labor Rights Are Civil Rights: Mexican American Workers in Twentieth-Century America* (Princeton, N.J.: Princeton University Press, 2005).

14. Carl Hayden to R. L. Webster, November 2, 1942, in Hayden Papers, ASU; Otey M. Scruggs, "Evolution of the Mexican Farm Labor Agreement of 1942," *Agricultural History* 34 (July 1960): 140–149; Department of State, Press Release, July 4, 1944, in "Mexican Labor—Rio Grande Valley," Box 111, Tom Connally Papers, MD, LC.

15. Sam Rayburn to Lee Simmons, September 5, 1940, in "1940 General," Box 3R281, Sam Rayburn Papers, BCAH (first quote); Drew Pearson, "Men Who Make the Senate Tick," *Washington Post*, October 23, 1949 (second quote); Philip Murray to Dear Senator, February 3, 1941 (third quote), and Elbert D. Thomas to Murray, February 5, 1941, both in "Miscellaneous and Correspondence C," 77th Congress, Senate 77A-F9, Box 157, Senate Committee on Education and Labor, RG 46, RUSS, NA; Howard W. Smith to Mary T. Norton, March 24, 1941, and Norton to Smith, March 26, 1941 (fourth quote), both in "Correspondence with Labor Committee—Mrs. Norton," Box 219, Smith Papers, UVA; Minutes, Twelfth Meeting, Committee on the Judiciary, House of Representatives, April 3, 1941, HR 77A-F21.3, House Committee on the Judiciary, RG 233, RUSHR, NA (remaining quotes).

16. William L. Green to Robert L. Doughton, April 19, 1941, and Doughton to Green, April 25, 1941, both in Robert L. Doughton Papers, SHC; Harry S Truman to Perrin D. McElroy, April 24, 1941, and Truman to Southern, September 9, 1941, both in "Labor Situation (March 1940–January 1942)," Box 73, S/VP Papers, HSTL.

17. Tom Connally, as told to Alfred Steinberg, *My Name Is Tom Connally* (New York: Crowell, 1954), 253 (quote); Nelson Lichtenstein, *Labor's War at Home: The CIO in World War II* (New York: Cambridge University Press, 1987), 28–32, 46.

18. Smith to T. Justin Moore, November 10, 1941 (first two quotes), Smith to Norton, November 19, 1941, and Smith to Dear Colleague, November 18, 1941, all in "H.R. 6066—Labor Bill—Correspondence," Box 2, Smith Papers, UVA; Press Release of Senator Tom Connally of Texas, November 17, 1941, in "S. 2054 Strikes," Box 140, Connally Papers, MD, LC (third quote); McNaughton to Bermingham, April 15, 1945, in "April 1945 and undated," Box 8, McNaughton Papers, HSTL (last quote).

19. Westbrook Pegler, "Fair Enough," *Washington Post*, November 26, 1941; Minutes, Thirty-Sixth Meeting, Committee on the Judiciary, House of Representatives, November 26, 1941, HR 77A-F21.3, House Committee on the Judiciary, RG 233, RUSHR, NA; Henry N. Dorris, "A Sweeping Bill: Majority of Democrats Join 123 Republicans in 252–136 Vote," *NYT*, December 4, 1941; Lichtenstein, *Labor's War at Home*, 70, 96; Gallup, *The Gallup Poll*, 304; Hadley Cantril, ed., *Public Opinion, 1935–1946* (Princeton, N.J.: Princeton University Press, 1951), 393–395.

20. Harry F. Byrd to Elbert Thomas, December 6, 1941, in "Letter to Senator Elbert D. Thomas, December 6, 1941," Box 400, Harry F. Byrd Papers, UVA.

21. "Labor Legislation and National Defense," December 7, 1941, *The American Forum of the Air*, in "1941, September–December," Box 315, Theodore Granik Papers, MD, LC.

22. McNaughton to David Hulburd, January 2, 1942, in "January 1–15, 1942," Box 2, McNaughton Papers, HSTL (first four quotes); Smith, "What Laws Should be Passed to Prevent Strikes in Defense Industries," *American Bar Association Journal* 28 (January 1942): 4, in "American Bar Association Journal," Box 191, Smith Papers, UVA (last quote).

23. "Should The Forty-Hour Week Law Be Repealed?" March 22, 1942, *The American Forum of the Air*, in "1942, January–June," Box 315, Granik Papers, MD, LC.

24. "Congressman's Mail: His Finger on Public Pulse," *St. Louis Post-Dispatch*, March 29, 1942 (first four quotes), William Bewley to Thomas, March 30, 1942, and L. B. Eames to Thomas, March 31, 1942 (last quote), all in "Letters, 1942," 77th Congress, Senate 77A-F9, Box 161, Senate Committee on Education and Labor, RG 46, RUSS, NA.

25. "How Shall We Provide for Displaced War Industry Workers?" February 22, 1942, *The American Forum of the Air*, in "1942, January–June," Box 315, Granik Papers, MD, LC.

26. "America's Manpower Problem," October 18, 1942, *The American Forum of the Air*, in "1942, July–December," Box 315, Granik Papers, MD, LC (first two quotes); Bruno Stein, "Labor's Role in Government Agencies during World War II," *Journal of Economic History* 17 (September 1957): 403–404; James W. Wadsworth to Grenville Clark, April 15, 1942, and Wadsworth to Clark, July 13, 1942 (remaining quotes), both in "Austin-Wadsworth Bill, April 4, 1942–January 25, 1943," Box 21, James W. Wadsworth Papers, MD, LC.

27. Address of Robert A. Taft at the National Republican Club, "Profits, Pickets, and Parity" [c. 1943], in "Labor—Connally Bill, 1943," Box 675, Robert A. Taft Papers, MD, LC.

28. Clark to Franklin D. Roosevelt, December 30, 1943, in "Austin-Wadsworth Bill, January 7, 1944–January 27, 1944," Box 21, Wadsworth Papers, MD, LC.

29. "America's Manpower," *NYT*, November 14, 1942 (first quote); C. P. Trussell, "Congress Leaders Ask One-Man Rule of the Home Front," *NYT*, November 15, 1942 (remaining quotes); Koistinen, "Mobilizing the World War II Economy," 454–455; James MacGregor Burns, *Roosevelt: The Soldier of Freedom* (New York: Harcourt Brace Jovanovich, 1970), 340.

30. McNaughton to James McConaughy, March 6, 1943, in "March 1–15, 1943," Box 5, McNaughton Papers, HSTL; Frederick R. Barkley, "Manpower Demand Is Raised Again," *NYT*, February 7, 1943; George Q. Flynn, *The Mess in Washington: Manpower Mobilization in World War II* (Westport, Conn.: Greenwood Press, 1979), 82; Transcript of Truman interview with Nover, c. April 1943, in "National Defense Committee, April 1943," Box 121, S/VP Papers, HSTL; Clare E. Hoffman to Mary I. Miller, May 5, 1943, in "Manpower Mobilization," Box 26, Clare Hoffman Papers, BHL.

31. Wadsworth to Albert L. Cox, February 12, 1943, in "Austin-Wadsworth Bill, February 1, 1943–March 1, 1943" (first three quotes), and Wadsworth to Emil G. Tschanz, July 5, 1943, in "Austin-Wadsworth Bill, April 7, 1943–August 19, 1943" (fifth quote), both in Box 21, Wadsworth Papers, MD, LC; Koistinen, "Mobilizing the World War II Economy" 458 (fourth quote).

32. McNaughton to Johnson, July 6, 1943, in "July 1943," Box 5, McNaughton Papers, HSTL. There were over twenty hearings in the Senate Committee on Military Affairs. See for example, U.S. Congress, Senate, Committee on Military Affairs, *Manpower (National War Service Bill)*, part 22, 78th Congress, 1st session, 1943. Wadsworth to Clark, July 9, 1943 (first quote), Wadsworth to Glenn W. Herrick, August 18, 1943 (second and third quotes), both in "Austin-Wadsworth Bill, April 7, 1943–August 19, 1943," and Clark to Wadsworth, October 9, 1943, in "Austin-Wadsworth Bill, September 10, 1943–November 30, 1943" (last quote), all in Box 21, Wadsworth Papers, MD, LC.

33. Wadsworth to A. G. Thacher, November 11, 1943, in "Austin-Wadsworth Bill, September 10, 1943–November 30, 1943," Box 21, Wadsworth Papers, MD, LC; Koistinen, "Mobilizing the World War II Economy," 458.

34. Allen Drury, *A Senate Journal, 1943–1945* (New York: McGraw-Hill, 1963), 46 (first quote); Clark to Roosevelt, December 30, 1943, in "Austin-Wadsworth Bill, January 7, 1944–January 27, 1944," and Joint Statement by Senator Warren R. Austin of Vermont, and Representative James W. Wadsworth of New York, re Proposed National War Service Act of 1943, in "Austin-Wadsworth Bill, January 27, 1944–March 1, 1944" (remaining quotes), both in Box 21, Wadsworth Papers, MD, LC.

35. Kersten, *Race, Jobs, and the War,* 37–38; Anthony S. Chen, *The Fifth Freedom: Jobs, Politics, and Civil Rights in the United States, 1941–1972* (Princeton, N.J.: Princeton University Press, 2009), 39; Louis Ruchames, *Race, Jobs and Politics: The Story of FEPC* (New York: Columbia University Press, 1953), 57–72; Reed, *Seedtime for the Modern Civil Rights Movement,* 51–76; Wright Patman to Sam Rayburn, December 30, 1942, in "Mr. Patman's Personal File—1943," Box 129A, Wright Patman Papers, LBJL; FEPC Fund "Pittance" Out of 98 Billions, NAACP Tells Senators, June 8, 1944, in Reel 12, Part 13, Series B, NAACP Papers, MD, LC; Russell to Cobb C. Torrance, May 31, 1944, in "File #2, FEPC 1944–1949," Box 108, Series V, Russell Papers, RBRL.

36. Chen, *The Fifth Freedom,* 39–40; Kersten, *Race, Jobs, and the War,* 41–46; Reed, *Seedtime for the Modern Civil Rights Movement,* 77–116; Kennedy, *Freedom from Fear,* 775; FEPC Wholly without Funds, NAACP Reveals, July 2, 1943, in Reel 12, Part 13, Series B, NAACP Papers, MD, LC.

37. Hugh Fulton, Memorandum to Members of the Committee, March 30, 1943, in File 1, Box 3, Homer Ferguson Papers, BHL.

38. Lichtenstein, *Labor's War at Home,* 157–177; "Reject New Lewis Pay Demand," *Chicago Daily Tribune,* June 2, 1943 (first quote); Kennedy, *Freedom from Fear,* 642–644 (second quote); Doris Kearns Goodwin, *No Ordinary Time: Franklin and Eleanor Roosevelt: The Home Front in World War II* (New York: Simon & Schuster, 1994), 441 (last quote); Joel Isaac Seidman, *American Labor from Defense to Reconversion* (Chicago: University of Chicago Press, 1953), 188–189; Sparrow, *Warfare State,* 194–195.

39. Gallup, *The Gallup Poll,* 383; *Congressional Record,* 78th Congress, 1st session, 3806–3813, 3881–3910; McNaughton to Hulburd, May 7, 1943, in "May 1943," Box 5, McNaughton Papers, HSTL (first two quotes); U.S. Congress, Senate, Committee on the Judiciary, Report, *Defense Plants,* 78th Congress, 1st session; Press Release—Connally Anti-Strike Bill, May 5, 1943, in "Anti-Strike Bill," Box 140, Connally Papers, MD, LC; *Congressional Record,* 78th Congress, 1st session, 3969–3995; C. P. Trussell, "House Group Seeks Rigid Strike Curbs," *NYT,* May 8, 1943 (last quote).

40. McNaughton to Hulburd, May 7, 1943 (first and third quotes), McNaughton to McConaughy, May 28, 1943 (second quote), and McNaughton to Johnson, May 14, 1943, all in "May 1943," Box 5, McNaughton Papers, HSTL; U.S. Congress, House of Representatives, Committee on Military Affairs, Report, *Use and Operation of War Plants in Prosecution of War,* 78th Congress, 1st session (fourth quote); Rayburn to Amon G. Carter, May 28, 1943, in "1943 General Miscellaneous, A-CA," Box 3R299, Rayburn Papers, BCAH (last quote).

41. McNaughton to McConaughy, May 28, 1943, in "May 1943," Box 5, McNaughton Papers, HSTL (quotes); *Congressional Record,* 78th Congress, 1st session, 5172–5172, 5221–5252, 5294–5348, 5387–5392.

42. McNaughton to Johnson, May 14, 1943, in "May 1943," Box 5, McNaughton Papers, HSTL; Connally, *My Name Is Tom Connally,* 253 (quote).

43. U.S. Congress, House of Representatives, Conference Report, *Use and Operation of War Plants in Prosecution of War,* June 10, 1943, 78th Congress, 1st session; McNaughton to Johnson, June 11, 1943, in "June 1943," Box 5, McNaughton Papers, HSTL; Seidman, *American Labor,* 189.

44. McNaughton to Johnson, June 26, 1943, in "June 1943," Box 5, McNaughton Papers, HSTL (quote); *War Labor Disputes Act—Veto Message from the President of the United States, June 25, 1943,* Senate, 78th Congress, 1st session.

45. McNaughton to Johnson, June 26, 1943, in "June 1943," Box 5, McNaughton Papers, HSTL; Lowell Turrentine and Sam D. Thurman Jr., "Wartime Federal Legislation," *California Law Review* 34 (June 1946): 321; Harold G. Vatter, *The U.S. Economy in World War II* (New York: Columbia University Press, 1985), 124–125.

46. McNaughton to Johnson, June 26, 1943, in "June 1943," Box 5, McNaughton Papers, HSTL (quote); W. H. Lawrence, "Congress Rebels," *NYT,* June 26, 1943; *Congressional Record,* 78th Congress, 1st session, 6487–6489, 6545–6549; Kennedy, *Freedom from Fear,* 644; Gallup, *The Gallup Poll,* 395.

47. McNaughton to Johnson, June 26, 1943, in "June 1943," Box 5, McNaughton Papers, HSTL (first quote); Doughton to C. A. Cannon, June 29, 1943 (last quote), Doughton Papers, SHC.

48. Connally, *My Name Is Tom Connally,* 253; McNaughton to Johnson, July 6, 1943, in "July 1943," and McNaughton to Johnson, September 2, 1943, in "September 1943," both in Box 5, McNaughton Papers, HSTL.

49. Report of the Acting Secretary, for the February [1944] Meeting of the Board, in Reel 19, Part 16, Board of Directors, Correspondence and Committee Materials, Series B, NAACP Papers, MD, LC (first quote); Kersten, *Race, Jobs, and the War,* 127–128; White to Dear Senator, March 1, 1944, and Roy Wilkins to My Dear, March 3, 1944, both in Reel 19, Part 13, Series B, NAACP Papers, MD, LC; "Agency Bill Tests Congress Revolt," *NYT,* February 28, 1944 (last quote); Reed, *Seedtime for the Modern Civil Rights Movement,* 156–157; Charles E. Egan, "Congress on Warpath for Executive Agencies," *NYT,* April 30, 1944.

50. Wilkins to George M. Johnson, March 3, 1944 (first quote), Wilkins to Carter Glass, March 7, 1944 (second–fourth quotes), both in Reel 19, and Senators Are Quizzed on Abolishing FEPC, March 3, 1944, in Reel 12 (last quote), all in Part 13, Series B, NAACP Papers, MD, LC.

51. Chapman Revercomb to Wilkins, March 10, 1944, in Reel 19, Part 13, Series B, NAACP Papers, MD, LC.

52. Harold Burton to Wilkins, May 11, 1944, in Reel 12, Part 13, Series B, NAACP Papers, MD, LC (first quote); Kersten, *Race, Jobs, and the War,* 128–129; *Congressional Record,* 78th Congress, 2nd session, 5016–5068 (second quote); C. P. Trussell, "House Votes Bill with

FEPC Funds," *NYT*, May 27, 1944; Reed, *Seedtime for the Modern Civil Rights Movement*, 158; Telegram from White, June 1, 1944, in Reel 14, Part 13, Series B, NAACP Papers, MD, LC (last quote).

53. Telegram from White, June 11, 1944, in Reel 14, Part 13, Series B, NAACP Papers, MD, LC (quote); Reed, *Seedtime for the Modern Civil Rights Movement*, 158–159; Memorandum to Mr. White, June 12, 1944, in Reel 12, Part 13, Series B, NAACP Papers, MD, LC.

54. Senate Reaches New Low Insulting Negroes, Jews, in Fight on FEPC, June 22, 1944, in Reel 12, Part 13, Series B, NAACP Papers, MD, LC (first two quotes); *Congressional Record*, 78th Congress, 2nd session, 6257–6264 (remaining quotes); Reed, *Seedtime for the Modern Civil Rights Movement*, 159–161; "Agency Bill Voted with FEPC Funds," *NYT*, June 21, 1944; Kersten, *Race, Jobs, and the War*, 126–130; Ruchames, *Race, Jobs and Politics*, 87–99; Only Vigorous Action Will Aid Passage of FEPC, August 24, 1944, in Reel 12, Part 13, Series B, NAACP Papers, MD, LC.

55. "What Is America's Present Manpower Problem?" January 16, 1945, *The American Forum of the Air*, in "What Is America's Present Manpower Situation," Box 257, Granik Papers, MD, LC.

56. Ibid. (quotes); Flynn, *The Mess in Washington*, 91–94.

57. Koistinen, "Mobilizing the World War II Economy," 459; Drury, *A Senate Journal*, 338 (first quote); McNaughton to Bermingham, January 20, 1945, in "January 16–31, 1945," Box 8, McNaughton Papers, HSTL (second quote).

58. McNaughton to Bermingham, January 26, 1945, in "January 16–31, 1945" (first three quotes), and McNaughton to Bermingham, February 3, 1945, in "February 1945," both in Box 8, McNaughton Papers, HSTL; *Congressional Record*, 79th Congress, 1st session, 643–665 (fourth quote), 704–748; Flynn, *The Mess in Washington*, 94.

59. Statement by Senator Joseph C. O'Mahoney (D, Wyo.) on the Proposed Work or Fight Legislation, February 3, 1945, in "Committees, 1945, Military Affairs Committee, Work or Fight Bill #2," Box 217, Joseph C. O'Mahoney Papers, AHC; Doings in Congress, February 7, 1945, in File 2, Box 28, William Lemke Papers, UND.

60. *Congressional Record*, 79th Congress, 1st session, 1918; Typescript, March 8, 1945, File 15, Box 31, Subseries A, Series III, Russell Papers, RBRL (first quote); McNaughton to Bermingham, March 9, 1945, in "March 1–16, 1945," Box 8, McNaughton Papers, HSTL (second and third quotes); Flynn, *The Mess in Washington*, 99; Wadsworth to George Patton, March 13, 1945, in "Austin-Wadsworth Bill, April 4, 1944–March 14, 1945," Box 21, Wadsworth Papers, MD, LC (remaining quotes).

61. Drury, *A Senate Journal*, 386–387 (quotes); McNaughton to Bermingham, March 24, 1945, in "March 17–31, 1945," McNaughton to Bermingham, April 6, 1945, and McNaughton to Bermingham, April 15, 1945, both in "April 1945 and undated," all in Box 8, McNaughton Papers, HSTL; Byrnes Report Sustains Senate on Manpower, March 31, 1945, in "Committees, 1945, Military Affairs Committee, Work or Fight Bill #3," Box 217, and Roosevelt to Elbert Thomas, March 28, 1945, in "Legislation, 1945, War Manpower Act of 1945," Box 243, both in O'Mahoney Papers, AHC; *Congressional Record*, 79th Congress, 1st session, 2937–2959; Robert Ramspeck, March 24, 1945, in "Whip, House of Representatives, 1945," Box 18, Brent Spence Papers, UKL; Seidman, *American Labor*, 164; Flynn, *The Mess in Washington*, 99–102.

62. NAACP Asks for Promised Action Now on FEPC Bill, February 1, 1945, in Reel 12, Hastie to Wilkins, February 5, 1945, Taft to Theodore M. Berry, February 8, 1945, and Wilkins to Herbert Brownell, February 8, 1945, all in Reel 20, all in Part 13, Series B, NAACP Papers, MD, LC.

63. Reed, *Seedtime for the Modern Civil Rights Movement,* 164–167; pp. 218–220 in "Norton, Mary T.: manuscript, Madam Congresswoman the Memoirs of Mary T. Norton of New Jersey," Box 17, Hickock Papers, FDRL (quotes).

64. Report of the Secretary, for the July 1945 Meeting of the Board, in Reel 19, Part 16, Series B, NAACP Papers, MD, LC (quote); Reed, *Seedtime for the Modern Civil Rights Movement,* 167–168; Drury, *A Senate Journal,* 442–443.

65. Memorandum from RR to Mr. White, June 6, 1945, in Reel 14, and Emergency Action, June 13, 1945, in Reel 12, both in Part 13, Series B, NAACP Papers, MD, LC; "Fair Practice Bill Held in Committee," *NYT,* June 7, 1945 (first quote); "Truman Backs Bill for Fair Job Policy," *NYT,* June 6, 1945; p. 225, in "Norton, Mary T.: manuscript, Madam Congresswoman the Memoirs of Mary T. Norton of New Jersey," Box 17, Hickock Papers, FDRL (last quote).

66. McNaughton to Bermingham, June 28, 1945, in "June 28–30, 1945," Box 9, McNaughton Papers, HSTL (first quote); Embittered Negro GI's Protest Eastland Smear and Nazi Tactics, July 26, 1945, in Reel 12, Part 13, Series B, NAACP Papers, MD, LC (remaining quotes).

67. White to *NYT, Herald Tribune, Washington Post, San Francisco Chronicle, Chicago Sun, Chicago Tribune, Chicago Daily News, St. Louis Post-Dispatch, Philadelphia Inquirer, Kansas City Star, Detroit Free Press, Cleveland Plain Dealer,* and *Christian Science Monitor,* June 30, 1945, in Reel 12, Part 13, Series B, NAACP Papers, MD, LC (first quote); *Congressional Record,* 79th Congress, 1st session, 7050–7068 (second quote); "Senate Backs FEPC; House Vote Held Up," *NYT,* July 1, 1945 (remaining quotes).

68. McNaughton to Jack Beal, July 5, 1945, in "July 1945," Box 9, McNaughton Papers, HSTL; Report of the Secretary, for the July 1945 Meeting of the Board, in Reel 19, Part 16, Series B, NAACP Papers, MD, LC; Kersten, *Race, Jobs, and the War,* 131–133; Ruchames, *Race, Jobs and Politics,* 121–136; Reed, *Seedtime for the Modern Civil Rights Movement,* 169–172; William S. White, "Congress Extends FEPC with $250,000 for Year," *NYT,* July 13, 1945.

69. War Production and Compulsory Labor, February 8, 1945, in "Committees, 1945, Military Affairs Committee, Work or Fight Bill #2," Box 217, O'Mahoney Papers, AHC.

70. William Haber, "Some Problems of Manpower Allocation," *American Economic Review* 42 (May 1952): 396.

5. "THE DREGS OF EUROPE": A CONFLICTED
REFUGEE POLICY

1. "Edelstein Dies after House Talk," *NYT,* June 5, 1941. The nativism on display in Congress during the 1940s is not dissimilar to that John Higham first recounted in *Strangers in the Land: Patterns of American Nativism, 1860–1925* (New Brunswick, N.J.: Rutgers University Press, 1955).

2. "Praised by Colleagues," *NYT*, June 5, 1941 (quote); Martha Gardner, *The Qualities of a Citizen: Women, Immigration, and Citizenship, 1870–1965* (Princeton, N.J.: Princeton University Press, 2005), 199–219; Mark A. Raider, *The Emergence of American Zionism* (New York: New York University Press, 1998), 210.

3. Alan Brinkley, *The End of Reform: New Deal Liberalism in Recession and War* (New York: Alfred A. Knopf, 1995); Carl J. Bon Tempo, *Americans at the Gate: The United States and Refugees during the Cold War* (Princeton, N.J.: Princeton University Press, 2008), 17–18.

4. Aaron Berman, *Nazism, the Jews, and American Zionism, 1933–1948* (Detroit, Mich.: Wayne State University Press, 1990), 127–128; Bon Tempo, *Americans at the Gate*, 17; American Palestine Committee, Statement by Senator Robert F. Wagner, March 27, 1941, File 6, Box 302, Series 1, James E. Murray Papers, KRTA.

5. Henry L. Feingold, *Bearing Witness: How America and Its Jews Responded to the Holocaust* (Syracuse, N.Y.: Syracuse University Press, 1995), 190; Frank McNaughton to David Hulburd, September 12, 1941, in "September 1–15, 1941," Box 1, Frank McNaughton Papers, HSTL (quotes).

6. Raider, *The Emergence of American Zionism*, 1–68, 172–216 (see p. 214 for the quote); Joint Statement by Senator Robert F. Wagner of New York and Robert A. Taft of Ohio on a Survey made by Elmo Roper of the American Jewish Opinion on a Jewish state in Palestine [late 1945], Folder 30, Box 2, PA Series, Robert Wagner Papers, GU.

7. Richard Breitman and Alan M. Kraut, *American Refugee Policy and European Jewry, 1933–1945* (Bloomington: Indiana University Press, 1987), 58; David S. Wyman, *The Abandonment of the Jews: America and the Holocaust, 1941–1945* (New York: Pantheon Books, 1984), 14; Feingold, *Bearing Witness*, 86. For more on American anti-Semitism during the war years, see James T. Sparrow, *Warfare State: World War II Americans and the Age of Big Government* (New York: Oxford University Press, 2011), 89–94.

8. James Madison, "The Federalist No. 10," in Alexander Hamilton, James Madison, and John Jay, *The Federalist*, edited by Terence Ball (New York: Cambridge University Press, 2003), 40–46.

9. Feingold, *Bearing Witness*, 261, 187; Wyman, *The Abandonment of the Jews*, 8; David S. Wyman, *Paper Walls America and the Refugee Crisis, 1938–1941* (Amherst: University of Massachusetts Press, 1968).

10. Hadley Cantril, ed., *Public Opinion, 1935–1946* (Princeton, N.J.: Princeton University Press, 1951), 381–388. (Following *Kristallnacht*, American approval of Hitler's treatment of Jews fell significantly, down to just 6 percent.)

11. Feingold, *Bearing Witness*, 261, 187; Wyman, *The Abandonment of the Jews*, 8; Wyman, *Paper Walls*.

12. Historians have worked on the topic of whiteness for over a decade. Some of the most important texts include Eric L. Goldstein, *The Price of Whiteness: Jews, Race, and American Identity* (Princeton, N.J.: Princeton University Press, 2006); Matthew Frye Jacobson, *Whiteness of a Different Color: European Immigrants and the Alchemy of Race* (Cambridge, Mass.: Harvard University Press, 1999); Kevin M. Schultz, *Tri-Faith America: How Catholics and Jews Held Postwar America to Its Protestant Promises* (New York: Oxford University Press, 2011). Other important studies of whiteness focus on the concept in the

South, home to many of the most outspoken restrictionists. See for example, Michelle Brattain, *The Politics of Whiteness: Race, Workers, and Culture in the Modern South* (Princeton, N.J.: Princeton University Press, 2001); Grace Elizabeth Hale, *Making Whiteness: The Culture of Segregation in the South, 1890–1940* (New York: Pantheon Books, 1998).

13. McNaughton to Hulburd, September 12, 1941, in "September 1–15, 1941," Box 1, McNaughton Papers, HSTL (first quote); Samuel Dickstein Oral History, January 1972, Columbia University Oral History Project, 19; Dale Kramer, "The American Fascists," *Harpers Magazine* (September 1940): 381 (second quote).

14. McNaughton to Bill Johnson, September 2, 1943, in "September 1943," Box 5, and McNaughton to Hulburd, September 12, 1941, in "September 1–15, 1941," Box 1 (quote), both in McNaughton Papers, HSTL.

15. McNaughton to Hulburd, September 12, 1941, in "September 1–15, 1941," Box 1, McNaughton Papers, HSTL.

16. Jeffrey Scott Demsky, "Going Public in Support: American Discursive Opposition to Nazi Anti-Semitism, 1933–1944" (Ph.D. dissertation, University of Florida, 2007), 28–64; Bat-Ami Zucker, *In Search of Refuge: Jews and US Consuls in Nazi Germany, 1933–1941* (London and Portland, Ore.: Vallentine Mitchell, 2001); [Alben] Barkley—Cleveland—Jan. 18th, 1941, excerpted in "Barkley Speeches, Excerpts from Address made in Cleveland, Ohio, January 18, 1941," Alben Barkley Papers, UKL; Alben W. Barkley, *That Reminds Me* (Garden City, N.Y.: Doubleday, 1954), 96; Address by Senator Alben W. Barkley on the Twenty-Fourth Anniversary of the Balfour Declaration, at Carnegie Hall, New York City, Saturday evening, November 1, 1941, in "Barkley Speeches, November 1, 1941, Carnegie Hall, New York City, Twenty-Fourth Anniversary, Balfour Declaration," Barkley Papers, UKL.

17. Joseph C. O'Mahoney to William Veta, December 10, 1938, in "Legislation—Jews," Box 73, Joseph C. O'Mahoney Papers, AHC (quotes); "Alien Deportation Bill Is Approved by House Group," *Washington Evening Star*, March 15, 1939; Sarah A. Ogilviet and Scott Miller, *Refuge Denied: The* St. Louis *Passengers and the Holocaust* (Madison, Wis.: University of Wisconsin Press, 2006); Lucy S. Dawidowicz, *The War against the Jews, 1933–1945*, 10th anniversary ed. (New York: Bantam Books, 1986); Arthur D. Morse, *While Six Million Died: A Chronicle of American Apathy* (New York: Random House, 1967).

18. "Recent Anti-Alien Legislative Proposals," *Columbia Law Review* 39 (November 1939): 1207; "Recent Federal Legislation against Subversive Influences," *Columbia Law Review* 41 (January 1941): 159–171; Martin Dies to Franklin D. Roosevelt, William B. Bankhead, Alben W. Barkley, Sam Rayburn, June 1, 1940, in "1942 Committee on Un American Activities," Box 3R290, Sam Rayburn Papers, BCAH (first quote). For more recent treatments of citizenship and immigration, see for example, Thomas J. Curran, *Xenophobia and Immigration, 1820–1930* (Boston, Mass.: Twayne Publishers, 1975); Gary Gerstle and John Mollenkopf, eds., *E Pluribus Unum? Contemporary and Historical Perspectives on Immigrant Political Incorporation* (New York: Russell Sage Foundation, 2001); Kenneth L. Karst, *Belonging to America: Equal Citizenship and the Constitution* (New Haven, Conn.: Yale University Press, 1989); David M. Ricci, *Good Citizenship in America* (New York: Cambridge University Press, 2004); Peter Schuck and Rogers M. Smith, *Citizenship without Consent: Illegal Aliens in the American Polity* (New Haven, Conn.: Yale

University Press, 1985); Cheryl Shanks, *Immigration and the Politics of American Sovereignty, 1890–1990* (Ann Arbor: University of Michigan Press, 2001); Rogers M. Smith, *Civic Ideals: Conflicting Visions of Citizenship in U.S. History* (New Haven, Conn.: Yale University Press, 1997); Aristide R. Zolberg, *A Nation by Design: Immigration Policy in the Fashioning of America* (New York: Russell Sage Foundation, 2006); Michael R. Belknap, *Cold War Political Justice: The Smith Act, the Communist Party, and American Civil Liberties* (Westport, Conn.: Greenwood Press, 1977), 22–27; Howard Worth Smith to Earl Godwin, July 31, 1939, in "Alien Registration—Support of Organizations," Box 1, Howard Worth Smith Papers, UVA; Bruce Dierenfield, *Keeper of the Rules: Congressman Howard W. Smith of Virginia* (Charlottesville: University Press of Virginia, 1987), 77–79 (second and third quotes); *Congressional Record,* 76th Congress, 3rd session, 8344 (fourth quote); "Congress Moves to Control Aliens," *NYT,* May 28, 1940; Roosevelt, Statement on Signing the Alien Registration Act, June 29, 1940, in John T. Woolley and Gerhard Peters, *The American Presidency Project* [online], Santa Barbara, Calif.: University of California (hosted), Gerhard Peters (database), http://www.presidency.ucsb.edu/ws/?pid=15973 (last quote); Mark A. Sheft, "The End of the Smith Act Era: A Legal and Historical Analysis of *Scales v. United States,*" *American Journal of Legal History* 36 (April 1992): 164–167. The legislation gained its infamy in the postwar era when it became a tool of the anti-Communists. This turn of events revealed the merger of wartime and postwar political time.

19. Sharon Kay Smith, "Elbert D. Thomas and America's Response to the Holocaust" (Ph.D. dissertation, Brigham Young University, 1991), 24, 41–51; Sol Bloom, *The Autobiography of Sol Bloom* (New York: Putnam's, 1948), 302–303 (quote).

20. State Department Release on Help for German Refugees, March 24, 1938, in Woolley and Peters, *The American Presidency Project* (first quote); Phone Message from Robert Wagner, October 14, 1938, OF 700, January–October 15, 1938, FDRL (last quote).

21. Zucker, *In Search of Refuge,* 171; Martin Gilbert, *Kristallnacht: Prelude to Destruction* (New York: HarperCollins Publishers, 2006), 13–15; Roosevelt, Statement on Refugees in Palestine, November 23, 1938, in Woolley and Peters, *The American Presidency Project*; Zucker, *In Search of Refuge,* 13, 47–48; Feingold, *Bearing Witness,* 61, 193.

22. Wyman, *The Abandonment of the Jews,* 100, 151; Breitman and Kraut, *American Refugee Policy,* 229; Wyman, *Paper Walls,* 67–71, 6; Henry L. Feingold, *Politics of Rescue: The Roosevelt Administration and the Holocaust, 1938–1945* (New Brunswick, N.J.: Rutgers University Press, 1970), 149.

23. Saha Bastami, "American Foreign Policy and the Question of Palestine, 1856–1939" (Ph.D. dissertation, George Washington University, 1989), 397; Emmanuel Celler to Louis Rittenberg, March 25, 1938, in "Israel (Palestine) Correspondence, 1930–1946," Box 23, Emmanuel Celler Papers, MD, LC (first two quotes); James E. Murray to Cordell Hull, October 15, 1938, in File 5, Box 302, Series 1, James E. Murray Papers, KRTA (last quote).

24. Wagner to Carter Glass, February 5, 1941, in "Wagner, Hon. Robert F.," Box 398, Carter Glass Papers, UVA; Memorandum of the American Palestine Committee, in File 6, Box 302, Series 1, Murray Papers, KRTA; Wagner to Edwin M. Watson, April 23, 1941, File 10, Box 1, and American Palestine Committee Press Release, December 11, 1942, File 20, Box 2, both in PA Series, Wagner Papers, GU; Berman, *Nazism,* 126–127.

25. Monty Noam Penkower, *Decision on Palestine Deferred: America, Britain and Wartime Diplomacy, 1939–1945* (London and Portland, Ore.: Frank Cass, 2002), 73–74, 171; Faris S. Malouf and Shukry E. Khoury to Murray, April 22, 1941 (quotes) and Murray to Malouf, April 29, 1941, both in File 6, Box 302, Series 1, Murray Papers, KRTA.

26. U.S. Congress, House of Representatives, Committee on Immigration and Naturalization, "Admission of German Refugee Children," unpublished hearings, 76th Congress, 1st session, July 19, 1939 (first and second quotes); McNaughton to James McConaughy, May 26, 1943, in "May 1943," Box 5, McNaughton Papers, HSTL (last quote).

27. U.S. Congress, House of Representatives, Committee on Immigration and Naturalization, "Isaac Zarembsky," unpublished hearings, 76th Congress, 1st session, May 17, 1939; Wyman, *The Abandonment of the Jews,* 14. For more on nonquota and nonimmigrant visas, see Zucker, *In Search of Refuge,* 112–132.

28. See the many case files in Boxes 64, 65, and 66, S/VP Papers, HSTL.

29. Lister Hill to Isadore Weil, July 29, 1940, Weil to Hill, November 8, 1940 (first quote), Hill to Weil, November 13, 1940 (second quote), Hill to Weil, May 6, 1941, all in File 6, Box 161. This case is just one example of the material in Hill's files. W. H. Holcombe to Hill, September 21, 1938; Herbert H. Lyons to Hill, March 3, 1939; and Hill to Lyons, March 6, 1939 (last quote), all in File 8, Box 161, all in Lister Hill Papers, WSHSC.

30. Mae M. Ngai, *Impossible Subjects: Illegal Aliens and the Making of Modern America* (Princeton, N.J.: Princeton University Press, 2004), 21–55 (first quote, p. 22); Dickstein Oral History, 63 (remaining quotes); for analysis of whether or not the legislation creating the quota system was designed to be anti-Semitic, see Feingold, *Bearing Witness,* 61–62.

31. Hamilton Fish, *Memoir of an American Patriot* (Washington: Regnery Gateway, 1991), 135–136, 139–141 (first four quotes); Penkower, *Decision on Palestine Deferred,* 22–23 (last quote).

32. Zucker, *In Search of Refuge,* 80–111; Dickstein Oral History, 20–21 (quotes); Melissa Jane Taylor, "'Experts in Misery'?: American Consuls in Austria, Jewish Refugees and Restrictionist Immigration Policy, 1938–1941" (Ph.D. dissertation, University of South Carolina, 2006), 1, 322–323; Wyman, *The Abandonment of the Jews,* 316–317.

33. "Jobs for Aliens," n.p., n.d., in "Newspaper Clippings," 79th Congress, Senate 79A-F11, Box 122, Senate Committee on Immigration, RG 46, RUSS, NA.

34. Ralph Smith, "Crackerland in Washington, Greatest Congressional Bother—Immigration," *Atlanta Journal,* February 18, 1939 (first three quotes); Carl Hayden to Hattie E. Bittenfield, April 5, 1940, in Carl Hayden Papers, ASU (last quote).

35. Wyman, *Paper Walls,* 75; "Aid to Child Exiles in U.S. Is Mapped," *NYT,* March 31, 1939; Wagner speech, June 7, 1939, File 8, Box 1, PA Series, Wagner Papers, GU (first quote); Breitman and Kraut, *American Refugee Policy,* 232 (last quote).

36. "Urge Bill to Admit Refugee Children," *NYT,* April 21, 1939; Daniel J. Tichenor, *Dividing Lines: The Politics of Immigration Control in America* (Princeton, N.J.: Princeton University Press, 2002), 164; "Home and Homeland," *Christian Science Monitor,* February 17, 1939; Breitman and Kraut, *American Refugee Policy,* 73; Wyman, *Paper Walls,* 82; "Refugee Child Bill Formally Reported," *NYT,* May 6, 1939; "Bill to Shut Out Aliens Is Reported," *NYT,* July 1, 1939; "Congress Winds Up on or Near July 15 Again Is Predicted,"

NYT, July 3, 1939; Wagner Press Release, July 3, 1939, Volume 2, Part 2, 76th Congress, Box 121, BB Series, Wagner Papers, GU; J. Joseph Huthmacher, *Senator Robert F. Wagner and the Rise of Urban Liberalism* (New York: Atheneum, 1968), 269; Feingold, *Bearing Witness,* 173.

37. Wyman, *Paper Walls,* 99–115. The statistics are drawn from my count of the hearings listed in the index to the unpublished hearings of Congress. Some named individuals in these private bills were the subject of more than one hearing. In such cases I only included the person/private bill in my count one time unless the private bill was carried forward or reintroduced in a subsequent Congress or unless there was a second private bill for that person that also named another person, either a spouse, parent, or child.

38. U.S. Congress, House of Representatives, Committee on Immigration and Naturalization, "H.R. 6546, A Bill for the Relief of Benno von Mayrhauser and Oskar von Mayrhauser," unpublished hearings, 76th Congress, 1st session, July 19, 1939 (first quote); U.S. Congress, House of Representatives, Committee on Immigration and Naturalization, "H.R. 8295," unpublished hearings, 76th Congress, 2nd session, February 21, 1940 (second quote); *Congressional Record,* 76th Congress, 1st session, 5167 (third quote).

39. U.S. Congress, House of Representatives, Committee on Immigration and Naturalization, "A Bill to Record the Lawful Admission for Permanent Residence of Kurt Wessely," unpublished hearings, 76th Congress, 1st session, February 15, 1939 (first quote); U.S. Congress, House of Representatives, Committee on Immigration and Naturalization, "H.R. 9027, A Bill for the Relief of Doctor Gustav Weil, Irma Weil, and Marion Weil," unpublished hearings, 76th Congress, 2nd session, May 29, 1940 (remaining quotes).

40. U.S. Congress, House of Representatives, Committee on Immigration and Naturalization, "H.R. 3266, H.R. 3165, and H.R. 5716," unpublished hearings, 76th Congress, 1st session, May 18, 1939 (first two quotes); Typescript transcript of hearings for H.R. 1541, H.R. 1542, and H.R. 2716, Wednesday, February 12, 1941, House Committee on Immigration and Naturalization, in HR 77A-F15.1, Box 286, House Committee on Immigration and Naturalization, RG 233, RUSHR, NA (next two quotes); U.S. Congress, House of Representatives, Committee on Immigration and Naturalization, "H.R. 3315," unpublished hearings, 77th Congress, 1st session, July 9, 1941 (last quote).

41. Wagner to Glass, January 23, 1942, in "Wagner, Hon. Robert F.," Box 398, Glass Papers, UVA (first quote); Press Release Draft, n.d., in Folder 2, Box 1, PA Series, Wagner Papers, GU (second quote); Andrew L. Somers to Harry S Truman, January 26, 1942, and Truman to Somers, January 28, 1942 (third quote) both in "Jews," Box 71, S/VP Papers, HSTL; "Zionist Rally Here Asks Jewish Army," *NYT,* February 5, 1942 (last quote).

42. Gabriel A. Wechsler to Bloom, November 24, 1942, in "B-C," HR 77A-F14.1, Box 284, House Committee on Foreign Affairs, RG 233, RUSHR, NA (quote); Harold R. Schradzke to Truman, May 14, 1943, in "Jews," Box 71, S/VP Papers, HSTL.

43. Truman to William Rosenwald, April 24, 1942 (first quote) and Truman to Mr. and Mrs. Arthur Karbank, March 3, 1943, both in "Jews," Box 71, S/VP Papers, HSTL; Sol Bloom to A. Marschak, March 17, 1943, in "Mc–Q" (second quote) and Bloom to Genevieve M. Hubbard, March 19, 1943 (remaining quotes) both in 78th Congress, House of Representatives 78A-F15.1, Box 267, House Committee on Immigration and Naturalization, RG 233, RUSHR, NA.

44. Smith, "Elbert D. Thomas," 99 (quote); McNaughton to McConaughy, March 12, 1943, in "March 1–15, 1943," Box 5, McNaughton Papers, HSTL.

45. Breitman and Kraut, *American Refugee Policy,* 140 (quote); Roosevelt to Samuel Dickstein [April 1943], in 'OF 3186, Political Refugees, 1943, Box 3, FDRL; McNaughton to McConaughy, April 16, 1943, in "April 1–22, 1943," Box 5, McNaughton Papers, HSTL; Smith, "Elbert D. Thomas," 103.

46. Advertisement, "To 5,000,000 Jews in the Nazi Death-Trap Bermuda Was a 'Cruel Mockery,'" *NYT,* May 4, 1943, in "Jews," Box 71, S/VP Papers, HSTL (first four quotes); Truman to Stephen S. Wise, June 1, 1943, Folder 24, Box 2, PA Series, Wagner Papers, GU (last three quotes).

47. *Congressional Record,* 78th Congress, 1st session, 4044–4047, 4140–4141, first quote on 4045 and third quote on 4141; "Refugee Parley 'Ad' Criticized in Senate," *NYT,* May 7, 1943 (second quote); Truman to Wise, June 1, 1943, in Folder 24, Box 2, PA Series, Wagner Papers, GU (fourth and fifth quotes); Edwin C. Johnson to Peter Bergson, May 6, 1943, in "Jews," Box 71, S/VP Papers, HSTL; Wyman, *The Abandonment of the Jews,* 143 (last quote).

48. "Quick Aid Is Asked for Europe's Jews," *NYT,* July 21, 1943; Berman, *Nazism,* 125.

49. Allen Drury, *A Senate Journal, 1943–1945* (New York: McGraw-Hill, 1963), 30; Penkower, *Decision on Palestine Deferred,* 253; Feingold, *Bearing Witness,* 145; The American Press and the Rescue Resolution, in "1943 Jewish Literature," Box 51, Elbert D. Thomas Papers, USHS; "Relief Unit Scored by Jewish Group," *NYT,* December 31, 1943; Jeffery C. Livingston, "Ohio Congressman John M. Vorys: A Republican Conservative Nationalist and Twentieth Century American Foreign Policy" (Ph.D. dissertation, University of Toledo, 1989), 142–144; Robert G. Spivack, "The New Anti-Alien Drive," *New Republic* 109 (November 29, 1943): 740–741 (quote); Mark A. Raider, "'Irresponsible, Undisciplined Opposition': Ben Halpern on the Bergson Group and Jewish Terrorism in Pre-State Palestine," *American Jewish History* 92 (September 2004): 318; Berman, *Nazism,* 119–121.

50. Wyman, *The Abandonment of the Jews,* 193–206 (first quote on 195, second quote on 198); The American Press and the Rescue Resolution, in "1943 Jewish Literature," Box 51, Thomas Papers, USHS; "Time Races Death What Are We Waiting For?" *NYT,* December 17, 1943.

51. Wyman, *The Abandonment of the Jews,* 193–206 (first quote on 200; next three quotes on 201); Maurice R. Davie, with the collaboration of Sarah W. Cohn et al., *Refugees in America: Report of the Committee for the Study of Recent Immigration from Europe* (Westport, Conn.: Greenwood Press, 1974), 12; Feingold, *Bearing Witness,* 145.

52. A. M. Levin to Truman, February 7, 1944, Truman to Levin, February 16, 1944, and M. J. Slonim to Truman, February 22, 1944, all in "Jews," Box 71, S/VP Papers, HSTL; Press Release, February 1, 1944, File 26, Box 2, PA Series, Wagner Papers, GU (first quote); Robert M. La Follette phone message, February 28, 1944, in "Committee Correspondence, Etc., Confidential Material Removed," 78th Congress, Senate 78A-F11, Box 125, Senate Committee on Foreign Relations Papers, RG 46, RUSS, NA; Arthur Krock, "Reliance on Marshall," *NYT,* March 8, 1944; Vandenberg to Philip Slomovitz, March 14, 1944, in Roll 3, Arthur Vandenberg Papers on Microfilm, BHL (second quote); Penkower, *Decision on Palestine Deferred,* 265–268; Address of Robert A. Taft at Testimonial Dinner for Dr. Abba

Hillel Silver, March 21, 1945, Hotel Commodore, New York City, in "Palestine and the Jews, 1944–1945," Box 734, Robert A. Taft Papers, LC (last two quotes).

53. Nancy MacLennan, "Roosevelt Backs Palestine Plan as Homeland for Refugee Jews," *NYT*, March 10, 1944; Vandenberg to Slomovitz, March 23, 1944, in Roll 3, Vandenberg Papers, BHL (quote); I. F. Stone, "Palestine Run-Around," *The Nation* 158 (March 18, 1944): 326–328.

54. Rayburn to Roosevelt, March 7, 1944, OF 700, 1944, FDRL (first two quotes); "Senate Expected to Defer Vote on Palestine Immigration Issue," *NYT*, March 6, 1944 (third quote); "Defers House Vote on Palestine Issue," *NYT*, March 18, 1944 (last quote).

55. Taft to Henry L. Stimson, September 12, 1944, in "Palestine and the Jews, 1944," Box 734, Taft Papers, LC (first quote); Cordell Hull to Roosevelt, August 30, 1944, OF 700, 1944, FDRL; Stimson to Taft, October 10, 1944, in "78-2, H.Res. 418 and 419 on Palestine Report," 78th Congress, Senate 78A-F11, Box 124, Senate Committee on Foreign Relations, RG 46, RUSS, NA; U.S. Congress, House of Representatives, Committee on Foreign Affairs, *The Jewish Homeland in Palestine: Report to Accompany H.Res. 418,* 78th Congress, 2nd session, 1944 (next two quotes); Penkower, *Decision on Palestine Deferred,* 315–319; Wagner to Roosevelt, December 2, 1944, File 28, Box 2, PA Series, Wagner Papers, GU (fourth quote); Roosevelt to Wagner, December 3, 1944, in "78-2, H.Res. 418 and 419 on Palestine Report," 78th Congress, Senate 78A-F11, Box 124, Senate Committee on Foreign Relations, RG 46, RUSS, NA (remaining quotes).

56. Penkower, *Decision on Palestine Deferred,* 315–319; Senator Tom Connally, Chairman Senate Committee on Foreign Relations, Submitted to the Committee: "Statement by the State Department, December 8, 1944," in "78-2, H.Res. 418 and 419 on Palestine Report," 78th Congress, Senate 78A-F11, Box 124, Senate Committee on Foreign Relations, RG 46, RUSS, NA; Vandenberg to Slomovitz, December 9, 1944, in Roll 3, Vandenberg Papers, BHL (quotes); [Abba Hillel] Silver to Taft, December 11, 1944, in "Palestine and the Jews," Box 734, Taft Papers, MD, LC; Vandenberg to Slomovitz, December 12, 1944, in Roll 3, Vandenberg Papers, BHL.

57. Translation of a Note Dated December 21, 1944 from the Iraqi Foreign Office to the American Legation, Baghdad, in "78-2, H.Res. 418 and 419 on Palestine Report," 78th Congress, Senate 78A-F11, Box 124, Senate Committee on Foreign Relations, RG 46, RUSS, NA.

58. See for example, Martin Gilbert, *The Holocaust: A History of the Jews of Europe during the Second World War* (New York: Henry Holt, 1985).

59. *Congressional Record,* 79th Congress, 1st session, 3946, 3952, 3990, 4576–4577.

60. Gilbert, *The Holocaust,* 62, 792; United States Holocaust Memorial Museum, "Buchenwald," *Holocaust Encyclopedia,* http://www.ushmm.org/wlc/en/article.php?Module Id=10005198, United States Holocaust Memorial Museum, "Dora-Mittelbau," *Holocaust Encyclopedia,* http://www.ushmm.org/wlc/en/article.php?ModuleId=10005322, United States Holocaust Memorial Museum, "Dachau," *Holocaust Encyclopedia,* http://www .ushmm.org/wlc/en/article.php?ModuleId=10005214.

61. Statement for the Press, May 8, 1945, in "Barkley Speeches, Atrocities in German Concentration Camps, Statements," Barkley Papers, UKL.

62. Ibid.

63. Smith, "Elbert D. Thomas," 113–114 (first quote); Livingston, "Ohio Congressman John M. Vorys," 146 (remaining quotes).

64. M. Grossman to Louis Lipsky, May 11, 1945, in "Immigration Correspondence, 1945–1946," Box 15, Celler Papers, MD, LC.

65. McNaughton to Don Bermingham, May 17, 1945, in "May 16–31, 1945," Box 8, McNaughton Papers, HSTL (remaining quotes); *Congressional Record,* 79th Congress, 1st session, 4576–4584, 4610–4616, first quote on 4578.

66. Andrew L. Somers to Dear Colleague, May 9, 1945, in File 8, Box 145, Langer Papers, UND; "House Group Backs Senate on Palestine," *NYT,* December 19, 1945; "Aid to Jews Held Needed for Peace," *NYT,* December 24, 1945.

67. Wagner and Taft to Dear Senator, May 18, 1945, in File 8, Box 145, Langer Papers, UND (first quote); Thomas C. Hart Oral History, Columbia University Oral History Project, 262–264 (remaining quotes); An Investigation by the Committee on Immigration and Naturalization of the House of Representatives of the Congress of the United States, of Conditions at the Refugee Shelter at Fort Ontario, Oswego, New York, June 25–26, 1945, in "Subcommittee Hearing No. VI, June 25, Ft. Ontario, Oswego, New York, 1945," 79th Congress, House of Representatives 79A-F16.2, House Committee on Immigration and Naturalization, RG 233, RUSHR, NA.

68. An Investigation by the Committee on Immigration and Naturalization of the House of Representatives of the Congress of the United States, of Conditions at the Refugee Shelter at Fort Ontario, Oswego, New York, June 25–26, 1945, in "Subcommittee Hearing No. VI, June 25, Ft. Ontario, Oswego, New York, 1945," 79th Congress, House of Representatives 79A-F16.2, House Committee on Immigration and Naturalization, RG 233, RUSHR, NA; Dickstein Oral History, 73–74 (quotes); for more on the Oswego camp, see Wyman, *The Abandonment of the Jews,* 265–276. Conditions at Oswego previewed the huge role displaced persons would play in postwar politics. For more on the postwar policies for displaced persons (DPs), see Leonard Dinnerstein, *America and the Survivors of the Holocaust* (New York: Columbia University Press, 1982); Haim Genizi, *America's Fair Share: The Admission and Resettlement of Displaced Persons, 1945–1952* (Detroit: Wayne State University Press, 1993); Arieh J. Kochavi, *Post-Holocaust Politics: Britain, the United States and Jewish Refugees, 1945–1948* (Chapel Hill: University of North Carolina Press, 2001); Gil Loescher and John A. Scanlan, *Calculated Kindness: Refugees and America's Half-Open Door, 1945 to the Present* (New York: Free Press, 1986); Mark Wyman, *DP: Europe's Displaced Persons, 1945–1951* (Philadelphia: Balch Institute Press, 1989).

69. N. M. Mason to Dickstein, June 6, 1941, in "[blank folder title]," HR 77A-F15.2, Box 290, House Committee on Immigration and Naturalization, RG 233, RUSHR, NA.

6. a "virtual black-out of civil liberties" and the politics of prejudice

1. "Address of Senator Alben W. Barkley at the Charter Day Celebration of Howard University," *Howard University Bulletin* 21 (April 1, 1942): 5–10, in "Barkley Speeches,

Address at Charter Day Dinner Howard University, Washington, D.C., March 2, 1942," Alben Barkley Papers, UKL.

2. Allen Drury, *A Senate Journal, 1943–1945* (New York: McGraw-Hill, 1963), 8 (first quote); John E. Rankin Speech, August 24, 1942, in 77th Congress, House of Representatives 77A-F39.1, Box 335, House Committee on World War Veterans Legislation, RG 233, RUSHR, NA (remaining quotes); Alexander Keyssar, *The Right to Vote: The Contested History of Democracy in the United States* (New York: Basic Books, 2000), 244–245; Kimberly Johnson, *Reforming Jim Crow: Southern Politics and State in the Age before Brown* (New York: Oxford University Press, 2010), 1–18. For more on the argument about the southern Senate strategy of delay, see Keith M. Finley, *Delaying the Dream: Southern Senators and the Fight against Civil Rights, 1938–1965* (Baton Rouge: Louisiana State University Press, 2008), 1–14, 56–96.

3. Harvard Sitkoff, "Racial Militancy and Interracial Violence in the Second World War," *Journal of American History* 58 (December 1971): 661–681; Justin Hart, "Making Democracy Safe for the World: Race, Propaganda, and the Transformation of U.S. Foreign Policy during World War II," *Pacific Historical Review* 73 (February 2004): 49–84; Johnson, *Reforming Jim Crow*, 46; Beth Tompkins Bates, "A New Crowd Challenges the Agenda of the Old Guard in the NAACP, 1933–1941," *American Historical Review* 102 (April 1997): 340–377; Cheryl Lynn Greenberg, *"Or Does It Explode?" Black Harlem in the Great Depression* (New York: Oxford University Press, 1991); Jennings Perry, *Democracy Begins at Home: The Tennessee Fight on the Poll Tax* (Philadelphia: Lippincott, 1944), 260 (quote); Elizabeth Borgwardt, *A New Deal for the World: America's Vision for Human Rights* (Cambridge, Mass.: Harvard University Press, 2005); Carol Anderson, *Eyes off the Prize: The United Nations and the African American Struggle for Human Rights, 1944–1955* (New York: Cambridge University Press, 2003).

4. Gilbert C. Fite, *Richard B. Russell, Jr., Senator from Georgia* (Chapel Hill: University of North Carolina Press, 1991); William Gellermann, *Martin Dies* (New York: John Day, 1944); Bruce Dierenfield, *Keeper of the Rules: Congressman Howard W. Smith of Virginia* (Charlottesville: University Press of Virginia, 1987); Drew Pearson, "Men Who Make the Senate Tick," *Washington Post*, October 23, 1949 (quote).

5. W. E. B. DuBois, "Race Relations in the United States, 1917–1947," *Phylon* 9 (Third Quarter 1948): 237; Walter White to Charles T. Brackins, April 6, 1940, in Reel 33, Part 7, Anti-Lynching Campaign, Series B, NAACP Papers, MD, LC (quote); "Roosevelt Asked for Lynching Curb," *NYT*, December 17, 1933; Jacquelyn Dowd Hall, *Revolt against Chivalry: Jessie Daniel Ames and the Women's Campaign against Lynching*, rev. ed., (New York: Columbia University Press, 1993); Patricia A. Schechter, *Ida B. Wells-Barnett and American Reform, 1880–1930* (Chapel Hill: University of North Carolina Press, 2001); Jessie Daniel Ames to Tom Connally, October 8, [1938], in "Hearings—Anti-Lynching," Box 126, Tom Connally Papers, MD, LC; "Gallup and Fortune Polls," *Public Opinion Quarterly* 4 (June 1940): 351; Johnson, *Reforming Jim Crow*, 46–48, gives much lower numbers for southern lynchings, just 196 between 1910 and 1954; Kevin McMahon, *Reconsidering Roosevelt on Race: How the Presidency Paved the Road to Brown* (Chicago, Ill.: University of Chicago Press, 2004).

6. Richard B. Russell to John Boykin, January 21, 1938, in "File #3, Antilynch Material, January 1938–February 1939," Box 2, Series X, Richard B. Russell Papers, RBRL (first quote); Record of Senators on Cloture on Anti-Lynching Bill, December 6, 1938, in "Newspaper Clippings, Articles, Pictures, Anti-Lynching," Box 126, Connally Papers, MD, LC; Perry, *Democracy Begins at Home,* 255 (second and third quotes); Joseph F. Guffey, *Seventy Years on the Red-Fire Wagon; from Tilden to Truman, through New Freedom and New Deal* (n.p., 1952), 152 (remaining quotes). For the classic treatment of the so-called conservative coalition, see James T. Patterson, *Congressional Conservatism and the New Deal: The Growth of the Conservative Coalition in Congress, 1933–1939* (Lexington: For the Organization of American Historians by the University of Kentucky Press, 1967).

7. Tom Connally, as told to Alfred Steinberg, *My Name Is Tom Connally* (New York: Crowell, 1954), 169–170 (first quote); White to James E. Chappell, February 14, 1940, in Reel 32, Part 7, Series B, NAACP Papers, MD, LC (second and third quotes); Record of Senators on Cloture on Anti-Lynching Bill, December 6, 1938, in "Newspaper Clippings, Articles, Pictures, Anti-Lynching," Box 126, Connally to Tuskegee Institute, January 20, 1939, in "Anti-Lynching Bill—Correspondence Regarding, 1930–1944," Box 127 (fourth quote), and Allen J. Ellender to Connally, February 13, 1939, in "Civil Rights," Box 126, all in Connally Papers, MD, LC.

8. Connally to W. E. Neely, April 3, 1940 (quotes), and Connally to Neely, June 4, 1940, both in "Anti-Lynching Bill—Correspondence Regarding, 1930–1944," Box 127, Connally Papers, MD, LC.

9. Connally to Ames, September 29, 1939 (first quote), Connally to Mrs. J. F. Lane and Mrs. F. A. Dobbins, February 16, 1940 (second quote), and Connally to George L. Allen, May 23, 1940 (remaining quotes), all in "Hearings—Anti-Lynching," Box 126, Connally Papers, MD, LC.

10. Lynching Goes Underground: A Report on a New Technique, January 1940, in Reel 34, Part 7, Series B, NAACP Papers, MD, LC (quotes). For more on the public spectacle of lynching in the early twentieth century, see Amy Louise Wood, *Lynching and Spectacle: Witnessing Racial Violence in America, 1890–1940* (Chapel Hill: University of North Carolina Press, 2009).

11. "Says Republicans Try to 'Buy' Negro," *NYT,* January 10, 1940 (quotes); Nancy Weiss, *Farewell to the Party of Lincoln: Black Politics in the Age of FDR* (Princeton, N.J.: Princeton University Press, 1983); Alan Brinkley, *The End of Reform: New Deal Liberalism in Recession and War* (New York: Alfred A. Knopf, 1995), 164–170.

12. Antilynching Report to accompany H.R. 801, April 8, 1940, 76th Congress, 3rd session, Senate, in Reel 24, Part 13, The NAACP and Labor, 1940–1955, Series B, and Barkley to White, April 22, 1940, in Reel 32, Part 7, Series B (quotes), both in NAACP Papers, MD, LC.

13. White to Barkley, April 23, 1940, in Reel 32, Part 7, Series B, NAACP Papers, MD, LC.

14. White to P. B. Young, May 3, 1940 (first three quotes), and White to Chicago Defender, September 23, 1940 (last quote) both in Reel 32, Part 7, Series B, NAACP Papers, MD, LC.

15. Radio Broadcast, Senator Robert F. Wagner, April 29, 1942, in Reel 32, and NAACP

Demands Lynch Probe, October 23, 1942, in Reel 35, both in Part 7, Series B, NAACP Papers, MD, LC.

16. Frances Saylor, "The Poll Tax Kills Democracy," *The Crisis* (May 1942): 162, 173.

17. Frederic D. Ogden, *The Poll Tax in the South* ([University, Ala.]: University of Alabama Press, 1958), 244–246; Harold H. Burton to White, November 19, 1942, and Rabaut Urges Abolition of Poll Tax [May 24, 1943], both in Reel 12, Part 4, Voting Rights Campaign, NAACP Papers, MD, LC; Alfred O. Hero Jr., "Liberalism-Conservatism Revisited: Foreign vs. Domestic Federal Policies, 1937–1967," *Public Opinion Quarterly* 33 (Autumn 1969): 399–408; Linda Reed, *Simple Decency and Common Sense: The Southern Conference Movement, 1938–1963* (Bloomington: University of Indiana Press, 1991), 67–69; Saylor, "The Poll Tax Kills Democracy," *The Crisis*, 162, 173. At least one scholar of Jim Crow has argued that white southern political support for poll tax reform had less to do with race and more to do with expanding the poor white voting base, which was also disenfranchised by the tax, in order to preserve the New Deal. See Johnson, *Reforming Jim Crow*, 91–115. When looked at from the perspective of Congress, the anti–poll tax debate remained a fight about racial discrimination, but one where non-southern white liberals challenged southern racial conservatives.

18. George H. Gallup, *The Gallup Poll, Public Opinion, 1935–1971*, vol. 1, *1935–1948* (New York: Random House, 1972), 271.

19. Carter Glass to Raymond E. Bottom, June 30, 1941, in "Poll Tax," Box 394, Carter Glass Papers, UVA; Burnet R. Maybank to W. H. Miller, November 5, 1942, in Reel 12, Part 4, NAACP Papers, MD, LC.

20. Claude Pepper to George Norris, March 10, 1942, in "Poll Tax, 1942," Box 324, George Norris Papers, MD, LC; Frank McNaughton to James McConaughy, October 14, 1942, in "October 1–15, 1942," Box 3, Frank McNaughton Papers, HSTL (first two quotes); Chester M. Morgan, *Redneck Liberal: Theodore G. Bilbo and the New Deal* (Baton Rouge: Louisiana State University Press, 1985); John Sparkman to Gessner T. McCorvey, October 19, 1942, in "Poll Tax File," Box 41, John Sparkman Papers, WSHSC (last quote).

21. "Senate Passes Bill for Soldier Vote," *NYT*, August 26, 1942 (quote); *Congressional Record*, 77th Congress, 2nd session, 6923–6938, 6951–6972; Finley, *Delaying the Dream*, 59–60.

22. McNaughton to McConaughy, June 26, 1942, in "June 1942," Box 3, McNaughton Papers, HSTL; Claude Pepper to Clare Boothe Luce, August 25, 1942, in File 5, Box 350, Clare Boothe Luce Papers, MD, LC (first quote); McNaughton to David Hulburd, August 28, 1942, in "July–August 1942," Box 3, McNaughton Papers, HSTL (remaining quotes).

23. Bill Roy to Sam Rayburn, August 31, 1942, in "1942 Congressman N–R (except Q)," Box 3R290, Sam Rayburn Papers, BCAH (first quote); "Agree on Details of Soldier Voting," *NYT*, September 2, 1942 (remaining quotes); "Soldier Vote Bill Accepted by House," *NYT*, September 10, 1942; *Congressional Record*, 77th Congress, 2nd session, 7063–7079; Ira Katznelson, Kim Geiger, and Daniel Kryder, "Limiting Liberalism: The Southern Veto in Congress, 1933–1950," *Political Science Quarterly* 108 (Summer 1993): 297–298; James MacGregor Burns, *Roosevelt: The Soldier of Freedom* (New York: Harcourt Brace Jovanovich, 1970), 430; Keyssar, *The Right to Vote*, 246–247.

24. Clyde Herring to White, September 12, 1942, in Reel 12, Part 4, NAACP Papers, MD, LC; Burns, *Roosevelt: The Soldier of Freedom*, 430; Keyssar, *The Right to Vote*, 246–247.

25. Replies from Representatives in the U.S. Congress to Letter of June 20, 1942, Urging Signatures to Discharge Petition No. 1, on the Geyer Anti-Poll Tax Bill (H.R. 1024), July 25, 1942, in Reel 35, Part 7, Series B (quotes), and Report of the Secretary, for the September 1942 Meeting of the Board, in Reel 19, Part 16, Board of Directors, Correspondence and Committee Materials, Series B, both in NAACP Papers, MD, LC.

26. McNaughton to McConaughy, September 24, 1942, in "September 1942," Box 3, McNaughton Papers, HSTL.

27. Milton Kemnitz to Sol Bloom, September 29, 1942, in "K–S" (first quote), Jeanette Modell to Bloom, October 6, 1942, in "Mc–M" (second quote), Virginia Foster Durr to Bloom, October 3, 1942 (third quote), and Bloom to Durr, October 7, 1942 (fourth quote), both in "N–P," all in 77th Congress, House of Representatives 77A-F14.1, Box 285, and Sol Bloom to Jonah J. Goldstein, October 13, 1942, in "G," 77th Congress, House of Representatives 77A-F14.1, Box 284 (fifth quote), all in House Committee on Foreign Affairs, RG 233, RUSHR, NA; "House by 254 to 84 Votes to Outlaw Southern Poll Tax," *NYT*, October 14, 1942 (last quote); *Congressional Record*, 77th Congress, 2nd session, 8120–8175.

28. Joseph C. O'Mahoney to John F. Finerty, October 14, 1942, in "Anti-Poll Tax Correspondence," Box 67 (first quote), The Pepper Bill Is Unconstitutional, Article written by JCOM for Washington Post, November 19, 1942, in "November 19, 1942, 'The Pepper Bill Is Unconstitutional,'" Box 244 (second quote), and O'Mahoney to Arthur Garfield Hays, November 13, 1943, in "Committees, 1943—Judiciary—Anti-Poll Tax," Box 130, all in Joseph C. O'Mahoney Papers, AHC (last quote).

29. Replies from Senators in the U.S. Senate to Inquiries from National Office and Branches October, 1942, re Supporting Pepper Anti-Poll Tax Bill When It Comes before the Senate, November 12, 1942, in Reel 12, Part 4, NAACP Papers, MD, LC; *Congressional Record*, 77th Congress, 2nd session, 8839 (quote); McNaughton to McConaughy, January 8, 1943, in "January 1–15, 1943," Box 4, McNaughton Papers, HSTL.

30. White to Charles McNary, November 19, 1942, in Reel 8, Part 13, Series B (first quote), and Republican Filibuster Plot to Kill Anti-Poll Tax Bill Charged, November 20, 1942, in Reel 12, Part 4 (remaining quotes), both in NAACP Papers, MD, LC; Perry, *Democracy Begins at Home*, 263.

31. Perry, *Democracy Begins at Home*, 262.

32. McNaughton to McConaughy, November 21, 1942, in "November 20–30, 1942," Box 4, McNaughton Papers, HSTL.

33. Frederick R. Barkley, "Poll Tax Upheld as Senate Defeats Closure, 41 to 37," *NYT*, November 24, 1942; *Congressional Record*, 77th Congress, 2nd session, 9060–9072; Arthur Capper to White, December 11, 1942, in Reel 12, Part 4, NAACP Papers, MD, LC; McNary to Mr. and Mrs. J. H. Meyer, December 19, 1942, in "December 1942," Box 20, Charles McNary Papers, MD, LC.

34. "Maps New Poll Tax Fight," *NYT*, January 4, 1943; "Naming Marcantonio on

Committee Stirs House Democrats to Revolt," *NYT*, January 16, 1943; McNaughton to McConaughy, January 21, 1943, in "January 16–31, 1943," Box 4, McNaughton Papers, HSTL (quotes); Clarence A. Berdahl, "American Government and Politics: Some Notes on Party Membership in Congress, III," *American Political Science Review* 43 (August 1949): 728–729.

35. White to Durr, March 15, 1943, Durr to White, March 18, 1943 (quotes), Memorandum on the Board of the National Committee to Abolish the Poll Tax Meeting Held April 8, 1943, and Sylvia Beitscher to White, March 19, 1943, all in Reel 12, Part 4, NAACP Papers, MD, LC.

36. John J. Cochran to White, March 29, 1943, and J. Percy Priest to White, March 29, 1943, both in Reel 33, Part 7, Series B, NAACP Papers, MD, LC.

37. George H. Bender to White, April 15, 1943, and Note penned on Bender to White, April 15, 1943, both in Reel 33, Part 7, Series B, NAACP Papers, MD, LC.

38. Memorandum on Conference with Congressmen James V. Heidinger (R. of Illinois) and Chauncey W. Reed (R. of Illinois), April 21, 1943, in Reel 33, Part 7, Series B, NAACP Papers, MD, LC (first two quotes); Katznelson, et al., "Limiting Liberalism," 298 (last quote).

39. Memorandum to Mr. White from Mr. Perry, May 5, 1943 (first quote), and Bender to White, May 7, 1943 (second quote), both in Reel 12, Part 4, NAACP Papers, MD, LC.

40. Frederick R. Barkley, "Anti-Poll Tax Bill Is Adopted by House 265 Votes to 110," *NYT*, May 26, 1943; *Congressional Record*, 78th Congress, 1st session, 4844–4889; McNaughton to McConaughy, May 28, 1943, in "May 1943," Box 5, McNaughton Papers, HSTL (quotes); "Five Senators Threaten Poll Tax Filibuster," *Chicago Defender*, June 5, 1943. Jones's race was not noted in leading national papers, only in the *Chicago Defender*, an African American newspaper.

41. Vito Marcantonio to Dear Friend, May 28, 1943, Bender to White, June 4, 1943, and Joseph Clark Baldwin to White, June 17, 1943, all in Reel 12, Part 4, and Thurgood Marshall to Ira Lewis, November 17, 1943, in Reel 8, Part 13, Series B, all in NAACP Papers, MD, LC.

42. Nat Brandt, *Harlem at War: The Black Experience in World War II* (Syracuse, N.Y.: Syracuse University Press, 1996), 137–143; Luis Alvarez, *The Power of the Zoot: Youth Culture and Resistance during World War II* (Berkeley: University of California Press, 2008), 155–199, 204–211.

43. White to Friendly Congressmen, June 18, 1943, in Reel 35, Part 7, Series B, NAACP Papers, MD, LC.

44. Brandt, *Harlem at War*, 144–149; Thomas J. Sugrue, *The Origins of the Urban Crisis: Race and Inequality in Postwar Detroit* (Princeton, N.J.: Princeton University Press, 1996), 29 (quote), 55; Matthew C. Ehrlich, *Radio Utopia: Postwar Audio Documentary in the Public Interest* (Urbana: University of Illinois Press, 2011), 17–19.

45. John W. McCormack to Rayburn, April 2, 1943, in "1943 Congressmen, J–M," Box 3R299, Rayburn Papers, BCAH.

46. Drury, *A Senate Journal*, 12 (first quote); Charles W. Vursell to Robert A. Taft, November 19, 1943, in "Soldier Vote, 1943," Box 866, Robert A. Taft Papers, MD, LC;

Richard Polenberg, *War and Society: The United States, 1941–1945* (Philadelphia: Lippincott, 1972), 195, 196–197; O'Mahoney to Lester C. Hunt, January 4, 1944, in "War Department—Soldiers Vote," Box 87, O'Mahoney Papers, AHC; McNaughton to Bill Johnson, January 8, 1944, in "January–March, 1944" (second quote), and Ray Brecht to Johnson, December 10, 1943, in "December 1943" (remaining quotes), both in Box 6, McNaughton Papers, HSTL.

47. Drury, *A Senate Journal*, 17.

48. O'Mahoney to Margaret R. McCullough, December 16, 1943, in "Committees, 1944—Judiciary—Poll Tax," Box 277, O'Mahoney Papers, AHC (first two quotes); McNaughton to Johnson, December 17, 1943, in "December 1943," Box 6, McNaughton Papers, HSTL (last quote).

49. O'Mahoney to Hunt, January 4, 1944 (first quote), O'Mahoney to Arthur B. Langlie, January 5, 1944, and Scott W. Lucas to O'Mahoney, January 10, 1944 (second quote), all in "War Department—Soldiers Vote," Box 87, O'Mahoney Papers, AHC; Polenberg, *War and Society*, 196–197; See Memorandum, Total replies received, in "Governor Replies, Soldier Vote," Box 348, Theodore Francis Green Papers, MD, LC; Barkley to O'Mahoney, January 13, 1944, O'Mahoney to Lucas, January 5, 1944 (third quote), McCormack to O'Mahoney, January 18, 1944 (last quote), and Rayburn to O'Mahoney, January 10, 1944, all in "War Department—Soldiers Vote," Box 87, O'Mahoney Papers, AHC.

50. "New Bills Offered for Soldier Voting," *NYT*, January 12, 1944; "Fights State Rule of Soldiers Vote," *NYT*, January 16, 1944 (quotes); C. P. Trussell, "Senate Committee Votes Compromise on Soldier Voting," *NYT*, January 21, 1944; C. P. Trussell, "Senate Foes Fight Compromise Plan on Soldier Voting," *NYT*, January 25, 1944; Polenberg, *War and Society*, 195.

51. C. P. Trussell, "President Calls Vote Bill 'Fraud,'" *NYT*, January 27, 1944 (first two quotes); Burns, *Roosevelt: The Soldier of Freedom*, 431 (last quote).

52. C. P. Trussell, "Two Houses Split on Soldier Vote," *NYT*, January 30, 1944; Burns, *Roosevelt: The Soldier of Freedom*, 431.

53. Polenberg, *War and Society*, 197; Petition dated January 25, 1944, and Letter of explanation from Clinton Anderson, January 26, 1944, both in "Worley Soldier Vote Bill," Box 463, Clinton Anderson Papers, MD, LC; Robert L. Doughton to Josephus Daniels, February 1, 1944, in Robert L. Doughton Papers, SHC (first quote); Roland Young, *Congressional Politics in the Second World War* (New York: Columbia University Press, 1956), 86–87; *Congressional Record*, 78th Congress, 1st session, 1169–1230; "Roll-Call in House Defeats Vote Bill President Sought," *NYT*, February 4, 1944 (last quote).

54. Arthur Krock, "Vote Bill Prospects," *NYT*, February 9, 1944; "Compromise Near on Soldier Vote," *NYT*, February 22, 1944; Paul W. Ward, "Soldier Vote Held Up Again; Rankin Recants Approval of Worley Compromise," *Baltimore Sun*, February 23, 1944 (first quote); Drury, *A Senate Journal*, 82 (last quote).

55. "Compromise Reached on Service Vote," *Baltimore Sun*, March 1, 1944 (quote); "President's Aides for Ballot Veto," *NYT*, March 5, 1944; C. P. Trussell, "Soldier Voting Battle Has a Political Tinge," *NYT*, March 19, 1944; "42 of States Answer on Service Vote," *Hartford Courant*, March 20, 1944.

56. Drury, *A Senate Journal*, 104.

57. Philip Murray to My Dear Congressman, March 4, 1944, in "CIO and Affiliates—Miscellaneous Communications from," Box 4, Clare Hoffman Papers, BHL (first quote); *Congressional Record*, 78th Congress, 2nd session, 2639; Frank Burt Freidel, *Franklin D. Roosevelt: A Rendezvous with Destiny* (Boston, Mass.: Little Brown, 1990), 503 (second quote); Floyd M. Riddick, "The Second Session of the Seventy-Eighth Congress," *American Political Science Review* 39 (April 1945): 335; "Findings and Recommendations of the Special Committee on Service Voting," *American Political Science Review* 46 (June 1952): 512–523; Polenberg, *War and Society*, 197.

58. Drury, *A Senate Journal*, 152.

59. Connally to E. R. Strong, April 28, 1944, in "Negro: Supreme Court Decision," Box 126, Connally Papers, MD, LC (first quote); McNaughton to Johnson, April 14, 1944, in "April 1–15, 1944," Box 6, McNaughton Papers, HSTL (remaining quotes).

60. Russell to Mother, May 5, 1944, in "Family Parents, 1944," Box 42, Winder Series, Russell Papers, RBRL (first two quotes); C. P. Trussell, "Poll Tax Repealer Taken Up in Senate," *NYT*, May 10, 1944; C. P. Trussell, "Wagner Hits Talk of Poll Tax 'Deals,' Insists Fight Go On," *NYT*, May 13, 1944 (remaining quotes). Smith's words were sanitized once they appeared in the *Congressional Record*: "I have stood for the Constitution, for the rights of my State, and for white supremacy. Those who do not like it, by George, can lump it. Those who want to vote for me, I shall be glad to have do so. The remainder can go to heaven." See *Congressional Record*, 78th Congress, 2nd session, 4403.

61. David Brinkley, *Washington Goes to War* (New York: Alfred A. Knopf, 1988), 203; Connally, *My Name Is Tom Connally*, 172 (first quote); McNaughton to Johnson, May 12, 1944, in "May 1–15, 1944," Box 6, McNaughton Papers, HSTL (remaining quotes).

62. McNaughton to Johnson, May 15, 1944, in "May 1–15, 1944," Box 6, McNaughton Papers, HSTL (first three quotes); C. P. Trussell, "Senate Vote Bars Poll Tax Closure; Bill Is Set Aside," *NYT*, May 16, 1944; *Congressional Record*, 78th Congress, 2nd session, 4465–4470; *Detroit Free Press*, June 14, 1945, in Weekly Summary of Editorials about or Concerning Negroes from 25 Daily Newspapers throughout the Country, June 29, 1945, in Reel 12, Part 13, Series B, NAACP Papers, MD, LC; Rayburn to E. E. Cox, July 10, 1944, in "1944 Congressman Correspondence With," Box 3R309, Rayburn Papers, BCAH (last quote).

63. Taft to Harry E. Davis, August 4, 1944, in "Negro Issue, 1944–1945," Box 726, Taft Papers, MD, LC.

64. "Apology from 'Dago' Demanded by Bilbo," *NYT*, July 25, 1945 (first and last quotes); "Bilbo Refuses Apology to Brooklyn Woman for Addressing Her as 'My Dear Dago,'" *NYT*, July 24, 1945 (second, third, fifth, sixth, and seventh quotes); Adwin Wigfall Green, *The Man Bilbo* (Baton Rouge: Louisiana State University Press, 1963), 102 (fourth quote).

65. Theodore G. Bilbo to My Dear Colleague, September 4, 1945, in File 26, Box 140, Lister Hill Papers, WSHSC.

66. Fred H. M. Turner to Russell, July 28, 1945, in "File #6, FEPC Material 1945," Box 58, Subseries A, Series III, Russell Papers, RBRL; Capper to Mrs. Judd Spray, August 6, 1945, in "B (General)," Box 3, Arthur Capper Papers, KSHS.

67. McNaughton to Johnson, September 2, 1943, in "September 1943," Box 5, McNaughton Papers, HSTL.

7. "SAVING AMERICA FOR AMERICANS": THE FASCISTIC ORIGINS OF THE SECOND RED SCARE

1. Joe Starnes to Robert Stripling, June 29, 1942, in "Starnes, Joe, 1942," Box 2, House Special Committee on Un-American Activities, RG 233, RUSHR, NA (quote); Dennis Kay McDaniel, "Martin Dies of Un-American Activities: His Life and Times" (Ph.D. dissertation, University of Houston, 1988), 1–340; David Caute, *The Great Fear: The Anti-Communist Purge under Truman and Eisenhower* (New York: Simon and Schuster, 1978); John Joseph Gladchuk, "Reticent Reds: HUAC, Hollywood, and the Evolution of the Red Menace, 1935–1950" (Ph.D. dissertation, University of California, Riverside, 2006); Kai Bird and Martin J. Sherwin, *American Prometheus: The Triumph and Tragedy of J. Robert Oppenheimer* (New York: Vintage Books, 2006); Richard M. Fried, *Nightmare in Red: The McCarthy Era in Perspective* (New York: Oxford University Press, 1990). More recent work, albeit by neoconservative historians, has suggested the Soviet Union maintained an active espionage program in the United States during the 1930s and 1940s. See Harvey Klehr, John Earl Haynes, and Fridrikh Igorevich Firsov, *The Secret World of American Communism* (New Haven, Conn.: Yale University Press, 1995); John Earl Haynes, Harvey Klehr, and Alexander Vassiliev, *Spies: The Rise and Fall of the KGB in America* (New Haven, Conn.: Yale University Press, 2009). Francis MacDonnell, *Insidious Foes: The Axis Fifth Column and the American Home Front* (New York: Oxford University Press, 1995), hints at the anti–New Deal component of Dies's work, but he is not the focus of this book's analysis.

2. Thomas C. Reeves, *The Life and Times of Joe McCarthy: A Biography* (New York: Stein and Day, 1982), 657 (first two quotes); Kenneth O'Reilly, "A New Deal for the FBI: The Roosevelt Administration, Crime Control, and National Security," *Journal of American History* 69 (December 1982): 650; Kenneth Franklin Kurz, "Franklin Roosevelt and the Gospel of Fear: The Responses of the Roosevelt Administration to Charges of Subversion" (Ph.D. dissertation, University of California at Los Angeles, 1995), 1–2 (last quote). For a dismissive portrait of Dies, one that also notes the argument from the 1930s that there was no difference between anti-communism and fascism, see Richard Gid Powers, *Not without Honor: The History of American Anticommunism* (New York: Free Press, 1995), 129, 154. William Gellermann, *Martin Dies* (New York: John Day, 1944), 3 (third and fourth quotes).

3. Martin Dies, *Martin Dies' Story* (New York: Bookmailer, 1963), 11 (first quote), 17 (second quote), 140; Ellen Schrecker, *Many Are the Crimes: McCarthyism in America* (Boston, Mass.: Little, Brown, 1998), 91; Frank McNaughton to David Hulburd, February 13, 1942, in "February 1942," Box 2, Frank McNaughton Papers, HSTL. Landon R. Y. Storrs in *The Second Red Scare and the Unmaking of the New Deal Left* (Princeton, N.J.: Princeton University Press, 2012), argues that the architects of the second red scare attacked New Deal liberalism not only because of the welfare state but also because of left-feminism.

4. McNaughton to Hulburd, February 13, 1942, in "February 1942," Box 2, McNaughton Papers, HSTL (quotes); Martin Dies to Franklin D. Roosevelt, September 6, 1941, OF 4403 Office of Price Administration, September–December 1941, Box 1, FDRL; Dies speech [1941], "Communism—Opponents of, House Un–American Activities Committee, 1941," Box 21, Westbrook Pegler Papers, HHPL.

5. Stripling to Dies, April 23, 1941, in "Dies, Martin, 1941," Box 1, House Special Committee on Un–American Activities, RG 233, RUSHR, NA; Guenter Lewy, *The Cause That Failed: Communism in American Political Life* (New York: Oxford University Press, 1990), 179.

6. Robert Griffith, *The Politics of Fear: Joseph R. McCarthy and the Senate* (Lexington: University Press of Kentucky, 1970), 32–33 (first five quotes); Caute, *The Great Fear*, 100–101 (sixth and seventh quotes); Arthur Vandenberg to John Milliken, January 8, 1942, in Roll 3, Arthur Vandenberg Papers on Microfilm, BHL; David Oshinsky, *A Conspiracy So Immense: The World of Joe McCarthy* (New York: Free Press, 1983), 93; John E. Rankin Speech, August 24, 1942, in 77th Congress, House of Representatives 77A-F39.1, Box 335, House Committee on World War Veterans Legislation, RG 233, RUSHR, NA (last quote).

7. O'Reilly, "A New Deal for the FBI," 656 (quotes); Clyde R. Miller, "Foreign Efforts to Increase Disunity," *Annals of the American Academy of Political and Social Science* 223 (September 1942): 173–181.

8. MacDonnell, *Insidious Foes*, 49–71; McDaniel, "Martin Dies of Un-American Activities," 264–265, 352–356, 362 (first quote); McNaughton to Hulburd, February 13, 1942, in "February 1942," Box 2, McNaughton Papers, HSTL (second and third quotes); D. A. Saunders, "The Dies Committee: First Phase," *Public Opinion Quarterly* 3 (April 1939): 224, 225 (fourth quote); Jay Franklin, "We, the People: Dies Probe Itself Treads on Field of Un-Americanism," *Washington Star*, August 31, 1938, in "Newspaper Clippings," Senate 79A-F11, Box 122, Senate Committee on Immigration, RG 46, RUSS, NA (fifth quote); *Congressional Record*, 78th Congress, 1st session, A2763; Dies, *Martin Dies' Story*, 59–61 (sixth quote), 77 (seventh quote), 107–108, 140; *Congressional Record*, 75th Congress, 2nd session, 7567–7586.

9. Jerold Simmons, *Operation Abolition: The Campaign to Abolish the House Un-American Activities Committee, 1938–1975* (New York and London: Garland Publishing, 1986), 2–5; Fried, *Nightmare in Red*, 47–49; Schrecker, *Many are the Crimes*, 108–109; Jerry Voorhis, *Confessions of a Congressman* (Garden City, N.Y.: Doubleday, 1947), 209 (quotes). See Dies to Dear Colleague, November 17, 1944, in "Legislation, Dies Committee, 1943–1944," Box 9, Brent Spence Papers, UKL, for an accounting of the committee's activities written from Dies's perspective.

10. MacDonnell, *Insidious Foes*, 174–177 (first two quotes); Memorandum, December 9, 1940, and Memorandum, November 25, 1940 (third quote), both in Roll 1, Microfilm Edition of the FBI File on the House Committee on Un–American Activities.

11. Kurz, "Franklin Roosevelt and the Gospel of Fear," 70–86; Nancy Lynn Lopez, "'Allowing Fears to Overwhelm Us': A Re-examination of the House Special Committee on Un-American Activities, 1938–1944" (Ph.D. dissertation, Rice University, 2002), 665, 669–670; O'Reilly, "A New Deal for the FBI," 651; The President's Conference with

Representative Martin Dies, November 29, 1940, PPF 3458, FDRL (first three quotes); Washington News Service, November 29, 1940, in Roll 1, Microfilm Edition of the FBI File on the House Committee on Un-American Activities; Dies to Roosevelt, December 4, 1940, OF 320 Dies Committee, 1940–1941, Box 4, FDRL (fourth quote); Dies, *Martin Dies' Story*, 144–146 (remaining quotes).

12. Powers, *Not without Honor*, 125; Oshinsky, *A Conspiracy So Immense*, 92 (quote).

13. Dies, *Martin Dies' Story*, 62; Robert E. Stripling, *The Red Plot against America* (Drexel Hill, Pa.: Bell, 1949), 22–23; Frank J. Donner, *The Un-Americans* (New York: Ballantine Books, 1961), 14; Oshinsky, *A Conspiracy So Immense*, 118 (quote); Kenneth O'Reilly and Athan G. Theoharis, "The FBI, the Congress, and McCarthyism," in *Beyond the Hiss Case: The FBI, Congress, and the Cold War*, Athan G. Theoharis, ed. (Philadelphia: Temple University Press, 1982), 375, 404 n. 34; J. B. Matthews to Pegler, April 24, 1944, "Commission—Opponents of House Un-American Activities Committee, 1942–1968 and undated," Box 21, Pegler Papers, HHPL; Powers, *Not without Honor*, 25–26; Caute, *The Great Fear*, 101–102; Harold M. Nelson, *Libel: In News of Congressional Investigating Committees* (Minneapolis: University of Minnesota Press, 1961), 83.

14. Schrecker, *Many Are the Crimes*, 109–110 (quote); James Rowe Jr. to S. T. Early, January 4, 1940, OF 320, Dies Committee, 1940–1941, Box 4, FDRL; Lopez, "'Allowing Fears to Overwhelm Us,'" 683–684; Robert E. Cushman, "Civil Liberties," *American Political Science Review* 37 (February 1943): 49–56; "Dies Charges 1,124 Federal Aids Are Reds," *New York Herald Tribune* [October 19, 1941], in "Communism—HUAC, 1941," Box 21, in Pegler Papers, HHPL; Griffith, *The Politics of Fear*, 32; Allen Weinstein, *Perjury: The Hiss-Chambers Case* (New York: Random House, 1997); R. Bruce Craig, *Treasonable Doubt: The Harry Dexter White Spy Case* (Lawrence: University Press of Kansas, 2004).

15. Kurz, "Franklin Roosevelt and the Gospel of Fear," 87–117, 148–151; Federal Bureau of Investigation Report, August 22, 1942, in "Dies Committee," Box 859, Clinton Anderson Papers, MD, LC; Dies, *Martin Dies' Story*, 75; Voorhis, *Confessions of a Congressman*, 224 (quote); Cushman, "Civil Liberties," 51–52; To the Senate and House of Representatives of the United States of America in Congress Assembled, November 20, 1942, in "Reports and Correspondence," 77th Congress, Senate 77A-F2, Box 36, Senate Committee on Appropriations, RG 46, RUSS, NA; O'Reilly, "A New Deal for the FBI," 654.

16. Lopez, "'Allowing Fears to Overwhelm Us,'" 324–484, 674, 706, 712–714; McNaughton to Hulburd, February 13, 1942, in "February 1942," Box 2, McNaughton Papers, HSTL; Margaret A. Blanchard, *Revolutionary Sparks: Freedom of Expression in Modern America* (New York: Oxford University Press, 1992), 164.

17. Memorandum for Mr. Early, January 9 [1940], OF 320 Dies Committee, 1940–1941, Box 4, FDRL (first quote); Untitled, undated typed note in "Dies, Martin, 1941," Box 1, House Special Committee on Un-American Activities, RG 233, RUSHR, NA (second and third quotes); Adolph Sabath to Edwin M. Watson, January 16, 1940, and Roosevelt to Pa, January 22, 1940 (last quote), both in OF 320 Dies Committee, 1940–1941, Box 4, FDRL.

18. McNaughton to Hulburd, February 13, 1942, in "February 1942," Box 2, McNaughton Papers, HSTL (quotes); James F. Byrnes to Roosevelt [January 1942], OF 133 Immigration, Box 1, FDRL.

19. U.S. Congress, House of Representatives, Special Committee on Un-American Activities, *Investigation of Un-American Propaganda Activities in the United States,* 76th Congress, 3rd session, 1940, 7207–7208, 7216–7219, 7332–7333.

20. Thomas to Stripling, December 26, 1942 (quotes), and Thomas to Stripling, December 29, 1942, both in "Thomas, J. Parnell, 1942," Box 3, House Special Committee on Un-American Activities, RG 233, RUSHR, NA. Nudism proved something of a fad among certain liberal intellectuals during this period.

21. "American Institute of Public Opinion—Surveys, 1938–1939," *Public Opinion Quarterly* 3 (October 1939): 595; "Gallup and Fortune Polls," *Public Opinion Quarterly* 4 (June 1940): 349; Saunders, "The Dies Committee," 224; Note for Pegler from Dies attached to Dies to Franklin D. Roosevelt, September 6, 1941, in "Communism—HUAC, 1941," Box 21, in Pegler Papers, HHPL; McDaniel, "Martin Dies of Un-American Activities," 383.

22. Simmons, *Operation Abolition,* 28 (first quote), 33; Roosevelt to Vito Marcantonio, February 24, 1942, OF 320 Dies Committee, 1942–1944, Box 4, FDRL (last quote).

23. Donner, *The Un-Americans,* 12; Sol Bloom to Selma Arnold, January 29, 1943, in HR78A-F15.1, Box 266, House Committee on Foreign Affairs, RG 233, RUSHR, NA; Robert L. Doughton to Clarence Cannon, February 13, 1942, Robert L. Doughton Papers, SHC.

24. *Congressional Record,* 78th Congress, 1st Session, 474–486 (first four quotes); Frederick L. Schuman, "'Bill of Attainder' in the Seventy-Eighth Congress," *American Political Science Review* 37 (October 1943): 819; Brent Spence to B. D. Gaskin, February 12, 1943, in "Legislation, Dies Committee, 1943–1944," Box 9, Spence Papers, UKL (fifth and sixth quotes); Fred E. Busbey to Martin Dies, February 3, 1943, in "Busbey, Hon. Fred E.," Box 1, House Special Committee on Un-American Activities, RG 233, RUSHR, NA (last two quotes).

25. Schuman, "'Bill of Attainder,'" 820–821; Arthur W. Macmahon, "Congressional Oversight of Administration: The Power of the Purse, I," *Political Science Quarterly* 58 (June 1943): 168–169; Henry N. Dorris, "House Votes, 302–94, for Dies Extension," *NYT,* February 11, 1943.

26. Kurz, "Franklin Roosevelt and the Gospel of Fear," 194–197.

27. Arthur Spingarn to John McCormack and Joseph W. Martin Jr., February 8, 1943, in "NAACP," Box 40, Harold H. Burton Papers, MD, LC.

28. Executive Session—Confidential, Alleged Subversive Activities of Employees of Executive Departments and Agencies of the Government, Friday, April 2, 1943, House of Representatives, Special Subcommittee on Subversive Activities of the Committee on Appropriations, 2–3 (first two quotes), and Executive Session—Confidential, Alleged Subversive Activities of Employees of Executive Departments and Agencies of the Government, Friday, May 28, 1943, House of Representatives, Special Subcommittee on Subversive Activities of the Committee on Appropriations, 900 (last quote), both in HR 78A-F3.2, Box 208, House Committee on Appropriations, RG 233, RUSHR, NA; O'Reilly, "A New Deal for the FBI," 656.

29. *Congressional Record,* 78th Congress, 1st session, A2763; Schuman, "'Bill of Attainder,'" 820–823.

30. *Congressional Record,* 78th Congress, 1st session, A2763 (first quote); Schuman, "'Bill

of Attainder,'" 820–823; Francis Biddle, "Subversives in Government," *Annals of the American Academy of Political and Social Science* 300 (July 1955): 51–61 (last quote, 54).

31. Schuman, "'Bill of Attainder,'" 820–823.

32. Joseph A. Facci to Cannon, February 9, 1943, in HR 78A-F3.2, Box 210, House Committee on Appropriations, RG 233, RUSHR, NA.

33. Irving E. Bender to James L. Fly, February 17, 1942, in "Letters and Telegrams re Goodwin Watson, February 1942," 77th Congress, Senate 77A-F2, Box 42, Senate Committee on Appropriations, RG 46, RUSS, NA (first quote); "Watson Denounces Report," *NYT*, April 22, 1943; Francis D. Culkin to John H. Kerr, February 11, 1943 (second quote), and A. Philip Randolph to Kerr, March 22, 1943 (last two quotes), both in HR 78A-F3.2, Box 209, House Committee on Appropriations, RG 233, RUSHR, NA.

34. Executive Session—Confidential, Alleged Subversive Activities of Employees of Executive Departments and Agencies of the Government, Friday, April 2, 1943, House of Representatives, Special Subcommittee on Subversive Activities of the Committee on Appropriations, 13–17, in HR 78A-F3.2, Box 208, House Committee on Appropriations, RG 233, RUSHR, NA.

35. *Congressional Record,* 78th Congress, 1st session, 3066–3067.

36. *Congressional Record,* 78th Congress, 1st session, 3067, 3068, 3069–3070, 3089.

37. Harold Ickes to Kerr, April 15, 1943, in HR 78A-F3.2, Box 210, House Committee on Appropriations, RG 233, RUSHR, NA.

38. Schuman, "'Bill of Attainder,'" 823 n. 5; Henry G. Alsberg to Kerr, April 22, 1943, in HR 78A-F3.2, Box 209, House Committee on Appropriations, RG 233, RUSHR, NA.

39. Executive Session—Confidential, Alleged Subversive Activities of Employees of Executive Departments and Agencies of the Government, Thursday, May 6, 1943, House of Representatives, Special Subcommittee on Subversive Activities of the Committee on Appropriations, 699, in HR 78A-F3.2, Box 208, House Committee on Appropriations, RG 233, RUSHR, NA.

40. Ibid., 779.

41. McDaniel, "Martin Dies of Un-American Activities," 469–471 (first quote); Executive Session—Confidential, Alleged Subversive Activities of Employees of Executive Departments and Agencies of the Government, Friday, May 28, 1943, House of Representatives, Special Subcommittee on Subversive Activities of the Committee on Appropriations, 906–920, 921–929, 933, 934, 947 (second and third quotes) in HR 78A-F3.2, Box 208, House Committee on Appropriations, RG 233, RUSHR, NA; Clinton P. Anderson to J. G. Luhrsen, June 19, 1943, in "Kerr Committee on Subversive Activities," Box 856, Anderson Papers, MD, LC (last quote).

42. *Congressional Record,* 78th Congress, 1st session, 4546 (first three quotes); Schuman, "'Bill of Attainder,'" 825–826; Macmahon, "Congressional Oversight of Administration," 168 (last quote); Lewy, *The Cause that Failed,* 179, suggests Lovett was a fellow traveler, but makes no mention of Watson or Dodd.

43. *Congressional Record,* 78th Congress, 1st session, 4553–4555; Schuman, "'Bill of Attainder,'" 828 (quote).

44. *Congressional Record,* 78th Congress, 1st session, 4582, 4583 (quotes), 4592, 4596, 4605.

45. Schuman, "'Bill of Attainder,'" 823–825; "Kerr Holds Fast on Loyalty Study," *NYT,* September 25, 1943; "Bill of Attainder," *NYT,* May 20, 1943 (first quote); "Ickes Denounces Lovett Removal," *NYT,* May 16, 1943 (last quote).

46. "Votes to Restore Pay for Lovett," *NYT,* May 26, 1943; Kenneth McKellar to Kerr, May 31, 1943, in HR 78A-F3.2, Box 217, House Committee on Appropriations, RG 233, RUSHR, NA (quotes); Schuman, "'Bill of Attainder,'" 823–825; "Kerr Holds Fast on Loyalty Study," *NYT,* September 25, 1943.

47. *Congressional Record,* 78th Congress, 1st session, A2763–A2764.

48. *Congressional Record,* 78th Congress, 1st session, 5920–5921.

49. Schuman, "'Bill of Attainder,'" 823–825; "Kerr Holds Fast on Loyalty Study," *NYT,* September 25, 1943.

50. Fred E. Busbey to Martin Dies, January 24, 1944, and Stripling to Busbey, July 18, 1944, both in "Busbey, Cong. Fred E.," Box 1, and J. Parnell Thomas to Ross Rizley, October 20, 1944, in "Thomas, J. Parnell, 1944," Box 3, all in House Special Committee on Un-American Activities, RG 233, RUSHR, NA; McNaughton to Bill Johnson, January 27, 1944, in "January–March 1944," Box 6, McNaughton Papers, HSTL (quotes); Dies, *Martin Dies' Story,* 82.

51. Lopez, "'Allowing Fears to Overwhelm Us,'" 696; Dies, *Martin Dies' Story,* 83 (first quote); McNaughton to Johnson, May 12, 1944, in "May 1–15, 1944," Box 6, McNaughton Papers, HSTL (remaining quotes); Martin Dies, *The Trojan Horse in America* (New York: Dodd, Mead, 1940); McDaniel, "Martin Dies of Un-American Activities," 406, 423, 425–441. Politicians typically netted between $300 and $500 per speech in the late 1930s and early 1940s. See Nancy Beck Young, *Wright Patman: Populism, Liberalism, and the American Dream* (Dallas: Southern Methodist University Press, 2000), 83.

52. Statement of Honorable J. Parnell Thomas, Ranking Republican Member of the Dies Committee, May 14, 1944, in "Thomas, J. Parnell, 1944," Box 3, House Special Committee on Un-American Activities, RG 233, RUSHR, NA.

53. Untitled, undated statement by Martin Dies, in "Dies, Chairman Martin, 1944," Box 1, House Special Committee on Un-American Activities, RG 233, RUSHR, NA.

54. McNaughton to Johnson, June 6, 1944, in "June 1–8, 1944," Box 6, McNaughton Papers, HSTL.

55. McNaughton to Johnson, April 21, 1944, in "April 16–30, 1944," Box 6, McNaughton Papers, HSTL (first two quotes); H. C. Nixon, "Politics of the Hills," *Journal of Politics* 2 (May 1946): 123–133; Donner, *The Un-Americans,* 15–19; McNaughton to Eleanor Welch, January 4, 1945, in "January 1–15, 1945," Box 8, McNaughton Papers, HSTL (third quote).

56. Dies to Colleague, November 17, 1944, in "Committee, 1942–1968 and undated," Box 21, Pegler Papers, HHPL; *Congressional Record,* 79th Congress, 1st session, 11–15 (quote).

57. McNaughton to A. F. Monroe, January 5, 1945, in "January 1–15, 1944," Box 8, McNaughton Papers, HSTL.

58. McNaughton to Johnson, September 2, 1943, in "September 1943," Box 5,

McNaughton Papers, HSTL; Dies to Pegler, April 21, 1945, in "Communists—Opposition of, House Un-American Activities Committee, 1942–1968 and undated," Box 21, Pegler Papers, HHPL (first quote); Donner, *The Un-Americans,* 8 (last quote).

EPILOGUE: THE WORLD THE WAR MADE

1. Frank McNaughton to Stephen Laird, August 5, 1944, in "July–August 1–20, 1944," Box 7, Frank McNaughton Papers, HSTL (first two quotes); Sam Rayburn to Harry L. Seay, February 19, 1945, in *"Speak Mr. Speaker"* (Bonham, Tex.: Sam Rayburn Foundation, 1978), 119 (third quote); George H. Gallup, *The Gallup Poll, Public Opinion, 1935–1971,* vol. 1, *1935–1948* (New York: Random House, 1972), 503; Robert Higgs, "From Central Planning to the Market: The American Transition, 1945–1947," *Journal of Economic History* 59 (September 1999): 600–623; William L. O'Neill, *A Democracy at War: America's Fight at Home and Abroad in World War II* (New York: Free Press, 1993), 393; Rayburn to Warren Andrews, June 6, 1944, in "1944 General Miscellaneous, A–F," Box 3R310, Sam Rayburn Papers, BCAH (last quote).

2. For an alternative view that suggests the war years were ones of continuity not change, see John W. Jeffries, *Wartime America: The World War II Home Front* (Chicago: Ivan R. Dee, 1996), 193–198.

3. McNaughton to Bill Johnson, September 2, 1943, in "September 1943," Box 5, McNaughton Papers, HSTL.

4. David R. B. Ross, *Preparing for Ulysses: Politics and Veterans during World War II* (New York: Columbia University Press, 1969), 91 (quote). For a thoughtful analysis of the long-privileged position of veterans in the U.S. welfare state, see Theda Skocpol, *Protecting Soldiers and Mothers: The Political Origins of Social Policy in the United States* (Cambridge, Mass.: Belknap Press of Harvard University Press, 1992). For more on the GI Bill see Michael J. Bennett, *When Dreams Came True: The GI Bill and the Making of Modern America* (McLean, Va.: Brassey's Publishing, 1996); Margot Canaday, "Building a Straight State: Sexuality and Social Citizenship under the 1944 G.I. Bill," *Journal of American History* 90 (December 2003): 935–957; Kathleen J. Frydl, *The GI Bill* (New York: Cambridge University Press, 2009); Suzanne Mettler, "The Creation of the G.I. Bill of Rights of 1944: Melding Social and Participatory Citizenship Ideals," *Journal of Policy History* 17 (2005): 345–374.

5. Address of Robert A. Taft before the Alabama Bar Association at Birmingham, Saturday, July 10, 1943, in "Mackinac Conference—Domestic," Box 158, Robert A. Taft Papers, MD, LC.

6. Robert L. Doughton to Gordon Canfield, July 15, 1941, in Robert L. Doughton Papers, SCH; Anthony J. Badger, *The New Deal: The Depression Years, 1933–1940* (New York: Hill and Wang, 1989), 227–235; McNaughton to David Hulburd, December 18, 1941, in "December 16–31, 1941," Box 2, McNaughton Papers, HSTL; *Congressional Record,* 78th Congress, 2nd Session, 4513; Lee E. Cooper, "New Law Gives Draftee the Right to Cancel Lease on Month's Notice," *NYT,* October 18, 1942.

7. "How Adequate Is the G.I. Bill of Rights?" *American Forum of the Air,* January 2, 1945,

"How Adequate Is the GI Bill of Rights," Box 257, Theodore Granik Papers, MD, LC; "The GI Bill of Rights," *The New Republic* 111 (October 23, 1944): 512; Skocpol, *Protecting Soldiers and Mothers*. For more on World War I veterans' benefits, see McNaughton to Johnson, January 8, 1944, in "January–March, 1944," Box 6, McNaughton Papers, HSTL (quote); *Congressional Record*, 78th Congress, 2nd Session, 4513; See for example, Roger Daniels, *The Bonus March: An Episode of the Great Depression* (Westport, Conn.: Greenwood Publishing, 1971); Jennifer D. Keene, *Doughboys, the Great War, and the Remaking of America* (Baltimore, Md.: Johns Hopkins University Press, 2001); Donald J. Lisio, *The President and Protest: Hoover, Conspiracy, and the Bonus Riot* (Columbia: University of Missouri Press, 1974); Stephen R. Ortiz, "Rethinking the Bonus March: Federal Bonus Policy, the Veterans of Foreign Wars, and the Origins of a Protest Movement," *Journal of Policy History* 18 (2006): 275–303; William Pencak, *For God and Country: The American Legion, 1919–1941* (Boston: Northeastern University Press, 1989); Nancy Beck Young, *Wright Patman: Politics, Liberalism, and the American Dream* (Dallas, Tex.: Southern Methodist University Press, 2000).

8. Henry L. Stimson to Albert J. Engel, January 11, 1941, in "Correspondence, 1941," Box 1, Albert J. Engel Papers, BHL; D. B. Hardeman and Donald C. Bacon, *Rayburn: A Biography* (Austin: Texas Monthly Press, 1987), 289–291; Rayburn interview by Bill Lawrence, July 16, 1961, in "Rayburn Interview, July 16, 1961, ABC Radio, 'Issues and Answers,'" Box 3U102, Rayburn Papers, BCAH (first quote); Joe Martin, as told to Robert J. Donovan, *My First Fifty Years in Politics* (New York: McGraw-Hill Book Company, 1960), 100–101 (second quote); Robert P. Patterson to Engel, November 5, 1943, in "Correspondence 1943," and Engel to Stimson, February 23, 1945, in "Correspondence, 1945," both Box 1, Engel Papers, BHL. For more information on funding the Manhattan Project, see Elmer Thomas, *Forty Years a Legislator*, edited by Richard Lowitt and Carolyn G. Hanneman (Norman: University of Oklahoma Press, 2007), 127, 133–135.

9. Julian Zelizer, *On Capitol Hill: The Struggle to Reform Congress and Its Consequences, 1948–2000* (New York: Cambridge University Press, 2004), 29–31.

10. *Building America*, vol. 10, no. 2, in "Congress—Maloney Committee, 1942–1945," Box 515, Taft Papers, MD, LC (quotes); Allen Drury, *A Senate Journal, 1943–1945* (New York: McGraw-Hill, 1963), 206.

11. Robert M. La Follette Jr. and Mike Monroney to Taft, March 5, 1945, Taft to Ray C. Sutliff, August 1, 1942, James F. Byrnes, "Streamlining Congress," all in "Congress—Maloney Committee, 1942–1945," Box 515, Taft Papers, MD, LC; Alexander Wiley to Harry F. Byrd, in "Legislation," 79th Congress, Senate 79A-F27, Box 163, Senate Committee on Rules Papers, RG 46, RUSS, NA.

12. Zelizer, *On Capitol Hill*, 31; Robert C. Byrd, ed., *The Senate, 1789–1989, Addresses on the History of the United States Senate*, vol. 1 (Washington, D.C.: U.S. Government Printing Office, 1988), 537–538 (first quote); *Building America*, vol. 10, No. 2, in "Congress—Maloney Committee, 1942–1945," Box 515, Taft Papers, MD, LC (second quote).

13. McNaughton to Hulburd, February 2, 1946, in "February 1946," Box 11, McNaughton Papers, HSTL (quotes); Stephen K. Bailey, *Congress Makes a Law: The Story behind the Employment Act of 1946* (New York: Vintage Books, 1964).

14. Lewis L. Gould and Nancy Beck Young, "The Speaker and the Presidents: Sam Rayburn, the White House, and the Legislative Process, 1941–1961," in *Masters of the House: Congressional Leaders over Two Centuries,* Roger H. Davidson, Susan Webb Hammond, and Raymond W. Smock, eds. (Boulder, Colo.: Westview Press, 1998), 191.

15. Susan M. Hartmann, *Truman and the 80th Congress* (Columbia: University of Missouri Press, 1971), 79–90; R. Alton Lee, *Truman and Taft-Hartley: A Question of Mandate* (Lexington: University of Kentucky Press, 1966); U.S. Congress, House of Representatives, Committee on Education and Labor, *Labor Management Relations Act, 1947,* House Report 245 to accompany H.R. 3020, 80th Congress, 1st session, 3–5, 64–65.

16. Hartmann, *Truman and the 80th Congress,* 72–78, 186–210; James T. Patterson, *Mr. Republican: A Biography of Robert A. Taft* (Boston: Houghton Mifflin, 1971), 323.

17. McNaughton to Bob Hagy, November 12, 1948, in "November 1948," and Jack Beal and McNaughton to Girvin for Fitzpatrick, October 27, 1948, in "October 1948," both in Box 16, McNaughton Papers, HSTL.

18. McNaughton and Beal to Don Bermingham, March 18, 1949, in "March 17–31, 1949," Box 17, McNaughton Papers, HSTL; Mary L. Dudziak, *Cold War Civil Rights: Race and the Image of American Democracy* (Princeton, N.J.: Princeton University Press, 2000), 275–277; Kevin McMahon, *Reconsidering Roosevelt on Race: How the Presidency Paved the Road to Brown* (Chicago: University of Chicago Press, 2004), 177–202; Donald R. McCoy, *Quest and Response: Minority Rights and the Truman Administration* (Lawrence: University Press of Kansas, 1973); William C. Berman, *The Politics of Civil Rights in the Truman Administration* (Columbus: Ohio State University Press, 1970).

19. Robert H. Ferrell, *Harry S Truman: A Life* (Columbia: University of Missouri Press, 1994), 285–291; Monte M. Poen, *Harry S Truman versus the Medical Lobby: The Genesis of Medicare* (Columbia: University of Missouri Press, 1979); Philip J. Funigiello, *Chronic Politics: Health Care Security from FDR to George W. Bush* (Lawrence: University Press of Kansas, 2005), 62–87; Colin Gordon, *Dead on Arrival: The Politics of Health Care in Twentieth-Century America* (Princeton, N.J.: Princeton University Press, 2003), 95 (quote).

20. McNaughton to Bermingham, August 26, 1949, in "August 16–31, 1949," McNaughton to Bermingham, October 20, 1949 (first quote), McNaughton to Bermingham, October 22, 1949 (second quote), McNaughton to Bermingham, October 19, 1949 (last quote) all in "October 1949," Box 19, McNaughton to Bermingham, January 28, 1949, in "January 16–31, 1949," Box 17, all in McNaughton Papers, HSTL.

21. Stephen Ambrose, *Eisenhower: The President* (New York: Simon and Schuster, 1984), 118 (quote); Geoffrey Kabaservice, *Rule and Ruin: The Downfall of Moderation and the Destruction of the Republican Party, from Eisenhower to the Tea Party* (New York: Oxford University Press, 2012), 10–18.

22. Rayburn Speech, September 10, 1954, in "Rayburn, Sam, correspondence, 1954–1961," Box 115, Post Presidential Files, Harry S Truman Papers, HSTL (first quote); Lyndon Johnson and Rayburn to Dwight D. Eisenhower, October 9, 1954, in "Speech of October 8, 1954," Box 638, White House Central Files—President's Personal Files, Dwight D. Eisenhower Library, Abilene, Kansas (remaining quotes).

23. Helen Thomas, *Thanks for the Memories, Mr. President: Wit and Wisdom from the Front Row at the White House* (New York: Scribner, 2002), 137 (first quote); Robert Dallek, *Lone Star Rising: Lyndon Johnson and His Times, 1908–1960* (New York: Oxford University Press, 1991), 480–482 (last quote).

24. Dallek, *Lone Star Rising,* 493–496, 510, 517–527 (first quote on 526); Memorandum, n.d., in "Reedy: Memos, Fall 1956," Box 419, Lyndon B. Johnson Senate Papers, LBJL (second quote).

25. Zelizer, *On Capitol Hill,* 53; Meeting of Republican Leaders, June 4, 1957, in "L-39 (3), June 4, 1957," Box 4, Legislative Meetings Series, Records of the Office of the Staff Secretary, Eisenhower Library.

26. Gould and Young, "The Speaker and the Presidents," 208–213; "It's Up to Mr. Sam," *The New Republic* 142 (February 8, 1960): 3–4 (quote).

27. Richard Bolling, *House Out of Order* (New York: Dutton, 1966), 208–212; Richard Bolling Oral History, January 26, 1980, Box 3U99, Rayburn Papers, BCAH; Gould and Young, "The Speaker and the Presidents," 208–213; James N. Giglio, *The Presidency of John F. Kennedy* (Lawrence: University Press of Kansas, 1991), 37; Tom Wicker, *JFK and LBJ: The Influence of Personality upon Politics* (Chicago: Ivan R. Dee, 1991), 30–39.

28. Rayburn to Clarence Cannon, December 2, 1960, Cannon to Rayburn, December 8, 1960, both in "Congressmen, Miscellaneous," Box 3U44, Rayburn to Clifford Davis, December 7, 1960, in "Congressmen, Miscellaneous," Box 3U45, all in Rayburn Papers, BCAH; *NYT,* November 13, 1960; Hardeman and Bacon, *Rayburn,* 451 (second quote), 454, 456 (first quote), 459 (last quote); *NYT,* December 20, 1960, January 9, 1961, January 12, 1961, January 13, 1961, January 18, 1961, January 19, 1961, January 25, 1961, January 26, 1961, January 29, 1961, February 1, 1961, February 2, 1961; Bolling, *House Out of Order,* 213; Transcript, Lawrence O'Brien Oral History Interview #1, September 18, 1985, by Michael L. Gillette, 39–43; Transcript, Richard Bolling Oral History, February 27, 1969, by Paige Mulhollan, 4, 17, both in LBJL; Carl Albert to Philip J. Philbin, January 23, 1961, Albert to Jim Wright, January 23, 1961, Albert to Thaddeus J. Dulsk, January 23, 1961, Albert to William A. Burrett, January 24, 1961, Albert to Robert Nix, January 24, 1961, and Whip Polls, all in Folder 80, Box 58, "Anticipated Democratic Votes against Rules Change" [January 25, 1961], in Folder 76, Box 53, all in Legislative Series, Carl Albert Papers, Carl Albert Congressional Research and Studies Center Congressional Archives, University of Oklahoma; Neil MacNeil, *Forge of Democracy: The House of Representatives* (New York: David McKay, 1963), 429, 438; *Congressional Record,* 87th Congress, 1st session, 1580.

29. Bolling Oral History, February 27, 1969, p. 27, LBJL; Hardeman and Bacon, *Rayburn,* 451 (first quote); Bolling, *House Out of Order,* 220 (second quote); Tip O'Neill with William Novak, *Man of the House: The Life and Political Memoirs of Speaker Tip O'Neill* (New York: Random House, 1987), 138; Giglio, *The Presidency of John F. Kennedy,* 97–187, 255–275.

30. Randall Woods, *LBJ: Architect of American Ambition* (New York: Free Press, 2006), 434–436.

31. Lyndon B. Johnson, *The Vantage Point: Perspectives of the Presidency, 1963–1969*

(New York: Holt, Rinehart and Winston, 1971), 157 (quote); G. Calvin Mackenzie and Robert Weisbrot, *The Liberal Hour: Washington and the Politics of Change in the 1960s* (New York: Penguin Books, 2009), 160–161.

32. Don Oberdorfer, *Senator Mansfield: The Extraordinary Life of a Great American Statesman and Diplomat* (Washington, D.C.: Smithsonian Books, 2003), 226–234 (first quote); Johnson, *The Vantage Point*, 159 (remaining quotes).

33. Telephone conversation, Lyndon B. Johnson and Hubert H. Humphrey, May 2, 1964, in Michael Beschloss, ed., *Taking Charge: The Johnson White House Tapes, 1963–1964* (New York: Simon and Schuster, 1997), 340.

34. Johnson, *The Vantage Point*, 158; Byron C. Hulsey, *Everett Dirksen and His Presidents: How a Senate Giant Shaped American Politics* (Lawrence: University Press of Kansas, 2000), 192–195 (first two quotes); Gilbert C. Fite, *Richard B. Russell, Jr.: Senator from Georgia* (Chapel Hill: University of North Carolina Press, 1991), 409–414 (remaining quotes).

35. J. J. Pickle and Peggy Pickle, *Jake* (Austin: University of Texas Press, 1997), 92–95; Tracy Roof, *American Labor, Congress, and the Welfare State, 1935–2010* (Baltimore: Johns Hopkins University Press, 2011), 83–146.

36. Robert Dallek, *Flawed Giant: Lyndon Johnson and His Times, 1961–1973* (New York: Oxford University Press, 1998), 211–221, 335–339.

37. Ibid., 400–425, 438–442, 513–536, 550–564; Zelizer, *On Capitol Hill*, 72–73.

38. Zelizer, *On Capitol Hill*, 5–8; Melvin Small, *The Presidency of Richard Nixon* (Lawrence: University Press of Kansas, 1999), 185–194; Joan Hoff, *Nixon Reconsidered* (New York: Basic Books, 1994), 17–49, 115–144; Irwin F. Gellman, *The Contender, Richard Nixon: The Congress Years, 1946–1952* (New York: Free Press, 1999); Rick Perlstein, *Nixonland: The Rise of a President and the Fracturing of America* (New York: Scribner, 2008); David Greenberg, *Nixon's Shadow: The History of an Image* (New York: W. W. Norton, 2003).

39. Kabaservice, *Rule and Ruin*, 32–251; Doug Rossinow, *Visions of Progress: The Left-Liberal Tradition in America* (Philadelphia: University of Pennsylvania Press, 2008), 233–260; Michael Kazin, *American Dreamers: How the Left Changed a Nation* (New York: Alfred A. Knopf, 2011), 209–251.

40. Young, *Wright Patman*, 288–301; Zelizer, *On Capitol Hill*, 156–176; John Jacobs, *A Rage for Justice: The Passion and Politics of Phillip Burton* (Berkeley: University of California Press, 1995), 248–279; Nelson W. Polsby, *How Congress Evolves: Social Bases of Institutional Change* (New York: Oxford University Press, 2004), 3–108.

41. Zelizer, *On Capitol Hill*, 1–2.

42. Michael S. Sherry, *In the Shadow of War: The United States since the 1930s* (New Haven, Conn.: Yale University Press, 1995).

Essay on Sources

Writing about Congress is challenging for institutional and archival reasons. Congress is composed of two separate institutions, and though there is a clear leadership structure in each chamber, centers of power shift from issue to issue. Compared with presidential topics, there is not one centralized archive containing the bulk of the primary material needed to write a book. Committee records for the various standing, special, and select congressional committees are available in Washington, D.C., at the Center for Legislative Archives, National Archives, but the richness of the material varies from committee to committee and Congress to Congress. The personal papers of the members, if they are extant, are crucial but also cannot stand alone for topics that are not biographical. Beyond the archival repositories, successful study of Congress requires thorough exploration of the *Congressional Record*, the official record of floor debate in the House and the Senate, and the printed transcripts of relevant congressional committee hearings. The extent of this research increases exponentially in parallel with the scope of the problem being considered.

For *Why We Fight* my obstacles were greater because I did not limit this study to a particular issue or constellation of issues, instead examining the entirety of Congress for a crucial period of transformation. As such I devised the following research strategy: I sought out the archival collections for members who played a leadership role in Congress or at least were significant figures in one or two key policy bailiwicks. Next I relied on the materials in the Center for Legislative Archives, which highlight institutional processes much more than the internal thinking of lawmakers. Between the two—lawmakers' personal papers and official committee records—some clear patterns emerged, helping me to formulate my overarching thesis about the centrality of moderates in preserving the New Deal. I augmented this work with research in the relevant presidential libraries: Franklin D. Roosevelt and Harry S Truman. At final count I consulted over 100 manuscript collections located in twenty-eight different repositories, making *Why We Fight* the most comprehensively sourced analysis of Congress during World War II.

At the Truman Library I was especially lucky to find the papers of Frank McNaughton, a reporter and copywriter for *Time* magazine. McNaughton's opinions are valuable because he maintained close relationships with key members of Congress. They trusted him and frequently spoke at length off the record about the interior workings of Congress, making his memoranda valuable sources for understanding the legislative process during the war years. The sometimes gossipy, sometimes confidential nature of McNaughton's reports from lawmakers exposes legislative strategy, personal animus, and the culture of Congress in ways not possible from other sources.

I augmented my work in archival sources with some basic statistical analysis of congressional roll call votes, which I used to prepare the charts in this manuscript. I have entered the roll call votes for the key pieces of legislation analyzed in this manuscript into a comprehensive database. Included are the votes about the Revenue Act of 1941, the Revenue Act of 1943, the Revenue Act of 1944, various measures pertaining to price control and the Office of Price Administration, antistrike legislation, the Fair Employment Practices Committee, anti–poll tax legislation, anti-lynching legislation, soldiers' vote legislation, and activities of the Dies Committee. I also included some roll call votes regarding the rescission of a few key New Deal programs in 1943. I chose the roll calls in conjunction with a careful read of the congressional debates. Sometimes preliminary votes on a particular amendment or to invoke cloture were more revealing than votes on final passage, and I used the revealing votes not the pro forma votes. With just one exception—the votes in February 1944 to override Roosevelt's veto of the tax bill, the first ever of a president for a general revenue measure—I excluded votes that were near unanimous based on the argument that such roll calls do not speak so much to ideology but to a decision already made and only being formalized. Comparative analysis of roll call voting patterns on economic policy and social justice policy combined with careful description and evaluation of the key differences in liberal and moderate behavior in these two large policy domains reveals why parts of the New Deal vision were jettisoned.

I narrowed the database by querying for the following factors: economic conservatism, social conservatism, economic moderation, social moderation, economic liberalism, social liberalism, tax conservatism, tax moderation, and tax liberalism. I also organized the database by partisan and regional identification as well as tenure in Congress. Finally, because so few roll call votes from the 79th Congress are evaluated in the text of *Why We Fight* there proved to be insufficient data to make accurate assessments of voting ideology for this Congress, though I do include analysis of individual roll calls from all three of the war congresses where pertinent in the chapters.

For the 77th Congress there were four House chamber economic policy votes evaluated: one on the removal of the joint returns provision from the 1941 tax bill (nay was pro-administration/liberal), to pass the price control bill (yea was pro-administration/liberal), to pass the conference committee report on the price control bill (yea was pro-administration/liberal), and to pass the Smith antistrike bill (nay was pro-administration/liberal). Only 322 members voted on all four of these measures, and another 74 voted on three of the four. I excluded those lawmakers with participation rates under 75 percent. Those not included span the regional and partisan divisions within Congress. Of the 452 men and women who sat in the House at some point during the 77th Congress, 71.2 percent voted on all four of these roll calls, 16.3 percent on three of the roll calls, 5.3 percent on two of the roll calls, 2.8 percent on one of the roll calls, and 4.4 percent on none of the roll calls. (Here and throughout the total number of members who served in each chamber for each Congress was greater than the seats apportioned—435 for the House and 96 for the Senate—because of deaths, resignations, and replacements. I have chosen to make my calculations based on the total number who served in each chamber, not the seat allocation, because there is no good way to test ideological consistency between the departing members and their replacements.) To be counted as either a liberal or a conservative the voting division needed to be 4–0 or 3–1 out of the four roll calls or at least 3–0 or 2–1 when absent for one of the roll calls. I coded those with a 2–2 vote division as moderate.

Senate votes in the 77th Congress pertaining to economic policy included the Bankhead amendment to the price control bill (nay was pro-administration/liberal) and the conference committee report for the price control bill (yea was pro-administration/liberal). Because I only had two votes with which to work, I included all members who voted at least once, 16, as well as those who voted on both measures, 74, for a total of 90 members. Of the 109 men and women who sat in the Senate at some point during the 77th Congress, 67.9 percent voted on both these roll calls, 14.7 percent on one of the roll calls, and 17.4 percent on none of the roll calls. Those whose votes were ideologically consistent were coded accordingly and those who split were coded as moderates.

I examined two social justice roll calls in the House in 1941 and 1942 for purposes of evaluating ideological divisions, the vote to discharge the anti–poll tax bill from the Rules Committee (yea was pro-administration/liberal) and passage of the anti–poll tax bill (yea was pro-administration/liberal). Because I only had two votes with which to work, I included all members who voted at least once. There were a total of 354 members who participated in these social justice policy votes, and there were 319 who voted on both roll calls. Of the 452 men and women who sat in the House at some point during the 77th Congress, 70.6 percent voted on both these roll calls, 7.7 percent on one of the roll calls, and 21.7 percent on none of the roll calls. Those whose votes were ideologically consistent were coded accordingly and those who split were coded as moderates.

Senators in the 77th Congress voted on few social justice policy concerns, including an amendment to remove the poll tax requirement from the soldiers' vote bill (yea was pro-administration/liberal) and cloture on the anti–poll tax bill (yea was pro-administration/liberal). Because I only had two votes with which to work, I included all members who voted at least once, 45, as well as those who voted twice, 43, for a total of 88 members. Of the 109 men and women who sat in the Senate at some point during the 77th Congress, 39.4 percent voted on both these roll calls, 41.3 percent on one of the roll calls, and 19.3 percent on none of the roll calls. Those whose votes were ideologically consistent were coded accordingly and those who split were coded as moderates.

The bulk of congressional work on wartime economic policy occurred in the 78th Congress, and there were 10 record votes in the House that I judged to be key to this policy domain: rejection of the Ruml Plan on March 30, 1943 (nay was pro-administration/liberal), rejection of the Carlson bill regarding tax collection on May 4, 1943 (nay was pro-administration/liberal), recommitting the Ways and Means Committee tax bill on May 4, 1943 (yea was pro-administration/liberal), passage of the dark horse tax bill later that same day (nay was pro-administration/liberal), defeat of the Senate tax bill on May 18, 1943 (nay was pro-administration/liberal), preservation of the Rural Electrification Administration on June 23, 1943 (yea was pro-administration/liberal), passage of the Smith-Connally bill (nay was pro-administration/liberal), overriding FDR's veto of Smith-Connally (nay was pro-administration/liberal), sustaining FDR's veto of amendments to the OPA (nay was pro-administration/liberal), and overriding FDR's veto of the tax bill in 1944 (nay was pro-administration/liberal). While 217 members voted on all ten of these measures, I also included those who voted eight and nine times, adding another 154 members to my analysis of economic voting trends in the 78th Congress for the House of Representatives. There is scant deviation between members included and excluded according to ideological and partisan and regional divisions. Of the 451 men and women who sat in the House at some point during the 78th Congress, 48.1 percent voted on all ten of these roll calls, 23.5 percent on nine of the roll calls, 10.6 percent on eight of the roll calls, 7.1 percent on seven of the roll calls, 3.9 percent on six of the roll calls, 1.1 percent on five of the roll calls, 1 percent on four of the roll calls, 0.4 percent on three of the roll calls, 0.2 percent on two of the roll calls, 1.9 percent on one of the roll calls, and 2.2 percent on none of the roll calls. To be counted as either a liberal or a conservative the voting division needed to be 10–0, 9–1, 8–2, or 7–3 out of the ten roll calls or 9–0, 8–1, 7–2, 6–3, 8–0, 7–1, or 6–2 when absent for one or two of the roll calls. I coded the following vote divisions as moderate: 5–5, 4–6, 6–4, 5–4, 4–5, 4–4, 5–3, 3–5.

These numbers, though, do not tell the full story of ideological behavior regarding economic voting patterns because six of the roll calls pertain to tax votes—necessary if the war was to be funded—and the remaining four are divided as follows: two regarding antistrike legislation, and one each regarding price control and retention of a New Deal program. Members could and did vote consistently in a liberal fashion on tax policy matters but not on the other economic issues in the 78th Congress. As such, I have looked separately at the six economic policy votes to determine who were the tax liberals, moderates, and conservatives. I omitted from my statistical analysis those who voted less than 67 percent of the time. On these six votes 325 of the members voted each time, and another 84 voted at least four times, meaning that I have captured 409 House members. Of the 451 men and women who sat in the House at some point during the 78th Congress, 72.1 percent voted on six of the roll calls, 16 percent on five of the roll calls, 2.6 percent on four of the roll calls, 2.9 percent on three of the roll calls, 2.2 percent on two of the roll calls, 2 percent on one of the roll calls, and 2.2 percent on none of the roll calls. To be counted as either a liberal or a conservative the voting division needed to be 6–0, 5–1, or 4–2 out of the six roll calls or 3–1 or 4–1 when absent for one or two of the roll calls. I coded the following vote divisions as moderate: 3–3, 3–2, and 2–2.

In the Senate there were seven economic policy votes, but there was not such a large dichotomy between voting patterns on economic policy generally and tax policy specifically so I did not subdivide the Senate votes as I did the House votes in this domain. The seven roll call votes included passage of the Ruml inspired tax bill (nay was pro-administration/liberal), passage of legislation to eliminate the National Youth Administration (nay was pro-administration/liberal), recommitting the antistrike bill to committee (yea was pro-administration/liberal), passage of the antistrike bill (nay was pro-administration/liberal), overriding Roosevelt's veto of Smith-Connally (nay was pro-administration/liberal), rejection of the Russell amendment to limit funding for the FEPC (nay was pro-administration/liberal), and overriding Roosevelt's veto of the tax bill in 1944 (nay was pro-administration/liberal). I have included in my sample the 85 senators who voted four or more times. Of that number, 28 voted on all seven roll calls. Of the 104 men and women who sat in the Senate at some point during the 78th Congress, 26.9 percent on seven of the roll calls, 27.8 percent on six of the roll calls, 15.4 percent on five of the roll calls, 11.5 percent on four of the roll calls, 7.7 percent on three of the roll calls, 2 percent on two of the roll calls, 2 percent on one of the roll calls, and 6.7 percent on none of the roll calls. To be counted as either a liberal or a conservative the voting division needed to be 7–0, 6–1, or 5–2 out of the seven roll calls or 6–0, 5–1, 4–2, 5–0, 4–1, 4–0, or 3–1 when absent for one or two of the roll calls. I coded the following vote divisions as moderate: 4–3, 3–3, 3–2, 2–3, and 2–2.

Social justice policy votes in the House in the 78th Congress included passage of the anti–poll tax bill (yea was pro-administration/liberal), recommitting the states' rights soldiers' vote bill and passing the federal bill instead (yea was pro-administration/liberal), voting to extend the life of the Dies Committee (nay was pro-administration/liberal), and voting to deny appropriation of salary to individuals charged with being Communist (nay was pro-administration/liberal) in the House. To be considered for this comparative analysis I excluded lawmakers who voted twice or less on these four roll calls. A total of 289 members voted on all four of these measures, and another 102 voted on three of the four. Of the 451 men and women who sat in the House at some point during the 78th Congress, 64.1 percent on four of the roll calls, 22.6 percent on three of the roll calls, 7.3 percent on two of the roll calls, 2.9 percent on one of the roll calls, and 3.1 percent on none of the roll calls. Those not included span the regional and partisan divisions within Congress. To be counted as either a liberal or a conservative the voting division needed to be 4–0 or 3–1 out of the four roll calls or at least 3–0 or 2–1 when absent for one of the roll calls. I coded those with a 2–2 vote division as moderate.

The key social justice bills with Senate roll call votes included passage of a states' rights soldiers' vote bill (nay was pro-administration/liberal), passage of a federalized soldiers' vote bill (yea was pro-administration/liberal), and to deny salaries to individuals named by the Dies Committee as Communists (nay was pro-administration/liberal). To be considered for comparative analysis senators needed to vote on at least two of these measures. If consistent, 3-0 or 2-0, or if one vote off when voting all three times (2-1), I coded the member as either liberal or conservative. When the vote was split 1-1, I coded the member as moderate. A total of 61 senators voted on all three of these measures, and another 28 voted on two of the three. Those not included span the regional and partisan divisions within Congress. Of the 104 men and women who sat in the Senate at some point during the 78th Congress, 58.7 percent on three of the roll calls, 26.9 percent on two of the roll calls, 4.8 percent on one of the roll calls, and 9.6 percent on none of the roll calls.

There are also historiographic challenges for scholars who write about Congress simply because the topic has been understudied vis-à-vis the presidency. What follows is not a complete historiographical analysis of all the secondary sources used for *Why We Fight*, but instead is a treatment of the key categories that frame this book: works on Congress, the World War II home front, liberalism, modern conservatism, consensus, and the New Deal. At least since Arthur M. Schlesinger Jr. wrote *The Imperial Presidency* (Boston: Houghton Mifflin, 1973), historians have contended that the White House was the center of national politics. Such interpretations have oversimplified American politics while also making the president either the hero or the villain in ideological struggles between left and right. This approach ignores the centrality of Congress. Indeed, lawmakers represented both conservative and liberal views and in their fighting came much closer than a single president ever could to reflecting the diversity of thought within the nation about public policy questions. While little work from this perspective has been done on any era in modern American politics, analysis must begin with the 1930s and 1940s because these years proved to be a key transition point toward a more powerful and more centralized federal government. Liberal and leftist historians either celebrate FDR or criticize him for not being liberal enough at a moment they contend was ripe for introducing socialism into the United States. As such, these works either overlook or lambast the role of Congress in the politics of the interwar years. By contrast, conservative scholars defended Congress and the separation of powers, perhaps best reflected in James Burnham's *Congress and the American Tradition* (Chicago: H. Regnery, 1959). A more balanced, Congress-centered study of this key era is needed.

Because ideological wars are often fought in Congress, this institution must be privileged as the political scientist and historian Ira Katznelson has argued in the study of both national politics and political ideology if scholars are ever going to untangle the nation's complex political past. See Ira Katznelson, "The Possibilities of Analytical Political History," in *The Democratic Experiment: New Directions in American Political History,* Meg Jacobs, William J. Novak, and Julian E. Zelizer, eds. (Princeton, N.J.: Princeton University Press, 2003), 381–400. An early contribution to this effort, James T. Patterson's *Congressional Conservatism and the New Deal: The Growth of the Conservative Coalition in Congress, 1933–1939* (Lexington: For the Organization of American Historians by the University of Kentucky Press, 1967), argued that southern Democrats and Republicans formed a conservative coalition in the late 1930s that thwarted the passage of further liberal legislation.

Students of American political development have made tremendous headway over the past decade in filling the void in the literature about modern American politics with more titles on congressional topics. See for example, Karen Orren and Stephen Skowronek, "Regimes and Regime Building in American Government: A Review of the Literature on the 1940s," *Political Science Quarterly* 113 (Winter 1998–1999): 689–702. Elizabeth Sanders has shown that Progressive Era lawmakers representing laborers and farmers took their ideas for regulatory laws from elite intellectuals. See Sanders, *Roots of Reform: Farmers, Workers, and the American State, 1877–1917* (Chicago: University of Chicago Press, 1999). Still more scholarship ranges from analysis of tax-making policy to postwar institutional reform. For example, Julian Zelizer and others deftly show how Congress responded to the limitations of the seniority system to reinvent and modernize its procedures. See Zelizer, *Taxing America: Wilbur D. Mills, Congress and the State, 1945–1975* (New York: Cambridge University Press, 1998); Zelizer, *On Capitol Hill: The Struggle to Reform Congress and Its Consequences, 1948–2000* (New York: Cambridge University Press, 2004); and Eric Schickler, *Disjointed Pluralism: Institutional Innovation and the Development of the U.S. Congress* (Princeton, N.J.: Princeton University Press, 2001). For a thoughtful and theoretical treatment of why partisanship has been an essential force in American politics, see Sarah Binder, *Minority Rights, Majority Rule: Partisanship and the Development of Congress* (New York: Cambridge University Press, 1997).

Because *Why We Fight* contends Congress remained relevant to domestic politics, consideration of the political science literature suggesting a weakened Congress is necessary. See Jeffrey E. Cohen, "The Impact of the Modern Presidency on Presidential Success in the

U.S. Congress," *Legislative Studies Quarterly* 7 (November 1982): 515–532; Thomas E. Cronin, "A Resurgent Congress and the Imperial Presidency," *Political Science Quarterly* 95 (Summer 1980): 209–237; Harvey G. Zeidenstein, "The Reassertion of Congressional Power: New Curbs on the President," *Political Science Quarterly* 93 (Autumn 1978): 393–409. Other scholars have suggested the continued relevance of Congress in the making of public policy since 1940. See for example Ronald C. Moe and Steven C. Teel, "Congress as Policy-Maker: A Necessary Reappraisal," *Political Science Quarterly* 85 (September 1970): 443–470. Still other scholars have called into question the executive-legislative dichotomy with regard to public policy formation. See for example George C. Edwards III and B. Dan Wood, "Who Influences Whom? The President, Congress, and the Media," *American Political Science Review* 93 (June 1999): 327–344.

More recent contributions have shown congressional leadership in policy bailiwicks as diverse as the Cold War, civil rights, and environmental protection. See David M. Barrett, *The CIA and Congress: The Untold Story from Truman to Kennedy* (Lawrence: University Press of Kansas, 2005); Robert David Johnson, *Congress and the Cold War* (New York: Cambridge University Press, 2006); and Keith M. Finley, *Delaying the Dream: Southern Senators and the Fight against Civil Rights, 1938–1965* (Baton Rouge: Louisiana State University Press, 2008). All these works reveal the multiple ways Congress mattered.

In comparison with the paucity of generalized political history foregrounding Congress, the biographical literature about members of Congress is vast. For treatments of key representatives and senators from the New Deal and World War II era, see James K. Libbey, *Dear Alben: Mr. Barkley of Kentucky* (Lexington: University Press of Kentucky, 1979); Polly Ann Davis, *Alben W. Barkley, Senate Majority Leader and Vice President* (New York: Garland Publishing, 1979); Virginia Van der Veer Hamilton, *Lister Hill: Statesman from the South* (Chapel Hill: University of North Carolina Press, 1987); Richard Coke Lower, *A Bloc of One: The Political Career of Hiram W. Johnson* (Stanford, Calif.: Stanford University Press, 1993); Patrick J. Maney, *"Young Bob" La Follette: A Biography of Robert M. La Follette, Jr., 1895–1953* (Columbia: University of Missouri Press, 1978); James J. Kenneally, *A Compassionate Conservative: A Political Biography of Joseph W. Martin, Jr., Speaker of the U.S. House of Representatives* (Lanham, Md: Lexington Books, 2003); Steve Neal, *McNary of Oregon: A Political Biography* (Portland, Ore.: Western Imprints, 1985); Donald E. Spritzer, *Senator James E. Murray and the Limits of Post-War Liberalism* (New York: Garland, 1985); Richard Lowitt, *George W. Norris: The Making of a Progressive, 1861–1912* (Syracuse, N.Y.: Syracuse University Press, 1963); Lowitt, *George W. Norris: The Persistence of a Progressive, 1913–1933* (Urbana: University of Illinois Press, 1971); Lowitt, *George W. Norris: The Triumph of a Progressive, 1933–1944* (Urbana: University of Illinois Press, 1978); Wayne S. Cole, *Senator Gerald P. Nye and American Foreign Relations* (Minneapolis: University of Minnesota Press, 1962); D. B. Hardeman and Donald C. Bacon, *Rayburn: A Biography* (Austin: Texas Monthly Press, 1987); Lewis L. Gould and Nancy Beck Young, "The Speaker and the Presidents: Sam Rayburn, the White House, and the Legislative Process, 1941–1961," in *Masters of the House: Congressional Leadership over Two Centuries,* Roger H. Davidson, Susan Webb Hammond, Raymond W. Smock, eds. (Boulder, Colo.: Westview Press, 1998), 181–221; James T. Patterson, *Mr. Republican: A Biography of Robert A. Taft* (Boston: Houghton Mifflin, 1972); Donald H. Riddle, *The Truman Committee: A Study in Congressional Responsibility* (New Brunswick, N.J.: Rutgers University Press, 1964); C. David Tompkins, *Senator Arthur H. Vandenberg: The Evolution of a Modern Republican, 1884–1945* (Lansing: Michigan State University Press, 1970); J. Joseph Huthmacher, *Senator Robert F. Wagner and the Rise of Urban Liberalism* (New York: Atheneum, 1968).

Just as there has been insufficient examination of the congressional role in American political history, until the early twenty-first century scholars have not been terribly interested in wartime politics, viewing it as less compelling than the New Deal years that preceded it or the era of McCarthyism that followed. In an important historiographic essay, Neil A. Wynn in "The 'Good War': The Second World War and Postwar American Society," *Journal of Contemporary History* 31 (July 1996): 463–482, argues that while World War II, not the New Deal, should be viewed as the time period when modern America emerged, he downplays the importance of the government in this process. The omission of wartime politics from histories of the 1940s is ironic because scholars have considered the domestic politics of earlier wars. Examples of past legislative-executive conflict in wartime occurred in the Mexican War with Whigs discounting the Democratic president's explanation that Mexican aggression had triggered the hostilities, in the Civil War with the failed congressional committee on the conduct of the war, and in World War I with the destructive Senate fight over the Treaty of Versailles and the League of Nations. See Steven E. Woodworth, *Manifest Destinies: America's Westward Expansion and the Road to the Civil War* (New York: Alfred A. Knopf, 2010); Bruce Tap, *Over Lincoln's Shoulder: The Committee on the Conduct of the War* (Lawrence: University Press of Kansas, 1998); John Milton Cooper Jr., *Breaking the Heart of the World: Woodrow Wilson and the Fight for the League of Nations* (New York: Cambridge University Press, 2001).

For World War II, few scholars have addressed domestic politics. The one book on Congress during the war is both dated and narrow in its research methodology, citing primarily the *Congressional Record* and overlooking all archival research. See Roland A. Young, *Congressional Politics in the Second World War* (New York: Columbia University Press, 1956). Scholars have produced a rich literature on the home front, though. In a scholarly outpouring that began in the 1970s, historians have examined whether or not World War II was a watershed for the home front, typically in synthetic works with little new archival research. Too often, though, legislative deliberations are omitted from treatments of war era politics. See John W. Jeffries, *Wartime America: The World War II Home Front* (Chicago: Ivan R. Dee, 1996), and Allan M. Winkler, *Home Front, U.S.A.: America during World War II*, 2nd ed. (Wheeling, Ill.: Harlan Davidson, 2000). Other titles include John Morton Blum, *V was for Victory: Politics and American Culture during World War II* (New York: Harcourt Brace Jovanovich, 1976); David M. Kennedy, *Freedom from Fear: The American People in Depression and War, 1929–1945* (New York: Oxford University Press, 1999); Richard R. Lingeman, *Don't You Know There's a War On? The American Home Front, 1941–1945* (New York: G. P. Putnam's Sons, 1970); William L. O'Neill, *A Democracy at War: America's Fight at Home and Abroad in World War II* (New York: Free Press, 1993); Geoffrey Perrett, *Days of Sadness, Years of Triumph: The American People, 1939–1945* (New

York: Coward, McCann, and Geoghegan, 1973); and Richard Polenberg, *War and Society: The United States, 1941–1945* (Philadelphia: Lippincott, 1972).

In the last few years, there has been a discernable shift in interest toward the study of wartime politics, but the historiographic implications are not yet fully apparent. Elizabeth Borgwardt, working at the intersection of domestic policy accomplishments with foreign policy innovations, contends that war era politicians used the conflict to construct an international edifice for human rights, one that would make the New Deal international. See Borgwardt, *A New Deal for the World: America's Vision for Human Rights* (Cambridge, Mass.: Harvard University Press, 2005). James T. Sparrow conversely explores the genesis of so-called big government in World War II domestic politics by showing how nationalism and liberalism merged. His book reveals that the interplay between political elites and average Americans was a prerequisite for the emergence of big government. Citizens had to accept big government as necessary and good for it to become a permanent fixture. See Sparrow, *Warfare State: World War II Americans and the Age of Big Government* (New York: Oxford University Press, 2011).

Thoughtful scholarship, some of it synthetic and intended for undergraduates, has debated the notion of a good war. See especially Michael C. C. Adams, *The Best War Ever: America and World War II* (Baltimore, Md.: Johns Hopkins University Press, 1994); Paul Fussell, *Wartime: Understanding and Behavior in the Second World War* (New York: Oxford University Press, 1989); and Studs Terkel, *"The Good War": An Oral History of World War II* (New York: Pantheon Books, 1984). A more recent book, Robert B. Westbrook, *Why We Fought: Forging American Obligations in World War II* (Washington, D.C.: Smithsonian, 2010), contends that personal, familial motivations, not nationalism and citizenship moved Americans to fight this war. This important cultural study provides a fresh read on the good war debate.

Biographies of the president and books about FDR's administration provide a necessary foundation upon which more nuanced treatments of domestic politics using Congress as a main actor can be built. Among the more essential and recent works is Susan Dunn, *Roosevelt's Purge: How FDR Fought to Change the Democratic Party* (Cambridge, Mass.: Belknap Press of Harvard University Press, 2010). Her argument that Roosevelt wanted to remake the Democratic party into a purely liberal party and to see the Republicans become the purely conservative party supports what I am attempting in *Why We Fight*. Roosevelt failed in 1937, but the 1942 midterm congressional elections did push Congress in that direction, suggesting the importance of moderates as kingmakers in the legislative arena. Roosevelt the manipulator should have appreciated this development more than he did. Leaving Dunn aside, many of the key texts on FDR often depict Roosevelt as the central political figure in wartime America and sometimes have little to say about the legislative branch. See for example James MacGregor Burns, *Roosevelt: The Soldier of Freedom* (New York: Harcourt Brace Jovanovich, 1970); Matthew J. Dickinson, *Bitter Harvest: FDR, Presidential Power, and the Growth of the Presidential Branch* (New York: Cambridge University Press, 1996); Thomas Fleming, *The New Dealers' War: FDR and the War within World War II* (New York: Basic Books, 2001); Frank Burt Freidel, *Franklin D. Roosevelt: A Rendezvous with Destiny* (Boston: Little, Brown, 1990); Doris Kearns Goodwin, *No Ordinary Time: Franklin and Eleanor Roosevelt: The Home Front in World War II* (New York: Simon & Schuster, 1994); George T. McJimsey, *The Presidency of Franklin Delano Roosevelt* (Lawrence: University Press of Kansas, 2000). Intersecting presidential history with legislative history is difficult to do, especially when there are few books focusing on Congress as an institution. McJimsey more than most works the legislative branch into his assessment of FDR's administration. Taken together, this presidency-centered scholarship exacerbates the notion of the 1940s as devoid of meaningful presidential conflict with Congress focusing instead on FDR's skills as a wartime leader. Without sufficient attention to congressional politics our understanding of the policy process is incomplete.

Much of the remaining literature has looked at the home front from a social or a cultural perspective, revealing wartime conflict and lack of consensus regarding questions of race, class, and gender. For some of the most important works in this category, see Karen Anderson, *Wartime Women: Sex Roles, Family Relations, and the Status of Women during World War II* (Westport, Conn.: Greenwood Press, 1981); Roger Daniels, *Concentration Camps U.S.A.: Japanese Americans in World War II* (New York: Holt, Rinehart, and Winston, 1971); Maureen Honey, *Creating Rosie the Riveter: Class, Gender, and Propaganda during World War II* (Amherst: University of Massachusetts Press, 1984); Nelson Lichtenstein, *Labor's War at Home: The CIO in World War II* (New York: Cambridge University Press, 1987); August Meier and Elliott Rudwick, *CORE: A Study in the Civil Rights Movement, 1942–1968* (New York: Oxford University Press, 1973); Merl E. Reed, *Seedtime for the Modern Civil Rights Movement: The President's Committee on Fair Employment Practice, 1941–1946* (Baton Rouge: Louisiana State University Press, 1991); Greg Robinson, *By Order of the President: FDR and the Internment of Japanese Americans* (Cambridge, Mass.: Harvard University Press, 2001). As yet, though, no one has extrapolated the findings of conflict from these books and used this interpretation to test the level of conflict in national politics.

For an account of the vital center liberalism see Arthur M. Schlesinger, *The Vital Center: The Politics of Freedom* (Boston: Houghton Mifflin, 1949). Other treatments of the relationship between the New Deal and postwar liberalism include Jonathan Bell, *The Liberal State on Trial: The Cold War and American Politics in the Truman Years* (New York: Columbia University Press, 2004); H. W. Brands, *The Strange Death of American Liberalism* (New Haven, Conn.: Yale University Press, 2001); Alan Brinkley, *Liberalism and Its Discontents* (Cambridge, Mass.: Harvard University Press, 1998); William Henry Chafe, ed., *The Achievement of American Liberalism: The New Deal and Its Legacies* (New York: Columbia University Press, 2003); Steve Fraser and Gary Gerstle, eds., *The Rise and Fall of the New Deal Order, 1930–1980* (Princeton, N.J.: Princeton University Press, 1989); Steven M. Gillon, *Politics and Vision: The ADA and American Liberalism, 1947–1985* (New York: Oxford University Press, 1987); Alonzo L. Hamby, *Beyond the New Deal: Harry S Truman and American Liberalism* (New York: Columbia University Press, 1973); Richard H. Pells, *The Liberal Mind in a Conservative Age: American Intellectuals in the 1940s and 1950s* (New York: Harper & Row, 1985); Jason Scott Smith, *Building New Deal Liberalism: The Political Economy of Public Works, 1933–1956* (New York: Cambridge University Press, 2006).

Consideration of the historiography of modern conservatism is also relevant to *Why We*

Fight. The evolving partisan ideology in the 1940s provided a foundation for this late twenti-eth-century development. My location of modern conservatism in war era politics is in sym-metry with Kim Phillips-Fein, who argues in her book, *Invisible Hands: The Businessmen's Crusade against the New Deal* (New York: W. W. Norton, 2010), ix–52, that members of the business community had been critiquing New Deal liberalism, especially its economic phi-losophy, since the 1930s. See Patterson, *Congressional Conservatism and the New Deal* for an astute accounting of the range of conservative views present in Congress in the 1930s. He contends that opposition to New Deal domestic programs was the one unifying factor among an otherwise disparate faction of politicians. For more on modern conservatism, see for example, Dan T. Carter, *The Politics of Rage: George Wallace, the Origins of the New Con-servatism, and the Transformation of American Politics* (New York: Simon & Schuster, 1995); Donald T. Critchlow, *The Conservative Ascendancy: How the GOP Right Made Political His-tory* (Cambridge, Mass.: Harvard University Press, 2007); Ronald P. Formisano, *Boston against Busing: Race, Class, and Ethnicity in the 1960s and 1970s* (Chapel Hill: University of North Carolina Press, 2004); and Lisa McGirr, *Suburban Warriors: The Origins of the New American Right* (Princeton, N.J.: Princeton University Press, 2001). This literature is sugges-tive of the richness that has been produced in the last two decades on modern conservatism and also the multiple interpretations proffered of its origins and focus.

To find works that link modern conservatism with the war era or the postwar era, one must start with scholarship from the 1950s. See Daniel Bell, *The New American Right* (New York: Criterion Books, 1955) and Richard Hofstadter, "The Pseudo-Conservative Revolt," *American Scholar* 24 (Winter 1954–1955): 11–17. More recent titles include Jefferson R. Cowie, *Capital Moves: RCA's Seventy-Year Quest for Cheap Labor* (Ithaca, N.Y.: Cornell University Press, 1999); Sara Diamond, *Roads to Dominion: Right-Wing Movements and Political Power in the United States* (New York: The Guilford Press, 1995); Thomas W. Evans, *The Education of Ronald Reagan: The General Electric Years and the Untold Story of His Conversion to Conservatism* (New York: Columbia University Press, 2006); Elizabeth A. Fones-Wolf, *Selling Free Enterprise: The Business Assault on Labor and Liberalism, 1945–1960* (Urbana: University of Illinois Press, 1994); Michael Kimmage, *The Conservative Turn: Lionel Trilling, Whittaker Chambers, and the Lessons of Anti-Communism* (Cam-bridge, Mass.: Harvard University Press, 2009); and John E. Moser, *Right Turn: John T. Flynn and the Transformation of American Liberalism* (New York: New York University Press, 2005). Other scholars have found the roots of modern conservatism in the 1920s or earlier. See the following for examples: Rosemary Feurer, *Radical Unionism in the Midwest, 1900–1950* (Urbana: University of Illinois Press, 2006); Beverly Gage, *The Day Wall Street Exploded: A Story of America in Its First Age of Terror* (New York: Oxford University Press, 2009); Allan J. Lichtman, *White Protestant Nation: The Rise of the American Conservative Movement* (New York: Atlantic Monthly Press, 2008); and Kim E. Nielsen, *Un-American Womanhood: Antiradicalism, Antifeminism, and the First Red Scare* (Columbus: Ohio State University Press, 2001).

Moderates have been overlooked outside of the biographical literature. The closest that scholars have come to studying moderates is the now outdated consensus school of U.S. historiography, which emerged in the 1950s. See for example, Daniel Boorstin, *Genius in*

American Politics (Chicago: University of Chicago Press, 1953); Louis Hartz, *The Liberal Tradition in America* (New York: Harcourt, Brace, 1955); Richard Hofstadter, *The American Political Tradition and the Men Who Made It* (New York: Alfred A. Knopf, 1948); Schlesinger, *The Vital Center.* More recently Geoffrey Kabaservice in *Rule and Ruin: The Downfall of Moderation and the Destruction of the Republican Party, from Eisenhower to the Tea Party* (New York: Oxford University Press, 2012) has looked at the collapse of moderates in the GOP. He argues that this process dates to the end of the Eisenhower presidency. Laura Jane Gifford in *The Center Cannot Hold: The 1960 Presidential Election and the Rise of Modern Conservatism* (DeKalb: Northern Illinois University Press, 2009), finds the roots of the moderate declension in presidential politics. For other views on the 1960 presidential election see W. J. Rorabaugh, *The Real Making of the President: Kennedy, Nixon, and the 1960 Election* (Lawrence: University Press of Kansas, 2009). Rorabaugh concentrates on other significant transformations that occurred during this contest, namely the emergence of racial liberalism, the power of television, and the decline of political conventions in favor of presidential primaries.

Scholars recently have developed the once conventional idea about consensus in provocative ways. For example, Wendy Wall argues that business, political, and cultural leaders purposefully manufactured consensus in the 1930s in response to the Great Depression and concerns about fascism and communism, but she also acknowledges that ideological conflict remained present beneath the surface. Focusing too much on consensus ignores other prescient truths, namely that war era partisanship was a tool to effect legislative compromise. This dominant characteristic of lawmaker discourse did not at all minimize the tone, the intensity, or even the vitriol of the rhetoric, but it did govern the context, the understanding of, and the definition of wartime partisanship. See Wendy L. Wall, *Inventing the "American Way": The Politics of Consensus from the New Deal to the Civil Rights Movement* (New York: Oxford University Press, 2008), 103–159. Other scholars have found important conflicts in the 1940s and 1950s. See for example, Thomas J. Sugrue, *The Origins of the Urban Crisis: Race and Inequality in Postwar Detroit* (Princeton, N.J.: Princeton University Press, 1996). In this landmark book, Sugrue argues liberals never reached consensus on race policy, meaning that there was never a triumphal liberal moment but instead messy disagreement about the meanings of and access to democracy.

The rich and vast literature on the New Deal also underpins *Why We Fight.* New Deal liberalism took on new characteristics in the war years, namely a departure from the anticapitalism of the early 1930s in favor of an alliance between big government and big business alongside a nascent concern for individual rights based on the premise most Americans could better be defined as consumers, not producers. See Alan Brinkley, *The End of Reform: New Deal Liberalism in Recession and War* (New York: Alfred A. Knopf, 1995). For standard treatments of the New Deal, see for example, Arthur M. Schlesinger Jr., *The Age of Roosevelt,* 3 vols. (Boston: Houghton Mifflin, 1957–1960), and William E. Leuchtenburg, *Franklin D. Roosevelt and the New Deal, 1932–1940* (New York: Harper & Row, 1963).

Scholars have sought numerous ways to understand the complexity of the New Deal.

Some have categorized it according to the relief, recovery, reform schema while others have focused on the chronological notion of two or three New Deals. Still others have explicated it according to constituencies—agriculture, business, and labor. Some of the most important works on the New Deal era include: Anthony J. Badger, *The New Deal: The Depression Years, 1933–40* (Chicago: Ivan R. Dee, 2002); Gary Dean Best, *Pride, Prejudice, and Politics: Roosevelt versus Recovery, 1933–1938* (New York: Praeger, 1991); Paul K. Conkin, *The New Deal,* 3rd ed. (Wheeling, Ill.: Harlan Davidson, 1992); Kenneth Finegold and Theda Skocpol, *State and Party in America's New Deal* (Madison: University of Wisconsin Press, 1995); Colin Gordon, *New Deals: Business, Labor, and Politics in America, 1920–1935* (New York: Cambridge University Press, 1994); Otis L. Graham Jr., *An Encore for Reform: The Old Progressives and the New Deal* (New York: Oxford University Press, 1967); Ellis W. Hawley, *The New Deal and the Problem of Monopoly: A Study in Economic Ambivalence* (New York: Fordham University Press, 1995); David M. Kennedy, *Freedom from Fear: The American People in Depression and War, 1929–1945* (New York: Oxford University Press, 1999); William E. Leuchtenburg, *Franklin D. Roosevelt and the New Deal, 1932–1940* (New York: Harper & Row, 1963); Rhonda F. Levine, *Class Struggle and the New Deal: Industrial Labor, Industrial Capital, and the State* (Lawrence: University Press of Kansas, 1988); Donald R. McCoy, *Angry Voices: Left-of-Center Politics in the New Deal Era* (Lawrence: University Press of Kansas, 1958); Patrick D. Reagan, *Designing a New America: The Origins of New Deal Planning, 1890–1943* (Amherst: University of Massachusetts Press, 2000); Theodore Saloutos, *The American Farmer and the New Deal* (Ames: Iowa State University Press, 1982); and Jordan A. Schwarz, *The New Dealers: Power Politics in the Age of Roosevelt* (New York: Alfred A. Knopf, 1993).

Scholars have recently debated whether the New Deal was an exceptional moment in American politics. See Jefferson Cowie and Nick Salvatore, "The Long Exception: Rethinking the Place of the New Deal in American History," *International Labor and Working-Class History* 74 (Fall 2008): 3–32; Kevin Boyle, "Why Is There No Social Democracy in America?" *International Labor and Working-Class History* 74 (Fall 2008): 33–37; Michael Kazin, "A Liberal Nation in Spite of Itself," *International Labor and Working-Class History* 74 (Fall 2008): 38–41; Jennifer Klein, "A New Deal Restoration: Individuals, Communities, and the Long Struggle for the Collective Good," *International Labor and Working-Class History* 74 (Fall 2008): 42–48; Nancy MacLean, "Getting New Deal History Wrong," *International Labor and Working-Class History* 74 (Fall 2008): 49–55; David Montgomery, "The Mythical Man," *International Labor and Working-Class History* 74 (Fall 2008): 56–62; Jefferson Cowie and Nick Salvatore, "History, Complexity, and Politics: Further Thoughts," *International Labor and Working-Class History* 74 (Fall 2008): 63–69.

Historiographical assessment of the various threads I have woven together reveals just how much more room there is for reconsidering midcentury politics. *Why We Fight* begs for more scholars to use Congress as the primary lens to reconsider the key themes in modern political history: conservatism and liberalism; race, ethnicity, and gender; the politics of consumption; the welfare state; the economy; urbanization and suburbanization; energy and the environment; social movement activism and political reform;

federalism; and war and society, for example. Yet since this period is well trod historiographic ground, conducting such work is challenging. I have used Congress to address when and how New Deal liberalism morphed into a more moderate, pragmatic mode of governance, work that also reveals some of the origins of modern conservatism. Other scholars should continue the study of Congress both as an end point and as a means to do more big history.

Bibliography

MANUSCRIPT COLLECTIONS

Abraham Lincoln Presidential Library, Springfield, IL
    Scott W. Lucas Papers
Arizona State University, Department of Archives and Manuscripts, Tempe, AZ
    Carl Hayden Papers
Brigham Young University, Special Collections, Provo, UT
    Abe Murdock Papers
Carl Albert Congressional Research and Studies Center Congressional Archives, University of Oklahoma, Norman, OK
    Carl Albert Papers
Dwight D. Eisenhower Library, Abilene, KS
    Dwight D. Eisenhower Papers
        White House Central Files—President's Personal Files
    Records of the Office of the Staff Secretary
        Legislative Meetings Series
FBI File on the House Committee on Un-American Activities, Microfilm Edition, Franklin D. Roosevelt Library, Hyde Park, NY
    Lorena Hickock Papers
    Franklin D. Roosevelt Papers
        Official File
        President's Personal File
        President's Secretary's File
Georgetown University, Special Collections, Washington, D.C.
    Leon Keyserling Papers
    Robert Wagner Papers
Harry S Truman Library, Independence, MO
    Hugh Fulton Papers
    Frank McNaughton Papers
    Harold G. Robinson Papers
    Harry S Truman Papers
        Papers as Senator and Vice President
        Post-Presidential Files
        President's Secretary's Files
Herbert Hoover Presidential Library, West Branch, IA
    Herbert Hoover Papers
        Post-Presidential Individuals File Series

Gerald Nye Papers
Westbrook Pegler Papers
Indiana University, Lilly Library, Bloomington, IN
    Charles Halleck Papers
    Louis Ludlow Papers
Kansas State Historical Society, Topeka, KS
    Arthur Capper Papers
Library of Congress, Manuscript Division, Washington, D.C.
    Clinton P. Anderson Papers
    Harold H. Burton Papers
    Emanual Celler Papers
    Tom Connally Papers
    Theodore Granik Papers
    Theodore Francis Green Papers
    Harold Ickes Papers
    Robert M. LaFollette Jr. Papers
    Clare Boothe Luce Papers
    Charles McNary Papers
    National Association for the Advancement of Colored People Papers on Microfilm,
        Part 4, Voting Rights Campaign
        Part 7, Anti-Lynching Campaign, Series B
        Part 13, The NAACP and Labor, 1940–1955, Series B
        Part 16, Board of Directors, Correspondence and Committee Materials, Series B
    George Norris Papers
    Robert A. Taft Papers
    James W. Wadsworth Papers
Lyndon Baines Johnson Presidential Library, Austin, TX
    LBJA, Lyndon B. Johnson Papers
    Lyndon B. Johnson Senate Papers
    Wright Patman Papers
National Archives, Washington, D.C.
    Department of State, Press Releases, Microfilm Edition
    RG 46 Committee on Agriculture and Forestry, Senate
    RG 46 Committee on Appropriations, Senate
    RG 46 Committee on Banking and Currency, Senate
    RG 46 Committee on Commerce, Senate
    RG 46 Committee on Education and Labor, Senate
    RG 46 Committee on Finance, Senate
    RG 46 Committee on Foreign Relations, Senate
    RG 46 Committee on Immigration, Senate
    RG 46 Committee on the Judiciary, Senate
    RG 46 Committee on Military Affairs, Senate
    RG 46 Committee on Naval Affairs, Senate

RG 46 Committee on Rules, Senate

RG 233 Committee on Agriculture, House of Representatives

RG 233 Committee on Appropriations, House of Representatives

RG 233 Committee on Banking and Currency, House of Representatives

RG 233 Committee on Education, House of Representatives

RG 233 Committee on Expenditures in the Executive Department, House of Representatives

RG 233 Committee on Foreign Affairs, House of Representatives

RG 233 Committee on Immigration and Naturalization, House of Representatives

RG 233 Committee on Indian Affairs, House of Representatives

RG 233 Committee on Interstate and Foreign Commerce, House of Representatives

RG 233 Committee on the Judiciary, House of Representatives

RG 233 Committee on Labor, House of Representatives

RG 233 Committee on Military Affairs, House of Representatives

RG 233 Committee on Naval Affairs, House of Representatives

RG 233 Committee on Rules, House of Representatives

RG 233 Committee on Ways and Means, House of Representatives

RG 233 Committee on World War Veterans' Legislation, House of Representatives

RG 233 Special Committee on Un-American Activities, House of Representatives

University of Alabama at Tuscaloosa, W. S. Hoole Special Collections, Tuscaloosa, AL
    Lister Hill Papers
    Samuel Francis Hobbs Papers
    John J. Sparkman Papers

University of Colorado, University Archives Political Collections, Boulder, CO
    J. Edgar Chenoweth Papers
    Eugene Donald Millikin Papers

University of Georgia, Richard B. Russell Library for Political Research and Studies, Athens, GA
    Richard B. Russell Papers

University of Kentucky Libraries, Special Collections and Archives, Lexington, KY
    Alben Barkley Papers
    A. B. "Happy" Chandler Papers
    Brent Spence Papers

University of Michigan, Bentley Historical Library, Ann Arbor, MI
    Prentiss Brown Papers
    Albert J. Engel Papers
    Homer Ferguson Papers
    Clare Hoffman Papers
    Arthur Vandenberg Papers

University of Montana, K. Ross Toole Archives and Special Collections, Missoula, MT
    James E. Murray Papers

University of North Carolina, Southern Historical Collection, Chapel Hill, NC
    Robert L. Doughton Papers

University of North Dakota, Chester Fritz Library, Grand Forks, ND
    Usher L. Burdick Papers
    William Langer Papers
    William Lemke Papers
University of Texas at Austin, Dolph Briscoe Center for American History, Austin, TX
    Sam Rayburn Papers
University of Virginia, Alderman Library, Charlottesville, VA
    Harry Flood Byrd Papers
    Carter Glass Papers
    Howard W. Smith Papers
University of Wyoming, American Heritage Center, Laramie, WY
    Joseph C. O'Mahoney Papers
    Robert E. Kennedy Papers
Utah State Historical Society, Salt Lake City, UT
    Elbert D. Thomas Papers
Washington and Jefferson College, Washington, PA
    Joseph Guffey Papers
Woolley, John T., and Gerhard Peters. The American Presidency Project [online at http://www.presidency.ucsb.edu/index.php]. Santa Barbara, Calif.: University of California (hosted), Gerhard Peters (database).

NEWSPAPERS

Atlanta Journal
Baltimore Sun
Chicago Defender
Chicago Tribune
Christian Science Monitor
Hartford Courant
Los Angeles Times
New York Times
St. Louis Post Dispatch
Wall Street Journal
Washington Evening Star
Washington Post

ORAL HISTORY

Transcript, Richard Bolling Oral History, February 27, 1969, by Paige Mulhollan. Lyndon B. Johnson Presidential Library.
Samuel Dickstein Oral History. January 1972. Columbia University Oral History Project.
Thomas C. Hart Oral History. Columbia University Oral History Project.
Transcript, Lawrence O'Brien Oral History Interview #1, September 18, 1985, by Michael L. Gillette. Lyndon B. Johnson Presidential Library.

BOOKS, ARTICLES, AND PUBLISHED DOCUMENTS

Aberbach, Joel D., and Mark A. Peterson, eds. *The Executive Branch.* New York: Oxford University Press, 2005.

Ackerman, Bruce. *We The People: Foundations.* Cambridge, Mass.: Harvard University Press, 1991.

———. *We The People: Transformations.* Cambridge, Mass.: Harvard University Press, 1998.

Adams, Michael C. C. *The Best War Ever: America and World War II.* Baltimore, Md.: Johns Hopkins University Press, 1994.

Altman, O. R. "First Session of the Seventy-Fifth Congress, January 5, 1937, to August 21, 1937." *American Political Science Review* 31 (December 1937): 1071–1093.

———. "Second and Third Sessions of the Seventy-Fifth Congress, 1937–38." *American Political Science Review* 32 (December 1938): 1099–1123.

———. "Second Session of the Seventy-Fourth Congress, January 3, 1936, to June 20, 1936." *American Political Science Review* 30 (December 1936): 1086–1107.

Alvarez, Luis. *The Power of the Zoot: Youth Culture and Resistance during World War II.* Berkeley: University of California Press, 2008.

Ambrose, Stephen. *Eisenhower: The President.* New York: Simon and Schuster, 1984.

Ambrosius, Lloyd E. *Wilsonian Statecraft: Theory and Practice of Liberal Internationalism during World War I.* Wilmington, Del.: SR Books, 1991.

"American Institute of Public Opinion—Surveys, 1938–1939." *Public Opinion Quarterly* 3 (October 1939): 581–607.

Anderson, Carol. *Eyes off the Prize: The United Nations and the African American Struggle for Human Rights, 1944–1955.* New York: Cambridge University Press, 2003.

Anderson, Karen. *Wartime Women: Sex Roles, Family Relations, and the Status of Women during World War II.* Westport, Conn.: Greenwood Press, 1981.

Badger, Anthony J. *The New Deal: The Depression Years, 1933–1940.* Chicago: Ivan R. Dee, 2002.

Bailey, Stephen K. *Congress Makes a Law: The Story behind the Employment Act of 1946.* New York: Vintage Books, 1964.

Baker, Richard A., and Roger H. Davidson, eds. *First among Equals: Outstanding Senate Leaders of the Twentieth Century.* Washington, D.C.: Congressional Quarterly, 1991.

Ballard, James Stokes. *The Shock of Peace: Military and Economic Demobilization after World War II.* Washington, D.C.: University Press of America, 1983.

Balogh, Brian. *A Government Out of Sight: The Mystery of National Authority in Nineteenth-Century America.* New York: Cambridge University Press, 2009.

Barber, Lucy G. *Marching on Washington: The Forging of an American Political Tradition.* Berkeley: University of California Press, 2002.

Barkley, Alben W. *That Reminds Me.* Garden City, N.Y.: Doubleday, 1954.

Barkley, Jane R. *I Married the Veep.* New York: Vanguard Press, 1958.

Barrett, David M. *The CIA and Congress: The Untold Story from Truman to Kennedy.* Lawrence: University Press of Kansas, 2005.

Bartels, Andrew H. "The Office of Price Administration and the Legacy of the New Deal, 1939–1946." *Public Historian* 5 (Summer 1983): 5–29.

Bastami, Saha. "American Foreign Policy and the Question of Palestine, 1856–1939." Ph.D. dissertation, George Washington University, 1989.

Bates, Beth Tompkins. "A New Crowd Challenges the Agenda of the Old Guard in the NAACP, 1933–1941." *American Historical Review* 102 (April 1997): 340–377.

Belknap, Michael R. *Cold War Political Justice: The Smith Act, the Communist Party, and American Civil Liberties.* Westport, Conn.: Greenwood Press, 1977.

Bell, Daniel. *The New American Right.* New York: Criterion Books, 1955.

Bell, Jonathan. *The Liberal State on Trial: The Cold War and American Politics in the Truman Years.* New York: Columbia University Press, 2004.

Bennett, David Harry. *Demagogues in the Depression: American Radicals and the Union Party, 1932–1936.* New Brunswick, N.J.: Rutgers University Press, 1969.

Bennett, Michael J. *When Dreams Came True: The GI Bill and the Making of Modern America.* McLean, Va.: Brassey's Publishing, 1996.

Bentley, Amy. *Eating for Victory: Food Rationing and the Politics of Domesticity.* Urbana: University of Illinois Press, 1998.

Berdahl, Clarence A. "American Government and Politics: Some Notes on Party Membership in Congress, III." *American Political Science Review* 43 (August 1949): 721–734.

Berman, Aaron. *Nazism, the Jews, and American Zionism, 1933–1948.* Detroit, Mich.: Wayne State University Press, 1990.

Berman, William C. *The Politics of Civil Rights in the Truman Administration.* Columbus: Ohio State University Press, 1970.

Bernstein, Barton J. "Clash of Interests: The Postwar Battle between the Office of Price Administration and the Department of Agriculture." *Agriculture History* 41 (January 1967): 45–58.

Beschloss, Michael, ed. *Taking Charge: The Johnson White House Tapes, 1963–1964.* New York: Simon and Schuster, 1997.

Best, Gary Dean. *Pride, Prejudice, and Politics: Roosevelt versus Recovery, 1933–1938.* New York: Praeger, 1991.

Biddle, Francis. "Subversives in Government." *Annals of the American Academy of Political and Social Science* 300 (July 1955): 51–61.

Binder, Sarah A. *Minority Rights, Majority Rule: Partisanship and the Development of Congress.* New York: Cambridge University Press, 1997.

Binder, Sarah A., and Steven S. Smith. *Politics or Principle? Filibustering in the United States Senate.* Washington, D.C.: Brookings Institution, 1997.

Bird, Kai, and Martin J. Sherwin. *American Prometheus: The Triumph and Tragedy of J. Robert Oppenheimer.* New York: Vintage Books, 2006.

Black, John D., and Charles A. Gibbons. "The War and American Agriculture." *Review of Economics and Statistics* 26 (February 1944): 3–55.

Blanchard, Margaret A. *Revolutionary Sparks: Freedom of Expression in Modern America.* New York: Oxford University Press, 1992.

Bloom, Sol. *The Autobiography of Sol Bloom.* New York: Putnam's, 1948.

Blum, John Morton. *Roosevelt and Morgenthau.* Boston: Houghton Mifflin, 1972.

———. *V Was for Victory: Politics and American Culture during World War II.* New York: Harcourt Brace Jovanovich, 1976.

Bolling, Richard. *House Out of Order.* New York: Dutton, 1966.

Bon Tempo, Carl J. *Americans at the Gate: The United States and Refugees during the Cold War.* Princeton, N.J.: Princeton University Press, 2008.

Borgwardt, Elizabeth. *A New Deal for the World: America's Vision for Human Rights.* Cambridge, Mass.: Harvard University Press, 2005.

Boyle, Kevin. "Why Is There No Social Democracy in America?" *International Labor and Working-Class History* 74 (Fall 2008): 33–37.

Brands, H. W. *The Strange Death of American Liberalism.* New Haven, Conn.: Yale University Press, 2001.

Brandt, Nat. *Harlem at War: The Black Experience in World War II.* Syracuse, N.Y.: Syracuse University Press, 1996.

Brattain, Michelle. *The Politics of Whiteness: Race, Workers, and Culture in the Modern South.* Princeton, N.J.: Princeton University Press, 2001.

Breitman, Richard, and Alan M. Kraut. *American Refugee Policy and European Jewry, 1933–1945.* Bloomington: Indiana University Press, 1987.

Brinkley, Alan. *The End of Reform: New Deal Liberalism in Recession and War.* New York: Alfred A. Knopf, 1995.

———. *Liberalism and Its Discontents.* Cambridge, Mass.: Harvard University Press, 1998.

Brinkley, David. *Washington Goes to War.* New York: Alfred A. Knopf, 1988.

Brinton, Crane. *The Anatomy of Revolution.* New York: W. W. Norton, 1938.

Brownlee, W. Elliot. *Federal Taxation in America: A Short History,* 2nd ed. New York and Washington, D.C.: Cambridge University Press and Woodrow Wilson Center Press, 2004.

Bruce, Robert B. *A Fraternity of Arms: America and France in the Great War.* Lawrence: University Press of Kansas, 2003.

Buckwalter, Doyle W. "The Congressional Concurrent Resolution: A Search for Foreign Policy Influence." *Midwest Journal of Political Science* 14 (August 1970): 434–458.

Burke, Robert E. "A Friendship in Adversity: Burton K. Wheeler and Hiram W. Johnson." *Montana* 36 (Winter 1986): 12–25.

Burnham, James. *Congress and the American Tradition.* Chicago: H. Regnery, 1959.

Burns, James MacGregor. *Roosevelt: The Soldier of Freedom.* New York: Harcourt Brace Jovanovich, 1970.

Byrd, Robert C., ed. *The Senate, 1789–1989, Addresses on the History of the United States Senate,* vol. 1. Washington, D.C.: U.S. Government Printing Office, 1988.

Cameron, Donald John. "Burton K. Wheeler as Public Campaigner, 1922–1942." Ph.D. dissertation, Northwestern University, 1960.

Campbell, D'Ann. *Women at War with America.* Cambridge, Mass.: Harvard University Press, 1984.

Canaday, Margot. "Building a Straight State: Sexuality and Social Citizenship under the 1944 G.I. Bill." *Journal of American History* 90 (December 2003): 935–957.

Cantril, Hadley, ed. *Public Opinion, 1935–1946.* Princeton, N.J.: Princeton University Press, 1951.

Capt, J. C. "The Method and Procedure of the Apportionment of Representatives in Congress." *Estadistica, Journal of the Inter-American Statistical Institute* 1 (June 1943): 94–102.

Carter, Dan T. *The Politics of Rage: George Wallace, the Origins of the New Conservatism, and the Transformation of American Politics.* New York: Simon & Schuster, 1995.

Caute, David. *The Great Fear: The Anti-Communist Purge under Truman and Eisenhower.* New York: Simon and Schuster, 1978.

Chadwin, Mark Lincoln. *The Hawks of World War II.* Chapel Hill: University of North Carolina Press, 1968.

Chafe, William Henry, ed. *The Achievement of American Liberalism: The New Deal and Its Legacies.* New York: Columbia University Press, 2003.

Champagne, Anthony. *The Austin-Boston Connection: Five Decades of House Democratic Leadership, 1937–1989.* College Station: Texas A & M University Press, 2009.

———. *Congressman Sam Rayburn.* New Brunswick, N.J.: Rutgers University Press, 1984.

Chen, Anthony S. *The Fifth Freedom: Jobs, Politics, and Civil Rights in the United States, 1941–1972.* Princeton, N.J.: Princeton University Press, 2009.

Clifford, J. Garry, and Samuel R. Spencer Jr. *The First Peacetime Draft.* Lawrence: University Press of Kansas, 1986.

Coffman, Edward M. *The War to End All Wars: The American Military Experience in World War I.* New York: Oxford University Press, 1968.

Cohen, Deborah. *Braceros: Migrant Citizens and Transnational Subjects in the Postwar United States and Mexico.* Chapel Hill: University of North Carolina Press, 2011.

Cohen, Jeffrey E. "The Impact of the Modern Presidency on Presidential Success in the U.S. Congress." *Legislative Studies Quarterly* 7 (November 1982): 515–532.

Cohen, Lizabeth. *A Consumers' Republic: The Politics of Mass Consumption in Postwar America.* New York: Alfred A. Knopf, 2003.

Cohen, Robert. *When the Old Left Was Young: Student Radicals and America's First Mass Student Movement, 1929–1941.* New York: Oxford University Press, 1993.

Cole, Wayne S. *America First: The Battle against Intervention, 1940–1941.* Madison: University of Wisconsin Press, 1953.

———. *Charles A. Lindbergh and the Battle against American Intervention in World War II.* New York: Harcourt Brace Jovanovich, 1974.

———. *Senator Gerald P. Nye and American Foreign Relations.* Minneapolis: University of Minnesota Press, 1962.

Congressional Directory, 77th Congress–79th Congress.

Congressional Record, 75th Congress–79th Congress.

Conkin, Paul K. *The New Deal,* 3rd ed. Wheeling, Ill.: Harlan Davidson, 1992.

Connally, Thomas T., as told to Alfred Steinberg. *My Name Is Tom Connally.* New York: Thomas T. Crowell Company, 1954.

Coombs, Frank Alan. "Joseph Christopher O'Mahoney: The New Deal Years." Ph.D. dissertation, University of Illinois at Urbana-Champaign, 1968.

Cooper, John Milton, Jr. *Breaking the Heart of the World: Woodrow Wilson and the Fight for the League of Nations.* New York: Cambridge University Press, 2001.

Cowie, Jefferson R. *Capital Moves: RCA's Seventy-Year Quest for Cheap Labor.* Ithaca, N.Y.: Cornell University Press, 1999.

Cowie, Jefferson R., and Nick Salvatore. "History, Complexity, and Politics: Further Thoughts." *International Labor and Working-Class History* 74 (Fall 2008): 63–69.

———. "The Long Exception: Rethinking the Place of the New Deal in American History." *International Labor and Working-Class History* 74 (Fall 2008): 3–32.

Craig, R. Bruce. *Treasonable Doubt: The Harry Dexter White Spy Case.* Lawrence: University Press of Kansas, 2004.

Critchlow, Donald T. *The Conservative Ascendancy: How the GOP Right Made Political History.* Cambridge, Mass.: Harvard University Press, 2007.

Cronin, Thomas E. "A Resurgent Congress and the Imperial Presidency." *Political Science Quarterly* 95 (Summer 1980): 209–237.

Curran, Thomas J. *Xenophobia and Immigration, 1820–1930.* Boston: Twayne Publishers, 1975.

Cushman, Robert E. "Civil Liberties." *American Political Science Review* 37 (February 1943): 49–56.

Dallek, Robert. *Flawed Giant: Lyndon Johnson and His Times, 1961–1973.* New York: Oxford University Press, 1998.

———. *Lone Star Rising: Lyndon Johnson and His Times, 1908–1960.* New York: Oxford University Press, 1991.

Danese, Tracy E. *Claude Pepper and Ed Ball: Politics, Purpose, and Power.* Gainesville: University Press of Florida, 2000.

Daniel, Edward Oda. "Sam Rayburn: Trials of a Party Man." Ph.D. dissertation, North Texas State University, 1979.

Daniels, Roger. *The Bonus March: An Episode of the Great Depression.* Westport, Conn.: Greenwood Publishing, 1971.

———. *Concentration Camps U.S.A.: Japanese Americans in World War II.* New York: Holt, Rinehart, and Winston, 1971.

Darilek, Richard E. *A Loyal Opposition in Time of War: The Republican Party and the Politics of Foreign Policy from Pearl Harbor to Yalta.* Westport, Conn.: Greenwood Press, 1976.

Davidson, Roger H. "The Advent of the Modern Congress: The Legislative Reorganization Act of 1946." *Legislative Studies Quarterly* 15 (August 1990): 357–373.

Davidson, Roger H., Susan Webb Hammond, Raymond W. Smock, eds. *Masters of the House: Congressional Leadership over Two Centuries.* Boulder, Colo.: Westview Press, 1998.

Davie, Maurice R., with the collaboration of Sarah W. Cohn et al. *Refugees in America: Report of the Committee for the Study of Recent Immigration from Europe.* Westport, Conn.: Greenwood Press, 1974.

Davis, Kenneth S. *FDR, the War President, 1940–1943: A History.* New York: Random House, 2000.

Davis, Polly Ann. *Alben W. Barkley, Senate Majority Leader and Vice President.* New York: Garland Publishing, 1979.

Dawidowicz, Lucy S. *The War against the Jews, 1933–1945,* 10th anniversary ed. New York: Bantam Books, 1986.

Dawley, Alan. *Changing the World: American Progressives in War and Revolution.* Princeton, N.J.: Princeton University Press, 2003.

Demsky, Jeffrey Scott. "Going Public in Support: American Discursive Opposition to Nazi Anti-Semitism, 1933–1944." Ph.D. dissertation, University of Florida, 2007.

Diamond, Sara. *Roads to Dominion: Right-Wing Movements and Political Power in the United States.* New York: The Guilford Press, 1995.

Dickinson, Matthew J. *Bitter Harvest: FDR, Presidential Power, and the Growth of the Presidential Branch.* New York: Cambridge University Press, 1996.

Dickson, Paul, and Thomas B. Allen. *The Bonus Army: An American Epic.* New York: Walker and Company, 2004.

Dierenfield, Bruce. *Keeper of the Rules: Congressman Howard W. Smith of Virginia.* Charlottesville: University Press of Virginia, 1987.

Dies, Martin. *Martin Dies' Story.* New York: Bookmailer, 1963.

———. *The Trojan Horse in America.* New York: Dodd, Mead, 1940.

Dimock, Wai-chee. *Empire for Liberty: Melville and the Poetics of Individualism.* Princeton, N.J.: Princeton University Press, 1989.

Dinnerstein, Leonard. *America and the Survivors of the Holocaust.* New York: Columbia University Press, 1982.

Divine, Robert A. *The Illusion of Neutrality.* Chicago: University of Chicago Press, 1962.

———. *Roosevelt and World War II.* New York: Penguin Books, 1970.

Donnelly, Mark. *Britain in the Second World War.* New York: Routledge, 1999.

Donner, Frank J. *The Un-Americans.* New York: Ballantine Books, 1961.

Dorough, C. Dwight. *Mr. Sam.* New York: Random House, 1962.

Drinnon, Richard. *Keeper of Concentration Camps: Dillon S. Myer and American Racism.* Berkeley: University of California Press, 1987.

Drummond, Donald Francis. *The Passing of American Neutrality, 1937–1941.* Ann Arbor: University of Michigan Press, 1955.

Drury, Allen. *A Senate Journal, 1943–1945.* New York: McGraw-Hill, 1963.

DuBois, W. E. B. "Race Relations in the United States, 1917–1947." *Phylon* 9 (Third Quarter 1948): 234–247.

Dudziak, Mary L. *Cold War Civil Rights: Race and the Image of American Democracy.* Princeton, N.J.: Princeton University Press, 2000.

———. *War-Time: An Idea, Its History, Its Consequences.* New York: Oxford University Press, 2012.

Dunn, Susan. *Roosevelt's Purge: How FDR Fought to Change the Democratic Party.* Cambridge, Mass.: Belknap Press of Harvard University Press, 2010.

Eagles, Charles W. *Democracy Delayed: Congressional Reapportionment and Urban-Rural Conflict in the 1920s.* Athens: University of Georgia Press, 1990.

Edwards, George C. III, and B. Dan Wood. "Who Influences Whom? The President, Congress, and the Media." *American Political Science Review* 93 (June 1999): 327–344.

Edwards, Lee. *Missionary for Freedom: The Life and Times of Walter Judd.* New York: Paragon House, 1990.

Ehrlich, Matthew C. *Radio Utopia: Postwar Audio Documentary in the Public Interest.* Urbana: University of Illinois Press, 2011.

Evans, Thomas W. *The Education of Ronald Reagan: The General Electric Years and the Untold Story of His Conversion to Conservatism.* New York: Columbia University Press, 2006.

Feingold, Henry L. *Bearing Witness: How America and Its Jews Responded to the Holocaust.* Syracuse, N.Y.: Syracuse University Press, 1995.

———. *Politics of Rescue: The Roosevelt Administration and the Holocaust, 1938–1945.* New Brunswick, N.J.: Rutgers University Press, 1970.

Ferrell, Robert H. *Harry S Truman: A Life.* Columbia: University of Missouri Press, 1994.

———. *Woodrow Wilson and World War I, 1917–1921.* New York: Harper & Row, 1985.

Feurer, Rosemary. *Radical Unionism in the Midwest, 1900–1950.* Urbana: University of Illinois Press, 2006.

"Findings and Recommendations of the Special Committee on Service Voting." *American Political Science Review* 46 (June 1952): 512–523.

Finegold, Kenneth, and Theda Skocpol. *State and Party in America's New Deal.* Madison: University of Wisconsin Press, 1995.

Finley, Keith M. *Delaying the Dream: Southern Senators and the Fight against Civil Rights, 1938–1965.* Baton Rouge: Louisiana State University Press, 2008.

Fish, Hamilton. *Memoir of an American Patriot.* Washington, D.C.: Regnery Gateway, 1991.

Fite, Gilbert C. *Richard B. Russell, Jr., Senator from Georgia.* Chapel Hill: University of North Carolina Press, 1991.

Flamm, Michael W. "The National Farmers Union and the Evolution of Agrarian Liberalism, 1937–1946." *Agricultural History* 68 (Summer 1994): 54–80.

Fleissner, James P. "August 11, 1938: A Day in the Life of Senator Walter F. George." *Journal of Southern Legal History* 9 (2001): 55–101.

Fleming, Thomas. *The New Dealers' War: FDR and the War within World War II.* New York: Basic Books, 2001.

Flynn, George Q. *The Mess in Washington: Manpower Mobilization in World War II.* Westport, Conn.: Greenwood Press, 1979.

Fones-Wolf, Elizabeth A. *Selling Free Enterprise: The Business Assault on Labor and Liberalism, 1945–1960.* Urbana: University of Illinois Press, 1994.

Formisano, Ronald P. *Boston against Busing: Race, Class, and Ethnicity in the 1960s and 1970s.* Chapel Hill: University of North Carolina Press, 2004.

Fosher, Kerry B. *Under Construction: Making Homeland Security at the Local Level.* Chicago: University of Chicago Press, 2009.

Fraser, Steve, and Gary Gerstle, eds. *The Rise and Fall of the New Deal Order, 1930–1980.* Princeton, N.J.: Princeton University Press, 1989.

Freidel, Frank Burt. *Franklin D. Roosevelt: A Rendezvous with Destiny*. Boston: Little Brown, 1990.

French, Michael. *U.S. Economic History since 1945*. Manchester, England: Manchester University Press, 1997.

Fried, Richard M. *Nightmare in Red: The McCarthy Era in Perspective*. New York: Oxford University Press, 1990.

Fromkin, David. *Europe's Last Summer: Who Started the Great War in 1914?* New York: Alfred A. Knopf, 2004.

Frydl, Kathleen J. *The GI Bill*. New York: Cambridge University Press, 2009.

Funigiello, Philip J. *Chronic Politics: Health Care Security from FDR to George W. Bush*. Lawrence: University Press of Kansas, 2005.

Fussell, Paul. *Wartime: Understanding and Behavior in the Second World War*. New York: Oxford University Press, 1989.

F. V. L., Jr. "The Nationality Act of 1940." *Virginia Law Review* 27 (February 1941): 531–543.

Gage, Beverly. *The Day Wall Street Exploded: A Story of America in Its First Age of Terror*. New York: Oxford University Press, 2009.

Gaglielmo, Thomas A. "Fighting for Caucasian Rights: Mexicans, Mexican Americans, and the Transnational Struggle for Civil Rights in World War II Texas." *Journal of American History* (March 2006): 1212–1237.

Galbraith, John Kenneth. *A Life in Our Times: Memoirs*. Boston: Houghton Mifflin, 1981.

Galloway, George B. "Leadership in the House of Representatives." *Western Political Quarterly* 12 (June 1959): 417–441.

Gallup, George H. *The Gallup Poll, Public Opinion, 1935–1971*, vol. 1, *1935–1948*. New York: Random House, 1972.

"Gallup and Fortune Polls." *Public Opinion Quarterly* 4 (June 1940): 339–363.

"Gallup and Fortune Polls." *Public Opinion Quarterly* 6 (Autumn 1942): 475–494.

Gardner, Martha. *The Qualities of a Citizen: Women, Immigration, and Citizenship, 1870–1965*. Princeton, N.J.: Princeton University Press, 2005.

Garfinkel, Herbert. *When Negroes March: The March on Washington Movement in the Organizational Politics for FEPC*. Glencoe, Ill.: Free Press, 1959.

Gellermann, William. *Martin Dies*. New York: John Day, 1944.

Gellman, Irwin F. *The Contender, Richard Nixon: The Congress Years, 1946–1952*. New York: Free Press, 1999.

Genizi, Haim. *America's Fair Share: The Admission and Resettlement of Displaced Persons, 1945–1952*. Detroit, Mich.: Wayne State University Press, 1993.

Gerstle, Gary, and John Mollenkopf, eds. *E Pluribus Unum? Contemporary and Historical Perspectives on Immigrant Political Incorporation*. New York: Russell Sage Foundation, 2001.

"The GI Bill of Rights." *The New Republic* 111 (October 23, 1944): 512.

Gifford, Laura Jane. *The Center Cannot Hold: The 1960 Presidential Election and the Rise of Modern Conservatism*. DeKalb: Northern Illinois University Press, 2009.

Giglio, James N. *The Presidency of John F. Kennedy*. Lawrence: University Press of Kansas, 1991.

Gilbert, Martin. *The Holocaust: A History of the Jews of Europe during the Second World War*. New York: Henry Holt, 1985.

———. *Kristallnacht: Prelude to Destruction*. New York: HarperCollins Publishers, 2006.

Gillon, Steven M. *Politics and Vision: The ADA and American Liberalism, 1947–1985*. New York: Oxford University Press, 1987.

Gladchuk, John Joseph. "Reticent Reds: HUAC, Hollywood, and the Evolution of the Red Menace, 1935–1950." Ph.D. dissertation, University of California, Riverside, 2006.

Goldstein, Eric L. *The Price of Whiteness: Jews, Race, and American Identity*. Princeton, N.J.: Princeton University Press, 2006.

Goodno, Floyd Russel. "Walter H. Judd: Spokesman for China in the United States House of Representatives." Ed.D., Oklahoma State University, 1962.

Goodwin, Doris Kearns. *No Ordinary Time: Franklin and Eleanor Roosevelt, The Home Front in World War II*. New York: Simon and Schuster, 1994.

Gordon, Colin. *Dead on Arrival: The Politics of Health Care in Twentieth-Century America*. Princeton, N.J.: Princeton University Press, 2005.

———. *New Deals: Business, Labor, and Politics in America, 1920–1935*. New York: Cambridge University Press, 1994.

Gordon, Lester I. "John McCormack and the Roosevelt Era." Ph.D. dissertation, Boston University, 1976.

Gould, Lewis L. *Progressives and Prohibitionists: Texas Democrats in the Wilson Era*. Austin and London: University of Texas Press, 1973.

Graham, Otis L., Jr. *An Encore for Reform: The Old Progressives and the New Deal*. New York: Oxford University Press, 1967.

Green, Adwin Wigfall. *The Man Bilbo*. Baton Rouge: Louisiana State University Press, 1963.

Greenberg, Cheryl Lynn. *"Or Does It Explode?" Black Harlem in the Great Depression*. New York: Oxford University Press, 1991.

Greenberg, David. *Nixon's Shadow: The History of an Image*. New York: W. W. Norton, 2003.

Griffin, John D., and Michael Keane. "Are African Americans Effectively Represented in Congress?" *Political Research Quarterly* 64 (March 2011): 145–156.

Griffith, Robert. *The Politics of Fear: Joseph R. McCarthy and the Senate*. Lexington: University Press of Kentucky, 1970.

Guffey, Joseph F. *Seventy Years on the Red-Fire Wagon; from Tilden to Truman, through New Freedom and New Deal*. n.p., 1952.

Guinsburg, Thomas N. *The Pursuit of Isolationism in the United States Senate from Versailles to Pearl Harbor*. New York: Garland Publishing, 1982.

Gulick, Merle L. "Tom Connally as a Founder of the United Nations." Ph.D. dissertation, Georgetown University, 1955.

Haber, William. "Some Problems of Manpower Allocation." *American Economic Review* 42 (May 1952): 385–398.

Hair, William Ivy. *The Kingfish and his Realm: The Life and Times of Huey P. Long*. Baton Rouge: Louisiana State University Press, 1991.

Hairgrove, Kenneth D. "Sam Rayburn: Congressional Leader, 1940–1952." Ph.D. dissertation, Texas Tech University, 1974.

Hale, Grace Elizabeth. *Making Whiteness: The Culture of Segregation in the South, 1890–1940.* New York: Pantheon Books, 1998.

Hall, Jacquelyn Dowd. *Revolt against Chivalry: Jessie Daniel Ames and the Women's Campaign against Lynching,* rev. ed. New York: Columbia University Press, 1993.

Halt, Charles, "Joseph F. Guffey, New Deal Politician From Pennsylvania." Ph.D. dissertation, Syracuse University, 1965.

Hamby, Alonzo L. *Beyond the New Deal: Harry S Truman and American Liberalism.* New York: Columbia University Press, 1973.

Hamilton, Alexander, James Madison, and John Jay. *The Federalist,* edited by Terence Ball. New York: Cambridge University Press, 2003.

Hamilton, Virginia Van der Veer. *Lister Hill: Statesman from the South.* Chapel Hill: University of North Carolina Press, 1987.

Hardeman, D. B., and Donald C. Bacon. *Rayburn: A Biography.* Austin: Texas Monthly Press, 1987.

Hart, Justin. "Making Democracy Safe for the World: Race, Propaganda, and the Transformation of U.S. Foreign Policy during World War II." *Pacific Historical Review* 73 (February 2004): 49–84.

Hartmann, Susan M. *Truman and the 80th Congress.* Columbia: University of Missouri Press, 1971.

Hartz, Louis. *The Liberal Tradition in America.* New York: Harcourt, Brace, 1955.

Hasenfus, William A. "Managing Partner: Joseph W. Martin, Jr., Republican Leader of the United States House of Representatives, 1939–1959." Ph.D. dissertation, Boston College, 1986.

Hawley, Ellis W. *The Great War and the Search for Modern Order: A History of the American People and their Institutions, 1917–1933,* 2nd ed. New York: St. Martin's Press, 1992.

———. *The New Deal and the Problem of Monopoly: A Study in Economic Ambivalence.* New York: Fordham University Press, 1995.

Hayashi, Brian Masaru. *Democratizing the Enemy: The Japanese American Internment.* Princeton, N.J.: Princeton University Press, 2004.

Haynes, John Earl, Harvey Klehr, and Alexander Vassiliev. *Spies: The Rise and Fall of the KGB in America.* New Haven, Conn.: Yale University Press, 2009.

Heinrichs, Waldo. *Threshold of War: Franklin D. Roosevelt and American Entry into World War II.* New York: Oxford University Press, 1988.

Hendrickson, Kenneth E., Jr., and Michael L. Collins, eds. *Profiles in Power: Twentieth-Century Texans in Washington.* Arlington Heights, Ill.: Harlan Davidson, 1993.

Hero, Alfred O., Jr. "Liberalism-Conservatism Revisited: Foreign vs. Domestic Federal Policies, 1937–1967." *Public Opinion Quarterly* 33 (Autumn 1969): 399–408.

Herring, E. Pendleton. "First Session of the Seventy-Fourth Congress, January 3, 1935, to August 26, 1935." *American Political Science Review* 29 (December 1935): 985–1005.

Herzstein, Robert. *Henry R. Luce: A Political Portrait of the Man Who Created the American Century.* New York: Scribner's, 1994.

Hibbing, John R., and Elizabeth Theiss-Morse. *Congress as Public Enemy: Public Attitudes toward American Political Institutions.* New York: Cambridge University Press, 1995.

Hietala, Thomas. *Manifest Design: American Exceptionalism and Empire*, rev. ed. Ithaca, N.Y.: Cornell University Press, 2003.

Higgs, Robert. *Crisis and Leviathan: Critical Episodes in the Growth of American Government.* New York: Oxford University Press, 1987.

———. "From Central Planning to the Market: The American Transition, 1945–1947." *Journal of Economic History* 59 (September 1999): 600–623.

Higham, John. *Strangers in the Land: Patterns of American Nativism, 1860–1925.* New Brunswick, N.J.: Rutgers University Press, 1955.

Hinckley, Barbara. *The Seniority System in Congress.* Bloomington: Indiana University Press, 1972.

Hinds, Asher C. *Hinds' Precedents of the House of Representatives of the United States, Including References to Provisions of the Constitution, the Laws, and Decisions of the United States Senate.* Washington, D.C.: Government Printing Office, 1907–1908.

Hirsch, Julius. "Evaluation of Our Wartime Price Control." *Journal of Marketing* 8 (January 1944): 281–288.

Hoff, Joan. *Nixon Reconsidered.* New York: Basic Books, 1994.

Hoffmann, Stanley. "The Effects of World War II on French Society and Politics." *French Historical Studies* 2 (Spring 1961): 28–63.

Hofstadter, Richard. *The American Political Tradition and the Men Who Made It.* New York: Alfred A. Knopf, 1948.

———. "The Pseudo-Conservative Revolt." *American Scholar* 24 (Winter 1954–1955): 11–17.

Hogansen, Kristen. *Fighting for American Manhood: How Gender Politics Provoked the Spanish-American and Philippine-American Wars.* New Haven, Conn.: Yale University Press, 1998.

Honey, Maureen. *Creating Rosie the Riveter: Class, Gender, and Propaganda during World War II.* Amherst: University of Massachusetts Press, 1984.

Horowitz, David A. *Beyond Left and Right: Insurgency and the Establishment.* Urbana: University of Illinois Press, 1997.

———. "Senator Borah's Crusade to Save Small Business from the New Deal." *Historian* 55 (Summer 1993): 693–708.

Horsman, Reginald. *Race and Manifest Destiny: The Origins of American Racial Anglo-Saxonism.* Cambridge, Mass.: Harvard University Press, 1981.

Howard, John. *Concentration Camps on the Home Front: Japanese Americans in the House of Jim Crow.* Chicago: University of Chicago Press, 2008.

Hulsey, Byron C. *Everett Dirksen and His Presidents: How a Senate Giant Shaped American Politics.* Lawrence: University Press of Kansas, 2000.

Hunt, Michael. *Ideology and U.S. Foreign Policy.* New Haven, Conn.: Yale University Press, 1987.

Huntington, E. V. "The Apportionment of Representatives in Congress." *Transactions of the American Mathematical Society* 30 (1928): 85–110.

———. "A New Method of Apportionment of Representatives." *Journal of the American Statistical Association* 17 (September 1921): 859–887.

Huthmacher, J. Joseph. *Senator Robert F. Wagner and the Rise of Urban Liberalism.* New York: Atheneum, 1968.

Hyman, Harold M. *American Singularity: The 1787 Northwest Ordinance, the 1862 Homestead and Morrill Acts, and the 1944 G.I. Bill.* Athens: University of Georgia Press, 1987.

Irons, Peter H. *Justice at War.* New York: Oxford University Press, 1983.

"It's Up to Mr. Sam." *The New Republic* 142 (February 8, 1960): 3–4.

Jacobs, John. *A Rage for Justice: The Passion and Politics of Phillip Burton.* Berkeley: University of California Press, 1995.

Jacobs, Meg. "'How About Some Meat?': The Office of Price Administration, Consumption Politics, State Building from the Bottom Up, 1941–1946." *Journal of American History* 84 (December 1997): 910–941.

———. *Pocketbook Politics: Economic Citizenship in Twentieth-Century America.* Princeton, N.J.: Princeton University Press, 2005.

Jacobs, Meg, William J. Novak, and Julian E. Zelizer, eds. *The Democratic Experiment: New Directions in American Political History.* Princeton, N.J.: Princeton University Press, 2003.

Jacobson, Matthew Frye. *Whiteness of a Different Color: European Immigrants and the Alchemy of Race.* Cambridge, Mass.: Harvard University Press, 1999.

Janeway, Michael. *Fall of the House of Roosevelt: Brokers of Ideas and Power from FDR to LBJ.* New York: Columbia University Press, 2004.

Jeffries, John W. *Wartime America: The World War II Home Front.* Chicago: Ivan R. Dee, 1996.

Johnson, Kimberly. *Reforming Jim Crow: Southern Politics and State in the Age before Brown.* New York: Oxford University Press, 2010.

Johnson, Lyndon B. *The Vantage Point: Perspectives of the Presidency, 1963–1969.* New York: Holt, Rinehart and Winston, 1971.

Johnson, Robert David. *Congress and the Cold War.* New York: Cambridge University Press, 2006.

Jonas, Manfred. *Isolationism in America, 1935–1941.* Ithaca, N.Y.: Cornell University Press, 1966.

Jones, Jesse H., and Carl H. Pforzheimer. *Fifty Billion Dollars: My Thirteen Years with the RFC, 1932–1945.* New York: Macmillan, 1951.

Kabaservice, Geoffrey. *Rule and Ruin: The Downfall of Moderation and the Destruction of the Republican Party, from Eisenhower to the Tea Party.* New York: Oxford University Press, 2012.

Karst, Kenneth L. *Belonging to America: Equal Citizenship and the Constitution.* New Haven, Conn.: Yale University Press, 1989.

Katznelson, Ira, Kim Geiger, and Daniel Kryder. "Limiting Liberalism: The Southern Veto in Congress, 1933–1950." *Political Science Quarterly* 108 (Summer 1993): 283–306.

Kazin, Michael. *American Dreamers: How the Left Changed a Nation.* New York: Alfred A. Knopf, 2011.

————. "A Liberal Nation in Spite of Itself." *International Labor and Working-Class History* 74 (Fall 2008): 38–41.

Keene, Jennifer D. *Doughboys, the Great War, and the Remaking of America.* Baltimore, Md.: Johns Hopkins University Press, 2001.

Kelley, Robin D. G. *Hammer and Hoe: Alabama Communists during the Great Depression.* Chapel Hill: University of North Carolina Press, 1990.

Kenneally, James J. *A Compassionate Conservative: A Political Biography of Joseph W. Martin, Jr., Speaker of the U.S. House of Representatives.* Lanham, Md.: Lexington Books, 2003.

Kennedy, David M. *Freedom from Fear: The American People in Depression and War, 1929–1945.* New York: Oxford University Press, 1999.

————. *Over Here: The First World War and American Society.* New York: Oxford University Press, 1980.

Kennedy, William P. *America's Fighting Congress.* S. Doc. no. 78–94. Washington, D.C.: Government Printing Office, 1943.

Kersten, Andrew Edmund. *Race, Jobs, and the War: The FEPC in the Midwest, 1941–46.* Urbana: University of Illinois Press, 2000.

Kessler-Harris, Alice. *In Pursuit of Equity: Women, Men, and the Quest for Economic Citizenship in 20th-Century America.* New York: Oxford University Press, 2001.

Keyssar, Alexander. *The Right to Vote: The Contested History of Democracy in the United States.* New York: Basic Books, 2000.

Kimball, Warren F. *The Juggler: Franklin Roosevelt as Wartime Statesman.* Princeton, N.J.: Princeton University Press, 1991.

————. *The Most Unsordid Act: Lend-Lease, 1939–1941.* Baltimore, Md.: Johns Hopkins University Press, 1969.

Kimmage, Michael. *The Conservative Turn: Lionel Trilling, Whittaker Chambers, and the Lessons of Anti-Communism.* Cambridge, Mass.: Harvard University Press, 2009.

Klehr, Harvey, John Earl Haynes, and Fridrikh Igorevich Firsov. *The Secret World of American Communism.* New Haven, Conn.: Yale University Press, 1995.

Klein, Jennifer. "A New Deal Restoration: Individuals, Communities, and the Long Struggle for the Collective Good." *International Labor and Working-Class History* 74 (Fall 2008): 42–48.

Kloppenberg, James T. *Uncertain Victory: Social Democracy and Progressivism in European and American Thought, 1870–1920.* New York: Oxford University Press, 1986.

Knock, Thomas J. *To End All Wars: Woodrow Wilson and the Quest for a New World Order.* New York: Oxford University Press, 1992.

Kochavi, Arieh J. *Post-Holocaust Politics: Britain, the United States and Jewish Refugees, 1945–1948.* Chapel Hill: University of North Carolina Press, 2001.

Koistinen, Paul A. C. "Mobilizing the World War II Economy: Labor and the Industrial-Military Alliance." *Pacific Historical Review* 42 (November 1973): 443–478.

Kramer, Dale. "The American Fascists." *Harpers Magazine* (September 1940): 380–393.

Kryder, Daniel. *Divided Arsenal: Race and the American State in World War II.* New York: Cambridge University Press, 2000.

Kurz, Kenneth Franklin. "Franklin Roosevelt and the Gospel of Fear: The Responses of the Roosevelt Administration to Charges of Subversion." Ph.D. dissertation, University of California at Los Angeles, 1995.

Lash, Joseph P. *Dealers and Dreamers: A New Look at the New Deal.* New York: Doubleday, 1988.

Lee, R. Alton. *Truman and Taft-Hartley: A Question of Mandate.* Lexington: University of Kentucky Press, 1966.

LeFeber, Walter. *The New Empire: An Interpretation of American Expansion, 1860–1898.* Ithaca, N.Y.: Cornell University Press, 1963.

Leff, Mark H. "The Politics of Sacrifice on the American Home Front in World War II." *Journal of American History* 77 (March 1991): 1296–1318.

———. "Taxing the 'Forgotten Man': The Politics of Social Security Finance in the New Deal." *Journal of American History* 70 (September 1983): 359–381.

Leong, Karen J. "Foreign Policy, National Identity, and Citizenship: The Roosevelt White House and the Expediency of Repeal." *Journal of American Ethnic History* 22 (Summer 2003): 3–30.

Leuchtenburg, William E. *Franklin D. Roosevelt and the New Deal, 1932–1940.* New York: Harper & Row, 1963.

Levine, Rhonda F. *Class Struggle and the New Deal: Industrial Labor, Industrial Capital, and the State.* Lawrence: University Press of Kansas, 1988.

Lewy, Guenter. *The Cause That Failed: Communism in American Political Life.* New York: Oxford University Press, 1990.

Libbey, James K. *Dear Alben: Mr. Barkley of Kentucky.* Lexington: University Press of Kentucky, 1979.

Lichtenstein, Nelson. *Labor's War at Home: The CIO in World War II.* New York: Cambridge University Press, 1987.

Lichtman, Allan J. *White Protestant Nation: The Rise of the American Conservative Movement.* New York: Atlantic Monthly Press, 2008.

Lieberman, Robert C. *Shifting the Color Line: Race and the American Welfare State.* Cambridge, Mass.: Harvard University Press, 1998.

Lingeman, Richard R. *Don't You Know There's a War On? The American Home Front, 1941–1945.* New York: G. P. Putnam's Sons, 1970.

Lisio, Donald J. *The President and Protest: Hoover, Conspiracy, and the Bonus Riot.* Columbia: University of Missouri Press, 1974.

Little, Dwayne Lee. "The Political Leadership of Speaker Sam Rayburn, 1940–1961." Ph.D. dissertation, University of Cincinnati, 1970.

Livingston, Jeffery C. "Ohio Congressman John M. Vorys: A Republican Conservative Nationalist and Twentieth Century American Foreign Policy." Ph.D. dissertation, University of Toledo, 1989.

Lodge, Henry Cabot. *The Senate and the League of Nations.* New York: C. Scribner's Sons, 1925.

Loescher, Gil, and John A. Scanlan. *Calculated Kindness: Refugees and America's Half-Open Door, 1945 to the Present.* New York: Free Press, 1986.

Lopez, Nancy Lynn. "'Allowing Fears to Overwhelm Us': A Re-examination of the House Special Committee on Un-American Activities, 1938–1944." Ph.D. dissertation, Rice University, 2002.

Lorence, James J. *Gerald J. Boileau and the Progressive-Farmer-Labor Alliance: Politics of the New Deal.* Columbia: University of Missouri Press, 1994.

Lower, Richard Coke. *A Bloc of One: The Political Career of Hiram W. Johnson.* Stanford, Calif.: Stanford University Press, 1993.

Lowi, Theodore J. *The End of Liberalism: The Second Republic of the United States,* 2nd ed. New York: W. W. Norton, 1979.

Lowitt, Richard. *George W. Norris: The Making of a Progressive, 1861–1912.* Syracuse, N.Y.: Syracuse University Press, 1963.

———. *George W. Norris: The Persistence of a Progressive, 1913–1933.* Urbana: University of Illinois Press, 1971.

———. *George W. Norris: The Triumph of a Progressive, 1933–1944.* Urbana: University of Illinois Press, 1978.

Ma, Xiaohua. "The Sino-American Alliance during World War II and the Lifting of the Chinese Exclusion Acts." *American Studies International* 38 (June 2000): 39–61.

MacDonnell, Francis. *Insidious Foes: The Axis Fifth Column and the American Home Front.* New York: Oxford University Press, 1995.

Mackenzie, G. Calvin, and Robert Weisbrot. *The Liberal Hour: Washington and the Politics of Change in the 1960s.* New York: Penguin Books, 2009.

MacLean, Nancy. "Getting New Deal History Wrong." *International Labor and Working-Class History* 74 (Fall 2008): 49–55.

Macmahon, Arthur W. "Congressional Oversight of Administration: The Power of the Purse, I." *Political Science Quarterly* 58 (June 1943): 161–190.

MacNeil, Neil. *Forge of Democracy: The House of Representatives.* New York: David McKay, 1963.

Maney, Patrick J. *"Young Bob" La Follette: A Biography of Robert M. La Follette Jr., 1895–1953.* Columbia: University of Missouri Press, 1978.

Margulies, Herbert F. *The Mild Reservationists and the League of Nations Controversy in the Senate.* Columbia: University of Missouri Press, 1989.

Martin, Joe, as told to Robert J. Donovan. *My First Fifty Years in Politics.* Westport, Conn.: Greenwood Press, 1975.

Matheny, David Leon. "A Comparison of Selected Foreign Policy Speeches of Senator Tom Connally." Ph.D. dissertation, University of Oklahoma, 1965.

McCoy, Donald R. *Angry Voices: Left of Center Politics in the New Deal Era.* Lawrence: University Press of Kansas, 1958.

———. *Quest and Response: Minority Rights and the Truman Administration.* Lawrence: University Press of Kansas, 1973.

McDaniel, Dennis Kay. "Martin Dies of Un-American Activities: His Life and Times." Ph.D. dissertation. University of Houston, 1988.

McGirr, Lisa. *Suburban Warriors: The Origins of the New American Right.* Princeton, N.J.: Princeton University Press, 2001.

McJimsey, George. *The Presidency of Franklin Delano Roosevelt.* Lawrence: University Press of Kansas, 2000.

McKean, David. *Tommy the Cork: Washington's Ultimate Insider from Roosevelt to Reagan.* Hanover, N.H.: Steerforth Press, 2004.

McKenna, Marian C. *Borah.* Ann Arbor: University of Michigan Press, 1961.

McMahon, Kevin. *Reconsidering Roosevelt on Race: How the Presidency Paved the Road to Brown.* Chicago: University of Chicago Press, 2004.

McMillan, James E. "Father of the GI Bill: Ernest W. McFarland and Veterans' Legislation." *Journal of Arizona History* 35 (1994): 357–376.

McMillen, Neil R. *Remaking Dixie: The Impact of World War II on the American South.* Jackson: University Press of Mississippi, 1997.

Meier, August, and Elliott Rudwick. *CORE: A Study in the Civil Rights Movement, 1942–1968.* New York: Oxford University Press, 1973.

Mellichamp, Josephine. *Senators from Georgia.* Huntsville, Ala.: Strode Publishers, 1976.

Mettler, Suzanne. "Bringing the State Back in to Civic Engagement: Policy Feedback Effects of the G.I. Bill for World War II Veterans." *American Political Science Review* 96 (June 2002): 351–365.

———. "The Creation of the G.I. Bill of Rights of 1944: Melding Social and Participatory Citizenship Ideals." *Journal of Policy History* 17 (2005): 345–374.

———. "'The Only Good Thing Was the G.I. Bill': Effects of the Education and Training Provisions on African-American Veterans' Political Participation." *Studies in American Political Development* 19 (Spring 2005): 31–52.

Michel, Sonya. *Children's Interests/Mothers' Rights: The Shaping of America's Child Care Policy.* New Haven, Conn.: Yale University Press, 1999.

Miller, Clyde R. "Foreign Efforts to Increase Disunity." *Annals of the American Academy of Political and Social Science* 223 (September 1942): 173–181.

Mitchell, Gary. "Women Standing for Women: The Early Political Career of Mary T. Norton." *New Jersey History* 96 (Spring-Summer 1978): 27–42.

Mize, Ronald L., and Alicia C. S. Swords. *Consuming Mexican Labor: From the Bracero Program to NAFTA.* Toronto: University of Toronto Press, 2011.

Moe, Ronald C., and Steven C. Teel. "Congress as Policy-Maker: A Necessary Reappraisal." *Political Science Quarterly* 85 (September 1970): 443–470.

Montgomery, David. "The Mythical Man." *International Labor and Working-Class History* 74 (Fall 2008): 56–62.

Mooney, Booth. *Roosevelt and Rayburn: A Political Partnership.* Philadelphia: Lippincott, 1971.

Morgan, Chester M. *Redneck Liberal: Theodore G. Bilbo and the New Deal.* Baton Rouge: Louisiana State University Press, 1985.

Morse, Arthur D. *While Six Million Died: A Chronicle of American Apathy.* New York: Random House, 1967.

Moser, John E. *Right Turn: John T. Flynn and the Transformation of American Liberalism.* New York: New York University Press, 2005.

Mouré, Kenneth, and Martin S. Alexander, eds. *Crisis and Renewal in France, 1918–1962.* New York: Berghahn Books, 2002.

Mulder, Ronald A. "The Progressive Insurgents in the United States Senate, 1935–1936: Was There a Second New Deal?" *Mid-America* 57 (April 1975): 106–125.

Muller, Eric L. *American Inquisition: The Hunt for Japanese American Disloyalty in World War II.* Chapel Hill: University of North Carolina Press, 2007.

Mundt, Karl. "A Strong Opposition Is Needed." *Vital Speeches of the Day* 7 (September 1, 1941): 696–698.

Nash, Gerald D. *World War II and the West: Reshaping the Economy.* Lincoln: University of Nebraska Press, 1990.

National Archives. "Federal Register, Administration of Franklin D. Roosevelt (1933–1945)." http://www.archives.gov/federal-register/executive-orders/roosevelt.html.

Neal, Steve. *McNary of Oregon: A Political Biography.* Portland, Ore.: Western Imprints, 1985.

Nelson, Donald M. *Arsenal of Democracy: The Story of American War Production.* New York: Harcourt, Brace, 1946.

Nelson, Garrison. "Irish Identity Politics: The Reinvention of Speaker John W. McCormack of Boston." *New England Journal of Public Policy* 15 (Fall/Winter 1999/2000): 7–34.

Nelson, Harold M. *Libel: In News of Congressional Investigating Committees.* Minneapolis: University of Minnesota Press, 1961.

Ngai, Mae M. *Impossible Subjects: Illegal Aliens and the Making of Modern America.* Princeton, N.J.: Princeton University Press, 2004.

Nielsen, Kim E. *Un-American Womanhood: Antiradicalism, Antifeminism, and the First Red Scare.* Columbus: Ohio State University Press, 2001.

Nixon, H. C. "Politics of the Hills." *Journal of Politics* 2 (May 1946): 123–133.

Noyes, C. E. "Spending vs. Economy: A Ten-Year Record." *Editorial Research Reports 1940,* vol. 1. Washington, D.C.: CQ Press, 1940.

Oberdorfer, Don. *Senator Mansfield: The Extraordinary Life of a Great American Statesman and Diplomat.* Washington, D.C.: Smithsonian Books, 2003.

Ogden, Frederic D. *The Poll Tax in the South.* [University, Ala.]: University of Alabama Press, 1958.

Ogilviet, Sarah A., and Scott Miller. *Refuge Denied: The* St. Louis *Passengers and the Holocaust.* Madison: University of Wisconsin Press, 2006.

O'Leary, Kevin. *Saving Democracy: A Plan for Real Representation in America.* Stanford, Calif.: Stanford University Press, 2006.

O'Leary, Paul M. "Wartime Rationing and Governmental Organization." *American Political Science Review* 39 (December 1945): 1089–1106.

Olson, Keith W. *The G.I. Bill, the Veterans, and the Colleges.* Lexington: University Press of Kentucky, 1974.

O'Neill, Tip, with William Novak. *Man of the House: The Life and Political Memoirs of Speaker Tip O'Neill.* New York: Random House, 1987.

O'Neill, William L. *A Democracy at War: America's Fight at Home and Abroad in World War II.* New York: Free Press, 1993.

Onkst, David H. "'First a Negro . . . Incidentally a Veteran': Black World War Two Veterans and the G.I. Bill of Rights in the Deep South, 1944–1948." *Journal of Social History* 31 (Spring 1998): 517–543.

O'Reilly, Kenneth. "A New Deal for the FBI: The Roosevelt Administration, Crime Control, and National Security." *Journal of American History* 69 (December 1982): 638–658.

Orren, Karen, and Stephen Skowronek. "Regimes and Regime Building in American Government: A Review of the Literature on the 1940s." *Political Science Quarterly* 113 (Winter 1998–1999): 689–702.

Ortiz, Stephen R. "Rethinking the Bonus March: Federal Bonus Policy, the Veterans of Foreign Wars, and the Origins of a Protest Movement." *Journal of Policy History* 18 (2006): 275–303.

Oshinsky, David. *A Conspiracy So Immense: The World of Joe McCarthy.* New York: Free Press, 1983.

Parker, Richard. *John Kenneth Galbraith: His Life, His Politics, His Economics.* Chicago: University of Chicago Press, 2007.

Patenaude, Lionel V. "Garner, Sumners, and Connally: The Defeat of the Roosevelt Court Bill in 1937." *Southwestern Historical Quarterly* 74 (July 1970): 36–51.

Patterson, James T. *Congressional Conservatism and the New Deal: The Growth of the Conservative Coalition in Congress, 1933–1939.* Lexington: For the Organization of American Historians by the University of Kentucky Press, 1967.

———. *Mr. Republican: A Biography of Robert A. Taft.* Boston: Houghton Mifflin, 1972.

Paxton, Robert O. *Vichy France: Old Guard and New Order, 1940–1944.* New York: Columbia University Press, 2001.

Pearson, Kathryn. "Demographic Change and the Future of Congress." *PS: Political Science & Politics* 43 (April 2010): 235–238.

Pells, Richard H. *The Liberal Mind in a Conservative Age: American Intellectuals in the 1940s and 1950s.* New York: Harper & Row, 1985.

———. *Radical Visions and American Dreams: Culture and Social Thought in the Depression Years.* New York: Harper & Row, 1973.

Pencak, William. *For God and Country: The American Legion, 1919–1941.* Boston: Northeastern University Press, 1989.

Penkower, Monty Noam. *Decision on Palestine Deferred: America, Britain and Wartime Diplomacy, 1939–1945.* London and Portland, Ore.: Frank Cass, 2002.

Pepper, Claude D., with Hays Gorey. *Pepper, Eyewitness to a Century.* San Diego, Calif.: Harcourt Brace Jovanovich, 1987.

Perlstein, Rick. *Nixonland: The Rise of a President and the Fracturing of America.* New York: Scribner, 2008.

Perrett, Geoffrey. *Days of Sadness, Years of Triumph: The American People, 1939–1945.* New York: Coward, McCann, and Geoghegan, 1973.

Perry, Donald R. "Aliens in the United States." *Annals of the American Academy of Political and Social Science* 223 (September 1942): 1–9.

Perry, Jennings. *Democracy Begins at Home: The Tennessee Fight on the Poll Tax.* Philadelphia: Lippincott, 1944.

Phillips-Fein, Kim. *Invisible Hands: The Businessmen's Crusade against the New Deal.* New York: W. W. Norton, 2010.

Pickle, J. J., and Peggy Pickle. *Jake.* Austin: University of Texas Press, 1997.

Pleasants, Julian M. *Buncombe Bob: The Life and Times of Robert Rice Reynolds.* Chapel Hill: University of North Carolina Press, 2000.

Plotke, David. *Building a Democratic Political Order: Reshaping American Liberalism in the 1930s and 1940s.* New York: Cambridge University Press, 1996.

Poen, Monte M. *Harry S Truman versus the Medical Lobby: The Genesis of Medicare.* Columbia: University of Missouri Press, 1979.

Polenberg, Richard. *War and Society: The United States, 1941–1945.* Philadelphia: Lippincott, 1972.

Polsby, Nelson W. *How Congress Evolves: Social Bases of Institutional Change.* New York: Oxford University Press, 2004.

Pope, Robert Dean. "Senatorial Baron: The Long Political Career of Kenneth C. McKellar." Ph.D. dissertation, Yale University, 1975.

Porter, David L. *Congress and the Waning of the New Deal.* Port Washington, N.Y.: Kennikat Press, 1980.

———. *The Seventy-Sixth Congress and World War II, 1939–1940.* Columbia: University of Missouri Press, 1979.

Powers, Richard Gid. *Not without Honor: The History of American Anticommunism.* New York: Free Press, 1995.

Raider, Mark A. *The Emergence of American Zionism.* New York: New York University Press, 1998.

———. "'Irresponsible, Undisciplined Opposition': Ben Halpern on the Bergson Group and Jewish Terrorism in Pre-State Palestine." *American Jewish History* 92 (September 2004): 313–360.

Rawls, W. Lee. *In Praise of Deadlock: How Partisan Struggle Makes Better Laws.* Washington, D.C.: Woodrow Wilson Center Press, 2009.

Reagan, Patrick D. *Designing a New America: The Origins of New Deal Planning, 1890–1943.* Amherst: University of Massachusetts Press, 2000.

"Recent Anti-Alien Legislative Proposals." *Columbia Law Review* 39 (November 1939): 1207–1223.

"Recent Federal Legislation against Subversive Influences." *Columbia Law Review* 41 (January 1941): 159–171.

"Record of the 79th Congress (First Session), 1945." *Editorial Research Reports 1945*, vol. 2. Washington, D.C.: CQ Press, 1945.

Reed, Linda. *Simple Decency and Common Sense: The Southern Conference Movement, 1938–1963.* Bloomington: University of Indiana Press, 1991.

Reed, Merl E. *Seedtime for the Modern Civil Rights Movement: The President's Committee on Fair Employment Practice, 1941–1946.* Baton Rouge: Louisiana State University Press, 1991.

Reeves, Thomas C. *The Life and Times of Joe McCarthy: A Biography.* New York: Stein and Day, 1982.

Rehfeld, Andrew. *The Concept of Constituency: Political Representation, Democratic Legitimacy, and Institutional Design.* New York: Cambridge University Press, 2005.

Reynolds, David. *From Munich to Pearl Harbor: Roosevelt's America and the Origins of the Second World War.* Chicago: Ivan R. Dee, 2001.

Ricci, David M. *Good Citizenship in America.* New York: Cambridge University Press, 2004.

Riddick, Floyd M. "American Government and Politics: Third Session of the Seventy-Sixth Congress, January 3, 1940, to January 3, 1941." *American Political Science Review* 35 (April 1941): 284–303.

———. "The Second Session of the Seventy-Eighth Congress." *American Political Science Review* 39 (April 1945): 317–336.

Riddle, Donald H. *The Truman Committee: A Study in Congressional Responsibility.* New Brunswick, N.J.: Rutgers University Press, 1964.

Riggs, Fred Warren. *Pressures on Congress: A Study of the Repeal of Chinese Exclusion.* New York: King's Crown Press, 1950.

Riley, Susan E. "Caring for Rosie's Children: Federal Child Care Policies in the World War II Era." *Polity* 4 (Summer 1994): 655–675.

Ritchie, Donald A. *James M. Landis: Dean of the Regulators.* Cambridge, Mass.: Harvard University Press, 1980.

Ritchie, Donald A., ed. *Minutes of the U.S. Senate Democratic Conference, 1903–1964, Fifty-Eighth Congress through Eighty-Eighth Congress.* Washington, D.C.: U.S. Government Printing Office, 1998.

Robertson, David. *Sly and Able: A Political Biography of James F. Byrnes.* New York: W. W. Norton, 1994.

Robinson, George W. "Alben Barkley and the 1944 Tax Veto." *Register of the Kentucky Historical Society* 67 (July 1969): 197–210.

Robinson, Greg. *By Order of the President: FDR and the Internment of Japanese Americans.* Cambridge, Mass.: Harvard University Press, 2001.

Roof, Tracy. *American Labor, Congress, and the Welfare State, 1935–2010.* Baltimore, Md.: Johns Hopkins University Press, 2011.

Rorabaugh, W. J. *The Real Making of the President: Kennedy, Nixon, and the 1960 Election.* Lawrence: University Press of Kansas, 2009.

Rose, Elizabeth. *A Mother's Job: The History of Day Care, 1890–1960.* New York: Oxford University Press, 1999.

Rosenof, Theodore. "The Political Education of an American Radical: Thomas R. Amlie in the 1930s." *Wisconsin Magazine of History* 58 (Autumn 1974): 19–30.

Ross, David R. B. *Preparing for Ulysses: Politics and Veterans during World War II.* New York: Columbia University Press, 1969.

Rossinow, Doug. *Visions of Progress: The Left-Liberal Tradition in America.* Philadelphia: University of Pennsylvania Press, 2008.

Ruchames, Louis. *Race, Jobs and Politics: The Story of FEPC.* New York: Columbia University Press, 1953.

Ruetten, Richard T. "Burton K. Wheeler of Montana: A Progressive between the Wars." Ph.D. dissertation, University of Oregon, 1961.

Saloutos, Theodore. *The American Farmer and the New Deal.* Ames: Iowa State University Press, 1982.

Sanders, Elizabeth. *Roots of Reform: Farmers, Workers, and the American State, 1877–1917.* Chicago: University of Chicago Press, 1999.

Saunders, D. A. "The Dies Committee: First Phase." *Public Opinion Quarterly* 3 (April 1939): 223–238.

Saylor, Frances. "The Poll Tax Kills Democracy." *The Crisis* (May 1942): 162, 173.

Schaffer, Howard B. *Chester Bowles: New Dealer in the Cold War.* Cambridge, Mass.: Harvard University Press, 1993.

Schapsmeier, Edward L., and Frederick H. Schapsmeier. "Farm Policy from FDR to Eisenhower: Southern Democrats and the Politics of Agriculture." *Agricultural History* 53 (January 1979): 352–371.

Schechter, Patricia A. *Ida B. Wells-Barnett and American Reform, 1880–1930.* Chapel Hill: University of North Carolina Press, 2001.

Schickler, Eric. *Disjointed Pluralism: Institutional Innovation and the Development of the U.S. Congress.* Princeton, N.J.: Princeton University Press, 2001.

Schlesinger, Arthur M., Jr. *The Age of Roosevelt,* 3 vols. Boston: Houghton Mifflin, 1957–1960.

———. *The Imperial Presidency.* Boston: Houghton Mifflin, 1973.

———. *The Vital Center: The Politics of Freedom.* Boston: Houghton Mifflin, 1949.

Schlesinger, Arthur M., Jr., and Roger Bruns, eds. *Congress Investigates: A Documented History, 1792–1974,* vol. 4. New York: Chelsea House Publishers, 1975.

Schrecker, Ellen. *Many Are the Crimes: McCarthyism in America.* Boston: Little, Brown, 1998.

Schuck, Peter, and Rogers M. Smith. *Citizenship without Consent: Illegal Aliens in the American Polity.* New Haven, Conn.: Yale University Press, 1985.

Schultz, Kevin M. *Tri-Faith America: How Catholics and Jews Held Postwar America to Its Protestant Promises.* New York: Oxford University Press, 2011.

Schuman, Frederick L. "'Bill of Attainder' in the Seventy-Eighth Congress." *American Political Science Review* 37 (October 1943): 819–829.

Schwarz, Jordan A. *The New Dealers: Power Politics in the Age of Roosevelt.* New York: Alfred A. Knopf, 1993.

Scruggs, Otey M. "Evolution of the Mexican Farm Labor Agreement of 1942." *Agricultural History* 34 (July 1960): 140–149.

Seidman, Joel Isaac. *American Labor from Defense to Reconversion.* Chicago: University of Chicago Press, 1953.

Shanks, Cheryl. *Immigration and the Politics of American Sovereignty, 1890–1990.* Ann Arbor: University of Michigan Press, 2001.

Sheft, Mark A. "The End of the Smith Act Era: A Legal and Historical Analysis of *Scales v. United States.*" *American Journal of Legal History* 36 (April 1992): 164–202.

Sherry, Michael S. *In the Shadow of War: The United States since the 1930s.* New Haven, Conn.: Yale University Press, 1995.

Simmons, Jerold. *Operation Abolition: The Campaign to Abolish the House Un-American Activities Committee, 1938–1975.* New York and London: Garland Publishing, 1986.

Sitkoff, Harvard. "Racial Militancy and Interracial Violence in the Second World War." *Journal of American History* 58 (December 1971): 661–681.

Skocpol, Theda. *Protecting Soldiers and Mothers: The Political Origins of Social Policy in the United States.* Cambridge, Mass.: Belknap Press of Harvard University Press, 1992.

Skowronek, Stephen. *Building a New American State: The Expansion of National Administrative Capacities, 1877–1920.* New York: Cambridge University Press, 1982.

Small, Melvin. *The Presidency of Richard Nixon.* Lawrence: University Press of Kansas, 1999.

Smith, Geoffrey S. *To Save a Nation: American Extremism, the New Deal, and the Coming of World War II.* Chicago: Elephant Paperbacks, 1992.

Smith, Jason Scott. *Building New Deal Liberalism: The Political Economy of Public Works, 1933–1956.* New York: Cambridge University Press, 2006.

Smith, Rogers M. *Civic Ideals: Conflicting Visions of Citizenship in U.S. History.* New Haven, Conn.: Yale University Press, 1997.

Smith, Sharon Kay. "Elbert D. Thomas and America's Response to the Holocaust." Ph.D. dissertation, Brigham Young University, 1991.

Smyrl, Frank Herbert. "Tom Connally and the New Deal." Ph.D. dissertation, University of Oklahoma, 1968.

Sparrow, Bartholomew H. *From the Outside In: World War II and the American State.* Princeton, N.J.: Princeton University Press, 1996.

Sparrow, James T. *Warfare State: World War II Americans and the Age of Big Government.* New York: Oxford University Press, 2011.

"Speak Mr. Speaker." Bonham, Tex.: Sam Rayburn Foundation, 1978.

Spivack, Robert G. "The New Anti-Alien Drive." *New Republic* 109 (November 29, 1943): 740–741.

Spritzer, Donald E. *Senator James E. Murray and the Limits of Post-War Liberalism.* New York: Garland, 1985.

St. Clair, James E., and Linda C. Gugin. *Chief Justice Fred M. Vinson of Kentucky: A Political Biography.* Lexington: University Press of Kentucky, 2002.

Stein, Bruno. "Labor's Role in Government Agencies during World War II." *Journal of Economic History* 17 (September 1957): 389–408.

Steinberg, Alfred. *Sam Rayburn: A Biography.* New York: Hawthorn Books, 1975.

Stephanson, Anders. *Manifest Destiny: American Expansion and the Empire of Right.* New York: Hill and Wang, 1995.

Stoltzfus, Emilie. *Citizen, Mother, Worker: Debating Public Responsibility for Child Care after the Second World War.* Chapel Hill: University of North Carolina Press, 2003.

Stone, I. F. "Palestine Run-Around." *The Nation* 158 (March 18, 1944): 326–328.

Stone, Ralph. *The Irreconcilables: The Fight against the League of Nations.* Lexington: University Press of Kentucky, 1970.

Storrs, Landon R. Y. *Civilizing Capitalism: The National Consumers' League, Women's Activism, and Labor Standards in the New Deal Era.* Chapel Hill: University of North Carolina Press, 2000.

———. *The Second Red Scare and the Unmaking of the New Deal Left.* Princeton, N.J.: Princeton University Press, 2012.

Stripling, Robert E. *The Red Plot against America*. Drexel Hill, Pa.: Bell, 1949.

Sugrue, Thomas J. *The Origins of the Urban Crisis: Race and Inequality in Postwar Detroit*. Princeton, N.J.: Princeton University Press, 1996.

Swain, Martha H. *Pat Harrison: The New Deal Years*. Jackson: University Press of Mississippi, 1978.

Takaki, Ronald. *Double Victory: A Multicultural History of America in World War II*. Boston: Little, Brown, 2000.

Tap, Bruce. *Over Lincoln's Shoulder: The Committee on the Conduct of the War*. Lawrence: University Press of Kansas, 1998.

Taylor, Melissa Jane. "'Experts in Misery'?: American Consuls in Austria, Jewish Refugees and Restrictionist Immigration Policy, 1938–1941." Ph.D. dissertation, University of South Carolina, 2006.

Terkel, Studs. *"The Good War": An Oral History of World War II*. New York: Pantheon Books, 1984.

Theoharis, Athan G., ed. *Beyond the Hiss Case: The FBI, Congress, and the Cold War*. Philadelphia: Temple University Press, 1982.

Thomas, Elmer. *Forty Years a Legislator*, edited by Richard Lowitt and Carolyn G. Hanneman. Norman: University of Oklahoma Press, 2007.

Thomas, Helen. *Thanks for the Memories, Mr. President: Wit and Wisdom from the Front Row at the White House*. New York: Scribner, 2002.

Tichenor, Daniel J. *Dividing Lines: The Politics of Immigration Control in America*. Princeton, N.J.: Princeton University Press, 2002.

Tobin, Maurice B., and Joan Shaffer. *Hidden Power: The Seniority System and Other Customs of Congress*. New York: Greenwood Press, 1986.

Tompkins, C. David. *Senator Arthur H. Vandenberg: The Evolution of a Modern Republican, 1884–1945*. Lansing: Michigan State University Press, 1970.

Tucker, Robert W., and David Hendrickson. *Empire of Liberty: The Statecraft of Thomas Jefferson*. New York: Oxford University Press, 1990.

Tugwell, Rexford G. *The Democratic Roosevelt: A Biography of Franklin D. Roosevelt*. Garden City, N.Y.: Doubleday, 1957.

Turrentine, Lowell, and Sam D. Thurman Jr. "Wartime Federal Legislation." *California Law Review* 34 (June 1946): 277–330.

Tuttle, William M. *Daddy's Gone to War: The Second World War in the Lives of America's Children*. New York: Oxford University Press, 1993.

U.S. Congress. House of Representatives. Committee on Banking and Currency. *Price Control Bill*, pt. 1. 77th Congress, 1st session, 1941.

U.S. Congress. House of Representatives. Committee on Banking and Currency. *Price Control Bill*, pt. 2. 77th Congress, 1st session, 1941.

U.S. Congress. House of Representatives. Committee on Education and Labor. *Labor Management Relations Act*, House Report 245 to accompany H.R. 3020. 80th Congress, 1st session, 1947.

U.S. Congress. House of Representatives. Committee on Foreign Affairs. *American Neutrality Policy*. 74th Congress, 2nd session, 1936.

U.S. Congress. House of Representatives. Committee on Foreign Affairs. *American Neutrality Policy.* 76th Congress, 1st session, 1939.

U.S. Congress. House of Representatives. Committee on Foreign Affairs. *The Jewish Homeland in Palestine: Report to Accompany H.Res. 418.* 78th Congress, 2nd session, 1944.

U.S. Congress. House of Representatives. Committee on Immigration and Naturalization. "A Bill to Record the Lawful Admission for Permanent Residence of Kurt Wessely." Unpublished Hearings. 76th Congress, 1st session, February 15, 1939.

U.S. Congress. House of Representatives. Committee on Immigration and Naturalization. "Admission of German Refugee Children." Unpublished Hearings. 76th Congress, 1st session, July 19, 1939.

U.S. Congress. House of Representatives. Committee on Immigration and Naturalization. "H.R. 3266, H.R. 3165, and H.R. 5716." Unpublished Hearings. 76th Congress, 1st session, May 18, 1939.

U.S. Congress. House of Representatives. Committee on Immigration and Naturalization. "H.R. 3315." Unpublished Hearings. 77th Congress, 1st session, July 9, 1941.

U.S. Congress. House of Representatives. Committee on Immigration and Naturalization. "H.R. 6546, A Bill for the Relief of Benno von Mayrhauser and Oskar von Mayrhauser." Unpublished Hearings. 76th Congress, 1st session, July 19, 1939.

U.S. Congress. House of Representatives. Committee on Immigration and Naturalization. "H.R. 8295." Unpublished Hearings. 76th Congress, 2nd session, February 21, 1940.

U.S. Congress. House of Representatives. Committee on Immigration and Naturalization. "H.R. 9027, A Bill for the Relief of Doctor Gustav Weil, Irma Weil, and Marion Weil." Unpublished Hearings. 76th Congress, 2nd session, May 29, 1940.

U.S. Congress. House of Representatives. Committee on Immigration and Naturalization. "Isaac Zarembsky." Unpublished Hearings. 76th Congress, 1st session, May 17, 1939.

U.S. Congress. House of Representatives. Committee on Military Affairs. Report. *Use and Operation of War Plants in Prosecution of War.* 78th Congress, 1st session, 1943.

U.S. Congress. House of Representatives. Committee on Military Affairs. *Women's Army Auxiliary Corps.* 77th Congress, 2nd session, 1942.

U.S. Congress. House of Representatives. Committee on Ways and Means. *Individual Income Tax.* 78th Congress, 1st session, 1943.

U.S. Congress. House of Representatives. Committee on Ways and Means. *Revenue Revision of 1941,* vol. 1. 77th Congress, 1st session, 1941.

U.S. Congress. House of Representatives. Committee on Ways and Means. *Revenue Revision of 1941,* vol. 2. 77th Congress, 1st session, 1941.

U.S. Congress. House of Representatives. Conference Report. *Use and Operation of War Plants in Prosecution of War,* June 10, 1943. 78th Congress, 1st session, 1943.

U.S. Congress. House of Representatives. Special Committee on Un-American Activities. *Investigation of Un-American Propaganda Activities in the United States,* vols. 1–4, *Executive Hearings.* 76th Congress, 3rd session, 1939, 1940.

U.S. Congress. Senate. Committee on Banking and Currency. *Emergency Price Control Act.* 77th Congress, 1st session, 1941.

U.S. Congress. Senate. Committee on Banking and Currency. *Stabilizing the Cost of Living.* 77th Congress, 2nd session, 1942.

U.S. Congress. Senate. Committee on Finance. *Current Tax Payment Act of 1943.* 78th Congress, 1st session, 1943.

U.S. Congress. Senate. Committee on the Judiciary. Report. *Defense Plants.* 78th Congress, 1st session, 1943.

U.S. Congress. Senate. Committee on Military Affairs. *Manpower (National War Service Bill),* part 22. 78th Congress, 1st session, 1943.

United States Holocaust Memorial Museum. "Buchenwald." *Holocaust Encyclopedia.* http://www.ushmm.org/wlc/en/article.php?ModuleId=10005198.

United States Holocaust Memorial Museum. "Dachau." *Holocaust Encyclopedia.* http://www.ushmm.org/wlc/en/article.php?ModuleId=10005214.

United States Holocaust Memorial Museum. "Dora-Mittelbau." *Holocaust Encyclopedia.* http://www.ushmm.org/wlc/en/article.php?ModuleId=10005322.

Vandenberg, Arthur H., Jr., ed. *The Private Papers of Senator Vandenberg.* Boston: Houghton Mifflin, 1952.

Vargas, Zaragosa. *Labor Rights Are Civil Rights: Mexican American Workers in Twentieth-Century America.* Princeton, N.J.: Princeton University Press, 2005.

Vatter, Harold G. *The U.S. Economy in World War II.* New York: Columbia University Press, 1985.

Vaughn, Stephen. *Holding Fast the Inner Lines: Democracy, Nationalism, and the Committee on Public Information.* Chapel Hill: University of North Carolina Press, 1980.

Virginia Office of Civil Defense Committee on Child Care. *The War and Virginia's Children.* Richmond, Va.: Virginia Committee on Child Care, Office of Civilian Defense, 1944.

Voorhis, Jerry. *Confessions of a Congressman.* Garden City, N.Y.: Doubleday, 1947.

Waddell, Brian. *The War against the New Deal: World War II and American Democracy.* DeKalb: Northern Illinois University Press, 2001.

Wall, Wendy L. *Inventing the "American Way": The Politics of Consensus from the New Deal to the Civil Rights Movement.* New York: Oxford University Press, 2008.

Waller, Robert A. *Rainey of Illinois: A Political Biography, 1903–34.* Urbana: University of Illinois Press, 1977.

Wallis, John. "American Government Finance in the Long Run, 1790–1990." *Journal of Economic Perspectives* 14 (Winter 2000): 61–82.

"War and Peace: Follow What Leader?" *Time* (October 6, 1941): 18–20.

War Labor Disputes Act—Veto Message from the President of the United States, June 25, 1943. Senate. 78th Congress, 1st session.

Ware, Caroline F. *The Consumer Goes to War: A Guide to Victory on the Home Front.* New York and London: Funk and Wagnalls, 1942.

Waterman, Richard W. "Institutional Realignment: The Composition of the U.S. Congress." *Western Political Quarterly* 43 (March 1990): 81–92.

Wawro, Gregory J., and Eric Schickler. *Filibuster: Obstruction and Lawmaking in the U.S. Senate.* Princeton, N.J.: Princeton University Press, 2006.

Wayman, Dorothy G. *David I. Walsh: Citizen Patriot.* Milwaukee, Wisc.: Bruce Publishing, 1952.

Weinstein, Allen. *Perjury: The Hiss-Chambers Case.* New York: Random House, 1997.

Weisman, Steven R. *The Great Tax Wars: Lincoln to Wilson: The Fierce Battles over Money and Power That Transformed the Nation.* New York: Simon and Schuster, 2002.

Weiss, Nancy. *Farewell to the Party of Lincoln: Black Politics in the Age of FDR.* Princeton, N.J.: Princeton University Press, 1983.

Weiss, Stuart L. "Maury Maverick and the Liberal Bloc." *Journal of American History* 57 (March 1971): 880–895.

———. "Thomas Amlie and the New Deal." *Mid-America* 59 (January 1977): 19–38.

Westbrook, Robert B. *Why We Fought: Forging American Obligations in World War II.* Washington, D.C.: Smithsonian, 2010.

Wicker, Tom. *JFK and LBJ: The Influence of Personality upon Politics.* Chicago: Ivan R. Dee, 1991.

Williams, William Appleman. "The Legend of Isolationism in the 1920s." *Science and Society* 18 (Winter 1954): 1–20.

Wills, George Stockton. "Mr. Speaker and the Call to Arms: The Role of Sam Rayburn in the 1941 Extension of the Selective Service Act." M.A. thesis, University of Virginia, 1962.

Winkler, Allan M. *Home Front, U.S.A.: America during World War II,* 2nd ed. Wheeling, Ill.: Harlan Davidson, 2000.

———. *The Politics of Propaganda: The Office of War Information, 1942–1945.* New Haven, Conn.: Yale University Press, 1978.

Wood, Amy Louise. *Lynching and Spectacle: Witnessing Racial Violence in America, 1890–1940.* Chapel Hill: University of North Carolina Press, 2009.

Woods, Randall. *LBJ: Architect of American Ambition.* New York: Free Press, 2006.

Woodward, David R. *Trial by Friendship: Anglo-American Relations, 1917–1918.* Lexington: University Press of Kentucky, 1993.

Woodworth, Steven E. *Manifest Destinies: America's Westward Expansion and the Road to the Civil War.* New York: Alfred A. Knopf, 2010.

Wyman, David S. *The Abandonment of the Jews: America and the Holocaust, 1941–1945.* New York: Pantheon Books, 1984.

———. *Paper Walls: America and the Refugee Crisis, 1938–1941.* Amherst: University of Massachusetts Press, 1968.

Wyman, Mark. *DP: Europe's Displaced Persons, 1945–1951.* Philadelphia: Balch Institute Press, 1989.

Wynn, Neil A. "The 'Good War': The Second World War and Postwar American Society." *Journal of Contemporary History* 31 (July 1996): 463–482.

Yellin, Emily. *Our Mothers' War: American Women at Home and at the Front during World War II.* New York: Free Press, 2004.

Young, Nancy Beck. "'Do Something for the Soldier Boys': Congress, the G.I. Bill of Rights, and the Contours of Liberalism." In *Veterans' Policy, Veterans' Politics: New*

Perspectives on Veterans in the Modern United States. Stephen R. Ortiz, editor. Gainesville: University Press of Florida, 2012.

————. *Wright Patman: Populism, Liberalism, and the American Dream.* Dallas, Tex.: Southern Methodist University Press, 2000.

Young, Roland A. *Congressional Politics in the Second World War.* New York: Columbia University Press, 1956.

Zeidenstein, Harvey G. "The Reassertion of Congressional Power: New Curbs on the President." *Political Science Quarterly* 93 (Autumn 1978): 393–409.

Zeigler, Luther Harmon, Jr. "Senator Walter George's 1938 Campaign." *Georgia Historical Quarterly* 43 (December 1959): 333–352.

Zelizer, Julian E. *On Capitol Hill: The Struggle to Reform Congress and Its Consequences, 1948–2000.* New York: Cambridge University Press, 2004.

————. *Taxing America: Wilbur D. Mills, Congress, and the State, 1945–1975.* New York: Cambridge University Press, 1998.

Zieger, Robert H. *America's Great War: World War I and the American Experience.* Lanham, Md.: Rowman & Littlefield, 2000.

Zimmerman, Joseph F., and Wilma Rule. "A More Representative United States House of Representatives?" *PS: Political Science & Politics* 31 (March 1998): 5–10.

Zolberg, Aristide R. *A Nation by Design: Immigration Policy in the Fashioning of America.* New York: Russell Sage Foundation, 2006.

Zucker, Bat-Ami. *In Search of Refuge: Jews and US Consuls in Nazi Germany, 1933–1941.* London and Portland, Ore.: Vallentine Mitchell, 2001.

Index